2024 RUGBY ALMANACK

Edited by Clive Akers, Adrian Hill
& Campbell Burnes

Cover Photographs

Front: : Outstanding All Blacks halfback Aaron Smith who retired from international rugby at the end of the 2023 Rugby World Cup. (Photo by Getty)

A catalogue record for this book is available from the National Library of New Zealand

A Mower Book
Published in 2024 by Upstart Press Ltd
26 Greenpark Road, Penrose, Auckland, New Zealand

978-1-77694-062-2

Typesetting and design by CVD Limited (www cvdgraphics nz)
Printed by Printlink Ltd, Wellington

2024 RUGBY ALMANACK

The editors welcome notification of any errors or omissions

Please correspond directly with the editors:

Clive Akers
Opiki
RD4
Palmerston North 4474
Phone: 06 329 1822
email: akers@xtra co nz

Campbell Burnes
2/37 Grotto Street
Onehunga
Auckland 1061
Phone: 021 717 150
email: cmburnes@hotmail com

Adrian Hill
1/212 Grove Road
Hastings 4122
email: adhill@xtra co nz

ACKNOWLEDGEMENTS

the publishers and editors acknowledge the assistance of the New Zealand Rugby Union and appreciate their co-operation and the co-operation of the 26 rugby unions in compiling the *2024 Rugby Almanack*

KEY

In team record charts

BSC	Bruce Steel Cup
HS	Hanan Shield
RS	Ranfurly Shield
H	Bunnings NPC Heartland Championship

In individual appearance charts

15	fullback
14	right wing
13	centre
12	second five-eighth
11	left wing
10	first five-eighth
9	halfback
8	number eight
7	open-side flanker
6	blind-side flanker
5	right lock
4	left lock
3	right (tighthead) prop
2	hooker
1	left (loosehead) prop
*	retired injured or substituted
s	substitute
t	includes penalty try

CONTENTS

EDITORIAL

Another busy year for rugby in New Zealand culminated in the All Blacks' run to the Rugby World Cup final, where they fell, narrowly and possibly unluckily, to old foe South Africa.

The All Blacks' 2023 campaign as a whole was a very good one, returning a 9-3 record, locking away the Bledisloe Cup for a 20th year and claiming a 20th Rugby Championship/Tri Nations championship. Six rookies were blooded and money was banked from the Qatar Airways Cup Test at Twickenham against the Springboks.

However, the clear highlight was a pulsating 28-24 RWC quarter-final victory over world No 1 Ireland in which captain Sam Cane and World Rugby and New Zealand Kelvin R Tremain player of the year Ardie Savea stood tall. It was some turnaround after the travails of July/August 2022 and leaves outgoing head coach Ian Foster with a decent, if inconsistent, legacy to look back on.

New Zealand Rugby made the groundbreaking call to go early (March) with its appointment of new All Blacks coach Scott Robertson from 2024 through until at least 2027. It was not a universally popular decision, but was rooted in logic after the issues from the 2019 changeover of coaches. Few can argue with Robertson's Super Rugby record of seven straight titles, so we now eagerly await what his new team can produce.

The momentum from the joyous Women's Rugby World Cup on these shores in 2022 could not be maintained, but that was not the fault of the top women's players.

A dramatic and high quality Sky Super Rugby Aupiki final in Hamilton drew only around 4000 fans and, while the Black Ferns played some expansive rugby in their seven Tests, the crowds during spring's Global WXV1 tournament were disappointing, perhaps due to the clash with the business end of the men's World Cup in France. In short, just a year out from the next women's World Cup, the Black Ferns need more matches, especially at home, to be more visible to fans.

Happily, Aupiki is being expanded to a double-round in 2024 and there is more preparation time for our leading professionals.

The Farah Palmer Cup, presented by Bunnings Warehouse, has its own niche and the Auckland Storm wound back the clock to win a 16th title in fine style in the Christchurch Premiership final. This competition is not professional, but is still crucial and produces prime young talent.

Both our national sevens teams bounced back strongly from the disappointments of 2022 to win World Series titles. The All Blacks Sevens do not get enough credit for their work on an increasingly competitive circuit and much kudos has to go to 2017-23 coach Clark Laidlaw, who laid solid foundations until his departure mid-year to take up the reins at the Hurricanes.

The Black Ferns Sevens were able to successfully gel the promotion of youth with the nous of the veterans to again hit the high notes. Both teams look well equipped to perform strongly at July's Paris Olympics.

DHL Super Rugby Pacific has its challenges, not the least of which is losing leading players to sabbaticals in Japan, but its rule variations are at least more in line with aiding fan and player experience, while it is heartening to see the competition expanding its horizons in 2024, Moana Pasifika taking a home match to Tonga.

An independent review into New Zealand Rugby's governance highlighted concerns around the Bunnings NPC and just how and where it sits in the landscape. While financially it is problematic and crowds are dwindling, the NPC is vital to the game and must be continued in some meaningful and viable form. The sight of 14,000 packing Yarrow Stadium in New Plymouth to see a rousing final, won by Taranaki, should hold meaning.

The Heartland Championship, presented by Bunnings Warehouse, which has no trouble with its identity, went from strength to strength in 2023, South Canterbury and West Coast, the latter for the first time, taking the silverware.

The New Zealand Under 20s placed only seventh at their first Junior World Championship since 2019. This is an important national team and the balance between player development and results needs to be better managed. In mitigation, the Under 20s were playing catch-up after being isolated from international play during the Covid-19 pandemic.

Financially, New Zealand Rugby announced record revenue of $271m at April's AGM, though that was countered by $277m expenditure. However, that was due to Silver Lake payouts and historical Covid-related costs. Cash reserves look healthy.

In 2024, we would like to see Olympic glory for our sevens teams, the Māori All Blacks back in action, the All Blacks to kick-start the Scott Robertson tenure, more eyeballs on the top of the women's game and the number of overall registered players to remain healthy, plus a vibrant grassroots scene for our clubs and schools. The pressures, however, are myriad.

Our deep appreciation again goes to New Zealand Rugby and the team managers of the national sides, franchises and provincial unions for assisting us with information and checking statistics. The accuracy of this is the foundation upon which the Almanack is built and should never be taken for granted.

Several individuals contributed vital information and copy, in particular Chris Jansen (referees), John Lea (overseas players), Adam Julian (schools), Paul Neazor, Geoff Miller, Lindsay Knight, Brent Drabble, Matt Shaw, Kelly Plummer, David Ormrod, Jeremy Sutherland and Matthew McQuilkin.

Clive Akers, Adrian Hill, Campbell Burnes
January 2024

FROM THE PUBLISHERS

A SALUTE TO CLIVE AKERS

This edition of the Rugby Almanack *will be the last for Clive Akers as a full-time editor. After 30 years in the role, Clive is taking a step back and will instead become a contributor to future editions. Here, highly respected sports journalist and author LINDSAY KNIGHT pays tribute to Clive's outstanding contribution to not only the* Almanack, *but to the game itself.*

When he joined the *Rugby Almanack* in 1994 Clive Akers followed in a long line of admirable servants in chronicling New Zealand rugby. But Clive didn't just maintain the standards set since the *Almanack*'s inception in 1935 by Arthur Swan, Arthur Carman, Read Masters, Neville McMillan and Rod Chester. He enhanced them. Not only was he as meticulous a statistician as his predecessors but he brought a more literary touch to some of the prose than what had been the case previously, especially in the *Almanack*'s earlier years.

Though not a professional journalist Clive was a competent writer, as was shown in his many other publications as well as his various *Almanack* pieces. There is a certain irony to the years in which Clive has been so closely involved with producing the *Almanack*. For they have coincided, almost within a year, of rugby's lurch towards undiluted professionalism, which has been traumatic for so many because it has caused a diminution of many of the structures which once underpinned the game.

Adapting to the challenges posed by professionalism would have been particularly daunting for Clive as he exemplified many of those values which have come under such threat. By his own description he was a player without distinction, but he developed a deep love for the game through his involvement in the first XVs of his Masterton boarding schools and his membership of clubs in Manawatu, Hawke's Bay and King Country. His affinity for the game at its various levels, particularly in its rural environment, have been reflected in his editorship of the *Almanack*. Clive has always ensured that provincial and Heartland rugby, club, age-groups and, more recently, women's rugby have enjoyed almost as equal focus as the All Blacks and the Super competitions.

This writer for one will always appreciate Clive's respect for the giants of the past and under his direction the *Almanack*'s obituaries have been expanded to do them justice. Before joining the *Almanack* Clive was a stalwart of that other great institution which has also done much to preserve New Zealand rugby's history and heritage, Palmerston North's New Zealand Rugby Museum, of which he has been curator, chairman and life member.

Clive himself has been a prolific author, with histories on Manawatu, Horowhenua, a biography on New Zealand rugby's founder CJ Monro, another on rugby-playing war-time heroes and his extraordinary *Rugby Register*, which records every single player who has appeared in New Zealand first class rugby. It is a reference book without parallel, the product of monumental research and a definitive argument settler.

That Clive has been able to achieve so much is remarkable, because his real job is as a farmer and successful stud breeder of Cheviot sheep. He also has actively followed the notable careers in equestrian sport of his five daughters.

There may have been times when, like others battling to preserve those strands which were the basis of New Zealand rugby, Clive has felt it was an exercise in whistling against the wind. But to his credit, he kept the faith and rugby in this country is in his debt.

Clive was made a Member of the New Zealand Order of Merit (MNZM) in the 2018 Queen's Birthday Honours for services to rugby and historical research.

UNION DIRECTORY

New Zealand Rugby Union
Auckland office:
3B, 125 The Strand, Parnell, Auckland
Postal: PO Box 2453, Shortland Street, Auckland 1140
Telephone: 09 300 4995
Wellington office:
New Zealand Rugby House, Level 4, 100 Molesworth Street, Wellington
Postal: PO Box 2172, Wellington 6140
Telephone: 04 499 4995
email: info@nzrugby.co.nz
Websites: www.allblacks.com
www.nzrugby.co.nz

Auckland RU
Office: Eden Park, Walters Road, Auckland
Postal: PO Box 56-152, Dominion Road, Auckland 1446
Telephone: 09 815 4850
email: info@aucklandrugby.co.nz
Website: www.aucklandrugby.co.nz

Bay of Plenty RFU
Office: High Performance Centre, Blake Park, 52 Miro Street, Mt Maunganui
Postal: PO Box 4058, Mt Maunganui South 3149
Telephone: 07 574 2037
Fax: 07 574 2046
email: reception@boprugby.co.nz
Website: www.boprugby.co.nz

Buller RFU
Office: Craddock Park, Domett Street, Westport
Postal: PO Box 361, Westport 7866
Telephone: 027 789 8330
email: office@bullerrugby.co.nz
Website: www.bullerrugby.co.nz

Canterbury RFU
Office: Rugby Park, Malvern Street, St Albans, Christchurch
Postal: PO Box 755, Christchurch 8140
Telephone: 03 379 8300
email: info@crfu.co.nz
Website: www.canterburyrugby.co.nz

Counties Manukau RFU
Office: Navigation Homes Stadium, Stadium Drive, Pukekohe
Postal: PO Box 175, Pukekohe 2340
Telephone: 09 237 0033
email: admin@steelers.co.nz
Website: www.steelers.co.nz

Ngati Porou East Coast RFU
Office: Whakarua Park, Ruatoria
Postal: PO Box 106, Ruatoria 4032
Telephone: 06 864 8812
Fax: 06 864 8813
email: admin@npec.co.nz
Website: www.npec.co.nz

Hawke's Bay RFU
Office: 3 Orotu Drive, Poraiti, Napier
Postal: PO Box 201, Napier 4140
Telephone: 06 835 7617
email: admin@hbrugby.co.nz
Website: www.hbmagpies.co.nz

Horowhenua Kapiti RFU
Office: 15-19 Bristol Street, Levin
Postal: PO Box 503, Levin 5540
Telephone: 06 367 8059
email: office@hkrfu.co.nz
Website: www.hkrfu.co.nz

King Country RFU
Office: Cotter Street, Te Kuiti
Postal: PO Box 159, Te Kuiti
Telephone: 07 878 7545
email: office@kingcountryrugby.co.nz
Website: www.sporty.co.nz/kcrfu

Manawatu RU
Office: 30 Waldegrave Street, Palmerston North
Postal: PO Box 1729, Palmerston North 4440
Telephone: 06 357 2633
email: info@manawaturugby.co.nz
Website: www.manawaturugby.co.nz

Mid Canterbury RU
Office: A&P Showgrounds, Brucefield Avenue, Ashburton
Postal: PO Box 98, Ashburton 7740
Telephone: 03 308 8718
email: admin@midcanterburyrugby.co.nz
Website: www.midcanterburyrugby.co.nz

North Harbour RU
Office: North Harbour Stadium, Stadium Drive, Albany
Postal: PO Box 300 492, Albany 0752
Telephone: 09 447 2100
email: harbour@harbourrugby.co.nz
Website: www.harbourrugby.co.nz

North Otago RFU
Office: Shop 6a Thames Arcade, 203 Thames Street, Oamaru
Postal: PO Box 102, Oamaru 9444
Telephone: 03 434 2053 *Fax:* 03 434 2054
email: admin@northotagorugby.co.nz
Website: www.northotagorugby.co.nz

Northland RU
Office: 136 Riverside Drive, Whangarei
Postal: PO Box 584, Whangarei 0140
Telephone: 09 438 4743
email: reception@northlandrugby.co.nz
Website: www.taniwha.co.nz

Otago RFU
Office: Forsyth Barr Stadium, Anzac Avenue, Dunedin
Postal: PO Box 691, Dunedin 9054
Telephone: 03 477 0928
email: orfu@orfu.co.nz
Website: www.orfu.co.nz

Poverty Bay RFU
Office: River Oak Mews
74 Grey Street, Gisborne
Postal: PO Box 520, Gisborne 4040
Telephone: 06 868 9968
email: info@povertybayrugby.co.nz
Website: www.povertybayrugby.co.nz

Rugby Southland
Office: 120a Leet Street, Invercargill
Postal: PO Box 291, Invercargill 9840
Telephone: 03 216 8694
email: reception@rugbysouthland.co.nz
Website: www.rugbysouthland.co.nz

South Canterbury RFU
Office: 226 Evans Street, Timaru
Postal: PO Box 787, Timaru 7910
Telephone: 03 688 8653
email: jason@scrfu.co.nz
Website: www.scrfu.co.nz

Taranaki RFU
Office: Sport Taranaki, Maratahu Street, New Plymouth
Postal: PO Box 5004, New Plymouth 4343
Telephone: 06 759 0167
email: jimmy@trfu.co.nz
Website: www.trfu.co.nz

Tasman RU
Office: Trafalgar Park Lane, Nelson
Postal: PO Box 7157, Nelson 7042
Telephone: 03 548 7030
email: info@tasmanrugby.co.nz
Website: www.tasmanrugby.co.nz

Thames Valley RFU
Office: 140a Normanby Road, Paeroa
Postal: PO Box 245, Paeroa 3600
Telephone: 07 862 6352
email: admin@tvrfu.co.nz
Website: www.thamesvalleyswampfoxes.co.nz

Waikato RU
Office: FMG Stadium,
128 Seddon Road, Hamilton
Postal: PO Box 9507, Hamilton 3240
Telephone: 07 839 5675
Fax: 07 838 1713
email: admin@mooloo.co.nz
Website: www.mooloo.co.nz

Wairarapa Bush RFU
Office: Trust House, Memorial Park,
149 Dixon Street, Masterton
Postal: PO Box 372, Masterton 5840
Telephone: 06 378 8369
email: webadmin@waibush.co.nz
Website: www.waibush.co.nz

Wellington RFU
Office: 30 Somme Road, Trentham, Upper Hutt
Postal: PO Box 7201, Wellington South 6242
Telephone: 04 389 0020
email: mail@wrfu.co.nz
Website: www.wrfu.co.nz

West Coast RFU
Office: 123 Main South Road, Greymouth
Postal: PO Box 31, Greymouth 7840
Telephone: 03 768 7822
email: wcrugbynz@gmail.com
Website: www.westcoastrfu.co.nz

Whanganui RFU
Office: 40 Maria Place Extn, Whanganui
Postal: PO Box 4213, Whanganui 4541
Telephone: 06 349 2313
email: info@whanganuirugby.co.nz
Website: *www.*whanganuirugby.co.nz

New Zealand Rugby Museum
326 Main Street, Palmerston North
Postal: PO Box 36, Palmerston North 4440
Telephone: 06 358 6947
Fax: 06 358 6947
email: info@rugbymuseum.co.nz
Website: www.rugbymuseum.co.nz

NEW ZEALAND RUGBY UNION

OFFICE BEARERS

2023–2024

Patron

I.A. (Ian) Kirkpatrick MBE

President

M.G. (Max) Spence (*Nelson*)

Vice-president

M.J.A. (Matthew) Cooper MNZM (*Waikato*)

Chair

Dame Patsy Reddy

Deputy chair

Dame Farah Palmer and B.N. Mackey (jointly)

Board

Elected members: Ajit Balasingham (*Northland*), B.N. (*Bailey*) Mackey (*Auckland*), S.M. (*Stuart*) Mather (*Auckland*), W.A. (*Wayne*) Young (*Marlborough*).

Appointed members: R.K. (*Rowena*) Davenport (*Otago*), M.R. (*Mark*) Hutton (*Auckland*), C.M. (*Catherine*) Savage (*Wellington*), Dame Patsy Reddy GNZM CVO QSO DStJ (*Wellington*)

Maori representative: Dame Farah Palmer DNZM ONZM (*Manawatu*)

Chief Executive Officer

M.P. (Mark) Robinson

Life Members

R.A. (Richie) Guy ONZM; R.A. (Rob) Fisher ONZM;
J.A. (John) Sturgeon ONZM, MBE; A.R. (Andy) Leslie MNZM;
Sir Graham Henry KNZM; M.T. (Mike) Eagle ONZM;
Sir Bryan Williams KNZM, MBE; G.N.K. (Graham) Mourie MBE.

2023 HONOURS
THE ALMANACK NEW ZEALAND XV

Beauden Barrett
Blues

Will Jordan *Crusaders* | Rieko Ioane *Blues* | Mark Telea *Blues*

Jordie Barrett
Hurricanes

Richie Mo'unga
Crusaders

Aaron Smith
Highlanders

Ardie Savea
Hurricanes

Sam Cane *Chiefs* | Scott Barrett *Crusaders* | Brodie Retallick *Chiefs* | Shannon Frizell *Highlanders*

Tyrel Lomax *Hurricanes* | Codie Taylor *Crusaders* | Ethan de Groot *Highlanders*

Reserves –

Samisoni Taukei'aho (*Chiefs*), Tamaiti Williams (*Crusaders*), Fletcher Newell (*Crusaders*), Sam Whitelock (*Crusaders*), Dalton Papali'i (*Blues*), Cameron Roigard (*Hurricanes*), Damian McKenzie (*Chiefs*), Leicester Fainga'anuku (*Crusaders*).

COMMENTS

The following comment on leading players is on those involved in Super Rugby, being the basis of selection for the All Blacks.

Fullback: Beauden Barrett (Blues) did not produce the form expected of him at first five-eighth for his club, however in the test arena at fullback he was very accomplished with his running game from the back and exit options with the boot.

Shaun Stevenson (Chiefs) was a highly consistent performer in Super Rugby and unlucky to miss All Black selection although he remained on the periphery as injury cover and did play against Australia at Dunedin. Will Jordan (Crusaders) also excelled in this position for his club but was picked again at international level on the wing. He had one test at fullback v Australia.

Josh Moorby (Hurricanes), Zarn Sullivan (Blues) gave good service to their clubs while Sam Gilbert (Highlanders) was one of his team's best players in their disappointing season.

Wing threequarters: Will Jordan (Crusaders) again showed his tremendous attacking skill in the tests and Mark Telea (Blues) was in outstanding form throughout the year, regularly demonstrating the ability to beat a man.

Leicester Fainga'anuku (Crusaders) was the top try scorer in NZ first class rugby for 2023 with his powerful running but was unable to cement a regular test spot and will spend the next two years playing in France. Emoni Narawa (Chiefs) made an assured test debut against Argentina but suffered a back injury during it, and a reaggravation in training at the World Cup before the opening game saw him invalided out of the tournament without playing a game.

Caleb Clarke (Blues) is still a leading wing but found himself overtaken in the All Blacks lineups.

The Hurricanes pairing of Kini Naholo and Salesi Rayasi was a productive one and Etene Nanai-Seturo (Chiefs) also impressed. Sevu Reece (Crusaders) suffered a knee injury in March which ruled him out of all rugby for the remainder of the year.

Centre threequarter: Rieko Ioane (Blues) was far and away the best player in this position. On the test stage he was sharp on attack, provided try assists and was strong defensively, although his attacking threat was contained by South Africa in all three tests.

Braydon Ennor (Crusaders), Alex Nankivell (Chiefs) and Billy Proctor (Hurricanes) were all strong midfielders for their clubs. Ennor suffered an ACL injury against Australia at Dunedin which ended his season while Proctor and Nankivell made the All Blacks XV tour to Japan. Daniel Rona (Chiefs) looked handy in his first season.

Second five-eighth: Jordie Barrett (Hurricanes) cemented this position after his shift here from fullback last year. He carried and tackled well, and his ability to kick the ball a long distance out of hand or for goal is an extra asset. His partnership with Rieko Ioane looks set to continue for the foreseeable future.

Anton Lienert-Brown's (Chiefs) experience and defensive play made him a reliable bench option for the All Blacks and appeared in all seven games at the World Cup. Bryce Heem (Blues) had his best season yet while Roger Tuivasa-Sheck's (Blues) three-year involvement with rugby came to an end and is to return to rugby league next year.

Another to depart is Jack Goodhue (Crusaders), who is heading to France after 19 tests for New Zealand, the last of which was in 2020, in a career that has been blighted by injury since. David Havili (Crusaders) had an injury affected year but made the World Cup squad while Dallas McLeod (Crusaders) benefited from playing more on the wing than his customary midfield position, due to this log-jam of talent, and gained a surprise selection in the All Blacks squad for the Rugby Championship.

Quinn Tupaea (Chiefs) missed the entire Super Rugby season due to the ACL injury he sustained playing against Australia last year but took the field for Waikato in the NPC.

First five-eighth: Richie Mo'unga (Crusaders) played to his usual high standard and as the established first choice in the All Blacks his acceptance of a three-year contract in Japan while still in his prime years came as a surprise to many.

Damian McKenzie (Chiefs) enjoyed a successful season for his club and was understudy to Mo'unga in the tests while the Hurricanes new signing, one-test All Black, Brett Cameron had a frustrating season due to injury which allowed Aidan Morgan to build on last year's efforts.

Halfback: Aaron Smith (Highlanders) ended his career in New Zealand and will leave a large gap in the position. Eleven years after his test debut there was still no diminishing of performance at the highest level and will be ranked as one of the best All Blacks halfbacks.

Cameron Roigard (Hurricanes), one of our five players of the year, made a huge advance during the year with some outstanding displays to deservedly gain All Black honours. Finlay Christie (Blues) was favoured by the national selectors in what must have been a very close decision ahead of Brad Weber (Chiefs) who was another unlucky player after some consistently good performances for the Super Rugby beaten finalists.

Mitchell Drummond (Crusaders) continues to serve his club well while TJ Perenara

(Hurricanes) missed the whole year due to the achilles tendon injury he suffered on last year's end of season All Blacks tour. Noah Hotham (Crusaders) looks a capable understudy.

Number eight: Ardie Savea (Hurricanes) had no peer in this position. His contribution to the All Blacks and Hurricanes was immense and took over the captaincy in the World Cup final after Sam Cane's early red card and almost led the team to an unlikely victory with 14 men.

Luke Jacobson (Chiefs) had a good year for his club to regain test selection and Hugh Renton was one of the few Highlanders to advance his claims in 2023. Cullen Grace (Crusaders) had another season punctuated by injury and Christian Lio-Willie fitted in well when taking over in his debut season at the club.

Hoskins Sotutu (Blues) had a disappointing season and did not even make the All Blacks XV selection for its tour of Japan.

Flankers: If the All Blacks captain Sam Cane (Chiefs) felt under pressure for his place he responded positively to the challenge. He played and led well, getting through a tremendous amount of work in his games, having an outstanding game in the tense quarter-final win over Ireland. After a lengthy period of time being in and out of the test squad, Shannon Frizell (Highlanders) finally delivered the consistency hoped for as blindside flanker and is now going to be lost to the All Blacks having signed to play in Japan.

As understudy to Cane, Dalton Papali'i (Blues) did not make the same impact in the tests as he did on last year's end of season tour although he performed well against Italy. Ethan Blackadder (Crusaders) endured another injury plagued season but was called to France as an injury replacement for Emoni Narawa. Samipeni Finau's (Chiefs) performances in Super Rugby earned a call up to the All Blacks and a highly satisfactory debut v Australia.

Billy Harmon (Highlanders) and Du Plessis Kirifi (Hurricanes) gained deserved recognition with their selection into the All Blacks XV and Tom Christie (Crusaders) gave sterling service to the champions in playing all 17 games with high tackle and turnover counts. Adrian Choat (Blues) prospered when given a chance and Devan Flanders (Hurricanes) established himself as a starting blindside flanker.

Pita Gus Sowakula (Chiefs) and Akira Ioane (Blues) were not favoured by the All Blacks selectors with Sowakula taking up a contract in France.

Locks: The outstanding careers of Sam Whitelock (Crusaders) and Brodie Retallick (Chiefs) in New Zealand rugby came to an end at the conclusion of the World Cup with their subsequent moves to play in France and Japan respectively. They have been automatic selections since their debuts and started together in a world record 66 tests for a locking pair.

Scott Barrett (Crusaders) was a dominant figure throughout the season with his lineout skills, work around the field and priceless ability to remain injury free. Going forward for the All Blacks he will be a key player.

The Chiefs pair of Tupou Vaa'i and Josh Lord, 23 and 22 years old respectively, will be favoured to step up with their already acquired accumulated test experience, albeit mainly off the bench. Cameron Suafoa (Blues) emerged this year and Quinten Strange (Crusaders) and Isaia Walker-Leawere (Hurricanes) played consistently throughout the season.

Patrick Tuipulotu (Blues), James Blackwell (Hurricanes) and Josh Dickson (Highlanders) have all given solid service to their clubs for a number of years and the latter two have now accepted contracts overseas.

Props: Ethan De Groot (Highlanders) and Tyrel Lomax (Hurricanes) solidified their standing throughout the year and lost nothing in comparison with any of the international opposition they faced.

Tamaiti Williams (Crusaders) made big strides with a most promising debut season at international level. At 140kg a building of more mobility would enhance his credentials even more, particularly as he can play both sides of the scrum. Fletcher Newell was injured in the Crusaders opening match of the year in February. His next match after that was the test against Australia at Dunedin six months later and at season's end had justified the national selectors faith in him after last year's impressive debut.

The experienced Blues pair Ofa Tu'ungafasi and Nepo Laulala were steady without being imposing in the test arena and Laulala has now taken up a contract in France. Jermaine Ainsley (Highlanders) and Aidan Ross (Chiefs) are also experienced players who gave excellent service to their clubs.

Chiefs team mates Ollie Norris and George Dyer are two young developing props who were rewarded with selection in the All Blacks XV.

Joe Moody (Crusaders) was first choice All Blacks loosehead just two seasons ago and injury for the second year in a row ruined his chance of selection. George Bower (Crusaders), an All Black since 2021, had a season ending injury in April, and it will be interesting to see whether these two can regain their positions next year in competition with the current crop of younger talents.

Hooker: As one of our five players of the year Codie Taylor (Crusaders) was the form hooker and regained the starting position in the All Blacks. Samisoni Taukei'aho (Chiefs) lost some of his edge compared to last year while Dane Coles (Hurricanes) played with typical vigour and commitment in his final year. Coles' decision to retire leaves a vacancy in the All Blacks squad with Asafo Aumua (Hurricanes) having the inside running as his replacement.

Tyrone Thompson (Chiefs) is a fast progressing hooker and Ricky Riccitelli and Kurt Eklund are both accomplished players at the Blues.

FIVE PLAYERS OF THE YEAR

Cameron Dane Roigard (*Counties Manukau/Hurricanes*) was a big mover in 2023. Any doubts the Hurricanes might struggle without their long-standing first choice halfback, TJ Perenara for the season due to injury, were quickly dispelled with Roigard's outstanding form seeing him appear in 14 of the 15 matches, all but one of them being starts.

As well as serving the backline confidently and kicking well, he proved to be adept at spotting opportunities and his running game netted him nine tries and saw him finish as equal top try scorer for the Hurricanes. His efforts had many pundits picking him to be one of the three halfbacks named in the All Blacks squad, a prediction that proved to be accurate. He finished the year with five appearances in the 12 Tests, scoring four tries along the way.

Cameron Roigard was born on November 16, 2000 at Onewhero. He was educated at Karapiro school and St Peter's school, Cambridge, having three years in the St Peter's first XV 2016–2018. Signed by the Counties Manukau academy for 2019, he joined the Onewhero club, going straight into their premier side and represented the Counties Manukau under 19 team.

The following year he was picked in the Chiefs under 20 team and made his first-class debut with seven appearances for Counties Manukau in the NPC. This led to him joining the Hurricanes for 2021 as an injury replacement for Jamie Booth, making his first four appearances for the club. This was sufficient for the Hurricanes to offer him a full contract for 2022.

He had an outstanding NPC season with Counties Manukau in 2022, securing their Player of the Year award, his form earning him selection in the All Blacks XV team for its end-of-year tour.

Ardie Suemalo Savea (*Wellington/Hurricanes*) was again a dominant figure in New Zealand rugby in 2023 with his play for the All Blacks and Hurricanes. The outstanding number eight was the recipient of both the World Rugby Player of the Year award for his appearances in the Test arena and the Kelvin Tremain Memorial Trophy award for New Zealand Player of the Year.

Ardie Savea was an Almanack Promising Player of the year for 2012 and an Almanack Player of the Year four times previously.

Aaron Luke Smith (*Manawatu/Highlanders*) showed no sign of a tapering off in his play as he finished his All Blacks career in 2023 as he had started it in 2012 with quick positioning behind the ball and an instant, accurate, pass to the backline, while the variations in kicking or running were still well executed. He scored a fine individual try in the World Cup semi-final and was unlucky to have had a try ruled out in the final.

Aaron Smith has been an Almanack Player of the Year five times previously.

Codie Joshua Dane Taylor (*Canterbury/Crusaders*) was a reinvigorated player in 2023, back to his best form for both the Crusaders and All Blacks with accurate lineout throwing, running well with ball in hand and competing at the breakdown. For the Crusaders, he scored 12 tries in his 14 appearances and by the end of the year had reclaimed the number one hooking spot in the All Blacks with strong performances at the World Cup tournament in France.

Codie Taylor was previously an Almanack Player of the Year for 2017.

Mark Evander Telea (*North Harbour/Blues*) ended the year with World Rugby's Breakthrough Player of the Year award for his efforts at Test level. Throughout the year for both the Blues and the All Blacks he always looked dangerous when given a bit of room and numerous times he showed the ability to beat a defender, notably in the World Cup final when not many other All Blacks did. He was the All Blacks first choice left wing at the World Cup and scored four tries in his seven Tests this year, which followed a standout season for the Blues where he scored 12 tries in 14 matches and was their Player of the Year.

Mark Telea was born at Auckland on December 6, 1996, and educated at Massey High School 2010–2014, having two years in the first XV. He joined Massey Rugby Club in 2015 and represented North Harbour under 19s. In 2016, he played for the Blues under 20s and made his first-class debut for North Harbour in the NPC.

He had a six-week stint with the Hurricanes in 2019 as temporary injury cover but did not appear for the club and was named in the Blues for 2020. His debut Super Rugby season ended with him being awarded the Blues Rookie of the Year award and he followed this by signing for Tasman who went on to win the NPC title that year.

Last year Telea was called into the All Blacks as injury cover for the home three-Test series against Ireland but did not make any match-day selection. He then returned to North Harbour, from Tasman, for the NPC competition. At the end of the season he gained selection in the inaugural All Blacks XV squad for their two-match tour. Due to injuries in the All Blacks, who were touring at the same time, Telea left the All Blacks XV squad without appearing for them to join the All Blacks and eventually made his Test debut against Scotland, scoring two tries. He finished the year playing against England the following week.

PROMISING PLAYERS OF THE YEAR

Qualification for consideration is usually players in their debut season at first-class level or first full season.

Austin Richard Charles Anderson (*Waikato*) established a regular starting place in the Waikato team in his debut season at first-class level. The 19-year-old, 1.86m, 94kg, second-five proved adept at advancing past the gain line with footwork rather than running straight ahead into contact, and delivered accurate, well-timed passes. He received Waikato Emerging men's player of the year award for his season's efforts and rounded out the year with a two-year contract with the Brumbies for Super Rugby Pacific 2024–2025 after having been in their 2023 Elite Development squad.

Austin Anderson was born at Perth, Western Australia on November 18, 2003. He attended Quinns Beach primary school 2009–2015 followed by three years at Aranmore Catholic College 2016–2018. During this time his main playing position was first-five and he represented the West Australia under 15 teams at both rugby and rugby league in 2018 and during that year signed a three-year junior contract with the North Queensland Cowboys rugby league team.

His family moved to New Zealand in 2019 and he attended Rotorua Boys' High School, going straight into the first XV, and the Bay of Plenty under 16 team, at first-five. He had two years at Hamilton Boys' High School 2020–2021 making the first XV both years, mostly at fullback the first year and at second-five in his second year. During this time he was selected in the Chiefs under 18 team (2020 and 2021), the New Zealand Schools rugby league team (2020) and the New Zealand Schools rugby team (2021).

In 2022, he joined the Te Awamutu Rugby and Sports Club and represented the Chiefs under 20 and Brumbies under 19 teams.

Tahlor Myles Cahill (*Canterbury*) gained a three-year contract with the Crusaders at the end of 2023 after a very good season with the New Zealand under 20 and Canterbury teams. He was a standout in the New Zealand under 20 team which had a disappointing campaign at the World Championship, finishing seventh of 12 teams. The strongly built 1.98m, 113kg, 20-year-old, lock shone with his lineout work and all-round game. The youngest and least experienced of the five locks named in the Canterbury NPC squad, he established himself with equal game time with his seven appearances.

Born at Christchurch on June 8, 2003, Tahlor Cahill started playing rugby at the age of four with Christchurch Rugby Club and attended Our Lady of Fatima primary school. In 2011, after the Christchurch earthquake, the family moved to Brisbane. In 2014, he played for the Brisbane under 12 team at number eight and lock and gained a scholarship to Ipswich Grammar School for 2015–2016.

The family returned to Christchurch for 2017 and Tahlor enrolled at Shirley Boys' High School through to 2020, making the first XV in his final two years. During that time he made the Canterbury under 14, under 15 and under 16 teams, while in his final year he was selected in the Junior Crusaders (U18) team. He chose to go Hamilton Boys' High School as a boarder for 2021 and from their first XV was selected into the New Zealand Schools team and the Junior Crusaders again.

In 2022, he joined the Marist Albion club and entered Canterbury University to study sports coaching. He missed selection in the Crusaders team for the Super Rugby under 20 tournament at Taupo but was subsequently picked in the NZ Barbarians team for the same event. At the conclusion of the week-long tournament, Cahill received the DJ Graham Award for player of the tournament. He made his first-class debut for the New Zealand under 20 team at the Oceania Championship on Australia's Sunshine Coast and finished the year representing the Canterbury under 19s.

Billy Guyton, who represented North Otago, Tasman, Hurricanes, Crusaders, Blues and Maori All Blacks, is a cousin.

In something of a comeback **Joshua Sidney Tuala Gray** (*Counties Manukau*) scored six tries for his province in seven appearances in the NPC. The 1.80m, 92kg 24-year-old wing proved to be an excellent finisher of opportunities that came his way, including a couple of spectacular one-handed touchdowns in the corner with his body in the air over the sideline.

As a result of his exploits, he finished the year with an appearance in the NZ Barbarians team and an invite to pre-Christmas training with the Chiefs.

Joshua Gray was born at Otahuhu on April 18, 1999, and educated at St Mary's Papakura primary school before attending Sacred Heart College from 2010–2016 where he made the first XV in his final year.

Upon leaving school he joined the Ardmore Marist club playing for the under 21 side and representing Counties Manukau under 19s. In 2018, he was promoted to his club's premier side which won the McNamara Cup that year, and had another season with the Counties Manukau under 19s. The following year he was picked in the Counties Manukau B team, but due to injuries in the Steelers' NPC squad he got the opportunity to play two first-class matches off the bench.

In 2022 he joined Auckland club Manukau Rovers who won the Gallaher Shield, but for 2023 he returned to the Counties Manukau fold and played for the Patumahoe club.

Although he had a season limited by injury, **Blair James Murray** (*Canterbury*) created a favourable impression for Canterbury in the NPC. In their opening four matches the fast, elusive wing scored six tries, including three against Wellington but then went off injured later in the match. The 1.73m, 83kg 21-year-old missed the next five games and completed the NPC season with seven tries in seven appearances.

He had started the year in the Crusaders Development team and was selected in the New Zealand Universities team for their tour of Japan in May. He played at first-five in the sole first-class fixture of the tour, kicking four conversions and a penalty goal in the match against Japan under 20s. In November, although he missed out on a full contract with the Crusaders for Super Rugby Pacific next year, it was announced he would be an injury-cover addition to the squad.

Blair Murray was born at Hawera on October 9, 2001. He attended Turuturu primary school and Hawera Intermediate before starting at New Plymouth Boys High School in 2015. He played for the first XV 2017–2019, appearing in both the halfback and first-five positions in his first year and fullback in his final two years. He represented the Taranaki under 13, under 14, under 16 teams all at halfback, and the Chiefs under 16 (halfback) and under 18 teams (fullback). In 2018 and 2019 he was selected in the New Zealand Schools team and was awarded the Rugby News Jerry Collins Memorial Bronze Boot in 2018 for the best New Zealand player in their series of matches.

In 2020, he enrolled at Canterbury University to undertake a Bachelor of Commerce degree and played for the University club. After appearances for Canterbury under 19, Canterbury B, Crusaders under 20 and Crusaders Development teams, he made his first-class debut for Canterbury in 2022 against North Harbour in his only NPC match of that year.

Blair was a New Zealand under 16 touch rugby rep and in April 2019 he placed first in the long jump and triple jump events at the North Island Secondary Schools athletic championships.

At just 20-years of age **Rohan Nicholas Wingham** (*Otago*) grasped his opportunity well in the rigours of the front row for Otago in the NPC. The 1.87m, 115kg loosehead prop appeared in nine of their ten matches, and although the team had a disappointing season, the scrum was a real strength, his scrummaging ability showing up well against all opponents.

Rohan Wingham was born at Dunedin on November 4, 2002. He was educated at St Clair primary school and Tahuna Normal Intermediate before arriving at King's High School in 2016. He was in the first XV for three years 2018–2020, and in his final year he captained the side and was selected into the New Zealand Schools team. During his time at King's High he represented Otago under 14s, under 16s, under 18s and the Highlanders under 18 team.

Upon leaving school, he joined the Dunedin club and in 2021 and 2022 played for the Highlanders under 20 team at the annual tournament in Taupo. Later in 2022 he made his first-class debut for North Otago, appearing in four Heartland Championship matches as a loan player.

Rohan attended Otago University for two years studying chemistry and physics, and is currently a teacher aide at Carisbrook school.

RESULTS FROM 2023 FIRST-CLASS SEASON

Key:		
	RC	SANZAAR Rugby Championship
	SRP	Super Rugby Pacific
	P	Bunnings NPC Premier
	RS	Ranfurly Shield
	H	Heartland Championship
	MC	Meads Cup (Heartland Championship)
	LC	Lochore Cup (Heartland Championship)
	OT	Osborne Taonga
	qf	Quarter-final
	sf	Semi-final
	f	Final
	*	not first class
	aet	after extra time
	W20	World Under 20 Championship

Winning team listed first

January								
Sat-Sun	21-22	*	2022-2023 World Series Sevens		Round Four		Hamilton
Fri-Sun	27-29	*	2022-2023 World Series Sevens		Round Five		Sydney
February							
Fri	24	SRP	Chiefs	31	Crusaders	10	Christchurch
Sat	25	SRP	Fijian Drua	36	Moana Pasifika	34	Auckland
	25	SRP	Blues	60	Highlanders	20	Dunedin
	25	SRP	Hurricanes	47	Reds	13	Townsville
Sat-Sun	25-26	*	2022-2023 World Series Sevens		Round Six		Los Angeles
March							
Fri	3	SRP	Crusaders	52	Highlanders	15	Melbourne
	3	SRP	Hurricanes	39	Rebels	33	Melbourne
Fri-Sun	3-5	*	2022-2023 World Series Sevens		Round Seven		Vancouver
Sat	4	SRP	Chiefs	52	Moana Pasifika	29	Melbourne
Sun	5	SRP	Brumbies	25	Blues	20	Melbourne
Fri	10	SRP	Chiefs	28	Highlanders	7	Hamilton
Sat	11	SRP	Fijian Drua	25	Crusaders	24	Lautoka
	11	SRP	Blues	25	Hurricanes	19	Wellington
	11	SRP	Force	21	Moana Pasifika	18	Perth
Fri	17	SRP	Hurricanes	34	Waratahs	17	Wellington
Sat	18	SRP	Chiefs	44	Rebels	25	Hamilton
	18	SRP	Crusaders	34	Blues	28	Auckland
	18	SRP	Brumbies	62	Moana Pasifika	36	Canberra

Sun	19	SRP	Highlanders	43	Force	35	Invercargill
Fri	24	SRP	Crusaders	35	Brumbies	17	Christchurch
	24	SRP	Chiefs	24	Waratahs	14	Sydney
Sat	25	SRP	Highlanders	57	Fijian Drua	24	Dunedin
	25	SRP	Hurricanes	59	Moana Pasifika	0	Auckland
Sun	26	SRP	Blues	30	Force	17	Auckland
Fri	31	SRP	Highlanders	45	Moana Pasifika	17	Auckland
	31	SRP	Crusaders	25	Reds	12	Brisbane
Fri-Sun	31-2	*	2022-2023 World Series Sevens		Round Eight		Hong Kong
April							
Sat	1	SRP	Chiefs	20	Blues	13	Hamilton
Sun	2	SRP	Hurricanes	45	Force	42	Palmerston North
Fri	7	SRP	Crusaders	38	Moana Pasifika	21	Christchurch
Sat	8	SRP	Hurricanes	29	Highlanders	14	Dunedin
	8	SRP	Blues	54	Rebels	17	Melbourne
Sat-Sun	8-9	*	2022-2023 World Series Sevens		Round Nine		Singapore
Fri	14	SRP	Reds	40	Moana Pasifika	28	Apia
Sat	15	SRP	Chiefs	33	Hurricanes	17	Wellington
Fri	21	SRP	Chiefs	50	Fijian Drua	17	Hamilton
	21	SRP	Crusaders	43	Rebels	27	Melbourne
Sat	22	SRP	Blues	55	Waratahs	21	Auckland
	22	SRP	Force	30	Highlanders	17	Perth
Fri	28	SRP	Hurricanes	32	Brumbies	27	Wellington
	28	SRP	Waratahs	21	Highlanders	20	Sydney
Sat	29	SRP	Blues	30	Fijian Drua	14	Lautoka
	29	SRP	Rebels	43	Moana Pasifika	33	Auckland
	29	SRP	Chiefs	34	Crusaders	24	Hamilton
May							
Fri	5	SRP	Chiefs	52	Highlanders	28	Dunedin
Sat	6	SRP	Fijian Drua	27	Hurricanes	24	Suva
	6	SRP	Crusaders	48	Force	13	Christchurch
	6	SRP	Blues	31	Moana Pasifika	30	Auckland
Fri	12	SRP	Reds	25	Chiefs	22	New Plymouth
Fri-Sun	12-14	*	2022-2023 World Series Sevens		Round Ten		Toulouse
Sat	13	SRP	Hurricanes	71	Moana Pasifika	22	Wellington
	13	SRP	Crusaders	15	Blues	3	Christchurch
Sun	14	SRP	Brumbies	48	Highlanders	32	Canberra
Fri	19	SRP	Crusaders	41	Moana Pasifika	7	Auckland
	19	SRP	Blues	45	Reds	26	Brisbane
Sat	20	SRP	Highlanders	20	Rebels	17	Dunedin
	20	SRP	Chiefs	23	Hurricanes	12	Hamilton
Sat-Sun	20-21	*	2022-2023 World Series Sevens		Round Eleven		London
Wed	24	*	Hanshin Barbarians	52	New Zealand Universities	38	Osaka
Fri	26	SRP	Highlanders	35	Reds	30	Dunedin
Sat	27		Japan Under 20	52	New Zealand Universities	46	Tokyo
	27	SRP	Fijian Drua	47	Moana Pasifika	46	Lautoka

	27	SRP	Crusaders	42	Waratahs	18	Christchurch
	27	SRP	Blues	36	Hurricanes	25	Auckland
	27	SRP	Chiefs	31	Brumbies	21	Canberra
Mon	29	*	Australia Under 20	34	New Zealand Under 20	26	Upper Hutt
June							
Fri	2	SRP	Blues	16	Highlanders	9	Auckland
Sat	3		Poverty Bay	29	NP East Coast	17	Gisborne
	3	*	New Zealand Under 20	19	Australia Under 20	18	Wellington
	3	SRP	Hurricanes	27	Crusaders	26	Wellington
	3	SRP	Moana Pasifika	33	Waratahs	24	Sydney
	3	SRP	Chiefs	43	Force	19	Perth
Fri	9	SRP qf	Blues	41	Waratahs	12	Auckland
Sat	10	SRP qf	Chiefs	29	Reds	20	Hamilton
	10	SRP qf	Crusaders	49	Fijian Drua	8	Christchurch
	10	SRP qf	Brumbies	37	Hurricanes	33	Canberra
Fri	16	SRP sf	Crusaders	52	Blues	15	Christchurch
Sat	17	SRP sf	Chiefs	19	Brumbies	6	Hamilton
Sat	24	SRP f	Crusaders	25	Chiefs	20	Hamilton
Sun	25	W20	New Zealand Under 20	27	Wales Under 20	26	Paarl
Thurs	29	W20	France Under 20	35	New Zealand Under 20	14	Paarl
July							
Wed	5	W20	New Zealand Under 20	62	Japan Under 20	19	Stellenbosch
Sat	8		All Blacks XV	38	Japan XV	6	Tokyo
	8	RC	New Zealand	41	Argentina	12	Mendoza
Sun	9	W20 5-8	Australia Under 20	44	New Zealand Under 20	35	Cape Town
Wed	12	RS	Wellington	68	Horowhenua Kapiti	7	Levin
Fri	14	W20 7-8	New Zealand Under 20	50	Georgia Under 20	26	Stellenbosch
Sat	15	RC	New Zealand	35	South Africa	20	Auckland
	15		All Blacks XV	41	Japan	27	Kumamoto
Wed	19	RS	Wellington	67	South Canterbury	21	Lower Hutt
Sat	29	RC	New Zealand	38	Australia	7	Melbourne
August							
Fri	4	P	Tasman	27	Otago	15	Nelson
		P	Taranaki	37	Counties Manukau	29	New Plymouth
Sat	5		New Zealand	23	Australia	20	Dunedin
	5	P	Hawke's Bay	23	North Harbour	21	Napier
	5	P	Wellington	22	Manawatu	6	Palmerston North
	5	P	Canterbury	43	Northland	11	Whangarei
Sun	6	P	Auckland	32	Bay of Plenty	30	Tauranga
	6	P	Waikato	29	Southland	21	Invercargill
Wed	9	P	Taranaki	28	Northland	13	Whangarei
Fri	11	P	Hawke's Bay	25	Counties Manukau	24	Pukekohe
Sat	12	P	Bay of Plenty	19	Waikato	15	Tauranga
	12	H	North Otago	43	Mid Canterbury	24	Ashburton
	12	H	Poverty Bay	52	Buller	33	Gisborne
	12	H	South Canterbury	48	Horowhenua Kapiti	14	Waimate
	12	H	Wairarapa Bush	32	Ngati Porou East Coast	31	Masterton
	12	H	Thames Valley	36	Whanganui	33	Whanganui
	12	H	West Coast	40	King Country	9	Greymouth

	12	P		Wellington	28	Otago	5	Dunedin
	12	P		Tasman	24	Auckland	12	Blenheim
Sun	13	P		Canterbury	28	North Harbour	24	Onewa
	13	P		Southland	15 aet	Northland	15 aet	Invercargill
	13	P		Taranaki	26	Manawatu	17	Palmerston North
Wed	16	P		Hawke's Bay	35	Waikato	32	Napier
Fri	18	P		Counties Manukau	32	Bay of Plenty	19	Pukekohe
Sat	19	H	OT	Ngati Porou East Coast	19	Mid Canterbury	8	Ruatoria
	19	P		Auckland	43	North Harbour	21	Onewa
	19	P	RS	Wellington	39	Southland	17	Lower Hutt
	19	H		Whanganui	13	Buller	5	Westport
	19	H		West Coast	48	Horowhenua Kapiti	28	Levin
	19	H		South Canterbury	45	King Country	21	Taupo
	19	H		North Otago	50	Wairarapa Bush	3	Oamaru
	19	H		Thames Valley	24	Poverty Bay	17	Te Aroha
	19	P		Canterbury	68	Manawatu	26	Christchurch
	19	P		Northland	32	Tasman	5	Whangarei
Sun	20	P		Hawke's Bay	33	Otago	32	Napier
	20	P		Taranaki	29	Waikato	17	Hamilton
Wed	23	P	RS	Wellington	7	Tasman	0	Wellington
Fri	25	P		Manawatu	31	Northland	30	Palmerston North
	25			South Africa	35	New Zealand	7	London
Sat	26	H	OT	Ngati Porou East Coast	38	North Otago	29	Ruatoria
	26	P		Auckland	41	Hawke's Bay	22	Auckland
	26	H		King Country	23	Whanganui	17	Taumarunui
	26	H		Mid Canterbury	43	Horowhenua Kapiti	14	Ashburton
	26	H		South Canterbury	56	Buller	0	Geraldine
	26	H		Wairarapa Bush	30	Poverty Bay	24	Masterton
	26	H		Thames Valley	30	West Coast	22	Greymouth
	26	P		Bay of Plenty	29	Taranaki	26	New Plymouth
	26	P		Otago	31	Southland	21	Dunedin
Sun	27	P		Wellington	36	Canterbury	31	Christchurch
	27	P		Tasman	20 aet	North Harbour	15 aet	Nelson
	27	P		Waikato	37	Counties Manukau	15	Hamilton
Wed	30	P		Manawatu	33	Auckland	31	Auckland
September								
Fri	1	P		Northland	44	Hawke's Bay	21	Whangarei
Sat	2	H		Horowhenua Kapiti	24	Wairarapa Bush	19	Levin
	2	P		Bay of Plenty	38	Otago	14	Rotorua
	2	P		Canterbury	29	Taranaki	28	Rangiora
	2	H		Ngati Porou East Coast	24 aet	Buller	21aet	Westport
	2	H		South Canterbury	26	North Otago	22	Oamaru
	2	H		Mid Canterbury	23	Poverty Bay	20	Gisborne
	2	H		Thames Valley	27	King Country	21	Thames
	2	H		Whanganui	36	West Coast	12	Whanganui
	2	P		North Harbour	39	Waikato	17	Albany
	2	P	RS	Wellington	56	Counties Manukau	25	Wellington

Sun	3	P	Auckland	41	Southland	13	Invercargill
	3	P	Tasman	58	Manawatu	19	Nelson
Wed	6	P	North Harbour	27	Otago	24	Albany
Fri	8	P	Wellington	41	Waikato	24	Hamilton
	8	WC	France	27	New Zealand	13	Saint Denis
Sat	9	H OT	Ngati Porou East Coast	31	Poverty Bay	11	Ruatoria
	9	H	Horowhenua Kapiti	33	Buller	22	Levin
	9	H	Thames Valley	34	Mid Canterbury	31	Ashburton
	9	H	Whanganui	34	North Otago	19	Oamaru
	9	H	South Canterbury	39	West Coast	26	Fairlie
	9	H	Wairarapa Bush	35	King Country	26	Masterton
	9	P	Counties Manukau	39	Southland	29	Pukekohe
	9	P	Bay of Plenty	38	Hawke's Bay	35	Napier
	9	P	Auckland	36	Canterbury	29	Auckland
Sun	10	P	Tasman	29	Taranaki	18	New Plymouth
	10	P	North Harbour	48	Manawatu	29	Palmerston North
	10	P	Otago	30	Northland	15	Dunedin
Wed	13	P	Counties Manukau	31	Canterbury	29	Pukekohe
Fri	15	P	Hawke's Bay	57	Manawatu	7	Napier
	15	WC	New Zealand	71	Namibia	3	Toulouse
Sat	16	P	Waikato	27	Auckland	12	Pakuranga
	16	H	Buller	27	Wairarapa Bush	20	Westport
	16	H	King Country	31	Horowhenua Kapiti	27	Te Kuiti
	16	H	North Otago	50	Poverty Bay	43	Gisborne
	16	H	South Canterbury	36	Thames Valley	31	Whangamata
	16	H	Whanganui	40	Ngati Porou East Coast	24	Whanganui
	16	H	West Coast	32 aet	Mid Canterbury	29 aet	Greymouth
	16	P	North Harbour	50	Northland	31	Albany
	16	P	Taranaki	36	Otago	17	Dunedin
Sun	17	P	Wellington	26	Bay of Plenty	14	Rotorua
	17	P	Canterbury	29	Southland	14	Christchurch
	17	P	Tasman	27	Counties Manukau	17	Blenheim
Fri	22	P	Bay of Plenty	32	Northland	26	Whangarei
Sat	23	H OT	Ngati Porou East Coast	29	King Country	11	Ruatoria
	23	H	South Canterbury	50	Mid Canterbury	35	Christchurch
	23	P	Counties Manukau	46	Manawatu	19	Pukekohe
	23	P	Hawke's Bay	33	Southland	7	Invercargill
	23	H	Poverty Bay	31	Horowhenua Kapiti	17	Levin
	23	H	North Otago	34	Thames Valley	33	Maheno
	23	H	Whanganui	36	Wairarapa Bush	18	Masterton
	23	P	Canterbury	30	Tasman	28	Christchurch
	23	P	Taranaki	18	Auckland	16	New Plymouth
	23	H	Buller	29	West Coast	11	Christchurch
Sun	24	P RS	Wellington	26	North Harbour	6	Porirua
	24	P	Waikato	47	Otago	7	Hamilton
Wed	27	P	Bay of Plenty	25	Southland	23	Invercargill
Fri	29	P	Auckland	27	Northland	26	Auckland
Sat	30	WC	New Zealand	96	Italy	17	Lyon

	30	H		Thames Valley	31	Ngati Porou East Coast	26	Waihi
	30	H		Wairarapa Bush	33	Mid Canterbury	28	Ashburton
	30	H		South Canterbury	41	Poverty Bay	31	Patutahi
	30	P		Waikato	37	Canterbury	35	Hamilton
	30	P	RS	Hawke's Bay	20	Wellington	18	Wellington
	30	H		King Country	33	Buller	28	Taupo
	30	H		West Coast	27	North Otago	12	Greymouth
	30	H		Whanganui	55	Horowhenua Kapiti	19	Whanganui
	30	P		Taranaki	54	North Harbour	21	New Plymouth
October								
Sun	1	P		Bay of Plenty	41	Tasman	12	Tauranga
	1	P		Otago	38	Counties Manukau	22	Dunedin
	1	P		Southland	37	Manawatu	12	Palmerston North
Thurs	5	WC		New Zealand	73	Uruguay	0	Lyon
Fri	6	P	qf	Canterbury	29	Auckland	24	Christchurch
Sat	7	MC	sf	Whanganui	38	Thames Valley	3	Whanganui
	7	LC	sf	Poverty Bay	40	North Otago	35	Oamaru
	7	LC	sf	West Coast	33	Wairarapa Bush	27	Masterton
	7	MC	sf	South Canterbury	34	Ngati Porou East Coast	17	Pleasant Point
	7	P	qf	Wellington	32	Waikato	28	Wellington
	7	P	qf	Taranaki	34	Tasman	18	New Plymouth
Sun	8	P	qf	Hawke's Bay	38	Bay of Plenty	28	Tauranga
Fri	13	P	sf	Taranaki	23	Canterbury	16	New Plymouth
Sat	14	MC	f	South Canterbury	40	Whanganui	30	Temuka
	14	P	sf	Hawke's Bay	25	Wellington	24	Wellington
	14	WC	qf	New Zealand	28	Ireland	24	Saint Denis
Sun	15	LC	f	West Coast	23	Poverty Bay	20	Greymouth
Fri	20	WC	sf	New Zealand	44	Argentina	6	Saint Denis
Sat	21	P	f	Taranaki	22	Hawke's Bay	19	New Plymouth
Sat	28	WC	f	South Africa	12	New Zealand	11	Saint Denis
November								
Wed	1	*		NZ Heartland	43	Canterbury Development	17	Methven
Sat	4			NZ Barbarians	49	NZ Heartland	26	Oamaru
	4			Wales	49	UK Barbarians	26	Cardiff
December								
Sat-Sun	2-3	*		2023-2024 World Series Sevens		Round One		Dubai
Sat-Sun	9-10	*		2023-2024 World Series Sevens		Round Two		Cape Town

224 First-class matches

NEW ZEALAND REPRESENTATIVES 2023

Of the 39 All Blacks used in the 12 Test matches of 2023, six were making their debuts, two less than in 2022.

Details of the six new All Blacks are:

NARAWA, Emoni Rokomoce *born Suva (Fiji), July 13, 1999*
All Blacks #1208
Bay of Plenty (Tauranga Sports) 2018 (1), 2019 (12), 2020 (8), 2021 (6) 2022 (10); Blues 2020 (6), 2021 (1); Chiefs 2022 (9), 2023 (13); New Zealand 2023 (1)

WILLIAMS, Tamaiti Patariki Thomas *born Whangarei, August 10, 2000*
All Blacks #1209
Canterbury (Burnside) 2020 (8), 2021 (2), 2022 (10), Crusaders 2021 (7), 2022 (15), 2023 (16); NZ Under 20 (Canterbury) 2019 (5); NZ Maori 2020 (1), 2021 (2), 2022 (2); All Blacks XV 2022 (2); New Zealand 2023 (8)

ROIGARD, Cameron Dane *born Onewhero, November 16, 2000*
All Blacks #1210
Counties Manukau (Onewhero) 2020 (7), 2021 (1), 2022 (9); Hurricanes 2021 (7), 2022 (6), 2023 (14); All Blacks XV 2022 (1); New Zealand 2023 (5)

FINAU, Samipeni Uaine *born Nuku'alofa (Tonga) May 10, 1999*
All Blacks #1211
Waikato (Hamilton Old Boys) 2019 (5), 2020 (11), 2021 (6), 2022 (6), 2023 (3); Chiefs 2021 (6), 2022 (12), 2023 (14); Moana Pasifika 2020 (1); NZ Under 20 (Waikato) 2019 (6); New Zealand 2023 (1)

STEVENSON, Shaun Tualaulelei *born North Shore, November 14, 1996*
All Blacks #1212
Waikato (Hamilton Old Boys) 2015 (10), 2016 (1); North Harbour (Marist) 2017 (11), 2018 (10), 2019 (9), 2020 (10), (Northcote) 2021 (2), 2022 (11), 2023 (7); Chiefs 2016 (6), 2017 (18), 2018 (9), 2019 (11), 2020 (8), 2021 (10), 2022 (5), 2023 (17); UK Barbarians 2019 (1), 2023 (1); NZ Under 20 (Waikato) 2016 (5); NZ Maori 2017 (2), 2018 (3), 2019 (2), 2020 (1), 2021 (2), 2022 (2); All Blacks XV 2022 (2); New Zealand 2023 (1)

McLEOD, Dallas Alexander Marcon *born Christchurch, April 30, 1999*
All Blacks #1213
Canterbury (Christchurch) 2019 (9), 2020 (6), 2021 (9), 2022 (12), 2023 (11); Crusaders 2020 (2), 2021 (10), 2022 (1), 2023 (14); NZ Under 20 (Canterbury) 2019 (7); New Zealand 2023 (1)

ALL BLACKS MANAGEMENT 2023

Head Coach/selector:	Ian Foster
Assistant Coach/Selector (Forwards):	Jason Ryan
Assistant Coach/Selector (Backs):	Joe Schmidt
Assistant Coach (Defence):	Scott McLeod
Assistant Coach (Scrum):	Greg Feek
Kicking Coach:	David Hill
Skills Coach:	Andrew Strawbridge
Manager (Business and Operations):	Darren Shand
Manager (Leadership):	Gilbert Enoka
Strength and Conditioning Coach:	Dr Nic Gill
Assistant Strength and Conditioning Coach:	Kim Simperingham
Performance Analyst:	Jamie Hamilton
Assistant Performance Analyst:	Hayden Chapman
Doctor:	Dr James McGarvey
Physiotherapist:	Peter Gallagher
Manual Therapist:	George Duncan
Nutritionist:	Katrina Darry
Operations Manager:	Bianca Thiel
Operations Co-ordinator:	Paula Powlesland
Media Manager:	Matt Manukia
Assistant Media Manager:	Jo Malcolm
Logistics Manager:	James Iversen

Photo by Bruce Jarvis Photographic Services Ltd

ALL BLACKS

2023 Rugby World Cup Runners-up

Back row: N. Gill (*S&C Coach*), M. Manukia (*Comms Manager*), J. Garvey (*Doctor*), S. Frizell, J. Barrett, T. Vaa'I, T. Williams, S. McLeod (*Asst Coach*), D. Shand (*Manager — Business & Operations*). ***Fourth row:*** J. Iversen (*Logistics Manager*), A. Strawbridge (*Skills Coach*), G. Enoka (*Manager — Leadership*), N. Laulala, F. Newell, L. Jacobson, L. Fainga'anuku, W. Jordan, E. de Groot, G. Feek (*Scrum Coach*), K. Simperingham (*Asst S&C Coach*). ***Third row:*** K. Darry (*Nutritionist*), J. Schmidt (*Asst Coach*), E. Narawa, A. Lienert-Brown, C. Clarke, S. Taukei'aho, M. Telea, D. Papali'i, D. Havili, D. Hill (*Kicking Coach*), J. Malcolm (*Comms Advisor*), P. Powlesland (*Business Manager*). ***Second row:*** J. Hamilton (*Analyst*), B. Thiel (*Operations Manager*), J. Ryan (*Asst Coach*), F. Christie, R. Mo'unga, C. Roigard, T. Lomax, D. McKenzie, H. Chapman (*Analyst*), G. Duncan (*Muscle Therapist*), P. Gallagher (*Physio*). ***Front row:*** C. Taylor, R. Ioane, D. Coles, B. Barrett, A. Smith, S. Cane (*Captain*), I. Foster (*Head Coach*), S. Whitelock, B. Retallick, O. Tu'ungafasi, S. Barrett, A. Savea. ***Inset:*** E. Blackadder.

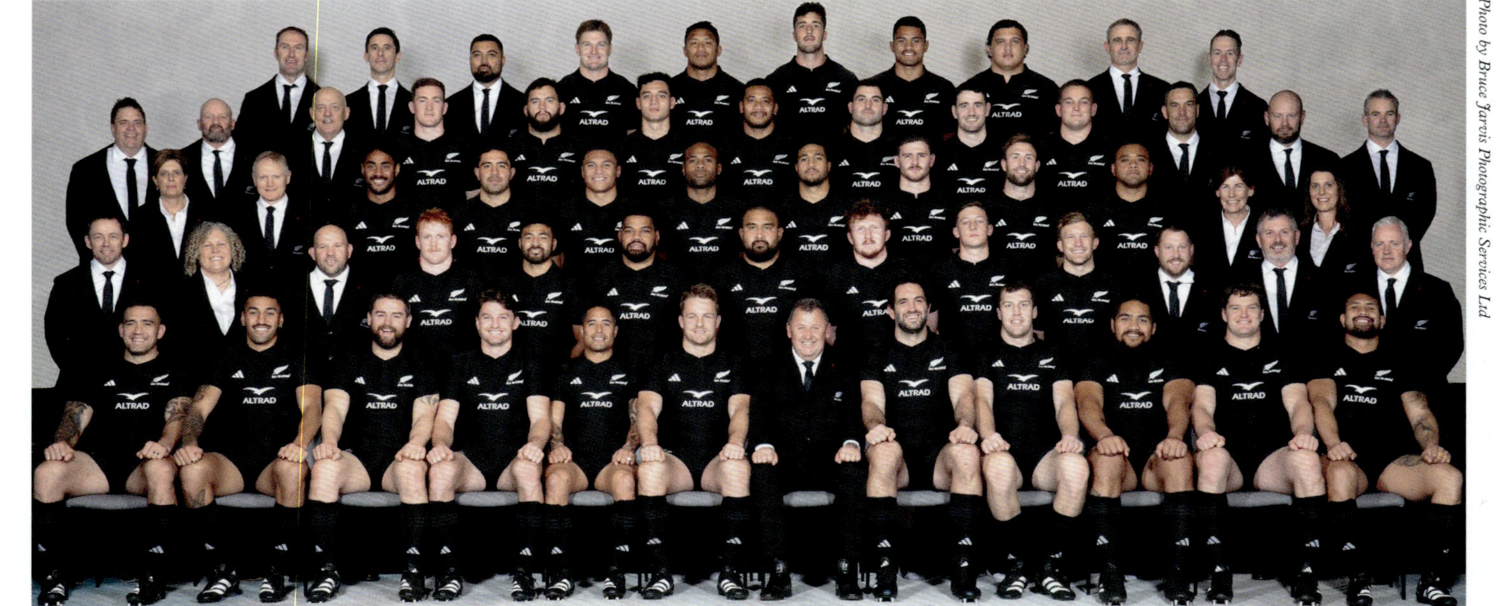

Photo by Bruce Jarvis Photographic Services Ltd

ALL BLACKS

2023 Lipovitan-D Rugby Championship Winners & Bledisloe Cup Holders

Back row: N. Gill (*S&C Coach*), J. McGarvey (*Doctor*), M. Manukia (*Comms Manager*), J. Barrett, S. Finau, J. Lord, T. Vaa'i, T. Williams, S. McLeod (*Asst Coach*), D. Shand (*Manager — Business & Operations*). ***Fourth row:*** J. Iversen (*Logistics Manager*), A. Strawbridge (*Skills Coach*), G. Enoka (*Manager — Leadership*), D. McLeod, T. Lomax, S. Stevenson, S. Frizell, L. Jacobson, W. Jordan, E. de Groot, D. Hill (*Kicking Coach*), G. Feek (*Scrum Coach*), K. Simperingham (*Asst S&C Coach*). ***Third row:*** K. Darry (*Nutritionist*), J. Schmidt (*Asst Coach*), E. Narawa, A. Lienert-Brown, C. Clarke, M. Telea, L. Fainga'anuku, D. Papali'i, B. Ennor, T. Mafile'o, (*Communications Advisor*), P. Powlesland (*Business Manager*). ***Second row:*** J. Hamilton (*Analyst*), B. Thiel (*Operations Manager*), J. Ryan (*Asst Coach*), F. Christie, R. Mo'unga, S. Taukei'aho, N. Laulala, F. Newell, C. Roigard, D. McKenzie, H. Chapman (*Analyst*), G. Duncan (*Muscle Therapist*), P. Gallagher (*Physio*). ***Front row:*** C. Taylor, R. Ioane, D. Coles, B. Barrett, A. Smith, S. Cane (*Captain*), I Foster (*Head Coach*), S. Whitelock, B. Retallick, O. Tu'ungafasi, S. Barrett, A. Savea.

BLACK FERNS

2023 WXV1 Squad v France, Wales and England

Back row: C. Shalfoon (*IMG Analyst*), P. Talaapitaga (*Scrum Coach*), T. Jackson (*Assistant S&C*), L. Sae, P. Maliepo, K. Henwood, C. Smith, S. Fisher, C. Bremner, T. Kalounivale, M. Paul, L. Connor, K. Murray, C. Viliko, A. Rule, K. Fowke (*Physio*), J. Chappell (*Team Liaison*). ***Second row:*** C. Kaua (*World Rugby Coaching Intern*), C. Twentyman (*S&C*), R. Holmes, A. du Plessis, L. Jenkins, A. Bayler, R. Kelly, G. Gago, I. Hohaia, S. Brunt, M. Matele, K. Vahaakolo, J. Ardagh (*Asst Physio*), A. Meade (*Media Manager*), A. Cameron (*Doctor*), L. Posthumus (*Nutritionist*), R. Runciman (*Analyst*). ***Front Row:*** N. Strickland (*Manager*), T. Christie (*Asst Coach*), L. Mikaele Tu'u, M. Roos, G. Ponsonby, R. Demant (*Co-captain*), A. Bunting (*Director of Rugby*), K. Simon (*Co-captain*), R. Tui, A. Bremner, A. Marino-Tauhinu, S. Jackson (*Asst Coach*), M. Delany (*Asst Coach*), I. Saunders (*Mental Skills Coach*). Absent: A. Parrott (*Asst S&C*).

www.kenbakerphotography.com

MATATŪ

2023 Super Rugby Aupiki Champions

Back row: C. Nelles, M. Palu, S. Naiqama. ***Third row:*** N. Groube (*S&C*), A. Tiplady (*Doctor*), G. Brooker, G. Ponsonby, E. Doyle, M. Parkes, E. Dermody, C. Poko, P. Love, J. Hansen (*Performance Psychologist*), L. Roden (*Lead Analyst*). ***Second row:*** D. Cron (*Coach*), R. Archibald (*Manager*), A. du Plessis, L. Jenkins, N. Delamere, A. Rule, M. Mataele, C. Cunningham, G. Steinmetz, J. Ardagh (*Lead Physio*), W. Hansen (*Coach*), T. Christie (*Coach*). ***Front row:*** R. Kelly, D. Hiini, A. Lolohea, K. Reynolds (*Vice-captain*), A. Bremner (*Captain*), B. Baxter (*Head Coach*), R. Holmes (*Vice-captain*), T. Gapper, C. Robins-Reti, L. Miles, G. Cormick. Absent: C. Chalfoon, H. Peta. ***Insets:*** S. Te-Ohaere Fox, S. Munro (*General Manager Professional Rugby*).

www.kenbakerphotography.com

CRUSADERS

2023 Super Rugby Pacific Champions

Back row: E. Blackadder, D. Gardiner, M. Dunshea, Z. Gallagher, J. Hannah, Q. Strange, C. Grace. ***Fifth row:*** S. Curry (*Physical Performance*), C. Fihaki, W. Gualter, L. Fainga'anjku, W. Jordan, D. McLeod, M. Nanai, O. Jager, L. Surridge (*Sports Science*), H. Dewar (*Sports Science*). ***Fourth row:*** J. Roche (*Lead Physio*), M. Swan (*Doctor*), N. Tucker (*Physio*), T. Christie, S. Calder, C. Lio-Willie, F. Brewis, C. Kellow, T. Williams (*Operations Manager*), V. Peterson (*Analyst*), B. Christie (*Physio*). ***Third row:*** J. Miles (*Logistics Manager*), V. Le Bas (*PDM*), A. Turner, R. O'Neill, F. Newell, S. Talitui, B. McAlister, G. Bower, K. Sykes-Martin, F. Burke, R. Archibald (*High Performance Administrator*), S. van Gruting (*Physical Performance*). ***Second row:*** J. Marshall (*Coach*), D. Perrin (*Coach*), S. Hansen (*Coach*), S. Hickey, L. Chapman, Q. MacDonald, J. Afoa, P. Patafilo, G. Bell, N. Hotham, K. Tylee (*High Performance Administrator*), G. Duder (*Lead Physical Performance*), S. Fletcher (*Manager*). ***Front row:*** S. Reece, B. Ennor, J. Goodhue, J. Moody, C. Taylor (*Vice-captain*), S. Robertson (*Head Coach*), S. Barrett (*Captain*), S. Whitelock (*Vice-captain*), D. Havili (*Vice-captain*), W. Heinz, M. Drummond, R. Mo'unga. ***Insets*** (*left to right*): T. Williams, T. Kemara, M. Springer, I. Moananu, T. Ellison (*Coach*), J. Lam.

Photo by Farrelly Photos

AUCKLAND STORM

2023 Farah Palmer Cup Premiership Winners

Back row: A. Vahai, M. Vaipulu, C Tuli-Fale, M. Kaipo, P. Maliepo, C. Viliko, K. Vahaakolo. ***Third row:*** D. Nankivell, D. Fesolai, S. Kaipo, E. Moimoi, B. Sorensen-McGee, S. Halafihi, M. Vaea, R. Demant. ***Second row:*** K. Moratti (*Asst S&C*), A. Thomas (*PDM*), M. Puckett, A. Po'oi, M. Ieremia, G. Fa'aumu, S. Brunt, A. Courtney (*Manager*), R. Alilles (*Asst S&C*). ***Front row:*** E. Itunu (*Support*), A. Itunu, W. Walker (*Head Coach*), M. Roos, E. Blackwell (*Captain*), S. Fisher, L. Mikaele-Tu'u, M. Hooper (*Asst Coach*), Z. Papali'i. Absent: A. Richards (*Asst Coach*), C. Wilson (*Physio*), A. Parrott (*S&C Coach*), J. Dermody, C. Tofa, F. Bloomfield, M. Kataoka, N. Moors, N. Nagata, P. Elliot.

Photo by About Image

TARANAKI BULLS

2023 Bunnings NPC Premiership Champions

Back row: J. Potroz, A. Lennox, J. Jacomb, M. Mckenzie, B. Kooman, L. Blyde. ***Third Row:*** N. Lawrence (*Asst Analyst*), M. Burgess (*S&C Asst*), S. Ritchie (*S&C*), K. Stewart, H. Bedwell Curtis, H. Cunningham, B. Northcott-Hill, M. Sandle (*CEO*), B. Cooper (*Asst Coach*). ***Second Row:*** A. Moore (*Manager*), P. Riley (*Doctor*), K. Naholo, A. Poliko, D. Rona, S. Jury, J. Lord, T. Franklin, J. Parete, M. Grindlay, M. Loft, N. Barnes (*Coach*), J. Hoeata (*Asst Coach*). ***Front Row:*** N. Milby (*Physio*), K. Fuglistaller (*PDM*), S. Perofeta, R. Riccitelli, M. Bent, R. O'Neill, L. Crowley (*Co-captain*), K. Boshier (*Co-captain*), J. Proffit, T. Florence, B. Slater, T. Walden, C. Blyde (*President*), D. Radcliffe (*Chairman*). Absent: B. Barrett, B. Preston (*Analyst*), D. Brighouse, F. Sa, J. Ratumaitavuki-Kneepkens, J. Barrett, L. Nawai, M. Sanerivi, M. O'Neill, P. Marsh (*Asst Analyst*), P. Gus Sowakula, S. Barrett, T. Vaa'i, V. Tikoisolomone, W. Ratu.

Photo by Bruce Jarvis Photographic Services Ltd

NEW ZEALAND UNDER 20

World Rugby Championship, Cape Town 2023

Back row: C. Dunlea (*Asst coach*), T. Hurst (*S&C Coach*), I. Hutchinson, R. Williams, V. Bason, R. Tuputupu, A. Tuivailala, X. Taele, A. Faleafaga, J. Viljoen, L. Roden (*Analyst*), M. Bourke (*Asst Coach*). ***Second row:*** J. Fleming (*Asst Physio*), R. Marsden (*Physio*), W. Clarke (*Asst Coach*), C. Tangitau, G. Robinson, B. Ake, T. Allen, C. Clark, H. Morrison, M. Wrampling-Alec, Codemeru Vai, M. Hala, C. Flanders, L. Wharetohunga (*Doctor*), M. Sexton (*Campaign Manager*). ***Front row:*** C. Laidlaw (*Head Coach*), H. Godfrey, S. Hainsworth-Fa'aofo, W. Stodart, M. Springer, T. Kemara (*Vice-captain*), N. Hotham (*Captain*), P. Lakai (*Vice-captain*), J. Taylor, L. Gordon, T. Cahill, S. Lauaki, R. Everiss (*Manager*). ***Insets:*** W. Martin, H. Fahey

TEST MATCH RECORDS OF 2023 NEW ZEALAND REPRESENTATIVES

ALL BLACKS CAREER RECORDS TO JANUARY 1, 2024

	Debut	*Tests*	*Starts*	*Wins*	*Winning %*	*Tries*	*Conversions*	*Penalty Goals*	*Dropped Goals*	*Points*
Beauden Barrett	2012	123	83	101	82.1	43	168	58	3	734
Jordie Barrett	2017	57	46	41	71.9	24	47	26	–	292
Scott Barrett	2016	69	45	52	75.3	7	–	–	–	35
Ethan Blackadder	2021	10	5	8	80	–	–	–	–	0
Sam Cane	2012	95	73	76	80	16	–	–	–	80
Finlay Christie	2021	21	4	17	80.9	1	–	–	–	5
Caleb Clarke	2020	20	16	15	75	6	–	–	–	30
Dane Coles	2012	90	58	73	81.1	23	–	–	–	115
Ethan de Groot	2021	22	17	16	72.7	3	–	–	–	15
Braydon Ennor	2019	9	4	9	100	1	–	–	–	5
Leicester Fainga'anuku	2022	7	6	5	71.4	5	–	–	–	25
Samipeni Finau	2023	1	1	1	100	1	–	–	–	5
Shannon Frizell	2018	33	26	25	75.7	6	–	–	–	30
David Havili	2017	27	17	18	66.7	9	–	–	–	45
Rieko Ioane	2016	69	59	49	71	36	–	–	–	180
Luke Jacobson	2019	18	9	15	83.3	5	–	–	–	25
Will Jordan	2020	31	27	21	67.8	31	–	–	–	155
Nepo Laulala	2015	53	36	41	77.3	–	–	–	–	0
Anton Lienert-Brown	2016	70	40	53	75.7	14	–	–	–	70
Tyrel Lomax	2018	32	18	23	71.8	–	–	–	–	0
Josh Lord	2021	4	2	3	75	–	–	–	–	0
Damian McKenzie	2016	47	28	38	80.8	20	30	2	–	166
Dallas McLeod	2023	1	–	1	100	–	–	–	–	0
Richie Mo'unga	2018	56	39	39	69.6	11	144	41	–	466
Emoni Narawa	2023	1	1	1	100	1	–	–	–	5
Fletcher Newell	2022	13	–	10	76.9	1	–	–	–	5
Dalton Papali'i	2018	32	18	24	75	8	–	–	–	40
Brodie Retallick	2012	109	91	92	84.4	9	–	–	–	45
Cam Roigard	2023	5	2	4	80	4	–	–	–	20
Ardie Savea	2016	81	56	59	72.3	24	–	–	–	120
Aaron Smith	2012	125	114	100	80	29	1	–	–	147
Shaun Stevenson	2023	1	1	1	100	1	–	–	–	5
Samisoni Taukei'aho	2021	30	10	22	73.3	10	–	–	–	50
Codie Taylor	2015	85	43	65	76.4	20	–	–	–	100
Mark Telea	2022	9	9	5	55.5	6	–	–	–	30
Ofa Tuungafasi	2016	57	13	44	77.1	1	–	–	–	5
Tupou Vaa'i	2020	25	7	17	68	3	–	–	–	15
Sam Whitelock	2010	153	127	125	81.6	7	–	–	–	35
Tamaiti Williams	2023	8	1	6	75	1	–	–	–	5

ALL BLACKS IN RUGBY CHAMPIONSHIP, BLEDISLOE CUP AND ENGLAND 2023

ALL BLACKS APPEARANCES, 2023

	Franchise	*Date of Birth*	*Height*	*Weight*	*Tests at 7/9/23*
B.J. (Beauden) Barrett	Blues	27-05-91	1.87	91	116
J.M. (Jordie) Barrett	Hurricanes	17-02-97	1.96	101	52
S.K. (Scott) Barrett	Crusaders	20-11-93	1.97	111	62
E.J. (Ethan) Blackadder	Crusaders	22-03-95	1.91	107	9
S.J. (Sam) Cane (capt)	Chiefs	13-01-92	1.89	106	90
F.T. (Finlay) Christie	Blues	19-09-95	1.77	84	17
C.D. (Caleb) Clarke	Blues	29-03-99	1.87	103	18
D.S. (Dane) Coles	Hurricanes	10-12-86	1.84	110	87
E.L. (Ethan) de Groot	Highlanders	22-07-98	1.9	122	17
L.O.K.W.P. (Leicester) Fainga'anuku	Crusaders	11-10-99	1.88	103	3
S.M. (Shannon) Frizell	Highlanders	11-02-94	1.95	108	28
D.K. (David) Havili	Crusaders	23-12-94	1.84	95	25
R.E. (Rieko) Ioane	Blues	18-03-97	1.89	103	63
L.B. (Luke) Jacobson	Chiefs	20-04-97	1.91	107	15
W.T. (Will) Jordan	Crusaders	24-02-98	1.88	91	25
N.E. (Nepo) Laulala	Blues	06-11-91	1.84	116	49
A.R. (Anton) Lienert-Brown	Chiefs	15-04-95	1.85	96	63
T.S. (Tyrel) Lomax	Hurricanes	16-03-96	1.92	127	27
D.S. (Damian) McKenzie	Chiefs	20-04-95	1.75	82	42
R. (Richie) Mo'unga	Crusaders	25-05-94	1.76	88	49
E.R. (Emoni) Narawa	Chiefs	13-07-99	1.84	94	1
F.D. (Fletcher) Newell	Crusaders	01-03-00	1.83	119	8
D.R. (Dalton) Papali'i	Blues	11-10-97	1.9	105	26
B.A. (Brodie) Retallick	Chiefs	31-05-91	2.04	120	103
C.D. (Cam) Roigard	Hurricanes	16-11-00	1.83	88	2
A.S. (Ardie) Savea	Hurricanes	14-10-93	1.88	102	75
A.L. (Aaron) Smith	Highlanders	21-11-88	1.71	83	119
S.F.S. (Samisoni) Taukei'aho	Chiefs	08-08-97	1.83	115	25
C.J.D. (Codie) Taylor	Crusaders	31-03-91	1.83	106	79
M.E. (Mark) Telea	Blues	06-12-96	1.86	94	5
A.O.H.M. (Ofa) Tuungafasi	Blues	19-04-92	1.95	122	53
T.P.O. (Tupou) Vaa'i	Chiefs	27-01-00	1.97	118	22
S.L. (Sam) Whitelock	Crusaders	12-10-88	2.02	122	146
T.P.T. (Tamaiti) Williams	Crusaders	10-08-00	1.94	140	3

ALL BLACKS 2023	Argentina	South Africa (1)	Australia (1)	Australia (2)	South Africa (2)	TOTALS
B. Barrett	15	15	15	–	15	**4**
Jordan	–	14	14	15	14	**4**
Stevenson	–	–	–	14	–	**1**
Narawa	14	–	–	–	–	**1**
Telea	–	11	11	–	11	**3**
Clarke	11	s	s	–	–	**3**
Fainga'anuku	–	–	–	11	–	**1**
R. Ioane	13	13	13	–	13	**4**
Ennor	s	s	–	13	–	**3**
McLeod	–	–	–	s	–	**1**
Lienert-Brown	–	–	s	12	s	**3**
J. Barrett	12	12	12	–	12	**4**
McKenzie	10	–	–	10	–	**2**
Mo'unga	s	10	10	s	10	**5**
Smith	9	9	9	s	9	**5**
Christie	s	s	–	9	–	**3**
Roigard	–	–	s	–	s	**2**
Savea	8	8	8	8	8	**5**
Papali'i	s	s	7	–	s	**4**
Cane	7	7	–	7	7	**4**
Jacobson	–	–	s	s	6	**3**
Finau	–	–	–	6	–	**1**
Frizell	6	6	6	–	–	**3**
S. Barrett	4	5	5	–	4	**4**
Lord	5	–	–	–	s	**2**
Whitelock	–	–	s	5	5	**3**
Retallick	–	4	4	4	–	**3**
Vaa'i	s	s	–	s	s	**4**
Laulala	s	s	s	3	–	**4**
Lomax	3	3	3	–	3	**4**
Newell	–	–	–	s	s	**2**
Williams	–	s	–	1	s	**3**
Tuungafasi	s	–	s	s	–	**3**
De Groot	1	1	1	–	1	**4**
Coles	2	–	–	s	2	**3**
Taylor	s	2	2	–	–	**3**
Taukei'aho	–	s	s	2	s	**4**

INDIVIDUAL SCORING

	Tries	Con	PG	DG	Points
Mo'unga	1	9	5	–	38
McKenzie	–	4	1	–	11
Frizell	2	–	–	–	10
Ioane	2	–	–	–	10
Jordan	2	–	–	–	10
Smith	2	–	–	–	10
B. Barrett	1	–	–	–	5
J. Barrett	1	–	–	–	5
Clarke	1	–	–	–	5
Coles	1	–	–	–	5
Finau	1	–	–	–	5
Narawa	1	–	–	–	5
Roigard	1	–	–	–	5
Savea	1	–	–	–	5
Stevenson	1	–	–	–	5
Taylor	1	–	–	–	5
Telea	1	–	–	–	5
Totals	***20***	***13***	***6***	***0***	***144***
Opposition scored	*13*	*10*	*3*	*0*	*94*

ALL BLACKS IN RUGBY CHAMPIONSHIP, BLEDISLOE CUP AND ENGLAND 2023

Played 5 ***Won 4*** ***Lost 1*** ***Points For 144*** ***Points Against 94***

Date	Opponent	Location	Score	Tries	Con	PG	DG	Referee
July 8	Argentina (RC)	Mendoza	41–12	Coles, Savea. J. Barrett, Ioane, Smith, B. Barrett, Narawa	McKenzie (3)			A. Gardner (AUS)
July 15	South Africa (RC)	Auckland	35–20	Smith, Frizell, Jordan, Mo'unga	Mo'unga (3)	Mo'unga (3)		M. Raynal (FRA)
July 29	Australia (RC, BC)	Melbourne	38–7	Frizell, Taylor, Jordan, Clarke, Ioane, Telea	Mo'unga (4)			W. Barnes (ENG)
August 5	Australia (BC)	Dunedin	23–20	Stevenson, Finau	McKenzie, Mo'unga	Mo'unga (2), McKenzie		K. Dickson (ENG)
August 25	South Africa	London	7–35	Roigard	Mo'unga			M. Carley (ENG)

LIPOVITAN-D RUGBY CHAMPIONSHIP 2023

In this truncated Rugby Championship in a Rugby World Cup year, the All Blacks comfortably retained the Freedom Cup and Bledisloe Cup and won their 20th Rugby Championship/Tri Nations crown.

Results

Date	Winning team				Venue
July 8	South Africa	43	Australia	12	Pretoria
July 8	New Zealand	41	Argentina	12	Mendoza
July 15	New Zealand	35	South Africa	20	Auckland
July 15	Argentina	34	Australia	31	Sydney
July 29	New Zealand	38	Australia	7	Melbourne
July 29	South Africa	22	Argentina	21	Johannesburg

Final standings

Team	*P*	*W*	*D*	*L*	*For*	*Against*	*Bonus*	*Total*
New Zealand	3	3	-	-	114	39	2	14
South Africa	3	2	-	1	85	68	1	9
Argentina	3	1	-	2	67	94	1	5
Australia	3	-	-	3	50	115	1	1

Scoring distribution

			FOR					***AGAINST***		
Team	*T*	*C*	*PG*	*DG*	*Pts*	*T*	*C*	*PG*	*DG*	*Pts*
New Zealand	17	10	3	-	114	6	3	1	-	39
South Africa	12*	6	3	-	85	8	5	6	-	68
Argentina	8	6	5	-	67	14	9	2	-	94
Australia	7	6	1	-	50	16*	11	3	-	115
TOTALS	***44***	***28***	***12***	***0***	***316***	***44***	***28***	***12***	***0***	***316***

**Includes two penatly tries (14 points)*

NEW ZEALAND v ARGENTINA

Rugby Championship

Test #626 | **Estadio Malvinas Argentinas, Mendoza** | **July 8, 2023**

New Zealand won 41–12

NEW ZEALAND		*ARGENTINA*
Beauden Barrett	15	Emiliano Boffelli
Emoni Narawa	14	Sebastian Cancelliere
Rieko Ioane	13	Matias Moroni
Jordie Barrett	12	Lucio Cinti
Caleb Clarke	11	Mateo Carreras
Damian McKenzie	10	Santiago Carreras
Aaron Smith	9	Gonzalo Bertranou
Ardie Savea	8	Rodrigo Bruni
Sam Cane (capt)	7	Juan Martin Gonzalez
Shannon Frizell	6	Pablo Matera
Josh Lord	5	Tomas Lavanini
Scott Barrett	4	Matias Alemanno
Tyrel Lomax	3	Lucio Sordoni
Dane Coles	2	Julian Montoya (capt)
Ethan de Groot	1	Thomas Gallo
Codie Taylor (rep 2, 47m)	16	Agustin Creevy (rep 2, 69m)
Ofa Tuungafasi (rep 1, 54m)	17	Mayco Vivas (rep 1, 65m)
Nepo Laulala (rep 3, 61m)	18	Eduardo Bello (rep 3, 65m)
Tupou Vaa'i (rep 5, 54m)	19	Pedro Rubiolo (rep 5, 62m)
Dalton Papali'i (rep 6, 67m)	20	Santiago Grondona (rep 7, 61m)
Finlay Christie (rep 9, 61m)	21	Lautaro Bazan Velez (rep 9, 65m)
Richie Mo'unga (rep 15, 61m)	22	Nicolas Sanchez (rep 14, 54m)
Braydon Ennor (rep 13, 69m)	23	Matias Orlando (rep 13, 54m)
Coles, Savea, J. Barrett, Ioane Smith, B. Barrett, Narawa	Tries	Sordoni, Creevy,
McKenzie (3)	Cons	Boffelli

Kickoff: 4:10pm ***Attendance:*** 42,500 ***Conditions:*** Fine

Referee: Angus Gardner (*Australia*)
Assistant referees: Jordan Way (*Australia*), Nic Berry (*Australia*)
TMO: Brett Cronan (*Australia*)

Scoring:
First half: 5m Coles try 5–0, 8m Savea try 10–0, 11m J. Barrett try, McKenzie conversion 17–0, 29m R. Ioane try, McKenzie conversion 24–0, Smith try, McKenzie conversion 31–0
Second half: 52m Sordoni try 31–5, 56m B. Barrett try 36–5, 75m Narawa try 41–5, 80m Creevy try, Boffelli conversion 41–12

All Black Test debuts: Narawa (*All Blacks No 1208*)
Yellow card: Bruni 38m

*This was the All Blacks' first Test match in Mendoza.
*This was Bertranou's 50th Test match for Argentina.

NEW ZEALAND v SOUTH AFRICA

Rugby Championship/Freedom Cup

Test #627 | **Go Media Stadium Mt Smart, Auckland** | **July 15, 2023**

New Zealand won 35–20

NEW ZEALAND		*SOUTH AFRICA*
Beauden Barrett	15	Willie Le Roux
Will Jordan	14	Cheslin Kolbe
Rieko Ioane	13	Lukhanyo Am
Jordie Barrett	12	Damian de Allende
Mark Telea	11	Makazole Mapimpi
Richie Mo'unga	10	Damian Willemse
Aaron Smith	9	Faf de Klerk
Ardie Savea	8	Jasper Wiese
Sam Cane (capt)	7	Franco Mostert
Shannon Frizell	6	Kwagga Smith
Scott Barrett	5	Lood de Jager
Brodie Retallick	4	Eben Etzebeth (capt)
Tyrel Lomax	3	Frans Malherbe
Codie Taylor	2	Bongi Mbonambi
Ethan de Groot	1	Steven Kitshoff
Samisoni Taukei'aho (rep 2, 47m)	16	Malcolm Marx (rep 2, 44m)
Tamaiti Williams (rep 1, 60m)	17	Thomas du Toit (rep 1, 60m)
Nepo Laulala (rep 3, 55m)	18	Vincent Koch (rep 3, 60m)
Tupou Vaa'i (rep 6, 72m)	19	RG Snyman (rep 5, 44m)
Dalton Papali'i (rep 7, 40m)	20	Pieter-Steph du Toit (rep 7, 45m)
Finlay Christie (rep 9, 60m)	21	Duane Vermeulen (rep 8, 47m)
Braydon Ennor (rep 13, 67m)	22	Grant Williams (rep 9, 52m)
Caleb Clarke (rep 11, 72m)	23	Manie Libbok (rep 11, 63m)
Smith, Frizell, Jordan, Mo'unga	Tries	Marx, Kolbe, Smith
Mo'unga (3)	Cons	Kolbe
Mo'unga (3)	Pens	De Klerk

Kickoff: 7.05pm ***Attendance:*** 31,261 ***Conditions:*** Fine

Referee: Mathieu Raynal (*France*)
Assistant referees: Angus Gardner (*Australia*), Pierre Brousset (*France*)
TMO: Ben Whitehouse (*Wales*)

Scoring:
First half: 5m A. Smith try, Mo'unga conversion 7–0, 10m Mo'unga conversion 10–0, 15m Frizell try, Mo'unga conversion 17–0, 35m De Klerk penalty 17–3, 38m Mo'unga penalty 20–3
Second half: 53m Marx try, Kolbe conversion 20–10, 60m Mo'unga penalty 23–10, 62m Kolbe try 23–15, 69m Jordan try, Mo'unga conversion 30–15, 77m Mo'unga try 35–15, 80m K. Smith try 35–20

All Blacks Test debuts: Williams (All Blacks No 1209)

*This was Jordie Barrett's 50th Test match.
*This was South Africa's first Test match at Mt Smart Stadium.

NEW ZEALAND v AUSTRALIA

Bledisloe Cup/Rugby Championship

Test #628 | **Melbourne Cricket Ground, Melbourne** | **July 29, 2023**

New Zealand won 38–7

NEW ZEALAND		AUSTRALIA
Beauden Barrett	15	Andrew Kellaway
Will Jordan	14	Mark Nawaqanitawase
Rieko Ioane	13	Jordan Petaia
Jordie Barrett	12	Samu Kerevi
Mark Telea	11	Marika Koroibete
Richie Mo'unga	10	Carter Gordon
Aaron Smith	9	Tate McDermott
Ardie Savea (capt)	8	Rob Valetini
Dalton Papali'i	7	Tom Hooper
Shannon Frizell	6	Jed Holloway
Scott Barrett	5	Will Skelton
Brodie Retallick	4	Nick Frost
Tyrel Lomax	3	Allan Alaalatoa (capt)
Codie Taylor	2	Dave Porecki
Ethan de Groot	1	Angus Bell (rep 7, 62m, temp) (rep 18, 69m)
Samisoni Taukei'aho (rep 2, 51m)	16	Jordan Uelese (rep 2, 48m)
Ofa Tuungafasi (rep 1, 51m)	17	James Slipper (rep 1, 48m)
Nepo Laulala (rep 3, 54m)	18	Taniela Tupou (rep 3, 38m)
Sam Whitelock (rep 4, 51m)	19	Richie Arnold (rep 5, 48m)
Luke Jacobson (rep 6, 66m)	20	Rob Leota (rep 6, 48m)
Cam Roigard (rep 9, 61m)	21	Nic White (rep 9, 51m)
Anton Lienert-Brown (rep 12, 63m)	22	Quade Cooper (rep 10, 50m)
Caleb Clarke (rep 15, 58m)	23	Izaia Perese (rep 13, 68m)
Frizell, Taylor, Jordan, Clarke, Telea, Ioane	Tries	Valetini
Mo'unga (4)	Cons	Gordon

Kickoff: 8.00pm ***Attendance:*** 83,944 ***Conditions:*** Fine

Referee: Wayne Barnes (*England*)
Assistant referees: Karl Dickson (*England*), Christopher Ridley (*England*)
TMO: Tom Foley (*England*)

Scoring:
First half: 3m Frizell try 5–0, 7m Valetini try, Gordon conversion 5–7, 34m Taylor try, Mo'unga conversion 12–7, 40m Jordan try, Mo'unga conversion 19–7
Second half: 59m Clarke try, Mo'unga conversion 26–7, 64m Telea try 31–7, 68m Ioane try, Mo'unga conversion 38–7

All Black Test debut: Roigard (All Blacks No 1210)

Yellow cards: Koroibete 25m, Tupou 57m

*The All Blacks retain the Bledisloe Cup for a 21st straight season and retain the Rugby Championship, last ceded in 2019.

NEW ZEALAND v AUSTRALIA

Bledisloe Cup

Test #629	Forsyth Barr Stadium, Dunedin	August 5, 2023

New Zealand won 23–20

NEW ZEALAND		*AUSTRALIA*
Will Jordan	15	Andrew Kellaway
Shaun Stevenson	14	Mark Nawaqanitawase
Braydon Ennor	13	Jordan Petaia
Jordie Barrett	12	Samu Kerevi
Leicester Fainga'anuku	11	Marika Koroibete
Damian McKenzie	10	Carter Gordon
Finlay Christie	9	Tate McDermott (capt)
Ardie Savea	8	Rob Valetini
Sam Cane (capt)	7	Fraser McReight
Samipeni Finau	6	Tom Hooper
Sam Whitelock	5	Richie Arnold
Brodie Retallick	4	Nick Frost
Nepo Laulala	3	Pone Fa'amausili
Samisoni Taukei'aho	2	Dave Porecki
Tamaiti Williams	1	Angus Bell
Dane Coles (rep 2, 53m)	16	Matt Faessler (rep 2, 14m)
Ofa Tuungafasi (rep 1, 49m)	17	James Slipper (rep 1, 56m)
Fletcher Newell (rep 3, 49m)	18	Zane Nonggorr (rep 3, 68m)
Tupou Vaa'i (rep 4, 25m)	19	Will Skelton (rep 5, 50m)
Luke Jacobson (rep 7, 71m)	20	Rob Leota (rep 7, 60m)
Aaron Smith (rep 9, 53m)	21	Nic White (rep 9, 65m)
Richie Mo'unga (rep 10, 49m)	22	Quade Cooper (rep 10, 65m)
Dallas McLeod (rep 13, 58m)	23	Izaia Perese (rep 13, 71m)
Stevenson, Finau	Tries	Koroibete, Hooper
McKenzie, Mo'unga	Cons	Gordon (2)
Mo'unga (2), McKenzie	Pens	Gordon, Cooper

Kickoff: 2:35pm ***Attendance:*** 28,000 ***Conditions:*** Under roof

Referee: Karl Dickson (*England*)
Assistant referees: Wayne Barnes (*England*), Christopher Ridley (*England*)
TMO: Marius Jonker (*South Africa*)

Scoring:
First half: 3m Koroibete try, Gordon conversion 0–7, 7m Hooper try, Gordon conversion 0–14, 14m McKenzie penalty 3–14, 22m Gordon penalty 3–17
Second half: 43m Stevenson try, McKenzie conversion 10–17, 57m Mo'unga penalty 13–17, 63m Finau try, Mo'unga conversion 20–17, 72m Cooper penalty 20–20, 79m Mo'unga penalty 23–20

All Black Test debuts: Finau (All Blacks No 1211), Stevenson (1212), McLeod (1213)

NEW ZEALAND v SOUTH AFRICA

Qatar Airways Cup/RWC warm-up

Test #630	Twickenham, London	August 25, 2023

South Africa won 35–7

NEW ZEALAND		*SOUTH AFRICA*
Beauden Barrett	15	Damian Willemse
Will Jordan	14	Kurt-Lee Arendse
Rieko Ioane	13	Canan Moodie
Jordie Barrett	12	Andre Esterhuizen
Mark Telea	11	Makazole Mapimpi
Richie Mo'unga	10	Manie Libbok
Aaron Smith	9	Faf de Klerk
Ardie Savea	8	Duane Vermeulen
Sam Cane (capt)	7	Pieter-Steph du Toit
Luke Jacobson	6	Siya Kolisi (capt)
Sam Whitelock	5	Franco Mostert
Scott Barrett	4	Eben Etzebeth
Tyrel Lomax	3	Frans Malherbe
Dane Coles	2	Malcolm Marx
Ethan de Groot	1	Steven Kitshoff
Samisoni Taukei'aho (rep 2, 40m)	16	Bongi Mbonambi (rep 2, 48m)
Tamaiti Williams (rep 1, 51m)	17	Ox Nche (rep 1, 48m)
Fletcher Newell (rep 3, 13m)	18	Trevor Nyakane (rep 3, 48m)
Tupou Vaa'i (rep 6, 39m)	19	Jean Kleyn (rep 5, 48m)
Josh Lord (rep 5, 51m)	20	RG Snyman (rep 4, 48m)
Dalton Papali'i (rep 7, 63m)	21	Marco van Staden (rep 6, 48m)
Cam Roigard (rep 9, 62m)	22	Cobus Reinach (rep 11, 63m)
Anton Lienert-Brown (rep 14, 65m)	23	Kwagga Smith (rep 8, 48m)
Roigard	Tries	Kolisi, Arendse, Marx, Mbonambi, Smith
Mo'unga	Cons	Libbok (5)

Kickoff: 7.30pm ***Attendance:*** 80,827 ***Conditions:*** Fine

Referee: Matthew Carley (*England*)
Assistant referees: Christoher Ridley (England), Craig Evans (*Wales*)
TMO: Tom Foley (*England*)

Scoring:
First half: 18m Kolisi try, Libbok conversion 0–7; 33m Arendse try, Libbok conversion 0–14
Second half: 42m Marx try, Libbok conversion 0–21; 59m Mbonambi try, Libbok conversion 0–28; 66m Smith try, Libbok conversion 0–35; 70m Roigard try, Mo'unga conversion 7–35

Yellow cards: S. Barrett 13m, Cane 16m, Du Toit 52m
Red card: S. Barrett 39m (second yellow card)

*This was the All Blacks' heaviest defeat by margin.

2023 RUGBY WORLD CUP RESULTS

POOL A

	P	W	D	L	TF	PF	PA	BP	Pts
France	**4**	**4**	**–**	**–**	**27**	**210**	**32**	**2**	**18**
New Zealand	**4**	**3**	**–**	**1**	**38**	**253**	**47**	**3**	**15**
Italy	4	2	–	2	15	114	181	2	10
Uruguay	4	1	–	3	9	65	164	1	5
Namibia	4	–	–	4	3	37	255	–	0

Date	*Winner*		*Loser*		*Venue*	*Referee*
September 8	France	27	New Zealand	13	Paris	J. Peyper (RSA)
September 9	Italy	52	Namibia	8	St Etienne	A. Brace (IRE)
September 14	France	27	Uruguay	12	Lille	B. O'Keeffe (NZL)
September 15	New Zealand	71	Namibia	3	Toulouse	L. Pearce (ENG)
September 20	Italy	38	Uruguay	17	Nice	A. Gardner (AUS)
September 21	France	96	Namibia	0	Marseille	M. Carley (ENG)
September 27	Uruguay	36	Namibia	26	Lyon	M. Raynal (FRA)
September 29	New Zealand	96	Italy	17	Lyon	M. Carley (ENG)
October 5	New Zealand	73	Uruguay	0	Lyon	W. Barnes (ENG)
October 6	France	60	Italy	7	Lyon	K. Dickson (ENG)

POOL B

	P	W	D	L	TF	PF	PA	BP	Pts
Ireland	**4**	**4**	**–**	**–**	**27**	**190**	**46**	**3**	**19**
South Africa	**4**	**3**	**–**	**1**	**22**	**151**	**34**	**3**	**15**
Scotland	4	2	–	2	21	146	71	2	10
Tonga	4	1	–	3	13	96	177	1	5
Romania	4	–	–	4	4	32	287	–	0

Date	*Winner*		*Loser*		*Venue*	*Referee*
September 9	Ireland	82	Romania	8	Bordeaux	N. Amashukeli (GEO)
September 10	South Africa	18	Scotland	3	Marseille	A. Gardner (AUS)
September 16	Ireland	59	Tonga	16	Nantes	W. Barnes (ENG)
September 17	South Africa	76	Romania	0	Bordeaux	M. Raynal (FRA)
September 23	Ireland	13	South Africa	8	Paris	B. O'Keeffe (NZL)
September 24	Scotland	45	Tonga	17	Nice	K. Dickson (ENG)
September 30	Scotland	84	Romania	0	Lille	W. Barnes (ENG)
October 1	South Africa	49	Tonga	18	Marseille	L. Pearce (ENG)
October 7	Ireland	36	Scotland	14	Paris	N. Berry (AUS)
October 8	Tonga	45	Romania	24	Lille	A. Gardner (AUS)

POOL C

	P	W	D	L	TF	PF	PA	BP	Pts
Wales	**4**	**4**	**–**	**–**	**17**	**143**	**59**	**3**	**19**
Fiji	**4**	**2**	**–**	**2**	**9**	**88**	**83**	**3**	**11**
Australia	4	2	–	2	11	90	91	3	11
Portugal	4	1	1	2	8	64	103	–	6
Georgia	4	–	1	3	7	64	113	1	3

Date	Winner		Loser		Venue	Referee
September 9	Australia	35	Georgia	15	Paris	L. Pearce (ENG)
September 10	Wales	32	Fiji	26	Bordeaux	M. Carley (ENG)
September 16	Wales	28	Portugal	8	Nice	K. Dickson (ENG)
September 17	Fiji	22	Australia	15	St Etienne	A. Brace (IRE)
September 23	Georgia	18	Portugal	18	Toulouse	P. Williams (NZL)
September 24	Wales	40	Australia	6	Lyon	W. Barnes (ENG)
September 30	Fiji	17	Georgia	12	Bordeaux	K. Dickson (ENG)
October 1	Australia	34	Portugal	14	St Etienne	N. Amashukeli (GEO)
October 7	Wales	43	Georgia	19	Nantes	M. Raynal (FRA)
October 8	Portugal	24	Fiji	23	Toulouse	L. Pearce (ENG)

POOL D

	P	W	D	L	TF	PF	PA	BP	Pts
England	**4**	**4**	**–**	**–**	**17**	**150**	**39**	**2**	**18**
Argentina	**4**	**3**	**–**	**1**	**15**	**127**	**69**	**2**	**14**
Japan	4	2	–	2	12	109	107	1	9
Samoa	4	1	–	3	11	92	75	3	7
Chile	4	–	–	4	4	27	215	–	4

Date	Winner		Loser		Venue	Referee
September 9	England	27	Argentina	10	Marseille	M. Raynal (FRA)
September 10	Japan	42	Chile	12	Toulouse	N. Berry (AUS)
September 16	Samoa	43	Chile	10	Bordeaux	P. Williams (NZL)
September 17	England	34	Japan	12	Nice	N. Amashukeli (GEO)
September 22	Argentina	19	Samoa	10	St Etienne	N. Berry (AUS)
September 23	England	71	Chile	0	Lille	J. Peyper (RSA)
September 28	Japan	28	Samoa	22	Toulouse	J. Peyper (RSA)
September 30	Argentina	59	Chile	5	Nantes	P. Williams (NZL)
October 7	England	18	Samoa	17	Lille	A. Brace (IRE)
October 8	Argentina	39	Japan	27	Nantes	B. O'Keeffe (NZL)

PLAYOFFS

QUARTER-FINALS

October 14, Marseille, 5pm
Argentina 29 (Sclavi, Sanchez tries; Boffelli 2 conversions, 4 penalty goals, Sanchez penalty goal) defeated **Wales 17** (Biggar, Williams tries; Biggar 2 conversions, penalty goal)
Referee: Jaco Peyper (South Africa)

October 14, Paris, 9pm
New Zealand 28 (Fainga'anuku, Savea, Jordan tries; J. Barrett conversion, 2 penalty goals, Mo'unga conversion, penalty goal) defeated **Ireland 24** (Aki, Gibson-Park tries, penalty try; Sexton 2 conversions, penalty goal)
Referee: Wayne Barnes (England)

October 15, Marseille, 5pm
England 30 (Tuilagi, Marchant tries; Farrell conversion, 5 penalty goals, dropped goal) defeated **Fiji 24** (Mata, Ravai, Botitu tries, Kuruvoli 2 conversions, Lomani conversion, Lomani penalty goal)
Referee: Mathieu Raynal (France)

October 15, Paris, 9pm
South Africa 29 (Arendse, De Allende, Kolbe, Etzebeth tries; Libbok 2 conversions, Pollard conversion, penalty goal) defeated **France 28** (Baille 2, Mauvaka tries; Ramos 2 conversions, 3 penalty goals)
Referee: Ben O'Keeffe (New Zealand)

SEMIFINALS

October 20, Paris, 9pm
New Zealand 44 (Jordan 3, Frizell 2, J. Barrett, Smith tries; Mo'unga 3 conversions; penalty goal) defeated **Argentina 6** (Boffelli 2 penalty goals)
Referee: Angus Gardner (Australia)

October 21, Paris, 9pm
South Africa 16 (Snyman try; Pollard conversion, 2 penalty goals, Libbok penalty goal) defeated **England 15** (Farrell 4 penalty goals, dropped goal)
Referee: Ben O'Keeffe (New Zealand)

BRONZE FINAL

October 27, Paris, 9pm
England 26 (Earl, Dan tries; Farrell 2 conversions, 4 penalty goals) defeated **Argentina 23** (Cubelli, S. Carreras tries; Boffelli 2 conversions, 2 penalty goals, Sanchez penalty goal)
Referee: Nic Berry (Australia)

FINAL

October 28, Stade de France, Paris, 9pm
South Africa 12 (Pollard 4 penalty goals) defeated **New Zealand 11** (B. Barrett try; Mo'unga 2 penalty goals)
Referee: Wayne Barnes (England)

NEW ZEALAND AT RUGBY WORLD CUP 2023

ALL BLACKS APPEARANCES

	Franchise	*Date of Birth*	*Height*	*Weight*	*Tests at 1/1/24*
B.J. (Beauden) Barrett	Blues	27-05-91	1.87	91	123
J.M. (Jordie) Barrett	Hurricanes	17-02-97	1.96	101	57
S.K. (Scott) Barrett	Crusaders	20-11-93	1.97	111	69
E.J. (Ethan) Blackadder	Crusaders	22-03-95	1.91	107	10
S.J. (Sam) Cane (capt)	Chiefs	13-01-92	1.89	106	95
F.T. (Finlay) Christie	Blues	19-09-95	1.77	84	21
C.D. (Caleb) Clarke	Blues	29-03-99	1.87	103	20
D.S. (Dane) Coles	Hurricanes	10-12-86	1.84	110	90
E.L. (Ethan) de Groot	Highlanders	22-07-98	1.9	122	22
L.O.K.W.P. (Leicester) Fainga'anuku	Crusaders	11-10-99	1.88	103	7
S.M. (Shannon) Frizell	Highlanders	11-02-94	1.95	108	33
D.K. (David) Havili	Crusaders	23-12-94	1.84	95	27
R.E. (Rieko) Ioane	Blues	18-03-97	1.89	103	69
L.B. (Luke) Jacobson	Chiefs	20-04-97	1.91	107	18
W.T. (Will) Jordan	Crusaders	24-02-98	1.88	91	31
N.E. (Nepo) Laulala	Blues	06-11-91	1.84	116	53
A.R. (Anton) Lienert-Brown	Chiefs	15-04-95	1.85	96	70
T.S. (Tyrel) Lomax	Hurricanes	16-03-96	1.92	127	32
D.S. (Damian) McKenzie	Chiefs	20-04-95	1.75	82	47
R. (Richie) Mo'unga	Crusaders	25-05-94	1.76	88	56
E.R. (Emoni) Narawa	Chiefs	13-07-99	1.84	94	1
F.D. (Fletcher) Newell	Crusaders	01-03-00	1.83	119	13
D.R. (Dalton) Papali'i	Blues	11-10-97	1.9	105	32
B.A. (Brodie) Retallick	Chiefs	31-05-91	2.04	120	109
C.D. (Cam) Roigard	Hurricanes	16-11-00	1.83	88	5
A.S. (Ardie) Savea	Hurricanes	14-10-93	1.88	102	81
A.L. (Aaron) Smith	Highlanders	21-11-88	1.71	83	125
S.F.S. (Samisoni) Taukei'aho	Chiefs	08-08-97	1.83	115	30
C.J.D. (Codie) Taylor	Crusaders	31-03-91	1.83	106	85
M.E. (Mark) Telea	Blues	06-12-96	1.86	94	9
A.O.H.M. (Ofa) Tuungafasi	Blues	19-04-92	1.95	122	57
T.P.O. (Tupou) Vaa'i	Chiefs	27-01-00	1.97	118	25
S.L. (Sam) Whitelock	Crusaders	12-10-88	2.02	122	153
T.P.T. (Tamaiti) Williams	Crusaders	10-08-00	1.94	140	8

NB. Narawa was ruled out befure the first match and was replaced by Blackadder.

2023 ALL BLACKS

	France	Namibia	Italy	Uruguay	Ireland (QF)	Argentina (SF)	South Africa (F)	Totals
B. Barrett	15	15*	15	s	15	15*	15	**7**
Jordan	14	–	14	14	14	14	14*	**6**
Clarke	–	14	–	s	–	–	–	**2**
Telea	11*	–	11	–	–	11	11	**4**
Fainga'anuku	s	11	–	11	11*	–	–	**4**
R. Ioane	13	s	13	–	13	13*	13	**6**
Havili	s	12	–	–	–	–	–	**2**
Lienert-Brown	12*	13*	s	13	s	s	s	**7**
J. Barrett	–	–	12*	12*	12	12	12	**5**
McKenzie	–	10	s	15	–	s	s	**5**
Mo'unga	10	s	10*	10*	10	10	10*	**7**
Smith	9*	s	9*	–	9	9*	9*	**6**
Christie	s	–	–	s	–	s	s	**4**
Roigard	–	9*	s	9*	–	–	–	**3**
Savea	8	8*	8	–	8	8	8	**6**
Cane	–	–	s	7	7*	7*	7	**5**
Papali'i	7	7	7*	–	s	s	s	**6**
Jacobson	s	6*	–	8	–	–	–	**3**
Blackadder	–	–	–	s	–	–	–	**1**
Frizell	–	–	6*	6*	6*	6	6*	**5**
S. Barrett	5	s	5	s	5	5	5	**7**
Vaa'i	6*	s	–	5	–	–	–	**3**
Whitelock	4*	5	s	4*	s	4*	s	**7**
Retallick	s	4*	4	–	4	s	4*	**6**
Laulala	3*	3*	3*	–	–	–	s	**4**
Lomax	–	–	s	3*	3*	3*	3*	**5**
Newell	s	s	–	s*	s	s	–	**5**
Williams	–	–	s	s	s	s	s	**5**
Tuungafasi	s	1*	1*	1*	–	–	–	**4**
De Groot	1*	s	–	–	1*	1*	1*	**5**
Coles	–	s	s	–	s	–	–	**3**
Taylor	2*	–	2*	2*	2*	2*	2*	**6**
Taukei'aho	s	2*	–	s	–	s	s	**5**

INDIVIDUAL SCORING

	Tries	*Con*	*PG*	*DG*	*Points*
Mo'unga	1	19	5	–	58
McKenzie	5	13	–	–	51
Jordan	8	–	–	–	40
Fainga'anuku	5	–	–	–	25
Smith	4	–	–	–	20
Roigard	3	–	–	–	15
Savea	3	–	–	–	15
Telea	3	–	–	–	15
J. Barrett	1	1	2	–	13
Coles	2	–	–	–	10
Frizell	2	–	–	–	10
Lienert-Brown	2	–	–	–	10
Papali'i	2	–	–	–	10
B. Barrett	1	2	–	–	9
Clarke	1	–	–	–	5
De Groot	1	–	–	–	5
Havili	1	–	–	–	5
Ioane	1	–	–	–	5
Newell	1	–	–	–	5
Retallick	1	–	–	–	5
Williams	1	–	–	–	5
Totals	***49***	***35***	***7***	***0***	***336***
Opposition scored	*7**	*5*	*14*	*0*	*89*

** Includes one penalty try*

NEW ZEALAND AT RUGBY WORLD CUP 2023

TEAM RECORD 2023

Played 7 **Won 5** **Lost 2** **Points For 336** **Points Against 89**

Date	*Opponent*	*Location*	*Score*	*Tries*	*Con*	*PG*	*DG*	*Referee*
September 8	France	Paris	13–27	Telea (2)		Mo'unga		J. Peyper (RSA)
September 15	Namibia	Toulouse	71–3	Roigard (2), McKenzie (2), Fainga'anuku, Lienert-Brown, De Groot, Havili, Papali'i, Clarke, Ioane	McKenzie (7), Mo'unga			L. Pearce (ENG)
September 29	Italy	Lyon	96–17	Smith (3), Savea (2), Coles (2), Jordan (2), Telea, Retallick, Papali'i, Lienert-Brown, McKenzie	Mo'unga (9), McKenzie (4)			M. Carley (ENG)
October 05	Uruguay	Lyon	73–0	Fainga'anuku (3), McKenzie (2), Jordan (2), Newell, Williams, Mo'unga, Roigard	Mo'unga (5), McKenzie (2), B. Barrett (2)			W. Barnes (ENG)
October 14	Ireland (QF)	Paris	28–24	Fainga'anuku, Savea, Jordan	Mo'unga, J. Barrett	J. Barrett (2), Mo'unga		W. Barnes (ENG)
October 20	Argentina (SF)	Paris	44–6	Jordan (3), Frizell (2), J. Barrett, Smith	Mo'unga (3)	Mo'unga		A. Gardner (AUS)
October 28	South Africa (F)	Paris	11–12	B. Barrett		Mo'unga (2)		W. Barnes (ENG)

RUGBY WORLD CUP

NEW ZEALAND v FRANCE

Test #631 | Stade de France, Paris | September 8, 2023

France won 27–13

NEW ZEALAND		*FRANCE*
Beauden Barrett	15	Thomas Ramos
Will Jordan	14	Damian Penaud
Rieko Ioane	13	Gael Fickou
Anton Lienert-Brown	12	Yoram Moefana
Mark Telea	11	Gabin Villiere
Richie Mo'unga	10	Matthieu Jalibert
Aaron Smith	9	Antoine Dupont (capt)
Ardie Savea (capt)	8	Gregory Alldritt
Dalton Papali'i	7	Charles Ollivon
Tupou Vaa'i	6	Francois Cros
Scott Barrett	5	Thibaud Flament
Sam Whitelock	4	Cameron Woki
Nepo Laulala	3	Uini Atonio
Codie Taylor	2	Julien Marchand
Ethan de Groot	1	Reda Wardi
Samisoni Taukei'aho (rep 2, 57m)	16	Peato Mauvaka (rep 2, 12m)
Ofa Tuungafasi (rep 1, 53m)	17	Jean-Baptiste Gros (rep 1, 53m)
Fletcher Newell (rep 3, 53m)	18	Dorian Aldegheri (rep 3, 53m)
Brodie Retallick (rep 4, 69m)	19	Romain Taofifenua (rep 4, 49m)
Luke Jacobson (rep 6, 57m)	20	Paul Boudehent (rep 6, 63m)
Finlay Christie (rep 9, 63m)	21	Maxime Lucu (rep 9, 76m)
David Havili (rep 12, 63m)	22	Arthur Vincent (rep 12, 58m)
Leicester Fainga'anuku (rep 11, 72m)	23	Melvyn Jaminet (rep 15, 76m)
Telea (2)	Tries	Penaud, Jaminet
	Cons	Ramos
Mo'unga	Pens	Ramos (5)

Kickoff: 9:15pm ***Attendance:*** 80,000 ***Conditions:*** Fine, warm

Referee: Jaco Peyper (*South Africa*)
Assistant referees: Christopher Ridley (*England*), Karl Dickson (*England*)
TMO: Tom Foley (*England*)

Scoring:
First half: 1m Telea try 5–0; 5m Ramos penalty 5–3; 19m Ramos penalty 5–6; 25m Mo'unga penalty 8–6; 28m Ramos penalty 8–9
Second half: 42m Telea try 13–9; 55m Penaud try, Ramos conversion 13–16; 64m Ramos penalty 13–19; 73m Ramos penalty 13–22; 77m Jaminet try 13–27

Yellow card: Will Jordan 57m

*This was the All Blacks' first pool defeat in Rugby World Cup history.

RUGBY WORLD CUP

NEW ZEALAND v NAMIBIA

Test #632	Stade de Toulouse, Toulouse	September 15, 2023

New Zealand won 71–3

NEW ZEALAND		NAMIBIA
Beauden Barrett	15	Cliven Loubser
Caleb Clarke	14	Gerswin Mouton
Anton Lienert-Brown	13	Johan Deysel (capt)
David Havili	12	Le Roux Malan
Leicester Fainga'anuku	11	Divan Rossouw
Damian McKenzie	10	Tiaan Swanepoel
Cam Roigard	9	Damian Stevens
Ardie Savea (capt)	8	Richard Hardwick
Dalton Papali'i	7	Prince Gaoseb
Luke Jacobson	6	Wian Conradie
Sam Whitelock	5	Tjiuee Uanivi
Brodie Retallick	4	Johan Retief
Nepo Laulala	3	Aranos Coetzee
Samisoni Taukei'aho	2	Torsten van Jaarsveld
Ofa Tuungafasi (rep 6, 74m)	1	Jason Benade
Dane Coles (rep 2, 52m)	16	Louis van der Westhuizen (rep 2, 50m)
Ethan de Groot (rep 1, 48m)	17	Des Sethie (rep 1, 50m)
Fletcher Newell (rep 3, 48m)	18	Haitembu Shifuka (rep 3, 53m)
Scott Barrett (rep 4, 57m)	19	PJ van Lill (rep 6, 50m)
Tupou Vaa'i (rep 8, 64m)	20	Adriaan Booysen (rep 8, 59m)
Aaron Smith (rep 9, 67m)	21	Max Katjijeko (rep 7, 69m)
Richie Mo'unga (rep 15, 60m)	22	Jacques Theron (rep 9, 79m)
Rieko Ioane (rep 13, 69m)	23	JC Greyling (rep 12, 18m)
Roigard (2), McKenzie (2), Lienert-Brown, Clarke, Ioane, Papali'i, De Groot, Havili, Fainga'anuku	Tries	
McKenzie (7), Mo'unga	Cons	
	Pens	Swanepoel

Kickoff: 9.00pm ***Attendance:*** 31,996 ***Conditions:*** Mild, some rain

Referee: Luke Pearce (*England*)
Assistant referees: Andrew Brace (Ireland), Jordan Way (*Australia*)
TMO: Brian MacNeice (*Ireland*)

Scoring:
First half: 2m Roigard try, McKenzie conversion 7–0; 7m Roigard try 12–0; 11m Swanepoel penalty 12–3; 19m McKenzie try, conversion 19–3; 24m Fainga'anuku try 24–3; 35m Lienert-Brown try, McKenzie conversion 31–3; 38m McKenzie try, conversion 38–3
Second half: 48m De Groot try 43–3; 54m Papali'i try, McKenzie conversion 50–3; 57m Havili try, McKenzie conversion 57–3; 67m Clarke try, McKenzie conversion 64–3; 77m Ioane try, Mo'unga conversion 71–3

Yellow card: De Groot 71m (upgraded to red by bunker)

*Whitelock equalled Richie McCaw as the most capped All Black with 148 Tests.

RUGBY WORLD CUP

NEW ZEALAND v ITALY

Test #633 | OL Stadium, Lyon | September 29, 2023

New Zealand won 96–17

NEW ZEALAND		*ITALY*
Beauden Barrett	15	Tommaso Allan
Will Jordan	14	Ange Capuozzo
Rieko Ioane	13	Juan Ignacio Brex
Jordie Barrett	12	Luca Morisi
Mark Telea	11	Monty Ioane
Richie Mo'unga	10	Paolo Garbisi
Aaron Smith	9	Stephen Varney
Ardie Savea (capt)	8	Lorenzo Cannone
Dalton Papali'i	7	Michele Lamaro (capt)
Shannon Frizell	6	Sebastian Negri
Scott Barrett	5	Federico Ruzza
Brodie Retallick	4	Dino Lamb
Nepo Laulala	3	Marco Riccioni
Codie Taylor	2	Giacomo Nicotera
Ofa Tuungafasi	1	Danilo Fischetti
Dane Coles (rep 2, 57m)	16	Hame Faiva (rep 2, 50m)
Tamaiti Williams (rep 1, 49m)	17	Ivan Nemer (rep 1, 18m)
Tyrel Lomax (rep 3, 49m)	18	Simone Ferrari (rep 3, 46m)
Sam Whitelock (rep 6, 49m)	19	Niccolo Cannone (rep 4, 41m)
Sam Cane (rep 7, 57m)	20	Manuel Zuliani (rep 6, 50m)
Cam Roigard (rep 9, 49m)	21	Toa Halafihi (rep 7, 65m)
Damian McKenzie (rep 10, 64m)	22	Martin Page-Relo (rep 9, 49m)
Anton Lienert-Brown (rep 12, 64m)	23	Paolo Odogwu (rep 15, 61m)
Smith (3), Jordan (2), Savea (2), Coles (2), Lienert-Brown, Papali'i, McKenzie, Retallick, Telea	Tries	Capuozzo, M. Ioane
Mo'unga (9), McKenzie (4)	Cons	Allan, Garbisi
	Pens	Allan

Kickoff: 9.00pm | ***Attendance:*** 57,200 | ***Conditions:*** Fine

Referee: Matthew Carley (*England*)
Assistant referees: Nic Berry (*Australia*), Christopher Ridley (*England*)
TMO: Brett Cronan (*Australia*)

Scoring:
First half: 6m Jordan try, Mo'unga conversion 7–0; 9m Allan penalty 7–3; 16m Smith try, Mo'unga conversion 14–3; 18m Telea try, Mo'unga conversion 21–3; 22m Savea try, Mo'unga conversion 28–3; 26m Smith try, Mo'unga conversion 35–3; 33m Smith try, Mo'unga conversion 42–3; 44m Savea try, Mo'unga conversion 49–3
Second half: 48m Capuozzo try, Allan conversion 49–10; 50m Retallick try, Mo'unga conversion 56–10; 55m Papali'i try, Mo'unga conversion 63–10; 61m Coles try 68–10; 66m McKenzie try, conversion 75–10; 69m Jordan try, McKenzie conversion 82–10; 73m Coles try, McKenzie conversion 89–10; 75m Lienert-Brown try, McKenzie conversion 96–10; 81m M. Ioane try, Garbisi conversion 96–17

*Sam Whitelock, in his 149th Test, surpassed Richie McCaw as the most capped All Black.

RUGBY WORLD CUP

NEW ZEALAND v URUGUAY

Test #634	OL Stadium, Lyon	October 5, 2023

New Zealand won 73–0

NEW ZEALAND		*URUGUAY*
Damian McKenzie	15	Rodrigo Silva
Will Jordan	14	Gaston Mieres
Anton Lienert-Brown	13	Tomas Inciarte
Jordie Barrett	12	Andres Vilaseca (capt)
Leicester Fainga'anuku	11	Nicolas Freitas
Richie Mo'unga	10	Felipe Etcheverry
Cam Roigard	9	Santiago Arata
Luke Jacobson	8	Manuel Diana
Sam Cane (capt)	7	Lucas Bianchi
Shannon Frizell	6	Manuel Ardao
Tupou Vaa'i	5	Manuel Leindekar
Sam Whitelock	4	Ignacio Dotti
Tyrel Lomax	3	Diego Arbelo
Codie Taylor	2	German Kessler
Ofa Tuungafasi (rep 18, 74m)	1	Mateo Sanguinetti
Samisoni Taukei'aho (rep 2, 46m)	16	Guillermo Pujadas (rep 2, 63m)
Tamaiti Williams (rep 1, 46m)	17	Matias Benitez (rep 1, 64m)
Fletcher Newell (rep 3, 9m)	18	Ignacio Peculo (rep 3, 58m)
Scott Barrett (rep 4, 63m)	19	Juan Manuel Rodriguez (rep 4, 47m)
Ethan Blackadder (rep 6, 54m)	20	Santiago Civetta (rep 8, 55m)
Finlay Christie (rep 9, 53m)	21	Agustin Ormaechea (rep 9, 60m)
Beauden Barrett (rep 10, 63m)	22	Felipe Berchesi (rep 10, 50m)
Caleb Clarke (rep 12, 53m)	23	Juan Manuel Alonso (rep 14, 58m)
Fainga'anuku (3), Jordan (2), McKenzie (2), Mo'unga, Roigard, Newell, Williams	Tries	
Mo'unga (5), McKenzie (2), B. Barrett (2)	Cons	

Kickoff: 9.00pm ***Attendance:*** 57,672 ***Conditions:*** Fine

Referee: Wayne Barnes (*England*)
Assistant referees: Jordan Way (*Australia*), Matthew Carley (*England*)
TMO: Marius Jonker (*South Africa*)

Scoring:
First half: 16m McKenzie try, Mo'unga conversion 7–0; 25m Mo'unga try, conversion 14–0; 33m Jordan try, Mo'unga conversion 21–0; 38m Roigard try 26–0
Second half: 44m Newell try 31–0; 48m Fainga'anuku try, Mo'unga conversion 38–0; 52m McKenzie try, Mo'unga conversion 45–0; 64m Jordan try, McKenzie conversion 52–0; 67m Fainga'anuku try, McKenzie conversion 59–0; 72m Williams try, B. Barrett conversion 66–0; 76m Fainga'anuku try, B. Barrett conversion 73–0

*This was the first official Test match between New Zealand and Uruguay.

RUGBY WORLD CUP – QUARTER-FINAL

NEW ZEALAND v IRELAND

Test #635 | Stade de France, Paris | October 14, 2023

New Zealand won 28–24

NEW ZEALAND		*IRELAND*
Beauden Barrett	15	Hugo Keenan
Will Jordan	14	Mack Hansen
Rieko Ioane	13	Garry Ringrose
Jordie Barrett	12	Bundee Aki
Leicester Fainga'anuku	11	James Lowe
Richie Mo'unga	10	Johnny Sexton (capt)
Aaron Smith	9	Jamison Gibson-Park
Ardie Savea	8	Caelan Doris
Sam Cane (capt)	7	Josh van der Flier
Shannon Frizell	6	Peter O'Mahony
Scott Barrett	5	Iain Henderson
Brodie Retallick	4	Tadhg Beirne
Tyrel Lomax	3	Tadhg Furlong
Codie Taylor	2	Dan Sheehan
Ethan de Groot	1	Andrew Porter
Dane Coles (rep 4, 65m, temp) (rep 2, 75m)	16	Ronan Kelleher (rep 2, 64m)
Tamaiti Williams (rep 1, 64m)	17	Dave Kilcoyne (rep 1, 76m)
Fletcher Newell (rep 3, 64m)	18	Finlay Bealham (rep 3, 53m)
Sam Whitelock (rep 6, 59m)	19	Joe McCarthy (rep 5, 59m)
Dalton Papali'i (rep 7, 75m)	20	Jack Conan (rep 7, 59m)
Finlay Christie	21	Conor Murray (rep 9, 61m)
Damian McKenzie	22	Jack Crowley
Anton Lienert-Brown (rep 11, 64m)	23	Jimmy O'Brien (rep 14, 56m)
Fainga'anuku, Savea, Jordan	Tries	Aki, Gibson-Park, penalty try
Mo'unga, J. Barrett	Cons	Sexton (2)
J. Barrett (2), Mo'unga	Pens	Sexton

Kickoff: 9.00pm ***Attendance:*** 78,000 ***Conditions:*** Fine

Referee: Wanye Barnes (*England*)
Assistant referees: Matthew Carley (*England*), Christopher Ridley (*England*)
TMO: Tom Foley (*England*)

Scoring:
First half: 7m Mo'unga penalty 3–0; 14m J. Barrett penalty 6–0; 19m Fainga'anuku try, Mo'unga conversion 13–0; 22m Sexton penalty 13–3; 26m Aki try, Sexton conversion 13–10; 33m Savea try 18–10; 38m Gibson-Park try, Sexton conversion 18–17
Second half: 52m Jordan try, J. Barrett conversion 25–17; 63m: Penalty try Ireland 25–24; 69m: J. Barrett penalty 28–24

Yellow cards: Smith 36m, Taylor 63m

*This was the second straight RWC quarter-final between the two nations.
* The All Blacks ended Ireland's 17-match winning streak.

RUGBY WORLD CUP – SEMIFINAL

NEW ZEALAND v ARGENTINA

Test #636 | Stade de France, Paris | October 20, 2023

New Zealand won 44–6

NEW ZEALAND		*ARGENTINA*
Beauden Barrett	15	Juan Cruz Mallia
Will Jordan	14	Emiliano Boffelli
Rieko Ioane	13	Lucio Cinti
Jordie Barrett	12	Santiago Chocobares
Mark Telea	11	Matteo Carreras
Richie Mo'unga	10	Santiago Carreras
Aaron Smith	9	Gonzalo Bertranou
Ardie Savea	8	Facundo Isa
Sam Cane (capt)	7	Marcos Kremer
Shannon Frizell	6	Juan Martin Gonzalez
Scott Barrett	5	Tomas Lavinini
Sam Whitelock	4	Guido Petti
Tyrel Lomax	3	Francisco Gomez Kordela
Codie Taylor	2	Julian Montoya (capt)
Ethan de Groot	1	Thomas Gallo
Samisoni Taukei'aho (rep 2, 51m)	16	Agustin Creevy (rep 2, 64m)
Tamaiti Williams (rep 1, 56m)	17	Joel Sclavi (rep 1, 67m)
Fletcher Newell (rep 3, 56m)	18	Eduardo Bello (rep 3, 51m)
Brodie Retallick (rep 4, 61m)	19	Matias Alemanno (rep 5, 41m)
Dalton Papali'i (rep 7, 65m)	20	Rodrigo Bruni (rep 8, 19m, temp) (rep 8, 64m)
Finlay Christie (rep 9, 56m)	21	Lautaro Bazan Velez (rep 9, 61m)
Damian McKenzie (rep 15, 56m)	22	Nicolas Sanchez (rep 10, 66m)
Anton Lienert-Brown (rep 13, 61m)	23	Matias Moroni (rep 12, 64m)
Jordan (3), Frizell (2), J. Barrett, Smith,	Tries	
Mo'unga (3)	Cons	
Mo'unga	Pens	Boffelli (2)

Kickoff: 9.00pm ***Attendance:*** 80,000 ***Conditions:*** Showers

Referee: Angus Gardner (*Australia*)
Assistant referees: Nic Berry (*Australia*), Karl Dickson (*England*)
TMO: Ben Whitehouse (*Wales*)

Scoring:
First half: 4m Boffelli penalty 0–3; 10m Jordan try, Mo'unga conversion 7–3; 16m J. Barrett try 12–3; 34m Boffelli penalty 12–6; 37m Mo'unga penalty 15–6; 39m Frizell try 20–6
Second half: 42m Smith try, Mo'unga conversion 27–6; 48m: Frizell try, Mo'unga conversion 34–6; 62m Jordan try 39–6; 73m Jordan try 44–6

Yellow card: S. Barrett 65m

*This was the first All Blacks-Pumas meeting in a RWC semifinal.
*The All Blacks opted to play the last five minutes with 14 men.

RUGBY WORLD CUP – FINAL

NEW ZEALAND v SOUTH AFRICA

Test #637 | Stade de France, Paris | October 28, 2023

South Africa won 12–11

NEW ZEALAND		*SOUTH AFRICA*
Beauden Barrett	15	Damian Willemse
Will Jordan	14	Kurt-Lee Arendse
Rieko Ioane	13	Jesse Kriel
Jordie Barrett	12	Damian de Allende
Mark Telea	11	Cheslin Kolbe
Richie Mo'unga	10	Handre Pollard
Aaron Smith	9	Faf de Klerk
Ardie Savea	8	Duane Vermeulen
Sam Cane (capt)	7	Pieter-Steph du Toit
Shannion Frizell	6	Siya Kolisi (capt)
Scott Barrett	5	Franco Mostert
Brodie Retallick	4	Eben Etzebeth
Tyrel Lomax	3	Frans Malherbe
Codie Taylor	2	Bongi Mbonambi
Ethan de Groot	1	Steven Kitshoff
Samisoni Taukei'aho (rep 2, 66m)	16	Deon Fourie (rep 2, 4m)
Tamaiti Williams (rep 1, 66m)	17	Ox Nche (rep 1, 52m)
Nepo Laulala (rep 3, 66m)	18	Trevor Nyakane (rep 3, 66m)
Sam Whitelock (rep 6, 55m)	19	Jean Kleyn (rep 4, 58m)
Dalton Papali'i (rep 4, 71m)	20	RG Snyman (rep 5, 52m)
Finlay Christie (rep 9, 66m)	21	Kwagga Smith (rep 8, 58m)
Damian McKenzie (rep 10, 75m)	22	Jasper Wiese (rep 6, 73m)
Anton Lienert-Brown (rep 14, 71m)	23	Willie le Roux (rep 15, 66m)
B. Barrett	Tries	
	Cons	
Mo'unga (2)	Pens	Pollard (4)

Kickoff: 9.00pm ***Attendance:*** 80,000 ***Conditions:*** Wet

Referee: Wayne Barnes (*England*)
Assistant referees: Matthew Carley (*England*), Karl Dickson (*England*)
TMO: Tom Foley (*England*)

Scoring:
First half: 2m Pollard penalty 0–3; 12m Pollard penalty 0–6; 16m Mo'unga penalty 3–6; 19m Pollard penalty 3–9; 34m Pollard penalty 3–12; 38m Mo'unga penalty 6–12
Second half: 58m B. Barrett try 11–12

Yellow card: Frizell 2m, Cane 28m (upgraded to red), Kolisi 45m, Kolbe 73m

* This was the second RWC final between these two nations after the 1995 event.
* South Africa won a record fourth RWC title and second straight Webb Ellis Cup.

NEW ZEALAND UNDER 20

New Zealand failed to make the semifinals at the World Rugby Under 20 Championship held in South Africa. France was clearly the dominant team, being undefeated while scoring an average 51 points per game. In the semifinals, Ireland defeated South Africa 31–12 and France defeated England 52–31. In the final, France defeated Ireland 50–14.

New Zealand's failure was not helped by a lack of discipline, resulting in a number of cards being issued, mainly for careless tackling. Against Wales (Robinson yellow), France (Springer yellow), Australia (Allen red in the 13th minute, Wrampling-Alec and Taele yellow), Georgia (Ake and Wrampling-Alec yellow). Against Australia, in a semifinal for fifth place, New Zealand had only 13 minutes with 15 players before Allen was red-carded and for the remainder of the game the side was twice reduced to 13 players due to players spending 10 minutes in the bin.

Prior to the tournament an enlarged squad played two unofficial games against Australia.

	Union	*Date of Birth*	*Height*	*Weight*
B.J. (Ben) Ake	Auckland	24-02-03	1.91	104
T.G. (Tom) Allen	Hawke's Bay	23-07-04	1.97	114
V. (Vernon) Bason	Manawatu	10-10-04	1.80	106
T.M. (Tahlor) Cahill	Canterbury	08-06-03	1.98	113
C.P.J. (Che) Clark	Auckland	22-04-03	1.94	101
H.J. (Hunter) Fahey	Southland	14-05-03	1.90	125
A.J. (Ajay) Faleafaga	Otago	02-02-03	1.91	89
C.G. (Cooper) Flanders	Hawke's Bay	31-08-03	1.87	104
H.G.R. (Harry) Godfrey	Hawke's Bay	03-01-03	1.78	86
L.D. (Leo) Gordon	Auckland	22-04-03	1.84	101
S.J.T. (Sam) Hainsworth-Fa'aofo	Auckland	20-04-03	1.84	100
M.H. (Malakai) Hala	Manawatu	07-01-03	1.84	125
N.R.F. (Noah) Hotham (capt)	Tasman	23-05-03	1.80	96
I.J. (Isaac) Hutchinson	Canterbury	02-03-04	1.80	93
T. (Taha) Kemara	Waikato	17-04-03	1.79	86
P.R.J. (Peter) Lakai	Wellington	04-03-03	1.85	110
S.G. (Siale) Lauaki	Wellington	30-05-03	1.90	125
W.P. (Will) Martin	Waikato	09-12-04	1.89	115
H.F. (Hunter) Morrison	Hawke's Bay	11-01-03	1.97	114
G.R. (Gabe) Robinson	Waikato	22-08-03	1.84	116
M.R. (Macca) Springer	Tasman	29-03-03	1.90	100
W.R. (Will) Stodart	Otago	03-10-03	1.95	115
X.A. (Xavi) Taele	Auckland	19-12-04	1.82	90
C.L. (Caleb) Tangitau	Auckland	19-03-03	1.87	98
J.J.K. (Jack) Taylor	Southland	25-06-03	1.80	106
G.A.M. (Aki) Tuivailala	Waikato	24-09-04	1.86	98
R. (Raymond) Tuputupu	Manawatu	11-04-03	1.83	106
C.M. (Codemeru) Vai	Bay of Plenty	25-02-04	1.88	84
J.K. (Jordi) Viljoen	Manawatu	14-10-03	1.69	76
R.O (Riley) Williams	Auckland	08-01-04	1.78	86
M.I.R.T. (Malachi) Wrampling-Alec	Waikato	15-04-04	1.92	112

Cahill, Godfrey, Hotham, Lakai, Lauaki, Springer and Tuputupu were members of the 2022 squad. Toby Bell (Canterbury), Maliu Niuafe (Auckland), Cody Nordstrom (Waikato), Fiti Sa (Taranaki) and Payton Spencer (Auckland) were unavailable for selection due to injury.
Original selection Bradley Crichton (Wellington) did not travel.
Martin was injured and returned home. He was replaced by Fahey.

Head coach: Clark Laidlaw
Assistant coaches: Marty Bourke (backs), Wesley Clarke (forwards), Craig Dunlea (scrum)
Campaign manager: Matt Sexton
Team manager: Ross Everiss
Physio: Richie Marsden
Doctor: Lincoln Wharetohunga
S&C coach: Tim Hurst
Analyst: Luca Roden
Assistant physio: James Fleming (South Africa based)

Late in May two unofficial (not first-class) 'tests' were played against Australia Under 20 at Wellington to assist in the final selection for the Under 20 Championship in South Africa. In each game both sides used 25 players. Results were:

May 29, at NZ Campus of Innovation and Sport, Upper Hutt. Lost 26–34.
Wrampling-Alec, Hutchinson, Vai, Hurley tries; Williams 3 conversions. Referee: Reuben Keane (Australia).

June 3, at Sky Stadium, Wellington. Won 19–18.
Tangitau (2), Springer tries; Kemara 2 conversions. Referee: Angus Mabey.

Players who took part in one, or both, games but did not visit South Africa were: Finn Hurley (Otago), Maliu Niuafe (Auckland), Dominic Ropeti (Wellington), Nic Shearer (Canterbury), Payton Spencer (Auckland), Essendon Tuitupou (Auckland) and Rory Woods (Northland).

Of the squad that went to South Africa, Fahey, Gordon, Lauaki, Martin, Stodart and Viljoen did not appear against Australia.

INDIVIDUAL SCORING

	Tries	Con	PG	DG	Points
Kemara	2	12	2	1	43
Springer	5	–	–	–	25
Tangitau	5	–	–	–	25
penalty tries	2	–	–	–	14
Godfrey	–	4	1	–	11
Clark	2	–	–	–	10
Hainsworth-Fa'aofo	2	–	–	–	10
Lakai	2	–	–	–	10
Stodart	2	–	–	–	10
Wrampling-Alec	2	–	–	–	10
Flanders	1	–	–	–	5
Hotham	1	–	–	–	5
Hutchinson	1	–	–	–	5
Taylor	1	–	–	–	5
Totals	***28****	***16***	***3***	***1***	***188***
Opposition scored	*23*	*16*	*1*	*0*	*150*

NEW ZEALAND UNDER 20

	Wales	France	Japan	Australia	Georgia	TOTALS
Godfrey	15	15	15	15	15	**5**
Tangitau	14*	14	–	14*	14	**4**
Vai	s	s	s	s	s	**5**
Hutchinson	–	–	14*	–	–	**1**
Springer	11	11	11	11	11	**5**
Tuivailala	13	13	–	13	13*	**4**
Taele	–	–	13*	s	s	**3**
Faleafaga	12*	s	12*	–	12*	**4**
Gordon	s	12*	s	12*	–	**4**
Kemara	10	10*	10	10	10	**5**
Hotham	9*	9*	9	9*	9*	**5**
Viljoen	s	s	–	s	s	**4**
Williams	–	–	s	–	–	**1**
Lakai	8	7	–	8	8*	**4**
Wrampling-Alec	s	8	8	6*	s	**5**
Hainsworth-Fa'aofo	7*	–	7	7*	–	**3**
Flanders	–	s	s	–	7	**3**
Clark	6	6	–	s	s	**4**
Stodart	5	s	6	5	6	**5**
Allen	s	5*	s	4	–	**4**
Morrison	–	–	5*	–	5*	**2**
Cahill	4*	4*	4*	s	4	**5**
Lauaki	3*	3*	s	3*	3*	**5**
Robinson	s	s	3*	s	–	**4**
Ake	1*	1*	1*	–	1*	**4**
Hala	s	s	–	1*	s	**4**
Martin	–	–	s	–	–	**1**
Fahey	–	–	–	s	s	**2**
Taylor	2*	2*	2*	2*	2*	**5**
Tuputupu	s	s	–	–	s	**3**
Bason	–	–	s	s	–	**2**

NEW ZEALAND U20 TEAM RECORD 2023

Played 5 Won 3 Lost 2 Points for 175 Points against 26

Date	*Opponent*	*Location*	*Score*	*Tries*	*Con*	*PG*	*DG*	*Referee*
June 24	Wales	Paarl	27–26	Tangitau, Springer, Hainsworth-Fa'aofo, Clark	Kemara (2)	Godfrey		A. Woodthorpe (ENG)
June 29	France	Paarl	14–35	penalty try, Lakai	Kemara			D. Schneider (ARG)
July 4	Japan	Stellenbosch	62–19	Springer (3), Kemara (2), Hutchinson, Hainsworth-Fa'aofo, Wrampling-Alec, Flanders, Stodart	Godfrey (4), Kemara (2)			R. Keane (AUS)
July 9	Australia (semifinal for 5th)	Cape Town	35–44	Tangitau (2), Springer, Wrampling-Alec, Taylor	Kemara (2)	Kemara	Kemara	T. Namekawa (JPN)
July 14	Georgia(playoff for 7th place)	Stellenbosch	50–26	Tangitau (2), Stodart, Lakai, Hotham, Clark, penalty try	Kemara (5)	Kemara		A. Woodthorp (ENG)

Venues: Paarl Gimnasium, Paarl; Danie Craven Stadium, Stellenbosch; Athlone Sports Stadium, Cape Town.

ALL BLACKS XV

The All Blacks XV undertook a two-match tour of Japan in July.

	Super Rugby Club/Union	*Date of Birth*	*Height*	*Weight*
N.S. (Naitoa) Ah Kuoi	Chiefs / Bay of Plenty	07/10/99	1.96	116
J.M.L. (Jermaine) Ainsley	Highlanders / Otago	08/08/95	1.81	122
Asafo Aumua	Hurricanes / Wellington	05/05/97	1.77	108
G.D.E. (George) Bell	Crusaders / Canterbury	29/01/02	1.83	107
B.D. (Brett) Cameron	Hurricanes / Manawatu	04/10/96	1.71	83
G.E. (George) Dyer	Chiefs / Waikato	22/10/99	1.89	124
F.M.N. (Folau) Fakatava	Highlanders / Hawke's Bay	16/12/99	1.77	80
S.J. (Sam) Gilbert	Highlanders / Otago	23/01/99	1.89	98
E.J. (Jack) Goodhue	Crusaders / Northland	13/06/95	1.88	100
W.K. (Billy) Harmon (co-capt)	Highlanders / Canterbury	23/12/94	1.87	104
A.L. (Akira) Ioane	Blues / Auckland	16/06/95	1.94	118
O.G.J.T. (Oli) Jager	Crusaders / Canterbury	05/07/95	1.92	127
D.P.A. (Du Plessis) Kirifi	Hurricanes / Wellington	03/03/97	1.80	101
AJ (Alexander) Lam	Blues / Auckland	29/07/98	1.92	105
C.J. (Christian) Lio-Willie	Crusaders / Otago	26/08/98	1.87	105
Ruben Love	Hurricanes / Wellington	28/04/01	1.83	90
E.W.P.S. (Etene) Nanai-Seturo	Chiefs / Counties Manukau	20/08/99	1.83	92
A.P. (Alex) Nankivell	Chiefs / Tasman	25/10/96	1.88	98
J.M. (Jona) Nareki	Highlanders / Otago	27/12/97	1.75	83
O.M. (Ollie) Norris	Chiefs / Waikato	11/12/99	1.95	126
X.S. (Xavier) Numia	Hurricanes / Wellington	29/11/98	1.89	111
Stephen Perofeta	Blues / Taranaki	12/03/97	1.81	85
B.D. (Billy) Proctor	Hurricanes / Wellington	14/05/99	1.87	96
P.G. (Pouri) Rakete-Stones	Hurricanes / Hawke's Bay	17/06/97	1.83	118
J.R. (Ricky) Riccitelli	Blues / Taranaki	03/02/95	1.78	110
Aidan Ross	Chiefs / Bay of Plenty	25/10/95	1.89	111
P.G.N. (Pita Gus) Sowakula	Chiefs / Taranaki	26/10/94	1.90	117
Q.J. (Quinten) Strange	Crusaders / Tasman	21/08/96	1.99	114
C.J.T.S. (Cameron) Suafoa	Blues / North Harbour	23/04/98	1.96	116
B.W.M. (Bailyn) Sullivan	Hurricanes / Waikato	03/09/98	1.88	98
T.T.W.J. (Tyrone) Thompson	Chiefs / Hawke's Bay	28/05/00	1.86	111
I.E.T. (Isaia) Walker-Leawere	Hurricanes / Hawke's Bay	16/04/97	1.97	122
B.M. (Brad) Weber (co-capt)	Chiefs / Hawke's Bay	17/01/91	1.72	75

Selectors: Ian Foster, Jason Ryan, Joe Schmidt
Head coach: Leon MacDonald (Blues)
Assistant coaches: Scott Hansen (Crusaders), Clayton McMillan (Chiefs)

Before assembly, original selections Tevita Mafileo (Hurricanes/North Harbour) and Aidan Ross withdrew. Mafileo went to the All Blacks squad as injury cover. They were replaced by Ollie Norris and Pouri Rakete-Stones. George Bell, George Dyer and Aidan Ross joined the squad after the first match as replacements for Asafo Aumua, Oli Jager and Isaia Walker-Leawere who had all returned home without playing a match.

ALL BLACKS XV 2023

Played 2 Won 2 Lost 0 Points for 79 Points against 33

Date	*Opponent*	*Location*	*Score*	*Tries*	*Con*	*PG*	*DG*	*Referee*
July 8	Japan XV	Tokyo	38–6	Perofeta, Goodhue, Nanai-Seturo, Nankivell, Fakatava	Perofeta, Cameron	Perofeta (3)		Mike Adamson (Scotland)
July 15	Japan	Kumamoto	41–27	Proctor (4), Perofeta, Lam	Perofeta (4)	Perofeta		Tual Trainini (France)

Japan held a world ranking of 10th at the time of the match

ALL BLACKS XV 2023

	Japan XV	Japan	**Totals**
Love	15	15*	**2**
Sullivan	14	–	**1**
Nanai-Seturo	11	–	**1**
Lam	–	14	**1**
Nareki	–	11	**1**
Nankivell	13	s	**2**
Proctor	–	13	**1**
Goodhue	12*	12*	**2**
Gilbert	s	s	**2**
Perofeta	10*	10	**2**
Cameron	s	–	**1**
Weber	9*	9*	**2**
Fakatava	s	s	**2**
Lio-Willie	8*	s	**2**
Harmon	s	7	**2**
Sowakula	–	8*	**1**
Kirifi	7*	–	**1**
Suafoa	s	s	**2**
Ioane	6	6	**2**
Strange	5	5	**2**
Ah Kuoi	4	4*	**2**
Ainsley	3*	3*	**2**
Numua	1*	–	**1**
Norris	s	s	**2**
Rakete-Stones	s	–	**1**
Ross	–	1*	**1**
Dyer	–	s	**1**
Riccitelli	2*	–	**1**
Thompson	s	s	**2**
Bell	–	2*	**1**

**Replaced during match*

INDIVIDUAL SCORING

	Tries	*Con*	*PG*	*DG*	*Points*
Perofeta	2	5	4	–	32
Proctor	4	–	–	–	20
Goodhue	1	–	–	–	5
Nanai-Seturo	1	–	–	–	5
Nankivell	1	–	–	–	5
Fakatava	1	–	–	–	5
Lam	1	–	–	–	5
Cameron	–	1	–	–	2
Totals	***11***	***6***	***4***	***–***	***79***
Opposition scored	*3*	*3*	*4*	*–*	*33*

UK BARBARIANS

The club played a match against Wales that included appearances by Asafo Aumua, Joe Moody and Shaun Stevenson. Their involvement gained them each a New Zealand first-class appearance. All Blacks coach elect Scott Robertson co-coached the Barbarians along with Australian Eddie Jones. Wales did not award caps for the match. Crowd 53,271.

v WALES

Principality Stadium, Cardiff — **November 4, 2023**

UK Barbarians lost 49–26

UK BARBARIANS

15	Ilasia Droasese (*Fiji*)
14	**Shaun Stevenson** (*New Zealand*)
13	Len Ikitau (*Australia*)
12	Izaia Perese (*Australia*)
11	Selestino Ravutaumada (*Fiji*)
10	Nicolas Sanchez (*Argentina*)
9	Simione Kuruvoli (*Fiji*)
8	Rob Valetini (*Australia*)
7	Michael Hooper (*Australia*)
6	Justin Tipuric (*Wales*)
5	Alun Wyn Jones (*capt.*) (*Wales*)
4	Rob Leota (*Australia*)
3	Taniela Tupou (rep 18, 62m)(*Australia*)
2	Tevita Ikanivere (rep 7, 67-74m)(*Fiji*)
1	**Joe Moody** (*New Zealand*)
16	**Asafo Aumua (rep 2, h/t)** (*New Zealand*)
17	Angus Bell (rep 1, h/t) (*Australia*)
18	Peni Ravai (rep 3, 32-62m) (*Fiji*)
19	Aaron Shingler (rep 8, 60m) (*Wales*)
20	Tom Hooper (rep 4, 50m) (*Australia*)
21	Lautaro Bazan Velez (rep 9, 65m) (*Argentina*)
22	Ben Donaldson (rep 10, 65m) (*Australia*)
23	Andrew Kellaway (rep 15, 60m) (*Australia*)
Tries	Kuruvoli (2), Jones, T. Hooper
Cons	Sanchez (2), Donaldson

Referee: Andrea Piardi (Italy)

NB. Aumua received a yellow card for a late tackle after 61 minutes. Ikanivere returned to the field after 67 minutes replacing M. Hooper until Aumua's time in the sin bin was completed.

NEW ZEALAND UNIVERSITIES

The New Zealand Universities men's side made its first tour of Japan since 2018, playing two matches. The first, against Hanshin Barbarians, was lost 52–38 on May 24 in Osaka, in a non first-class match. The team then faced Japan Under 20s in Tokyo, a first-class fixture, with details below.

JAPAN UNDER 20s v NZ UNIVERSITIES

Prince Chichibu Memorial Stadium, Tokyo **May 27, 2023**

Japan Under 20s won 52–46

NZ UNIVERSITIES

15	Jermaine Pepe (Otago University)
14	Cooper Roberts (Canterbury University)
13	Noah Foster (Auckland University)
12	Levi Reweti (Waikato University)
11	Jeremiah Asi (Otago University)
10	Blair Murray (Canterbury University)
9	Brian Lealiifano (Lincoln University)
8	Julian Goerke (Massey University)
7	Aaron Withy (Otago University)
6	Xavier Saifoloi (Waikato University)
5	Master Aho (Otago University)
4	Charlie Murray (Lincoln University)
3	Sam Lester (Auckland University)
2	Te Ariki Te Puni (Auckland University)
1	Nick Grogan (Massey University, capt)
16	Harrison Dakin (Lincoln University) (rep 2, 55m)
17	Thomas Polo (Canterbury University) (rep 3, 60m)
18	Samson Koneferenisi (Old Boys-University) rep 1,50m)
19	Jonathan Lee (Lincoln University) (rep 6, 55m)
20	Joshua Retter (Auckland University) (rep 7, 55m)
21	Ngakete George (Auckland University) (rep 9, 60m)
22	Te Wehi Wright (Old Boys-University) (rep 15, 60m)
23	Isaac Leota (Canterbury University) (rep 13, 50m)
Tries	Asi (3), Te Puni (2), Dakin, Aho
Cons	Murray (4)
PG	Murray

Manager: Braeden Saul
Head coach: Jason McLean
Assistant coach: Tyrone Elkington-MacDonald
Physio: Harley Matthews
Doctor: Jamie Jolly

NB. Other playing squad members were Ty Poe (Old Boys-University, Victoria) and Mason Allison (Lincoln University).

NEW ZEALAND HEARTLAND

The New Zealand Heartland team played two matches in November, against a Canterbury Development team and New Zealand Barbarians. Only the fixture against New Zealand Barbarians carries first-class status.

v NZ BARBARIANS

Whitestone Contracting Stadium, Oamaru **November 4, 2023**

NZ Heartland lost 26-49

NZ HEARTLAND

15	Renata Roberts-Te Nana (*Ngati Porou East Coast*)
14	Peceli Malanicagi (*Whanganui*)
13	Shayne Anderson (*West Coast*)
12	Paula Fifita (*South Canterbury*)
11	Fletcher Morgan (*Thames Valley*)
10	Sam Briggs (*South Canterbury*)
9	Willie Wright (capt.) (*South Canterbury*)
8	Douglas Horrocks (*Whanganui*)
7	Finlay Joyce (*South Canterbury*)
6	Kaleb Foote (*King Country*)
5	Peter-Travis Hay-Horton (*Whanganui*)
4	Joshua Clark (*North Otago*)
3	Tyler Kearns (*West Coast*)
2	Connor Anderson (*South Canterbury*)
1	Tokoma'ata Fakatava (*South Canterbury*)
16	Leopino Maupese (rep 2, 45m) (*Buller*)
17	Vaka Taelega (rep 1, 45m) (*South Canterbury*)
18	Adam Williamson (rep 3, 45m) (*Mid Canterbury*)
19	Keanu Taumata (rep 7, 55m) (*Poverty Bay*)
20	Loni Toumohunui (rep 5, 55m) (*South Canterbury*)
21	Uluifalefesi Fakatoufifita (rep 8, 57m) (*North Otago*)
22	Leroy Neels (rep 12, 60m) (*Thames Valley*)
23	Dane Whale (rep 14, h/t) (*Whanganui*)
Tries	Neels (2), Roberts-Te Nana, Morgan
Cons	Briggs (3)

Referee: Fraser Hannon

Original selection Saimone Samate (North Otago) played only against Canterbury Development. Lindsay Horrocks (Whanganui) withdrew from the squad after original selection and replaced by Leroy Neels. Loni Toumohunui was added to the squad as injury cover.

NZ Heartland management
Head Coach: Nigel Walsh (*South Canterbury*)
Assistant Coach: Miah Nikora (*Poverty Bay*)
Manager: Thomas Zimmerman (*Horowhenua Kapiti*)
Observer Coach: Jason Forrest (*North Otago*)
Team Doctor: Coll Campbell (*Poverty Bay*)
Team Physio: Geoff Thompson (*South Canterbury*)
Team Trainer: Slade King (*Rotorua*)

In the non-first-class match v Canterbury Development, played at Methven, November 1, the New Zealand Heartland team won 43–17. The team was (15–1): Roberts-Te Nana (Samate), Malanicagi, Anderson, Fifita (Whale), Samate (Morgan), Briggs, Wright (capt.) (Neels), Fakatoufifita (Taumata), Joyce (Toumohunui), Horrocks, Hay-Horton, Foote, Kearns (Williamson), Anderson (Maupese), Fakatava (Taelega).

Tries: Roberts-Te Nana (2), Williamson (2), Anderson, Malanicagi, Morgan
Conversions: Briggs (4)
Referee: Jackson Henshaw
NZ Heartland won 43-17.

NEW ZEALAND BARBARIANS

The club played one first-class match in 2023, against the NZ Heartland team.

v NZ HEARTLAND

Whitestone Contracting Stadium, Oamaru **November 4, 2023**

NZ Barbarians won 49–26

NZ BARBARIANS

15 Rory Van Vugt (*Southland*)
14 Joshua Gray (*Counties Manukau*)
13 Amanaki Savieti (*Manukau Rovers RFC*)
12 Joe Cooke (*Dunedin RFC*)
11 Jeremiah Asi (*Otago*)
10 Byron Smith (*Grammar TEC RFC*)
9 Kieran McClea (*Otago*)
8 George Risale (*Tawa RFC*)
7 Harry Taylor (*Otago*)
6 Lui Naeata (*Toyota Industries, Japan*)
5 Antonio Shalfoon (*Tasman*)
4 Alefosio Aho (*Otago University RFC*)
3 Mosese Mafi (*Thames Valley*)
2 Quentin MacDonald (*capt.*) (*Tasman*)
1 Joseph Walsh (*Southland*)

16 Monu Moli (rep 2, 45m) (*Tasman*)
17 Jack Sexton (rep 1, 45m) (*Lincoln University RFC/Southland-loan*)
18 Quinn Harrison-Jones (rep 3, 47m) (*Southland*)
19 Lucas Casey (rep 7, 47m) (*Kaikorai RFC/North Otago-loan*)
20 Cameron Rowland (rep 4, 53m) (*Valley RFC*)
21 Jahvis Wallace (rep 9, 49m) (*Southland*)
22 Coby Miln (rep 10, 45m) (*Randwick RFC, Sydney*)
23 Mefi Tupoi (rep 13, 49m) (*Kaikorai RFC*)

Tries: Savieti (2), Mafi, Naeata, Cooke, Casey, Van Vugt
Conv: Smith (5), Miln (2)

Referee: Fraser Hannon

NZ Barbarians management
Coaches: Dave Dillon (*Highlanders*), Ryan Bambry (*Otago*), Carl Hoeft (*Hamilton*)
Manager: Richard Smith (*Southland*)
Team Physio: Alex Gough (*Dunedin*)
Strength and Conditioning: Luke Bradley (*Gisborne*), Cam McClea (*Highlanders*)
Team Analyst: Regan Bennett (*Southland*)

DHL SUPER RUGBY PACIFIC 2023

The second edition of Super Rugby Pacific was, happily, largely unaffected by Covid-19 and it ended in yet another Crusaders' championship, their 14th in 28 seasons.

It seemed like the competition was copping it from all sides during the season and when Sir Wayne Smith admitted, in a throwaway line that went viral, that he had switched channels when the Force and Highlanders were playing out a snore-fest in Perth, there were some alarm bells ringing.

But mostly the rugby held its quality, despite the usual plethora of lineout-driven tries, and this was helped by some law variations, including some that limited the power of the TMO and allowed matches to play out faster. There were fewer red cards dished out for accidental head clashes, which was welcome. Crowds were an issue across the board, but TV viewership remained sound.

There seemed to be growing competitiveness amongst the Australian 'conference' teams, and there were 13 victories from those sides, including the Fijian Drua, over their Kiwi counterparts, up one from 2022, and four teams making the playoffs, again up one from 2022.

The Drua were the heartwarming success of the season, winning six games and defeating the Crusaders and Hurricanes on home soil. They engendered unmatched atmosphere at their home fixtures and proved hellishly tough to beat in Fiji.

The Crusaders' victory in the final might just top the lot of the seven titles from the Scott Robertson era, given their horrendous injury toll. The Chiefs had a tremendous season and played some high calibre rugby.

Moana Pasifika needs more support to be more competitive, though there are signs of potential in the franchise. The Highlanders were largely disappointing and missed the playoffs.

There will be many changes to Super Rugby Pacific in 2024, from coaching staff to top players, many of whom are departing, so we await a fresh-look to a competition that still holds vital importance, commercially and rugby-wise, to New Zealand, Australia and the Pacific nations.

ALMANACK SUPER RUGBY PACIFIC NEW ZEALAND XV

Shaun Stevenson
Chiefs

Mark Telea
Blues

Rieko Ioane
Blues

Leicester Fainga'anuku
Crusaders

David Havili
Crusaders

Damian McKenzie
Chiefs

Cam Roigard
Hurricanes

Ardie Savea
Hurricanes

Sam Cane
Chiefs

Scott Barrett
Crusaders

Brodie Retallick
Chiefs

Samipeni Finau
Chiefs

Tamaiti Williams
Crusaders

Codie Taylor
Crusaders

Ethan de Groot
Highlanders

Reserves –

Samisoni Taukei'aho (Chiefs), Aidan Ross (Chiefs), Jermaine Ainsley (Highlanders), Tupou Vaa'i (Chiefs), Luke Jacobson (Chiefs), Brad Weber (Chiefs), Richie Mo'unga (Crusaders), Emoni Narawa (Chiefs)

PREVIOUS WINNERS

1996	Auckland Blues	**2011**	Reds
1997	Auckland Blues	**2012**	Chiefs
1998	Crusaders	**2013**	Chiefs
1999	Crusaders	**2014**	Waratahs
2000	Crusaders	**2015**	Highlanders
2001	Brumbies	**2016**	Hurricanes
2002	Crusaders	**2017**	Crusaders
2003	Blues	**2018**	Crusaders
2004	Brumbies	**2019**	Crusaders
2005	Crusaders	**2020**	Crusaders (Super Rugby Aotearoa)
2006	Crusaders	**2021**	Crusaders (Super Rugby Aotearoa)
2007	Bulls	**2021**	Blues (Super Rugby Trans-Tasman)
2008	Crusaders	**2022**	Crusaders (Super Rugby Pacific)
2009	Bulls	**2023**	Crusaders (Super Rugby Pacific)
2010	Bulls		

NB. The Brumbies (2020) and Reds (2021) were winners of the Super Rugby AU competition.

SUPER RUGBY PACIFIC FINAL STANDINGS

Team	P	W	D	L	F	A	TF	TA	+/-	BP	Pts
Chiefs	14	13	–	1	487	261	65	38	226	7	59
Crusaders	14	10	–	4	457	278	65	36	179	8	48
Blues	14	10	–	4	446	292	60	39	154	6	46
Brumbies	14	10	–	4	474	393	66	52	81	6	46
Hurricanes	14	9	–	5	480	338	70	47	142	5	41
Waratahs	14	6	–	8	387	408	54	53	-21	7	31
Fijian Drua	14	6	–	8	370	492	54	73	-122	2	26
Reds	14	5	–	9	391	451	54	61	-60	4	24
Highlanders	14	5	–	9	362	459	48	60	-97	4	24
Force	14	5	–	9	346	494	46	70	-148	2	22
Rebels	14	4	–	10	406	484	57	68	-78	5	21
Moana Pasifika	14	1	–	13	354	610	50	92	-256	4	8
TOTALS	**84**	**84**	**–**	**84**	**4960**	**4960**	**689**	**689**			

**Leading the individual points tally was Damian McKenzie (Chiefs) with 191, and leading the individual tries tally was Leicester Fainga'anuku (Crusaders) with 13.*

F — *Points for*
A — *Points against*
TF — *Tries for*
TA — *Tries against*
+/- — *Points differential*
BP — *Bonus points*
Pts — *Competition points*

Points: 4 for a win
2 for a draw
Bonus points were for: a loss by seven points or fewer (1) and/or for scoring three tries more than opponent (1)

SUPER RUGBY PACIFIC RESULTS

	Winning team				Venue
February					
24	Chiefs	31	Crusaders	10	Christchurch
24	Brumbies	31	Waratahs	25	Sydney
25	Fijian Drua	36	Moana Pasifika	34	Auckland
25	Blues	60	Highlanders	20	Dunedin
25	Hurricanes	47	Reds	13	Townsville
25	Force	34	Rebels	27	Perth
March					
3	Crusaders	52	Highlanders	15	Melbourne
3	Hurricanes	39	Rebels	33	Melbourne
4	Chiefs	52	Moana Pasifika	29	Melbourne
4	Waratahs	46	Fijian Drua	17	Melbourne
5	Brumbies	25	Blues	20	Melbourne
5	Reds	71	Force	20	Melbourne
10	Chiefs	28	Highlanders	7	Hamilton
10	Rebels	34	Waratahs	27	Melbourne
11	Fijian Drua	25	Crusaders	24	Lautoka
11	Blues	25	Hurricanes	19	Wellington
11	Brumbies	23	Reds	17	Canberra
11	Force	21	Moana Pasifika	18	Perth
17	Hurricanes	34	Waratahs	17	Wellington
18	Chiefs	44	Rebels	25	Hamilton
18	Crusaders	34	Blues	28	Auckland
18	Brumbies	62	Moana Pasifika	36	Canberra
19	Highlanders	43	Force	35	Invercargill
19	Reds	27	Fijian Drua	24	Brisbane
24	Crusaders	35	Brumbies	17	Christchurch
24	Chiefs	24	Waratahs	14	Sydney
25	Highlanders	57	Fijian Drua	24	Dunedin
25	Hurricanes	59	Moana Pasifika	0	Auckland
25	Rebels	40	Reds	34	Melbourne
26	Blues	30	Force	17	Auckland
31	Highlanders	45	Moana Pasifika	17	Dunedin
31	Crusaders	25	Reds	12	Brisbane

	Winning team				Venue
April					
1	Fijian Drua	38	Rebels	28	Suva
1	Chiefs	20	Blues	13	Hamilton
1	Brumbies	40	Waratahs	36	Canberra
2	Hurricanes	45	Force	42	Palmerston North
7	Crusaders	38	Moana Pasifika	21	Christchurch
7	Brumbies	52	Reds	24	Brisbane
8	Hurricanes	29	Highlanders	14	Dunedin
8	Blues	54	Rebels	17	Melbourne
14	Reds	40	Moana Pasifika	28	Apia
14	Brumbies	43	Fijian Drua	28	Canberra
15	Chiefs	33	Hurricanes	17	Wellington
15	Waratahs	36	Force	16	Sydney
21	Chiefs	50	Fijian Drua	17	Hamilton
21	Crusaders	43	Rebels	27	Melbourne
22	Blues	55	Waratahs	21	Auckland
22	Force	30	Highlanders	17	Perth
28	Hurricanes	32	Brumbies	27	Wellington
28	Waratahs	21	Highlanders	20	Sydney
29	Blues	30	Fijian Drua	14	Lautoka
29	Rebels	43	Moana Pasifika	33	Auckland
29	Chiefs	34	Crusaders	24	Hamilton
29	Reds	31	Force	17	Brisbane
May					
5	Chiefs	52	Highlanders	28	Dunedin
6	Fijian Drua	27	Hurricanes	24	Suva
6	Crusaders	48	Force	13	Christchurch
6	Blues	31	Moana Pasifika	30	Auckland
6	Waratahs	32	Reds	24	Townsville
7	Brumbies	33	Rebels	26	Melbourne
12	Reds	25	Chiefs	22	New Plymouth
12	Force	34	Fijian Drua	14	Perth
13	Hurricanes	71	Moana Pasifika	22	Wellington
13	Crusaders	15	Blues	3	Christchurch

	Winning team				*Venue*
13	Waratahs	38	Rebels	20	Sydney
14	Brumbies	48	Highlanders	32	Canberra
19	Crusaders	41	Moana Pasifika	7	Auckland
19	Blues	45	Reds	26	Brisbane
20	Highlanders	20	Rebels	17	Dunedin
20	Chiefs	23	Hurricanes	12	Hamilton
20	Waratahs	32	Fijian Drua	18	Sydney
20	Force	24	Brumbies	19	Perth
26	Highlanders	35	Reds	30	Dunedin
26	Rebels	52	Force	14	Melbourne
27	Fijian Drua	47	Moana Pasifika	46	Lautoka
27	Crusaders	42	Waratahs	18	Christchurch
27	Blues	36	Hurricanes	25	Auckland
27	Chiefs	31	Brumbies	21	Canberra
June					
2	Blues	16	Highlanders	9	Auckland
2	Brumbies	33	Rebels	17	Canberra
3	Fijian Drua	41	Reds	17	Suva
3	Hurricanes	27	Crusaders	26	Wellington
3	Moana Pasifika	33	Waratahs	24	Sydney
3	Chiefs	43	Force	19	Perth
Quarter-finals					
9	Blues	41	Waratahs	12	Auckland
10	Chiefs	29	Reds	20	Hamilton
10	Crusaders	49	Fijian Drua	8	Christchurch
10	Brumbies	37	Hurricanes	33	Canberra
Semifinals					
16	Crusaders	52	Blues	15	Christchurch
17	Chiefs	19	Brumbies	6	Hamilton
Final					
24	Crusaders	25	Chiefs	20	Hamilton

BLUES

Postal address: 32 Campbell Crescent,
Auckland 1051
Telephone: (09) 846 5425
Email: info@blues.rugby
Home venue: Eden Park, Auckland
Colours: Blue
Chairman: D.A. (Don) Mackinnon
Chief executive: A.J. (Andrew) Hore

Played 390, Won 213, Lost 170, Drew 7

	Tries	Conv	Pen	DG	Points
For	1287	876	758	14	10,515
Against	1061	734	826	28	9349

RECORDS — TEAM

Most points in a game	74	*v Stormers, 1998*
Most points in a season	534	*2022*
Biggest winning margin	53	*60–7 v Hurricanes, 2002*
Most tries in a game	11	*v Stormers, 1998*
		v Rebels, 2022
Most tries in a season	72	*2022*

RECORDS — INDIVIDUAL

Most points in a game	29	*G.W. Anscombe v Bulls, 2012*
Most points in a season	180	*A.R. Cashmore, 1998*
Most points in a career	641	*A.R. Cashmore, 1996-2000*
Most tries in a game	4	*J. Vidiri v Bulls, 2000*
		D.C. Howlett v Hurricanes, 2002
		J.M. Muliaina v Bulls, 2002
		R.E. Ioane v Sunwolves, 2019
		M.E. Telea v Hurricanes, 2023
Most tries in a season	12	*D.C. Howlett, 2003*
		M.E. Telea, 2023
Most tries in a career	55	*D.C. Howlett, 1999-2007*
Most conversions in a game	8	*S. Perofeta v Rebels, 2022*
Most conversions in a season	38	*S. Perofeta, 2022*
Most conversions in a career	120	*C.J. Spencer*
Most penalty goals in a game	6	*A.R. Cashmore v Chiefs, 1998*
		A.R. Cashmore v Hurricanes, 1999
		J.A. Arlidge v Bulls, 2001
		S.A. Brett v Bulls, 2010
		C.M. Noakes v Stormers, 2013
Most penalty goals in a season	34	*A.R. Cashmore, 1999*
Most penalty goals in a career	114	*A.R. Cashmore*
Most dropped goals in a game	1	*on 14 occasions*
Most dropped goals in a season	2	*O. Ai'i, 2000*
Most dropped goals in a career	3	*C.J. Spencer*
Most games	164	*K.F. Mealamu, 2000-2015*

After being the best team throughout most of the 2022 season, until the decider, the 2023 Blues produced spotty rugby and a pockmarked record.

They started on fire, however, destroying the Highlanders in Dunedin, but thereafter inconsistency bedevilled them, and they should have lost their Auckland derby to Moana Pasifika. That said, the narrow defeat to the Crusaders at Eden Park was one of the games of the regular season.

Placing third on the table, they cast aside the Waratahs before imploding in the semifinals against the Crusaders, easily their worst display of the season. The forwards, who had made such progress under Tom Coventry since 2019, did not fire when it counted.

The best player was right wing Mark Telea, who equalled the franchise record of 12 tries, while Rieko Ioane, who joined his brother Akira in reaching the 100-game milestone, was also mostly in fine touch.

Roger Tuivasa-Sheck played well early in the season, but was then hit by injury and lost his place. We think Harry Plummer, who usurped him for the No 12 jersey, is not a natural in that position.

Cameron Suafoa, who played all bar one of the 16 games, was the big mover in the pack, slotting into lock to cover injuries and performing so well he made the All Blacks XV. Ofa Tuungafasi, Dalton Papali'i and Kurt Eklund did not perform as consistently as in 2022. Tom Robinson, one of several who are departing, including head coach Leon MacDonald to the All Blacks, was strangely marginalised.

The hope is that incoming head coach Vern Cotter will inject some starch into the forwards in 2024 which will, in turn, hopefully allow the backline to flourish.

BLUES INDIVIDUAL SCORING

	Tries	*Con*	*PG*	*DG*	*Points*		*Tries*	*Con*	*PG*	*DG*	*Points*
Barrett	3	32	12	–	115	Suafoa	2	–	–	–	10
Telea	12	–	–	–	60	Tuungafasi	2	–	–	–	10
Clarke	7	–	–	–	35	Penalty try	1	–	–	–	7
Perofeta	1	6	6	–	35	Eklund	1	–	–	–	5
Riccitelli	7	–	–	–	35	Funaki	1	–	–	–	5
Plummer	–	9	5	–	33	A. Ioane	1	–	–	–	5
Sullivan	5	1	–	–	27	Laulala	1	–	–	–	5
R. Ioane	4	–	–	–	20	Renata	1	–	–	–	5
Christie	3	–	–	–	15	Robinson	1	–	–	–	5
Darry	3	–	–	–	15	Tuivasa-Sheck	1	–	–	–	5
Papali'i	3	–	–	–	15						
Tuipulotu	3	–	–	–	15	***Totals***	***67***	***48***	***23***	***0***	***502***
Ratumaitavuki-Kneepkens	2	–	–	–	10						
Sotutu	2	–	–	–	10	*Opposition scored*	*47**	*31*	*19*	*0*	*356*

*Includes one penalty try

Player	Union	Date of birth	Height	Weight	Blues games	Blues points
B.J. (Beauden) Barrett	Taranaki	27-05-91	1.86	92	30	199
A.J. (Adrian) Choat	Auckland	20-11-97	1.9	102	32	5
F.T. (Finlay) Christie	Tasman	19-09-95	1.77	84	45	60
C.D. (Caleb) Clarke	Auckland	29-03-99	1.87	103	49	110
S.G. (Sam) Darry	Canterbury	18-07-00	2.03	110	23	30
K.A.N. (Kurt) Eklund	Bay of Plenty	05-01-92	1.8	103	51	70
C.T. (Corey) Evans	Auckland	11-01-01	1.81	96	6	5
S.T. (Taufa) Funaki	Auckland	29-07-00	1.79	91	13	5
J. (Josh) Fusitu'a	Auckland	01-05-01	1.8	116	6	–
B.I. (Bryce) Heem	Auckland	18-01-89	1.93	104	33	35
A.T.O.A. (Alex) Hodgman	Auckland	16-07-93	1.9	119	57	–
A.L. (Akira) Ioane	Auckland	16-06-95	1.94	113	105	135
R.E. (Rieko) Ioane	Auckland	18-03-97	1.88	103	100	250
A.J. (Alexander) Lam	Auckland	29-07-98	1.92	105	29	50
J.M. (James) Lay	Auckland	16-12-93	1.78	116	11	–
J.A. (Jordan) Lay	Auckland	05-11-91	1.84	115	20	–
N.E. (Nepo) Laulala	Counties Manukau	06-11-91	1.84	116	38	10
S.J. (Sam) Nock	Northland	18-06-96	1.78	85	62	5
D.R. (Dalton) Papali'i (captain)	Counties Manukau	11-10-97	1.93	113	68	75
S. (Stephen) Perofeta	Taranaki	12-03-97	1.81	85	56	298
H.R.J. (Harry) Plummer	Auckland	19-06-98	1.84	94	58	126
T. (Taine) Plumtree	Wellington	09-03-00	1.97	111	6	10
J.W.J. (Jacob) Ratumaitavuki-Kneepkens	Taranaki	03-08-01	1.88	89	13	10
M.T. (Marcel) Renata	Auckland	24-02-94	1.87	121	38	10
J.R. (Ricky) Riccitelli	Taranaki	03-02-95	1.78	110	24	45
T.N. (Tom) Robinson	Northland	10-11-94	1.98	110	55	45
R.H.T. (Rob) Rush	Northland	14-11-00	1.93	110	1	–
A. (Anton) Segner	Tasman	24-07-01	1.92	108	16	–
H.C.R (Hoskins) Sotutu	Counties Manukau	12-07-98	1.92	106	50	75
C.J.T.S. (Cameron) Suafoa	North Harbour	23-04-98	1.96	116	18	15
Z. (Zarn) Sullivan	Auckland	07-10-00	1.93	101	32	45
C.L. (Caleb) Tangitau	Auckland	19-03-03	1.93	110	1	–
M.E. (Mark) Telea	North Harbour	06-12-96	1.86	94	52	130
T.R. (Tanielu) Tele'a	Auckland	16-06-98	1.87	107	21	20
J.F. (James) Tucker	Waikato	05-08-94	1.97	111	23	5
P.T. (Patrick) Tuipulotu	Auckland	23-01-93	1.98	120	99	75
R. (Roger) Tuivasa-Sheck	Auckland	05-06-93	1.82	96	18	10
A.O.H.M. (Ofa) Tuungafasi	Northland	19-04-92	1.95	129	134	35
S.M. (Soane) Vikena	Auckland	01-07-01	1.83	112	18	10

NB. Tele'a did not appear in 2023.

Manager: Richard Fry
Coach: Leon MacDonald
Assistant coaches: Tom Coventry, Daniel Halangahu, Paul Tito, Craig McGrath, Tana Umaga

BLUES 2023	Highlanders	Brumbies	Hurricanes	Crusaders	Force	Chiefs	Rebels	Waratahs	Drua	Moana Pasifika	Crusaders	Reds	Hurricanes	Highlanders	Waratahs (QF)	Crusaders (SF)	**TOTALS**
Sullivan	–	–	–	s	15	s	15	s	15	s	15	15	15	15	15	15	**13**
Perofeta	15	15	15	15	10	15	–	15	–	–	–	–	s	10	s	s	**11**
Telea	14	14	–	14	11	–	14	14	14	–	14	14	14	14	14	14	**13**
Tangitau	–	–	–	–	–	–	s	–	–	–	–	–	–	–	–	–	**1**
Ratumaitavuki-Kneepkens	–	s	s	–	14	14	–	–	–	15	–	s	–	–	–	–	**6**
Lam	s	–	14	–	–	–	–	–	s	14	s	11	–	s	11	–	**8**
Clarke	11	11	11	11	–	11	11	11	11	11	11	–	11	11	–	11	**13**
R. Ioane	13	13	13	13	–	13	13	13	13	s	13	–	13	13	13	13	**14**
Heem	s	s	s	s	13	–	–	s	s	13	s	13	12	–	12	12	**13**
Tuivasa-Sheck	12	12	12	12	–	–	–	–	–	12	–	s	–	s	–	–	**7**
Evans	–	–	–	–	s	–	s	–	–	–	–	–	–	–	–	–	**2**
Plummer	–	–	–	–	12	12	12	12	12	10	12	12	10	12	s	s	**12**
Barrett	10	10	10	10	–	10	10	10	10	–	10	10	–	–	10	10	**12**
Christie	9	9	9	9	–	9	9	9	9	s	9	–	9	9	9	9	**14**
Funaki	s	s	s	s	s	–	–	–	–	9	–	s	–	–	–	–	**7**
Nock	–	–	–	–	9	s	s	s	s	–	s	9	s	s	s	s	**11**
Sotutu	8	8	8	8	8	8	–	8	8	–	8	8	8	–	8	8	**13**
Choat	s	s	s	6	7	–	6	7	6	–	6	7	7	–	–	s	**12**
Segner	–	–	–	–	6	6	8	6	–	s	–	s	s	7	s	–	**9**
Papali'i (capt)	7	7	7	7	–	7	7	–	7	7	7	–	–	8	7	7	**12**
Plumtree	–	–	–	s	s	–	–	–	–	–	–	–	–	–	–	–	**2**
A. Ioane	6	–	–	–	–	–	–	s	s	6	s	6	6	s	6	6	**10**
Rush	–	–	–	–	–	–	–	–	–	–	–	–	–	s	–	–	**1**
Suafoa	5	5	5	5	5	4	s	s	4	8	s	5	5	–	s	s	**15**
Robinson	–	6	6	s	s	s	s	–	–	s	–	–	–	6	4	4	**10**
Tuipulotu	4	4	4	–	–	s	4	4	–	–	4	4	4	4	–	–	**10**
Tucker	s	s	s	4	4	–	–	–	s	4	–	s	s	5	5	5	**12**
Darry	–	–	–	–	s	5	5	5	5	5	5	–	–	–	–	–	**7**
Laulala	3	s	s	s	–	3	3	3	–	–	–	s	3	3	3	3	**12**
Renata	s	–	–	–	s	–	–	–	3	3	3	3	s	s	s	s	**10**
Tuungafasi	1	s	–	–	3	s	s	1	1	1	1	–	1	1	1	1	**13**
James Lay	–	3	3	3	–	s	s	s	s	s	s	–	–	–	–	–	**9**
Fusitu'a	s	1	1	–	1	–	–	–	–	–	–	s	–	–	–	–	**5**
Jordan Lay	–	–	–	s	s	1	1	s	s	–	s	1	s	s	s	s	**12**
Hodgman	–	–	s	1	–	–	–	–	–	–	–	–	–	–	–	–	**2**
Eklund	2	s	s	s	2	s	–	–	–	2	s	s	s	s	s	s	**13**
Riccitelli	s	2	2	2	s	2	2	2	s	–	2	2	2	2	2	2	**15**
Vikena	–	–	–	–	–	–	s	s	2	–	–	–	–	–	–	–	**3**

BLUES TEAM RECORD 2023

Played 16 **Won 1`1** **Lost 5** **Points for 502** **Points against 356**

Date	Opponent	Location	Score	Tries	Con	PG	DG	Referee
February 25	Highlanders	Dunedin	60–20	Telea (2), R. Ioane (2), Papali'i, Barrett, Clarke, Renata	Barrett (7)	Barrett (2)		Paul Williams
March 5	Brumbies	Melbourne	20–25	Riccitelli, Robinson	Barrett (2)	Barrett (2)		Ben O'Keeffe
March 11	Hurricanes	Wellington	25–19	Tuipulotu, Sotutu, Clarke	Perofeta (2)	Perofeta (2)		Nic Berry
March 18	Crusaders	Auckland	28–34	Clarke, Tuivasa-Sheck, Telea, Perofeta	Barrett (4)			James Doleman
March 26	Force	Auckland	30–17	Tuungafasi, Telea, Riccitelli, Ratumaitavuki-Kneepkens	Perofeta (2)	Perofeta (2)		Ben O'Keeffe
April 1	Chiefs	Hamilton	13–20	Riccitelli, Clarke		Barrett		Angus Gardner
April 8	Rebels	Melbourne	54–17	Christie (2), Telea (2), Riccitelli, Darry, Papali'i, Sullivan, Tuungafasi	Barrett (3)	Barrett		Reuben Keane
April 22	Waratahs	Auckland	55–21	Riccitelli (2), Sullivan (2), Clarke, Darry, Suafoa	Barrett (6), Perofeta	Perofeta (2)		Paul Williams
April 29	Fijian Drua	Lautoka	30–14	Suafoa, Papali'i, R. Ioane	Barrett (3)	Barrett (2), Plummer		Ben O'Keeffe
May 6	Moana Pasifika	Auckland	31–30	Eklund, Darry, A. Ioane, Clarke, penalty try	Plummer, Sullivan			Graham Cooper
May 13	Crusaders	Christchurch	3–15			Barrett		Nic Berry
May 19	Reds	Brisbane	45–26	Tuipulotu, Barrett, Telea, Sullivan, Funaki, Ratumaitavuki-Kneepkens	Plummer (4), Barrett (2)	Barrett		Jordan Way
May 27	Hurricanes	Auckland	36–25	Telea (4), Sotutu, R. Ioane	Plummer (2), Perofeta			Angus Gardner
June 2	Highlanders	Auckland	16–9	Tuipulotu	Plummer	Plummer (3)		Ben O'Keeffe
June 9	Waratahs (QF)	Auckland	41–12	Riccitelli, Laulala, Christie, Telea, Sullivan	Barrett (4), Plummer	Barrett, Plummer		Ben O'Keeffe
June 16	Crusaders (SF)	Christchurch	15–52	Barrett, Clarke	Barrett	Barrett		Angus Gardner

CHIEFS

Postal address: Box 4292, Hamilton East 3247
Telephone: (07) 853 0231
Email: info@chiefs.co.nz
Home venue: FMG Stadium Waikato, Hamilton
Colours: black base with yellow and red, black shorts
Chairman: W.M. (Bill) Osborne
Chief executive: S.A. (Simon) Graafhuis

Played 394, Won 217, Lost 167, Drew 10

	Tries	*Conv*	*Pen*	*DG*	*Points*
For	1233	906	816	10	10,478
Against	1101	780	829	28	9652

RECORDS — TEAM

Most points in a game	72	*v Lions, 2010*
Most points in a season	560	*2016*
Biggest winning margin	51	*(61-10) v Sunwolves, 2018*
Most tries in a game	9	*v Force, 2007; v Blues, 2009; v Lions, 2010; v Force, 2016; v Sunwolves, 2018; v Moana Pasifika, 2022*
Most tries in a season	76	*2016*

RECORDS — INDIVIDUAL

Most points in a game	32	*S.R. Donald v Lions, 2010*
Most points in a season	251	*A.W. Cruden, 2012*
Most points in a career	1070	*D.S. McKenzie, 2015–2023*
Most tries in a game	5	*S.T. Wainui v Waratahs, 2021*
Most tries in a season	12	*R.Q. Randle, 2002* *S.T. Stevenson, 2023*
Most tries in a career	42	*S.W. Sivivatu, 2003-2011*
Most conversions in a game	9	*S.R. Donald v Lions, 2010*
Most conversions in a season	43	*A.W. Cruden, 2012* *D.S. McKenzie 2016* *D.S. McKenzie 2023*
Most conversions in a career	214	*D.S. McKenzie*
Most penalty goals in a game	6	*G.W. Jackson v Reds, 2001* *S.R. Donald v Crusaders, 2007*
Most penalty goals in a season	50	*A.W. Cruden, 2012*
Most penalty goals in a career	158	*D.S. McKenzie*
Most dropped goals in a game	1	*on ten occasions*
Most dropped goals in a season	2	*I.D. Foster, 1996*
Most dropped goals in a career	2	*I.D. Foster* *G.W. Jackson*
Most games	183	*L.J. Messam, 2006-2021*

It was a case of so close, yet so far, for the Chiefs in 2023.

Like the Blues in 2022, they were clearly the best team during the season, but did not win enough big moments and had a call or two go against them in the final in Hamilton, allowing the Crusaders to edge home. But a 15–2 overall record, including two wins over the Crusaders, is something to be proud of, and the platform was laid by an industrious forward pack led by co-captain Sam Cane, Luke Jacobson and Brodie Retallick, the brilliance (and 191 points) of Damian McKenzie, and the 20 tries between Shaun Stevenson and Emoni Narawa, which gave the Chiefs a real cutting edge out wide.

The Chiefs reeled off 10 straight victories before falling, surprisingly, to the Reds in New Plymouth. They righted the ship but never recaptured that sparkling form and will regret that decider when they did not play poorly.

Centre Daniel Rona made the biggest impression for a rookie in the midfield during Anton Lienert-Brown's absence, while Rameka Poihipi had his best Super Rugby season yet, offering a skilled playmaker option outside McKenzie. The latter was in superb touch for most of the season, and combined well with Brad Weber.

As a rule, the forwards were muscular and accurate, Jacobson thriving at No 8 and tackling with his usual venom. Naitoa Ah Kuoi kept recalled All Black Josh Lord out of the match-day 23 during the playoffs with his consistent and high work-rate.

The front-row was led by Samisoni Taukei'aho, whose form was top-notch, while Irish import tighthead prop John Ryan more than filled his contract by appearing in all 17 games, one of four Chiefs to do so.

CHIEFS INDIVIDUAL SCORING

	Tries	*Con*	*PG*	*DG*	*Points*		*Tries*	*Con*	*PG*	*DG*	*Points*
McKenzie	3	43	30	–	191	Tauke'iaho	2	–	–	–	10
Stevenson	12	–	–	–	60	Thompson	2	–	–	–	10
Narawa	8	–	–	–	40	Boshier	1	–	–	–	5
Nanai-Seturo	5	–	–	–	25	Cane	1	–	–	–	5
Poihipi	2	5	1	–	23	Dyer	1	–	–	–	5
Gatland	1	5	2	–	21	Ioane	1	–	–	–	5
Ratima	4	–	–	–	20	Jacobson	1	–	–	–	5
Retallick	4	–	–	–	20	McWhannell	1	–	–	–	5
Finau	3	–	–	–	15	Nankivell	1	–	–	–	5
Rona	3	–	–	–	15	Tahuriorangi	1	–	–	–	5
Sowakula	3	–	–	–	15						
Vaa'i	3	–	–	–	15	***Totals***	**70**	**53**	**33**	**0**	**555**
Weber	3	–	–	–	15						
Coombes-Fabling	2	–	–	–	10	*Opposition scored*	*44**	*26*	*11*	*1*	*312*
Lienert-Brown	2	–	–	–	10						

*Includes two penalty tries

Player	*Union*	*Date of birth*	*Height*	*Weight*	*Chiefs games*	*Chiefs points*
N.S. (Naitoa) Ah Kuoi	Bay of Plenty	07-10-99	1.96	116	49	10
S. (Solomon) Alaimalo	Southland	27-12-95	1.96	103	48	90
K.L. (Kaylum) Boshier	Taranaki	09-04-99	1.89	102	17	10
S.J. (Sam) Cane (co-captain)	Bay of Plenty	13-01-92	1.89	105	150	85
L.A. (Liam) Coombes-Fabling	Waikato	07-07-98	1.8	83	4	10
G.E. (George) Dyer	Waikato	22-10-99	1.88	118	22	5
S.U. (Samipeni) Finau	Waikato	10-05-99	1.93	109	32	15
B.E.C. (Bryn) Gatland	North Harbour	05-10-95	1.78	88	32	176
J.R. (Josh) Ioane	Otago	11-07-95	1.76	85	17	44
L.B. (Luke) Jacobson	Waikato	20-04-97	1.91	107	63	65
L. (Lalomilo) Lalomilo	Bay of Plenty	02-12-99	1.76	98	2	–
A.R. (Anton) Lienert-Brown	Waikato	15-04-95	1.87	103	106	85
J.M.J. (Josh) Lord	Taranaki	17-01-01	2.02	119	19	–
P. (Peniasi) Malimali	Counties Manukau	08-12-96	1.82	98	3	–
D.S. (Damian) McKenzie	Waikato	20-04-95	1.75	82	111	1070
L.E. (Laghlan) McWhannell	Waikato	20-10-98	1.98	114	7	5
A. (Atu) Moli	Tasman	12-06-95	1.89	125	55	15
E.W.P.S (Etene) Nanai-Seturo	Counties Manukau	20-08-99	1.83	92	44	75
A.P. (Alex) Nankivell	Tasman	25-10-96	1.88	98	70	65
E.R. (Emoni) Narawa	Bay of Plenty	13-07-99	1.84	94	22	65
O.M. (Ollie) Norris	Waikato	11-12-99	1.94	120	45	5
S.C. (Simon) Parker	Waikato	06-05-00	1.93	109	8	–
R.H. (Rameka) Poihipi	Canterbury	14-10-98	1.87	105	30	28
J.P. (Jared) Proffit	Taranaki	14-09-93	1.83	112	4	–
N.G.J. (Ngane) Punivai	Canterbury	30-08-98	1.91	100	1	–
C.P. (Cortez) Ratima	Waikato	22-03-01	1.79	87	26	35
R.W.M. (Rivez) Reihana	Northland	25-05-00	1.87	93	9	5
B.A. (Brodie) Retallick	Hawke's Bay	31-05-91	2.04	121	128	100
X.O. (Xavier) Roe	Waikato	13-12-98	1.79	86	17	5
D.K. (Daniel) Rona	Taranaki	10-04-00	1.87	91	9	15
A. (Aidan) Ross	Bay of Plenty	25-10-95	1.89	111	74	10
J.W. (John) Ryan	Overseas	02-08-88	1.83	120	17	–
M.W.H. (Manaaki) Selby-Rickit	Bay of Plenty	05-06-96	2	112	5	–
B.A. (Bradley) Slater	Taranaki	23-09-98	1.81	112	48	10
P-G.N. (Pita-Gus) Sowakula	Taranaki	10-10-94	1.95	110	69	60
S.T. (Shaun) Stevenson	North Harbour	14-11-96	1.93	95	84	140
A. (Angus) Ta'avao-Matau	Auckland	22-03-90	1.94	124	62	30
T.T.H. (Te Toiroa) Tahuriorangi	Bay of Plenty	31-03-95	1.74	84	50	20
S.F.S. (Samisoni) Taukei'aho	Waikato	08-08-97	1.83	115	78	65
T.T.W.J. (Tyrone) Thompson	Wellington	28-05-00	1.86	111	15	15
S.M. (Solomone) Tukuafu	Waikato	25-10-96	1.83	122	2	–
Q.P.C. (Quinn) Tupaea	Waikato	10-05-99	1.86	97	34	30
T.P.O. (Tupou) Vaa'i	Taranaki	27-01-00	1.97	118	44	35
B.M. (Brad) Weber (co-captain)	Hawke's Bay	17-01-91	1.75	75	123	139
G.T. (Gideon) Wrampling	Waikato	26-07-01	1.88	102	2	–

N.B. Roe, Ta'avao-Matau and Tupaea did not appear in 2023.

Manager: Martyn Vercoe
Head coach: Clayton McMillan
Assistant coaches: Roger Randle, David Hill, Nick White, Ross Filipo, Paul Feeney

CHIEFS 2023	Crusaders	Moana Pasifika	Highlanders	Rebels	Waratahs	Blues	Hurricanes	Drua	Crusaders	Highlanders	Reds	Hurricanes	Brumbies	Force	Reds (QF)	Brumbies (SF)	Crusaders (F)	TOTALS
Narawa	–	–	–	–	–	–	14	–	14	14	14	14	14	–	14	14	14	**13**
Stevenson	15	15	15	15	s	15	15	14	15	15	15	15	s	15	15	15	15	**17**
Coombes-Fabling	14	14	–	–	–	s	–	–	–	–	–	–	–	14	–	–	–	**4**
Alaimalo	11	–	–	–	–	–	–	–	–	–	–	–	–	–	–	–	–	**1**
Nanai-Seturo	–	11	11	11	11	11	11	11	11	–	11	11	11	11	11	11	11	**15**
Malimali	–	–	–	s	–	–	s	–	–	11	–	–	–	–	–	–	–	**3**
Wrampling	–	–	–	–	–	–	–	s	–	–	–	–	–	–	–	–	–	**1**
Punivai	–	s	–	–	–	–	–	–	–	–	–	–	–	–	–	–	–	**1**
Nankivell	13	13	13	13	13	–	–	–	–	s	s	13	13	13	–	13	13	**12**
Lalomilo	–	–	–	–	–	–	–	–	s	–	–	–	–	s	–	–	–	**2**
Rona	–	–	s	–	s	13	13	13	13	13	–	–	s	–	s	–	–	**9**
Lienert-Brown	12	–	–	–	–	–	–	–	–	12	13	12	–	12	13	12	12	**8**
Poihipi	s	12	12	12	12	12	12	12	12	–	12	s	12	10	12	s	s	**16**
Ioane	s	–	s	–	–	–	–	–	–	–	s	s	10	–	s	s	s	**8**
Reihana	–	–	–	–	–	–	–	–	–	–	–	–	–	s	–	–	–	**1**
McKenzie	10	10	10	s	15	10	10	15	10	10	10	10	15	–	10	10	10	**16**
Gatland	–	s	–	10	10	s	s	10	s	s	–	–	–	–	–	–	–	**8**
Tahuriorangi	–	–	–	s	–	–	–	s	–	–	s	–	–	9	–	–	–	**4**
Ratima	s	s	s	9	s	s	s	9	s	s	9	s	s	s	s	s	s	**17**
Weber	9	9	9	–	9	9	9	–	9	9	–	9	9	–	9	9	9	**13**
Parker	–	s	–	–	–	–	–	s	–	–	8	s	–	7	–	–	–	**5**
Sowakula	6	6	s	8	8	s	6	8	s	6	–	6	6	s	8	s	6	**16**
Cane	7	7	7	–	7	7	7	–	7	7	–	7	7	–	7	7	7	**13**
L. Jacobson	8	8	8	7	–	8	8	–	8	8	7	8	8	–	s	8	8	**14**
Boshier	–	–	–	s	s	–	–	7	–	s	–	–	–	–	–	–	–	**4**
Vaa'i	5	5	5	–	–	5	5	s	5	4	4	5	–	5	–	5	5	**13**
Finau	s	–	s	6	6	6	s	6	6	–	6	–	s	8	6	6	s	**14**
Retallick	4	4	4	–	4	4	4	4	4	–	–	4	4	–	4	4	4	**13**
Ah Kuoi	s	–	6	4	s	s	s	–	s	5	s	s	s	6	s	s	s	**15**
Lord	–	–	–	–	–	–	–	s	–	s	5	–	–	–	5	–	–	**4**
Selby-Rickit	–	–	–	5	5	–	–	5	–	–	s	–	–	s	–	–	–	**5**
McWhannell	–	s	–	s	–	–	–	–	–	–	–	–	5	4	–	–	–	**4**
Dyer	3	3	s	s	s	s	3	–	3	3	–	3	3	–	s	3	3	**14**
Ryan	s	s	3	3	3	3	s	3	s	s	3	s	s	3	3	s	s	**17**
Moli	–	–	–	–	–	–	–	–	–	–	s	–	–	s	–	–	–	**2**
Tukuafe	–	–	–	–	–	–	–	s	–	–	–	–	–	–	–	–	–	**1**
Norris	s	1	s	s	s	1	s	1	s	s	s	s	s	1	s	s	s	**17**
Proffit	–	s	–	–	–	–	–	s	–	–	1	–	–	s	–	–	–	**4**
Ross	1	–	1	1	1	s	1	–	1	1	–	1	1	–	1	1	1	**13**
Taukei'aho	2	2	2	s	s	2	2	2	2	2	–	2	2	–	2	2	2	**15**
Slater	s	–	s	–	2	–	s	–	–	s	2	–	s	s	s	–	–	**9**
Thompson	–	s	–	2	–	s	–	s	s	–	s	s	–	2	–	s	s	**10**

CHIEFS TEAM RECORD 2023

Played 17 **Won 15** **Lost 2** **Points for 555** **Points against 312**

Date	Opponent	Location	Score	Tries	Con	PG	DG	Referee
February 24	Crusaders	Christchurch	31–10	Retallick, Cane, Nankivell, Ratima	McKenzie (4)	McKenzie		Ben O'Keeffe
March 4	Moana Pasifika	Melbourne	52–29	Stevenson (3), Weber (2), McKenzie, Poihipi, Coombes-Fabling	McKenzie (5), Gatland			Angus Gardner
March 10	Highlanders	Hamilton	28–7	Stevenson (2), Nanai-Seturo, Finau	McKenzie	McKenzie (2)		Paul Williams
March 18	Rebels	Hamilton	44–25	Stevenson (2), Nanai-Seturo, Thompson, Poihipi, Narawa	Gatland (4)	Gatland (2)		Dan Waenga
March 24	Waratahs	Sydney	24–14	Narawa (2), Gatland	McKenzie (3)	McKenzie		Jordan Way
April 1	Blues	Hamilton	20–13	Narawa (2)	McKenzie (2)	McKenzie (2)		Angus Gardner
April 15	Hurricanes	Wellington	33–17	Rona, Sowakula, Ratima, McKenzie	McKenzie (2)	McKenzie (3)		Jordan Way
April 21	Fijian Drua	Hamilton	50–17	Taukei'aho, Retallick, Boshier, Ratima, Nanai-Seturo, Stevenson, McKenzie, Vaa'i	McKenzie (5)			Brendon Pickerill
April 29	Crusaders	Hamilton	34–24	Retallick, Stevenson, Thompson	McKenzie (2)	McKenzie (5)		Angus Gardner
May 5	Highlanders	Dunedin	52–28	Rona (2), Dyer, Weber, Lienert-Brown, Narawa, Stevenson	McKenzie (7)	McKenzie		Ben O'Keeffe
May 12	Reds	New Plymouth	22–25	Nanai-Seturo (2), Finau	McKenzie (2)	McKenzie		Paul Williams
May 20	Hurricanes	Hamilton	23–12	Vaa'i (2), Taukei'aho	McKenzie	McKenzie (2)		James Doleman
May 27	Brumbies	Canberra	31–21	Jacobson, Ioane, Ratima, Stevenson	McKenzie (4)	McKenzie		Nic Berry
June 3	Force	Perth	43–19	McWhannell, Lienert-Brown, Coombes-Fabling, Finau, Sowakula, Tahuriorangi	Poihipi (5)	Poihipi		Nic Berry
June 10	Reds (QF)	Hamilton	29–20	Sowakula, Narawa	McKenzie (2)	McKenzie (5)		Angus Gardner
June 17	Brumbies (SF)	Hamilton	19–6	Retallick	McKenzie	McKenzie (4)		Nic Berry
June 24	Crusaders (F)	Hamilton	20–25	Narawa, Stevenson	McKenzie (2)	McKenzie (2)		Ben O'Keeffe

HURRICANES

Postal address: Box 7201, Wellington
Telephone: (04) 389 0020
Email: mail@hurricanes.co.nz
Home venues: SKY Stadium, Wellington;
Central Energy Trust Arena, Palmerston North;
Colours: yellow and black
Chairman: I. (Iain) Potter
Chief executive: A.D. (Avan) Lee

Played 392, Won 222, Lost 163, Drew 7

	Tries	Conv	Pen	DG	Points
For	1334	932	755	6	10821
Against	1075	748	831	26	9456

RECORDS — TEAM

Most points in a game	83	*v Sunwolves, 2017*
Most points in a season	691	*2017*
Biggest winning margin	66	*83-17 v Sunwolves, 2017*
Most tries in a game	13	*v Sunwolves, 2017*
Most tries in a season	101	*2017*

RECORDS — INDIVIDUAL

Most points in a game	30	*D.E. Holwell v Highlanders, 2001* *J.M. Barrett v Highlanders, 2021*
Most points in a season	223	*B.J. Barrett, 2016*
Most points in a career	1238	*B.J. Barrett, 2011-2019*
Most tries in a game	4	*M.B. Lam v Rebels, 2018* *K.H. Laumape v Blues, 2018*
Most tries in a season	16	*K.H. Laumape, 2017* *M.B. Lam, 2018*
Most tries in a career	62*	*S.J. Savea, 2011–18, 2021–23*
Most conversions in a game	9	*B.J. Barrett v Rebels, 2012* *O.W. Black v Sunwolves, 2017*
Most conversions in a season	50	*B.J. Barrett, 2016*
Most conversions in a career	249	*B.J. Barrett*
Most penalty goals in a game	7	*J.B. Cameron v Blues, 1996* *D.E. Holwell v Highlanders, 2001*
Most penalty goals in a season	40	*B.J. Barrett, 2013, 2014*
Most penalty goals in a career	189	*B. J. Barrett*
Most dropped goals in a game	1	*by six players*
Most dropped goals in a season	1	*by six players*
Most dropped goals in a career	1	*by six players*
Most games	153	*S.J. Savea, 2011–18, 2021–23*

*Savea's total includes two penalty tries.

The Hurricanes played some good rugby and returned a similar record to the 2022 side, but will be highly disappointed at losing a tight quarter-final in Canberra on a contentious decision when Ardie Savea looked to have scored the match-winner.

The good news was that the Hurricanes used only 40 players in 2023, not the 50 from 2022, and in halfback Cam Roigard, who more than filled TJ Perenara's big boots, and Savea the Younger, they had two of the best players in the competition.

The elder Savea, wing Julian, scored three tries to bring him to 62 in Super Rugby, a figure which includes two penalty tries. The official Sanzaar numbers have him at 60, which is equal with Israel Folau.

Kini Naholo was a star turn in the backs, scoring nine tries from 10 outings on the wing, and finally underlining his qualities at this level.

Jordie Barrett did not star in midfield, but was solid enough. Injury to Ruben Love ruled him out for most of the season, while the No 10 jersey was never quite nailed down, but Brett Cameron was the better performer ahead of Aidan Morgan.

In the pack, Du'Plessis Kirifi, Isaia Walker-Leawere, Tyrel Lomax and Asafo Aumua were good value, while Dane Coles played strongly in his final campaign until injury scratched him for five games.

The Hurricanes had the wood on Moana Pasifika but, at other times, they clocked off defensively, allowing the Force to score 42 points in Palmerston North and the Blues 36 in Auckland, meaning they placed fifth and headed to Canberra for another playoffs clash.

Former All Blacks Sevens coach Clark Laidlaw takes the reins from 2024, replacing Jason Holland, who joins the All Blacks coaching staff.

HURRICANES INDIVIDUAL SCORING

	Tries	*Con*	*PG*	*DG*	*Points*		*Tries*	*Con*	*PG*	*DG*	*Points*
Barrett	2	36	12	–	118	Kirifi	2	–	–	–	10
Naholo	9	–	–	–	45	Lomax	2	–	–	–	10
Roigard	9	–	–	–	45	Penalty try	1	–	–	–	7
Cameron	1	12	4	–	41	Blackwell	1	–	–	–	5
A. Savea	8	–	–	–	40	Booth	1	–	–	–	5
Rayasi	7	–	–	–	35	Delany	1	–	–	–	5
Moorby	5	–	–	–	25	Devery	1	–	–	–	5
Iose	4	–	–	–	20	Lakai	1	–	–	–	5
Proctor	4	–	–	–	20	Numia	1	–	–	–	5
Flanders	3	–	–	–	15	Sullivan	1	–	–	–	5
J. Savea	3	–	–	–	15						
Morgan	2	1	–	–	12	***Totals***	***73***	***49***	***16***	***0***	***513***
Coles	2	–	–	–	10						
Faiva	2	–	–	–	10	*Opposition scored*	*52*	*35*	*15*	*0*	*375*

Player	Union	Date of birth	Height	Weight	Hurricanes games	Hurricanes points
A.J. (Asafo) Aumua	Wellington	05-05-97	1.77	108	56	50
J.M. (Jordie) Barrett	Taranaki	17-02-97	1.96	101	98	753
D.J. (Dominic) Bird	Wellington	09-04-91	2.06	112	5	–
J. (James) Blackwell	Wellington	01-04-95	1.9	107	73	20
J.P. (Jamie) Booth	North Harbour	14-09-94	1.71	92	49	20
B.D. (Brett) Cameron	Manawatu	04-10-96	1.72	83	7	41
D.S. (Dane) Coles	Wellington	10-12-86	1.84	110	141	145
C. (Caleb) Delany	Wellington	04-02-00	1.98	110	21	5
J.D. (Jacob) Devery	Hawke's Bay	21-10-98	1.8	103	7	5
E.U. (Hame) Faiva	Overseas	09-05-94	1.81	108	5	10
D.J. (Devan) Flanders	Hawke's Bay	20-07-99	1.9	98	40	30
O.T. (Owen) Franks	Wellington	23-12-87	1.85	121	16	–
H.G.R. (Harry) Godfrey	Hawke's Bay	03-01-03	1.75	85	8	–
L.E. (Logan) Henry	Manawatu	02-09-96	1.71	84	2	5
R.J. (Riley) Higgins	Wellington	10-09-02	1.8	95	4	–
R.(Riley) Hohepa	Counties Manukau	09-02-95	1.86	92	2	–
T.K. (Te Kamaka) Howden	Manawatu	28-01-01	1.93	109	14	–
B.D. (Brayden) Iose	Manawatu	26-08-98	1.88	105	25	35
D.A. (Du'Plessis) Kirifi	Wellington	03-03-97	1.8	101	65	35
P.A. (Peter) Lakai	Wellington	04-03-03	1.89	109	7	5
T. (Tyler) Laubscher	Manawatu	18-12-00	1.94	104	1	–
T.S. (Tyrel) Lomax	Tasman	16-03-96	1.92	127	50	20
R. (Ruben) Love	Wellington	28-04-01	1.83	90	18	27
T.T.P. (Tevita) Mafileo	Bay of Plenty	04-02-98	1.87	120	37	5
J.M. (Josh) Moorby	Northland	11-07-98	1.88	90	24	70
A. (Aidan) Morgan	Wellington	07-06-01	1.72	81	21	38
K.V. (Kini) Naholo	Taranaki	16-04-99	1.78	92	10	45
X.J.S (Xavier) Numia	Wellington	29-11-98	1.89	111	47	5
T.T.R. (TJ) Perenara	Wellington	23-01-92	1.84	91	150	292
H.J. (Hugo) Plummer	Wellington	25-08-00	1.98	110	1	–
R.J. (Reed) Prinsep	Canterbury	17-02-93	1.92	108	73	30
B.D. (Billy) Proctor	Wellington	14-05-99	1.87	96	49	70
P.G. (Pouri) Rakete-Stones	Hawke's Bay	17-06-97	1.81	113	30	5
S.T.M (Salesi) Rayasi	Auckland	25-09-96	1.93	105	39	110
C.D. (Cameron) Roigard	Counties Manukau	16-11-00	1.83	88	27	45
J.T. (Justin) Sangster	Bay of Plenty	30-11-96	1.98	114	13	5
A.S. (Ardie) Savea (captain)	Wellington	14-10-93	1.88	100	131	160
S.J. (Julian) Savea	Wellington	07-08-90	1.92	108	153	310*
D.P. (Daniel) Sinkinson	Waikato	08-02-01	1.85	92	3	–
B.W.M. (Bailyn) Sullivan	Waikato	03-09-98	1.87	93	17	30
V.P. (Pasilio) Tosi	Bay of Plenty	18-07-98	1.93	140	10	5
P.I.J. (Peter) Umaga-Jensen	Wellington	31-12-97	1.87	95	35	45
I.E.T. (Isaia) Walker-Leawere	Hawke's Bay	16-04-97	1.87	127	54	10

NB. Laubscher, Perenara and Prinsep did not appear in 2023.
*Julian Savea's 62 tries include two penalty tries.

Manager: Tony Ward
Coach: Jason Holland
Assistant coaches: Chris Gibbes, Cory Jane, Jamie Mackintosh, Tyler Bleyendaal

HURRICANES 2023	Reds	Rebels	Blues	Waratahs	Moana Pasifika	Force	Highlanders	Chiefs	Brumbies	Drua	Moana Pasifika	Chiefs	Blues	Crusaders	Brumbies (QF)	TOTALS
Moorby	15	15	15	15	15	–	15	15	15	15	s	15	15	15	15	**14**
Love	–	–	–	–	–	–	–	–	–	–	–	–	–	s	s	**2**
Godfrey	s	s	–	–	–	15	s	s	s	s	15	–	–	–	–	**8**
J. Savea	14	14	14	14	s	–	14	14	14	14	–	14	14	–	–	**11**
Rayasi	11	11	11	–	11	11	11	11	11	s	14	s	s	–	–	**12**
Naholo	–	–	–	11	14	s	–	–	s	11	11	11	11	11	11	**10**
Sinkinson	–	–	–	–	–	14	–	–	–	–	–	–	–	14	14	**3**
Sullivan	–	–	–	s	13	13	–	–	–	–	–	–	–	s	s	**5**
Proctor	13	13	13	13	12	–	13	–	–	13	13	13	13	13	13	**12**
Higgins	–	s	s	–	–	s	–	–	–	–	–	–	–	–	–	**3**
Umaga-Jensen	–	–	–	–	–	–	s	13	13	–	s	12	–	–	–	**5**
Barrett	12	12	12	12	–	12	12	12	12	12	12	–	12	12	12	**13**
Hohepa	–	–	–	–	s	–	–	–	–	–	–	s	–	–	–	**2**
Morgan	10	10	s	s	–	–	10	10	10	10	10	10	10	–	–	**11**
Cameron	–	–	10	10	10	10	–	–	–	–	–	–	s	10	10	**7**
Booth	s	s	s	s	s	9	s	s	s	s	9	s	s	s	s	**15**
Henry	–	–	–	–	–	–	–	–	–	–	s	–	–	–	–	**1**
Roigard	9	9	9	9	9	s	9	9	9	9	–	9	9	9	9	**14**
Iose	s	6	–	s	s	8	6	s	s	s	s	8	s	8	8	**14**
Lakai	7	s	8	–	7	s	s	s	–	–	–	–	–	–	–	**7**
A. Savea	8	8	–	8	8	–	8	8	8	8	8	–	8	7	7	**12**
Kirifi	s	7	7	7	–	7	7	7	7	7	7	7	7	–	s	**13**
Flanders	6	–	6	6	6	–	–	6	6	6	6	6	–	6	6	**11**
Howden	–	–	s	–	s	6	s	s	–	s	–	–	–	s	–	**7**
Delany	s	s	s	–	–	–	–	–	s	–	s	s	6	5	5	**9**
Bird	–	–	–	s	4	5	5	5	–	–	–	–	–	–	–	**5**
Plummer	–	–	–	–	–	s	–	–	–	–	–	–	–	–	–	**1**
Walker-Leawere	5	5	5	5	5	–	–	–	5	5	5	5	5	–	s	**11**
Sangster	–	–	–	–	–	–	–	–	–	4	–	s	s	s	–	**4**
Blackwell	4	4	4	4	–	4	4	4	4	–	4	4	4	4	4	**13**
Lomax	s	3	3	3	–	3	3	3	3	3	3	–	3	3	3	**13**
Tosi	–	–	s	s	s	–	–	s	–	–	s	s	–	–	–	**6**
Franks	3	s	–	–	3	s	s	–	s	s	–	3	s	s	s	**11**
Mafileo	s	s	–	–	s	s	–	s	s	s	1	s	s	1	s	**12**
Numia	1	1	1	1	1	–	1	1	1	1	–	1	1	–	1	**12**
Rakete-Stones	–	–	s	s	–	1	s	–	–	–	s	–	–	s	–	**6**
Aumua	s	s	s	2	2	–	s	2	2	2	–	–	2	–	s	**11**
Devery	–	–	–	–	–	–	–	–	s	s	2	2	–	s	–	**5**
Coles	2	2	2	s	–	2	2	s	–	–	–	–	–	2	2	**9**
Faiva	–	–	–	–	s	s	–	–	–	–	s	s	s	–	–	**5**

HURRICANES TEAM RECORD 2023

Played 15 **Won 9** **Lost 6** **Points for 513** **Points against 375**

Date	Opponent	Location	Score	Tries	Con	PG	DG	Referee
February 25	Reds	Townsville	47–13	Roigard, Proctor, J. Savea, Lomax, Booth, penalty try	Barrett (3)	Barrett (3)		Angus Gardner
March 3	Rebels	Melbourne	39–33	A. Savea (2), Rayasi, Barrett, Moorby	Barrett (4)	Barrett (2)		James Doleman
March 11	Blues	Wellington	19–25	Lomax, Rayasi, Moorby	Barrett (2)			Nic Berry
March 17	Waratahs	Wellington	34–17	Roigard (2), Naholo (2), Coles	Barrett (3)	Barrett		Brendon Pickerill
March 25	Moana Pasifika	Auckland	59–0	Rayasi (2), Lakai, A. Savea, Roigard, Cameron, Naholo, Moorby, Faiva	Cameron (7)			Reuben Keane
April 2	Force	Palmerston North	45–42	Iose (2), Naholo, Coles, Sullivan, Kirifi, Faiva	Barrett (5)			Paul Williams
April 8	Highlanders	Dunedin	29–14	Rayasi (2), Blackwell, Roigard	Barrett (3)	Barrett		Damon Murphy
April 15	Chiefs	Wellington	17–33	Flanders, Roigard	Barrett (2)	Barrett		Jordan Way
April 28	Brumbies	Wellington	32–27	Flanders, Roigard, A. Savea, Morgan	Barrett (3)	Barrett (2)		James Doleman
May 6	Fijian Drua	Suva	24–27	J. Savea (2), Kirifi, Numia	Barrett (2)			Jordan Way
May 13	Moana Pasifika	Wellington	71–22	A. Savea (3), Naholo (2), Devery, Morgan, Barrett, Proctor, Rayasi, Delany	Barrett (8)			Brendon Pickerill
May 20	Chiefs	Hamilton	12–23	Iose, Moorby	Morgan			James Doleman
May 27	Blues	Auckland	25–36	Naholo (2), Roigard, Proctor	Barrett	Barrett		Angus Gardner
June 3	Crusaders	Wellington	27–26	Proctor, Roigard, Moorby, Iose	Cameron (2)	Barrett		Brendon Pickerill
June 10	Brumbies (QF)	Canberra	33–37	Flanders, A. Savea, Naholo	Cameron (3)	Cameron (4)		Nic Berry

CRUSADERS

CRUSADERS™

Postal address: Box 755, Christchurch
Telephone: (03) 379 8300
Email: info@crfu.co.nz
Home venue: Orangetheory Stadium, Christchurch
Colours: red and black
Chairman: G.S. (Grant) Jarrold
Chief executive: C.S. (Colin) Mansbridge

Played 418, Won 299, Lost 111, Drew 8

	Tries	*Conv*	*Pen*	*DG*	*Points*
For	1523	1086	957	50	12,833
Against	973	688	800	30	8732

RECORDS — TEAM

Most points in a game	96	*v Waratahs, 2002*
Most points in a season	691	*2018*
Biggest winning margin	77	*96–19 v Waratahs, 2002*
Most tries in a game	14	*v Waratahs, 2002*
Most tries in a season	96	*2018*

RECORDS — INDIVIDUAL

Most points in a game	31	*T.J. Taylor v Stormers, 2012* *R. Mo'unga v Reds, 2021*
Most points in a season	221	*D.W. Carter, 2006*
Most points in a career	1708	*D.W. Carter, 2003-2015*
Most tries in a game	4	*C.S. Ralph v Waratahs, 2002* *S.D. Maitland v Brumbies, 2011*
Most tries in a season	15	*R.L. Gear, 2005* *G.C. Bridge 2018* *S.L. Reece, 2019*
Most tries in a career	52	*C.S. Ralph, 1999-2008*
Most conversions in a game	13	*A.P. Mehrtens v Waratahs, 2002*
Most conversions in a season	57	*R. Mo'unga, 2023*
Most conversions in a career	287	*D.W. Carter*
Most penalty goals in a game	8	*T.J. Taylor v Stormers, 2012*
Most penalty goals in a season	46	*C.R. Slade, 2014*
Most penalty goals in a career	307	*D.W. Carter*
Most dropped goals in a game	3	*A.P. Mehrtens v Highlanders, 1998*
Most dropped goals in a season	4	*A.P. Mehrtens, 1998, 1999, 2002*
Most dropped goals in a career	17	*A.P. Mehrtens*
Most games	203	*W.W.V. Crockett, 2006-2018*

Scott Robertson has signed off as the most successful coach in Super Rugby history with a 25–20 Crusaders' triumph over the Chiefs in a tight, compelling final in Hamilton.

Given a crippling injury toll, unusual for the franchise, that forced them to use 48 players, this might be the most special of the seven straight championships for the Crusaders.

Yet, after three rounds, the Crusaders were 1–2 and premature questions were being asked about Robertson and his group. They responded by winning 12 of their last 14 and demolishing the Blues in the semifinal, despite being depowered.

Sam Whitelock defied an Achilles injury and the wishes of the All Blacks' coaching staff to play the final, his last game of a long Super Rugby career. He delivered, as he has done on most occasions. The outstanding forward, though was Scott Barrett, who led from the front as captain. Other key figures were No 10 Richie Mo'unga, who showed his class again in the playoffs and scored 174 points, 12-try hooker Codie Taylor and 13-try wing Leicester Fainga'anuku.

Unsung heroes were loose forwards Christian Lio-Willie and Tom Christie, who were the only ones to appear in all 17 games.

There was a propping crisis, which saw 39-year-old John Afoa used for two games, but Tamaiti Williams stayed strong and went to the other side of the scrum, where he impressed.

Parsimonious defence was again a central plank in the Crusaders' strategy, only once conceding more than 20 in their last eight matches.

Matching the 2023 season will be a stiff challenge for the 2024 group and new head coach Rob Penney, especially with the exits of Robertson, Whitelock and Mo'unga.

Player	*Union*	*Date of birth*	*Height*	*Weight*	*Crusaders games*	*Crusaders points*
I.F. (John) Afoa	Overseas	16-10-83	1.83	119	2	–
S.K. (Scott) Barrett (captain)	Taranaki	20-11-93	1.98	116	112	85
G.D.E. (George) Bell	Canterbury	29-01-02	1.85	110	1	5
E.J. (Ethan) Blackadder	Tasman	22-03-95	1.91	107	37	35
G.G. (George) Bower	Otago	28-05-92	1.86	120	58	–
F.F. (Finlay) Brewis	Canterbury	10-02-00	1.88	124	6	–
F.W. (Fergus) Burke	Canterbury	03-09-99	1.89	85	34	118
S.A. (Seb) Calder	Canterbury	16-03-02	1.84	119	10	–
L.J. (Louie) Chapman	Tasman	01-05-00	1.79	84	1	–
T.M. (Tom) Christie	Canterbury	04-03-98	1.85	103	47	35
M.D. (Mitch) Drummond	Canterbury	15-12-94	1.8	86	132	102
M.T.W. (Mitch) Dunshea	Canterbury	18-11-95	1.96	114	38	15
B.M. (Braydon) Ennor	Canterbury	16-07-97	1.87	93	68	125
L.O.K.W.P (Leicester) Fainga'anuku	Tasman	11-10-99	1.88	103	55	150
L.C.V. (Chay) Fihaki	Canterbury	03-01-01	1.92	100	17	5
Z.W. (Zach) Gallagher	Canterbury	04-09-01	1.98	115	18	–
D.A. (Dominic) Gardiner	Canterbury	12-07-01	1.89	104	15	10
E.J. (Jack) Goodhue	Northland	13-06-95	1.86	98	81	65
W.G.(Wil) Gualter	Canterbury	05-06-01	1.86	95	5	–
J.L. (Jamie) Hannah	Canterbury	31-10-02	1.99	111	3	–
C.J. (Cullen) Grace	Canterbury	20-12-99	1.93	106	41	35
D.K. (David) Havili	Tasman	23-12-94	1.84	95	119	195
S.T. (Sione) Havili-Talitui	Tasman	25-01-98	1.85	104	35	30
W.A. (Willi) Heinz	Canterbury	24-11-86	1.79	88	68	37
N.R.F. (Noah) Hotham	Tasman	23-05-03	1.78	90	7	5
O.G.J.T. (Oli) Jager	Canterbury	05-07-95	1.92	120	53	10
W.T. (Will) Jordan	Tasman	24-02-98	1.88	91	52	190
C.J. (Corey) Kellow	Canterbury	25-05-01	1.89	107	12	–
T. (Taha) Kemara	Waikato	17-04-03	1.85	85	2	–

J.M. (Joel) Lam	Canterbury	17-05-02	1.75	83	1	–
C.J. (Christian) Lio-Willie	Otago	26-08-98	1.87	109	17	10
Q.J.R.W.J. (Quentin) MacDonald	Tasman	25-09-88	1.81	105	25	15
B.L. (Brodie) McAlister	Canterbury	17-06-97	1.84	109	37	30
D.A.M (Dallas) McLeod	Canterbury	30-04-99	1.88	99	27	15
I.T. (Ioane) Moananu	Counties Manukau	08-02-01	1.76	113	3	10
J.P.T. (Joe) Moody	Canterbury	16-09-88	1.88	120	116	20
R. (Richie) Mo'unga	Canterbury	25-05-94	1.76	86	109	1230
M. (Melani) Nanai	Bay of Plenty	03-08-93	1.92	92	1	–
F.D. (Fletcher) Newell	Canterbury	01-03-00	1.83	119	18	10
R.G. (Reuben) O'Neill	Taranaki	17-02-95	1.83	117	5	–
P. (Pepesana) Patafilo	Wellington	29-05-96	1.8	94	5	–
S.L. (Sevu) Reece	Tasman	13-02-97	1.78	92	59	230
M.R. (Macca) Springer	Tasman	29-03-03	1.89	95	9	20
Q.J. (Quinten) Strange	Tasman	21-08-96	1.99	112	56	20
K.J. (Kershawl) Sykes-Martin	Tasman	26-04-99	1.87	111	9	–
C.J. (Codie) Taylor	Canterbury	31-03-91	1.83	111	129	*210*
A. (Andrew) Turner	Overseas	16-02-02	1.86	115	2	–
S.L. (Sam) Whitelock	Canterbury	12-10-88	2.03	120	182	*45*
T.P.T. (Tamaiti) Williams	Canterbury	10-08-00	1.94	140	38	*25*

NB. Bell did not appear in 2023.

Manager: Shane Fletcher
Coach: Scott Robertson
Assistant coaches: Scott Hansen, Dan Perrin, Tamati Ellison, James Marshall

CRUSADERS INDIVIDUAL SCORING

	Tries	*Con*	*PG*	*DG*	*Points*		*Tries*	*Con*	*PG*	*DG*	*Points*
Mo'unga	3	57	14	1	174	Moananu	2	–	–	–	10
Fainga'anuku	13	–	–	–	65	Reece	2	–	–	–	10
Taylor	12	–	–	–	60	Penalty try	1	–	–	–	7
Burke	5	7	1	–	42	Blackadder	1	–	–	–	5
D. Havili	5	–	–	–	25	Drummond	1	–	–	–	5
McAlister	4	–	–	–	20	Fihaki	1	–	–	–	5
Springer	4	–	–	–	20	Grace	1	–	–	–	5
Ennor	3	–	–	–	15	Hotham	1	–	–	–	5
Heinz	3	–	–	–	15	Jager	1	–	–	–	5
Jordan	3	–	–	–	15	Moody	1	–	–	–	5
Barrett	2	–	–	–	10	Strange	1	–	–	–	5
Gardiner	2	–	–	–	10	Williams	1	–	–	–	5
S. Havili-Talitui	2	–	–	–	10						
Lio-Willie	2	–	–	–	10	***Totals***	***81***	***64***	***15***	***1***	***583***
MacDonald	2	–	–	–	10						
McLeod	2	–	–	–	10	*Opposition scored*	*41*	*28*	*20*	*0*	*321*

CRUSADERS 2023	Chiefs	Highlanders	Fijian Drua	Blues	Brumbies	Reds	Moana Pasifika	Rebels	Chiefs	Force	Blues	Moana Pasifika	Waratahs	Hurricanes	Drua (QF)	Blues (SF)	Chiefs (F)	**TOTALS**
Fihaki	–	–	15	–	s	s	–	–	–	s	–	14	14	s	s	s	s	**10**
Jordan	–	–	–	–	–	–	–	–	–	15	15	15	–	15	15	15	15	**7**
D. Havili	15	12	12	–	–	–	s	12	12	12	12	–	12	–	–	–	–	**9**
Reece	14	14	14	14	–	–	–	–	–	–	–	–	–	–	–	–	–	**4**
Nanai	–	–	–	–	–	–	s	–	–	–	–	–	–	–	–	–	–	**1**
Gualter	–	–	–	–	s	s	14	–	–	–	–	s	s	–	–	–	–	**5**
Patafilo	–	–	–	s	14	14	–	14	–	–	–	–	s	–	–	–	–	**5**
Springer	s	s	11	s	–	–	11	11	s	14	–	11	–	–	–	–	–	**9**
Fainga'anuku	11	11	–	11	11	11	–	–	11	11	11	–	13	11	11	11	11	**13**
Ennor	13	s	13	13	13	13	–	13	13	13	13	–	–	13	13	13	13	**14**
Goodhue	12	13	–	–	–	–	13	s	s	–	s	13	–	12	12	12	12	**11**
McLeod	–	–	s	12	12	12	12	s	14	–	14	12	11	14	14	14	14	**14**
Mo'unga	10	10	–	10	10	10	10	10	10	10	10	–	10	10	10	10	10	**15**
Burke	s	15	10	15	15	15	15	15	15	s	–	10	15	s	s	s	s	**16**
Kemara	–	–	s	–	–	–	–	–	–	–	–	s	–	–	–	–	–	**2**
Drummond	9	9	–	9	9	–	9	9	9	s	9	s	9	–	9	9	9	**14**
Chapman	–	–	–	–	–	–	–	–	–	–	–	–	–	9	–	–	–	**1**
Lam	–	–	–	–	–	–	–	–	–	–	–	–	–	s	–	–	–	**1**
Heinz	s	–	9	s	s	s	s	s	–	–	–	–	–	–	s	s	s	**10**
Hotham	–	s	s	–	–	9	–	–	–	9	s	9	s	–	–	–	–	**7**
Grace	8	–	–	–	–	–	–	s	8	8	8	8	8	–	–	–	–	**7**
Lio-Willie	s	8	8	s	s	8	8	8	s	s	6	6	6	8	8	8	8	**17**
Christie	7	7	7	7	7	7	s	7	7	7	7	s	7	7	7	7	7	**17**
S. Havili-Talitui	–	s	6	8	8	6	6	–	–	–	s	–	s	s	6	6	6	**12**
Kellow	–	–	s	–	–	s	7	–	–	–	–	7	–	–	–	s	–	**5**
Blackadder	6	6	–	6	6	–	–	–	–	–	–	–	–	–	s	–	–	**5**
Gardiner	–	–	–	–	5	5	5	6	6	6	–	s	–	–	–	s	s	**9**
Whitelock	–	5	5	5	–	–	–	5	5	–	–	–	5	5	–	–	5	**8**
Dunshea	5	–	–	–	–	–	–	–	–	–	–	–	–	–	–	–	–	**1**
Gallagher	s	s	s	s	–	–	–	–	–	s	s	5	s	s	s	–	–	**10**
Hannah	–	–	–	–	s	s	s	–	–	–	–	–	–	–	–	–	–	**3**
Strange	–	–	–	–	–	–	4	s	s	5	5	–	4	4	5	5	–	**9**
Barrett	4	4	4	4	4	4	–	4	4	4	4	4	–	6	4	4	4	**15**
Williams	s	3	3	3	3	3	3	3	3	3	3	3	–	1	1	1	1	**16**
Jager	–	–	–	–	–	–	–	–	s	s	s	–	–	–	3	3	3	**6**
Newell	3	–	–	–	–	–	–	–	–	–	–	–	–	–	–	–	–	**1**
Afoa	–	–	–	–	–	–	–	–	–	–	–	–	3	3	–	–	–	**2**
Calder	–	s	s	–	s	s	s	s	–	–	–	s	s	s	–	–	–	**9**
Bower	s	s	1	s	s	s	–	–	–	–	–	–	–	–	–	–	–	**6**
Brewis	–	–	–	–	–	–	s	s	–	–	–	–	–	–	–	–	–	**2**
Turner	–	–	–	–	–	–	–	–	–	s	–	s	–	–	–	–	–	**2**
O'Neill	–	–	–	–	–	–	–	–	–	–	–	–	s	s	s	s	s	**5**
Sykes-Martin	–	–	s	s	–	–	–	–	s	–	s	1	1	–	s	s	s	**9**
Moody	1	1	–	1	1	1	1	1	1	1	1	–	–	–	–	–	–	**10**
McAlister	s	s	–	s	s	s	s	2	s	2	s	2	s	s	s	s	–	**15**
Taylor	2	2	–	2	2	2	2	–	2	s	2	–	2	2	2	2	2	**14**
MacDonald	–	–	2	–	–	–	–	–	–	–	–	–	–	–	–	–	–	**1**
Moananu	–	–	s	–	–	–	–	s	–	–	–	s	–	–	–	–	–	**3**

CRUSADERS TEAM RECORD 2023

Played 17 **Won 13** **Lost 4** **Points for 583** **Points against 321**

Date	Opponent	Location	Score	Tries	Con	PG	DG	Referee
February 24	Chiefs	Christchurch	10–31	D. Havili	Mo'unga		Mo'unga	Ben O'Keeffe
March 3	Highlanders	Melbourne	52–15	Moody, Taylor, Mo'unga, Fainga'anuku, D. Havili, Reece, Burke	Mo'unga (7)	Mo'unga		Nic Berry
March 11	Fijian Drua	Lautoka	24–25	MacDonald (2), Reece, Moananu	Burke (2)			Brendon Pickerill
March 18	Blues	Auckland	34–28	Fainga'anuku (3), Blackadder, Burke	Mo'unga (3)	Mo'unga		James Doleman
March 24	Brumbies	Christchurch	35–17	Fainga'anuku (2), Ennor, Taylor, Lio-Willie	Mo'unga (5)			Brendon Pickerill
March 31	Reds	Brisbane	25–12	Gardiner, Fainga'anuku, Heinz	Mo'unga (2)	Mo'unga (2)		Damon Murphy
April 7	Moana Pasifika	Christchurch	38–21	Taylor (2), Gardiner, McLeod, Heinz	Mo'unga (5)	Mo'unga		James Doleman
April 21	Rebels	Melbourne	43–27	D. Havili (2), Springer, Moananu, Grace, McLeod	Mo'unga (5)	Mo'unga		Ben O'Keeffe
April 29	Chiefs	Hamilton	24–34	Williams, Burke, penalty try	Mo'unga (2)	Mo'unga		Angus Gardner
May 6	Force	Christchurch	48–13	McAlister (3), Fainga'anuku (2), Springer (2), Taylor	Mo'unga (4)			Brendon Pickerill
May 13	Blues	Christchurch	15–3	Strange, Fainga'anuku	Mo'unga	Mo'unga		Nic Berry
May 19	Moana Pasifika	Auckland	41–7	McAlister, Barrett, Lio-Willie, Hotham, Springer, Jordan	Burke (4)	Burke		Reuben Keane
May 27	Waratahs	Christchurch	42–18	Taylor, Drummond, Mo'unga, D. Havili, Burke, S. Havili	Mo'unga (6)			James Doleman
June 3	Hurricanes	Wellington	26–27	Fainga'anuku, Ennor, Taylor, Fihaki	Mo'unga (3)			Brendon Pickerill
June 10	Drua (QF)	Christchurch	49–8	Taylor (2), Jager, Barrett. S. Havili, Jordan, Heinz	Mo'unga (6), Burke			Brendon Pickerill
June 16	Blues (SF)	Christchurch	52–15	Fainga'anuku (2), Ennor, Jordan, Taylor, Burke	Mo'unga (5)	Mo'unga (4)		Angus Gardner
June 24	Chiefs (F)	Hamilton	25–20	Taylor (2), Mo'unga	Mo'unga (2)	Mo'unga (2)		Ben O'Keeffe

HIGHLANDERS

Postal address: Box 6070, Dunedin 9059
Telephone: (03) 479 9280
Email: contactus@highlanders.net.nz
Home venues: Forsyth Barr Stadium, Dunedin; Rugby Park Stadium, Invercargill
Colours: blue with gold and maroon
Chairman: P.N. (Peter) Kean
Chief executive: R.W. (Roger) Clark

Played 388, Won 186, Lost 198, Drew 4

	Tries	*Conv*	*Pen*	*DG*	*Points*
For	1114	782	827	28	9711
Against	1165	845	756	16	9837

RECORDS — TEAM

Most points in a game	65	*v Bulls, 1999*
Most points in a season	530	*2015*
Biggest winning margin	51	*61–10 v Force, 2022*
Most tries in a game	9	*v Bulls, 1999* *v Force, 2022*
Most tries in a season	64	*2017*

RECORDS — INDIVIDUAL

Most points in a game	28	*B.A. Blair v Sharks, 2005*
Most points in a season	191	*L.Z. Sopoaga, 2015*
Most points in a career	868	*L.Z. Sopoaga, 2011-2018*
Most tries in a game	3	*on 12 occasions*
Most tries in a season	13	*W.R. Naholo, 2015*
Most tries in a career	45	*W.R. Naholo, 2015-2019*
Most conversions in a game	8	*S.J. Gilbert v Force, 2022*
Most conversions in a season	41	*L.Z. Sopoaga 2018*
Most conversions in a career	163	*L.Z. Sopoaga*
Most penalty goals in a game	8	*W.C. Walker v Chiefs, 2003*
Most penalty goals in a season	34	*T.E. Brown, 2000*
Most penalty goals in a career	180	*T.E. Brown*
Most dropped goals in a game	1	*on 28 occasions*
Most dropped goals in a season	3	*L.Z. Sopoaga, 2015*
Most dropped goals in a career	6	*T.E. Brown*
Most games	185	*A.L. Smith, 2011-23*

Despite a solid scrum, the Highlanders will be mortified at a 5–9 return and the failure to reach the playoffs.

One more bonus point would have seen them scrape into the quarter-finals but they were always in catch-up mode after a poor start to the season. After a mini-revival which saw them rack up 145 points from three wins, they barely fired another shot, dropping six of their last eight games. In truth, had they made the playoffs, it would have been an injustice and a poster for doing away with the first round of the playoffs.

Still, there were several useful performers for the Highlanders.

Sam Gilbert, operating at fullback and second five, scored 122 points and ran with gusto.

Injuries again hampered the outside backs, though No 12 Thomas Umaga-Jensen delivered his best, most consistent, season at this level.

Englishman Freddie Burns and Mitch Hunt had their moments, but neither delivered consistent authority at No 10, while Aaron Smith played well but rarely dominated in his final season. Folau Fakatava never shrugged off his super-sub tag at halfback.

Injuries struck the pack but captain and openside flanker Billy Harmon manfully toiled away, as did his understudy Sean Withy. After a sketchy start, Shannon Frizell started to crank into gear and was playing more like his old self by the end of the campaign.

Jermaine Ainsley was the rock at tighthead prop, and the All Blacks selectors must have looked hard at him for promotion, but he did play for the All Blacks XV.

On the loosehead, Ethan de Groot was rarely bettered. Andrew Makalio shared the hooking duties with, mainly, Rhys Marshall.

	Tries	*Con*	*PG*	*DG*	*Points*		*Tries*	*Con*	*PG*	*DG*	*Points*
Gilbert	4	33	12	–	122	Ainsley	1	–	–	–	5
Renton	5	–	–	–	25	Frizell	1	–	–	–	5
Burns	–	6	2	–	18	Harmon	1	–	–	–	5
De Groot	3	–	–	–	15	Lienert-Brown	1	–	–	–	5
Garden-Bachop	3	–	–	–	15	Makalio	1	–	–	–	5
Hunt	3	–	–	–	15	Ma'u	1	–	–	–	5
Lowe	3	–	–	–	15	Mikaele-Tu'u	1	–	–	–	5
Smith	3	–	–	–	15	Paea	1	–	–	–	5
Timu	3	–	–	–	15	Parkinson	1	–	–	–	5
Bogado	2	–	–	–	10	Withy	1	–	–	–	5
Dawai	2	–	–	–	10						
Fakatava	2	–	–	–	10	***Totals***	***48***	***40***	***14***	***0***	***362***
Nareki	2	–	–	–	10						
Umaga-Jensen	2	–	–	–	10	*Opposition scored*	*60*	*45*	*23*	*0*	*459*
Millar	1	1	–	–	7						

Player	Union	Date of birth	Height	Weight	Highlanders games	Highlanders points
J. (Jermaine) Ainsley	Otago	08-08-95	1.81	122	27	5
L.C.A. (Leni) Apisai	Auckland	18-03-96	1.8	110	7	–
J.M. (James) Arscott	Otago	15-07-00	1.74	80	4	–
M. (Marty) Banks	Southland	19-09-89	1.9	90	51	243
J.J.G. (Josh) Bekhuis	Southland	26-04-86	2.01	116	84	10
M.G. (Martin) Bogado	Overseas	29-04-98	1.91	96	4	10
N.S.M. (Nikora) Broughton	Bay of Plenty	05-09-01	1.88	103	2	–
F.S. (Freddie) Burns	Overseas	13-05-90	1.83	90	9	18
M.R. (Mosese) Dawai	Waikato	29-06-98	1.93	101	13	20
E.L. (Ethan) de Groot	Southland	22-07-98	1.9	122	39	25
J.M. (Josh) Dickson	Otago	02-01-94	2	109	57	25
F.M.L.N. (Folau) Fakatava	Hawke's Bay	16-12-99	1.77	80	37	45
S.M. (Shannon) Frizell	Tasman	11-02-94	1.95	108	68	95
C.C. (Connor) Garden-Bachop	Wellington	04-02-00	1.89	94	28	30
S.J. (Sam) Gilbert	Otago	23-01-99	1.9	95	31	162
S.J. (Scott) Gregory	Southland	07-01-99	1.88	106	33	40
O. (Oliver) Haig	Otago	03-01-02	1.96	112	1	–
W.K. (Billy) Harmon (captain)	Canterbury	23-12-94	1.87	104	34	25
N. (Nathan) Hastie	Otago	27-04-01	1.77	87	1	–
K.M. (Kemara) Hauiti-Parapara	Otago	05-03-97	1.83	90	3	–
M.J.T. (Max) Hicks	Tasman	15-09-99	1.99	112	14	5
F.M. (Fabian) Holland	Otago	09-10-02	2.06	118	7	–
M.J. (Mitch) Hunt	Tasman	19-06-95	1.79	88	52	245
F.P. (Finn) Hurley	Otago	25-06-03	1.73	77	1	–
L.I. (Luca) Inch	Tasman	29-08-01	1.82	118	1	–
C.A. (Ayden) Johnstone	Waikato	24-10-96	1.84	120	44	5
V.T. (Vilimoni) Koroi	Otago	17-04-98	1.74	91	5	2
J.A.R. (James) Lentjes	Otago	16-01-91	1.88	104	68	35
D.P. (Daniel) Lienert-Brown	Canterbury	09-02-93	1.84	112	113	30
J.H. (Jonah) Lowe	Hawke's Bay	09-05-96	1.84	92	11	15
A. (Andrew) Makalio	Tasman	22-01-92	1.82	111	23	30
R.J.J. (Rhys) Marshall	Waikato	12-10-92	1.83	107	18	20
S. (Saula) Ma'u	Otago	29-04-00	1.93	140	22	5
M.E.R. (Marino) Mikaele-Tu'u	Hawke's Bay	06-11-97	1.93	114	48	30
C.G. (Cam) Millar	Otago	13-07-02	1.8	81	4	7
J.M. (Jona) Nareki	Otago	27-12-97	1.75	83	32	80
F.M.A. (Fetuli) Paea	Tasman	16-08-94	1.89	95	23	10
P.P.M. (Pari Pari) Parkinson	Tasman	12-09-96	2.04	119	36	10
H.T. (Hugh) Renton	Tasman	12-05-96	1.93	107	34	25
P.J. (PJ) Sheck	Wellington	10-03-00	1.93	122	1	–
A.L. (Aaron) Smith	Manawatu	21-11-88	1.71	83	185	175
J. (Jack) Taylor	Southland	25-06-03	1.8	107	1	–
J.O.W.(Jake) Te Hiwi	Otago	02-02-02	1.84	100	2	–
J.R. (Jeff) Thwaites	Bay of Plenty	22-11-92	1.9	115	14	–
J.C. (Josh) Timu	Otago	06-07-97	1.83	94	9	15
W.A. (Will) Tucker	Otago	16-03-98	2.02	114	6	–
T.N.M. (Thomas) Umaga-Jensen	Otago	31-12-97	1.87	95	32	25
M.A. (Matt) Whaanga	Southland	25-05-97	1.88	102	2	–
S.M. (Sean) Withy	Otago	01-02-01	1.91	108	15	5

NB. Banks, Inch, Koroi and Thwaites did not appear in 2023.

Manager: Paul McLaughlan
Coach: Clarke Dermody
Assistant coaches: Dave Dillon, Tom Donnelly, Riki Flutey, Richard Whiffin, Ben Smith

HIGHLANDERS 2023	Blues	Crusaders	Chiefs	Force	Fijian Drua	Moana Pasifika	Hurricanes	Force	Waratahs	Chiefs	Brumbies	Rebels	Reds	Blues	**TOTALS**
Gilbert	15	15	–	15	15	15	15	15	12	15	–	12	12	12	**12**
Hurley	–	–	–	s	–	–	–	–	–	–	–	–	–	–	**1**
Garden-Bachop	11	11	s	–	s	–	–	14	15	14	15	15	s	s	**11**
Dawai	–	s	11	–	–	14	14	–	–	–	–	–	–	–	**4**
Nareki	–	–	–	–	–	–	–	–	s	s	11	11	11	11	**6**
Bogado	s	–	14	14	14	–	–	–	–	–	–	–	–	–	**4**
Lowe	14	14	–	11	11	11	11	11	14	–	s	14	14	–	**11**
Te Hiwi	–	–	s	–	12	–	–	–	–	–	–	–	–	–	**2**
Timu	13	13	–	13	–	–	–	s	–	–	–	–	–	–	**4**
Whaanga	–	–	–	–	–	–	–	–	–	–	–	–	13	13	**2**
Paea	–	–	13	–	13	13	13	13	13	13	13	13	–	s	**10**
Umaga-Jensen	12	12	12	12	–	12	12	12	s	12	12	s	–	–	**11**
Gregory	–	–	–	–	–	–	s	–	11	11	14	–	s	14	**6**
Millar	–	–	–	s	s	s	10	–	–	–	–	–	–	–	**4**
Burns	s	10	15	–	–	–	–	s	–	10	10	10	10	10	**9**
Hunt	10	s	10	10	10	10	–	10	10	s	s	s	15	15	**13**
Smith	–	–	9	9	9	9	–	–	9	9	–	9	9	9	**9**
Hauiti-Parapara	s	9	s	–	–	–	–	–	–	–	–	–	–	–	**3**
Arscott	–	–	–	–	–	–	s	9	–	–	s	–	–	–	**3**
Hastie	–	–	–	–	–	–	–	s	–	–	–	–	–	–	**1**
Fakatava	9	s	–	s	s	s	9	–	s	s	9	s	s	s	**12**
Broughton	–	8	–	–	8	–	–	–	–	–	–	–	–	–	**2**
Renton	–	–	8	8	–	8	8	–	8	8	8	8	8	8	**10**
Lentjes	–	s	7	–	s	–	–	–	–	–	6	s	–	–	**5**
Haig	–	–	–	s	–	–	–	–	–	–	–	–	–	–	**1**
Harmon	7	6	–	7	7	7	7	7	–	7	7	7	7	7	**12**
Withy	s	7	s	6	6	6	s	s	7	s	s	6	s	s	**14**
Mikaele-Tu'u	8	–	–	–	–	s	s	8	s	s	s	s	s	s	**10**
Frizell	6	–	6	–	–	s	6	6	6	6	4	4	6	6	**11**
Dickson	5	–	5	–	–	–	5	–	–	5	5	–	–	–	**5**
Hicks	–	s	–	s	–	s	s	–	–	–	–	5	5	5	**7**
Parkinson	4	4	4	–	4	4	4	4	s	–	–	–	4	4	**10**
Bekhuis	–	–	–	5	s	–	–	–	–	–	–	–	–	–	**2**
Tucker	s	5	–	–	5	5	–	5	5	–	–	–	–	–	**6**
Holland	–	–	s	4	–	–	–	s	4	4	–	–	–	–	**5**
Ainsley	3	3	3	3	3	3	3	3	3	3	s	3	3	3	**14**
Sheck	–	–	–	s	–	–	–	–	–	–	–	–	–	–	**1**
Ma'u	s	s	s	–	s	s	s	s	s	s	3	s	s	s	**13**
Lienert-Brown	s	s	–	–	s	s	s	s	s	s	1	s	s	s	**12**
Johnstone	–	1	s	s	–	–	–	–	–	–	s	–	–	–	**4**
De Groot	1	–	1	1	1	1	1	1	1	1	–	1	1	1	**12**
Marshall	2	s	2	s	–	–	–	–	s	s	s	–	s	s	**9**
Makalio	s	2	–	2	–	s	2	2	2	2	2	2	2	2	**12**
Apisai	–	–	s	–	2	2	s	s	–	–	–	s	–	–	**6**
Taylor	–	–	–	–	s	–	–	–	–	–	–	–	–	–	**1**

HIGHLANDERS TEAM RECORD 2023

Played 14 **Won 5** **Lost 9** **Points for 362** **Points against 459**

Date	Opponent	Location	Score	Tries	Con	PG	DG	Referee
February 25	Blues	Dunedin	20–60	Hunt, Timu	Gilbert (2)	Gilbert (2)		Paul Williams
March 3	Crusaders	Melbourne	15–52	Timu (2)	Burns	Gilbert		Nic Berry
March 10	Chiefs	Hamilton	7–28	Dawai	Burns			Paul Williams
March 19	Force	Invercargill	43–35	Lowe (2), Withy, Renton, Hunt, Gilbert	Gilbert (5)	Gilbert		Angus Mabey
March 25	Fijian Drua	Dunedin	57–24	Bogado (2), Ainsley, Smith, Hunt, Lowe, Gilbert, de Groot, Millar	Gilbert (5), Millar			Paul Williams
March 31	Moana Pasifika	Auckland	45–17	Parkinson, Renton, Umaga-Jensen, Paea, Dawai, Gilbert, Mikaele-Tu'u	Gilbert (5)			Ben O'Keeffe
April 8	Hurricanes	Dunedin	14–29	Harmon, Renton	Gilbert (2)			Damon Murphy
April 22	Force	Perth	17–30	Makalio, Garden-Bachop	Gilbert (2)	Gilbert		Nic Berry
April 28	Waratahs	Sydney	20–21	Renton, Smith	Gilbert (2)	Gilbert (2)		Damon Murphy
May 5	Chiefs	Dunedin	28–52	Frizell, Smith, Gilbert, de Groot	Gilbert (4)			Ben O'Keeffe
May 14	Brumbies	Canberra	32–48	Lienert-Brown, Fakatava, Nareki, Umaga-Jensen	Burns (3)	Burns (2)		Graham Cooper
May 20	Rebels	Dunedin	20–17	De Groot, Garden-Bachop	Gilbert (2)	Gilbert (2)		Paul Williams
May 26	Reds	Dunedin	35–30	Renton, Nareki, Ma'u, Fakatava, Garden-Bachop	Gilbert (4), Burns			Brendon Pickerill
June 2	Blues	Auckland	9–16			Gilbert (3)		Ben O'Keeffe

MOANA PASIFIKA

Postal address: 12 Maurice Road, Penrose, Auckland 1061
Email: info@moanapasifika.co.nz
Home venues: Mt Smart Stadium, Auckland
Colours: ocean blue and white
Chairman: Sir M.N. (Michael) Jones
Chief executive: P. (Pelenato) Sakalia

Played 29, Won 3, Lost 26*

	Tries	*Conv*	*Pen*	*DG*	*Points*
For	89	62	23	0	642
Against	172	121	15	1	1152

*Includes 2020 match versus NZ Maori

RECORDS — TEAM

Most points in a game	46	*v Fijian Drua, 2023*
Most points in a season	354	*2023*
Biggest winning margin	10	*32–22 v Brumbies, 2022*
Most tries in a game	7	*v Fijian Drua, 2023*
Most tries in a season	50	*2023*

RECORDS — INDIVIDUAL

Most points in a game	16	*C.P. Lealiifano v Fijian Drua, 2023*
Most points in a season	90	*C.P. Lealiifano, 2023*
Most points in a career	148	*C.P. Lealiifano 2022–2023*
Most tries in a game	2	*on 9 occasions*
Most tries in a season	5	*L.J. T. Aumua, 2023* *M. T. Faiilagi, 2023* *F. Inisi, 2023* *T. T. Tavatavanawai, 2023*
Most tries in a career	8	*L.J. T. Aumua, A.A. Pole, 2022–2023*
Most conversions in a game	4	*on 5 occasions*
Most conversions in a season	20	*C.P. Lealiifano, 2023*
Most conversions in a career	34	*C.P. Lealiifano, 2022–2023*
Most penalty goals in a game	3	*C.P. Lealiifano v Blues, 2022*
Most penalty goals in a season	10	*C.P. Lealiifano, 2022*
Most penalty goals in a career	15	*C.P. Lealiifano, 2022–2023*
Most games	25	*W.L. Havili, E. V. Lindenmuth, 2022–23*

Hopes were high that the 2023 edition of Moana Pasifika would kick on after the insurmountable obstacles of the inaugural season.

There were signs of progress from the attack, Moana scoring 13 more tries and 87 more points in their second campaign. But the defence, an Achilles heel in 2022, again plagued them, as did ill-discipline.

They won just one match but could have won at least four more with an ounce of luck and accuracy, while they pushed the champion Crusaders hard in Christchurch and were unlucky not to topple the Blues at Eden Park in a nailbiting local derby. There was merit in the final round victory over the Waratahs in Sydney, but four games conceding in excess of 50 points were telling and costly.

One of the best finds was loose forward Miracle Faiilagi, who scored five trues and showed skill, work-rate and versatility. Solomone Funaki shouldered a heavy load as stand-in skipper for the injured Sekope Kepu, and manfully did his core tasks.

Midfielder Levi Aumua again proved to be the most penetrative back, closely followed by wing Timoci Tavatavanawai. Both scored five tries, as did Fine Inisi, who is starting to leaven his potential with more consistency.

Halves Christian Lealiifano and Ere Enari were again key and influential men, while there were good signs in the pack from the likes of Mike McKee, Ezekiel Lindenmuth and Sam Moli.

A good chunk of the roster appeared at Rugby World Cup 2023 for Samoa and Tonga, fulfilling a raison d'etre for this team.

Head coach Aaron Mauger resigned with a year left on his contract, and his successor was his old All Blacks midfield partner Tana Umaga, who comes across from the Blues.

MOANA PASIFIKA INDIVIDUAL SCORING

	Tries	*Con*	*PG*	*DG*	*Points*		*Tries*	*Con*	*PG*	*DG*	*Points*
Lealiifano	3	20	5	–	90	Penalty try	1	–	–	–	7
McClutchie	–	14	4	–	40	Apoua	1	–	–	–	5
Aumua	5	–	–	–	25	Curry	1	–	–	–	5
Faiilagi	5	–	–	–	25	Fainga'anuku	1	–	–	–	5
F. Inisi	5	–	–	–	25	Fomai	1	–	–	–	5
Tavatavanawai	5	–	–	–	25	Lindenmuth	1	–	–	–	5
Moli	4	–	–	–	20	Taefu	1	–	–	–	5
Pole	4	–	–	–	20	Tolai	1	–	–	–	5
Funaki	3	–	–	–	15	Tuitavuki	1	–	–	–	5
Toala	3	–	–	–	15						
Havili	2	–	–	–	10	***Totals***	**50**	**36**	**10**	**0**	**354**
Motuga	2	–	–	–	10						
Leuila	–	2	1	–	7	*Opposition scored*	*92**	*65*	*6*	*0*	*610*

*Includes one penalty try

Player	Union	Date of birth	Height	Weight	Moana Pasifika games	Moana Pasifika points
T. (Tomasi) Alosio	Tasman	26-01-92	1.87	89	4	10
S.J.L. (Joe) Apikotoa	Hawke's Bay	18-07-96	1.91	120	16	10
C. (Chris) Apoua	Southland	30-01-92	1.8	123	13	5
S. (Sue) Asomua	Counties Manukau	07-06-98	1.9	123	9	–
L.J.T. (Levi) Aumua	Tasman	09-10-94	1.85	108	22	40
M. (Michael) Curry	Tasman	02-03-94	1.96	115	17	10
E.C. (Ere) Enari	Hawke's Bay	30-05-97	1.78	85	24	–
M.T. (Miracle) Faiilagi	Overseas	31-08-99	1.93	108	12	25
L.T. (Tima) Fainga'anuku	Manawatu	26-04-97	1.88	105	14	20
P. (Penitoa) Finau	Bay of Plenty	17-12-93	1.85	97	7	–
N. (Neria) Fomai	Hawke's Bay	03-02-92	1.78	98	12	10
A.S. (Solomone) Funaki (captain)	Hawke's Bay	25-04-94	1.87	110	23	35
W.L. (William) Havili	Tasman	09-09-98	1.87	85	25	17
F. (Fine) Inisi	North Harbour	19-05-98	1.82	94	22	30
L. (Lotu) Inisi	North Harbour	26-04-99	1.87	110	7	5
N.A.D. (Niko) Jones	Auckland	22-07-00	1.87	101	2	–
S.M. (Sekope) Kepu	Counties Manukau	05-02-86	1.9	128	10	–
T. (Tau) Koloamatangi	Otago	03-01-95	1.77	128	10	5
J.T. (Jack) Lam	Waikato	18-11-87	1.87	105	6	–
C.P. (Christian) Lealiifano	Unattached	24-09-87	1.82	94	20	148
P.J. (Potu) Leavasa	Manawatu	10-01-96	1.94	106	6	–
A.D. (D'Angelo) Leuila	Waikato	18-01-97	1.74	100	6	9
E.V. (Ezekiel) Lindenmuth	Counties Manukau	14-07-97	1.87	116	25	10
J.D. (Jonah) Mau'u	Northland	28-07-98	1.83	102	10	–
L.F. (Lincoln) McClutchie	Hawke's Bay	12-04-99	1.74	84	20	58
M.J.F. (Mike) McKee	Southland	12-08-93	1.99	117	14	–
A.E. (Alex) McRobbie	Counties Manukau	14-02-00	1.96	111	17	5
S. (Sam) Moli	Tasman	24-12-98	1.85	114	23	20
A.L. (Alamanda) Motuga	Counties Manukau	11-09-94	1.81	96	18	20
M.A. (Mahonri) Ngakuru	Tasman	02-01-00	1.97	107	9	–
R.F. (Ray) Niuia	Manawatu	19-06-91	1.76	116	12	–
M. (Manu) Paea	Auckland	17-09-01	1.76	90	12	–
A.A. (Abraham) Pole	Otago	28-06-99	1.88	122	22	40
J.W. (Joe) Royal	Auckland	31-05-85	1.83	113	2	–
S.V. (Samuel) Slade	Counties Manukau	28-08-97	1.93	118	15	–
L.H. (Henry) Taefu	North Harbour	02-04-93	1.84	100	17	5
J.A. (Jonathan) Taumateine	Counties Manukau	28-09-96	1.77	82	16	–
T.T. (Timoci) Tavatavanawai	Tasman	14-02-98	1.75	95	20	35
D.S. (Danny) Toala	Hawke's Bay	23-03-99	1.76	95	18	20
L.H.V. (Luteru) Tolai	North Harbour	06-01-98	1.81	118	19	10
S. (Sione) Tu'ipulotu	Hawke's Bay	12-02-97	1.96	113	12	5
A.T.M. (Anzelo) Tuitavuki	Hawke's Bay	10-10-98	1.82	98	8	10
I.J. (Isi) Tu'ungafasi	Tasman	10-01-95	1.85	116	7	–
L. (Lolagi) Visinia	Hawke's Bay	17-01-93	1.93	109	5	–
S.A. (Sam) Wye	Auckland	11-11-00	1.78	89	1	–

*NB. Kepu and Lam did not appear in 2023.

Manager: Danny Gautasa
Coach: Aaron Mauger
Assistant coaches: Filo Tiatia, Dale MacLeod, Pauliasi Manu, Damian Karauna

MOANA PASIFIKA 2023

	Fijian Drua	Chiefs	Force	Brumbies	Hurricanes	Highlanders	Crusaders	Reds	Rebels	Blues	Hurricanes	Crusaders	Fijian Drua	Waratahs	TOTALS
Havili	15	s	15	15	15	15	15	15	15	15	s	15	15	15	**14**
Visinia	–	–	–	–	–	–	–	–	–	–	s	–	–	–	**1**
Leuila	–	–	–	–	s	s	s	s	–	12	–	–	–	–	**5**
Fainga'anuku	–	–	–	–	14	–	–	–	–	–	14	14	14	14	**5**
Alosio	–	–	–	–	–	–	–	–	–	–	15	–	–	–	**1**
Tavatavanawai	14	14	14	11	–	14	14	14	14	14	–	s	11	11	**12**
Tuitavuki	–	11	11	s	11	–	–	–	–	–	11	–	–	–	**5**
Fomai	11	–	–	–	–	11	11	11	11	11	–	11	–	–	**7**
Aumua	13	12	s	13	13	13	13	13	13	13	–	12	13	13	**13**
F. Inisi	s	13	13	14	s	s	s	s	s	s	–	13	s	s	**13**
Taefu	s	s	s	s	12	–	–	–	–	–	12	s	12	12	**9**
Toala	12	15	12	12	–	12	12	12	12	–	13	–	–	–	**9**
Lealiifano	10	10	–	10	10	–	–	–	10	10	–	10	10	10	**9**
McClutchie	–	–	10	–	–	10	10	10	s	s	10	–	–	s	**8**
Enari	9	s	9	9	9	9	9	9	9	9	–	9	s	s	**13**
Taumateine	–	–	–	–	–	–	–	–	s	s	9	s	9	9	**6**
Paea	s	9	s	s	s	s	s	s	–	–	–	–	–	–	**8**
Wye	–	–	–	–	–	–	–	–	–	–	s	–	–	–	**1**
Mau'u	8	8	s	–	–	s	s	–	7	s	s	s	s	–	**10**
L. Inisi	–	s	8	8	8	–	–	–	s	–	8	–	–	–	**6**
Tu'ipulotu	–	–	–	–	–	–	–	s	–	–	6	–	–	–	**2**
Fai'ilagi	–	6	6	6	s	6	6	6	6	6	–	6	s	6	**12**
Jones	–	–	–	–	–	–	–	7	–	–	–	–	–	–	**1**
Motuga	s	–	–	7	7	7	7	–	–	7	–	7	7	s	**9**
Funaki	7	7	7	s	6	8	8	8	8	8	–	8	8	8	**13**
Finau	–	–	–	–	–	–	–	–	–	–	7	–	6	7	**3**
McRobbie	–	–	4	s	–	–	–	–	s	s	4	4	–	–	**6**
Slade	4	4	–	–	4	5	5	–	–	–	–	–	–	5	**6**
Ngakuru	5	–	–	–	–	–	–	–	–	–	5	5	s	–	**4**
Leavasa	–	–	s	4	s	–	–	s	–	–	s	s	–	–	**6**
Curry	6	5	–	–	–	4	4	4	4	4	–	–	4	4	**9**
McKee	s	s	5	5	5	s	s	5	5	5	–	–	5	s	**12**
Apikotoa	–	–	–	–	–	s	3	–	–	–	–	s	3	3	**5**
Apoua	3	–	–	–	s	–	–	–	s	3	s	3	s	s	**8**
Lindenmuth	–	1	s	–	s	1	1	1	s	s	1	s	1	s	**12**
Asomua	s	3	3	3	3	3	–	s	–	–	–	–	–	–	**7**
Pole	1	s	1	1	1	s	s	s	1	1	–	1	s	1	**13**
Tu'ungafasi	–	s	s	s	–	–	s	3	3	–	3	–	–	–	**7**
Koloamatangi	s	–	–	s	–	–	–	–	–	s	s	–	–	–	**4**
Tolai	s	–	s	–	–	s	s	s	–	s	2	s	2	2	**10**
Moli	2	2	2	s	2	2	2	2	2	2	–	2	s	s	**13**
Niuia	–	s	–	2	s	–	–	–	s	–	–	–	–	–	**4**
Royal	–	–	–	–	–	–	–	–	–	–	s	–	–	–	**1**

MOANA PASIFIKA TEAM RECORD 2023

Played 14 **Won 1** **Lost 13** **Points for 354** **Points against 610**

Date	Opponent	Location	Score	Tries	Con	PG	DG	Referee
February 25	Fijian Drua	Auckland	34–36	Pole (2), Apoua, Curry, Toala	Lealiifano (3)	Lealiifano		James Doleman
March 4	Chiefs	Melbourne	29–52	Moli, Funaki, Tavatavanawai, penalty try	Lealiifano (2)	Lealiifano		Angus Gardner
March 11	Force	Perth	18–21	Moli, F. Inisi	McClutchie	McClutchie (2)		Jordan Way
March 18	Brumbies	Canberra	36–62	Motuga (2), Faiilagi, F. Inisi, Moli	Lealiifano (4)	Lealiifano		Graham Cooper
March 25	Hurricanes	Auckland	0–59					Reuben Keane
March 31	Highlanders	Auckland	17–45	Funaki, Aumua	McClutchie (2)	McClutchie		Ben O'Keeffe
April 7	Crusaders	Christchurch	21–38	Aumua (2), Tavatavanawai	McClutchie (3)			James Doleman
April 14	Reds	Apia	28–40	Fai'ilagi (2), Toala, Tolai	McClutchie (2), Leuila (2)			Brendon Pickerill
April 29	Rebels	Auckland	33–43	F. Inisi (2), Aumua, Fomai, Funaki	McClutchie (4)			Angus Mabey
May 6	Blues	Auckland	30–31	Pole, Lealiifano, Tavatavanawai, F. Inisi	Lealiifano (2)	Lealiifano, Leuila		Graham Cooper
May 13	Hurricanes	Wellington	22–71	Tuitavuki, Taefu, Toala	McClutchie (2)	McClutchie		Brendon Pickerill
May 19	Crusaders	Auckland	7–41	Fainga'anuku	Lealiifano			Reuben Keane
May 27	Fijian Drua	Lautoka	46–47	Havili (2), Lindenmuth, Lealiifano, Aumua, Moli, Pole	Lealiifano (4)	Lealiifano		Jordan Way
June 3	Waratahs	Sydney	33–24	Tavatavanawai (2), Faiilagi (2), Lealiifano	Lealiifano (4)			Graham Cooper

SUPER RUGBY AOTEAROA UNDER 20 TOURNAMENT

The third annual tournament was again held at Owen Delany Park, Taupo, and all matches were shown live on Sky TV. The matches are not of first-class status.

This year was notable for three innovations:
(1) Teams from Moana Pasifika and Fijian Drua were added.
(2) For the first time there was an actual competition with a tournament winner.
(3) The teams were able to use all 27 squad members in each game, with all 12 non-starters being available on the bench and able to come on as a substitute.

Nine players were making their third tournament appearance: Will Bason, Kyle Brown, Bradley Crichton, Harry Godfrey, Jordan Hutchings, Dayton Iobu, Dominic Ropeti, Feleti Sae-Ta'ufo'ou and Raymond Tuputupu.

March 19
Blues 51, Fijian Drua 7
Hurricanes 64, Moana Pasifika 19
NZ Barbarians 35, Crusaders 27
Highlanders 28, Chiefs 18

March 22
ranking Crusaders 50, Fijian Drua 22
ranking Chiefs 52, Moana Pasifika 20
semi-final Blues 51, NZ Barbarians 26
semi-final Hurricanes 36, Highlanders 26

March 25
7-8 Fijian Drua 33, Moana Pasifika 26
5-6 Chiefs 31, Crusaders 29
3-4 Highlanders 41, NZ Barbarians 22
final Blues 50, Hurricanes 36

SQUADS (APPEARANCES IN BRACKETS):

Blues: *Captain* — Sam Hainsworth-Fa'aofo (3) *Coach* — Steven Bates
Auckland: Ben Ake, Che Clark, Leo Gordon, Sam Hainsworth-Fa'aofo, Gage Jackson, Kurene Luamanuvae, King Maxwell, Maliu Nuiafe, Nathaniel Pole, Sika Pole, Byron Smith, Christian Stenhouse, Xavi Taele, Blair Tagi-Fuimaono, Valentino Taito, Caleb Tangitau, Xavier Tito-Harris, Hawkin Toeava, Ofa Topeni, Essendon Tuitupou, PJ (Poasa) Uiese, Josiah Unga, Chris Vunipola, Riley Williams. ***Northland:*** Tama Anderson*, JT (Junior) Pont-Bellamy, Kobe Walters, Rory Woods.

Chiefs: Captain — Fiti Sa (2), Cody Nordstrom (1) *Coach* — James Porter
Bay of Plenty: Tamiro Armstrong, Brayden Dew, Grady Forbes, Taine Kolose, Marley Murphy, Aoturoa Seeling, Te Hamana Te Aute, Codemeru Vai. ***Counties Manukau:*** Cohen Brady-Leatham, Esau Filimoehala, Josh Penney, Keran Van Staden. ***Taranaki:*** Fiti Sa, Peter Te Kahu. ***Waikato:*** Tai Cribb, Manahi Goulton, Senita Lauaki, William Martin, Jole Naufahu, Cody Nordstrom, Sean Ralph, Gabe Robinson, Waisake Salabiau, Jonty Short, Andrew Smith, Aki Tuivailala, Malachi Wrampling-Alec.
Original selection Perry Lawrence (Taranaki) withdrew before the tournament and replaced by Aoturoa Seeling.

Crusaders: *Captain* — Tahlor Cahill (2), James White (1) *Coach* — Alex Robertson
Canterbury: Toby Bell, Riley Brewis, Jae Broomfield, Angus Brown, Tahlor Cahill, Suliasi Faiva, Isaac Hutchinson, Liam Jack, Johnny Lee, Cody Lokotui, Moses McGoon, Anaru Paenga-Morgan, George Reeves, Cooper Roberts, Jayden Sa*, Nic Shearer, Dawson Smith, Hendrix Taylor, James White. ***Tasman:*** Penisimani Fihaki, Cooper Grant, Dylan Irvine, Joel Lauvale, Hunter Leppien, Matt Lowe, Brodie Robinson, Nic Sauira, Will Thornalley.

Highlanders: *Captain* — Will Stodart (3) *Coach* — Ryan Bambry
Otago: Jeremiah Asi, Cameron Burgess, Brad Campbell, Lucas Casey, Zack Cleaver-Donovan*, Ajay Faleafaga, Finn Hurley, Thomas Jackson, Fatai Koloi, Lawrence Leung-Wai, A One Lolofie, Fionn McKenna, Reuben Palmer, Kyan Rangitutia, Max Ratcliffe, Will Stodart, Moana Takataka, Jack Timu, Konrad Toleafoa, Mefi Tupou, Semisi Tupou-Ta'eiloa, Josh Whaanga, Aaron Withy. ***Southland:*** Hunter Areaiiti-Burgess, Hunter Fahey, Liam McIntosh, Jack Taylor, Caleb Williams.

Hurricanes: *Co-Captains* — Harry Godfrey, (3) Dominic Ropeti (3) *Coach* — Darren Larsen
Hawke's Bay: Tom Allen, Bryson Crawford-Pakoti*, Harry Godfrey, Bethel Malasia, Meni Manase, Mathew Monaghan, Hunter Morrison, Konradd Newland, Josiah Sakaria, Kusitino Savea. ***Manawatu:*** Isaiah Armstrong-Ravula, Vernon Bason, Sam Coles, Malakai Hala-Ngatai, Raymond Tuputupu, Jordi Viljoen, Epeli Waqa-Nalaqa. ***Wellington:*** Jeremiah Collins, Bradley Crichton, Tobias Crosby, Chicago Doyle, Sam Howling, Siale Lauaki, Jack O'Brien, Tofuka Paongo, Matolu Petaia, Dominic Ropeti, Senio Sanele.
Original selection Cooper Flanders (Hawke's Bay) withdrew before the tournament and was replaced by Jeremiah Collins.

NZ Barbarians: *Captain* — Te Rama Reuben (2), Will Bason (1) *Coach* — Steve Jackson
Auckland: Will Bason, Jordan Hutchings, Taeao Pomale-Time, Star Sami, Tito Tuipulotu
Canterbury: Jack Coulthard, Terrence Graham, Angus Hammett, Liam Pratt. ***Counties Manukau:*** Vaivaihefolau Kailahi. ***Hawke's Bay:*** Kade Manuel-Green*. ***Manawatu:*** Kyle Brown, Feleti Sae-Ta'ufo'ou. ***North Harbour:*** Siolo Freuan. ***Otago:*** Oliver Foote, Eric Peita, Filipo Whitehouse-Opetaia Tovio. ***Southland:*** Tupou Kaufononga. ***Tasman:*** Tylah Blake, Nelesoni Malalau. ***Thames Valley:*** Joshua Barker. ***Waikato:*** Zinzan Hansen, Jack Harding, Te Rama Reuben, Xavier Saifoloi. ***Wellington:*** Logan Love. ***West Coast:*** Jacob Lowe. ***Whanganui:*** Josh Brunger.

Fijian Drua: *Captain* — Motikai Murray (3) *Coach* — Ifereimi Rawaqa
Erami Baca, Philip Baseilala, Sikeli Basiyalo, Napolioni Batimala, Tevita Bukaniyava, Sakiusa Kama*, Joshua Kine, Tavite Kotobalavu, Breyton Legge, Isireli Masiwini, Nailani May, Motikai Murray, Joeli Nainoca, Emosi Natubailagi, Manieta Navonovono, Ibenizer Navula, Joeli Niubalavu, Tevita Sovau, Eroni Sarasau, Juda Saumaisue, Kavaia Tagiveitaua, Sitiveni Tamani, Lasaro Vuluma, Ponipate Tuberi, Waisea Tudulu, Tomasi Tuitatava, Maika Tuitubou, Mesake Vocevoce.

Moana Pasifika: *Captain* — Captain: Israel Otunuku (3) *Coach* — Gus Leger
Sam Asotasi, Calvin Fepulea'i, Tevita (Kini) Fonua, Laukau Halatonu*, Dayton Iobu, Jarius Iosefa, Uluaki Kale, Sonatane Kaufasi, Ofa Lea'amanu, Fatiauma Moeaha-Leota, Manase Mohuanga, Afa Moleli, Israel Otunuku, Lazarus Papalii, Paulo Paulo, Bless Perese-Elliott, Riki Reuben, John Samuelu, Kobie Scutt, Salesa Seumanugafai, Seuteni Seuteni, Bitner Tafili, Wally Tau, Kyren Taumoefolau, Brandon Televave, Maea Tema-Schmidt, Joe Tunumafono-Sale, Mikaele Vaeau.

**added to the squads during the tournament*

DJ Graham Award (player of the tournament)
Harry Godfrey (Hurricanes).

Leading Try Scorers
4 — Sean Ralph (Chiefs), Xavier Tito-Harris (Blues).

Leading Point Scorers
30 — Harry Godfrey (Hurricanes), Byron Smith (Blues).

Referees
Stu Catley (2), Tipene Cottrell (2), Andy Morton (2), Brandon Roberts (2), Cameron Stone (1), Mike Winter (1), Ben Woolerton (2).

NPC CHAMPIONSHIP WINNERS

	First Division	*Second Division (North)*	*Second Division (South)*
1976	Bay of Plenty	Taranaki	South Canterbury
1977	Canterbury	North Auckland	South Canterbury
1978	Wellington	Bay of Plenty	Marlborough
1979	Counties	Hawke's Bay	Marlborough
1980	Manawatu	Waikato	Mid Canterbury
1981	Wellington	Wairarapa Bush	South Canterbury
1982	Auckland	Taranaki	Southland
1983	Canterbury	Taranaki	Mid Canterbury
1984	Auckland	Taranaki	Southland

	First Division	*Second Division*	*Third Division*
1985	Auckland	Taranaki	North Harbour
1986	Wellington	Waikato	South Canterbury
1987	Auckland	North Harbour	Poverty Bay
1988	Auckland	Hawke's Bay	Thames Valley
1989	Auckland	Southland	Wanganui
1990	Auckland	Hawke's Bay	Thames Valley
1991	Otago	King Country	South Canterbury
1992	Waikato	Taranaki	Nelson Bays
1993	Auckland	Counties	Horowhenua
1994	Auckland	Southland	Mid Canterbury
1995	Auckland	Taranaki	Thames Valley
1996	Auckland	Southland	Wanganui
1997	Canterbury	Northland	Marlborough
1998	Otago	Central Vikings	Mid Canterbury
1999	Auckland	Nelson Bays	East Coast
2000	Wellington	Bay of Plenty	East Coast
2001	Canterbury	Hawke's Bay	South Canterbury
2002	Auckland	Hawke's Bay	North Otago
2003	Auckland	Hawke's Bay	Wanganui
2004	Canterbury	Nelson Bays	Poverty Bay
2005	Auckland	Hawke's Bay	Wairarapa Bush

	Air New Zealand Cup	*Meads Cup*	*Lochore Cup*
2006	Waikato	Wairarapa Bush	Poverty Bay
2007	Auckland	North Otago	Poverty Bay
2008	Canterbury	Wanganui	Poverty Bay
2009	Canterbury	Wanganui	North Otago

	ITM Cup	*Meads Cup*	*Lochore Cup*
2010	Canterbury	North Otago	Wairarapa Bush

	ITM Premiership	*ITM Championship*	*Meads Cup*	*Lochore Cup*
2011	Canterbury	Hawke's Bay	Wanganui	Poverty Bay
2012	Canterbury	Counties Manukau	East Coast	Buller

	ITM Cup		*PINK BATTS HEARTLAND CHAMPIONSHIP*	
	Premiership	***Championship***	***Meads Cup***	***Lochore Cup***
2013	Canterbury	Tasman	Mid Canterbury	South Canterbury
2014	Taranaki	Manawatu	Mid Canterbury	Wanganui
2015	Canterbury	Hawke's Bay	Wanganui	King Country

	MITRE 10 CUP/NPC		*MITRE 10 HEARTLAND CHAMPIONSHIP*	
	Premiership	***Championship***	***Meads Cup***	***Lochore Cup***
2016	Canterbury	North Harbour	Wanganui	North Otago
2017	Canterbury	Wellington	Wanganui	Mid-Canterbury
2018	Auckland	Waikato	Thames Valley	Horowhenua Kapiti
2019	Tasman	Bay of Plenty	North Otago	South Canterbury
2020	Tasman	Hawke's Bay	NR	NR

	BUNNINGS NPC		*BUNNINGS HEARTLAND CHAMPIONSHIP*	
	Premiership	***Championship***	***Meads Cup***	***Lochore Cup***
2021	Waikato	Taranaki	South Canterbury	Whanganui

	Premiership	***Meads Cup***	***Lochore Cup***
2022	Wellington	South Canterbury	Ngati Porou East Coast
2023	Taranaki	South Canterbury	West Coast

ALMANACK NPC FORM XV

Etene Nanai-Seturo
Counties Manukau

Jacob Ratumaitavuki-Kneepkens
Taranaki

Billy Proctor
Wellington

Heremaia Murray
Northland

Alex Nankivell
Tasman

Josh Jacomb
Taranaki

Brad Weber
Hawke's Bay

Kaylum Boshier (capt)
Taranaki

Du'Plessis Kirifi
Wellington

Manaaki Selby-Rickit
Bay of Plenty

Tom Parsons
Hawke's Bay

Billy Harmon
Canterbury

Tevita Mafileo
North Harbour

Tyrone Thompson
Hawke's Bay

Pouri Rakete-Stones
Hawke's Bay

Reserves –

Kurt Eklund (*Bay of Plenty*), Xavier Numia (*Wellington*), Reuben O'Neill (*Taranaki*), Naitoa Ah Kuoi (*Bay of Plenty*), Anton Segner (*Tasman*), Adam Lennox (*Taranaki*), Zarn Sullivan (*Auckland*), Roger Tuivasa-Sheck (*Auckland*)

BUNNINGS NPC PREMIER COMPETITION

Yet another format change for the Bunnings NPC Premiership occurred in 2023. Last year's Odds and Even Conferences were scrapped after just the one season and the tournament returned to what it had last been in 2010 – one competition table for all 14 teams.

Taranaki secured their second premiership title defeating Hawke's Bay 22–19 in the final. For Hawke's Bay it was their first ever appearance in the premiership final. Curiously, both teams had an identical run of results in the round robin — winning their first four matches, losing their next three matches, then winning their final three matches. They did not meet in the round robin.

Two matches went to golden point extra time, both scorelines being 15–15 after 80 minutes. Neither Southland or Northland could score in the ten minutes and the match finished 15–15, while Tasman scored a try in the second minute of extra time to win 20–15 v North Harbour.

ROUND ROBIN

										FOR					*AGAINST*		
	P	*W*	*D*	*L*	*TB*	*LB*	*Pts*	*T*	*C*	*PG*	*DG*	*Total*	*T*	*C*	*PG*	*DG*	*Total*
Wellington	10	9	0	1	6	1	**43**	40	27	15	0	299	22	10	6	0	148
Taranaki	10	7	0	3	8	2	**38**	44[1]	27	8	0	300	27	20	14	0	217
Canterbury	10	6	0	4	9	4	**37**	48[1]	35	13	0	351	37	22	14	0	271
Bay of Plenty	10	7	0	3	6	1	**35**	39	30	10	0	285	32[1]	20	13	0	241
Hawke's Bay	10	7	0	3	5	1	**34**	42[1]	31	10	0	304	35	25	13	0	264
Auckland	10	6	0	4	6	2	**32**	41	28	10	0	291	33[1]	20	11	1	243
Tasman	10	6	0	4	5	2	**31**	35	17	7	0	230	28	18	10	0	206
Waikato	10	5	0	5	7	2	**29**	43[1]	22	6	1	282	37	25	6	0	253
Counties Manukau	10	4	0	6	7	1	**24**	41[2]	22	9	0	280	47[2]	25	9	0	316
North Harbour	10	4	0	6	3	3	**22**	36	22	16	0	272	44	27	7	0	295
Otago	10	3	0	7	4	2	**18**	30	18	9	0	213	40	32	10	0	294
Northland	10	2	1	7	4	3	**17**	28	23	19	0	243	35[1]	27	17	0	282
Manawatu	10	2	0	8	4	0	**12**	30[1]	19	3	0	199	60[1]	41	13	0	423
Southland	10	1	1	8	2	1	**9**	25	15	14	0	197	45[1]	24	6	0	293
TOTALS								***522***	***336***	***149***	***1***	***3746***	***522***	***336***	***149***	***1***	***3746***

TB bonus points for four or more tries in a match.
LB bonus point for loss by seven or fewer points.

[1] *contains one penalty try (7 points)*
[2] *contains two penalty tries (14 points)*

PLAYOFF SUMMARY

Quarter-finals:
Canterbury **29** (4t,3c,pg) v Auckland **24** (4t,2c), at Christchurch
Wellington **32** (4t,3c,2pg) v Waikato **28** (4t,4c), at Wellington
Taranaki **34** (3t,pt,3c,2pg) v Tasman **18** (2t,c,2pg), at New Plymouth
Hawke's Bay **38** (6t,4c) v Bay of Plenty **28** (4t,4c), at Tauranga

Semi-finals:
Taranaki **23** (t,6pg) v Canterbury **16** (t,c,3pg), at New Plymouth
Hawke's Bay **25** (3t,2c,2pg) v Wellington **24** (3t,3c,pg), at Wellington

Final:
Taranaki **22** (3t,2c,pg) v Hawke's Bay **19** (3t,2c), at New Plymouth

RECORDS

BY THE TEAMS

In a Season

	BEST PERFORMANCES 2023		RECORD 1976–2023 First Division 1976–2005, Air New Zealand Cup 2006–2009, ITM Cup 2010–2015, Mitre 10 Cup 2016–2020, Bunnings NPC 2021–	
Most points	396	Canterbury	521	Otago, 1998
Most tries	54	Hawke's Bay	74	Wellington, 2017
Most conversions	39	Canterbury, Hawke's Bay	57	Canterbury, 2017
Most penalty goals	19	Northland	45	Otago, 2012
Most dropped goals	1	Waikato	12	Bay of Plenty, 1985

In a Match

Highest Score	68	Canterbury v Manawatu	97	Auckland v King Country, 1993
Biggest winning margin	50	Hawke's Bay v Manawatu, (57–7)	94	Auckland v King Country, 1993 (*97–3*)
Most tries	10	Canterbury v Manawatu	15	Auckland v King Country, 1993
Most conversions	9	Canterbury v Manawatu	12	Canterbury v Southland, 2012
Most penalty goals	6	Taranaki v Canterbury, October 13	9	Taranaki v Bay of Plenty, 2011
Most dropped goals	1	Waikato v Auckland	4	Bay of Plenty v Waikato, 1985

BY THE PLAYERS

	Best Performances 2023		Record 1976–2023 (First Division 1976–2005, Air New Zealand Cup 2006–2009, ITM Cup 2010–2015, Mitre 10 Cup 2016–2020, Bunnings NPC 2021–)	
In a Season				
Most points	125	L.F. McClutchie (Hawke's Bay)	196	T.E. Brown (*Otago*), 1998
Most tries	9	M.W.H. Selby-Rickit (Bay of Plenty)	15	T.J. Wright (*Auckland*), 1984 B.J. Laney (*Otago*), 1998
In a Match				
Most points	24	J.D. Jacomb (Taranaki) v North Harbour	37	B.A. Blair (*Canterbury*) v Counties Manukau, 1999
Most tries	3	Eight instances (eight players)	5	T.J. Wright (*Auckland*) v Manawatu, 1984 W.R. Gordon (*Waikato*) v Southland, 1990 C.J. Spencer (*Auckland*) v Otago, 1996 M.P. Robinson (*Taranaki*) v Southland, 1997 J. Maddock (*Canterbury*) v North Harbour, 2002 S.W. Sivivatu (*Waikato*) v Auckland, 2004 T. Li (*North Harbour*) v Taranaki, 2017
Most conversions	7	L.F. McClutchie (Hawke's Bay) v Manawatu, J.D. Jacomb (Taranaki) v North Harbour	12	T.J. Taylor (*Canterbury*) v Southland, 2012
Most penalty goals	5	A. Morgan (Wellington) v Manawatu	9	B.J. Barrett (*Taranaki*) v Bay of Plenty, 2011
Most dropped goals	1	T.P.A. Cook-Savage (Waikato) v Auckland	4	R.J. Preston (*Bay of Plenty*) v Waikato, 1985

Leading points-scorers in the 2023 Bunnings NPC Premiership:

L.F. McClutchie	*Hawke's Bay*	125
F.W. Burke	*Canterbury*	109
Z. Sullivan	*Auckland*	102
A. Morgan	*Wellington*	102
R.W.M. Reihana	*Northland*	86

Leading try-scorers in the 2023 Bunnings NPC Premiership:

M.W.H. Selby-Rickit	*Bay of Plenty*	9
H.W.W. Murray	*Northland*	8
B.J. Murray	*Canterbury*	7
L.F. Filipo	*Wellington*	7
C.J. Tiatia	*Hawke's Bay*	7

BUNNINGS HEARTLAND CHAMPIONSHIP 2023

South Canterbury won the Meads Cup to become Heartland champions for the third year in a row, and equal the feat of Whanganui 2015–2017. South Canterbury are currently on a winning streak, having won their last 31 consecutive Heartland Championship matches, a record for the competition.

West Coast's winning of the Lochore Cup was momentous for being the first time the union has ever won a national trophy.

For the third year in a row, South Canterbury, Thames Valley and Whanganui filled the top three positions in the round robin.

Two matches went to golden point extra time. Ngati Porou East Coast defeated Buller 24–21 with a penalty goal in the third minute of extra time, and West Coast defeated Mid Canterbury 32–29 with a penalty goal in the fifth minute of extra time.

South Canterbury's Siu Kakala became the fourth player to score a try/tries in all eight round robin matches. He also scored a try in the semi-final.

Four players reached the milestone of 100 games for their province during the Heartland Championship: Inia Katia (Wairarapa Bush), Verdon Bartlett (Ngati Porou East Coast), Lindsay Horrocks (Whanganui) and Roman Tutauha (Whanganui).

Ngati Porou East Coast successfully defended the Osborne Taonga in all four challenge matches:

Osborne Taonga matches:
August 19: Ngati Porou East Coast 19, Mid Canterbury 8, Ruatoria
August 26: Ngati Porou East Coast 38, North Otago 29, Ruatoria
September 9: Ngati Porou East Coast 31, Poverty Bay 11, Ruatoria
September 23: Ngati Porou East Coast 29, King Country 11, Ruatoria

ROUND ROBIN SUMMARY

								FOR					AGAINST				
	P	*W*	*D*	*L*	*TB*	*LB*	*Pts*	*T*	*C*	*PG*	*DG*	*Total*	*T*	*C*	*PG*	*DG*	*Total*
South Canterbury	8	8	0	0	8	0	**40**	53	35	2	0	341	25[1]	19	5	0	180
Whanganui	8	6	0	2	6	2	**32**	38	25	8	0	264	21	15	7	0	156
Thames Valley	8	6	0	2	5	2	**31**	32	22	14	0	246	33	23	3	0	220
Ngati Porou East Coast	8	5	0	3	5	2	**27**	30	24	8	0	222	21	12	18	0	183
North Otago	8	4	0	4	5	1	**22**	40	25	3	0	259	33	21	7	0	228
Wairarapa Bush	8	4	0	4	4	2	**22**	24	14	14	0	190	34	23	10	0	246
West Coast	8	4	0	4	5	0	**21**	30[1]	18	10	0	218	28	18	12	0	212
Poverty Bay	8	2	0	6	4	4	**16**	32	21	9	0	229	34	23	10	1	249
Mid Canterbury	8	2	0	6	5	3	**16**	30	19	10	1	221	35	23	8	0	245
King Country	8	3	0	5	3	1	**16**	23	18	8	0	175	34	24	10	0	248
Buller	8	2	0	6	5	2	**15**	24	15	5	0	165	35	26	5	0	242
Horowhenua Kapiti	8	2	0	6	2	1	**11**	24	16	8	0	176	47	25	4	0	297
TOTALS								***380***	***252***	***99***	***1***	***2706***	***380***	***252***	***99***	***1***	***2706***

TB bonus points for four or more tries in a match.
LB bonus point for loss by seven or fewer points.

[1] *contains one penalty try (7 points)*

North Otago and Wairarapa Bush both finished on 22 points. North Otago had the higher ranking due to winning their individual match.

Poverty Bay, Mid Canterbury and King Country all finished on 16 points. As the three teams did not all play each other, the determining ranking factor was points differential. Poverty Bay had the highest rank due to a differential of -20, followed by Mid Canterbury -24 and King Country -73.

PLAYOFF SUMMARY

MEADS CUP (1st–4th)

Semi-Finals: Whanganui **38** (5t, 2c, 2pg, dg) beat Thames Valley **3** (pg), at Whanganui; South Canterbury **34** (4t, 4c, 2pg) beat Ngati Porou East Coast **17** (t, pt, c, pg), at Pleasant Point.

Final: South Canterbury **40** (5t, 3c, 3pg) beat Whanganui **30** (4t ,2c, 2pg), at Temuka.

LOCHORE CUP (5th–8th)

Semi-Finals: Poverty Bay **40** (6t, 5c) beat North Otago **35** (4t,3c,3pg), at Oamaru; West Coast **33** (5t, 4c) beat Wairarapa Bush **27** (3t, 3c, 2pg), at Masterton.

Final: West Coast **23** (t, pt, c, 3pg) beat Poverty Bay **20** (4t), at Greymouth.

HEARTLAND CHAMPIONSHIP RECORDS

BY THE TEAMS

In a Season

	BEST PERFORMANCE 2023		*RECORD 2006–2023*	
Most points	415	South Canterbury	491	South Canterbury, 2022
Most tries	62	South Canterbury	69	South Canterbury, 2022
Most conversions	42	South Canterbury	46	South Canterbury, 2022
Most penalty goals	16	Wairarapa Bush	30	Wairarapa Bush, 2012
Most dropped goals	1	Mid Canterbury, Whanganui	2	on ten occasions (*eight teams*)

In a Match

	BEST PERFORMANCE 2023		*RECORD 2006–2023*	
Most points	56	South Canterbury v Buller	116	North Otago v East Coast, 2010
Biggest winning margin	56	South Canterbury v Buller (56–0)	113	North Otago v East Coast, 2010 (*116–3*)
Most tries	9	Whanganui v Horowhenua Kapiti	17	North Otago v East Coast, 2010
Most conversions	8	South Canterbury v Buller	14	North Otago v East Coast, 2010
Most penalty goals	4	West Coast v King Country Horowhenua Kapiti v Wairarapa Bush Thames Valley v Ngati Porou East Coast	7	Thames Valley v Mid Canterbury, 2009 Thames Valley v East Coast, 2011 Poverty Bay v Buller, 2013 Thames Valley v Wanganui, 2019
Most dropped goals	1	Mid Canterbury v Poverty Bay, Whanganui v Thames Valley, October 7	1	61 occasions

BY THE PLAYERS

	BEST PERFORMANCE 2023		RECORD 2006–2023	
In a Season				
Most points	116	F.R. Morgan (Thames Valley)	147	J.J. Lash (*Buller*), 2017
Most tries	13	A. Vakarorogo (Whanganui),S.I.F. Kakala (South Canterbury)	14	P. Fetuai (*Wanganui*), 2006
In a Match				
Most points	25	A. Vakarorogo (Whanganui) v Horowhenua Kapiti	35	S.C. Leighton (*Poverty Bay*) v Thames Valley, 2007
Most tries	5	A. Vakarorogo (Whanganui) v Horowhenua Kapiti	5	L.M. Herden (*North Otago*) v East Coast, 2010 S. Malatai (*Wairarapa Bush*) v Buller, 2018 A. Vakarorogo (*Whanganui*) v Horowhenua Kapiti, 2023
Most conversions	8	W.A. Wright (South Canterbury) v Buller	12	B.J. McCarthy (North Otago) v Horowhenua Kapiti
Most penalty goals	4	L.J. Ross (West Coast) v King Country J.T. Tatu-Robertsson (Horowhenua Kapiti) v Wairarapa Bush F.R. Morgan (Thames Valley) v Ngati Porou East Coast	7	D.P. Harrison (*Thames Valley*) v Mid Canterbury, 2009 J.R. Reynolds (*Thames Valley*) v East Coast, 2011 S.P. Parkes (*Poverty Bay*) v Buller, 2013 R.D. Crosland (*Thames Valley*) v Wanganui, 2019
Most dropped goals	1	T.J. Reekie (Mid Canterbury) v Poverty Bay D.J. Whale (Whanganui) v Thames Valley, October 7	1	on 61 occasions (*42 players*)

Leading points-scorers in the 2023 Championship:

F.R. Morgan	*Thames Valley*	116
L.J. Ross	*West Coast*	97
D.J. Whale	*Whanganui*	88
L.R.F. Ollion	*North Otago*	82
R. Patricio	*Poverty Bay*	82

Leading try scorers in the 2023 Championship:

A. Vakarorogo	*Whanganui*	13
S.I.U. Kakala	*South Canterbury*	13
U. Fakatoufifita	*North Otago*	9
L.P. Ralph	*Horowhenua Kapiti*	7
L. Simote	*South Canterbury*	7
K.V. Leatigaga	South Canterbury	7
C.J.D. Barrell	West Coast	7

AUCKLAND

2023 Status: Bunnings NPC
Founded 1883. Original member 1892
President: F.M. (Fiao'o) Faamausili
Chairman: B.G. (Brent) Metson
Chief executive officer: J.M. (Jarrod) Bear
Coach: C.E. (Craig) McGrath
Assistant coaches: S.P. (Steven) Bates, J.D. (Jono) Hickey, C.A. (Census) Johnston
Main ground: Eden Park, Auckland
Capacity: 47,000
Colours: Blue and white

RECORDS

Most appearances	192	*'Snow' White, 1950–63*
Most points	2746	*Grant Fox, 1982–93*
Most tries	112	*Terry Wright, 1984–93*
Most points in a season	322	*Grant Fox, 1990*
Most tries in a season	19	*Terry Wright, 1984*
Most conversions in a season	77	*Grant Fox, 1990*
Most penalty goals in a season	48	*Grant Fox, 1989, 1990*
Most dropped goals in a season	8	*Grant Fox, 1990*
Most points in a match	43	*Adrian Cashmore v Mid Canterbury, 1995*
Most tries in a match	8	*John Kirwan v North Otago, 1993*
Most conversions in a match	12	*Grant Fox v Marlborough, 1984*
		Brett Craies v Horowhenua, 1986
		Grant Fox v Nelson Bays, 1991
		Lachie Munro v North Otago, 2008
Most penalty goals in a match	7	*Grant Fox v Canterbury, 1990*
		Grant Fox v Waikato, 1992
Highest team score	139	*v North Otago, 1993*
Record victory (points ahead)	134	*139–5 v North Otago, 1993*
Highest score conceded	59	*v Waikato, 2004*
Record defeat (points behind)	48	*11–59 v Waikato, 2004*

Auckland was left to lament another inconsistent season, placing just sixth heading into the NPC playoffs and finishing with a 6-5 overall record.

And yet there were fine victories over North Harbour, Hawke's Bay and Canterbury (in the regular season) and a big second half to claim the John Drake Boot against Bay of Plenty. But those highs were pockmarked with a terrible first half against Tasman, a first loss to Manawatu at Eden Park since 1980 in what was virtually Auckland B v Manawatu B, a home defeat to a depleted Waikato and a scratchy last gasp win over struggling Northland. At least Auckland finished with a competitive display in the quarter-final in Christchurch, but a quarter-final exit was far from what this squad was capable of.

New head coach Craig McGrath will be as frustrated as anyone, with enough good rugby to give cause for hope, based on sound defence, but then clocking off at inopportune moments. However, he also had to deal with a bad injury toll amongst his senior players.

Incoming were Edward Annandale (France), Che Clark (sevens), Caleb Tangitau (sevens), Tanielu Tele'a (back from injury) and Kalani Thomas (Australia), while losses included Charlie Abel (retired), Robbie Abel (retired), Simon Hickey (Japan), Alex Hodgman (injured), Felix Kalapu (Australia), Jamie Lane (USA), Jordan Lay (Samoa, RWC), Manu Paea (RWC, Tonga), Jackson Pugh (Australia), Jordan Trainor (Northland), Connor Vest (Australia) and Sam Wye (Hawke's Bay).

Prop James Lay had originally tuned down Manu Samoa for personal reasons to play for Auckland but then, after just one game, answered an injury call-up to the Rugby World Cup.

Roger Tuivasa-Sheck fronted after resigning with the Warriors in the NRL and won plenty of respect for performing so well that he was one of the best fullbacks in the NPC and was one of seven to receive his blazer. His running game was incisive and his kicking game better than expected. Injury stymied the first foray into NPC rugby for Payton Spencer, but he will get his chance in 2024.

On the wings, Salesi Rayasi and AJ Lam scored 10 tries between them, but injury ruled the raw but promising Caleb Tangitau out of the second half of the campaign. Xavier Tito-Harris made a strong early impression, recording a hat-trick on debut versus Southland.

Bryce Heem and Corey Evans were solid enough in the midfield, while Tanielu Tele'a made a long-awaited return from injury. Captain Harry Plummer only turned out in five games due to injury.

Zarn Sullivan, for the most part, seized his chance in the No 10 jersey, cracking the 100-pomts mark and taking the ball hard to the line. Jock McKenzie made his Auckland debut 18 months after his Super Rugby debut for the Blues.

The sparky Kalani Thomas did very well at halfback, pushing ahead of Taufa Funaki in the pecking order.

Adrian Choat, operating in the No 6 jersey, was the best of the forwards with his strong defence and work over the ball, while Blake Gibson and Vaiolini Ekuasi also had their moments. Akira Ioane briefly assumed the captaincy until he was hit by injury. Rookie Che Clark, fresh from sevens, offered good impact off the pine.

Josh Beehre got through a lot of work at lock in place of the injured Patrick Tuipulotu, while Edward Annandale was an interesting new recruit later in the season, bringing height in the lineout.

Angus Ta'avao was the starting tighthead, ahead of Marcel Renata, with Josh Fusitu'a on the loosehead. Leni Apisai and Soane Vikena again shared the hooking duties, while veteran Joe Royal continued his prolific tryscoring club form by crossing for the winning try against Canterbury at Eden Park.

Auckland took the Mooloos game to the community, heading to Bell Park, home of the Pakuranga club in east Auckland, in what could be a pointer to the future, given the costs of playing at Eden Park.

Higher honours went to:

New Zealand:	C. Clarke, R. Ioane
New Zealand Sevens:	P. Spencer, X. Tito-Harris
All Blacks XV:	A. Ioane, AJ Lam
New Zealand Under 20:	B. Ake, C. Clark, L. Gordon, S. Hainsworth-Fa'aofo, X. Taele, C. Tangitau, R. Williams

AUCKLAND REPRESENTATIVES 2023

Name	Club	Date of birth	Height	Weight	For Union Debut	Games	Points
S.T. (Sione) Ahio	Waitemata	29-01-01	1.84	121	2021	15	0
B.J. (Ben) Ake	Waitemata	24-02-03	1.91	104	2023	6	0
E. (Edward) Annandale	Eden	18-01-01	2	115	2023	6	0
L.C.A. (Leni) Apisai	Ponsonby	08-03-96	1.8	111	2019	39	40
J.T. (Josh) Beehre	Grammar TEC	30-03-02	1.95	118	2022	14	20
A.J. (Adrian) Choat	Waitemata	20-11-97	1.9	103	2018	40	15
C.P.J. (Che) Clark	Grammar TEC	22-04-03	1.94	101	2023	10	5
J.H.C. (Joel) Cobb	Ponsonby	27-03-01	1.83	86	2020	8	5
P.Z. (Pele) Cowley	Ponsonby	16-04-93	1.75	84	2023	1	0
H. (Hamish) Dalzell	College Rifles	16-01-96	2.01	117	2020	31	5
V.P. (Vaiolini) Ekuasi	East Tamaki	11-10-01	1.85	107	2021	18	15
C.T. (Corey) Evans	Grammar TEC	11-01-01	1.81	97	2021	23	15
K.J. (Kalin) Felise	University	31-10-99	1.91	107	2023	1	0
S.T. (Taufa) Funaki	Marist	29-07-00	1.79	92	2020	28	2
J. (Josh) Fusitu'a	Grammar TEC	01-05-01	1.8	116	2022	14	0
B.T. (Blake) Gibson	Ponsonby	19-04-95	1.86	102	2014	61	50
B.I. (Bryce) Heem	Grammar TEC	18-01-89	1.93	109	2010	30	30
A.L. (Akira) Ioane	Ponsonby	16-06-95	1.94	113	2015	56	75
N.A.D. (Niko) Jones	Waitemata	22-07-00	1.87	101	2020	16	10
A.J. (Alexander) Lam	Grammar TEC	29-07-98	1.92	104	2019	38	105
J.M (James) Lay	University	16-12-93	1.78	116	2016	14	0
J.J (Jock) McKenzie	Grammar TEC	09-11-01	1.91	92	2023	4	13
H.R.J. (Harry) Plummer	Grammar TEC	19-06-98	1.84	99	2017	53	371
S.T.M. (Salesi) Rayasi	Marist	25-09-96	1.93	105	2018	52	200
M.C. (Marcel) Renata	University	24-02-94	1.87	121	2015	68	20
J.W. (Joe) Royal	Ponsonby	31-05-85	1.83	113	2020	5	5
P.C. (Payton) Spencer	Ponsonby	23-04-04	1.89	90	2023	3	0
Z. (Zarn) Sullivan	College Rifles	10-07-00	1.93	102	2020	23	116
A.W.F. (Angus) Ta'avao	Eden	22-03-90	1.94	124	2010	59	15
C.L. (Caleb) Tangitau	Grammar TEC	19-03-03	1.87	98	2023	5	15
T.R. (Tanielu) Tele'a	Marist	16-06-98	1.87	107	2018	25	20
K.W. (Kalani) Thomas	Overseas	18-04-02	1.78	84	2023	10	20
X.R. (Xavier) Tito-Harris	Manukau	05-01-05	1.79	91	2023	4	15
P.T. (Patrick) Tuipulotu	Ponsonby	23-01-93	1.98	120	2013	29	45
S. (Sione) Tuipulotu	Manukau[1]	12-02-97	1.96	113	2020	9	5
T.N.L. (Tito) Tuipulotu	Ponsonby	06-08-02	1.89	115	2023	1	0
R. (Roger) Tuivasa-Sheck	East Tamaki	05-06-93	1.82	96	2022	15	10
S.M. (Soane) Vikena	Waitemata	07-01-01	1.83	112	2020	26	15

1. Loaned by Hawke's Bay RFU

INDIVIDUAL SCORING

	Tries	Con	PG	DG	Points		Tries	Con	PG	DG	Points
Sullivan	4	26	10	–	102	Clark	1	–	–	–	5
Rayasi	6	–	–	–	30	Heem	1	–	–	–	5
Beehre	4	–	–	–	20	Ioane	1	–	–	–	5
Lam	4	–	–	–	20	Plummer	1	–	–	–	5
Thomas	4	–	–	–	20	Renata	1	–	–	–	5
Evans	3	–	–	–	15	Royal	1	–	–	–	5
Tangitau	3	–	–	–	15	Tuivasa-Sheck	1	–	–	–	5
Tito-Harris	3	–	–	–	15						
McKenzie	1	4	–	–	13	***Totals***	***45***	***30***	***10***	***0***	***315***
Apisai	2	–	–	–	10						
Ekuasi	2	–	–	–	10	*Opposition scored*	*37**	*23*	*13*	*1*	*275*
Vikena	2	–	–	–	10						

** includes one penalty try (7 points)*

AUCKLAND 2023	Bay of Plenty	Tasman	North Harbour	Hawke's Bay	Manawatu	Southland	Canterbury	Waikato	Taranaki	Northland	Canterbury (QF)	**Totals**
Tuivasa-Sheck	–	15	15	15	–	15	15	15	15	15	15	**9**
Spencer	–	–	–	–	15	s	s	–	–	–	–	**3**
Tangitau	14	11	s	s	14	–	–	–	–	–	–	**5**
Cobb	–	–	–	–	s	–	–	–	–	–	–	**1**
Tito-Harris	–	–	–	–	–	11	11	14	–	–	s	**4**
Lam	–	14	14	14	–	14	14	11	14	14	14	**9**
Rayasi	11	s	11	11	11	–	–	s	11	11	11	**9**
Heem	13	13	13	12	–	12	12	12	13	13	12	**10**
Tele'a	–	–	–	–	12	–	–	s	s	s	13	**5**
Evans	15	–	s	13	13	13	13	13	–	s	s	**9**
Plummer (capt)	12	12	12	–	–	–	–	–	12	12	–	**5**
Sullivan	10	10	10	10	–	10	10	10	10	10	10	**10**
McKenzie	s	–	–	s	10	s	–	–	–	–	–	**4**
Funaki	9	9	s	s	9	s	s	9	s	s	s	**11**
Cowley	–	–	–	–	s	–	–	–	–	–	–	**1**
Thomas	s	s	9	9	–	9	9	s	9	9	9	**10**
Ekuasi	8	–	–	–	s	8	s	8	s	8	8	**8**
Jones	–	–	–	–	7	–	–	s	–	s	s	**4**
Choat	6	6	6	6	–	6	6	6	6	–	–	**8**
Gibson	7	7	7	7	–	7	7	7	7	7	7	**10**
Ioane	–	8	8	8	8	–	8	–	–	–	–	**5**
Clark	s	s	s	s	6	s	–	s	8	6	6	**10**
S. Tuipulotu	–	–	–	s	5	–	–	–	–	–	–	**2**
Felise	–	–	–	–	s	–	–	–	–	–	–	**1**
Annandale	–	–	–	–	–	s	4	4	4	4	4	**6**
Beehre	5	5	5	5	–	5	5	–	5	5	5	**9**
P. Tuipulotu	–	4	4	4	–	4	–	–	–	–	–	**4**
Dalzell	4	s	s	–	4	–	s	5	s	s	s	**9**
Renata	–	–	–	–	1	s	–	–	s	s	s	**5**
Ahio	s	s	s	s	s	3	s	s	3	3	–	**10**
Ta'avao	3	3	3	3	3	–	3	3	–	s	3	**9**
T. Tuipulotu	–	–	–	–	–	–	–	–	–	–	s	**1**
Ake	–	s	s	s	–	s	s	s	–	–	–	**6**
Fusitu'a	s	1	1	1	–	1	1	1	1	1	1	**10**
Lay	1	–	–	–	–	–	–	–	–	–	–	**1**
Apisai	2	s	s	s	2	–	–	2	s	s	s	**9**
Vikena	s	2	2	2	–	2	2	–	2	2	2	**9**
Royal	–	–	–	–	s	s	s	s	–	–	–	**4**

AUCKLAND TEAM RECORD 2023

Played 11 **Won 6** **Lost 5** **Points for 315** **Points against 275**

Date	Opponent	Location	Score	Tries	Con	PG	DG	Referee
August 6	Bay of Plenty	Tauranga	32–30	Rayasi, Evans, Tangitau, Vikena	Sullivan (3)	Sullivan (2)		Dan Waenga
August 12	Tasman	Blenheim	12–24	Rayasi (2)	Sullivan			Stu Curran
August 19	North Harbour	Takapuna	43–21	Sullivan (2), Thomas, Lam, Plummer, Tangitau	Sullivan (5)	Sullivan		Cam Stone
August 26	Hawke's Bay	Auckland	41–22	Vikena, Evans, Beehre, Tuivasa-Sheck, Ioane, Lam	Sullivan (3), McKenzie	Sullivan		Mike Winter
August 30	Manawatu	Auckland	31–33	Apisai (2), Rayasi, McKenzie, Tangitau	McKenzie (3)			Nick Hogan
September 3	Southland	Invercargill	41–13	Tito-Harris (3), Lam, Sullivan, Thomas, Ekuasi	Sullivan (3)			Jackson Henshaw
September 9	Canterbury	Auckland	36–29	Thomas (2), Heem, Evans, Royal	Sullivan (4)	Sullivan		Dan Waenga
September 16	Waikato	Auckland	12–27	Ekuasi, Sullivan	Sullivan			Jono Bredin
September 23	Taranaki	New Plymouth	16–18	Rayasi	Sullivan	Sullivan (3)		Nick Briant
September 29	Northland	Auckland	27–26	Clark, Beehre, Renata	Sullivan (3)	Sullivan (2)		Dan Waenga
October 6	Canterbury (QF)	Christchurch	24–29	Beehre (2), Rayasi, Lam	Sullivan (2)			Nick Briant

BAY OF PLENTY

2023 Status: Bunnings NPC
Founded 1911. Affiliated 1911
President: D.A. (Don) Thwaites
Chairman: S.R.R. (Scott) Kahle
Chief executive officer: M.W. (Mike) Rogers
Coach: R.A. (Richard) Watt
Assistant coaches: James Porter, Pingi Tala'apitaga
Main grounds: Rotorua International Stadium; Tauranga Domain
Capacity: 20,000
Colours: Blue and gold.

RECORDS

Most appearances	161	*Greg Rowlands, 1969–82*
Most points	1008	*Greg Rowlands, 1969–82*
Most tries	62	*Graeme Moore, 1967–80*
Most points in a season	245	*Andrew Miller, 1996*
Most tries in a season	14	*Damon Kaui, 1995*
Most conversions in a season	53	*Andrew Miller, 1996*
Most penalty goals in a season	48	*Eion Crossan, 1991*
Most dropped goals in a season	13	*Ron Preston, 1985*
Most points in a match	36	*Adrian Cashmore v Thames Valley, 1993*
Most tries in a match	5	*Ian Backhouse v North Otago, 1965*
		Damon Kaui v Thames Valley, 1995
Most conversions in a match	9	*Eion Crossan v Poverty Bay, 1991*
Most penalty goals in a match	6	*Ron Preston v Poverty Bay, 1982*
		Eion Crossan v North Harbour, 1990
		Eion Crossan v Fiji President's XV, 1991
		Eion Crossan v Western Samoa, 1991
		Erin Cossey v Hawke's Bay, 1994
		Andrew Miller v Counties, 1995
		Andrew Miller v King Country, 1996
		Glen Jackson v Northland, 2001
		Glen Jackson v Otago, 2004
		Mike Delany v Waikato, 2009
Highest team score	88	*v East Coast, 1972*
Record victory (points ahead)	79	*88–9 v East Coast, 1972*
		82–3 v Thames Valley, 1995
Highest score conceded	93	*v New Zealand XV, 1993*
Record defeat (points behind)	88	*5–93 v New Zealand XV, 1993*

For the third year in a row the Steamers' season began with a new head coach. Richard Watts' team did remarkably well, finishing one game down on the previous year with a quarter-final exit. Of the eleven games played, seven were won with four losses.

The loss to Auckland came in the final minute from a lineout drive when a needless penalty was given away, while the loss to Counties Manukau at Pukekohe was a strange effort. Bay of Plenty conceded four tries in the first twelve minutes and the scoreline read 7–26. After that, only two penalty goals were conceded in the 19–32 defeat. The quarter-final loss to Hawke's Bay was a major disappointment. A wonderful first half saw four converted tries scored and, with a lead of nine points, the large crowd at Tauranga Domain was buzzing for what was to come in the second forty. But the second half saw hardly a shot fired.

On the positive side, a hard-earned victory over Waikato got the scoreboard ticking over. This was followed by excellent away wins over eventual champions Taranaki and Hawke's Bay. Bay of Plenty came through storm week at the end of the regulation season with three wins — against Northland, Southland and Tasman — the highlight being the comprehensive victory against Tasman, whom the Bay hadn't beaten since 2010.

Fullback Cole Forbes returned after a two-year break in Scotland. He showed plenty of speed and attacking flair and then, abruptly, in the process of scoring a long range try against Otago, he tore a hamstring which ended his season.

The wings were a contingent of NZ Sevens players and on the whole they didn't disappoint. Leroy Carter was once more a fire cracker who brought plenty to the table with his all-round pace, tigerish defence. He scored five tries. Ngarohi McGarvey Black was available for the first five games and was adventurous with plenty of dash. In his debut against Hawke's Bay, Fehi Fineanganofo was a huge standout with amazing pace and a strong defence which he brought to every game he played. Codemeru Vai, although not showing the same class, was steady and reliable and moved back to fullback when required.

At centre, in his debut season for the province, the experience of Melani Nanai Vai (brother of Codemeru) was much needed in the backline. He was always able to find space for his wingers. Reon Paul, plucked from club rugby, gave a great account of himself in the positions he was allocated and scored a wonderful solo try against Wellington. More should be seen of him next season.

Lalomilo Lalomilo and Seamus Bardoul shared the second-five position while Lucas Cashmore managed six games at first-five before injury shortened his season. Up until then, he showed an accurate line kick with good distance gained and was able to set his backline away quickly. Wharenui Hawera was then moved into the pivot position and looked more assured in his general play and goal kicking than last year.

At halfback Te Toiroa Tahuriorangi gave fine service, making a number of deceptive breaks and Richard Judd, who had last appeared in 2019, also performed well.

In the forwards, Nikora Broughton, at No 8, was again in good form until a mid-season injury took him out of play. Jacob Norris, who returned from overseas mid campaign, took over and didn't disappoint in the games he played.

Veveni Lasaqa played superbly on the openside flank and wasn't afraid to put his body on the line on many occasions. He only missed one game and was rewarded with the Bay Of Plenty Player of the year award. Semisi Paea had a short stint on the flank before being selected for the Tongan World Cup team. Naitoa Ah Kuoi, on the blindside flank, was again industrious in all that he did and he played all eleven games. For the first time, a player from Japan represented the province. Rysoke Funahashi played five games off the bench and the experience gained will be of great benefit upon his return to Japan.

At lock, Justin Sangster continues to progress while Manaaki Selby-Rickit was exceptional. He had a stellar season in all aspects of forward play, being in the thick of it at lineout, scrummaging, support play and, remarkably, scored nine tries to top the NPC try-scoring for 2023. His nine tries were also a record for a lock in an NPC season. In reserve, Etonia Waqa will have enjoyed the chance to gain more playing time in the ten games he participated in.

Of the seven props, Aidan Ross was used most, with Benet Kumeroa, Pasilio Tosi, John Afoa and Josh Bartlett all getting plenty of game time. It was Bartlett's first season as a regular and he impressed with his mobility and all round skills. When John Afoa debuted against Auckland he became the oldest player to represent the union, being just over two months short of his 40th birthday. His older brother James had represented the Bay in 2004–06.

In the hooking department, Kurt Eklund (captain) once again led from the front and Nathan Vella was enticed out of retirement as back-up. When injury took Vella out, Taine Kolose showed promise.

Of last season's players, notables who didn't return were Nigel Ah Wong (Tongan World Cup squad), Haereiti Hetet (Fiji), Joey Walton (New South Wales) ,Tevita Mafileo (North Harbour), Nic Souchon (Southland), Jeff Thwaites (retired), Emoni Narawa (New Zealand World Cup squad) and Kaleb Trask (Japan).

Higher honours went to:

New Zealand:	S. Cane, E. Narawa
All Blacks XV	N. Ah Kuoi, A. Ross
New Zealand Under 20:	C. Vai
New Zealand Sevens:	L. Carter, S. Curry, F. Fineanganofo, N.McGarvey-Black, R. Solo, C. Vai, R. Ware, J. Webber

INDIVIDUAL SCORING

	Tries	Con	PG	DG	Points		Tries	Con	PG	DG	Points
Hawera	–	19	6	–	56	Judd	1	–	–	–	5
Cashmore	2	15	4	–	52	Tanimo	1	–	–	–	5
Selby-Rickit	9	–	–	–	45	Sangster	1	–	–	–	5
Carter	5	–	–	–	25	Tosi	1	–	–	–	5
Eklund	4	–	–	–	20	Finau	1	–	–	–	5
Fineanganofo	3	–	–	–	15	Paul	1	–	–	–	5
Ah Kuoi	3	–	–	–	15	Nanai Vai	1	–	–	–	5
Tahuriorangi	2	–	–	–	10	Armstrong	1	–	–	–	5
C. Forbes	2	–	–	–	10						
McGarvey-Black	2	–	–	–	10	***Totals***	**43**	**34**	**10**	**0**	**313**
Bartlett	2	–	–	–	10						
Paea	1	–	–	–	5	*Opposition scored*	*38**	*24*	*13*	*0*	*279*

** includes one penalty try (7 points)*

BAY OF PLENTY REPRESENTATIVES 2023

Name	Club	Date of birth	Height	Weight	For Union Debut	Games	Points
I.F. "John" Afoa	overseas	16-10-83	1.83	121	2023	8	0
N.S. (Naitoa) Ah Kuoi	Whakarewarewa	07-10-99	1.96	116	2022	22	50
T.P.R. (Tamiro) Armstrong	Tauranga Sports	01-03-03	1.85	90	2023	5	5
S.R. (Seamus) Bardoul	Tauranga Sports	28-02-97	1.85	101	2022	10	0
J.C. (Josh) Bartlett	Tauranga Sports	28-12-02	1.82	115	2021	14	10
N.S.M. (Nikora) Broughton	Rangiuru	09-05-01	1.88	110	2021	23	15
L.B. (Leroy) Carter	Tauranga Sports	24-02-99	1.81	90	2019	29	60
L.H. (Lucas) Cashmore	Tauranga Sports	25-08-02	1.76	86	2021	16	97
K.A.N. (Kurt) Eklund	Mt Maunganui	01-05-92	1.80	105	2019	42	50
Penitoa Finau	Greerton Marist	17-12-93	1.86	105	2021	14	5
F.F. (Fatafehi) Fineanganofo	NZ Sevens	31-08-02	1.80	100	2023	5	15
C.D. (Cole) Forbes	Te Puke Sports	10-08-99	1.82	95	2018	9	15
G.C. (Grady) Forbes	Te Puke Sports				2023	1	0
Ryosuke Funahashi	overseas	05-01-97	1.85	106	2023	5	0
W.K.P. (Wharenui) Hawera	Hamilton Marist	22-05-93	1.81	94	2022	22	88
A.J.M. (Alex) Johnston	Te Puke Sports	23-08-95	1.84	113	2023	1	0
R.P. Richard Judd	overseas	18-05-92	1.78	90	2017	38	45
T.S. (Taine) Kolose	Rangiuru	25-02-03	1.87	120	2023	4	0
B.L.H. (Benet) Kumeroa	Rangiuru	25-06-00	1.84	120	2021	16	0
Lalomilo Lalomilo	Greerton Marist	12-02-99	1.80	98	2018	26	5
V.R.V.K. (Veveni) Lasaqa	Greerton Marist	04-06-02	1.82	101	2021	20	15
N.M. (Ngarohi) McGarvey-Black	Ruatoki	20-05-96	1.79	91	2023	5	10
M.H. (Melani) Nanai Vai	Mt Maunganui	08-03-93	1.93	99	2023	10	5
J.K. (Jacob) Norris	overseas	27-11-98	1.91	105	2022	15	0
S.F. (Semisi) Paea	overseas	17-04-99	1.93	112	2021	9	5
R.B. (Reon) Paul	Mt Maunganui	17-08-01	1.85	102	2023	5	5
C.T. (Carlos) Price	Mt Maunganui	30-09-98	1.79	88	2022	3	0
Aidan Ross	Te Puke Sports	25-10-95	1.89	114	2015	63	25
J.T. (Justin) Sangster	Te Puna	30-11-96	1.98	115	2021	29	30
M.W.H. (Manaaki) Selby-Rickit	Mt Maunganui	06-05-96	2.00	115	2021	31	57
T.T.H. (Te Toiroa) Tahuriorangi	Rotoiti	31-03-95	1.73	82	2020	39	25
Sekuini Tanimo	Greerton Marist	22-03-00	1.86	98	2021	10	10
V.P. (Pasilio) Tosi	Greerton Marist	18-07-98	1.90	140	2021	21	15
C.M. (Codemeru) Vai	NZ Sevens	25-02-04	1.88	86	2023	9	0
N.B. (Nathan) Vella	Mt Maunganui	10-02-90	1.86	108	2019	29	15
E.B. (Etonia) Waqa	Te Puna	02-06-99	1.97	105	2022	12	0

1. Waikato RU

BAY OF PLENTY 2023	Auckland	Waikato	Counties Manukau	Taranaki	Otago	Hawkes Bay	Wellington	Northland	Southland	Tasman	Hawkes Bay (qf)	**TOTALS**
C. Forbes	15	–	15	15	15	–	–	–	–	–	–	**4**
Tanimo	–	–	–	–	–	15	15	–	–	–	–	**2**
Armstrong	–	–	–	–	–	s	s	–	s	s	s	**5**
Carter	14	14	–	14	–	–	–	–	–	14	14	**5**
McGarvey-Black	11	11	11	11	11	–	–	–	–	–	–	**5**
Vai	–	s	14	–	14	14	14	s	14	15	15	**9**
Fineanganofo	–	–	–	–	–	11	11	11	11	–	11	**5**
Nanai Vai	13	13	13	13	13	13	13	13	–	13	13	**10**
Lalomilo	12	12	12	12	12	–	–	14	12	–	–	**7**
Bardoul	s	–	s	s	s	12	12	12	–	12	12	**9**
Paul	–	–	–	–	–	s	s	–	13	11	s	**5**
Cashmore	10	10	10	10	10	–	–	10	–	–	–	**6**
Hawera	s	15	s	s	s	10	10	15	15	10	10	**11**
Tahuriorangi	9	9	9	9	s	s	s	s	9	s	s	**11**
Judd	s	s	–	s	9	9	9	9	10	9	9	**10**
Price	–	–	s	–	–	–	–	–	–	–	–	**1**
Broughton	8	8	8	8	–	–	–	–	–	8	s	**6**
Lasaqa	7	7	s	7	7	7	7	7	7	–	7	**10**
Ah Kuoi	6	6	6	6	6	6	6	6	6	6	6	**11**
Paea	s	s	7	–	–	–	–	–	–	–	–	**3**
Finau	–	–	–	s	8	8	8	–	–	–	–	**4**
Funahashi	–	–	–	–	s	s	–	s	s	s	–	**5**
Norris	–	–	–	–	–	–	s	8	8	7	8	**5**
G. Forbes	–	–	–	–	–	–	–	–	–	s	–	**1**
Sangster	5	5	5	5	5	5	5	5	s	5	5	**11**
Selby-Rickit	4	4	4	4	4	4	4	4	4	4	4	**11**
Waqa	–	s	s	s	s	s	s	s	5	s	s	**10**
Afoa	3	3	3	3	–	–	–	s	s	s	s	**8**
Ross	1	1	1	1	1	1	1	1	–	1	1	**10**
Johnston	s	–	–	–	–	–	–	–	–	–	–	**1**
Kumeroa	s	s	s	s	3	3	s	–	s	3	–	**9**
Bartlett	–	s	s	s	s	s	s	s	1	s	s	**10**
Tosi	–	–	–	–	s	s	3	3	3	–	3	**6**
Eklund (capt.)	2	2	2	2	2	–	2	2	2	s	2	**10**
Vella	s	s	s	s	s	2	s	–	–	–	–	**7**
Kolose	–	–	–	–	–	s	–	–	s	2	s	**4**

Ross captained the side in the two matches Eklund did not play and start in.

BAY OF PLENTY TEAM RECORD 2023

Played 11 **Won 7** **Lost 4** **Points for 313** **Points against 279**

Date	Opponent	Location	Score	Tries	Con	PG	DG	Referee
August 6	Auckland	Tauranga	30–32	Carter (2), Selby-Rickit	Cashmore (3)	Cashmore (2), Hawera		Dan Waenga
August 12	Waikato	Tauranga	19–15	Carter, Tahuriorangi, Cashmore	Cashmore (2)			Brendon Pickerill
August 18	Counties Manukau	Pukekohe	19–32	C. Forbes, Eklund, Paea	Cashmore (2)			Marcus Playle
August 26	Taranaki	New Plymouth	29–26	McGarvey-Black (2), Eklund, Carter	Cashmore (3)	Cashmore		Stu Curran
September 2	Otago	Rotorua	38–14	Selby-Rickit (2), Judd, C. Forbes, Cashmore	Cashmore (5)	Cashmore		Jono Bredin
September 9	Hawke's Bay	Napier	38–35	Tanimo, Sangster, Tosi, Fineanganofo, Selby-Rickit	Hawera (5)	Hawera		Cam Stone
September 17	Wellington	Rotorua	14–26	Finau, Paul	Hawera (2)			Angus Mabey
September 22	Northland	Whangarei	32–26	Eklund, Selby-Rickit, Fineanganofo, Bartlett	Hawera (3)	Hawera (2)		Mike Winter
September 27	Southland	Invercargill	25–23	Fineanganofo, Selby-Rickit, Eklund, Ah Kuoi,	Hawera	Hawera		Fraser Hannon
October 1	Tasman	Tauranga	41–12	Ah Kuoi, Selby-Rickit, Bartlett, Nanai Vai, Tahuriorangi, Armstrong	Hawera (4)	Hawera		Jono Bredin
October 8	Hawke's Bay (qf)	Tauranga	28–38	Selby-Rickit (2), Ah Kuoi, Carter	Hawera (4)			Angus Mabey

BULLER

2023 Status: Heartland Championship
Founded 1894. Affiliated 1894
Chairman: H.W. (Hugh) McMillan
Chief Executive Officer: A.C. (Andrew) Duncan
Coach: N.J. (Nathan) Thompson
Assistant coaches: J.P. (Jon) Scanlon,
A.P. (Andrew) Stephens
Main ground: Victoria Square, Westport
Capacity: 5000
Colours: Cardinal and blue

RECORDS

Highest attendance	5000	*West Coast-Buller v South Africa, 1956*
Most appearances	174	*L.G. Brownlee, 1999-2018*
Most points	575	*D.J. Baird, 1981–91*
Most tries	45	*I. Tora*, 2013-2023*
Most points in a season	147	*J.J. Lash, 2017*
Most tries in a season	11	*I. Ravudra*, 2014*
Most conversions in a season	32	*J.J. Lash, 2016*
Most penalty goals in a season	27	*D.J. Baird, 1985*
Most dropped goals in a season	7	*D.J. Baird, 1984*
Most points in a match	27	*J.J. Lash v West Coast, 2019*
Most tries in a match	4	*J. Easton v Wellington Colts, 1935*
		T.J. Stuart v West Coast, 1992
		M. Taylor v East Coast, 2007
		I. Ravudra v Wairarapa Bush, 2014*
		S.T. Sauqaqa v Thames Valley, 2015
Most conversions in a match	7	*J.J. Lash v Wairarapa Bush, 2014*
		J.J. Lash v East Coast, 2017
		J.J. Lash v Ngati Porou East Coast, 2019
Most penalty goals in a match	6	*D.J. Baird v East Coast, 1987*
		C.J. Hart v East Coast, 1999
		S.N. Jack, v Wairarapa Bush, 2002
		A.P. Stephens v Horowhenua Kapiti, 2010
Highest team score	67	*v East Coast, 2014*
Record victory (points ahead)	61	*67–6 v East Coast, 2014*
Highest score conceded	83	*v Whanganui, 2022*
Record defeat (points behind)	76	*7–83 v Whanganui, 2022*

** I. Tora previously knowm as I. Ravudra*

With a record of two wins and six losses, Buller missed out on a playoff position. They were on the back foot early in the campaign with the opening five matches being lost, but it was only against South Canterbury that the side was outclassed. There was a stirring fightback against Poverty Bay after being 0–40 down to eventually lose 33–52, a spirited effort in the wind and rain against Whanganui, and a loss to Ngati Porou East Coast in golden point extra time.

The second half against West Coast was Buller's best 40 minutes of the season, coming from 3–11 down at halftime to win 29–11, while Buller led all the way in the win against Wairarapa Bush.

The outstanding forward was on loan No. 8 George Reeves. He was always prominent and top try scorer with five. Three of them came against Horowhenua Kapiti, including a superb 80-metre solo effort. Hooker Leopino Maupese, in his debut season, was not far behind to earn NZ Heartland selection, while the experience and versatility of captain Anthony Ellis was invaluable with his ability to play all three front row positions. Caleb Havili was another to turn in consistently good performances, and his partnership with Joel Everson made them a sound locking combination.

Injuries in the opening match ended Louis Devery's season and kept Jesse Pitman-Joass out until the last three matches. This necessitated a reshuffle in the backline, with Jesse Elley moving from halfback to fullback. Michael Stringer was still the danger man in the backline but had reduced opportunities compared to last year. Nevertheless his two tries against West Coast were outstanding efforts.

First-five Jack Parker showed up well in the win against Wairarapa Bush and wing Iliesa Tora ended the season as the top try scorer in Buller's history. His touchdown against King Country in the final match took him to 45, one ahead of Thomas Stuart.

A Seddon Shield challenge to Nelson Bays sub-union on August 5 at Murchison ended in a 39–22 defeat.

Higher honours went to:
New Zealand Heartland: L. Maupese

BULLER REPRESENTATIVES 2023

Name	Club	For Union Debut	Games	Points
T.K. (Tapiha) Allen	Westport	2022	15	0
T.G. (Taine) Brownlee	White Star	2022	14	0
S.R. (Stephen) Crackett	Westport	2009	61	0
B.M. (Brett) Cutbush	Reefton	2022	16	5
T.G. (Timothy) Dallison	Old Boys	2021	18	0
L.J.S. (Louis) Devery	Reefton	2019	6	10
G.A. (Glen) Duncan	Westport	2010	48	0
J.M. (Jesse) Elley	White Star	2013	37	28
A.W. (Anthony) Ellis	White Star	2015	65	40
J.R. (Joel) Everson	Nomads [1]	2022	9	0
J.G. (Joel) Hands	Westport	2018	24	17
C.T. (Caleb) Havili	Marist [2]	2021	15	15
Samuel Holman	Westport	2023	2	0
Mitieli Kaloudigibeci	Westport	2008	68	165
A.J. (Alex) Lean	Old Boys	2020	23	10
T.H. (Thor) Manawatu	Reefton	2015	32	13
L.D. (Leopino) Maupese	White Star	2023	7	10
B.R. (Blaine) Meikle	Old Boys	2023	7	5
R.G.O. (Rowan) Neilsen	White Star	2023	8	5
A.D. (Alan) Paterson	White Star	2022	5	0
J.A. (Jack) Parker	New Plymouth Old Boys [3]	2022	14	114
J.J. (Jesse) Pitman-Joass	Old Boys	2020	20	67
B.R. (Ben) Pratt	Old Boys	2020	18	0
G.J.L. (George) Reeves	Lincoln University [4]	2023	8	25
D.G. (Dylan) Rusbatch	White Star	2020	4	0
M.A. (Michael) Stringer	overseas	2022	16	35
K.J.S. (Kyle) Te Tai	Westport	2019	27	5
E.N. (Ehipa) Thompson	White Star	2022	9	0
Iliesa Tora	White Star	2013	77	227
R.P. (Rapture) Tuala-Tamalelagi	Reefton	2023	2	0
J.J. (Jacob) Wetere	Marist [2]	2021	7	0

1. Canterbury RU 2. Loaned by Tasman RU 3. Loaned by Taranaki RU 4. Loaned by Canterbury RU

	Tries	Con	PG	DG	Points
Parker	1	11	5	–	42
Reeves	5	–	–	–	25
Tora	4	–	–	–	20
Stringer	3	–	–	–	15
Havili	3	–	–	–	15
Maupese	2	–	–	–	10
Pitman-Joass	–	4	–	–	8
Hands	1	–	–	–	5
Te Tai	1	–	–	–	5
Cutbush	1	–	–	–	5
Meikle	1	–	–	–	5
Kaloudigibeci	1	–	–	–	5
Neilsen	1	–	–	–	5
Totals	**24**	**15**	**5**	**0**	**165**
Opposition scored	*35*	*26*	*5*	*0*	*242*

BULLER 2023	Poverty Bay	Whanganui	South Canterbury	Ngati Porou East Coast	Horowhenua Kapiti	Wairarapa Bush	West Coast	King Country	**TOTALS**
Pitman-Joass (co capt.)	15	–	–	–	–	s	s	15	**4**
Kaloudigibeci	14	14	14	s	14	–	s	s	**7**
Tora	11	11	11	11	11	11	11	11	**8**
Meikle	–	s	s	14	s	14	14	14	**7**
Stringer	13	15	12	15	13	13	13	13	**8**
Lean	s	13	13	13	s	s	s	s	**8**
Holman	–	s	s	–	–	–	–	–	**2**
Devery	12	–	–	–	–	–	–	–	**1**
Hands	s	12	–	12	12	12	12	12	**7**
Parker	10	10	10	10	10	10	10	–	**7**
Elley	9	9	15	s	15	15	15	10	**8**
Cutbush	s	s	9	9	9	9	9	9	**8**
Manawatu	–	–	–	–	s	–	–	–	**1**
Reeves	8	8	8	8	8	8	8	8	**8**
Pratt	–	–	s	–	s	6	s	–	**4**
Brownlee	7	7	7	7	7	s	7	7	**8**
Te Tai	6	6	6	6	s	7	6	6	**8**
Tuala-Tamalelagi	–	s	s	–	–	–	–	–	**2**
Havili	5	5	5	5	4	4	4	4	**8**
Neilsen	4	4	4	s	6	s	s	s	**8**
Everson	s	–	s	4	5	5	5	5	**7**
Rusbatch	–	s	–	–	–	–	–	–	**1**
Paterson	–	–	–	–	s	–	s	–	**2**
Allen	3	3	3	3	3	s	3	3	**8**
Ellis (co capt.)	1	1	1	–	2	3	1	1	**7**
Dallison	s	–	–	1	s	1	–	s	**5**
Crackett	s	s	s	s	s	s	s	–	**7**
Thompson	–	s	–	–	1	–	s	–	**3**
Wetere	–	–	–	–	–	–	–	s	**1**
Maupese	2	2	2	2	–	2	2	2	**7**
Duncan	s	s	–	s	–	–	–	–	**3**

BULLER TEAM RECORD 2023

Played 8 **Won 2** **Lost 6** **Points for 165** **Points against 242**

Date	*Opponent*	*Location*	*Score*	*Tries*	*Con*	*PG*	*DG*	*Referee*
August 12	Poverty Bay	Gisborne	33–52	Maupese, Stringer, Hands, Havili, Tora	Parker (4)			Katsuki Furuse (Japan)
August 19	Whanganui	Westport	5–13	Te Tai				Ben Alexander
August 26	South Canterbury	Geraldine	0–56					George Haswell
September 2	Ngati Porou East Coast	Westport	21–24 aet	Havili, Tora	Parker	Parker (3)		Dan Moore
September 9	Horowhenua Kapiti	Levin	22–33	Reeves (3), Cutbush	Parker			Will Johnston
September 16	Wairarapa Bush	Westport	27–20	Tora, Parker, Reeves, Meikle	Parker (2)	Parker		Ben Alexander
September 23	West Coast	Christchurch	29–11	Stringer (2), Havili, Kaloudigibeci	Parker (3)	Parker		Dan Moore
September 30	King Country	Taupo	28–33	Tora, Reeves, Neilsen, Maupese	Pitman-Joass (4)			Ben Woolerton

Buller played their home match v West Coast at Christchurch (see Happenings).

CANTERBURY

2023 Status: Bunnings NPC
Founded 1879. Affiliated 1894
President: J.E.A. (Julie) Patterson
Chairman: P.A. (Peter) Winchester
Chief executive officer: T.P. (Tony) Smail
Co-coaches: M.J. (Marty) Bourke
Assistant coaches: C.L. (Craig) Dunlea, A.T.G. (Alex) Robertson, M.B. (Matt) Todd
Main ground: Apollo Projects Stadium, Christchurch; Rangiora Showgrounds
Capacity: 17,000
Colours: Red and black

RECORDS

Most appearances	220	*Fergie McCormick, 1958–75*
Most points	1625	*Robbie Deans, 1979–90*
Most tries	93	*Paula Bale, 1989–96*
Most points in a season	279	*Robbie Deans, 1989*
Most tries in a season	24	*Paula Bale, 1989*
Most conversions in a season	52	*Greg Coffey, 1991*
		Ben Blair, 2001
Most penalty goals in a season	50	*Robbie Deans, 1989*
Most dropped goals in a season	10	*Andrew Mehrtens, 1994*
Most points in a match	44	*Jon Preston v West Coast, 1992*
Most tries in a match	7	*Bruce McPhail v Combined Services, 1959*
Most conversions in a match	20	*Jon Preston v West Coast, 1992*
Most penalty goals in a match	7	*Robbie Deans v Counties, 1984*
		Andrew Mehrtens v Fiji, 2003
		Cameron McIntyre v Wellington, 2003
Highest team score	128	*v West Coast, 1992*
Record victory (points ahead)	128	*128–0 v West Coast, 1992*
Highest score conceded	60	*v Wellington, 2017*
Record defeat (points behind)	46	*14–60 v Wellington, 2017*

Canterbury endured a funny old season, starting with a hiss and a roar from three straight wins, two of them demo jobs, and then winning just four of its last nine, and none by convincing margins, to dip out in the semifinals.

For all that, Canterbury played entertaining rugby, just once scoring less than 28 points, and often finishing some sweet set-piece moves, though four times it leaked more than 30.

The red and blacks provided five All Blacks to the Rugby World Cup squad and did have two more injured, but new international Dallas McLeod did appear in 11 of the 12 games, while former All Black Ryan Crotty gave good back-up in midfield.

Crotty was the sole major signing from abroad, returning from Japan, though Solomon Alaimalo returned to his schooling roots from Southland, while losses included Liam Allen (France), George Bridge (France), Owen Franks (France), Wil Gualter (Tasman), Shilo Klein

(North Harbour), Brodie McAlister (injury) and Isaiah Punivai (Japan).

After kicking off the NPC with 19 tries in its first three games, a stacked Canterbury came unstuck against an experimental Wellington side in Christchurch. The Taranaki game was taken to Rangiora, the first time, incredibly, that the red and blacks had played an NPC game outside the Garden City. There were two reverses in the northern region, including the first loss to Counties Manukau since 2016. Ferg Burke's boot was the difference against Tasman, but Canterbury did not exactly gallop into the playoffs after a defeat to Waikato. A tight quarter-final win over Auckland was followed by a narrow semifinal exit to Taranaki, Burke's injury a telling factor.

Chay Fihaki was the main man at fullback, scoring four tries and getting plenty of touches. Alaimalo seemed to enjoy his return to his home province, and alternated wings. Blair Murray was in sparkling, resourceful, form in his first full season, scoring seven tries, including a double against Northland and a triple against Wellington. Manasa Mataele, too, played with plenty of zip.

Rameka Poihipi was in good form at No 12, passing precisely and setting up much of the Canterbury attack. Alex Harford was again an able understudy to Ferg Burke, who was again one of the top first fives in the NPC. His loss via injury in the quarter-final was a tough blow for the team.

Halfback Mitch Drummond was always probing and had several try assists, while he reached 99 games for the union. Willi Heinz was a more than capable back-up.

Cullen Grace played eight games, most of them well, scoring the winning try against North Harbour and was always a lineout option. Billy Harmon was consistently Canterbury's best, be it in the No 8 or No 6 jerseys. The captain carried hard and was a tackling machine, as was fellow loose forward Tom Christie. Corey Kellow, Dom Gardner and Reed Prinsep all had injury issues.

Early on, there was a locking crisis, with several bone breaks, so the SOS went to the retired Luke Romano, still a smart lineout operator at 37. Tahlor Cahill played seven games and looked one of the most promising players in the competition.

Oli Jager and Seb Calder kept the tighthead side of the scrum up, while Daniel Lienert-Brown and Joe Moody, in the main, sorted the loosehead. Moody always bolstered the scrum, though he was on standby at times for the All Blacks.

Due to the season-ending injury to Brodie McAlister, George Bell emerged as the top rake, though he had good support from the veteran Ben Funnell, who scored four tries from lineout drives.

Three players raised the 50-game milestone for Canterbury in 2023 – Christie, Jager and Mitch Dunshea.

Higher honours went to:

New Zealand:	B. Ennor, D. McLeod, R. Mo'unga, F. Newell, C. Taylor, S. Whitelock, T. Williams
All Blacks XV:	B. Harmon
New Zealand Under 20:	T. Cahill, I. Hutchinson

CANTERBURY REPRESENTATIVES 2023

Name	Club	Date of birth	Height	Weight	For Union Debut	Games	Points
S. (Solomon) Alaimalo	Sydenham	27-12-95	1.96	103	2023	9	15
G.D.E. (George) Bell	Lincoln University	29-01-02	1.85	107	2022	19	20
J.J. (Joe) Brial	Lincoln University	07-01-02	1.9	111	2022	4	0
F.W. (Fergus) Burke	Canterbury University	03-09-99	1.86	94	2019	48	409
T.M. (Tahlor) Cahill	Marist-Albion	08-06-03	1.98	113	2023	7	5
S.A. (Seb) Calder	Lincoln University	16-03-02	1.84	121	2022	18	0
T.M. (Tom) Christie	Christchurch	04-03-98	1.86	104	2017	55	40
R.J. (Ryan) Crotty	New Brighton	23-09-88	1.81	94	2008	77	75
S.G. (Sam) Darry	HSOB	18-07-00	2.03	110	2020	35	20
M.D. (Mitch) Drummond	HSOB	15-02-94	1.79	88	2013	99	134
M.T.W. (Mitch) Dunshea	Hurunui	18-11-95	1.97	115	2015	56	35
L.C.V. (Chay) Fihaki	Belfast	03-01-01	1.92	100	2020	39	80
B.C.J. (Ben) Funnell	Hurunui	06-06-90	1.81	108	2011	91	85
Z.W. (Zach) Gallagher	Burnside	04-09-01	1.98	115	2020	14	0
D.A. (Dominic) Gardiner	Marist-Albion	12-07-01	1.93	105	2021	19	20
C.J. (Cullen) Grace	Lincoln University	20-12-99	1.93	105	2019	21	40
A.A. (Alex) Harford	HSOB	16-06-99	1.82	91	2021	13	68
W.K. (Billy) Harmon	New Brighton	23-12-94	1.82	107	2016	71	55
W.A. (Willi) Heinz	Linwood	24-11-86	1.79	88	2009	76	76
T.J. (Tom) Heywood	Canterbury University	02-08-97	1.87	115	2022	7	0
N.M.W. (Nick) Hyde	Glenmark-Cheviot	17-06-93	1.79	106	2023	2	0
O.G.J.T. (Oli) Jager	New Brighton	05-07-95	1.92	127	2016	56	15
C.J. (Corey) Kellow	Lincoln University	25-05-01	1.89	107	2021	28	15
J.M. (Joel) Lam	Burnside	17-05-02	1.75	83	2022	3	0
D.P. (Daniel) Lienert-Brown	HSOB	09-02-93	1.84	117	2014	75	20
M.M.B.T. (Manasa) Mataele	Marist-Albion	27-11-96	1.85	100	2020	29	70
D.A.M. (Dallas) McLeod	Christchurch	30-04-99	1.9	101	2019	47	75
J.P.T. (Joe) Moody	Lincoln	18-09-88	1.88	122	2011	42	15
J.F.K. (James) Mullan	Sydenham	20-11-02	1.85	107	2023	2	0
B.J. (Blair) Murray	Canterbury University	09-10-01	1.74	83	2022	8	35
R.H. (Rameka) Poihipi	Lincoln University	14-10-98	1.87	105	2019	47	59
R.J. (Reed) Prinsep	HSOB	17-02-93	1.92	109	2014	83	30
N.G.J. (Ngane) Punivai	Prebbleton	30-08-98	1.9	102	2017	47	60
L. (Luke) Romano	Hurunui	16-02-86	1.99	118	2009	85	60
J.M. (Jone) Rova	Lincoln University	12-07-02	1.85	96	2022	7	0
C.G. (Carisbrook) To'omalatai	New Brighton	23-09-93	1.75	126	2023	5	0

INDIVIDUAL SCORING

	Tries	Con	PG	DG	Points
Burke	3	29	12	–	109
Murray	7	–	–	–	35
Harford	1	7	4	–	31
Poihipi	4	3	1	–	29
Fihaki	4	–	–	–	20
Funnell	4	–	–	–	20
Alaimalo	3	–	–	–	15
Drummond	3	–	–	–	15
Grace	3	–	–	–	15
Mataele	3	–	–	–	15
McLeod	3	–	–	–	15
Bell	2	–	–	–	10
Christie	2	–	–	–	10
Gardiner	2	–	–	–	10
Punivai	2	–	–	–	10
Penalty try	1	–	–	–	7
Cahill	1	–	–	–	5
Harmon	1	–	–	–	5
Heinz	1	–	–	–	5
Jager	1	–	–	–	5
Kellow	1	–	–	–	5
Lienert-Brown	1	–	–	–	5
Totals	**53**	**39**	**17**	**0**	**396**
Opposition scored					*318*

CANTERBURY 2023	Northland	North Harbour	Manawatu	Wellington	Taranaki	Auckland	Counties Manukau	Southland	Tasman	Waikato	Auckland (QF)	Taranaki (SF)	**Totals**
Fihaki	15	15	15	15	15	15	15	15	15	–	15	15	**11**
Alaimalo	–	–	–	s	s	14	11	11	14	11	11	11	**9**
Murray	s	11	11	11	–	–	–	–	–	s	s	s	**7**
Mataele	11	14	14	14	–	–	–	–	11	14	14	14	**8**
Rova	–	s	–	–	–	s	13	s	s	s	–	–	**6**
Punivai	14	–	–	–	11	11	14	14	–	–	–	–	**5**
Crotty	13	–	s	s	13	s	s	13	–	–	s	s	**9**
McLeod	–	13	13	13	14	13	s	12	13	13	13	13	**11**
Poihipi	12	12	12	12	12	12	12	s	12	12	12	12	**12**
Harford	s	s	s	–	10	–	–	–	s	10	–	10	**7**
Burke	10	10	10	10	–	10	10	10	10	15	10	–	**10**
Drummond	s	s	9	9	9	9	s	9	9	s	9	9	**12**
Lam	–	–	–	–	–	–	–	–	–	9	–	–	**1**
Heinz	9	9	s	s	s	s	9	s	s	–	s	–	**10**
Grace	–	s	8	8	8	8	8	s	–	–	8	–	**8**
Brial	s	–	–	–	–	–	–	8	s	–	–	–	**3**
Harmon (capt)	8	8	6	6	6	6	6	–	8	8	6	6	**11**
Christie	–	7	7	7	7	7	s	7	7	7	7	7	**11**
Kellow	7	6	s	s	–	–	7	6	–	–	–	s	**7**
Prinsep	–	–	–	–	s	s	–	–	–	s	s	8	**5**
Gardiner	6	5	–	–	–	–	–	–	6	6	s	–	**5**
Cahill	5	–	5	5	–	–	s	5	s	–	–	s	**7**
Gallagher	–	–	–	–	s	s	4	s	–	–	4	4	**6**
Romano	4	4	s	–	4	–	–	4	–	s	–	–	**6**
Dunshea	s	s	4	4	–	4	–	–	4	4	–	–	**7**
Darry	–	–	–	s	5	5	5	–	5	5	5	5	**8**
Jager	–	s	3	–	s	3	3	–	–	s	3	3	**8**
Calder	3	3	s	3	3	s	s	s	s	–	s	s	**11**
To'omalatai	s	–	–	s	–	–	–	3	3	3	–	–	**5**
Lienert-Brown	1	1	s	–	s	s	1	–	s	s	1	1	**10**
Heywood	s	s	–	s	–	–	s	s	–	–	s	–	**6**
Moody	–	–	1	1	1	1	–	1	1	1	–	s	**8**
Funnell	s	2	2	2	2	s	2	–	s	s	s	s	**11**
Hyde	–	–	s	s	–	–	–	–	–	–	–	–	**2**
Mullan	–	s	–	–	–	–	–	2	–	–	–	–	**2**
Bell	2	–	–	–	s	2	s	s	2	2	2	2	**9**

CANTERBURY TEAM RECORD 2023

Played 12 **Won 7** **Lost 5** **Points for 396** **Points against 2318**

Date	Opponent	Location	Score	Tries	Con	PG	DG	Referee
August 5	Northland	Whangarei	43-11	Murray (2), Cahill, Funnell, Fihaki	Burke (3)	Burke (4)		Kutsuki Furuse (Japan)
August 13	North Harbour	Takapuna	28-24	Fihaki, Gardiner, McLeod, Grace	Burke	Burke (2)		Nick Briant
August 19	Manawatu	Christchurch	68-26	Mataele (2), Poihipi (2), Drummond (2), Burke, Murray, Kellow, Fihaki	Burke (6), Harford (3)			Fraser Hannon
August 27	Wellington	Christchurch	31-36	Murray (3), Grace, Funnell	Burke (3)			Jono Bredin
September 2	Taranaki	Rangiora	29-28	Harford, Punivai, Harmon, Poihipi	Harford (3)	Harford		Nick Briant
September 9	Auckland	Auckland	29-36	Burke, McLeod, Alaimalo, penalty try	Burke (2)	Burke		Dan Waenga
September 13	Counties Manukau	Pukekohe	29-31	Funnell, Lienert-Brown, Christie, Grace	Burke (3)	Burke		Nick Hogan
September 17	Southland	Christchurch	29-14	Burke, Punivai, Bell, Heinz	Burke (3)	Burke		Fraser Hannon
September 23	Tasman	Christchurch	30-28	Christie, Mataele, Alaimalo	Burke (3)	Burke (3)		Stu Curran
September 30	Waikato	Hamilton	35-37	Gardiner, McLeod, Jager, Drummond, Funnell	Burke (5)			Cam Stone
October 6	Auckland (QF)	Christchurch	29-24	Alaimalo, Bell, Fihaki, Murray	Poihipi (3)	Poihipi		Nick Briant
October 13	Taranaki (SF)	New Plymouth	16-23	Poihipi	Harford	Harford (3)		Stu Curran

COUNTIES MANUKAU

2023 Status: Bunnings NPC
Founded 1926 as South Auckland and affiliated to Auckland. Granted full union status as South Auckland Counties in 1955. Name changed to Counties 1956, to Counties Manukau 1996.
President: L.A.R.L. (Lee) Lidgard
Chairman: G.L. (Gary) Millington
General manager: A.B.D. (Aaron) Lawton
Coach: R. (Reon) Graham
Assistant coaches: J.T. (Jimmy) Maher, P. (Pauliasi) Manu, P.R. (Paul) Wheeler
Main ground: Navigation Homes Stadium, Pukekohe
Capacity: 18,000
Colours: Red, white and black

RECORDS

Most appearances	201	*Alan Dawson, 1976–89*
Most points	698	*Danny Love, 1993–96*
Most tries	58	*Alan Dawson, 1976–89*
Most points in a season	208	*Danny Love, 1995*
Most tries in a season	22	*Luke Erenavula, 1993*
Most conversions in a season	52	*Danny Love, 1993*
Most penalty goals in a season	47	*Stu Hollier, 1989*
Most dropped goals in a season	4	*Bob Lendrum, 1976*
		Joe Harvey, 1983
Most points in a match	37	*Jim Graham v East Coast, 1972*
Most tries in a match	5	*Koiatu Koiatu v King Country, 2004*
Most conversions in a match	14	*Jim Graham v East Coast, 1972*
Most penalty goals in a match	6	*Stu Hollier v France, 1989*
		Stu Hollier v Thames Valley, 1989
		Danny Love v Manawatu, 1994
		James Semple v Manawatu, 2011
		Baden Kerr v Auckland, 2012
		Riley Hohepa v Bay of Plenty, 2022
Highest team score	108	*v Horowhenua, 1994*
Record victory (points ahead)	103	*103–0 v Poverty Bay, 1993*
Highest score conceded	100	*v Auckland, 2004*
Record defeat (points behind)	85	*15–100 v Auckland, 2004*

It was a season of clear, if incremental, progress for the Counties Manukau Steelers.

While their final position of ninth was just outside the NPC playoffs, they recorded more wins (4) than in 2022, scored more points (280) and more tries (41) and conceded less points (316). This was a decent effort when you consider they lost several players to Rugby World Cup duty and won just one of their first five games.

They were agonisingly close to winning their first home clash, against Hawke's Bay, but were edged on a tough penalty try call against the pack. Then followed a very good display against Bay of Plenty, in what was close to their best of the season, before decisive defeats to Waikato and Wellington, its nemesis, in the Jonah Lomu Memorial Trophy. The Lions seem to have their number, but the Steelers still scored some fine tries in that one.

Then followed three victories in the next four games, which took them to the cusp of the playoffs. That included a rousing 31–29 win over Canterbury midweek in Pukekohe, their first win over the red and blacks since 2016. It was, therefore, disappointing to finish with a 38–22 loss to Otago in Dunedin.

The gains were Sione Molia (sevens), Toni Pulu (Australia), Viliami Taulani (England), James Thompson (Waikato), Jimmy Tupou (Japan) and Maama Vaipulu (France), the latter impressing again in club rugby.

The losses included Sekope Kepu (injury), Alamanda Motuga (Samoa, RWC), Jared Page (retired), Mark Royal (retired), Samuel Slade (Samoa, RWC), Viliame Rarasea, Jonathan Taumateine (Samoa, RWC) and Zuriel Togiatama (Fiji, RWC).

In all, 11 players made their debuts for the Steelers from 37 used, club form again a major factor in promotion, something the Steelers, with a limited budget for the salary cap, do better than most unions.

Etene Nanai-Seturo was the Steelers player of the year, and indeed the best fullback in the NPC, scoring six tries, some of them solo efforts, and making many clean breaks with his dangerous footwork. He deservedly won the Duane Monkley Medal.

Josh Gray, who also scored six tries, including a hat-trick against Southland, took his chances on the right wing, while Peniasi Malimali ran hard on the opposite flank. Injury hindered the veteran Toni Pulu, back for the first time since 2019.

Tevita Ofa cemented the centre position, and nervelessly kicked the winning conversion against Canterbury. Sione Molia slotted in wherever he was required, at fullback, wing or second five. Ahsee Tuala could get little traction in 2023, making just one start.

No 10 Riley Hohepa was not as accurate with his goalkicking, but looks comfortable at this level now. Liam Daniela claimed the No 9 jersey in lieu of the Steelers' two international halfbacks.

Hoskins Sotutu's presence for nine games was a bonus, and he performed well, winning the official player of the year at the CMRFU awards. He was not always dominant, but showed touches of class and a decent work-rate after his rejection by the All Blacks.

Captain Sean Reidy was the man of steel, the sole player to start all 10 matches. The loose forward support cast all had their moments.

Tupou and Thompson, the latter the defensive player of the year, formed a solid locking duo, even if the lineout, despite several tries from mauls, was again not always reliable.

Kauvaka Kaivelata made such progress at loosehead prop that he won a Super Rugby contract, one of 16 Steelers to be offered full contracts. Sue Asomua was the main man at tighthead.

Debutant hooker Ian West-Stevens impressed enough to be named rookie of the year, and on six occasions kept Ioane Moananu, who scored five tries, on the pine at kickoff.

Higher honours went to:

New Zealand:	N. Laulala, D. Papali'i, C. Roigard
New Zealand Sevens:	S. Molia

COUNTIES MANUKAU REPRESENTATIVES 2023

Name	Club	Date of birth	Height	Weight	For Union Debut	Games	Points
A.J.M. (AJ) Alatimu	Ardmore-Marist	25-03-93	1.73	100	2022	15	22
S. (Sue) Asomua	Karaka	06-07-98	1.87	125	2018	31	5
C.J. (Cohen) Brady-Leatham	Patumahoe	07-05-03	1.74	75	2023	8	0
A.R. (Adam) Brash	Bombay	07-09-99	1.87	99	2022	17	15
L.T. (Liam) Daniela	Patumahoe	18-10-94	1.78	93	2017	36	15
A.C.H. (Alex) Eruera	Patumahoe	16-01-95	1.79	82	2023	1	0
L.K. (Lionel) Evans	Patumahoe	12-12-99	1.76	112	2022	7	0
N.K. (Nikolai) Foliaki	Karaka	25-12-97	1.9	105	2019	26	5
W.R (Will) Furniss	Patumahoe	25-06-94	1.96	100	2022	13	0
J.S.T. (Josh) Gray	Patumahoe	14-04-99	1.79	92	2019	9	30
K.S. (Kanavale) Helu	Pukekohe	18-02-03	1.78	85	2023	2	0
R. (Riley) Hohepa	Patumahoe	09-02-95	1.86	92	2019	29	181
K.J. (Kauvaka) Kaivelata	Pukekohe	11-07-02	1.88	113	2022	15	15
J.A. (Jadin) Kingi	Pukekohe	19-08-02	1.98	108	2022	8	0
E.V. (Ezekiel) Lindenmuth	Ardmore-Marist	14-07-97	1.87	116	2020	29	0
B.A. (Blake) Makiri	Manurewa	22-06-02	1.85	96	2023	6	10
P. (Peniasi) Malimali	Karaka	08-12-96	1.82	98	2021	17	30
A.E. (Alex) McRobbie	Bombay	14-02-00	1.95	110	2021	17	10
I.T. (Ioane) Moananu	Manurewa	08-02-01	1.76	113	2022	17	40
S.L.J. (Sione) Molia	Karaka	05-09-93	1.86	95	2013	26	35
N.M. (Nicholas) Muli	Karaka	11-09-03	1.8	110	2023	1	0
E.W.P.S. (Etene) Nanai-Seturo	Karaka	20-08-99	1.83	92	2018	28	50
T.I. (Tevita) Ofa	Manurewa	18-01-02	1.86	90	2022	20	36
T.N. (Toni) Pulu	Bombay	28-11-89	1.85	95	2012	55	65
S. (Sean) Reidy	Patumahoe	10-05-89	1.82	104	2012	26	25
H.C.R. (Hoskins) Sotutu	Papakura	12-07-98	1.92	113	2021	13	5
V.T.H. (Viliami) Taulani	Manurewa	17-01-97	1.91	115	2016	21	10
J.M.P. (James) Thompson	Patumahoe	13-07-99	1.95	114	2023	9	5
A. (Ahsee) Tuala	Manurewa	23-08-89	1.91	95	2009	69	177
S.R. (Siate) Taupaki	Patumahoe	23-01-94	1.75	123	2023	2	0
S.G. (Salesi) Tuifua	Karaka	27-12-02	1.76	118	2023	8	0
S.M. (Sam) Tuifua	Karaka	23-02-02	1.82	112	2022	14	15
L.A. (Larenz) Tupaea-Thomsen	Manurewa	24-03-01	1.78	92	2023	1	0
S.S. (Jimmy) Tupou	Patumahoe	08-08-92	1.96	109	2012	64	32
M. (Ma'ama) Vaipulu	Pukekohe	21-07-89	1.9	112	2012	46	55
K.L. (Keran) van Staden	Pukekohe	16-04-03	1.89	120	2023	2	0
I.A.B. (Ian) West-Stevens	Pukekohe	24-05-98	1.83	96	2023	10	10

INDIVIDUAL SCORING

	Tries	Con	PG	DG	Points		Tries	Con	PG	DG	Points
Hohepa	2	10	6	–	48	Asomua	1	–	–	–	5
Gray	6	–	–	–	30	Brash	1	–	–	–	5
Nanai-Seturo	6	–	–	–	30	Malimali	1	–	–	–	5
Ofa	1	9	1	–	26	McRobbie	1	–	–	–	5
Moananu	5	–	–	–	25	Sotutu	1	–	–	–	5
Reidy	3	–	–	–	15	Thompson	1	–	–	–	5
Penalty tries	2	–	–	–	14	Sam Tuifua	1	–	–	–	5
Alatimu	–	3	2	–	12	Tupou	1	–	–	–	5
Daniela	2	–	–	–	10						
Kaivelata	2	–	–	–	10	***Totals***	***41***	***22***	***9***	***0***	***280***
Makiri	2	–	–	–	10						
West-Stevens	2	–	–	–	10	*Opposition scored*	*47**	*25*	*9*	*0*	*316*

** includes two penalty tries (14 points)*

COUNTIES MANUKAU 2023	Taranaki	Hawke's Bay	Bay of Plenty	Waikato	Wellington	Southland	Canterbury	Tasman	Manawatu	Otago	**Totals**
Nanai-Seturo	15	15	15	15	15	–	–	15	15	15	**8**
Molia	–	–	14	14	12	15	15	–	s	12	**7**
Ofa	s	13	13	13	13	13	13	13	13	13	**10**
Gray	14	11	–	–	–	14	14	11	14	14	**7**
Pulu	s	–	11	11	14	–	–	–	–	–	**4**
Makiri	–	s	s	–	–	s	s	14	–	s	**6**
Malimali	11	14	–	s	11	11	11	–	11	11	**8**
Foliaki	13	12	12	12	–	s	–	–	12	–	**6**
Tuala	–	–	s	s	–	–	–	12	s	s	**5**
Eruera	–	–	–	–	–	–	–	s	–	–	**1**
Alatimu	12	s	–	–	s	12	12	–	–	–	**5**
Tupaea-Thomsen	–	–	–	–	–	–	–	10	–	–	**1**
Hohepa	10	10	10	10	10	10	10	s	10	10	**10**
Helu	s	s	–	–	–	–	–	–	–	–	**2**
Brady-Leatham	–	–	s	s	s	s	s	9	s	s	**8**
Daniela	9	9	9	9	9	9	9	s	9	9	**10**
Sam Tuifua	s	–	6	6	s	s	s	8	–	–	**7**
Sotutu	8	8	8	8	8	8	8	–	8	8	**9**
Taulani	–	s	–	–	6	–	–	–	–	–	**2**
Reidy (capt)	7	7	7	7	7	7	7	7	7	7	**10**
Brash	–	–	s	s	s	6	s	s	s	s	**8**
Vaipulu	6	6	–	–	–	–	6	6	6	6	**6**
Tupou	4	4	–	–	–	4	4	4	4	4	**7**
Thompson	5	5	5	5	5	5	5	–	5	5	**9**
Kingi	–	–	s	s	–	–	–	–	–	–	**2**
Furniss	–	–	–	–	s	–	–	s	s	s	**4**
McRobbie	s	s	4	4	4	s	s	5	–	–	**8**
Evans	–	–	–	–	–	–	–	–	s	s	**2**
Salesi Tuifua	3	s	s	3	3	3	s	3	–	–	**8**
Van Staden	–	–	–	s	s	–	–	–	–	–	**2**
Asomua	s	3	3	–	–	s	3	s	3	3	**8**
Kaivelata	1	1	1	1	1	1	s	s	1	s	**10**
Taupaki	s	–	–	–	s	–	–	–	–	–	**2**
Lindenmuth	–	s	s	s	–	s	1	1	s	1	**8**
Moananu	2	–	s	s	2	s	2	s	s	s	**9**
West-Stevens	s	2	2	2	s	2	s	2	2	2	**10**
Muli	–	s	–	–	–	–	–	–	–	–	**1**

COUNTIES MANUKAU TEAM RECORD 2023

Played 10 Won 4 Lost 6 Points for 280 Points against 316

Date	*Opponent*	*Location*	*Score*	*Tries*	*Con*	*PG*	*DG*	*Referee*
August 4	Taranaki	New Plymouth	29–37	Nanai-Seturo, Kaivelata, McRobbie, Tupou	Hohepa (3)	Hohepa		Paul Williams
August 11	Hawke's Bay	Pukekohe	24–25	Sotutu, Reidy, Nanai-Seturo	Hohepa (3)	Hohepa		Mike Winter
August 18	Bay of Plerty	Pukekohe	32–19	Kaivelata, Sam Tuifua, Hohepa, penalty try	Hohepa (2)	Hohepa (2)		Marcus Playle
August 27	Waikato	Hamilton	15–37	Ofa, Nanai-Seturo	Hohepa	Hohepa		Angus Mabey
September 2	Wellington (RS)	Wellington	25–56	Moananu, Malimali, Daniela, Nanai-Seturo	Alatimu	Hohepa		Stu Curran
September 9	Southland	Pukekohe	39–29	Gray (3), Daniela, Hohepa, penalty try	Hohepa, Alatimu	Alatimu		Mike Winter
September 13	Canterbury	Pukekohe	31–29	Thompson, Moananu, Brash, Makiri	Ofa (3), Alatimu	Alatimu		Nick Hogan
September 17	Tasman	Blenheim	17–27	West-Stevens, Reidy	Ofa (2)	Ofa		Jackson Henshaw
September 23	Manawatu	Pukekohe	46–19	Gray (2), Moananu (2), Asomua, West-Stevens, Nanai-Seturo, Reidy	Ofa (3)			Jono Bredin
October 1	Otago	Dunedin	22–38	Gray, Nanai-Seturo, Moananu, Makiri	Ofa			Maggie Cogger-Orr

NGATI POROU EAST COAST

2023 Status: Heartland Championship
Founded 1921 as East Coast. Affiliated 1922.
Name changed to Ngati Porou East Coast 2017
President: C.W. (Campbell) Dewes
Chairman: V.S. (Val) Morrison
Chief executive officer: L.M. (Leroy) Kururangi
Coach: K.D. (Kahu) Tamatea
Assistant coaches: H.E. (Hosea) Gear, Kim Harris
Main ground: Whakarua Park, Ruatoria
Capacity: 3000
Colours: Sky blue

RECORDS

Highest attendance	4000	*v Poverty Bay (Div 3 final), 1999*
Most appearances	113	*E.M. Waitoa, 1979–2006*
	113	*C.F. Harrison, 2003-2017*
Most points	406	*E.J. Manuel, 1985–98*
Most tries	24	*J.R. Kururangi, 1979–96*
Most points in a season	145	*M.R. Flutey, 2000*
Most tries in a season	9	*S. Vorenasu, 2011*
Most conversions in a season	22	*T.R.H.H.H. Fraser, 2023*
Most penalty goals in a season	30	*M.R. Flutey, 2000*
Most dropped goals in a season	3	*M.R. Flutey, 2000*
Most points in a match	25	*T.R.H.H.H. Fraser v Buller, 2021*
Most tries in a match	3	*W. Peachy v Bush, 1954*
		T.M. Reedy v Horowhenua, 1958
		J.R. Kururangi v West Coast, 1992
		J. Higgins v Poverty Bay, 1993
		M. Vere v Buller, 1999
		T.W. Delamere v Horowhenua Kapiti, 2000
		H.F.Haerewa v Poverty Bay, 2012
		S.P. Destounis, v Poverty Bay, 2016
		S.P. Parkes v Horowhenua Kapiti, 2022
Most conversions in a match	8	*V.P. Taingahue v Buller, 1999*
Most penalty goals in a match	7	*M.R. Flutey v Nelson Bays, 2001*
Highest team score	74	*v Buller, 1999*
Record victory (points ahead)	69	*72–3 v West Coast, 1992*
Highest score conceded	116	*v North Otago, 2010*
Record defeat (points behind)	113	*3–116 v North Otago, 2010*

Ngati Porou East Coast's fortunes continued to rise with a top four finish in the Heartland Championship round robin for the first time since 2012. An unbeaten home record, including four successful defences of the Osborne Taonga, was the base that propelled the Coasters into the playoffs, while the win over Buller at Westport was achieved in golden point extra time. Two late penalty goal attempts missed against Wairarapa Bush in the one-point defeat.

In their Meads Cup semi-final they gave the all-conquering South Canterbury team an almighty scare, leading 17–3 after 44 minutes before succumbing to 31 unanswered points in the last 25 minutes. The conceding of two yellow cards in that time did not help.

The forward pack was a very experienced one with the rolling maul a very effective weapon. The front row of Hakarangi Tichborne, Joe Royal and Perrin Manuel anchored one of the best scrums in the competition, with Royal also a standout in general play. Finding a consistent locking combination was only solved in the second half of the season with Hoani Te Moana shifting from loose forward to partner Richard Green who, until then, had had a different partner in each game.

Ngati Porou East Coast had strength in the loose forward department, with Mitchell Crosswell, Will Bolingford, Hone Haerewa and Faifili Levave all doing sterling work although the latter two were not always available.

Renata Roberts-Te Nana was a highly accomplished fullback whose NZ Heartland selection was well earned. Te Rangi Fraser was also one of the best backs, proving an astute general. His excellent goalkicking form saw him set a new record for conversions in a season.

Sam Parkes had another fine season at halfback and his captaincy proved invaluable to the team. He now has 23 tries, just one short of the Ngati Porou East Coast record.

Verdon Bartlett became just the fourth centurion for the Union, playing his 100th game in the win against King Country.

Of the new players, Tevita Nabura (Counties Manukau/Highlanders) Renata Roberts-Te Nana (Northland) and Nick Crosswell (Manawatu/Chiefs/Highlanders/Hurricanes/NZ Maori) all had previous first-class experience.

After the King's Birthday fixture against Poverty Bay, Hosea Gear became Director of Rugby for the Union, and Kahu Tamatea took over as head coach. Black Fern Charmaine McMenamin, not playing in the Farah Palmer Cup due to a knee injury, was involved with the team as performance analyst.

Higher honours went to:
New Zealand Heartland: R. Roberts-Te Nana

INDIVIDUAL SCORING

	Tries	*Con*	*PG*	*DG*	*Points*		*Tries*	*Con*	*PG*	*DG*	*Points*
Fraser	2	22	8	-	78	Meihana	1	-	-	-	5
Roberts-Te Nana	4	4	1	-	31	Samupo	1	-	-	-	5
Royal	5	-	-	-	25	Palmer	1	-	-	-	5
Tichborne	3	-	-	-	15	Dearden	1	-	-	-	5
Parkes	3	-	-	-	15	Bartlett	1	-	-	-	5
Bolingford	2	-	-	-	10	More	1	-	-	-	5
Pewhalrangi	2	-	-	-	10	M. Crosswell	1	-	-	-	5
Levave	2	-	-	-	10						
Tangaere	2	-	-	-	10	***Totals***	**35**	**26**	**9**	**0**	**256**
Nabura	2	-	-	-	10						
Penalty Try	1	-	-	-	7	*Opposition scored*	*29*	*19*	*21*	*0*	*246*

NGATI POROU EAST COAST REPRESENTATIVES 2023

Name	Club	For Union Debut	Games	Points
S.M. (Semisi Akana	Uawa	2022	14	0
V.R.M. (Verdon) Bartlett	TVC	2008	101	46
W.C. (Will) Bolingford	Waiapu	2021	29	25
Manahi Brooking	Hicks Bay	2019	2	0
M.C. (Mitchell) Crosswell	–	2019	17	15
N.J. (Nick) Crosswell	–	2023	3	0
J.G. (Josh) Dearden	Uawa	2021	15	5
T.R.H.H.H. (Te Rangi) Fraser	Hicks Bay	2013	27	187
R.W. (Richard) Green	Waiapu	2015	39	5
H.T.R. (Hone) Haerewa	North Shore [2]	2015	57	44
Jayden Leiua-Pokia	Ruatoria City	2023	5	0
Faifili Levave	–	2021	14	10
P.J. (Perrin) Manuel [1]	Tech OB [3]	2013	64	41
Tipene Meihana	Hikurangi	2019	9	10
Hamuera Moana	Waiapu	2019	29	5
Jaya More	Whakarewarewa	2023	3	5
T.A.M. (Te Aho) Morice	Hikurangi	2020	8	0
Paora Mullany	Hicks Bay	2023	2	0
Tevita Nabura	Keri Keri [4]	2023	8	10
Taane Paki	Taniwharau [5]	2023	6	0
Karaitiana "Kris" Palmer	Hikurangi	2013	51	149
S.P. (Sam) Parkes	Keri Keri [4]	2012	71	161
A.M.T.W. (Apirana) Pewhairangi	Waima	2022	16	15
Jack Richardson	Ruatoria City	2018	27	10
R.C. (Renata) Roberts-Te Nana	Ruatoria City	2023	8	31
J.W. (Joe) Royal	Ponsonby [6]	2022	15	45
Pamona Samupo	Tokararangi	2013	30	20
T.M.T.I.W. (Tawhao) Stewart	Uawa	2019	20	30
BJ Sidney	Uawa	2010	16	12
F.C. (Frank) Taiapa	Hicks Bay	2012	18	0
J.T. (Jorian) Tangaere	Clive [3]	2020	30	40
G.C. (Gabriel) Te Kani	Waiapu	2021	9	5
Rico Te Kani	Waiapu	2023	6	0
H.J. (Hoani) Te Moana	TVC	2011	42	5
H.T.K. (Hakarangi) Tichborne	Waima	2018	26	55
Manahi Tipoki	Marist [2]	2023	1	0
J.K. (Jody) Tuhaka	Waiapu	2021	27	5
T.J.H. (Tutere) Waenga	TVC	2020	19	0
R.J.S. (Richard) Waitoa	Hicks Bay	2008	43	35

1. Player of Origin 2. Loaned by North Harbour RU 3. Hawke's Bay RU 4 Loaned by Northland RU
5 Waikato Rugby League 6 Loaned by Auckland RU

NGATI POROU EAST COAST 2023	Poverty Bay	Wairarapa Bush	Mid Canterbury	North Otago	Buller	Poverty Bay	Whanganui	King Country	Thames Valley	South Canterbury (sf)	TOTALS
Palmer	15	14	11	11	-	-	-	-	-	-	**4**
Roberts-Te Nana	-	15	15	-	15	15	15	15	15	15	**8**
Tipoki	14	-	-	-	-	-	-	-	-	-	**1**
Meihana	11	-	-	-	-	-	-	-	-	-	**1**
Nabura	-	11	12	12	11	12	12	-	11	11	**8**
Bartlett	-	s	s	s	s	s	s	11	-	s	**8**
Samupo	-	12	14	-	-	11	-	14	14	-	**5**
Sidney	-	-	-	14	14	-	14	-	-	-	**3**
Paki	-	-	-	s	12	-	11	s	s	14	**6**
Pewhairangi	13	13	13	13	13	13	-	13	13	13	**9**
Stewart	s	-	-	-	-	-	-	-	-	-	**1**
Waenga	-	-	s	-	-	-	13	12	12	12	**5**
Morice	12	-	-	s	s	14	-	s	s	-	**6**
Mullany	-	-	-	-	-	s	s	-	-	-	**2**
Fraser	10	10	10	10	10	10	10	10	10	10	**10**
Moana	9	-	-	-	-	-	s	-	-	-	**2**
Dearden	s	s	s	15	s	s	9	s	s	s	**10**
Parkes (capt.)	-	9	9	9	9	9	-	9	9	9	**8**
Haerewa	8	6	-	-	6	6	7	6	-	-	**6**
Te Moana	-	8	-	6	8	4	5	5	5	5	**8**
Bolingford	7	7	7	7	7	7	-	7	7	7	**9**
M. Crosswell	6	5	6	8	-	8	8	8	8	8	**9**
Richardson	s	-	-	s	s	-	s	-	s	-	**5**
Levave	-	s	8	-	-	-	6	-	6	6	**5**
R. Te Kani	-	-	s	4	-	s	s	-	s	s	**6**
Green	5	4	4	5	5	5	-	4	4	4	**9**
Taiapa	4	s	-	-	-	-	-	s	-	-	**3**
N. Crosswell	s	-	5	-	-	-	4	-	-	-	**3**
Waitoa	-	s	s	-	s	-	-	s	-	s	**5**
G. Te Kani	-	-	-	s	4	-	-	-	-	-	**2**
Tuhaka	3	s	-	-	s	s	1	-	s	s	**7**
Tichborne	1	1	1	1	1	1	s	1	1	1	**10**
Akana	s	3	-	-	-	s	-	s	-	-	**4**
More	s	-	3	-	-	-	s	-	-	-	**3**
Leiua-Pokia	-	-	s	s	-	s	s	s	-	-	**5**
Manuel	-	-	-	3	3	3	3	3	3	3	**7**
Brooking	-	-	-	s	-	-	-	-	-	-	**1**
Royal	2	2	2	2	-	-	-	2	2	2	**7**
Tangaere	-	s	-	s	2	2	2	s	s	s	**8**

Haerewa captained in first game v Poverty Bay;
M. Crosswell captained v Whanganui

NGATI POROU EAST COAST TEAM RECORD 2023

Played 10 **Won 5** **Lost 5** **Points for 256** **Points against 246**

Date	Opponent	Location	Score	Tries	Con	PG	DG	Referee
June 3	Poverty Bay *	Gisborne	17–29	Tichborne, Meihana, Bolingford	Fraser			Damian MacPherson
August 12	Wairarapa Bush	Masterton	31–32	Fraser, Pewhairangi, Samupo, Royal	Roberts-Te Nana (4)	Roberts-Te Nana		Nick Hogan
August 19	Mid Canterbury (OT)	Ruatoria	19–8	Royal, Levave, Parkes	Fraser (2)			Tipene Cottrell
August 26	North Otago (OT)	Ruatoria	38–29	Palmer, Parkes, Fraser, Dearden, Royal	Fraser (5)	Fraser		Andy Morton
September 2	Buller	Westport	24–21 aet	Tichborne, Roberts-Te Nana, Tangaere	Fraser (3)	Fraser		Dan Moore
September 9	Poverty Bay (OT)	Ruatoria	31–11	Roberts-Te Nana, Tangaere, Nabura, Bartlett	Fraser	Fraser (3)		Ben Woolerton
September 16	Whanganui	Whanganui	24–40	More, Nabura, Tichborne	Fraser (3)	Fraser		Stu Curran
September 23	King Country (OT)	Ruatoria	29–11	Royal (2), Roberts–Te Nana, Bolingford	Fraser (3)	Fraser		Tipene Cottrell
September 30	Thames Valley	Waihi	26–31	Parkes, M. Crosswell, Pewhairangi, Roberts-Te Nana	Fraser (3)			Andy Morton
October 7	South Canterbury (MC sf)	Pleasant Point	17–34	Penalty Try, Levave	Fraser	Fraser		Nick Hogan

** Non-Heartland Championship match*

HAWKE'S BAY

2023 Status: Bunnings NPC
Founded 1884. Original member 1892
President: M.R.M. (Mavis) Mullins
Chairman: B.J. (Brendon) Mahony
Chief executive officer: J.L. (Jay) Campbell
Coach: B.R. (Brock) James
Assistant coaches: F.J. (Francisco) Deformes, B.R. (Bryn) Evans, S.J. (Sam) McNicol
Main ground: McLean Park, Napier
Capacity: 16,500
Colours: Black and white

RECORDS

Most appearances	158	*N.W. Thimbleby, 1959–71*
Most points	998	*J.B. Cunningham, 90–98*
Most tries	73	*B.A. Grenside, 1919–31*
Most points in a season	237	*J.B. Cunningham, 94*
Most tries in a season	18	*B.A. Grenside, 1926*
		P.J. Cooke, 1986
Most conversions in a season	47	*J.B. Cunningham, 95*
Most penalty goals in a season	37	*M.W. Berquist, 2009*
Most dropped goals in a season	7	*B.D.M. Furlong, 1968*
		M.K. Sisam, 1979
Most points in a match	36	*M.K. Sisam v East Coast, 1979*
Most tries in a match	6	*R.P. Hunter v East Coast, 1979*
Most conversions in a match	13	*J.B. Cunningham v Cook Islands, 1995*
Most penalty goals in a match	7	*J.B. Cunningham v Manawatu, 1993*
		J.B. Cunningham v King Country, 1994
		R.G.E. Lewis v North Harbour, 2001
Highest team score	99	*v Cook Islands, 1995*
		v Mid Canterbury, 2003
Record victory (points ahead)	99	*99–0 v Cook Islands, 1995*
Highest score conceded	86	*v Waikato, 1999*
Record defeat (points behind)	86	*0–86 v Waikato, 1999*

Hawke's Bay went the closest they have ever been to becoming NPC champions. In their first ever Premiership final they lost to Taranaki at New Plymouth 22–19 in a match that was as tight as the scoreline suggests. A consolation was the regaining of the Ranfurly Shield from Wellington three weeks earlier to whom they had lost it to last year.

The Bay finished the round robin in fifth position with seven wins and three losses. Three of the victories came in the final minutes — Counties Manukau was defeated with a last-minute penalty try, the 35–32 win against Waikato (from 14–32 down) was achieved with a 78th-minute converted try, as was the Ranfurly Shield victory over Wellington.

In the quarter-final, the Magpies were 19–28 behind at halftime, then kept Bay of Plenty scoreless in the second half while the semi-final was more clearcut than the 25–24 score indicates as Hawke's Bay led 25–10 until the last four minutes when a yellow card reduced them down to 14 men.

The forward pack competed very well. Pouri Rakete-Stones, Tyrone Thompson and Joel Hintz formed one of the strongest front rows at scrum time, earning numerous penalties. Rakete-Stones and Thompson (Magpies player of the year) were also powerful ball carriers and Hintz had his best season yet. The return to first-class rugby of 2017 NZ Under 20 prop Tim Farrell after a three-year injury absence was pleasing to see.

Captain Tom Parsons and Geoff Cridge were two seasoned locks whose set piece work and all-round play were quite outstanding. Isaia Walker-Leawere only played once due to injury and 22-year-old Frank Lochore showed promise and should benefit from the extended game time he had. Hawke's Bay had outstanding loose forwards in Devan Flanders, Josh Kaifa, Marino Mikaele-Tu'u and Sam Smith. Flanders, in particular, produced some of his best form and Mikaele-Tu'u lived up to his reputation.

As expected, the All Blacks halfbacks Brad Weber and Folau Fakatava provided a fine service to the backline and proved troublesome to opposition teams when running. Weber must have been unlucky to miss World Cup selection. First-five Lincoln McClutchie handled well and proved himself an excellent general. With his accurate goal kicking, he topped the NPC competition points scoring.

Chase Tiatia and Nick Grigg were two contrasting midfield backs. Tiatia was constantly involved in the action and his three tries in the semi-final were fine efforts, while Grigg was a very steady player who rarely made a mistake. Jonah Lowe had a quieter season than usual on the wing while Ollie Sapsford, who started off in midfield, was shifted to the wing and finished off attacking movements well to score five tries.

Twenty-year-old Harry Godfrey looks to have a bright future. Although selected at fullback, he also has the ability to play first-five, which may well be where his future lies. Injury kept him out of action in the second half of the season and the Bay were able to rely on the experienced Lolagi Visinia who took over.

Regulars missing from last year were Ere Enari, Neria Fomai, Danny Toala (all Samoa World Cup squad), Joe Apikotoa, Solomone Funaki, Anzelo Tuitavuki (all Tonga World Cup squad), and Bryn Evans and Mark Braidwood both retired. New signings were Bo Abra (Western Force), Paula Balekana (New England Freejacks), Isaac Salmon (Tasman), Isileli Tu'ungafasi (Tasman) and Sam Wye (Auckland).

Higher honours went to:

New Zealand:	B. Retallick
All Blacks XV	F. Fakatava, P. Rakete-Stones, T. Thompson, B. Weber
New Zealand Under 20:	T. Allen, C. Flanders, H. Godfrey, H. Morrison

HAWKE'S BAY REPRESENTATIVES 2023

Name	Club	Date of birth	Height	Weight	For Union Debut	Games	Points
B.J. (Bowen) Abra	overseas	11-07-99	1.82	115	2023	8	0
T.G. (Tom) Allen	Havelock North	23-07-04	1.98	112	2023	1	0
S.J.L. (Joe) Apikotoa	Taradale	18-07-96	1.91	120	2018	43	5
P.C. (Paula) Balekana	overseas	18-05-93	1.80	96	2023	7	0
G.O. (Geoff) Cridge	overseas	06-02-95	1.99	112	2014	70	35
J.D. (Jacob) Devery	Hastings RS	21-10-98	1.80	103	2017	26	30
F.M.L.N. (Folau) Fakatava	Hastings RS	16-12-99	1.77	80	2018	45	40
T.J. (Tim) Farrell	Tech OB	23-06-98	1.92	125	2017	15	10
D.J. (Devan) Flanders	Havelock North	20-07-99	1.93	108	2018	63	55
J.W.J. (Josh) Gimblett	NOB Marist	08-06-00	1.91	105	2021	10	5
H.G.R. (Harry) Godfrey	Central HB	03-01-03	1.75	85	2021	11	43
N.J. (Nick) Grigg	overseas	18-09-92	1.75	92	2022	20	5
K.C. (Kienan) Higgins	Taradale	25-01-00	1.89	97	2021	11	30
J.N. (Joel) Hintz	overseas	11-07-96	1.74	108	2019	50	0
S.I.A. (Stacey) Ili	overseas	11-05-91	1.78	92	2018	61	30
Siosiua "Josh" Kaifa	Central HB	21-07-92	1.88	103	2018	55	60
K.L. (Kianu) Kereru-Symes	overseas	28-02-99	1.80	106	2018	52	35
F.W. (Frank) Lochore	Central HB	07-06-01	1.92	108	2021	17	0
J.H. (Jonah) Lowe	Clive	09-05-96	1.84	92	2015	73	137
C.L. (Caleb) Makene	overseas	20-04-96	1.80	85	2019	46	93
L.F. (Lincoln) McClutchie	Tamatea	12-04-99	1.74	84	2018	64	454
M.E.R. (Marino) Mikaele-Tu'u	Hastings RS	06-11-97	1.92	113	2016	62	77
H.F. (Hunter) Morrison	Taradale	11-01-03	1.95	114	2023	2	0
T.I. (Tom) Parsons	Central HB	25-06-90	1.98	113	2012	83	60
P.G. (Pouri) Rakete-Stones	Pirates	17-06-97	1.83	118	2017	76	55
I.A. (Isaac) Salmon	overseas	05-09-96	1.80	110	2023	3	0
O.R. (Ollie) Sapsford	overseas	07-10-95	1.91	104	2019	51	75
Hisamitsu Shimada	Clive	10-12-98	1.73	103	2023	2	5
S.H. (Sam) Smith	Havelock North	19-07-00	1.79	103	2022	20	30
T.T.W.J. (Tyrone) Thompson	Tech OB	28-05-00	1.88	115	2022	23	60
C.J. (Chase) Tiatia	overseas	14-10-95	1.81	93	2022	21	43
Isileli Tu'ungafasi	Grammar TEC[1]	10-01-95	1.85	116	2023	3	0
P.L. (Patrick) Tuifua	Hastings RS	25-08-04	1.91	113	2023	5	0
A.T.M. (Anzelo) Tuitavuki	Clive	10-10-98	1.82	98	2020	12	25
Lolagi Visinia	Clive	17-01-93	1.93	109	2020	37	75
I.E.T. (Isaia) Walker-Leawere	Clive	06-04-97	1.97	122	2019	34	20
B.M. (Brad) Weber	NOB Marist	17-01-91	1.72	75	2016	50	127
S.A. (Sam) Wye	Taradale	11-11-00	1.78	88	2023	5	5

1. Auckland RU

INDIVIDUAL SCORING

	Tries	Con	PG	DG	Points		Tries	Con	PG	DG	Points
McClutchie	3	37	12	–	125	Visinia	2	–	–	–	10
Tiatia	7	–	–	–	35	Penalty Try	1	–	–	–	7
Weber	5	–	–	–	25	Godfrey	1	1	–	–	7
Sapsford	5	–	–	–	25	Devery	1	–	–	–	5
Thompson	5	–	–	–	25	Shimada	1	–	–	–	5
Mikaele-Tu'u	4	–	–	–	20	Grigg	1	–	–	–	5
Smith	3	–	–	–	15	Wye	1	–	–	–	5
Lowe	3	–	–	–	15	Cridge	1	–	–	–	5
Rakete-Stones	2	–	–	–	10	Makene	–	1	–	–	2
Farrell	2	–	–	–	10						
Flanders	2	–	–	–	10	***Totals***	***54***	***39***	***12***	***0***	***386***
Parsons	2	–	–	–	10						
Kaifa	2	–	–	–	10	*Opposition scored*	*45*	*34*	*15*	*0*	*338*

HAWKE'S BAY 2023	North Harbour	Counties Manukau	Waikato	Otago	Auckland	Northland	Bay of Plenty	Manawatu	Southland	Wellington	Bay of Plenty (qf)	Wellington (sf)	Taranaki (f)	**TOTALS**
Godfrey	15	15	s	15	15	15	15	-	-	-	-	-	-	**7**
Makene	-	s	15	s	s	-	-	15	s	s	s	s	s	**10**
Lowe	14	14	14	-	-	-	14	14	14	14	14	14	14	**10**
Visinia	11	-	-	-	11	s	-	s	15	15	15	15	15	**9**
Tuitavuki	-	11	s	11	-	-	-	-	-	-	-	-	-	**3**
Balekana	-	-	11	14	14	14	s	s	s	-	-	-	-	**7**
Sapsford	13	12	-	13	13	11	11	11	11	11	11	11	11	**12**
Grigg	s	13	13	s	-	13	13	13	13	13	13	13	13	**12**
Higgins	-	-	-	-	-	s	-	-	-	-	-	-	-	**1**
Ili	-	-	-	-	s	12	s	-	-	s	s	s	s	**7**
Tiatia	12	s	12	12	12	-	12	12	12	12	12	12	12	**12**
McClutchie	10	10	10	10	10	10	10	10	10	10	10	10	10	**13**
Fakatava	9	s	s	9	9	9	s	-	s	s	s	9	s	**12**
Weber	s	9	9	-	-	-	9	9	9	9	9	-	9	**9**
Wye	-	-	-	s	s	s	-	s	-	-	-	s	-	**5**
Flanders	8	8	-	8	8	8	8	-	s	8	8	8	8	**11**
Kaifa	7	6	7	-	7	7	7	6	6	7	7	6	7	**12**
Mikaele-Tu'u	6	-	8	-	-	6	-	8	8	6	6	-	6	**8**
Smith	s	7	s	7	s	-	s	7	7	s	s	7	s	**12**
Tuifua	-	s	-	s	6	s	-	s	-	-	-	-	-	**5**
Gimblett	-	-	6	6	-	-	6	-	-	-	-	s	-	**4**
Parsons (capt.)	5	5	-	5	5	5	5	5	5	5	5	5	5	**12**
Lochore	4	4	4	-	s	4	s	s	s	s	s	s	s	**12**
Morrison	s	-	-	s	-	-	-	-	-	-	-	-	-	**2**
Walker-Leawere	-	s	-	-	-	-	-	-	-	-	-	-	-	**1**
Allen	-	-	5	-	-	-	-	-	-	-	-	-	-	**1**
Cridge	-	-	s	4	4	s	4	4	4	4	4	4	4	**11**
Hintz	3	3	s	-	-	3	3	3	3	3	3	3	3	**11**
Rakete-Stones	1	1	1	s	3	1	1	1	1	1	1	1	1	**13**
Salmon	s	s	3	-	-	-	-	-	-	-	-	-	-	**3**
Farrell	s	s	s	-	-	-	s	s	-	s	s	s	s	**9**
Apikotoa	-	-	-	3	-	-	-	-	-	-	-	-	s	**2**
Tu'ungafasi	-	-	-	1	1	-	-	-	s	-	-	-	-	**3**
Abra	-	-	-	-	s	s	s	s	s	s	s	s	-	**8**
Kereru-Symes	2	-	2	s	s	s	s	s	s	-	-	-	-	**8**
Devery	s	2	-	-	-	-	-	-	-	s	s	s	s	**6**
Thompson	-	s	s	2	2	2	2	2	2	2	2	2	2	**12**
Shimada	-	-	-	-	s	s	-	-	-	-	-	-	-	**2**

Weber captained v Waikato

HAWKE'S BAY TEAM RECORD 2023

Played 13 **Won 9** **Lost 4** **Points for 386** **Points against 338**

Date	Opponent	Location	Score	Tries	Con	PG	DG	Referee
August 5	North Harbour	Napier	23–21	Tiatia, Rakete-Stones	McClutchie (2)	McClutchie (3)		Stu Curran
August 11	Counties Manukau	Pukekohe	25–24	Devery, Tiatia, Penalty Try	McClutchie	McClutchie (2)		Mike Winter
August 16	Waikato	Napier	35–32	Farrell (2), Weber, Mikaele-Tu'u, Godfrey	McClutchie (5)			Angus Mabey
August 20	Otago	Napier	33–32	Flanders (2), Tiatia, Smith, Sapsford	McClutchie (4)			Nick Briant
August 26	Auckland	Auckland	22–41	McClutchie, Parsons, Shimada	McClutchie, Godfrey	McClutchie		Mike Winter
September 2	Northland	Whangarei	21–44	McClutchie (2), Thompson	McClutchie (3)			Maggie Cogger-Orr
September 9	Bay of Plenty	Napier	35–38	Sapsford (2), Thompson, Lowe, Weber	McClutchie (2)	McClutchie (2)		Cam Stone
September 15	Manawatu	Napier	57–7	Weber (2), Mikaele-Tu'u (2), Smith, Grigg, Sapsford, Wye	McClutchie (7)	McClutchie		Fraser Hannon
September 23	Southland	Invercargill	33–7	Kaifa (2), Thompson, Mikaele-Tu'u, Weber	McClutchie (3), Makene			Marcus Playle
September 30	Wellington (RS)	Wellington	20–18	Sapsford, Lowe, Smith	McClutchie	McClutchie		Nick Briant
October 8	Bay of Plenty (qf)	Tauranga	38–28	Thompson (2), Rakete-Stones, Lowe, Visinia, Tiatia	McClutchie (4)			Angus Mabey
October 14	Wellington (sf)	Wellington	25–24	Tiatia (3)	McClutchie (2)	McClutchie (2)		Cam Stone
October 21	Taranaki (f)	New Plymouth	19–22	Visinia, Parsons, Cridge	McClutchie (2)			Angus Mabey

HOROWHENUA KAPITI

2023 Status: Heartland Championship
Founded 1893. as Horowhenua. Affiliated 1893.
Name changed to Horowhenua Kapiti 1997.
President: L.E. (Lindsay) Walker
Chairman: John Cribb
Chief executive officer: C.J. (Corey) Kennett
Coach: P.A. (Aleni) Feagaiga
Assistant coach: A.J. (Anthony) Rehutai
Main ground: Levin Park Domain
Capacity: 12,000
Colours: Red, white and blue

RECORDS

Highest attendance	6500	*Hurricanes v Crusaders pre-season, 2014*
Most appearances	153	*P.M. Hirini, 1986–2000*
Most points	431	*C.W. Laursen, 1985–89*
Most tries	70	*D.C. Laursen, 1980–92*
		P.M. Hirini, 1986-2000
Most points in a season	136	*C.J. Spencer, 1993*
Most tries in a season	13	*D.C. Laursen, 1987*
		C.J. Kennett, 1993
Most conversions in a season	26	*C.J. Spencer, 1993*
		R.F. Aloe, 2008
Most penalty goals in a season	29	*C.W. Laursen, 1987*
Most dropped goals in a season	5	*M. Liddicoat, 1979*
Most points in a match	29	*J.P.M. Hamilton v West Coast, 2010*
		B.C. Laursen v Poverty Bay, 2015
Most tries in a match	5	*D.C. Laursen v West Coast, 1991*
Most conversions in a match	9	*D.P. Nepia v Buller, 1999*
	9	*R.F. Aloe v East Coast, 2008*
Most penalty goals in a match	6	*J. Proctor v Whanganui, 2009*
		J.S. So'oialo v Buller 2017
Highest team score	73	*v Buller, 1999*
		v East Coast, 2008
Record victory (points ahead)	73	*73–0 v Buller, 1999*
Highest score conceded	108	*v Counties, 1994*
Record defeat (points behind)	96	*12–108 v Counties, 1994*

With a record of two wins and six losses, Horowhenua Kapiti finished bottom of the Heartland Championship. The first win of the season, over Wairarapa Bush, was unexpected, given their respective positions on the Heartland Championship table at the time but Horowhenua Kapiti started well and led 24–0 early in the second half, before holding out to win 24–19.

In recent years the union has experienced a high turnover of players from year to year and 2023 was no exception. Just 13 of the 33 players used last year reappeared in 2023. Including the Ranfurly Shield challenge against Wellington, a total of 39 players were used, including 21 debutants. If the players used can be kept together then the union can hope for better results in 2024.

Of the newcomers, Aidan Champion and Jonathan Fuimaono had represented Wairarapa Bush, Jack Riley had played for NZ Universities and Regan Verney for Wellington and Taranaki. A loss from last year was the very experienced prop, Scott Cameron who was in Australia.

Newcomer Leighton Ralph showed considerable promise in his debut season of first-class football. Initially used off the bench, he finished the season as first-choice fullback and top try scorer with seven tries. Wing Willie Paia'aua showed up well and notched his 50th game in the last match of the season.

Of the other backs, Connor Paki has good individual performances at both wing and centre and Jack Tatu-Robertsson was an accomplished halfback. First-five was something of a problem position with four players tried.

Callum Watts-Pointer was always strong off the back of the scrum, and Aaron Lahmert continues to give fine service at flanker. At lock, Dallas Wiki improved markedly as the season went on, starting off the bench and he finished the season as a first-choice lock. The long-serving Ryan Shelford announced his retirement at the end of the season after 116 games for the union. His service as player and captain has been outstanding over 15 seasons.

In the front row, David McErlean was a top class scrummager and a hard worker in the tight, while hooker Tutangiora Mafi showed a great deal of promise.

INDIVIDUAL SCORING

	Tries	*Con*	*PG*	*DG*	*Points*		*Tries*	*Con*	*PG*	*DG*	*Points*
Tatu-Robertsson	–	14	7	–	49	Wiki	1	–	–	–	5
Ralph	7	–	–	–	35	Itielu	1	–	–	–	5
Masoe	4	–	–	–	20	Shelford	1	–	–	–	5
Paki	2	1	–	–	12	T. Winterburn	1	–	–	–	5
Mafi	2	–	–	–	10	McErlean	1	–	–	–	5
Watts-Pointer	2	–	–	–	10						
Paia'aua	2	–	–	–	10	***Totals***	**25**	**17**	**8**	**0**	**183**
Champion	–	2	1	–	7						
Lahmert	1	–	–	–	5	*Opposition scored*	*57*	*34*	*4*	*0*	*365*

HOROWHENUA KAPITI REPRESENTATIVES 2023

		For Union		
Name	Club	Debut	Games	Points
G.T. (Geordie) Bean	OB University [1]	2023	5	0
H.B. (Hamish) Buick	Rahui	2014	25	22
S.B. (Stephen) Burnell	Shannon	2023	1	0
A.M. (Aidan) Champion	OB Marist [2]	2023	4	7
M.M. (Morehu) Connor-Phillips	Rahui	2020	6	0
T.B.P (Teraiti) Donaghy	Rahui	2023	7	0
L.P. (Leon) Ellison	Rahui	2018	17	14
K.W.A. (Kale) Eriksson	Foxton	2022	14	0
H.F. (Henry) Fonoti	Levin COB	2022	4	0
Siosiua Fotu	Waikanae	2023	3	0
J.R. (Jonathan) Fuimaono	Rahui	2023	6	0
M.L.M. (Mikaere) Harvey	Foxton	2023	1	0
D.J. "Deejay" Hemopo	Shannon	2023	8	0
P.D. (Poleka) Itielu	Levin COB	2023	9	5
Samson Koneferenisi	OB University [1]	2023	1	0
Kolonio Koto	Waikanae	2021	13	0
A.D. (Aaron) Lahmert	Waikanae	2014	76	52
Z.A. (Zachary) Lemana	Paraparaumu	2023	1	0
T.K.I. (Tutangiora) Mafi	Foxton	2023	9	10
Malakai Masoe	Levin Wanderers	2023	7	20
D.J. (David) McErlean	Foxton	2011	75	55
W.E. (Willie) Paia'aua	Levin COB	2016	50	97
C.L. (Connor) Paki	Foxton	2020	22	14
O.M. (Oliver) Paotonu	Johnsonville [1]	2023	7	0
S.J. (Sean) Pape	Shannon	2019	8	0
J.C. (Jake) Quin	Rahui	2023	3	0
L.P. (Leighton) Ralph	Rahui	2023	9	35
J.T. (Joshua) Rauhihi	Shannon	2020	8	0
J.B. (Jack) Riley	OB University [1]	2023	5	0
D.G. (Dale) Sabbagh	Paremata-Plimmerton [1]	2023	3	0
S.V. (Slade) Salton	Shannon	2022	10	0
R.T. (Ryan) Shelford	Paraparaumu	2009	116	42
J.T. (Jack) Tatu-Robertsson	Rahui	2020	27	223
L.J. (Liam) Tooman	Rahui	2023	3	0
R.D. (Regan) Verney	Rahui	2023	6	0
C.J. (Callum) Watts-Pointer	Paraparaumu	2022	16	20
D.B. (Dallas) Wiki	Shannon	2020	11	5
J.K.M. (Joel) Winterburn	Rahui	2011	40	20
Treden Winterburn	Shannon	2023	8	5

1. Loaned by Wellington RU *2. Loaned by Manawatu*

HOROWHENUA KAPITI 2023	Wellington	South Canterbury	West Coast	Mid Canterbury	Wairarapa Bush	Buller	King Country	Poverty Bay	Whanganui	TOTALS
Connor-Phillips	15	–	s	15	–	–	–	–	–	**3**
Masoe	14	15	–	–	s	s	14	14	s	**7**
Fotu	11	s	–	s	–	–	–	–	–	**3**
Ralph	s	s	15	13	15	15	15	15	15	**9**
Paia'aua	–	11	11	11	11	11	11	11	11	**8**
Paki	13	14	14	14	14	13	13	–	s	**8**
Pape	–	–	–	–	s	14	–	s	14	**4**
Paotonu	–	13	13	12	13	12	–	13	13	**7**
Verney	12	12	–	–	12	–	12	12	12	**6**
Hemopo	s	s	12	s	–	s	s	s	s	**8**
Buick	10	–	s	10	–	–	–	–	–	**3**
Sabbagh	–	10	10	–	10	–	–	–	–	**3**
Champion	–	–	–	–	–	s	10	10	10	**4**
Ellison	9	–	–	–	–	–	–	–	–	**1**
Tatu-Robertsson	s	9	9	9	9	10	9	–	9	**8**
Rauhihi	–	–	s	s	s	9	s	9	s	**7**
Watts-Pointer	8	8	8	8	8	8	8	8	–	**8**
Harvey	–	–	–	–	–	–	–	–	8	**1**
Koto	–	–	–	–	s	–	s	s	6	**4**
Quin	7	7	7	–	–	–	–	–	–	**3**
Lahmert	6	6	6	6	s	6	6	7	7	**9**
T. Winterburn	s	s	s	s	6	s	s	6	–	**8**
Riley	5	–	–	7	7	7	7	–	–	**5**
J. Winterburn	–	–	–	–	–	–	–	s	–	**1**
Shelford (capt)	4	4	4	4	4	4	4	4	4	**9**
Wiki	s	s	s	5	5	5	5	5	–	**8**
Eriksson	–	5	5	s	–	s	–	–	5	**5**
Lemana	–	–	–	–	–	–	–	–	s	**1**
Koneferenisi	3	–	–	–	–	–	–	–	–	**1**
McErlean	1	s	3	1	1	1	1	1	1	**9**
Salton	s	–	–	–	–	–	–	–	–	**1**
Itielu	s	3	s	s	s	s	s	s	s	**9**
Bean	–	1	–	s	–	–	s	s	s	**5**
Donaghy	–	s	1	–	s	s	s	s	s	**7**
Fuimaono	–	–	–	3	3	3	3	3	3	**6**
Mafi	2	2	2	2	2	2	2	2	2	**9**
Burnell	s	–	–	–	–	–	–	–	–	**1**
Fonoti	–	s	s	–	–	s	–	–	–	**3**
Tooman	–	–	s	s	s	–	–	–	–	**3**

HOROWHENUA KAPITI TEAM RECORD, 2023

Played 9 ***Won 2*** ***Lost 7*** ***Points for 183*** ***Points against 365***

Date	*Opponent*	*Location*	*Score*	*Tries*	*Con*	*PG*	*DG*	*Referee*
July 12	Wellington (RS) *	Levin	7–68	Masoe	Paki			Natarsha Ganley
August 12	South Canterbury	Waimate	14–48	Lahmert, Ralph	Tatu-Robertsson (2)			Dan Moore
August 19	West Coast	Levin	28–48	Mafi, Watts-Pointer, Paki	Tatu-Robertsson (2)	Tatu-Robertsson (3)		Stu Catley
August 26	Mid Canterbury	Ashburton	14–43	Wiki, Itielu	Tatu-Robertsson (2)			Fraser Hannon
September 2	Wairarapa Bush	Levin	24–19	Ralph (2)	Tatu-Robertsson	Tatu-Robertsson (4)		Tipene Cottrell
September 9	Buller	Levin	33–22	Ralph, Shelford, Paki, Watts-Pointer, Mafi	Tatu-Robertsson (4)			Will Johnston
September 16	King Country	Te Kuiti	27–31	Masoe (3), Ralph, T. Winterburn	Tatu-Robertsson			Maggie Cogger-Orr
September 23	Poverty Bay	Levin	17–31	Ralph, Paia'aua	Champion (2)	Champion		Nick Hogan
September 30	Whanganui (BSC)	Whanganui	19–55	Ralph, McErlean, Paia'aua	Tatu-Robertsson (2)			Will Johnston

* non-Heartland Championship match BSC Bruce Steel Cup

KING COUNTRY

2023 Status: Heartland Championship
Founded 1922. Affiliated 1922
President: P.L. (Paul) Mitchell
Chairman: R.J. (Ron) Thomassen
General Manager: K.P. (Kurt) McQuilkin
Coach: C.W. (Craig) Jeffries (to July)
A.M. (Aarin) Dunster (from July)
Assistant coaches: C.J. (Charles) Hubbard, G.F. (Gene) Waller
Main grounds: Owen Delany Park, Taupo; Rugby Park, Te Kuiti
Capacity: 15,000; 5000
Colours: Gold and maroon

RECORDS

Highest attendance	12,000	*King Country v South Africa, 1994 (Taupo)*
Most appearances	146	*P.L. Mitchell, 1988–2001*
Most points	925	*H.C. Coffin, 1983–95*
Most tries	46	*M.R. Kidd, 1974–84*
Most points in a season	230	*H.C. Coffin, 1992*
Most tries in a season	11	*D.M. Flavell, 1981*
		S.J. Bradley, 1992
Most conversions in a season	40	*H.C. Coffin, 1992*
Most penalty goals in a season	45	*H.C. Coffin, 1992*
Most dropped goals in a season	8	*I.N. Ingham, 1966*
Most points in a match	33	*H.C. Coffin v Poverty Bay, 1992*
Most tries in a match	4	*C.A. Crossman v Auckland XV, 1936*
		J. Haitana & H. Dixon v Thames Valley, 1938
		T. Katene v Golden Bay-Motueka, 1955
		J.A.W. McIlroy v Horowhenua, 1965
		D.W. Koni v Taranaki, 1969
		D.M. Flavell v East Coast, 1979
		N.A. Harrison v East Coast, 1981
		N.A. Harrison v Horowhenua, 1984
		J.W. Wells v East Coast, 1992
Most conversions in a match	10	*H.C. Coffin v Poverty Bay, 1992*
Most penalty goals in a match	7	*L.W.T. Peina v Whanganui, 2000*
Highest team score	99	*v East Coast, 1992*
Record victory (points ahead)	99	*99–0 v East Coast, 1992*
Highest score conceded	97	*v Auckland, 1993*
Record defeat (points behind)	94	*3–97 v Auckland, 1993*

King Country's season began with controversy when head coach Craig Jeffries was released from the third year of his three-year contract just weeks before the Heartland Championship began. This decision raised a few eyebrows considering the Rams' effort in making the Meads Cup playoffs the previous year. Assistant coach Aarin Dunster took over the top job and focused on using local players wherever possible. There were a number of players missing from last year:

Carl Carmichael, Dan Ross (both retired), Dennis Andrews-Peters (Waikato), Josh Balme and Cruise Dunster (both injured), all crucial members of the tight five who proved difficult to replace. Strong running second-five Carlos Bellass and Joe Perawiti had also departed.

After an encouraging pre-season, including wins over Taranaki Maori and Waikato Harlequins, the Heartland campaign got off to the worst possible start in Greymouth against the resurgent West Coast. From there, the Rams faced the daunting prospect of South Canterbury, Whanganui, and Thames Valley in consecutive weeks. The side started well against South Canterbury but were eventually outclassed. Taumarunui was the venue for the Rams' best performance of the season, a victory over neighbours Whanganui bringing the Pinetree Log back home for just the second time. This was backed-up with a quality effort against the Swamp Foxes in a game which could have gone either way.Player resources were stretched in the final half of the competition and two good wins at home were offset by a couple of disappointing losses on the road. This resulted in a 10th place finish, equal on points with Mid Canterbury and Poverty Bay but missing out on a Lochore Cup spot due to points differential.

The backs all had their moments, but untimely injuries and unavailability meant that combinations couldn't develop. There was enough potential shown to suggest that a full-strength backline would have been a very dangerous proposition.

Zayn Tipping was again to the forefront, regularly producing big plays at key moments. Backup halfback Kane Tamou had another solid year, and the union was lucky to have depth in such a crucial position.First-five Quinn Collard was not as prominent as in 2022 but was still a classy operator and Kieron Rollinson, who had last appeared in 2017, was a more than useful alternative.

After sporadic appearances over the years, the versatile Cam Robinson found a home at second-five, and it was unfortunate that last year's promising player Zac Wickham-Darlington's season was injury-affected. Oliver Foote was on loan again and showed plenty of ability. He was on the fringes of the Otago squad, and it will be interesting to see how far he goes.

Logan Patterson was a promising newcomer who appeared in the final three games and looks to have a good future. Josevata Malimoce was a dangerous attacker and his line breaks led to a number of tries.The forwards were noticeably lighter than most of the packs they came up against and struggled at scrum time, propping depth being particularly tested with some notable omissions from last year. However, the pack's heart and effort could never be faulted.

Kaleb Foote was ever present at No. 8 and he was again selected for the NZ Heartland team. He was ably supported in the loose by openside Karney Dunster while Leveson Gower, Tamaki Kopa and George Birkett were all hard workers on the blindside flank.Lock Eli Winders had been spotted playing against King Country for the Waikato Harlequins in the pre-season match. He was quickly added to the squad and developed well during the year becoming one of the better performing forwards.Reeve Satherley and Bradly Jeffries were again regulars in the second row. At the age of 36, Gary Mansfield made his second appearance for the union in the Ngati Porou East Coast fixture at Ruatoria. His first appearance, back in 2016, had also been at Ruatoria where he scored a try, worth six points under the trial points scoring system then in place.

The best of the props was Irishman Ben Popplewell, son of former Lions international Nick. He scrummaged well and was a good ball carrier while newcomer Carey Cornelius-Peina improved as the season went on.

Charlie Henare had the misfortune to injure his calf in the captain's run before the opening game against West Coast and did not appear during the season. He is stranded on 24 first-class games for King Country, one short of his blazer. It is hoped he will be back for next season.

Hooker and captain Liam Rowlands had another great season and his omission from the NZ Heartland team was a surprise to many local supporters.

Higher honours went to:

New Zealand Heartland: K. Foote

KING COUNTRY REPRESENTATIVES 2023

Name	Club	For Union		
		Debut	Games	Points
P.P. (Piahana) Astle-Harris	Piopio	2018	13	5
M.R. (Mosese) Baravilala	Taupo Marist	2020	9	0
Jaide Barlow	Waitomo	2023	2	0
N.G. (Nick) Barnes	Taupo Sports	2017	22	10
G.D. (George) Birkett	Taumarunui RS	2022	14	0
B.L. (Baven) Brown	Waitete	2017	18	25
M.R.W. (Michael) Bryant	Taumarunui RS	2021	9	0
Q.J.T.T.T. (Quinn) Collard	Hamilton Marist [1]	2022	15	119
C.L.F. (Carey) Cornelius-Peina	Tongariro Utd	2023	7	0
J.W. (Joshua) Couper	Taumarunui RS	2023	1	0
C.T.A. (Conor) Dobbyn	Tongariro Utd	2022	8	10
K.K.A.M. (Karney) Dunster	Tongariro Utd	2019	30	10
K.M.J. (Kaleb) Foote	Piopio	2018	18	20
O.A. (Oliver) Foote	Kaikorai [2]	2022	13	15
L.A. (Leveson) Gower	Taumarunui Districts	2020	16	5
B.J. (Bradly) Jeffries	Piopio	2019	29	20
R.G. (Ryan) Joyes	Waitete	2023	1	0
Tamaki Kopa	Waitete	2023	6	0
Josevata Malimole	Taupo Sports	2020	17	15
Chedyn Mani	Taupo Sports	2023	3	10
G.R. (Gary) Mansfield	Taupo Sports	2016	2	6
L.G. (Logan) Patterson	Taupo Marist	2023	3	5
B.N. (Ben) Popplewell	Taupo Marist	2023	7	5
D.T.W. (Diego) Rangi	Waitete	2021	15	0
C.J. (Cameron) Robinson	Taupo Sports	2016	14	5
S.J. (Sam) Robinson	Taupo Marist	2020	8	0
K.J. (Kieron) Rollinson	Taupo Sports	2016	24	58
L.A. (Liam) Rowlands	Taupo Sports	2018	34	55
R.H. (Reeve) Satherley	Taupo Marist	2020	24	5
K.E.M. (Kane) Tamou	Tongariro Utd	2022	14	0
Z.J. (Zayn) Tipping	Taupo Sports	2013	71	248
J.P. (Jared) Van Rooyen	Taumarunui RS	2022	3	0
S.V. (Sisa) Vosaki	Taupo Sports	2017	32	25
Z.T.L. (Zacharia) Wickham-Darlington	Bush Utd	2022	13	28
E.J.S. (Eli) Winders	Hamilton Marist [1]	2023	8	10

1. Loaned by Waikato RU *2. Loaned by Otago RU*

INDIVIDUAL SCORING

	Tries	Con	PG	DG	Points		Tries	Con	PG	DG	Points
Collard	1	13	5	–	46	Jeffries	1	–	–	–	5
Rowlands	6	–	–	–	30	Brown	1	–	–	–	5
Tipping	1	5	3	–	24	Astle-Harris	1	–	–	–	5
O. Foote	2	–	–	–	10	Patterson	1	–	–	–	5
Winders	2	–	–	–	10	K. Foote	1	–	–	–	5
Mani	2	–	–	–	10						
C. Robinson	1	–	–	–	5	***Totals***	***23***	***18***	***8***	***0***	***175***
Popplewell	1	–	–	–	5						
Rollinson	1	–	–	–	5	*Opposition scored*	*34*	*24*	*10*	*0*	*248*
Vosaki	1	–	–	–	5						

KING COUNTRY 2023	West Coast	South Canterbury	Whanganui	Thames Valley	Wairarapa Bush	Horowhenua Kapiti	Ngati Porou East Coast	Buller	**TOTALS**
C. Robinson	15	12	12	12	12	–	12	10	**7**
O. Foote	–	–	15	15	15	15	15	–	**5**
Brown	14	14	–	–	11	14	–	s	**5**
Wickham-Darlington	11	15	13	–	–	–	11	–	**4**
Vosaki	s	11	11	14	14	–	14	14	**7**
Mani	–	–	–	11	9	11	–	–	**3**
Malimole	13	13	14	13	–	–	–	11	**5**
Rangi	–	–	s	–	s	s	s	–	**4**
Patterson	–	–	–	–	–	13	13	13	**3**
Dobbyn	–	–	–	–	–	s	–	–	**1**
Baravilala	12	–	–	–	–	12	s	12	**4**
Collard	10	10	–	s	13	10	10	15	**7**
Rollinson	s	s	10	10	10	–	–	s	**6**
Tipping	9	9	9	9	–	s	9	9	**7**
Tamou	s	s	s	s	–	9	s	–	**6**
Couper	–	–	–	–	s	–	–	–	**1**
K. Foote	8	8	8	8	8	8	8	8	**8**
Dunster	7	7	7	7	7	7	7	7	**8**
Birkett	6	s	s	s	s	–	–	–	**5**
Kopa	s	6	6	6	–	–	s	s	**6**
Gower	–	s	s	s	6	6	6	6	**7**
Winders	5	4	5	5	5	5	5	s	**8**
Jeffries	4	s	s	s	s	4	–	4	**7**
Barlow	s	5	–	–	–	–	–	–	**2**
Satherley	–	–	4	4	4	s	4	5	**6**
Mansfield	–	–	–	–	–	–	s	–	**1**
Cornelius-Peina	3	3	3	3	–	3	3	3	**7**
Popplewell	1	1	1	1	1	1	1	–	**7**
Joyes	s	–	–	–	–	–	–	–	**1**
Astle-Harris	–	s	s	s	3	s	s	1	**7**
Barnes	–	–	–	s	–	–	s	s	**3**
Van Rooyen	–	–	–	–	s	s	–	–	**2**
Bryant	–	–	–	–	s	–	–	–	**1**
Rowlands (capt)	2	2	2	2	2	2	2	2	**8**
S. Robinson	s	s	s	s	s	–	s	–	**6**

KING COUNTRY TEAM RECORD 2023

Played 8 **Won 3** **Lost 5** **Points for 175** **Points against 248**

Date	Opponent	Location	Score	Tries	Con	PG	DG	Referee
August 12	West Coast	Greymouth	9 –40			Collard (3)		Ben Alexander
August 19	South Carterbury	Taupo	21 –45	C. Robinson, Popplewell, Rollinson	Collard (3)			Ben Woolerton
August 26	Whanganui	Taumarunui	23 –17	O. Foote, Vosaki	Tipping (2)	Tipping (3)		Natarsha Ganley
September 2	Thames Valley	Thames	21 –27	Rowlands, O. Foote, Winders	Tipping (3)			Andy Morton
September 9	Wairarapa Bush	Masterton	26 –35	Rowlands (2), Mani, Jeffries	Collard (3)			Stu Catley
September 16	Horowhenua Kapiti	Te Kuiti	31 –27	Rowlands (2), Brown, Winders, Mani	Collard (3)			Maggie Cogger-Orr
September 23	Ngati Porou East Coast (OT)	Ruatoria	11 –29	Tipping		Collard (2)		Tipene Cottrell
September 30	Buller	Taupo	33 –28	Collard, Astle-Harris, Patterson, Rowlands, K. Foote	Collard (4)			Ben Woolerton

MANAWATU

2023 Status: Bunnings NPC
Founded 1886. Original member 1892
President: G.J. (Gary) Nesdale
Chairman: T.J. (Tim) Myers
Chief executive officer: A.M. (Andrea) Jackson
Coach: M.J.K. (Mike) Rogers
Assistant coaches: K.P. (Kent) Harris, N.R. (Nehe) Milner-Skudder, H.S. (Hayden) Triggs
Manager: D.A. (Duncan) Cameron
Main ground: Central Energy Trust Arena
Capacity: 17,000
Colours: Green and white

RECORDS

Highest attendance	17,100	Manawatu v British & Irish Lions, 2005
Most appearances	145	*G.A. Knight, 1975–86*
Most points	641	*J.J. Holland, 1991–96*
Most tries	66	*K.W. Granger, 1971–84*
Most points in a season	182	*J.M. Smith, 1991*
Most tries in a season	14	*P.L. Alston, 1991*
Most conversions in a season	38	*D.L. Rollerson, 1981*
		J.M. Smith, 1991
Most penalty goals in a season	27	*M.C. Finlay, 1984*
		A. McMaster, 1987
Most dropped goals in a season	9	*J.P.J. Carroll, 1978*
Most points in a match	35	*J.M. Smith v Horowhenua, 1992*
Most tries in a match	5	*J.P. Butt v Whanganui, 1944*
		N.J. Mears v Horowhenua, 1958
		G.P.D. Henare v Horowhenua, 1987
Most conversions in a match	11	*J.M. Smith v Poverty Bay, 1991*
Most penalty goals in a match	6	*M.R. Love v Waikato, 1983*
		M.C. Finlay v Whanganui, 1984
		A. McMaster v Waikato, 1987
		J.J. Holland v Counties, 1994
		I. Thompson v Northland, 2009
		B.D. Cameron v Counties Manukau 2021
Highest team score	94	*v Poverty Bay, 1991*
Record victory (points ahead)	87	*94–7 v Poverty Bay, 1991*
Highest score conceded	109	*v British & Irish Lions, 2005*
Record defeat (points behind)	103	*6–109 v British & Irish Lions, 2005*

Manawatu made a promising start by conceding only one try against Wellington but could not cross the line themselves. Two more losses followed including a thumping from Canterbury but then the team surprised the small home crowd with a one-point win over Northland, Manawatu's first win in 18 games. Five days later Manawatu stunned the nation by defeating Auckland at Eden Park, a midweek game in which both unions rested several key players. However, the improvement in effort was short-lived as the team returned to its old habits of leaky defence and suffered heavy losses in the following four games while conceding 32 tries. The final game of the disappointing season was against Southland, a side winless in its nine games and had not won away from home since 2015. The game was Manawatu's last chance to restore some pride but the southerners gave them a 37–12 hiding. It was apparent that the players had lost confidence in their ability during the latter half of the season.

New coach Mike Rogers, who had much success in the North American Major League, arrived to find some contracted players were not up to his expectations and 18 of the 40 players used were newcomers to the Turbos shirt, several of whom had played in America. While there are several talented local club players, many have yet to develop into seasoned NPC performers which forced Rogers to recruit from overseas.

The loose forward trio of Brayden Iose, TK Howden and Slade McDowall was a very efficient unit but suffered from a tight-five that lacked muscle in scrums and mauls. Inaccurate lineout throwing also cost possession.

Fullback Beaudein Waaka was the side's best attacking back. John Poland, from Ireland, impressed at halfback with NZ Under 20 representative Jordi Viljoen showing promise. Brett Cameron was hampered by injury and teenager Isaiah Armstrong-Ravula often filled the first five-eighth role. Young props Joseph Gavigan and Flyn Yates are still developing and had to contend with frequent changes of hooker, Canadian Andrew Quattrin eventually commanding the position. Canadian international Cole Keith was a regular coming off the bench. Three members of the 2023 NZ Under 20 squad appeared in the front row, 18-year-old hooker Vernon Bason, and props Malakai Hala-Ngatai and Raymond Tuputupu are youngsters showing promise. The locking pair of South African Johan Momsen and Dutchman Stan van den Hoven, both brought over from America, added to the multi-nations look of the squad.

Higher honours went to:
New Zealand: A.L. Smith

INDIVIDUAL SCORING

	Tries	Con	PG	DG	Points		Tries	Con	PG	DG	Points
Iose	5	–	–	–	25	Momsem	1	–	–	–	5
Armstrong-Ravula	–	12	–	–	24	Nalaga	1	–	–	–	5
Cameron	–	6	3	–	21	Peita	1	–	–	–	5
Howden	3	–	–	–	15	Quattrin	1	–	–	–	5
Gavigan	2	–	–	–	10	Tofa	1	–	–	–	5
McDowall	2	–	–	–	10	Tuputupu	1	–	–	–	5
Poland	2	–	–	–	10	Viljoen	1	–	–	–	5
Schwenke	2	–	–	–	10	Wild	1	–	–	–	5
penalty try	1	–	–	–	7	Yates	1	–	–	–	5
Waaka	1	1	–	–	7						
Brown	1	–	–	–	5	***Totals***	***30****	***19***	***3***	***0***	***199***
Goerke	1	–	–	–	5						
Milner-Skudder	1	–	–	–	5	*Opposition scored*	*60**	*41*	*13*	*0*	*423*

** includes one penalty try (7 points)*

MANAWATU REPRESENTATIVES 2023

Name	Club	Date of birth	Height	Weight	For Union Debut	Games	Points
I.S. (Isaiah) Armstrong-Ravula	College OB	07-01-04	1.72	84	2023	9	24
V. (Vernon) Bason	College OB	10-10-04	1.80	100	2023	5	0
K. (Kyle) Brown	Feilding	03-08-02	1.81	84	2023	5	5
C.D.G. (Chris) Cairns	OB Marist	12-02-97	1.80	104	2023	1	0
B.D. (Brett) Cameron	Te Kawau	04-10-96	1.71	83	2021	23	183
L.A. (Luke) Campbell	Kia Toa	16-02-95	1.77	84	2022	14	5
K.F. (Kegan) Christian-Goss	OB Marist	14-04-00	1.92	100	2022	10	0
E.F. (Elyjah) Crosswell	College OB	28-08-02	1.85	90	2022	6	0
J.W.C. (Jason) Emery	Kia Toa	21-09-93	1.73	90	2012	82	79
L.T. (Tima) Fainga'anuku	Kia Toa	26-04-97	1.88	104	2021	24	30
T.P. (Taniela) Filimone	Kia Toa	01-06-99	1.86	99	2021	12	5
J.B. (Johnny) Galloway	University	12-11-94	1.91	108	2019	40	25
J.R.G. (Joseph) Gavigan	Freyberg OB	05-11-01	1.87	117	2021	22	10
J.S. (Julian) Goerke	University	07-11-01	1.92	105	2023	3	5
M.H. (Malakai) Hala-Ngatai	Kia Toa	07-01-03	1.85	110	2023	7	0
Te K.D-M. (Te Kamaka) Howden	Feilding	28-01-01	1.93	109	2020	34	15
B.D. (Brayden) Iose	Kia Toa	26-08-98	1.88	102	2017	42	45
C.V. (Cole) Keith	Feilding	07-05-97	1.83	119	2023	8	0
S.R. (Slade) McDowall	Te Kawau	08-03-98	1.83	101	2022	10	10
D.T.P. (Darius) Mafile'o	Freyberg OB	22-07-01	1.90	129	2021	4	0
N.R. (Nehe) Milner-Skudder	University	15-12-90	1.75	88	2011	64	50
J.A. (Johan) Momsen	Te Kawau	21-08-95	1.98	113	2023	9	5
E.W. (Waqa) Nalaga	College OB	07-07-03	1.80	86	2023	3	5
S.B. (Sean) Paranihi	College OB	14-11-96	1.80	115	2017	29	0
T.M. (Terrell) Peita	Ponsonby[1]	23-04-00	1.89	106	2023	8	5
J.L. (John) Poland	Freyberg OB	21-11-96	1.70	79	2023	7	10
A.J. (Andrew) Quattrin	New England Free Jacks[2]	29-08-96	1.83	111	2023	5	5
F.F. (Feleti) Sae-Ta'ufo'au	Freyberg OB	17-06-02	1.90	112	2023	3	0
L.A. (Leif) Schwenke	College OB	15-10-95	1.80	102	2022	10	15
O.U.M.H. (Ofa) Tauatevalu	Kia Toa	29-10-00	1.99	112	2021	22	0
J.E.A. (Josh) Taula	University	05-04-02	1.98	124	2022	3	5
J. (James) Tofa	College OB	22-09-97	1.77	102	2018	36	25
R. (Raymond) Tuputupu	Freyberg OB	11-04-03	1.82	101	2023	5	5
P. (Pena) Va'a	Kia Toa	18-03-99	1.84	92	2023	3	0
S. (Stan) van den Hoven	University	22-11-98	2.03	115	2023	7	0
J.K. (Jordi) Viljoen	College OB	14-10-03	1.72	85	2023	9	5
B.R.T (Beaudein) Waaka	OB Marist	27-01-94	1.80	94	2023	9	7
T.W. (Te Rangatira) Waitokia	University	11-04-96	1.80	92	2017	28	10
D.R. (Drew) Wild	Feilding	14-07-00	1.77	86	2019	38	47
F.Z.R. (Flyn) Yates	University	25-05-00	1.88	125	2021	28	5

1. Auckland RU 2. USA

MANAWATU 2023	Wellington	Taranaki	Canterbury	Northland	Auckland	Tasman	North Harbour	Hawke's Bay	Counties Manukau	Southland	TOTALS
Waaka	15	–	15	15	s	15	15	15	15	15	**9**
Milner-Skudder	14	s	–	–	15	–	11	s	s	–	**6**
Wild	s	15	14	14	–	14	14	11	14	14	**9**
Fainga'anuku	11	11	11	11	–	–	–	14	–	–	**5**
Filimone	s	14	–	–	11	–	–	–	13	13	**5**
Nalaga	–	–	–	–	14	11	13	–	–	–	**3**
Va'a	–	–	–	–	s	–	–	–	11	11	**3**
Waitokia	13	–	s	13	–	13	–	–	–	–	**4**
Brown	12	13	13	12	–	s	–	–	–	–	**5**
Christian-Goss	–	–	–	–	13	–	–	13	–	–	**2**
Emery	–	12	12	s	–	12	–	s	s	s	**7**
Tofa	–	–	–	–	12	–	12	12	12	12	**5**
Cameron	10	10	10	10	–	10	10	–	–	10	**7**
Armstrong-Ravula	–	s	s	s	10	s	s	10	10	s	**9**
Campbell	9	9	–	–	–	–	–	s	–	s	**4**
Viljoen	s	s	9	9	s	9	s	9	s	–	**9**
Poland	–	–	s	s	9	s	9	–	9	9	**7**
Iose (captain)	8	8	8	8	–	8	8	8	8	8	**9**
McDowall	7	7	7	7	–	7	7	7	7	7	**9**
Crosswell	s	–	–	–	–	–	–	–	–	–	**1**
Galloway	–	–	–	–	7	s	s	s	s	s	**6**
Howden	6	–	–	6	6	6	6	6	6	6	**8**
Peita	–	s	6	s	8	s	s	s	s	–	**8**
Goerke	–	s	s	–	s	–	–	–	–	–	**3**
Momsen	5	6	5	5	s	5	5	–	5	5	**9**
Taula	s	–	–	–	5	–	–	–	–	–	**2**
Tauatevalu	4	4	4	s	4	4	s	5	–	s	**9**
van den Hoven	–	5	s	4	–	–	4	4	4	4	**7**
Sae-Ta'ufo'au	3	–	–	–	–	–	–	s	s	–	**3**
Paranihi	s	3	–	–	3	–	–	–	–	s	**4**
Yates	s	s	3	3	–	3	3	3	3	3	**9**
Gavigan	1	1	1	s	1	s	1	s	–	–	**8**
Mafile'o	–	s	–	–	–	–	–	–	–	–	**1**
Hala-Ngatai	–	–	s	1	s	1	s	–	1	1	**7**
Keith	–	–	s	s	s	s	s	1	s	s	**8**
Tuputupu	2	–	s	s	s	s	–	–	–	–	**5**
Bason	s	2	–	–	–	–	–	s	s	s	**5**
Schwenke	–	s	2	2	–	2	–	–	–	–	**4**
Quattrin	–	–	–	–	2	–	2	2	2	2	**5**
Cairns	–	–	–	–	–	–	s	–	–	–	**1**

Galloway was captain v Auckland

MANAWATU TEAM RECORD 2023

Played 10 ***Won 2*** ***Lost 8*** ***Points for 199*** ***Points against 423***

Date	*Opponent*	*Location*	*Score*	*Tries*	*Con*	*PG*	*DG*	*Referee*
August 4	Wellington	Palmerston North	6–22			Cameron (2)		Nick Hogan
August 13	Taranaki	Palmerston North	17–26	Yates, Iose	Cameron, Armstrong-Ravula	Cameron		Jono Bredin
August 19	Canterbury	Christchurch	26–68	Viljoen, Momsem, Brown, Tuputupu	Cameron (2), Armstrong-Ravula			Fraser Hannon
August 25	Northland	Palmerston North	31–30	Schwenke (2), Howden, penalty try, Iose	Cameron (2)			Cameron Stone
August 30	Auckland	Auckland	33–31	Peita, Nalaga, Gavigan, Howden, Goerke	Armstrong-Ravula (4)			Nick Hogan
September 3	Tasman	Nelson	19–58	McDowall, Gavigan, Poland	Armstrong-Ravula (2)			Marcus Playle
September 10	North Harbour	Palmerston North	29–48	Milner-Skudder, McDowall, Quattrin, Wild, Howden	Cameron, Armstrong-Ravula			Tipene Cottrell
September 15	Hawke's Bay	Napier	7–57	Waaka	Armstrong-Ravula			Fraser Hannon
September 23	Counties Manukau	Pukekohe	19–46	Iose (2), Tofa	Armstrong-Ravula (2)			Jono Bredin
October 1	Southland	Palmerston North	12–37	Poland, Iose	Waaka			Stu Catley

MID CANTERBURY

2023 Status: Heartland Championship
Founded 1904 as Ashburton sub-union affiliated to South Canterbury RU. Name changed to Ashburton County 1905 and affiliated to Canterbury RU 1905. Became a full union with affiliation to NZRU 1927.
Name changed to Mid Canterbury 1952.
President: M.J. (Mike) Hanham
Chairman: G.P. (Gerard) Rushton
Chief executive officer: T.J. (Tanya) Dearns
Coach: J.F. (John) Sherratt
Assistant coach: P.J. (Peter) Manson, G.B. (Grant) Polson
Main ground: Ashburton Showgrounds
Capacity: 10,000
Colours: Forest green and gold

RECORDS

Highest attendance	8656	*Mid Canterbury v British Isles, 1983*
Most appearances	158	*J.C. Ross, 1970–87*
Most points	598	*A.H.A. Smith, 1955–68*
Most tries	47	*G.R. Bryant, 1968–77*
Most points in a season	200	*S.R. Middleton, 1994*
Most tries in a season	13	*M.L. Sau, 2017*
Most conversions in a season	34	*S.R. Middleton, 1994*
		J.R. Percival, 2017
Most penalty goals in a season	44	*S.R. Middleton, 1994*
Most dropped goals in a season	12	*M.B. Roulston, 1982*
Most points in a match	22	*M.C. Williams v East Coast, 2014*
Most tries in a match	5	*G.R. Bryant v Nelson Bays, 1977*
Most conversions in a match	8	*S.R. Middleton v West Coast, 1998*
Most penalty goals in a match	6	*S.R. Middleton v Horowhenua Kapiti, 1998*
		D.J. Maw v West Coast, 2007
		M.C. Williams v Whanganui, 2014
Highest team score	90	*v West Coast, 1998*
Record victory (points ahead)	77	*90–13 v West Coast, 1998*
Highest score conceded	99	*v Hawke's Bay, 2003*
Record defeat (points behind)	91	*8–99 v Hawke's Bay, 2003*

With a record of two wins and six losses Mid Canterbury missed out on a playoff spot by the barest of margins. They were one of three teams to finish on 16 points, all vying to fill eighth spot in the Heartland Championship for a Lochore Cup semi-final. It came down to points differential over the season with Mid Canterbury's -24 being inferior to Poverty Bay's -20. In the end, Mid Canterbury had to settle for ninth position.

There was a dominant win over Horowhenua Kapiti and a 79th minute drop goal by Tom Reekie secured victory against Poverty Bay, however the last four matches were all lost, including to Thames Valley who scored a last-minute try, and to West Coast who won in golden point extra time.

The Hammers had a very settled team with 19 players appearing in all eight matches or missing just one, a base that probably should have led to a better win-loss record than was achieved. Inconsistency prevailed throughout the season with one particular trait seeing the side invariably conceding points quickly after having scored themselves, but Mid Canterbury could play some very capable rugby when they got things right.

Sam Pearce and Raitube Vasurakuta scored some fine tries, an exciting pair of outside backs with pace, strength and the ability to finish off try-scoring opportunities. Centre Isireli Masiwini got through a power of work in the midfield with strong running and outstanding defence. This key player was injured against Horowhenua Kapiti and did not reappear again, which was a big blow to the team.

Loan player Josh Jennings showed a lot of promise at first-five and was in good goalkicking form, while Liam McCormack — in for the unavailable Tyler Blackburn — was a halfback who delivered good ball to the backline and sniped around the rucks well.

Tighthead prop and captain Adam Williamson was the leading forward. He reached 50 games in the opening match and earned NZ Heartland selection again. Other capable performers in the pack were flanker Kaydis Hona, who was outstanding against Thames Valley, and Osea Baisagale who started on the bench and improved throughout the season to cement the starting loosehead prop position.

Higher honours went to:
New Zealand Heartland: A.C.J. Williamson

MID CANTERBURY REPRESENTATIVES 2023

Name	Club	For Union Debut	For Union Games	For Union Points
O.B. (Osea) Baisagale	Methven	2018	20	0
L.P. (Logan) Bonnington	Southern	2012	56	26
H.T.B. (Harry) Burgess	Celtic	2022	7	0
Callum Burrell	Southern	2020	21	15
Ben Dixon	Celtic	2023	4	0
J.L. (Jackson) Donlan 1	Shirley [2]	2013	62	26
Rory Duff	Linwood [3]	2023	8	0
H.R. (Hugh) Griffiths	Methven	2018	13	0
V.S. (Vainikolo) Halafihi	Shirley [3]	2023	6	15
C.R. (Cameron) Haynes	Mt Somers	2023	7	0
M.F. (Michael) Hennings	Methven	2021	25	30
Kaydis Hona	Celtic	2022	17	30
J.L. (Joshua) Jennings	Linwood [3]	2023	8	73
A.J. (Angus) MacKenzie	Rakaia	2022	17	0
H.I. (Hamish) Mackenzie	Southern	2017	10	0
Isireli Masiwini	Celtic	2017	34	50
A.T. (Ashton) McArthur	Celtic	2020	19	0
M.S. (Matthew) McAtamney	Southern	2019	15	15
L.T.N. (Liam) McCormack	Celtic	2021	16	15
H.C. (Henry) McManus	Celtic	2022	12	0
L.L. (Lote) Nasiga	Rakaia	2020	18	10
S.D. (Samuel) Pearce	Celtic	2023	8	20
T.J. (Tom) Reekie	Methven	2021	26	126
M.E. (Max) Stapleton	Celtic	2022	3	0
B.J. (Bradley) Tarbotton	Southern	2021	4	0
T.T. (Taualai) Tofilau	Celtic	2023	6	0
J.M. (Jonetani) Vasurakuta	Celtic	2022	12	25
R.M. (Raitube) Vasurakuta	Celtic	2020	31	90
A.C.J. (Adam) Williamson	Southern	2015	55	35

1. Player of Origin *2. Canterbury RU* *3. Loaned by Canterbury RU*

INDIVIDUAL SCORING

	Tries	Con	PG	DG	Points		Tries	Con	PG	DG	Points
Jennings	1	19	10	-	73	Reekie	1	-	-	1	8
R. Vasurakuta	4	-	-	-	20	McAtamney	1	-	-	-	5
Pearce	4	-	-	-	20	Donlan	1	-	-	-	5
Hona	4	-	-	-	20	Williamson	1	-	-	-	5
Halafihi	3	-	-	-	15						
J. Vasurakuta	3	-	-	-	15	***Totals***	**30**	**19**	**10**	**1**	**221**
Hennings	3	-	-	-	15						
Masiwini	2	-	-	-	10	*Opposition scored*	*35*	*23*	*8*	*0*	*245*
McCormack	2	-	-	-	10						

MID CANTERBURY 2023	North Otago	Ngati Porou East Coast	Horowhenua Kapiti	Poverty Bay	Thames Valley	West Coast	South Canterbury	Wairarapa Bush	TOTALS
Pearce	15	14	14	13	13	13	13	15	**8**
McAtamney	–	15	15	15	15	15	15	s	**7**
Griffiths	14	s	–	s	s	14	14	14	**7**
R. Vasurakuta	11	11	11	11	11	11	11	11	**8**
J. Vasurakuta	–	–	s	14	14	s	s	13	**6**
Masiwini	13	13	13	–	–	–	–	–	**3**
Reekie	12	12	s	s	s	12	12	12	**8**
H. Mackenzie	s	s	12	12	12	–	–	–	**5**
Jennings	10	10	10	10	10	10	10	10	**8**
McCormack	9	9	9	s	9	9	9	9	**8**
A. MacKenzie	s	s	s	9	s	s	s	s	**8**
Hennings	8	8	8	8	8	8	8	8	**8**
Hona	7	7	7	7	7	7	7	7	**8**
R. Duff	6	6	6	6	6	6	6	s	**8**
McArthur	s	s	s	–	s	s	s	6	**7**
Dixon	–	–	–	s	–	s	s	s	**4**
McManus	5	–	–	–	–	–	–	5	**2**
Nasiga	4	4	4	4	4	4	4	4	**8**
Bonnington	s	s	s	s	s	s	s	s	**8**
Halafihi	–	5	5	5	5	5	5	–	**6**
Williamson (capt.)	3	3	3	3	3	3	3	3	**8**
Haynes	1	s	s	–	s	s	s	1	**7**
Baisagale	s	s	1	1	1	1	1	–	**7**
Burgess	s	–	–	s	–	–	–	s	**3**
Tarbotton	–	1	–	–	–	–	–	–	**1**
Tofilau	–	–	s	s	s	s	s	s	**6**
Burrell	2	2	2	s	2	s	s	s	**8**
Donlan	s	–	s	2	s	2	2	2	**7**
Stapleton	–	s	–	–	–	–	–	–	**1**

MID CANTERBURY TEAM RECORD 2023

Played 8 Won 2 Lost 6 Points for 221 Points against 245

Date	Opponent	Location	Score	Tries	Con	PG	DG	Referee
August 12	North Otago	Ashburton	24–43	Masiwini (2), R. Vasurakuta	Jennings (3)	Jennings		George Haswell
August 19	Ngati Porou East Coast (OT)	Ruatoria	8–19	Halafihi		Jennings		Tipene Cottrell
August 26	Horowhenua Kapiti	Ashburton	43–14	Halafihi (2), McAtamney, R. Vasurakuta, Pearce, Hona, J. Vasurakuta	Jennings (4)			Fraser Hannon
September 2	Poverty Bay	Gisborne	23–20	Hennings (2)	Jennings (2)	Jennings (2)	Reekie	Stu Catley
September 9	Thames Valley	Ashburton	31–34	McCormack (2), Hona, Pearce, R. Vasurakuta	Jennings (3)			Ben Alexander
September 16	West Coast	Greymouth	29–32 aet	Hona (2), Pearce, R. Vasurakuta	Jennings (3)	Jennings		Josh Bamber
September 23	South Canterbury (HS)	Christchurch	35–50	Donlan, Pearce, Williamson, Jennings	Jennings (3)	Jennings (3)		George Haswell
September 30	Wairarapa Bush	Ashburton	28–33	J. Vasurakuta (2), Reekie, Hennings	Jennings	Jennings (2)		Jackson Henshaw

(HS) Hanan Shield

NORTH HARBOUR

2023 Status: Bunnings NPC
Founded 1985. Affiliated 1985
President: A.J. (Alan) Linstrom
Chairman: G.P. (Gerard) van Tilborg
Chief executive: A.M. (Adrian) Donald
Coach: D.K. (Daniel) Halangahu
Assistant coaches: K.J. (Kenny) Addison, B.T.P. (Ben) Afeaki
Main ground: North Harbour Stadium, Albany
Capacity: 25,000
Colours: White, black and cardinal

RECORDS

Most appearances	145	*Ron Williams, 1985–94*
		Walter Little, 1987–2000
Most points	1052	*Warren Burton, 1990–96*
Most tries	63	*Richard Kapa, 1985–93*
Most points in a season	258	*Warren Burton, 1995*
Most tries in a season	16	*Glenn Davis, 1999*
Most conversions in a season	53	*Warren Burton, 1991*
Most penalty goals in a season	47	*Warren Burton, 1995*
Most dropped goals in a season	3	*Jamie Cameron, 1991*
Most points in a match	34	*Frano Botica v Queensland Country, 1985*
Most tries in a match	5	*Glenn Davis v Poverty Bay-East Coast, 1999*
		Tevita Li v Taranaki, 2017
Most conversions in a match	10	*Frano Botica v Taranaki, 1989*
		Jamie Cameron v Marlborough, 1990
		Warren Burton v Whanganui, 1991
Most penalty goals in a match	7	*Bryn Gatland v Tasman, 2022*
Highest team score	99	*v Horowhenua Kapiti, 2008*
Record victory (points ahead)	93	*99–6 v Horowhenua Kapiti, 2008*
Highest score conceded	71	*v Auckland, 1995*
Record defeat (points behind)	55	*10–65 v Canterbury 2002*

North Harbour will be annoyed at missing out on playoffs rugby in October.

The season started with four straight losses, then came four straight wins, but the campaign fizzled with two straight defeats that saw them place 10th.

Daniel Halangahu's charges, however, were outclassed just twice – to Auckland in a damp Battle of the Bridge and to Taranaki in the final round. They were narrowly pipped in three of those first four games, including in extra time against the Tasman Mako. The 'Storm' week went well, three good wins against Waikato, Otago and Manawatu.

Due to North Harbour Stadium being out of commission due to the FIFA Women's World Cup, there was an old school return for two games to Onewa Domain for that ground's first first-class matches since 2002. In the first of those, North Harbour looked to have regained the Kevin Gimblett Memorial Trophy until a late try by Canterbury. They ran in seven tries in an entertaining Ian Jones Challenge Trophy victory over Northland and, while competitive in the Ranfurly Shield challenge, could not win the big moments to upset Wellington.

In general, North Harbour did not quite have the attacking cutting edge from 2022 (36 tries scored versus 53 in 2022) and much of that can be attributed to the absence of potent wings Tevita Li and Mark Telea.

Assistant coach Steve Jackson left earlier in the year to join the Black Ferns, while other exits included Danny Drake (Southland), Alex Fidow (Australia), Fine Inisi (Tonga, RWC), Felix Kalapu (Australia), Tevita Li (Japan), Isoa Nasilasila (Fiji, RWC), Denny Solomona (England) and Luteru Tolai (Samoa, RWC). Hooker Ray Niuia missed the cut for Manu Samoa but injury cut short his season after three games.

Incoming were Bryn Gordon (Manawatu), Ben Grant (USA), Shilo Klein (Canterbury), and the brothers Mafileo, Sione (back from injury), and Tevita (Bay of Plenty).

The union's newest All Black Shaun Stevenson played seven games, scored three tries and made 20 offloads, thus continuing his prime form for the province.

The big mover was right wing Kade Banks, the sole player to start all 10 games. He beat 51 defenders (second in the NPC), scored four tries, and won a Blues contract. No one nailed down the other wing berth, where veteran Alapati Leiua saw game time, as did Auckland loaner Sofai Maka and All Blacks Sevens rep Moses Leo.

Tom Barham, a solid defensive player, sewed up the centre position, in midfield partnership with Henry Taefu.

Captain designate Bryn Gatland was still rehabbing in the first half of the NPC, but he goalkicked with his usual accuracy upon his return, though still prone to kicking errors during play. Rookie Oscar Koller proved an able substitute, winning six starts and kicking well out of hand.

Jamie Booth was the main man at halfback, dictating the tempo, and his early understudy Aisea Halo won a Moana Pasifika contract.

In the pack, Lotu Inisi proved to be the supersub, invariably adding impact and scoring four tries. Captain Cam Suafoa filled the No 8 role to strong effect and won 10 turnovers.

There was no second-year syndrome for opensider Jed Melvin, the 2023 Almanack Promising Player of the Year. Only five made more than his 137 tackles. Karl Ruzich was a turnover merchant off the bench.

The top locks were tall timber Australian Ben Grant, who played his way into a Hurricanes contract and was not averse to stealing lineout ball, and former Mako Mahonri Ngakuru.

Shilo Klein took the No 2 jersey, having signed to get more game time. He was effective, as were the 1-2 Mafileo tighthead punch from Tevita, who was very solid, and Sione. Loosehead Nic Mayhew raised the 50-game milestone, though both he and Tevita Mafileo did cop more than their share of penalties (seven each).

Higher honours went to:

New Zealand:	S. Stevenson, M. Telea
All Blacks XV:	C. Suafoa
New Zealand Sevens:	M. Leo

NORTH HARBOUR REPRESENTATIVES 2023

Name	Club	Date of birth	Height	Weight	For Union Debut	Games	Points
K.J. (Kade) Banks	Mahurangi	09-06-00	1.83	90	2020	24	30
T.S. (Tom) Barham	Silverdale	03-06-99	1.88	98	2022	15	5
J.P. (Jamie) Booth	East Coast Bays	14-09-94	1.71	82	2022	21	30
C.P. (Cameron) Christie	Silverdale	06-06-04	1.96	107	2023	3	0
S.L. (Sam) Davies	North Shore	07-06-02	1.88	119	2022	5	0
J.A.J. (James) Fiebig	North Shore	13-12-97	1.95	114	2023	2	0
B.E.C. (Bryn) Gatland	Takapuna	10-05-95	1.79	88	2016	59	647
B. (Bryn) Gordon	Northcote	06-08-01	1.79	108	2023	7	0
B.W. (Ben) Grant	Overseas	18-05-98	2.04	115	2023	7	5
A.L. (Aisea) Halo	Takapuna	29-06-93	1.8	84	2021	6	0
L. (Lotu) Inisi	Takapuna	26-04-99	1.86	110	2019	30	30
S.I. (Shilo) Klein	East Coast Bays	05-05-99	1.81	107	2023	10	0
O.V.H. (Oscar) Koller	North Shore	04-11-00	1.83	97	2023	8	55
T.K.T. (Tevita) Langi	Massey	06-06-00	1.87	126	2022	19	5
A. (Alapati) Leiua	Overseas	21-09-88	1.81	99	2023	7	10
T.V. (Tika) Lelenga	Takapuna	14-03-98	1.84	92	2022	3	5
M.J. (Moses) Leo	Takapuna	11-08-97	1.85	94	2021	10	15
S.T. (Sione) Mafileo	North Shore	14-04-93	1.78	128	2014	75	15
T.T.P. (Tevita) Mafileo	North Shore	02-04-98	1.88	127	2023	9	15
S.J. (Sofai) Maka	Manukau[1]	02-05-91	1.81	94	2023	5	10
N.J. (Nic) Mayhew	Northcote	28-11-88	1.8	117	2010	58	10
T. (Tamarau) McGahan	Takapuna	08-12-99	1.88	102	2020	23	10
J.A.M. (Jed) Melvin	East Coast Bays	13-12-00	1.83	107	2022	19	5
D. (Danyon) Morgan-Puterangi	Takapuna	19-07-96	1.83	93	2023	5	20
M.A. (Mahonri) Ngakuru	Auckland University[2]	02-01-00	1.97	107	2023	9	0
S.T.K.H. (Siaosi) Nginingini	Kumeu	17-10-98	1.85	89	2022	16	5
R.F. (Ray) Niuia	Massey	19-06-91	1.75	118	2013	39	15
F.H.I. (Fatongia) Paea	Massey	09-04-99	1.83	125	2021	11	5
R.W.R. (Rex) Pollock	North Shore	01-12-92	1.92	106	2023	1	0
K.J. (Karl) Ruzich	Northcote	24-06-01	1.9	101	2022	11	0
W.B. (Wallace) Sititi	Massey	07-09-02	1.88	99	2022	10	5
S.T. (Shaun) Stevenson	Northcote	14-11-96	1.91	100	2017	60	129
C.J.T.S. (Cameron) Suafoa	Massey	23-04-98	1.94	115	2021	23	15
L.H. (Henry) Taefu	Northcote	02-04-93	1.84	103	2021	19	15
J.T.E. (John) Tapueluelu	Marist	07-04-96	1.83	89	2023	2	0

1. Loaned by Auckland RU *2. Auckland RU*

INDIVIDUAL SCORING

	Tries	Con	PG	DG	Points		Tries	Con	PG	DG	Points
Koller	1	7	12	–	55	Grant	1	–	–	–	5
Gatland	1	15	4	–	47	McGahan	1	–	–	–	5
Banks	4	–	–	–	20	Melvin	1	–	–	–	5
Inisi	4	–	–	–	20	Niuia	1	–	–	–	5
Morgan-Puterangi	4	–	–	–	20	Paea	1	–	–	–	5
T. Mafileo	3	–	–	–	15	Sititi	1	–	–	–	5
Stevenson	3	–	–	–	15	Taefu	1	–	–	–	5
Booth	2	–	–	–	10						
Leo	2	–	–	–	10	***Totals***	***36***	***22***	***16***	***0***	***272***
Leiua	2	–	–	–	10						
Maka	2	–	–	–	10	*Opposition scored*	*44*	*27*	*7*	*0*	*295*
Barham	1	–	–	–	5						

NORTH HARBOUR 2023	Hawke's Bay	Canterbury	Auckland	Tasman	Waikato	Otago	Manawatu	Northland	Wellington (RS)	Taranaki	**Totals**
Stevenson	–	–	15	15	15	15	–	15	15	15	**7**
Banks	15	15	14	14	14	14	15	14	14	14	**10**
Tapueluelu	s	s	–	–	–	–	–	–	–	–	**2**
Leiua	14	14	s	s	s	12	–	–	s	–	**7**
Maka	–	–	–	–	s	11	s	s	–	s	**5**
Lelenga	11	11	–	–	–	–	–	–	–	–	**2**
Leo	–	–	–	–	–	13	14	11	11	11	**5**
Barham	13	13	13	13	13	s	13	13	13	13	**10**
Morgan-Puterangi	–	s	11	11	11	–	11	–	–	–	**5**
Taefu	12	12	12	12	12	–	12	12	12	12	**9**
Gatland	–	–	–	–	–	s	10	10	10	10	**5**
Koller	10	10	10	10	10	10	s	s	–	–	**8**
Booth	9	9	9	9	9	s	9	9	9	9	**10**
Halo	s	s	s	s	–	–	–	–	–	–	**4**
Nginingini	–	–	–	–	s	9	s	s	s	s	**6**
L. Inisi	s	s	8	8	s	8	s	s	s	–	**9**
Sititi	s	s	s	6	–	6	s	–	–	s	**7**
McGahan	6	6	6	s	6	s	6	6	6	6	**10**
Ruzich	s	–	s	s	–	7	–	s	s	s	**7**
Melvin	7	7	7	7	7	–	7	7	7	7	**9**
Grant	4	4	–	4	4	–	4	4	4	–	**7**
Pollock	–	–	–	–	–	–	–	–	–	s	**1**
Christie	–	–	s	–	s	4	–	–	–	–	**3**
Ngakuru	–	5	5	s	5	5	5	5	5	5	**9**
Suafoa (capt)	8	8	4	5	8	s	8	8	8	8	**10**
Fiebig	5	–	–	–	–	–	–	–	–	4	**2**
T. Mafileo	3	3	3	3	3	–	3	3	3	1	**9**
S. Mafileo	s	s	s	s	s	s	s	s	s	3	**10**
Davies	–	–	–	–	–	–	–	–	–	s	**1**
Mayhew	s	1	1	s	1	3	1	1	1	–	**9**
Paea	–	–	–	–	–	s	s	–	–	–	**2**
Langi	1	s	s	1	s	1	–	s	s	s	**9**
Klein	2	2	2	2	2	s	2	2	2	2	**10**
Gordon	s	s	s	–	–	–	s	s	s	s	**7**
Niuia	–	–	–	s	s	2	–	–	–	–	**3**

NORTH HARBOUR TEAM RECORD 2023

Played 10 **Won 4** **Lost 6** **Points for 272** **Points against 295**

Date	Opponent	Location	Score	Tries	Con	PG	DG	Referee
August 5	Hawke's Bay	Napier	21–23	Leiua (2)	Koller	Koller (3)		Stu Curran
August 13	Canterbury	Takapuna	24–28	Booth, L. Inisi	Koller	Koller (4)		Nick Briant
August 19	Auckland	Takapuna	21–43	Morgan-Puterangi (2), Sititi		Koller (2)		Cam Stone
August 27	Tasman	Nelson	15–20 (ET)	T. Mafileo, Koller, Taefu				Dan Waenga
September 2	Waikato	Albany	39–17	Grant, T. Mafileo, Stevenson, Niuia, Morgan-Puterangi, L. Inisi	Koller (3)	Koller		Nick Hogan
September 6	Otago	Albany	27–24	Maka (2), Leo	Gatland (2), Koller	Koller (2)		Mike Winter
September 10	Manawatu	Palmerston North	48–29	Melvin, Leo, McGahan, Morgan-Puterangi, Gatland, Paea, Booth	Gatland (4), Koller	Gatland		Tipene Cottrell
September 16	Northland	Albany	50–31	Stevenson (2), Banks (2), L. Inisi (2), T. Mafileo	Gatland (6)	Gatland		Cam Stone
September 24	Wellington (RS)	Porirua	6–26			Gatland (2)		Dan Waenga
September 30	Taranaki	New Plymouth	21–54	Banks (2), Barham	Gatland (3)			Mike Winter

NORTH OTAGO

2023 Status: Heartland Championship
Founded 1904 as sub union affiliated to Otago RU.
Became a full union in 1927 with affiliation to NZRU.
President: D.I. (Duncan) Kingan
Chairman: W.L. (Warren) Prescott
Chief executive officer: C.S. (Colin) Jackson
Coach: J.A. (Jason) Forrest
Assistant coach: R.K. (Ralph) Darling, L.M. (Luke) Herden
Main ground: Whitestone Contracting Stadium, Oamaru
Capacity: 7000
Colours: Gold

RECORDS

Highest attendance	6500	*North Otago v Marlborough (Div 3 final), 1997*
Most appearances	123	*M.J. Mavor, 1995–2009*
Most points	431	*P.M. Ford, 1964–74*
Most tries	39	*V.T. Fifita, 2000–04*
Most points in a season	159	*S.M. Porter, 2002*
Most tries in a season	15	*V.T. Fifita, 2002*
Most conversions in a season	42	*M. Adair, 2005*
Most penalty goals in a season	30	*C.J.W. Finch, 1997*
		S.M. Porter, 2000
Most dropped goals in a season	4	*M.E. Kenworthy, 1986*
Most points in a match	29	*B.J. McCarthy v Horowhenua Kapiti, 2022*
Most tries in a match	5	*L.M. Herden v East Coast, 2010*
Most conversions in a match	12	*B.J. McCarthy v Horowhenua Kapiti, 2022*
Most penalty goals in a match	7	*C.J.W. Finch v South Canterbury, 1998*
Highest team score	116	*v East Coast, 2010*
Record victory (points ahead)	113	*116–3 v East Coast, 2010*
Highest score conceded	139	*v Auckland, 1993*
Record defeat (points behind)	134	*5–139 v Auckland, 1993*

The 2023 season started very promisingly for North Otago, but the season came to an end in the Lochore Cup semi-final. The side finished with a record of four wins and five losses, having ended the round robin in fifth place. It was all an exact repeat of the previous season.

There was a comprehensive win over Wairarapa Bush who finished the round robin just one place behind North Otago and on the same number of points. They led the eventual champions South Canterbury until conceding a try with just five minutes left, and registered a come from behind win against Thames Valley with a last-minute converted try.

But the season ended disappointingly with their two final performances. Needing a win in the last game of the round robin to give themselves a possibility of a fourth-place finish and a spot in the Meads Cup, North Otago led West Coast 12–10 at halftime but remained scoreless in the second half and lost the match 12–27. In the Lochore Cup semi-final, North Otago led 28–7 during the second half and eventually succumbed 35–40 to Poverty Bay.

Coach Jason Forrest had the use of some very experienced players, with 18 returning from last year's squad.

The inconsistent performances that resulted would have been a frustration for the side which was certainly capable of finishing higher than they did. Frontline local players absent from the previous season included halfback Jake Matthews (overseas), centre Hayden Todd (Otago), lock Manulua Taiti (retired) and Matthew Vocea (rugby league). Two arrivals into the province with previous first-class experience were Vilimoni Koroi (Otago/Highlanders/NZ Sevens) and Osea Qamasea (North Harbour).

North Otago had a good forward pack who were instrumental in securing a steady supply of possession. Rory Bartle, a former Welsh Under 20 rep, was handed the captaincy. He led by example and was outstanding. Seasoned lock Josh Clark showed he had lost none of his enthusiasm and his work in both set and broken play was of a high standard. Together they formed a first-rate locking partnership.

Number eight Uluifalefesi "Junior" Fakatoufifita was still a hard man to stop, always making ground with his crashing runs and topped the try scoring list with nine. Matt Duff remains a fine loose forward. Loan player Lucas Casey, who only came into the squad due to injuries to others, showed a lot of promise in his debut season at first-class level. Kelepi Funaki and Melikisua Kolinisau were two very strong props and Hayden Tisdall was an accomplished hooker and good all-round forward who scored a hat trick against Poverty Bay in the round robin.

Mataitini Feke was again a halfback of quality. His passing, running and covering were of the highest order. Vilimoni Koroi's presence at first-five, on loan from Otago, did not prove to be the boon it could have been. After playing both opening matches there was just one further appearance.

Saimone Samate and Osea Qamasea were two strong-running fast wings that were difficult to stop, although Samate, in particular, was under-used on occasions. Frenchman Lucas Ollion had an excellent season at fullback. He proved a dynamic attacking player, scoring six tries and also proved a good goalkicker.

Higher honours went to:
New Zealand Heartland: J. Clark, U. Fakatoufifita, S. Samate

INDIVIDUAL SCORING

	Tries	*Con*	*PG*	*DG*	*Points*		*Tries*	*Con*	*PG*	*DG*	*Points*
Ollion	6	17	6	-	82	Varu	1	-	-	-	5
Fakatoufifita	9	-	-	-	45	Bowring	1	-	-	-	5
Tisdall	5	-	-	-	25	Babiau	1	-	-	-	5
Qamasea	5	-	-	-	25	Kolinisau	1	-	-	-	5
Samate	4	-	-	-	20	Greenslade	1	-	-	-	5
Emery	1	3	-	-	11	Koroi	-	2	-	-	4
Morris-Lome	2	-	-	-	10	Phipps	-	1	-	-	2
Funaki	2	-	-	-	10						
Feke	2	-	-	-	10	***Totals***	***44***	***28***	***6***	***0***	***294***
Casey	2	-	-	-	10						
Davies	-	5	-	-	10	*Opposition scored*	*39*	*26*	*7*	*0*	*268*
Ravuvu	1	-	-	-	5						

NORTH OTAGO REPRESENTATIVES 2023

Name	Club	For Union Debut	Games	Points
Samuela Babiau	Excelsior	2020	12	5
R.O. (Rory) Bartle	Valley	2023	9	0
Temesia Bolavucu	Athletic Marist	2023	1	0
Jesse Bowring	Maheno	2023	8	5
L.D. (Lucas) Casey	Kaikorai [2]	2023	4	10
Will Clapham	Oamaru OB	2023	2	0
J.A. (Josh) Clark	Maheno	2013	51	5
Taylor Dale	Harbour [2]	2023	7	0
T.J. (Tyron) Davies	Excelsior	2012	23	22
M.R.V. (Matthew) Duff	Excelsior	2013	78	16
Levi Emery [1]	ENC Barbarians [3]	2021	23	51
Uluifalefesi "Junior" Fakatoufifita	Oamaru OB	2017	38	105
Mataitini Feke	Oamaru OB	2020	21	55
K.K. (Kelepi) Funaki	Oamaru OB	2018	50	40
J.S. (Jake) Greenslade	Valley	2015	41	20
Melikisua Kolinisau	Valley	2015	59	20
V.T. (Vilimoni) Koroi	Alhambra Union [2]	2023	3	4
R.E.V. (Ratu) Logavatu	Athletic Marist	2020	14	20
A.M. (Aleki) Morris-Lome	Overseas	2015	15	30
I.L. (Inoke) Naufahu	Oamaru OB	2015	31	47
L.R.F. (Lucas) Ollion	Kurow	2023	7	82
B.R. (Ben) Paton	Valley	2020	12	15
J.W.H. (Josh) Phipps	Excelsior	2020	15	50
Osea Qamasea	Athletic Marist	2023	5	25
Matia Qiolevu	Excelsior	2023	9	0
C.B. (Colati) "Tua" Ravula	Excelsior	2023	1	0
Asesela "Junior" Ravuvu	Valley	2021	12	10
S.F. (Saimone) Samate	Oamaru OB	2022	17	65
S.W. (Sam) Sturgess	Valley	2015	55	45
H.M. (Hayden) Tisdall	Maheno	2014	30	40
L.J. (Lisivani) Tuifua	Athletic Marist	2021	10	0
Petero Tuisiga	Excelsior	2023	2	0
S.I. (Sione) Tukala	Oamaru OB	2023	1	0
K.A. (Kasimila) Vaihu	Kurow	2023	6	0
L.M. (Leonard) Varu	Oamaru OB	2022	6	5
Josefa Veiogo	Valley	2023	5	0
Hikawera Waerea-Taikato	Excelsior	2023	2	0

1. Player of Origin 2. Loaned by Otago RU 2. Southland RU

NORTH OTAGO 2023	Mid Canterbury	Wairarapa Bush	Ngati Porou East Coast	South Canterbury	Whanganui	Poverty Bay	Thames Valley	West Coast	Poverty Bay (sf)	TOTALS
Ollion	15	15	15	15	–	–	15	15	15	**7**
Qiolevu	s	s	s	13	15	15	13	14	14	**9**
Emery	–	–	–	s	s	–	s	13	13	**5**
Ravula	14	–	–	–	–	–	–	–	–	**1**
Samate	11	–	11	11	11	11	11	11	11	**8**
Ravuvu	s	11	–	s	14	s	14	–	s	**7**
Qamasea	–	14	14	14	s	14	–	–	–	**5**
Paton	–	–	s	–	–	–	s	s	–	**3**
Clapham	–	–	–	–	–	s	–	s	–	**2**
Bowring	13	13	13	–	13	13	12	12	12	**8**
Morris-Lome	12	12	12	12	12	12	–	–	–	**6**
Koroi	10	10	–	–	10	–	–	–	–	**3**
Davies	s	s	s	10	9	10	10	10	10	**9**
Naufahu	–	s	10	–	–	s	–	–	–	**3**
Phipps	–	–	–	–	–	–	s	s	–	**2**
Feke	9	9	9	9	s	9	9	9	9	**9**
Fakatoufifita	8	8	8	–	8	8	8	8	8	**8**
Babiau	s	s	s	8	s	s	s	s	s	**9**
Duff	7	7	7	7	7	7	7	7	7	**9**
Vaihu	6	–	–	s	s	s	–	s	s	**6**
Logavatu	s	s	s	–	–	–	–	–	–	**3**
Dale	–	6	6	6	–	4	s	4	s	**7**
Casey	–	–	–	–	6	6	6	6	–	**4**
Tuisiga	–	–	–	–	–	–	–	s	6	**2**
Bartle (capt.)	5	5	5	5	5	5	5	5	5	**9**
Clark	4	4	4	4	4	–	4	–	4	**7**
Kolinisau	3	3	–	3	s	3	3	3	3	**8**
Funaki	1	1	3	1	1	1	1	1	1	**9**
Veiogo	s	s	1	s	s	–	–	–	–	**5**
Bolavucu	s	–	–	–	–	–	–	–	–	**1**
Waerea-Taikato	–	–	s	–	–	s	–	–	–	**2**
Tukala	–	–	s	–	–	–	–	–	–	**1**
Tuifua	–	–	–	–	–	s	s	s	s	**4**
Tisdall	2	2	–	–	2	2	2	2	2	**7**
Greenslade	s	s	2	s	3	–	s	s	s	**8**
Varu	–	s	s	2	–	s	–	–	–	**4**
Sturgess	–	–	–	s	s	–	–	–	–	**2**

NORTH OTAGO TEAM RECORD 2023

Played 9 Won 4 Lost 5 Points for 294 Points against 268

Date	Opponent	Location	Score	Tries	Con	PG	DG	Referee
August 12	Mid Canterbury	Ashburton	43–24	Fakatoufifita (2), Ollion (2), Samate (2), Tisdall	Ollion (2), Koroi (2)			George Haswell
August 19	Wairarapa Bush	Oamaru	50–3	Qamasea (2), Ollion (2), Fakatoufifita (2), Ravuvu, Varu	Ollion (5)			Dan Moore
August 26	Ngati Porou East Coast	Ruatoria	29–38	Fakatoufifita, Morris-Lome, Samate, Qamasea	Ollion (3)	Ollion		Andy Morton
September 2	South Canterbury (HS)	Oamaru	22–26	Qamasea, Samate, Funaki	Ollion, Emery	Ollion		Fraser Hannon
September 9	Whanganui	Oamaru	19–34	Morris-Lome, Feke, Qamasea	Emery (2)			Jackson Henshaw
September 16	Poverty Bay	Gisborne	50–43	Tisdall (3), Casey (2), Funaki, Fakatoufifita, Bowring	Davies (5)			Andy Morton
September 23	Thames Valley	Maheno	34–33	Fakatoufifita (2), Tisdall, Feke, Babiau	Ollion (2), Phipps	Ollion		Josh Bamber
September 30	West Coast	Greymouth	12–27	Ollion, Emery	Ollion			George Haswell
October 7	Poverty Bay (LC sf)	Oamaru	35–40	Fakatoufifita, Kolinisau, Ollion, Greenslade	Ollion (3)	Ollion (3)		Fraser Hannon

(HS) Hanan Shield

NORTHLAND

2023 Status: Bunnings NPC
Founded 1920 as North Auckland. Affiliated 1920.
Name changed to Northland 1994
President: B.R. (Bryce) Woodward
Chairman: A.J. (Andrew) Golightly
Chief executive officer: C.J. (Cameron) Bell
Coach: J.A. (John) Leslie
Assistant coaches: M. (Matt) Rolston,
R.G. (Ross) Wright, E.J. (Eric) Rush
Main ground: Semenoff Stadium, Whangarei
Capacity: 24,000
Colours: Cambridge blue

RECORDS

Most appearances	165	*Joe Morgan, 1967–81*
Most points	1656	*Warren Johnston, 1986–97*
Most tries	71	*Norman Berryman, 1991–2003*
Most points in a season	283	*David Holwell, 1997*
Most tries in a season	21	*Norman Berryman, 1994*
Most conversions in a season	85	*David Holwell, 1997*
Most penalty goals in a season	34	*Warren Johnston, 1989*
Most dropped goals in a season	10	*Eddie Dunn, 1979*
Most points in a match	38	*David Holwell v Thames Valley, 1997*
Most tries in a match	7	*Norman Berryman v Wairarapa Bush, 1994*
Most conversions in a match	14	*David Holwell v Thames Valley, 1997*
Most penalty goals in a match	6	*Chippie Semenoff v Thames Valley, 1978*
		Warren Johnston v Wairarapa Bush, 1993
		Warren Johnston v France, 1994
		Warren Johnston v Wairarapa Bush, 1995
		Ash Moeke v North Harbour, 2012
		Dan Hawkins v North Harbour, 2014
		Peter Breen v Otago, 2017
Highest team score	113	*v Thames Valley, 1997*
Record victory (points ahead)	99	*113–14 v Thames Valley, 1997*
Highest score conceded	84	*v Otago, 1998*
Record defeat (points behind)	74	*10–84 v Otago, 1998*

Twelfth place in the NPC was not where Taniwha fans wanted or envisaged their team finishing up in 2023 after the highs of 2022 and a playoffs berth.

And yet, on most occasions, Northland did not play like the 12th best team in the competition. Indeed, after the fine win over finalist Hawke's Bay, it was right in quarter-finals contention, but then fell away before almost engineering an upset win over Auckland at Eden Park in the last round.

The 'Storm' week to kick off the campaign stretched Northland and it only accrued two points from the draw in Invercargill. Then came the best win of the season, a 32–5 defeat of the Mako.

From thereon in, the Taniwha only once dipped under 20 points. There will be disappointment at the last gasp losses to Manawatu and Auckland, plus a 30–15 loss to Otago and shipping 50 points to North Harbour in the Ian Jones Challenge Trophy but, in the final analysis, the team was competitive in most matches. Four times they recorded a tryscoring bonus point. Discipline, however, was an ongoing issue.

There was disruption in May when incoming head coach Marty Veale left for personal reasons to return to the USA. Former Scotland, NZU, Highlanders and Otago second five John Leslie took the job, assisted by Matt Rolston, the freshly retired Ross Wright and former All Blacks wing Eric Rush, who had two boys in the team.

Losses from 2022 included Josh Goodhue (Japan), Jone Macilai (unavailable), Conan O'Donnell, Sila Puafisi, Tom Robinson (Japan) and Wright.

Gains were Chris Apoua (back from injury), Rob Cobb (Waikato), Jordan Olsen (back from break), Wilton Rebolo (Australia), Brady Rush (sevens), Jordan Trainor (Auckland) and Saimoni Uluinakauvadra (back from injury).

Of the 37 players used, 10 were new Northland caps.

Fullback Josh Moorby was not as potent as he was in 2022, but still had a hand in several tries. The seasoned Jordan Trainor only appeared in the last three games and showed glimpses of his attacking potential. Brady Rush finally made his Northland debut on the right wing and mostly acquitted himself well.

The star turn in the backs was left wing Heremaia Murray, who ran in eight tries in his 10 starts, including three doubles, and showed a nifty chip and chase. Pisi Leilua broke his arm in the first game against Canterbury.

The mainstay of the midfield was again Tamati Tua, while Jack Goodhue racked up eight games before heading to France. The former All Black was one of five Taniwha to bring up their blazer games (18). The old warhorse, centurion Rene Ranger, had six outings, mostly as an impact player.

Northland was well served at first five, where Rivez Reihana bult on his promising 2022. He was again accurate off the tee, as was his understudy, the veteran Dan Hawkins.

Halfback Sam Nock was plagued by injury, but was outstanding against Hawke's Bay, while the omnipresent Lisati Milo-Harris was more than capable in either the No 9 or 21 jerseys.

Co-captain Matt Matich led from the front, as ever, while opensider Jonah Mau'u made big strides after his maiden Super Rugby season. Co-captain Rob Rush, after being under-utilised by the Blues, was the sole forward to start every game.

The main locks used, Liam Hallam-Eames, Sam Caird and Allan Craig, were industrious.

The scrum had some very good moments, but was not always consistent. Injury to tighthead Chris Apoua, was unfortunate, so the first Brazilian to play Super Rugby, Wilton Rebolo, and Remsy Lemisio tried to fill his boots. Rob Cobb and Jarred Adams did the job on the loosehead.

Hooker was shared between two former Taniwha skippers. Matt Moulds and Jordan Olsen, with Bruce Kauika-Petersen as back-up.

Higher honours went to:

New Zealand:	O. Tuungafasi
All Blacks XV:	J. Goodhue
New Zealand Sevens:	B. Rush

NORTHLAND REPRESENTATIVES 2023

Name	Club	Date of birth	Height	Weight	For Union Debut	Games	Points
J.J. (Jarred) Adams	Waipu	26-09-96	1.81	120	2022	19	0
T.J. (Tama) Anderson	Hora Hora	14-10-03	1.8	85	2022	3	10
C. (Chris) Apoua	Mid Northern	30-01-92	1.8	123	2023	3	0
S.W. (Sam) Caird	Old Boys-Marist	18-03-97	2.02.	118	2019	41	5
R.L. (Rob) Cobb	Old Boys-Marist	08-04-99	1.92.	118	2023	10	5
A. (Allan) Craig	Mid Northern	19-04-02	1.96	112	2021	13	5
E.J. (Jack) Goodhue	Moerewa/United Kawakawa	13-06-95	1.87	100	2017	20	15
L.J. (Liam) Hallam-Eames	Hikurangi	20-08-95	1.99	115	2021	24	5
T.S.W. (Trent) Hape	Old Boys-Marist	27-06-98	1.7	80	2022	6	0
D.C. (Dan) Hawkins	Hora Hora	20-04-91	1.75	87	2013	80	454
B.M. (Blake) Hohaia	Kamo	10-06-95	1.78	93	2017	51	25
H.A. (Hayden) Jurlina	Eastern	24-10-96	1.9	107	2023	2	0
B. (Bruce) Kauika-Petersen	Hora Hora	16-04-97	1.85	110	2022	15	5
P. (Pisi) Leilua	Kamo	12-05-95	1.85	95	2019	32	15
R.J (Remsy) Lemisio	Mid Northern	20-01-02	1.86	124	2023	9	0
R.M. (Matt) Letoga	Hikurangi	09-09-99	1.89	125	2023	1	0
M.E.S. (Matt) Matich	Western Sharks	10-07-91	1.87	106	2016	65	55
J.D. (Jonah) Mau'u	Waipu	28-07-98	1.83	102	2021	25	20
S.J. (Sam) McNamara	Waipu	11-03-98	1.93	112	2018	44	10
L.M. (Lisati) Milo-Harris	Moerewa/United Kawakawa	05-10-96	1.81	90	2022	21	15
J.M. (Josh) Moorby	Wellsford	11-07-98	1.86	93	2022	16	30
M.G. (Matt) Moulds	Otamatea	15-05-91	1.88	105	2013	70	35
H.W.W. (Heremaia) Murray	Moerewa/United Kawakawa	11-01-00	1.88	90	2022	21	55
S.J. (Sam) Nock	Kerikeri	18-06-96	1.75	84	2015	78	97
J.D. (Jordan) Olsen	Mid Northern	27-04-92	1.8	103	2014	66	45
R.M.N. (Rene) Ranger	Wellsford	30-09-86	1.83	102	2006	118	110
W.J.M.(Wilton) Rebolo	Old Boys-Marist	02-08-95	1.82	118	2023	5	0
R.W.M. (Rivez) Reihana	Kamo	25-05-00	1.87	92	2021	29	168
B.J.K. (Brady) Rush	Mid Northern	24-04-99	1.89	100	2023	7	5
R.H.T. (Rob) Rush	Mid Northern	14-11-00	1.93	110	2020	29	20
K.M.M. (Kobie) Scutt	Mid Northern	25-01-03	1.86	91	2023	1	0
S.M.Y. (Sean) Sweetman	Wellsford	17-05-94	1.94	120	2015	11	5
C.J.W. (Coree) Te Whata-Colley	Panguru	13-01-95	1.96	147	2019	44	10
J.V. (Jordan) Trainor	Western Sharks	31-01-96	1.87	87	2023	3	5
T.R. (Tamati) Tua	Kamo	26-11-97	1.88	104	2016	61	40
S. (Samisoni) Uluinakauvadra	Waipu	07-05-98	1.87	102	2019	4	0
R.E. (Rory) Woods	Waipu	04-01-03	1.97	102	2023	4	0

INDIVIDUAL SCORING

	Tries	Con	PG	DG	Points		Tries	Con	PG	DG	Points
Reihana	1	18	15	–	86	Hallam-Eames	1	–	–	–	5
Murray	8	–	–	–	40	Milo-Harris	1	–	–	–	5
Hawkins	–	5	4	–	22	Olsen	1	–	–	–	5
Anderson	2	–	–	–	10	B. Rush	1	–	–	–	5
Mau'u	2	–	–	–	10	R. Rush	1	–	–	–	5
Moorby	2	–	–	–	10	Trainor	1	–	–	–	5
Moulds	2	–	–	–	10						
Nock	2	–	–	–	10	***Totals***	***28***	***23***	***19***	***0***	***243***
Tua	2	–	–	–	10						
Cobb	1	–	–	–	5	*Opposition scored*	*35**	*27*	*17*	*0*	*282*

** includes one penalty try (7 points)*

NORTHLAND 2023

	Canterbury	Taranaki	Southland	Tasman	Manawatu	Hawke's Bay	Otago	North Harbour	Bay of Plenty	Auckland	Totals
Moorby	–	–	15	15	15	15	15	15	15	–	**7**
Scutt	–	15	–	–	–	–	–	–	–	–	**1**
Trainor	–	–	–	–	–	–	–	14	14	15	**3**
Murray	15	11	11	11	11	11	11	11	11	11	**10**
Anderson	–	–	–	–	–	14	14	–	–	–	**2**
B. Rush	14	14	14	14	14	–	–	–	s	14	**7**
Leilua	11	–	–	–	–	–	–	–	–	–	**1**
Ranger	s	s	–	–	s	s	–	12	–	12	**6**
J. Goodhue	13	12	s	s	–	12	s	13	12	–	**8**
Tua	12	13	13	13	13	13	13	s	13	13	**10**
Hohaia	–	–	12	12	12	–	12	–	–	s	**5**
Reihana	10	s	10	10	10	10	10	10	10	10	**10**
Hawkins	s	10	–	s	s	s	s	s	s	s	**9**
Nock	9	–	–	–	–	9	9	–	–	9	**4**
Milo-Harris	s	9	9	9	9	s	s	9	9	s	**10**
Hape	–	s	s	s	s	–	–	–	s	–	**5**
Matich (co-capt)	8	8	7	s	8	s	s	8	7	8	**10**
McNamara	–	s	8	8	–	–	–	–	–	s	**4**
Mau'u	7	7	s	7	7	7	7	7	8	–	**9**
Letoga	–	–	–	–	–	–	–	s	–	–	**1**
Uluinakauvadra	s	–	–	–	–	–	–	–	–	7	**2**
Woods	–	–	–	–	s	6	6	–	s	–	**4**
R. Rush (co-capt)	6	6	6	6	6	8	8	6	6	6	**10**
Jurlina	–	–	–	s	5	–	–	–	–	–	**2**
Hallam-Eames	s	5	5	5	–	5	5	s	5	5	**9**
Sweetman	–	s	4	–	s	s	–	–	–	–	**4**
Craig	5	4	–	–	–	–	s	5	s	s	**6**
Caird	4	–	s	4	4	4	4	4	4	4	**9**
Te Whata-Colley	–	–	–	s	s	–	–	3	–	–	**3**
Rebolo	–	–	–	–	–	s	s	s	3	s	**5**
Apoua	3	3	s	–	–	–	–	–	–	–	**3**
Cobb	s	s	1	s	s	1	s	s	1	s	**10**
Lemisio	s	s	3	3	3	3	3	–	s	3	**9**
Adams	1	1	s	1	1	s	1	1	s	1	**10**
Moulds	2	s	2	s	2	2	–	2	2	2	**9**
Kauika-Petersen	s	–	s	2	s	–	2	–	–	–	**5**
Olsen	–	2	–	–	–	s	s	s	s	s	**6**

NORTHLAND TEAM RECORD 2023

Played 10 **Won 2** **Drawn 1** **Lost 7** **Points for 243** **Points against 282**

Date	Opponent	Location	Score	Tries	Con	PG	DG	Referee
August 5	Canterbury	Whangarei	11–43.	B. Rush		Reihana (2)		Katsuki Furuse (Japan)
August 9	Taranaki	Whangarei	13–28	Mau'u	Hawkins	Hawkins (2)		Angus Mabey
August 13	Southland	Invercargill	15–15	Murray (2)	Reihana	Reihana		Marcus Playle
August 19	Tasman	Whangarei	32–5	Murray (2), Hallam-Eames, Moulds	Reihana (2), Hawkins	Reihana (2)		Brendon Pickerill
August 25	Manawatu	Palmerston North	30–31	Moulds, Milo-Harris, Moorby	Reihana (2), Hawkins	Reihana (2), Hawkins		Cam Stone
September 1	Hawke's Bay	Whangarei	44–21	Nock (2), Anderson (2), Cobb	Reihana (4), Hawkins	Reihana (3)		Maggie Cogger-Orr
September 10	Otago	Dunedin	15–30	Murray (2)	Reihana	Reihana		Marcus Playle
September 16	North Harbour	Albany	31–50	Moorby, Murray, Reihana, Mau'u	Reihana (4)	Reihana		Cam Stone
September 22	Bay of Plenty	Whangarei	26–32	Tua, Murray	Reihana (2)	Reihana (3), Hawkins		Mike Winter
September 29	Auckland	Auckland	26–27	Trainor, R. Rush, Tua, Olsen	Reihana (2), Hawkins			Dan Waenga

OTAGO

2023 Status: Bunnings NPC
Founded 1881. Affiliated 1895
President: R.D. (Roy) Daniels
Chairman: P.R. (Peter) McCormack
Chief executive officer : R.P. (Richard) Kinley
Coach: T.J.S. (Tom) Donnelly
Assistant coaches: J.L. (Jamie) Mackintosh, B.R. (Ben) Smith
Main ground: Forsyth Barr Stadium, Dunedin
Capacity: 28,000
Colours: Dark blue

RECORDS

Most appearances	170	*Richard Knight, 1981–92*
Most points	1520	*Greg Cooper, 1984–96*
Most tries	73	*Paul Cooke, 1990–96*
Most points in a season	279	*Greg Cooper, 1991*
Most tries in a season	16	*John Timu, 1988*
		John Timu, 1990
		Paul Cooke, 1995
		Brendan Laney, 1998
Most conversions in a season	50	*Greg Cooper, 1989*
Most penalty goals in a season	54	*Greg Cooper, 1989*
Most dropped goals in a season	9	*Lee Smith, 1986*
Most points in a match	39	*Paul Turner v East Coast, 1986*
Most tries in a match	5	*George Owles v South Canterbury, 1920*
		Bill Meates v South Canterbury, 1948
		Bruce Hunter v Marlborough, 1969
		Graham Sims v West Coast, 1972
Most conversions in a match	14	*Paul Turner v East Coast, 1986*
Most penalty goals in a match	7	*Greg Cooper v NZ Combined Services, 1989*
		Greg Cooper v Canterbury, 1991
		Blair Feeney v Wellington, 2002
Highest team score	91	*v East Coast, 1986*
Record victory (points ahead)	85	*88–3 v North Otago, 1983*
Highest score conceded	68	*v Wellington, 2007*
Record defeat (points behind)	61	*7–68 v Wellington, 2007*

Otago regressed in 2023, finishing 11th with a record of three wins and seven losses. The season started off with three successive losses and the side never recovered, although the Hawke's Bay game could have been won if a last-minute sideline conversion had been successful. In later matches Otago were well beaten by Bay of Plenty and Taranaki, while the Waikato match was the low point of the season.

The win over Northland was the best performance of the season and the side finished on a high in the final match against Counties Manukau with a very good second half. Although Otago had a young team, it was still able to field 22 returnees from last season, including 13 players with fulltime contracts in Super Rugby in 2023.

Of last year's regulars, Josh Ioane (Waikato), Kemara Hauiti-Parapara (Wellington), and Freedom Vahaakolo (rugby league in Auckland) had moved on, Vilimoni Koroi was not wanted and played for North Otago in the Heartland Championship, Tau Koloamatangi was with Tonga at the World Cup, Josh Hohneck had retired while Oliver Haig, James Lentjes and Josh Timu all missed the entire NPC due to injury.

Former All Black Waisake Naholo and Tom Sanders (Canterbury/Crusaders/Chiefs) both returned from overseas.

Sam Gilbert's experience and confidence was valuable to a backline that at times had a lot of inexperience. He seems better suited to fullback, which he showed against Northland, but again was also required to be a utility, filling in at both five-eighths positions.

Jona Nareki had a mixed season on the wing. He could be a danger, as he showed by taking his chance to score against North Harbour and Taranaki but had an off game against Bay of Plenty and finished with a season-ending injury. Waisake Naholo, who only lasted 17 minutes, Thomas Umaga-Jensen and Cameron Millar also saw their seasons end prematurely through injury.

All these restricted appearances created opportunities for a number of young debutants to be introduced into the backline. Finn Hurley, Ajay Faleafaga, Jake Te Hiwi and Josh Whaanga had extended game time that would not have been expected at the start of the season and the experience gained can only be beneficial in the future. Of these, 19-year-old Whaanga was especially impressive. A strong runner, he top-scored with four tries and was the only player in the squad to start in all ten games.

Another newcomer who looks to have a bright future is Nathan Hastie who started the season as third choice halfback and finished it as first choice.

In the loose forwards, the absence of James Lentjes was felt, particularly at the breakdown. Sean Withy seemed to lack an edge after his exertions in Super Rugby but not so Christian Lio-Willie. With his strong carries, the No 8 showed excellent form and was Otago player of the year.

The tight five was a strength of the team and could be counted on for a solid shift. The locking trio of Josh Dickson, Will Tucker and Fabian Holland all worked well in the set pieces and general play. After 79, games Dickson is now heading off overseas to Japan while Holland continues to progress.

Saula Ma'u was a fine all-round prop who was strong in the scrum and hard to stop with ball in hand. After a handful of matches on loan to North Otago last year, newcomer Rowan Wingham had a very encouraging debut season for Otago. Just 20 years old, he showed good scrummaging ability. Jermaine Ainsley and Abraham Pole rounded out the position with all four props getting similar game time and starts. After his breakout season at hooker last year, Henry Bell continued the good form and Ricky Jackson was a very experienced replacement off the bench.

OTAGO REPRESENTATIVES 2023

Name	Club	Date of birth	Height	Weight	For Union Debut	Games	Points
J.M.L. (Jermaine) Ainsley	Alhambra Union	08-08-95	1.82	120	2021	26	5
J.M. (James) Arscott	Green Island	15-07-00	1.74	80	2019	34	0
J.P.C. (Jeremiah) Asi	University	10-09-03	1.85	104	2023	6	10
H.D.E. (Henry) Bell	overseas	22-08-99	1.78	103	2020	27	20
J.M. (Josh) Dickson	University	02-11-94	2.02	118	2014	79	55
A.J. (Ajay) Faleafaga	Dunedin	02-02-03	1.80	93	2023	7	5
S.H. (Sam) Fischli	overseas	02-04-98	1.88	103	2020	26	0
S.J. (Sam) Gilbert	Green Island	23-01-99	1.89	99	2021	26	73
N.M. (Nathan) Hastie	Harbour	27-04-01	1.77	88	2023	6	0
J.A. (Joshua) Hill	Taieri	22-04-99	1.95	110	2019	33	15
F.M. (Fabian) Holland	Dunedin	09-10-02	2.06	118	2021	23	20
F.P. (Finn) Hurley	Green Island	25-06-03	1.70	80	2023	10	29
R.D. (Ricky) Jackson	University	02-08-98	1.82	109	2017	41	10
C.G.D.B. (Caleb) Leef	Taieri				2022	3	0
J.M. (Jack) Leslie	Southern	25-07-00	1.84	92	2022	7	10
C.J. (Christian) Lio-Willie	Kaikorai	26-08-98	1.87	109	2021	23	5
B.F. (Benjamin) Lopas	Green Island				2023	3	0
Saula Ma'u	Harbour	29-04-00	1.94	140	2019	21	15
K.A. (Kieran) McClea	overseas	18-07-98	1.73	82	2022	8	5
C.G. (Cameron) Millar	Taieri	27-12-97	1.85	85	2021	15	95
W.;R. (Waisake) Naholo	Harbour	08-05-91	1.85	98	2023	1	0
J.M. (Jona) Nareki	Alhambra Union	27-12-97	1.75	83	2017	52	150
A.A. (Abraham) Pole	Harbour	28-05-92	1.88	123	2021	28	10
T.B. (Tom) Sanders	overseas	05-02-94	1.90	110	2023	7	0
W.R. (William) Stodart	University	03-10-03	1.87	112	2023	3	5
J.T.E.P. (John) Tapueluelu	Marist[1]	07-04-96	1.83	88	2022	9	10
H.M.J. (Harry) Taylor	Southern	06-12-01	1.85	107	2023	5	0
J.O.W. (Jake) Te Hiwi	Green Island	02-02-02	1.84	100	2022	10	10
W.A. (Will) Tucker	Kaikorai	16-03-98	2.02	114	2020	34	15
T.N.M. (Thomas) Umaga-Jensen	University	31-12-97	1.87	112	2020	11	10
J.R. (Josh) Whaanga	Taieri	15-03-04	1.93	98	2023	10	20
R.N. (Rohan) Wingham	Dunedin	04-12-02	1.89	117	2023	9	0
S.M. (Sean) Withy	University	01-02-01	1.91	108	2020	24	10

1. Loaned by North Harbour RU

INDIVIDUAL SCORING

	Tries	Con	PG	DG	Points		Tries	Con	PG	DG	Points
Gilbert	1	10	8	–	49	Holland	2	–	–	–	10
Hurley	2	8	1	–	29	Tapueluelu	2	–	–	–	10
Whaanga	4	–	–	–	20	Lio-Willie	1	–	–	–	5
Nareki	3	–	–	–	15	Faleafaga	1	–	–	–	5
Tucker	2	–	–	–	10	Ainsley	1	–	–	–	5
Te Hiwi	2	–	–	–	10	Stodart	1	–	–	–	5
Leslie	2	–	–	–	10						
Ma'u	2	–	–	–	10	***Totals***	***30***	***18***	***9***	***0***	***213***
Asi	2	–	–	–	10						
Dickson	2	–	–	–	10	*Opposition scored*	*40*	*32*	*10*	*0*	*294*

OTAGO 2023	Tasman	Wellington	Hawkes Bay	Southland	Bay of Plenty	North Harbour	Northland	Taranaki	Waikato	Counties Manukau	**TOTALS**
Hurley	15	15	s	15	15	15	s	s	15	15	**10**
Tapueluelu	–	–	–	s	s	11	s	s	14	14	**7**
Naholo	14	–	–	–	–	–	–	–	–	–	**1**
Nareki	11	11	11	11	11	s	11	11	–	–	**8**
Whaanga	13	14	14	14	14	14	14	14	13	13	**10**
Asi	–	–	s	s	s	s	–	–	11	11	**6**
Umaga-Jensen	s	12	13	13	12	–	–	–	–	–	**5**
Leef	s	–	–	–	–	–	–	–	–	s	**2**
Te Hiwi	12	13	–	–	13	13	13	13	12	–	**7**
Leslie	–	s	12	12	–	12	12	12	–	–	**6**
Gilbert (co–capt)	10	10	15	–	–	–	15	15	10	12	**7**
Millar	–	s	10	–	–	–	–	–	–	–	**2**
Faleafaga	–	–	–	10	10	10	10	10	s	10	**7**
Arscott	9	9	–	9	9	s	9	9	s	s	**9**
McClea	s	s	9	–	–	–	s	s	–	–	**5**
Hastie	–	–	s	s	s	9	–	–	9	9	**6**
Fischli	8	6	s	s	s	8	s	s	–	8	**9**
Lio-Willie	s	8	8	8	8	–	8	8	8	–	**8**
Withy (co-capt)	7	7	7	7	7	s	7	7	–	–	**8**
Taylor	s	s	–	–	–	7	–	–	7	7	**5**
Sanders	–	–	6	6	6	–	6	6	6	s	**7**
Stodart	–	–	–	–	–	6	–	–	s	s	**3**
Dickson	6	4	4	5	5	–	5	–	s	6	**8**
Tucker	5	5	5	–	s	s	4	4	4	4	**9**
Holland	4	s	s	4	4	4	s	5	5	5	**10**
Hill	–	–	–	s	–	5	–	s	s	s	**5**
Ma'u	3	3	3	s	s	3	3	3	s	s	**10**
Wingham	1	1	1	–	s	1	1	1	s	s	**9**
Ainsley	s	s	s	3	3	s	s	s	3	3	**10**
Lopas	s	–	s	s	–	–	–	–	–	–	**3**
Pole	–	s	–	1	1	s	s	s	1	1	**8**
Bell	2	2	2	2	2	s	2	2	2	2	**10**
Jackson	s	s	s	s	s	2	s	s	s	s	**10**

Hill captained v North Harbour

OTAGO TEAM RECORD 2023

Played 10 **Won 3** **Lost 7** **Points for 213** **Points against 294**

Date	*Opponent*	*Location*	*Score*	*Tries*	*Con*	*PG*	*DG*	*Referee*
August 4	Tasman	Nelson	15–27	Tucker, Te Hiwi	Gilbert	Gilbert		Angus Mabey
August 12	Wellington	Dunedin	5–28	Leslie				Jackson Henshaw
August 20	Hawke's Bay	Napier	32–33	Lio-Willie, Whaanga, Ma'u, Asi, Leslie	Gilbert, Hurley	Hurley		Nick Briant
August 26	Southland	Dunedin	31–21	Dickson (2), Whaanga, Faleafaga, Hurley	Hurley (3)			James Doleman
September 2	Bay of Plenty	Rotorua	14–38	Ainsley, Ma'u	Hurley (2)			Jono Bredin
September 6	North Harbour	Albany	24–27	Holland, Whaanga, Tapueluelu, Nareki	Hurley (2)			Mike Winter
September 10	Northland	Dunedin	30–15	Tucker, Nareki, Te Hiwi	Gilbert (3)	Gilbert (3)		Marcus Playle
September 16	Taranaki	Dunedin	17–36	Nareki		Gilbert (4)		Dan Waenga
September 24	Waikato	Hamilton	7–47	Holland	Gilbert			Angus Mabey
October 1	Counties Manukau	Dunedin	38–22	Hurley, Tapueluelu, Gilbert, Whaanga, Stodart, Asi	Gilbert (4)			Maggie Cogger-Orr

POVERTY BAY

2023 Status: Heartland Championship
Founded 1890. Affiliated 1893
President: T.R. (Tom) Crosby
Chairman: H.M. (Hayden) Swann
Chief executive officer: R.E. (Ray) Noble
Coach: M.N. (Miah) Nikora
Assistant coach: J.R. (James) Grogan
Main ground: Rugby Park, Gisborne
Capacity: 18,000
Colour: Scarlet

RECORDS

Highest attendance	15,000	*Poverty Bay-East Coast v British Isles, 1971*
Most appearances	150	*S.T. Ngatu, 2003–2018*
Most points	791	*S.C. Leighton, 2004–12*
Most tries	35	*P.S.R. Ransley, 1961–71*
Most points in a season	144	*S.C. Leighton, 2007*
Most tries in a season	11	*J. Moeke, 1997;* *J. Stewart, 2010* *J. Stewart, 2011*
Most conversions in a season	30	*S.C. Leighton, 2007*
Most penalty goals in a season	27	*D.M. Boyle, 1999*
Most dropped goals in a season	3	*G.B. Ross, 1976; J. Whittle, 1979*
Most points in a match	35	*S.C. Leighton v Thames Valley, 2007*
Most tries in a match	4	*J.L. Penny v Olympians Club, 1953* *K.A. Twigley v East Coast, 1966* *I.A. Kirkpatrick v East Coast, 1971* *K.D. Ferris v East Coast, 1983* *A.B. Hansen v North Otago, 1987*
Most conversions in a match	9	*R.P. Owen v East Coast, 1983*
Most penalty goals in a match	7	*S.P. Parkes v Buller, 2013*
Highest team score	75	*v East Coast, 1980*
Record victory (points ahead)	75	*75–0 v East Coast, 1980*
Highest score conceded	121	*v Waikato, 1998*
Record defeat (points behind)	121	*0–121 v Waikato, 1998*

Poverty Bay finished eighth on the Heartland Championship table on points differential, ahead of Mid Canterbury and King Country for a Lochore Cup semi-final by winning three of their eight matches.

After an opening win against Buller, when they scored six tries in the first 23 minutes, the Bay then lost five matches in a row, but in the last of those, against North Otago, they seemed to reach a turning point. Down 12–38 at halftime, they fought back to eventually lose 43–50.

A win over Horowhenua Kapiti got them back on track, then against the all-conquering South Canterbury side, in terrible conditions, Poverty Bay was only two points behind with 20 minutes left, before conceding a late penalty goal and a try. However, the bonus point earned for their four tries, and the defensive effort to limit their opponents to 36 points, proved just enough to hold on to eighth place and a playoff spot.

In the semi-final, the rematch with North Otago proved similar to their earlier encounter, but this time the comeback, from 7–28 down with 30 minutes left, was turned into a win, 40–35. With a chance of winning their first Heartland trophy since 2011, Poverty Bay travelled to Greymouth for the final. Into the strong wind and rain in the first half, the Bay were 0–23 down at halftime. The anticipated second half revival produced four tries but the side fell agonisingly short, 20–23.

Coach Miah Nikora used 36 players in the Heartland Championship, with injuries a big factor. The losses during the season, particularly of first-five Kelvin Smith and lock Dan Law, were never fully covered. When they clicked, Poverty Bay were a very dangerous side, but errors and a lack of patience with the ball were catalysts for inconsistent performances.

The forward pack made solid ground all season and usually managed to break even, but the scrum was under pressure from West Coast in the Lochore Cup final. Poverty Bay had two excellent loose forwards in Stuart Leach and Keanu Taumata. With just one game last year, Leach probably owed his chance to the unavailability of Adrian Wyrill who missed the Championship because of injury, and took it well, going from strength to strength. Taumata was impressive enough to earn NZ Heartland selection and in his three seasons to date he is yet to miss a game for Poverty Bay.

The experience of Morgan Reedy was needed at lock, with Law's season-ending injury. Prop was another position the Bay was fortunate to have a number of experienced players to call on when injuries struck, with Nehe Papuni and Jarryd Broughton being the preferred starters when available. Hooker and co-captain Shayde Skudder played every game.

After being mainly used off the bench last year, Ricardo Patricio was a revelation at fullback. An outstanding counter-attacker, he scored five tries, including a brilliant one against Mid Canterbury, and with good goalkicking finished with 91 points. Moses Christie, last year's fullback, spent most of the season coming off the bench, a reversal of his and Patricio's fortunes last year.

Taine Aupouri was in good form on the wing and when Ted Walters' season ended with injury, Aupouri was shifted into centre where he proved a good fit. Jacob Leaf played extremely well at second-five. He ran hard, covered well and his tackling was first rate. Ra Broughton was a high-class halfback with a very accurate kicking game.

Poverty Bay's home ground of Rugby Park was out of action during 2023 due to the rebuild of the John Heikell Grandstand. The grandstand had been closed in 2019 because of structural concerns, including of earthquake safety. Home matches this year were played at Gisborne Oval or at the Ngatapa club's ground at Patutahi.

Higher honours went to:
New Zealand Heartland: K. Taumata

POVERTY BAY REPRESENTATIVES 2023

		For Union		
Name	*Club*	*Debut*	*Games*	*Points*
T.K. (Taine) Aupouri	YMP	2021	20	25
Genesis Bartlett-Tamatea	YMP	2023	1	0
Jarryd Broughton [1]	Napier Pirates [2]	2020	23	35
R.S.B. (Rawiri) Broughton	YMP	2020	15	5
C.P.L. (Campbell) Chrisp	Ngatapa	2011	62	5
Moses Christie	OB Marist	2022	19	67
L.A. (Lance) Dickson	OB Marist	2014	26	0

Name	Club	For Union Debut	Games	Points
T.P.H.H. (Te Peehi) Fairlie	YMP	2015	41	90
J.W. (James) Higgins	Ngatapa	2021	23	15
Jimmy-Lee Hongara	Poneke [3]	2023	1	0
Harawira Kahukura	OB Marist	2023	3	0
J.J. (Jesse) Kapene	YMP	2018	25	20
Jordan Kingi	OB Marist	2023	9	0
D.M. (Dan) Law	Ngatapa	2021	24	5
S.R. (Stuart) Leach	YMP	2022	12	10
J.P. (Jacob) Leaf	Waikohu	2019	35	15
Kupu Lloyd	Waikohu	2022	8	0
S.A. (Seth) Lundon	YMP	2022	10	10
N.T.R. (Ngahiwi) Manuel	OB Marist	2022	9	5
Hunter Mokomoko	Te Puna [4]	2015	15	35
Nashwen Mouton	Ngatapa	2023	1	0
Hayze Nepia	YMP	2023	5	0
N.S. (Nehe) Papuni	YMP	2021	8	15
G.P. (Geoff) Pari	Waikohu	2013	33	5
Ricardo Patricio	Ngatapa	2022	19	106
Nik Patumaka	Tech OB [5]	2023	6	0
Matt Proffit	HSOB	2023	1	0
M.R. (Mitchell) Purvis	YMP	2022	18	25
M.J. (Morgan) Reedy	Northcote [6]	2019	16	0
F.H. (Fletcher) Scammell	HSOB	2020	25	0
S.P. (Shayde) Skudder	YMP	2015	48	45
K.M. (Kelvin) Smith	YMP	2011	70	194
Jonty Stewart	Napier OB Marist [5]	2023	5	9
W.T. "Willis" Tamatea	YMP	2008	40	5
Keanu Taumata	OB Marist	2021	31	50
Kayleb Te Whare	YMP	2023	8	5
Bosca "Joe" Tikicidre	YMP	2023	9	20
Ted Walters	Tech OB [5]	2021	16	15
Khian Westrupp	Ngatapa	2023	5	15
KC Wilson	Waikohu	2023	1	0

1. Player of Origin 2. Hawke's Bay RU 3. Loaned by Wellington RU 4. Loaned by Bay of Plenty RU
5. Loaned by Hawke's Bay RU 6. Loaned by North Harbour RU

INDIVIDUAL SCORING

	Tries	Con	PG	DG	Points		Tries	Con	PG	DG	Points
Patricio	5	21	8	-	91	Fairlie	2	-	-	-	10
Taumata	5	-	-	-	25	Stewart	1	2	-	-	9
Aupouri	4	-	-	-	20	Te Whare	1	-	-	-	5
Tikicidre	4	-	-	-	20	Papuni	1	-	-	-	5
Smith	1	3	2	-	17	Manuel	1	-	-	-	5
Westrupp	3	-	-	-	15	Lundon	1	-	-	-	5
Skudder	3	-	-	-	15	R. Broughton	1	-	-	-	5
J. Broughton	3	-	-	-	15	Purvis	1	-	-	-	5
Leaf	3	-	-	-	15						
Mokomoko	3	-	-	-	15	***Totals***	***46***	***29***	***10***	***0***	***318***
Christie	1	3	-	-	11						
Leach	2	-	-	-	10	*Opposition scored*	*43**	*28*	*16*	*1*	*324*

** includes one penalty try (7 points)*

POVERTY BAY 2023	Ngati Porou East Coast	Buller	Thames Valley	Wairarapa Bush	Mid Canterbury	Ngati Porou East Coast	North Otago	Horowhenua Kapiti	South Canterbury	North Otago (sf)	West Coast (f)	TOTALS
Patricio	15	15	15	s	15	15	15	15	15	15	15	**11**
Proffit	–	–	s	–	–	–	–	–	–	–	–	**1**
Tikicidre	14	14	14	11	s	–	–	11	11	11	11	**9**
Fairlie	11	11	13	–	11	11	11	–	14	14	14	**9**
Bartlett-Tamatea	s	–	–	–	–	–	–	–	–	–	–	**1**
Wilson	s	–	–	–	–	–	–	–	–	–	–	**1**
Christie	–	s	11	15	–	s	s	14	s	s	s	**9**
Mouton	–	–	s	–	–	–	–	–	–	–	–	**1**
Mokomoko	–	–	–	s	–	–	–	–	–	s	s	**3**
Aupouri	13	–	–	14	14	14	14	13	13	13	13	**9**
Walters	–	13	–	–	13	13	s	–	–	–	–	**4**
Purvis	12	s	–	13	s	10	13	s	s	10	s	**10**
Leaf	–	12	12	12	12	12	12	12	12	12	12	**10**
Smith (co capt.)	10	10	10	10	10	–	–	–	–	–	–	**5**
Stewart	–	–	–	–	–	s	10	10	10	–	10	**5**
R. Broughton	9	9	9	–	9	9	9	9	9	9	9	**10**
Te Whare	s	s	s	9	–	s	s	s	s	–	–	**8**
Hongara	–	–	–	s	–	–	–	–	–	–	–	**1**
Leach	8	8	8	8	8	8	8	8	8	7	8	**11**
Taumata	7	7	7	7	7	7	7	6	7	6	7	**11**
Westrupp	6	–	s	s	s	6	–	–	–	–	–	**5**
Lundon	s	6	6	s	–	s	s	7	6	–	–	**8**
Kapene	–	s	s	6	6	–	–	–	–	–	–	**4**
Kahukura	5	–	–	–	–	–	s	s	–	–	–	**3**
Tamatea	4	–	–	–	–	–	–	–	–	–	–	**1**
Scammell	s	–	–	–	–	–	–	–	–	–	–	**1**
Law	–	5	5	5	5	5	–	–	–	–	–	**5**
Reedy	–	4	–	–	4	–	–	5	5	5	5	**6**
Lloyd	–	s	–	–	–	s	6	s	s	s	s	**7**
Kingi	–	–	4	4	s	4	4	4	4	4	4	**9**
Dickson	3	–	s	3	s	s	1	s	s	s	1	**10**
Papuni	1	1	1	1	1	–	s	–	–	–	–	**6**
Chrisp	s	s	s	s	–	–	–	–	–	–	s	**5**
Nepia	s	–	–	–	–	–	–	s	s	8	6	**5**
J. Broughton	–	3	3	–	–	s	s	3	3	3	3	**8**
Higgins	–	s	–	s	3	3	3	s	s	s	s	**9**
Patumaka	–	–	–	–	s	1	5	1	1	1	–	**6**
Skudder (co capt.)	2	2	2	2	2	2	2	2	2	2	2	**11**
Pari	s	–	–	–	–	–	–	–	s	s	s	**4**
Manuel	–	s	s	s	–	s	s	s	–	s	s	**8**

POVERTY BAY TEAM RECORD 2023

Played 11 Won 4 Lost 7 Points for 318 Points against 324

Date	Opponent	Location	Score	Tries	Con	PG	DG	Referee
June 3	Ngati Porou East Coast *	Gisborne	29–17	Westrupp, Te Whare, Aupouri, Taumata	Patricio (3)	Patricio		Damian MacPherson
August 12	Buller	Gisborne	52–33	Tikicidre (2), Patricio (2), Skudder, Papuni, J. Broughton, Taumata	Patricio (6)			Katsuki Furuse (Japan)
August 19	Thames Valley	Te Aroha	17–24	Smith, Leaf, Westrupp	Patricio			Maggie Cogger-Orr
August 26	Wairarapa Bush	Masterton	24–30	Aupouri, Skudder, Westrupp	Smith (3)	Smith		Jack Sargentina
September 2	Mid Canterbury	Gisborne	20–23	Patricio (2)	Patricio (2)	Smith, Patricio		Stu Catley
September 9	Ngati Porou East Coast (OT)	Ruatoria	11–31	Manuel		Patricio (2)		Ben Woolerton
September 16	North Otago	Gisborne	43–50	Aupouri (2), Taumata (2), Stewart, Leaf, Lundon	Patricio (2), Stewart (2)			Andy Morton
September 23	Horowhenua Kapiti	Levin	31–17	Leach, J. Broughton, Taumata, Patricio	Patricio	Patricio (3)		Nick Hogan
September 30	South Canterbury	Patutahi	31–41	J. Broughton, Tikicidre, Leaf, Fairlie	Patricio (4)	Patricio		Tipene Cottrell
October 7	North Otago (LC sf)	Oamaru	40–35	Tikicidre, Skudder, R. Broughton, Purvis, Mokomoko, Christie	Christie (3), Patricio (2)			Fraser Hannon
October 15	West Coast (LC f)	Greymouth	20–23	Mokomoko (2), Fairlie, Leach				Jackson Henshaw

* Non-Heartland Championship match

SOUTH CANTERBURY

2023 Status: Heartland Championship
Founded 1888. Original member 1892
President: M.J.L. (Mick) Hobbs
Chairman: G.E. (Grant) Norton
Chief Executive Officer: C.W. (Craig) Calder (to February)
T.R. (Tim) Hyde-Smith (from February)
Coach: N.G. (Nigel) Walsh
Assistant coaches: S.P. (Shaun) Breen,
C.S. (Chris) Gard, Kelly Walsh
Main ground: Alpine Energy Stadium, Timaru
Capacity: 17,000
Colours: Emerald green and black

RECORDS

Highest attendance	17,000	*South Canterbury v France, 1961*
Most appearances	152	*S.J. Todd, 1986–2001*
Most points	1060	*B.J. Fairbrother, 1981–92*
Most tries	60	*S.J. Todd 1986–2001*
Most points in a season	175	*B.J. Fairbrother, 1991*
Most tries in a season	15	*S.I.F. Kakala, 2023*
Most conversions in a season	45	*S. Briggs, 2022*
Most penalty goals in a season	31	*B.J. Fairbrother, 1990*
Most dropped goals in a season	8	*B.J. Fairbrother, 1987*
		B.J. Fairbrother, 1991
Most points in a match	32	*G.I. Dempster v Wairarapa Bush, 1996*
Most tries in a match	4	on *10 occasions*
Most conversions in a match	9	*S. Briggs v Wairarapa Bush, 2022*
Most penalty goals in a match	7	*B.J. Fairbrother v East Coast, 1990*
Highest team score	100	*v Ngati Porou East Coast, 2018*
Record victory (points ahead)	93	*100–7 v Ngati Porou East Coast, 2018*
Highest score conceded	103	*v Canterbury, 2001*
Record defeat (points behind)	103	*0–103 v Canterbury, 2001*

South Canterbury's extraordinary run in the Heartland Championship continued in 2023 with the setting of more records. With a squad of 32 players — seven on debut — twelve players did not return with the notable absentees being captain Nick Strachan and Theo Davidson (both retired) and Henry Bryce (injured). Returning to the squad from 2021 were Taufa Hala'ufia and Fa'alele Iosua.The pre-season matches consisted of a non-first-class match against Otago 'B' at Waikouaiti, resulting in a 21–15 victory, and the Ranfurly Shield challenge against Wellington at the Hutt Recreation Ground. That match wasn't the spectacle enjoyed in 2022 against Hawkes Bay, but the team at least scored three converted tries against the NPC champions.

With Fraser Park (formerly Alpine Energy Stadium) out of action until the 2024 season, South Canterbury's home matches were again played at various venues around the province. The first of which was against Horowhenua Kapiti at Waimate's Manchester Park where South Canterbury eclipsed the Heartland record of 21 victories in a row set by Whanganui from 2015–17, with a 48–14 win.After further comfortable wins against King Country and Buller — which saw them retaining the Alan Strachan Cup — the next assignment was against North Otago at Oamaru. With the Hanan Shield, Direen & Gard Cups at stake, the match was a see-saw affair that had the crowd on the edge. With six minutes to go, Sireli Buliruarua scored after a breakout from inside the South Canterbury to put the side ahead 26–22. The next five minutes saw desperate attacks and defence from both sides, but on fulltime the North Otago first-five made a dash for the posts but was 'bear hugged' by Garret Casey and another South Canterbury forward, to which the referee decided that was the conclusion of the match.

The match against South Canterbury at Fairlie's Strathconan Park was another torrid affair for the locally significant Coalpit Trophy. South Canterbury were unable to shake the Coasters off until the remaining minutes when a late try sealed the win. Round six was played at Whangamata against Thames Valley and lived up to the top-of-the-table expectations. Both teams were unbeaten with South Canterbury keeping their noses in front throughout the second half.

The match against neighbours Mid Canterbury was played at Christchurch, with the Hanan Shield and the Frank Timblick Trophy at stake. It was a high-scoring game and South Canterbury only put the game away late in the match. The final round match saw yet another new venue in Patutahi (near Gisborne) against Poverty Bay and was played in the worst conditions seen in a number of seasons. At halftime, South Canterbury were comfortably ahead, but in the second half Poverty Bay attacked from all positions to seriously threaten the result, but yet again South Canterbury sealed the match with only minutes to go. With the round-robin completed, the team found themselves in the same position as 2021, unbeaten with 40 competition points, including the maximum eight bonus points. No other team has achieved this in the Heartland Championship. The semi-final saw a return to the Pleasant Point Domain for a match against Ngati Porou East Coast. At halftime the Green and Blacks found themselves down 3–17 but in the final quarter scored 31 unanswered points to earn their third Meads Cup final in a row.

The Meads Cup final was played at the Temuka Domain Oval in warm nor-west conditions. Whanganui took the early lead with the wind at their backs, but to the surprise of the 3,000 spectators it was South Canterbury that led at halftime.Kalavini Leatigaga's try just after halftime has been unofficially voted as the supporters' favourite for the season. It also left the local crowd with the feeling that the final was theirs. Whanganui refused to surrender, and twice came within three points in the last quarter.With five minutes, left Solomone Lavaka scored near the posts to put South Canterbury ahead by 40–30 and clinch a third consecutive Meads Cup victory.

Then other records were rolled out. On the basis of national provincial championship matches, South Canterbury's now 31 wins in a row surpassed Auckland's run of 27 consecutive wins from 1988–91. It was also the first time that South Canterbury had beaten Whanganui four times in a row, but more significantly it was the South Canterbury's 500th first class win.

Kalavini Leatigaga is the first player in the Heartland Championship to have scored 50 tries, and Siu Kakala had beaten the union's 22-year-old record for tries in a season, scoring in every match except the final, for a bag of 15. Co-captain Willie Wright showed all his 82-cap, 460 points experience as the kingpin between the squad's powerful forwards and very talented backline. For the third season in a row, the coaching team of Nigel Walsh and his assistants had the ability to make precise decisions in the last quarter of every match in regard to substitutions. This included their own version of the Springboks 'bomb squad', consisting of the physically imposing front row bench of Junior Fa'avae (back from injury), Garret Casey and Graison Dale. They ultimately ended East Coast's bid in the semi-final and did the same to Whanganui in the final.

Higher honours went to:

New Zealand Heartland: C. Anderson, S. Briggs, T. Fakatava, P. Fifita, F. Joyce, V. Taelega, L. Toumohunui, W. Wright

SOUTH CANTERBURY REPRESENTATIVES 2023

		For Union		
Name	*Club*	*Debut*	*Games*	*Points*
T.T.F. (Tevita) Ahokovi	Manukau Rovers [2]	2023	10	10
Anthony Amato	Waimate	2019	42	55
Conor Anderson	Celtic	2021	31	25
Sam Briggs	Celtic	2021	28	335
S.K. (Sireli) Buliruarua	Harlequins	2017	30	65
G.J. (Garret) Casey	Celtic	2015	36	25
Graison Dale	Celtic	2022	22	10
J.R. "Junior" Faavae	Temuka	2015	41	69
T.M.H.K. (Tokomaata) Fakatava	Waimate	2014	53	10
Paula Fifita	Harlequins	2013	42	130
L.U. (Lisiate) Folau	Harlequins	2022	14	35
Taufa Hala'ufia	Harlequins	2020	11	0
Faalele Iosua	Temuka	2019	16	53
F.R. (Finlay) Joyce	Temuka	2023	11	5
S.I.F. (Siu) Kakala	Harlequins	2019	43	180
S.P. (Solomone) Lavaka	Temuka	2018	37	30
K.V. (Kalavini) Leatigaga	Temuka	2016	60	276
P.P.I.N.H.V.F (Peala) Matakaiongo	Celtic	2023	3	15
Zac McKay	Kaiapoi [3]	2021	30	35
M.W. (Miles) Medlicott	Waimate	2011	70	38
Clarence Moli	Waimate	2019	21	60
P.L. (Paula) Moli	Waimate	2023	6	0
S.D. (Steve) Phillips [1]	Marist Albion [4]	2023	5	0
Z.C.C. (Zac) Saunders	Celtic	2018	50	100
Salesitangi Savelio	Temuka	2020	12	30
Liueli Simote	Temuka	2020	25	95
Vaka Taelega	Temuka	2020	28	25
A.T. (Apitoni) Toia	Harlequins	2023	1	0
Loni Toumohuni	Waimate	2013	48	85
M.D.T.K.T. (Maloni) Uhi	Harlequins	2023	1	0
Etienne Van Zyl	Temuka	2021	17	0
W.A. (William) Wright	Celtic	2011	82	460

1. Player of Origin *2. Loaned by Auckland RU* *3. Loaned by Canterbury RU* *4. Canterbury RU*

INDIVIDUAL SCORING

	Tries	*Con*	*PG*	*DG*	*Points*		*Tries*	*Con*	*PG*	*DG*	*Points*
Kakala	15	-	-	-	75	Ahokovi	2	-	-	-	10
Briggs	-	24	6	-	66	Lavaka	2	-	-	-	10
Wright	2	21	1	-	55	Amato	2	-	-	-	10
Simote	7	-	-	-	35	Joyce	1	-	-	-	5
Leatigaga	7	-	-	-	35	Taelega	1	-	-	-	5
Fifita	4	-	-	-	20	Saunders	1	-	-	-	5
McKay	4	-	-	-	20	Dale	1	-	-	-	5
C. Moli	4	-	-	-	20	Anderson	1	-	-	-	5
Matakaiongo	3	-	-	-	15						
Folau	3	-	-	-	15	***Totals***	***65***	***45***	***7***	***0***	***436***
Toumohuni	3	-	-	-	15						
Buliruarua	2	-	-	-	10	*Opposition scored*	*42 1*	*28*	*8*	*0*	*294*

** includes two penalty tries (14 points).*

SOUTH CANTERBURY 2023	Wellington	Horowhenua Kapiti	King Country	Buller	North Otago	West Coast	Thames Valley	Mid Canterbury	Poverty Bay	Ngati Porou East Coast (sf)	Whanganui (f)	TOTALS
Simote	15	15	–	15	15	–	–	–	15	15	15	**7**
Saunders	s	s	15	s	s	15	15	15	s	s	s	**11**
Folau	14	–	s	14	14	14	–	–	–	–	–	**5**
Leatigaga	11	–	–	s	–	11	11	11	11	11	11	**8**
Buliruarua	s	14	–	–	s	s	14	s	s	s	s	**9**
Matakaiongo	–	11	11	–	11	–	–	–	–	–	–	**3**
C. Moli	–	s	14	11	13	s	s	14	14	14	14	**10**
McKay	13	13	13	13	–	13	13	13	13	13	13	**10**
Fifita	12	12	12	12	–	12	12	12	–	12	12	**9**
Medlicott	–	–	s	–	12	–	s	s	12	–	–	**5**
Briggs	10	10	10	–	10	10	10	10	–	10	10	**9**
Wright (co capt.)	9	9	9	10	9	9	–	9	10	9	9	**10**
Iosua	s	s	s	9	–	s	9	s	9	–	–	**8**
Phillips	–	–	–	s	–	–	s	–	s	s	s	**5**
Toumohuni	8	s	s	s	s	6	6	6	6	6	6	**11**
Kakala	s	8	8	8	8	8	8	8	8	8	8	**11**
Joyce	7	7	7	7	7	7	7	7	7	7	7	**11**
Lavaka	6	6	s	6	6	–	–	s	s	s	s	**9**
Savelio	s	–	–	–	–	–	–	–	–	–	–	**1**
P. Moli	–	s	6	–	–	s	s	s	s	–	–	**6**
Uhi	–	–	–	–	–	–	s	–	–	–	–	**1**
Amato	5	4	–	4	4	4	4	4	4	4	4	**10**
Van Zyl	4	–	4	s	s	s	–	–	–	s	s	**7**
Ahokovi	–	5	5	5	5	5	5	5	5	5	5	**10**
Hala'ufia	3	3	3	–	3	–	3	3	–	3	–	**7**
Fakatava (co capt.)	1	1	1	1	1	1	1	1	3	1	3	**11**
Toia	s	–	–	–	–	–	–	–	–	–	–	**1**
Casey	s	s	–	s	s	3	s	s	s	s	s	**10**
Taelega	–	s	s	s	–	s	s	s	1	–	1	**8**
Dale	s	s	s	3	s	s	s	s	s	s	s	**11**
Anderson	2	2	2	2	2	2	2	2	2	2	2	**11**
Faavae	–	–	s	s	s	s	–	–	s	s	s	**7**

SOUTH CANTERBURY TEAM RECORD 2023

Played 11 Won 10 Lost 1 Points for 436 Points against 294

Date	Opponent	Location	Score	Tries	Con	PG	DG	Referee
July 19	Wellington (RS) *	Lower Hutt	21–67	Kakala (2), Fifita	Briggs (3)			Dan Waenga
August 12	Horowhenua Kapiti	Waimate	48–14	McKay (2), Simote, Fifita, Buliruarua, Kakala, Joyce, Taelega	Briggs (4)			Dan Moore
August 19	King Country	Taupo	45–21	Matakaiongo (3), Kakala, Ahokovi, Saunders, McKay	Wright (5)			Ben Woolerton
August 26	Buller	Geraldine	56–0	Folau (2), Kakala (2), Fifita, C. Moli, Lavaka, Simote	Wright (8)			George Haswell
September 2	North Otago (HS)	Oamaru	26–22	Kakala (2), Folau, Buliruarua	Wright (3)			Fraser Hannon
September 9	West Coast	Fairlie	39–26	Kakala (3), C. Moli (2), Fifita, Leatigaga,	Briggs, Wright			Dan Moore
September 16	Thames Valley	Whangamata	36–31	McKay, Toumohuni, Leatigaga, Kakala, Ahokovi	Briggs (4)	Briggs		Todd Petrie
September 23	Mid Canterbury (HS)	Christchurch	50–35	Leatigaga (3), Amato (2), Wright, Toumohuni, Kakala	Briggs (5)			George Haswell
September 30	Poverty Bay	Patutahi	41–31	Simote (3), C. Moli, Kakala, Dale	Wright (4)	Wright		Tipene Cottrell
October 7	Ngati Porou East Coast (MC sf)	Pleasant Point	34–17	Simote (2), Anderson, Kakala	Briggs (4)	Briggs (2)		Nick Hogan
October 14	Whanganui (MC f)	Temuka	40–30	Leatigaga (2), Toumohunui, Wright, Lavaka	Briggs (3)	Briggs (3)		Fraser Hannon

* Non-Heartland Championship match (HS) Hanan Shield

South Canterbury's home match against Mid Canterbury was played at Christchurch (see Happenings).

SOUTHLAND

2023 Status: Bunnings NPC
Founded 1887. Affiliated 1894
President: L.M. (Leicester) Rutledge
Chairman: M.D. (Murray) Brown
General Manager: S. (Steve) Mitchell
Coaches: D.G. (David) Hall, J.W.R. (James) Wilson
Assistant coach: D.E. (Daryl) Thompson
Main ground: Rugby Park Stadium, Invercargill
Capacity: 20,200
Colours: Maroon

RECORDS

Most appearances	143	*Jason Rutledge,* 2000–2020
Most points	976	*Simon Culhane, 1988–98*
Most tries	46	*Bruce Pascoe, 1983–89*
Most points in a season	194	*Simon Culhane, 1994*
Most tries in a season	13	*Simon Forrest, 1992*
Most conversions in a season	38	*Simon Culhane, 1997*
Most penalty goals in a season	41	*Eion Crossan, 1989*
Most dropped goals in a season	10	*Brian McKechnie, 1977*
Most points in a match	37	*Simon Culhane v Manawatu, 1994*
Most tries in a match	5	*Simon Forrest v Poverty Bay, 1992*
Most conversions in a match	11	*Simon Culhane v Malborough, 1997*
Most penalty goals in a match	8	*Simon Culhane v Manawatu, 1994*
Highest team score	92	*v Marlborough, 1997*
Record victory (points ahead)	74	*79–5 v Poverty Bay, 1992*
Highest score conceded	95	*v Waikato, 1998*
Record defeat (points behind)	88	*7–95 v Waikato, 1998*

Southland struggled again in 2023, with a solitary win and a draw in their ten matches to finish bottom of the Premiership. Injuries meant players in key positions were in and out of the side which prevented continuity of selection, combination and form, and there was an element of inexperience with an eye on selecting players for the future.

The Stags played well against Waikato and Bay of Plenty but were not able to land the winning score in either game. The draw against Northland was probably a fair result in an uninspiring match but they saved their best for last with a dominant second half against Manawatu to win 37–12.

Regulars missing from last year were Charles Alaimalo (overseas), Solomon Alaimalo (Canterbury), Caleb Aperahama (overseas), Matt James (overseas), Paula Latu (injured), Arese Poliko (Taranaki), Robbie Robinson (retired), Isaac Te Tamaki (overseas), and Viliami Tufui (Otago).

New players who arrived in with previous provincial experience were Jonah Aoina (Otago), Danny Drake (North Harbour), Noah Foster (Tasman), Gabriel Hamer-Webb (England U20/Bath), Dan Hollinshead (Bay of Plenty), Connor McLeod (Otago/Hawke's Bay), Dylan Nel (West Coast/Canterbury/Otago) and Ben Strang (Manawatu).

Michael Manson's six tries in six games underlined what a quality wing he is, and it was a blow that injury ended his season, while on the other wing Viliami Fine displayed powerful running and defended well.

Matt Whaanga had some fine games at both centre and second-five and Tevita Latu improved as the season progressed. At first-five, Marty Banks did not look the player of two years ago while at halfback Jay Renton was steady, but Connor McLeod looked more influential with his running game.

Southland had a youthful loose forward trio in Hayden Michaels (21 years of age), Blair Ryall (21) and Leroy Ferguson (22) who all should reap the benefit of this experience in the future. Ryall was outstanding, earning the Southland player of the year award. The very experienced Dylan Nel was an accomplished No 8 and his season ending early due to injury was another blow.

Josh Bekhuis led the team well, won his share of lineout ball and was a tireless worker around the field. Fellow lock Mike McKee also worked hard in the tight and passed 50 games during the season.

A large number of eight props were used during the season. First choice loosehead Joe Walsh's season ended prematurely with injury while Morgan Mitchell was invaluable at tighthead. After Southland's campaign ended, Mitchell was signed by Wellington as a loan player for their semi-final. New Zealand Under 20 hooker Jack Taylor looked a very good prospect in his debut season, appearing in all ten games, including starts in eight of them.

Higher honours went to

New Zealand:	E. De Groot
New Zealand Under 20:	H. Fahey, J. Taylor
New Zealand Sevens:	A.P. Nicole

INDIVIDUAL SCORING

	Tries	*Con*	*PG*	*DG*	*Points*		*Tries*	*Con*	*PG*	*DG*	*Points*
Hollinshead	–	9	5	–	33	Tupou Ta'eiloa	1	–	–	–	5
Manson	6	–	–	–	30	Ferguson	1	–	–	–	5
Banks	–	3	5	–	21	McKee	1	–	–	–	5
Dyer	–	3	4	–	18	Souchon	1	–	–	–	5
Latu	3	–	–	–	15	Drake	1	–	–	–	5
Renton	3	–	–	–	15						
Fine	2	–	–	–	10	***Totals***	**25**	**15**	**14**	**0**	**197**
Hamer-Webb	2	–	–	–	10						
Gregory	2	–	–	–	10	*Opposition scored*	*45**	*24*	*6*	*0*	*293*
Whaanga	2	–	–	–	10						

** includes one penalty try (7 points)*

SOUTHLAND REPRESENTATIVES 2023

Name	Club	Date of birth	Height	Weight	For Union Debut	Games	Points
J.T. (Jonah) Aoina	Woodlands	25-02-96	1.83	121	2023	7	0
Marty Banks	–	19-09-89	1.91	96	2021	21	148
J.J.G. (Josh) Bekhuis	Star	26-04-86	2.01	116	2006	134	55
J.H. (Jacob) Coghlan	ENC Barbarians	29-09-96	1.88	104	2020	13	0
D.J. (Danny) Drake	Northcote[1]	25-03-95	1.98	113	2023	7	5
G.I. (Greg) Dyer	Pirates OB	28-03-95	1.78	90	2016	36	62
H.J. (Hunter) Fahey	Dunedin[2]	14-05-03	1.89	118	2023	6	0
L.S. (Leroy) Ferguson	ENC Barbarians	03-08-01	1.84	97	2023	7	5
V.A.L.H.L. (Viliami) Fine	Woodlands	01-12-97	1.85	105	2022	20	25
N.W.S. (Noah) Foster	University[3]	17-08-99	1.80	95	2023	6	0
S.J. (Scott) Gregory	Marist	07-01-99	1.85	100	2022	13	10
G.M. (Gabriel) Hamer-Webb	overseas	07-11-00	1.83	95	2023	8	10
Q.J. (Quinn) Harrison-Jones	Marist	05-10-98	1.81	123	2022	13	5
D.C. (Dan) Hollinshead	overseas	07-06-95	1.83	95	2023	8	33
L.O. (Liam) Howley	Woodlands	14-01-96	1.78	86	2015	26	10
G.W. (Grayson) Knapp	Star	11-12-95	1.94	112	2021	17	0
T.H.M. (Tevita) Latu	Marist	15-12-98	1.83	108	2020	17	25
M.S.J. (Michael) Manson	Blues	05-07-01	1.81	87	2022	11	45
M.J.F. (Michael) McKee	ENC Barbarians	12-08-93	1.98	116	2015	51	10
C.M. (Connor) McLeod	overseas[4]	29-06-97	1.74	75	2023	4	0
H.G. (Hayden) Michaels	Kaikorai[2]	03-01-02	1.86	103	2021	16	0
M.D. (Morgan) Mitchell	overseas	20-07-93	1.80	122	2014	67	30
D.M. (Dylan) Nel	overseas	27-11-92	1.87	111	2023	3	0
J.W. (Jacob) Payne	Blues	08-08-00	1.76	105	2021	13	5
J.L. (Jay) Renton	Blues	16-03-98	1.79	84	2017	41	20
B.L. (Blair) Ryall	Woodlands	26-10-01	1.94	108	2022	15	5
J.M. (Jack) Sexton	Lincoln University[5]	17-05-01	1.89	110	2023	3	0
A.J. (Angus) Simmers	ENC Barbarians	07-12-99	1.84	95	2023	2	0
Shneil Singh	Fraser Tech[6]	02-02-97	1.97	107	2023	7	0
N.P. (Nic) Souchon	overseas	13-08-97	1.82	100	2023	5	5
S.D.G. (Shaun) Stodart	Marist	19-03-96	1.92	124	2016	30	0
B.M. (Ben) Strang	overseas	23-12-01	1.81	100	2023	4	0
Kaisei Tamura	Pirates OB	15-12-99	1.71	78	2023	2	0
J.J.K. (Jack) Taylor	Southern[2]	25-06-03	1.81	106	2023	10	0
H.T. (Hamdahn) Tuipulotu	overseas	21-03-00	1.89	118	2023	3	0
Semisi Tupou Ta'eiloa	Kaikorai[2]	25-11-03	1.85	112	2023	9	5
R.FA. (Rory) Van Vugt	Woodlands	08-10-97	1.87	93	2018	40	30
J.D. (Jahvis) Wallace	ENC Barbarians	22-09-96	1.72	80	2016	16	5
J.S. (Joseph) Walsh	Woodlands	23-07-93	1.90	121	2016	65	10
M.A. (Matt) Whaanga	Taieri[2]	25-05-97	1.89	103	2021	25	30

1 North Harbour RU 2 Otago RU 3 Auckland RU
4 Loaned by Hawke's Bay RU 5 Loaned by Canterbury RU 6 Waikato RU

SOUTHLAND 2023	Waikato	Northland	Wellington	Otago	Auckland	Counties Manukau	Canterbury	Hawkes Bay	Bay of Plenty	Manawatu	TOTALS
Van Vugt	15	–	15	–	–	–	s	15	15	15	**6**
Fine	14	s	14	14	14	14	13	14	14	14	**10**
Manson	11	11	–	11	11	11	11	–	–	–	**6**
Hamer-Webb	–	14	11	15	–	15	15	11	11	11	**8**
Latu	–	–	s	s	12	12	12	12	s	13	**8**
Whaanga	13	12	12	13	13	13	–	–	12	12	**8**
Foster	s	13	13	–	s	s	14	–	–	–	**6**
Gregory	12	15	–	12	–	–	–	13	13	s	**6**
Simmers	–	–	–	–	s	–	–	s	–	–	**2**
Dyer	10	s	10	–	15	s	s	10	–	–	**7**
Banks	s	10	–	s	–	–	–	–	10	10	**5**
Hollinshead	–	–	s	10	10	10	10	s	s	s	**8**
Renton	9	9	9	9	9	s	–	–	9	9	**8**
Howley	s	–	–	–	–	–	–	–	–	–	**1**
Tamura	–	s	s	–	–	–	–	–	–	–	**2**
Wallace	–	–	–	s	–	–	s	s	s	s	**5**
McLeod	–	–	–	–	s	9	9	9	–	–	**4**
Nel	8	8	8	–	–	–	–	–	–	–	**3**
Tupou Ta'eiloa	–	s	s	s	8	s	s	s	s	s	**9**
Michaels	7	7	–	6	7	7	s	6	7	–	**8**
Ryall	6	6	6	8	6	8	8	8	s	6	**10**
Ferguson	s	–	7	7	–	s	7	7	–	7	**7**
Knapp	–	–	s	–	–	–	–	–	–	–	**1**
Coghlan	–	–	–	–	s	–	–	–	8	8	**3**
Bekhuis (capt)	5	5	5	5	5	5	–	5	5	5	**9**
Drake	4	4	–	–	4	–	5	s	4	s	**7**
Singh	s	s	4	s	–	6	6	–	6	–	**7**
McKee	–	–	–	4	s	4	4	4	–	4	**6**
Mitchell	3	3	3	3	–	–	3	3	s	3	**8**
Walsh	1	1	1	1	–	1	–	–	–	–	**5**
Aoina	s	s	s	s	s	3	1	–	–	–	**7**
Harrison-Jones	s	s	s	s	3	–	–	s	3	–	**7**
Stodart	–	–	–	–	1	–	–	–	–	–	**1**
Fahey	–	–	–	–	s	s	s	1	s	s	**6**
Tuipulotu	–	–	–	–	–	s	s	–	–	s	**3**
Sexton	–	–	–	–	–	–	–	s	1	1	**3**
Payne	2	–	–	–	–	–	–	–	–	–	**1**
Taylor	s	2	2	2	2	2	s	2	2	2	**10**
Strang	–	s	s	s	–	s	–	–	–	–	**4**
Souchon	–	–	–	–	s	–	2	s	s	s	**5**

McKee captained v Canterbury

SOUTHLAND TEAM RECORD 2023

Played 10 Won 1 Drew 1 Lost 8 Points for 197 Points against 293

Date	*Opponent*	*Location*	*Score*	*Tries*	*Con*	*PG*	*DG*	*Referee*
August 6	Waikato	Invercargill	21–29	Manson, Fine	Dyer	Dyer (3)		Fraser Hannon
August 13	Northland	Invercargill	15–15 aet			Banks (4), Dyer		Marcus Playle
August 19	Wellington (RS)	Lower Hutt	17–39	Tupou Ta'eiloa, Ferguson, Hamer-Webb	Dyer			Ben O'Keeffe
August 26	Otago	Dunedin	21–31	Manson, Gregory, Whaanga	Hollinshead (3)			James Doleman
September 3	Auckland	Invercargill	13–41	Manson	Hollinshead	Hollinshead (2)		Jackson Henshaw
September 9	Counties Manukau	Pukekohe	29–39	Manson (3), McKee, Hamer-Webb	Hollinshead (2)			Mike Winter
September 17	Canterbury	Christchurch	14–29	Souchon, Drake	Hollinshead (2)			Fraser Hannon
September 23	Hawke's Bay	Invercargill	7–33	Latu	Dyer			Marcus Playle
September 27	Bay of Plenty	Invercargill	23–25	Renton, Fine, Latu	Hollinshead	Hollinshead (2)		Fraser Hannon
October 1	Manawatu	Palmerston North	37–12	Renton (2), Latu, Gregory, Whaanga	Banks (3)	Banks, Hollinshead		Stu Catley

TARANAKI

2023 Status: Bunnings NPC
Founded 1889. Original member 1892
President: C.D. (Cherry) Blyde
Chairman: D.J. (Daniel) Radcliffe
Chief executive officer: M.J. (Mike) Sandle
Coach: N.J. (Neil) Barnes
Assistant coaches: B.C. (Brad) Cooper, J.M.R.A. (Jarrad) Hoeata
Main ground: Yarrow Stadium, New Plymouth
Capacity: 3,000
Colours: Amber and black

RECORDS

Most appearances	222	*Ian Eliason, 1964–81*
Most points	1723	*Kieran Crowley, 1980–94*
Most tries	64	*Kieran Crowley, 1980–94*
Most points in a season	233	*Jamie Cameron, 1995*
Most tries in a season	13	*Charlie McAlister, 1985*
Most conversions in a season	49	*Kieran Crowley, 1983*
Most penalty goals in a season	39	*Jamie Cameron, 1995*
Most dropped goals in a season	11	*Ross Brown, 1964*
Most points in a match	34	*Jamie Cameron v Nelson Bays, 1995*
Most tries in a match	5	*George Loveridge v Whanganui, 1913*
		Dave Vesty v Thames Valley, 1971
		Mark Robinson v Southland, 1997
Most conversions in a match	13	*Kieran Crowley v East Coast, 1983*
Most penalty goals in a match	9	*Beauden Barrett v Bay of Plenty, 2011*
Highest team score	104	*v Nelson Bays, 1995*
Record victory (points ahead)	97	*97–0 v East Coast, 1983*
Highest score conceded	80	*v Otago, 1996*
Record defeat (points behind)	60	*16–76 v North Harbour, 1989*

The crowning of Taranaki as 2023 Bunnings NPC Champions was the icing on the cake for this union after an indifferent 2022 season. In a tense and thrilling final against Hawke's Bay, victory was sweet with the Bulls triumphing in front of their loyal and parochial supporters. They showed up in force in a welcome return to Yarrow Stadium, albeit at reduced capacity due to the rebuilding of the main stand.

A sellout crowd of 13,000 fans ensured the final was a great success with plenty of amber and black on display in the stands on a pleasant afternoon, proving that tribalism and passion for the NPC is still alive and kicking in some regions. Reminiscent of times past, it was a wonderful sight to see the masses storm onto the field at the end of the match to join the players in the celebrations of Taranaki's first NPC title win since 2014.

The catalyst for the team's success can largely be attributed to head coach Neil Barnes and the union for remaining loyal to many home-grown players who provided the nucleus of a strong core of talent in a largely settled squad. The team entered the season with a well-balanced roster of youth and experience and a clear intent and understanding around the style and brand of rugby they wanted to play. This, combined with good depth and few injuries, meant Barnes mostly had a full complement of front-line players to call on throughout the season.

Central to the team's philosophy was a real desire to make the province and their fans proud and this was evident every time the team took the field where several willing and committed performances were delivered. Wins in the first four matches over Counties-Manukau (home) and Northland, Manawatu, and Waikato (all away), offered encouraging signs.

The only setbacks during the regular season were the narrow losses to Bay of Plenty, Canterbury, and Tasman in successive weeks. Faith was quickly restored however, with good wins over Otago, Auckland, and North Harbour, all coming at the right time and giving the team good momentum and confidence going into the playoffs. A cornerstone of the team's success was undoubtedly its forward pack who out-scrummed, out-mauled, and outplayed virtually all their opponents. This, combined with ruthless and effective breakdown work, ensured that in the tight, Taranaki was rarely bettered. In particular, the scrum was a real attacking weapon.

Of those who were prominent, regular captain Kaylum Boshier led admirably from the front and was well supported by Bradley Slater, Tom Florence and Pita-Gus Sowakula who all delivered consistently good efforts. Front-rowers, Michael Bent, Jared Proffit, Reuben O'Neill and Ricky Riccitelli proved to be a tough quartet for most of their opponents.

NPC stalwart Tom Franklin quickly made himself at home in a Taranaki jersey, calling on all his experience in filling the locking stocks when Heyden Bedwell-Curtis and Jesse Parete were unavailable. All Blacks Josh Lord was a welcome addition for the business end of the season with his only appearances coming in the playoffs. Fita Sa was a new signing at lock and, at 20 years of age and standing 2.03m and weighing 125kgs, will be one to keep an eye on.

The backline profited from plenty of front-foot ball which set up the perfect platform for the team's deadly outside backs to unleash their pace and skills in the wider channels where some spectacular tries were scored from set moves and. on occasion, broken play.Jacob Ratumaitavuki-Kneepkens was the team's top try-scorer. He showed plenty of individual skills whether from fullback or wing, producing several great finishes. Kini Naholo also chimed in on occasion with his trademark powerful, destructive running proving a nightmare for defenders. Vereniki Tikoisolomone had another quiet season but otherwise gave a good account of himself in his appearances.

Meihana Grindlay had a good second season in the midfield, proving reliable and consistent and looking assured when working in tandem with the solid and dependable Daniel Rona. Matty McKenzie once again showed his value as a great utility option.

The young rookie pairing of halfback Adam Lennox and first-five Josh Jacomb was the real success story. Both were constant threats with ball in hand, showing quick acceleration off the mark, an eye for a gap and a sense for the big occasion, all beyond their years. The faith the selectors showed in elevating them to that of the team's starting pairing by the middle of the season was certainly justified and repaid. It would be wonderful if this pairing can be kept together.

Stephen Perofeta and Jayson Potroz each contributed valuable experience to the campaign by bringing a composure and steadiness to proceedings, often late in games which proved vital when calm heads were called for. Their role as the team's game drivers and their ability to read different situations and make good decisions proved invaluable in closing out some of the closer contests.

Overall, the season will be looked upon as a resounding success for both the union and the province and for all of those associated with the team. It is also pleasing to see that, in the professional age, a province outside of the traditional main centres and rugby franchises is still capable of winning the top silverware in New Zealand's premier domestic rugby competition.

Higher honours went to:

New Zealand:	B. Barrett, J. Barrett, S. Barrett, J. Lord, T. Vaa'i
All Blacks XV:	S. Perofeta, R. Riccitelli, P. Sowakula
New Zealand Sevens:	R. Featherstone, L. Ormond

TARANAKI REPRESENTATIVES 2023

Name	Club	Date of birth	Height	Weight	For Union Debut	Games	Points
H.K. (Heiden) Bedwell-Curtis	overseas	25-06-91	1.94	103	2012	17	5
M.R. (Michael) Bent	Southern	25-04-86	1.86	120	2009	69	10
L.G. (Liam) Blyde	Clifton	26-09-97	1.81	87	2018	28	25
K.L. (Kaylum) Boshier	NP OB	09-04-99	1.87	104	2018	44	45
D.I.M. (Donald) Brighouse	NP OB	29-03-93	1.81	132	2019	43	5
L.E. (Logan) Crowley	Coastal	04-04-96	1.74	79	2017	40	20
H.T. (Hemopo) Cunningham	Stratford-Eltham	11-08-01	1.87	100	2021	15	0
T.H.T. (Tom) Florence	overseas	20-05-98	1.89	106	2017	53	30
T.S.G. (Tom) Franklin	overseas	08-11-90	1.98	113	2023	7	5
M.J. (Meihana) Grindlay	Southern	07-04-91	1.88	107	2021	20	10
J.D. (Josh) Jacomb	Inglewood Utd	23-06-01	1.79	90	2021	13	76
B.A. (Brad) Kooman	Tukapa	01-12-99	1.87	82	2023	1	0
A.G. (Adam) Lennox	Stratford-Eltham	04-11-02	1.78	82	2022	19	25
M.P.J. (Michael) Loft	NP OB	11-11-99	1.88	101	2022	14	0
J.M.J. (Josh) Lord	Coastal	17-01-01	2.03	113	2019	22	0
M.R. (Matthew) McKenzie	Clifton	08-04-97	1.81	94	2019	20	16
K.N. (Kini) Naholo	Clifton	16-04-99	1.78	98	2018	32	95
B.K. (Brayton) Northcott-Hill	NP OB	21-03-98	1.86	94	2018	21	17
M.W. (Mitchell) O'Neill	NP OB	04-04-97	1.83	113	2022	14	0
R.G. (Reuben) O'Neill	NP OB	17-02-95	1.81	116	2015	62	10
J.W.Z. (Jesse) Parete	overseas	20-04-93	1.93	115	2014	30	10
Stephen Perofeta	Clifton	12-03-97	1.82	91	2016	63	340
Arese Poliko	Spotswood United	23-01-01	1.87	112	2023	3	0
J.P. (Jayson) Potroz	overseas	26-11-91	1.83	90	2018	47	177
J.P. (Jared) Proffit	Clifton	14-09-93	1.83	112	2015	75	15
W.G. (Willem) Ratu	Stratford-Eltham	28-03-01	1.80	95	2023	2	0
J.W.J. (Jacob) Ratumaitavuki-Kneepkens	Tukapa	03-08-01	1.86	93	2020	38	85
J.R. (Ricky) Riccitelli	Tukapa	03-02-95	1.81	110	2017	70	65
D.K. (Daniel) Rona	Clifton	10-04-00	1.87	91	2020	27	25
F.H.R.J.M. (Fitifiti) Sa	Shirley[1]	04-04-03	2.03	125	2023	7	0
M.L.T. (Millennium) Sanerivi	overseas	06-01-95	1.81	112	2021	19	0
B.A. (Bradley) Slater	NP OB	23-09-98	1.86	106	2017	51	35
P.G.N. (Pita Gus) Sowakula	Spotswood United	10-10-94	1.93	117	2017	59	35
K.L. (Kyle) Stewart	overseas	10-03-92	1.91	119	2018	37	0
V.W. (Vereniki) Tikoisolomone	overseas	24-11-98	1.82	90	2021	25	45
T.T. (Teihorangi) Walden	overseas	25-05-93	1.85	95	2018	49	40

1 Canterbury RU

INDIVIDUAL SCORING

	Tries	Con	PG	DG	Points		Tries	Con	PG	DG	Points
Jacomb	3	16	8	-	71	Slater	2	-	-	-	10
Perofeta	3	10	6	-	53	Florence	2	-	-	-	10
Ratumaitavuki-Kneepkens	6	-	-	-	30	Proffit	1	-	-	-	5
Potroz	1	6	3	-	26	Parete	1	-	-	-	5
Lennox	5	-	-	-	25	Bent	1	-	-	-	5
Boshier	4	-	-	-	20	Sowakula	1	-	-	-	5
Naholo	4	-	-	-	20	Crowley	1	-	-	-	5
Riccitelli	4	-	-	-	20	Franklin	1	-	-	-	5
Tikoisolomone	3	-	-	-	15	Rona	1	-	-	-	5
Penalty Try	2	-	-	-	14						
Walden	2	-	-	-	10	***Totals***	***52***	***32***	***17***	***0***	***379***
McKenzie	2	-	-	-	10						
Grindlay	2	-	-	-	10	*Opposition scored*	*33*	*24*	*19*	*0*	*270*

TARANAKI 2023	Counties Manukau	Northland	Manawatu	Waikato	Bay of Plenty	Canterbury	Tasman	Otago	Auckland	North Harbour	Tasman (qf)	Canterbury (sf)	Hawke's Bay (f)	**TOTALS**
Perofeta	15	15	-	15	10	15	15	10	-	-	-	15	15	**9**
Ratu	-	s	-	-	-	-	-	-	-	14	-	-	-	**2**
Ratumaitavuki-Kneepkens	14	14	14	14	14	14	14	15	15	15	15	14	14	**13**
Naholo	11	-	11	11	11	11	11	11	11	11	11	11	11	**12**
Tikoisolomone	s	11	s	-	-	s	s	14	14	-	14	s	s	**10**
Kooman	-	-	-	-	-	-	-	-	-	s	-	-	-	**1**
Grindlay	13	13	13	13	13	-	s	12	13	13	13	13	13	**12**
Walden	12	12	12	12	12	12	12	-	s	-	-	-	-	**8**
McKenzie	s	s	15	s	15	s	-	-	-	12	12	-	-	**8**
Rona	-	-	-	s	s	13	13	13	-	-	s	12	12	**8**
Northcott-Hill	-	-	-	-	-	-	-	s	12	-	-	-	-	**2**
Potroz	10	-	10	10	s	10	10	-	10	s	s	s	s	**11**
Jacomb	-	10	s	-	-	-	-	s	s	10	10	10	10	**8**
Crowley	9	9	9	9	-	-	9	9	9	-	-	-	s	**8**
Lennox	s	s	s	s	9	9	s	s	s	9	9	9	9	**13**
Blyde	-	-	-	-	s	s	-	-	-	s	s	s	-	**5**
Boshier (capt.)	8	6	6	6	8	8	8	8	-	8	-	8	8	**11**
Sowakula	-	8	8	8	6	6	6	6	8	6	6	6	6	**12**
Florence	7	7	s	7	7	7	7	7	7	-	7	7	7	**12**
Cunningham	6	5	5	5	5	-	-	-	-	-	-	-	-	**5**
Poliko	s	s	7	-	-	-	-	-	-	-	-	-	-	**3**
Sa	-	-	-	s	-	s	5	s	s	s	s	-	-	**7**
Bedwell-Curtis	5	-	-	-	-	s	s	-	5	5	s	s	s	**8**
Parete	4	4	4	4	4	4	4	4	-	-	-	-	-	**8**
Sanerivi	s	s	s	s	s	-	2	-	s	s	-	-	-	**8**
Franklin	-	-	-	-	s	5	-	5	-	4	4	4	4	**7**
Loft	-	-	-	-	-	-	s	s	4	7	8	s	s	**7**
Lord	-	-	-	-	-	-	-	-	-	-	5	5	5	**3**
Bent	3	-	-	3	s	s	s	s	s	3	s	s	s	**11**
Proffit	1	1	1	1	1	1	1	1	1	1	1	1	1	**13**
Stewart	s	s	s	s	-	-	-	-	-	-	-	-	-	**4**
M. O'Neill	s	s	s	-	-	-	-	-	-	s	-	-	-	**4**
R. O'Neill	-	3	3	s	3	3	3	3	3	-	3	3	3	**11**
Brighouse	-	-	-	-	s	s	s	s	s	s	s	s	s	**9**
Slater	2	s	s	2	s	2	-	2	6	2	2	2	2	**12**
Riccitelli	s	2	2	s	2	s	s	s	2	s	s	s	s	**13**

Crowley captained v Auckland; Slater captained v Tasman in the quarter-final

TARANAKI TEAM RECORD 2023

Played 13 Won 10 Lost 3 Points for 379 Points against 270

Date	Opponent	Location	Score	Tries	Con	PG	DG	Referee
August 4	Counties Manukau	New Plymouth	37-29	Boshier (2), Walden, Naholo, Ratumaitavuki-Kneepkens, Tikoisolomone	Perofeta (2)	Perofeta		Paul Williams
August 9	Northland	Whangarei	28-13	Boshier (2), Perofeta, Proffit	Jacomb (4)			Angus Mabey
August 13	Manawatu	Palmerston North	26-17	Parete, McKenzie, Grindlay, Penalty Try	Potroz (2)			Jono Bredin
August 20	Waikato	Hamilton	29-17	Naholo (2), Lennox (2), McKenzie	Potroz (2)			Dan Waenga
August 26	Bay of Plenty	New Plymouth	26-29	Perofeta, Naholo, Walden, Bent	Perofeta (3)			Stu Curran
September 2	Canterbury	Rangiora	28-29	Ratumaitavuki-Kneepkens, Riccitelli, Tikoisolomone, Perofeta	Potroz	Potroz (2)		Nick Briant
September 10	Tasman	New Plymouth	18-29	Potroz, Sowakula	Perofeta	Perofeta (2)		Angus Mabey
September 16	Otago	Dunedin	36-17	Crowley, Slater, Lennox, Ratumaitavuki-Kneepkens, Jacomb	Perofeta (4)	Perofeta		Dan Waenga
September 23	Auckland	New Plymouth	18-16	Riccitelli, Florence	Potroz	Potroz, Jacomb		Nick Briant
September 30	North Harbour	New Plymouth	54-21	Ratumaitavuki-Kneepkens (2), Jacomb (2), Riccitelli (2), Franklin, Slater	Jacomb (7)			Mike Winter
October 7	Tasman (qf)	New Plymouth	34-18	Tikoisolomone, Ratumaitavuki-Kneepkens, Florence, Penalty Try	Jacomb (3)	Jacomb (2)		Stu Curran
October 13	Canterbury (sf)	New Plymouth	23-16	Lennox		Jacomb (4), Perofeta (2)		Stu Curran
October 21	Hawke's Bay (f)	New Plymouth	22-19	Grindlay, Rona, Lennox	Jacomb (2)	Jacomb		Angus Mabey

TASMAN

2023 Status: Bunnings NPC
Founded and **affiliated 2005**
President: A.D. (Tony) Woodall
Chairman: B.A. (Baz) Henare
Chief executive officer: L.E. (Lyndon) Bray
Co-coaches: G.N. (Gray) Cornelius, D.M. (Dan) Perrin
Assistant coach: H.J. (Hoani) MacDonald
Main ground: Trafalgar Park, Nelson; Lansdowne Park, Blenheim
Capacity: 18,000
Colours: Navy blue and red

tasman rugbyunion

RECORDS

Most appearances	118	*Quentin MacDonald, 2008–23*
Most points	628	*Marty Banks, 2013–2016*
Most tries	25	*Robbie Malneek, 2006–2017*
Most points in a season	173	*Marty Banks, 2014*
Most tries in a season	10	*Peter Playford, 2006*
Most conversions in a season	37	*Marty Banks, 2014*
Most penalty goals in a season	33	*Marty Banks, 2016*
Most dropped goals in a season	1	*by five players*
Most points in a match	28	*Marty Banks v Northland, 2013*
Most tries in a match	4	*Peter Playford v Canada A, 2006*
		Peter Playford v Northland, 2006
Most conversions in a match	7	*Aaron Kimura v Northland, 2006*
		Marty Banks v Manawatu, 2013
Most penalty goals in a match	8	*Tom Marshall v Bay of Plenty, 2010*
Most dropped goals in a match	1	*by five players*
Highest team score	64	*v Waikato, 2013*
		v Manawatu, 2019
Record victory (points ahead)	61	*64-3 v Manawatu, 2019*
Highest score conceded	52	*v Counties Manukau, 2017*
		v Canterbury, 2022
Record defeat (points behind)	42	*7–49 v Auckland, 2007*

This was not to be the Tasman Mako's season, but they did at least return to playoffs rugby after the difficulties of 2022.

But there will be frustration at the topsy-turvy nature of their results, starting with two wins – the first stanza against Auckland was top shelf — then two losses, then four wins, before dropping their last three matches. They qualified seventh for the playoffs, and will feel that fourth or fifth was more than possible.

Again, a plethora of injuries and international commitments did not help the Mako, Ethan Blackadder and David Havili the only All Blacks to appear and, even then, just to prove fitness before getting the call-up to France.

Gains from 2022 included Wil Gualter (Canterbury), Feleti Kaitu'u (Australia), the hooker turning out to be very good value and taking rookie of the year, Tom Marshall (Japan), Tim O'Malley (Italy) and Paripari Parkinson (back from injury).

Losses included Fletcher Anderson (injured), Te Ahiwaru Cirikidaveta (Fiji, RWC), Noah Foster (Southland), Sione Havili (Tonga, RWC), Willy Havili (Tonga, RWC), Andrew Makalio (Japan), Sam Moli (Tonga, RWC), Viliami Napa'a (injured), Mahonri Ngakuru (North Harbour), Fetuli Paea (Italy), Campbell Parata (injured), Sevu Reece (injured), Isaac Salmon (Hawke's Bay), Braden Stewart (injured), Isi Tu'ungafasi (Hawke's Bay) and Te Rangitira Waitokia (Manawatu).

In general, the Mako defence was tight, at least until their last three games, but their attack, even with serious X-factor in their backs, could never consistently hit top gear, only once topping 30 points, in the blowout of the Turbos.

The 32–5 loss to Northland in Whangarei was described by captain Quin Strange as "horrific," while untimely errors were costly in the Ranfurly Shield challenge. The Mako got out of jail in extra time against North Harbour, while the 29–18 win over Taranaki in New Plymouth was probably the best of the season. The defeat to the Steamers was a bad look, and then the quarter-final against Taranaki possibly swung on a contentious yellow card call against Alex Nankivell, close to the best No 12 in the NPC, and a penalty try.

After passing 50 games, Tom Marshall hit injury, so Macca Springer, who ran in five tries, was fielded five times at the back. Timoci Tavatavanawai, strangely unwanted by Fiji, was one of five to start in all 11 games and he scored six tries, always proving tough to tackle.

Levi Aumua had a good campaign at centre, though the Mako could not always get him enough ball. Nankivell was very consistent one in.

Mitch Hunt never returned from injury until the last two games, so Taine Robinson filled in ably, though his goalkicking was not always metronomic. Loan player Shun Miyake enjoyed his first start against Manawatu, scoring 18 points. Halfback Noah Hotham scored a hat-trick in that game. He was mostly good, if not always dominant. Louie Chapman was an effective back-up.

Hugh Renton's progress was again stymied by injury at No 8, but Anton Segner carried a hefty load and did it so well he was named player of the year, while Max Hicks hustled and won his ball on the blindside. Seta Baker, one of 11 new Mako, showed real promise either off the bench or in the No 7 jersey. Strange was a model of consistency at lock, but Paripari Parkinson had just five outings.

Atu Moli's injury woes continued, meaning Sam Matenga and Luca Inch shared the tighthead duties. Ryan Coxon and new Crusader Kershawl Sykes-Martin had the loosehead covered.

Quentin MacDonald, who has now played well over half the Mako games since their 2006 inception, scored four tries from lineout drives and acted as a useful foil for Kaitu'u.

Higher honours went to:

New Zealand:	E. Blackadder, F. Christie, S. Frizell, W. Jordan, T. Lomax, L. Fainga'anuku
All Blacks XV:	A. Nankivell, D. Havili
New Zealand Under 20:	N. Hotham, M. Springer

TASMAN REPRESENTATIVES 2023

		Date of			For Union		
Name	Club	birth	Height	Weight	Debut	Games	Points
T. (Tomasi) Alosio	Renwick	26-01-92	1.85	92	2022	10	5
L.J.T. (Levi) Aumua	Kahurangi	09-10-94	1.85	108	2017	58	75
S.S.M.P. (Seta) Baker	Kahurangi	15-02-01	1.86	107	2023	7	5
E.J. (Ethan) Blackadder	Nelson	22-03-95	1.91	111	2016	46	40
L.J. (Louie) Chapman	Kahurangi	01-05-00	1.79	84	2020	34	0
R.C. (Ryan) Coxon	Nelson	30-09-97	1.83	118	2017	43	5

M. (Mike) Curry	Massey[1]	02-03-94	1.96	115	2018	13	0
A.W.D. (Angus) Fletcher	Kahurangi	21-06-00	1.96	107	2023	7	0
M.H. (Matt) Graham-Williams	Stoke	16-08-00	1.91	116	2021	8	0
J.B. (Jack) Gray	Kahurangi	07-03-00	1.86	92	2023	3	5
W.G. (Wil) Gualter	Central	05-06-01	1.86	95	2023	8	10
D.K. (David) Havili	Nelson	23-12-94	1.84	95	2014	65	154
M.J.T (Max) Hicks	Marist	15-09-99	1.99	112	2021	27	10
C.D. (Colm) Hogan	Stoke	14-01-97	1.87	100	2023	2	0
N.R.F (Noah) Hotham	Nelson	23-05-03	1.78	90	2021	23	50
M.J. (Mitch) Hunt	Stoke	19-06-95	1.79	88	2016	68	562
L.I. (Luca) Inch	Kahurangi	29-08-01	1.82	118	2021	21	0
A.T. (Feleti) Kaitu'u	Marist	30-12-94	1.81	105	2023	11	10
H.J. (Hunter) Leppien	Kahurangi	20-10-03	1.95	109	2023	1	0
Q.J.R.W.J (Quentin) MacDonald	Central	25-09-88	1.81	105	2008	118	100
T.G. (Tom) Marshall	Nelson	05-07-90	1.83	91	2010	52	124
S.I. (Samuel) Matenga	Kahurangi	08-05-98	1.86	116	2019	43	0
S. (Shun) Miyake	Marist-Albion[2]	28-12-01	1.72	90	2023	3	18
A. (Atu) Moli	Moutere	12-06-95	1.89	127	2019	15	0
L.H.A. (Monu) Moli	Moutere	19-08-02	1.82	105	2023	1	0
A.P. (Alex) Nankivell	Stoke	25-10-96	1.87	98	2015	81	65
T.P. (Tim) O'Malley	Waitohi	21-08-94	1.93	94	2016	49	92
P.P.M. (Paripari) Parkinson	Stoke	12-09-96	2.04	119	2016	44	5
H.T. (Hugh) Renton	Stoke	12-05-96	1.93	107	2020	30	0
T.J. (Taine) Robinson	Stoke	15-06-00	1.8	89	2021	18	92
A. (Anton) Segner	Nelson	24-07-01	1.92	108	2020	28	15
A.J. (Antonio) Shalfoon	Stoke	10-08-97	1.97	114	2021	15	0
T.J. (Tim) Sail	Kahurangi	21-05-98	1.9	105	2023	3	5
M.R. (Macca) Springer	Waimea Old Boys	29-03-03	1.89	95	2021	26	70
Q.J. (Quinten) Strange	Nelson	21-08-96	1.99	114	2016	69	40
K.J. (Kershawl) Sykes-Martin	Nelson	26-04-99	1.87	111	2020	18	0
T.T. (Timoci) Tavatavanawai	Central	14-02-98	1.75	111	2021	31	60
G.S. (Graham) Urquhart	Nelson	09-07-99	1.82	87	2023	1	0

1. Loaned by North Harbour RFU *2. Loaned by Canterbury RFU*

INDIVIDUAL SCORING

	Tries	*Con*	*PG*	*DG*	*Points*		*Tries*	*Con*	*PG*	*DG*	*Points*
Robinson	3	13	8	–	65	Segner	2	–	–	–	10
Tavatavanawai	6	–	–	–	30	Baker	1	–	–	–	5
Springer	5	–	–	–	25	Gray	1	–	–	–	5
MacDonald	4	–	–	–	20	Hicks	1	–	–	–	5
Miyake	1	5	1	–	18	Sail	1	–	–	–	5
Aumua	3	–	–	–	15						
Hotham	3	–	–	–	15	***Totals***	***37***	***18***	***9***	***0***	***248***
Gualter	2	–	–	–	10						
Kaitu'u	2	–	–	–	10	*Opposition scored*	*33**	*21*	*11*	*0*	*240*
Nankivell	2	–	–	–	10						

** includes one penalty try (7 points)*

TASMAN 2023	Otago	Auckland	Northland	Wellington (RS)	North Harbour	Manawatu	Taranaki	Counties Manukau	Canterbury	Bay of Plenty	Taranaki (QF)	**Totals**
Marshall	15	–	–	15	10	–	–	–	–	–	–	**3**
Robinson	10	10	s	10	–	–	10	10	10	15	15	**9**
Alosio	–	15	15	–	–	s	–	s	s	s	s	**7**
Tavatavanawai	14	14	14	14	14	14	14	14	14	14	14	**11**
Springer	11	11	11	11	15	15	15	15	15	11	11	**11**
Gray	–	–	–	–	11	s	s	–	–	–	–	**3**
Hogan	–	–	–	–	–	–	–	–	–	s	s	**2**
Gualter	–	s	s	s	13	11	11	11	11	–	–	**8**
Aumua	13	13	13	13	s	13	13	13	13	13	13	**11**
Nankivell	s	12	12	12	12	12	12	12	12	12	12	**11**
D. Havili	12	–	–	–	–	–	–	–	–	–	–	**1**
O'Malley	s	s	10	s	–	–	–	–	–	–	–	**4**
Hunt	–	–	–	–	–	–	–	–	–	10	10	**2**
Miyake	–	–	–	–	s	10	–	s	–	–	–	**3**
Hotham	s	9	9	9	s	9	9	9	9	9	9	**11**
Chapman	9	s	s	s	9	s	s	–	s	s	s	**10**
Urquhart	–	–	–	–	–	–	–	s	–	–	–	**1**
Renton	8	–	–	–	–	–	8	–	–	8	8	**4**
Blackadder	–	–	–	–	8	8	–	–	–	–	–	**2**
Fletcher	–	s	s	s	s	s	–	s	s	–	–	**7**
Baker	s	–	–	7	–	s	–	7	7	s	s	**7**
Segner	7	7	7	8	7	7	7	8	8	7	7	**11**
Hicks	6	6	6	6	6	6	6	6	6	6	6	**11**
Sail	s	8	8	–	–	–	–	–	–	–	–	**3**
Curry	–	–	4	–	–	5	s	5	–	s	s	**6**
Leppien	–	–	–	–	–	–	–	s	–	–	–	**1**
Shalfoon	–	s	–	4	s	–	–	–	s	5	5	**6**
Parkinson	5	5	–	–	5	–	5	–	5	–	–	**5**
Strange (capt)	4	4	5	5	4	4	4	4	4	4	4	**11**
Matenga	3	3	3	3	3	s	s	3	3	3	3	**11**
A. Moli	s	s	–	–	–	–	–	s	–	–	–	**3**
Coxon	s	1	1	s	1	1	s	1	s	s	s	**11**
Graham-Williams	–	s	–	–	s	s	–	s	–	–	–	**4**
Sykes-Martin	1	–	s	1	–	–	1	–	1	1	1	**7**
Inch	–	–	s	s	s	3	3	–	s	s	s	**8**
MacDonald	s	s	2	s	s	–	s	s	s	s	s	**10**
Kaitu'u	2	2	s	2	2	2	2	2	2	2	2	**11**
M. Moli	–	–	–	–	–	s	–	–	–	–	–	**1**

TASMAN TEAM RECORD 2023

Played 11 ***Won 6*** ***Lost 5*** ***Points for 248*** ***Points against 240***

Date	*Opponent*	*Location*	*Score*	*Tries*	*Con*	*PG*	*DG*	*Referee*
August 4	Otago	Nelson	27–15	Springer (2), Nankivell	Robinson (3)	Robinson (2)		Angus Mabey
August 12	Auckland	Blenheim	24–12	Aumua, Sail, Robinson, MacDonald	Robinson (2)			Stu Curran
August 19	Northland	Whangarei	5–32	MacDonald				Brendon Pickerill
August 23	Wellington (RS)	Wellington	0–7					James Doleman
August 27	North Harbour	Nelson	20–15 (ET)	Tavatavanawai (2), Kaitu'u, Springer				Dan Waenga
September 3	Manawatu	Nelson	58–19	Hotham (3), Segner, Kaitu'u, Springer, Miyake, Gualter, Gray	Miyake (5)	Miyake		Marcus Playle
September 10	Taranaki	New Plymouth	29–18	Aumua (2), Segner, Tavatavanawai	Robinson (3)	Robinson		Angus Mabey
September 17	Counties Manukau	Blenheim	27–17	Tavatavanawai, Robinson, Gualter, MacDonald, Baker	Robinson			Jackson Henshaw
September 23	Canterbury	Christchurch	28–30	Springer, Robinson, Tavatavanawai	Robinson (2)	Robinson (3)		Stu Curran
October 1	Bay of Plenty	Tauranga	12–41	Nankivell, MacDonald	Robinson			Jono Bredin
October 7	Taranaki (QF)	New Plymouth	18–34	Tavatavanawai, Hicks	Robinson	Robinson (2)		Stu Curran

THAMES VALLEY

2023 Status: Heartland Championship
Founded 1922. Affiliated 1922
President: R.M. (Ross) Cooper
Chairman: R.A. (Richard) Foster
Chief executive officer: S.L. (Scott) Penney (from January)
Co-Coaches: D.P. (David) Harrison, J.R. (Joe) Murray
Assistant coaches: L.E. (Leon) Holden, M.J. (Murray) Driver
Main ground: Paeroa Domain
Capacity: 3000
Colours: Gold and red

RECORDS

Highest attendance	7000	*Thames Valley v Auckland (Ranfurly Shield), 1989*
Most appearances	143	*B.C. Duggan, 1970–84*
Most points	665	*D.P. Harrison, 2004–15*
Most tries	42	*I.F. Campbell, 1981–94*
Most points in a season	130	*T. Doolan, 2021*
Most tries in a season	14	*I.F. Campbell, 1988*
Most conversions in a season	30	*D.B. McCallum, 1995*
Most penalty goals in a season	25	*J.R. Reynolds, 2011*
Most dropped goals in a season	4	*T.E. Shaw, 1962*
		R.W. Kemp, 1968
Most points in a match	27	*D.B. McCallum v East Coast, 1995*
		M. Griffin v King Country, 2003
Most tries in a match	4	*I.F. Campbell v North Otago, 1990*
		G.A. Ellis v North Otago, 1994
		G.W. McLiver v Marlborough, 1995
Most conversions in a match	8	*G.A. Ellis v West Coast, 1994*
		M.A. Handley v North Otago, 1994
Most penalty goals in a match	7	*D.P. Harrison v Mid Canterbury, 2009*
	7	*J.R. Reynolds v East Coast, 2011*
	7	*R.D. Crosland v Whanganui, 2019*
Highest team score	86	*v North Otago, 1994*
Record victory (points ahead)	79	*86–7 v North Otago, 1994*
Highest score conceded	113	*v Northland, 1997*
Record defeat (points behind)	99	*14–113 v Northland, 1997*

Coaches David Harrison and Joe Murray were presented with a major challenge when nine former representative players, who had played club rugby within the Valley during the 2023 season, were unavailable for the Swamp Foxes. To their credit, they overcame this setback and once again were able to produce one of the top four teams in the Heartland Championship. To support them, Leon Holden and Murray Driver came in as assistants to form a very experienced coaching group.

However, the going was not easy for Thames Valley and their biggest winning margin was only eight points over West Coast. The best and least impressive performances of the year were both against Whanganui in Whanganui. Thames Valley were easily the better team in the opening match of the Heartland Championship at Cook's Gardens but were completely outclassed at the same venue in the Meads' Cup semi–final. The 3–38 loss was Thames Valley's biggest defeat since 2016.

On the credit side, Thames Valley retained "The Game" trophy against West Coast and the Centurions Cup against King Country. Co–Captain, Sam McCahon and Harry Lafituanai, who both debuted for Thames Valley against East Coast in 2017, have now played fifty games for their province.

Thirty–six players were used during the season with 23 being new to first class rugby.

The inside back combination of Leroy Neels, Hendrix Beazley and McCahon started in all games with Neels having his best season so far, Beazley showing promise and McCahon again producing quality rugby. Declan Barnett, a former King Country and Bay of Plenty representative, was a real asset for the Swamp Foxes. He was greatly missed after being injured in the third game. Although he was closely marked Lafituanai , he was always dangerous on attack when he did have room to move.

The find of the year was Fletcher Morgan who had returned home to Waihi from Christchurch. He is a speedy wing and a capable fullback, as well as being an accurate left foot goal kicker. His 116 points in only eight games were key factors in Thames Valley's six victories, plus the narrow losses to South Canterbury and North Otago which were by five points and one point respectively. This is only the eighth time that a Thames Valley player has scored a century of points for his union in one season, and it was unfortunate that Morgan was called into a NZ Sevens Camp which clashed with the Meads Cup semi–final.

The other wing position was shared by Ethan Dromgool and Coel Kerr — two promising young players. Calum Wood made a very successful transition from wing to fullback by defending well and using his speed on attack.

Five different hookers were tried with Tyrell Kopua being the most promising. There is no doubt that the star front rower was the Hamilton Marist prop, Mosese Mafi. He was of great value to the forward pack and gained selection for the New Zealand Barbarians. Tui Paitai, and Brooklyn Toia also proved themselves to be worthy front row forwards. After a six–year gap, lock Tim Erceg returned to the Swamp Foxes where he became a key tight forward and enjoyed an excellent season. Co–Captain Cameron Dromgool interchanged between blindside flanker and lock, demonstrating his skills and durability in both positions. Loan players, Tayne Tupaea and Savelio Ropati are both strong and determined loose forwards who were well backed up by Richard Rosewarne and Guto Davies.

Leroy Neels (2) and Fletcher Morgan scored tries for the New Zealand Heartland team against the New Zealand Barbarians as did Mosese Mafi for the Barbarians. All three selections were well merited.

Higher honours went to:
New Zealand Heartland: F. Morgan, L. Neels

THAMES VALLEY REPRESENTATIVES 2023

Name	Club	For Union Debut	Games	Points
M.S. (Matt) Axtens	Mt Maunganui [2]	2019	17	15
J.M. (Joshua) Barker	Hauraki North	2023	1	0
D.G. (Declan) Barnett	overseas	2023	3	5
H.T.L. (Hendrix) Beazley	Paeroa	2023	9	3
R.M. (Ryan) Dafel	Hamilton Marist [3]	2023	1	0
S.A.J. (Shontayne) Dare-Johnson	College OB	2023	5	0
G.W. (Guto) Davies	Hauraki North	2023	9	5
C.M. (Cameron) Dromgool	College OB	2018	39	45
E.S. (Ethan) Dromgool	College OB	2022	7	5
T.M.A. (Tim) Erceg	Waihou	2016	17	5
P.F. (Patrick) Faapale	Hauraki North	2023	4	0
L.W. (Liam) Gilheany-Black [1]	Hamilton Marist [4]	2023	3	0
J.A.J. (Jahvani) Growe-Lolesi	College OB	2023	7	0
Mosese Halahuni	Paeroa	2023	7	0
D.J.M. (Dylan) Horne	Waihi Athletic	2023	1	0
Jacob Janson	Whangamata	2023	1	0
C.J. (Coel) Kerr	Paeroa	2023	4	0
T.C. (Tyrell) Kopua	College OB	2023	7	5
H.K. (Harry) Lafituanai	Waihou	2017	50	110
M.L. (Mosese) Mafi	Hamilton Marist [3]	2023	8	15
Taimua "Jay" Malielegaoi	Hauraki North	2023	5	0
Dane Mathew	Mercury Bay	2023	3	0
S.M. (Sam) McCahon	Waihou	2017	54	60
F.R. (Fletcher) Morgan	Waihi Athletic	2023	8	116
H.J.L. (Hayden) Mulgrew	Waihou	2023	2	0
L.T. (Leroy) Neels	College OB	2021	24	45
J.N. (Jake) O'Connor	Waihou	2023	8	0
T.T.M.M. (Tuakana) Paitai [1]	Morrinsville [4]	2022	14	0
S.N. (Sam) Pou	Hamilton Marist [3]	2023	4	0
T.J. (Tyler) Relph	Mercury Bay	2021	11	0
Savelio Ropati	Manukau Rovers [5]	2023	5	0
R.N.M. (Richard) Rosewarne	Hauraki North	2023	8	0
B.D.K.W. (Brooklyn) Toia	Paeroa	2019	10	0
T.L.T.R. (Tayne) Tupaea	Morrinsville	2022	16	15
N.G.M. (Nigel) Williams	Thames	2023	3	0
C.R.S. (Calum) Wood	Waihou	2022	16	25

1. Player of Origin 2. Loaned by Bay of Plenty RU 3. Loaned by Waikato RU
4. Waikato RU 5. Loaned by Auckland RU

INDIVIDUAL SCORING

	Tries	Con	PG	DG	Points		Tries	Con	PG	DG	Points
Morgan	6	22	14	-	116	Davies	1	-	-	-	5
Neels	6	-	-	-	30	Tupaea	1	-	-	-	5
Lafituanai	3	-	-	-	15	Erceg	1	-	-	-	5
Wood	3	-	-	-	15	E. Dromgool	1	-	-	-	5
Mafi	3	-	-	-	15	Beazley	-	-	1	-	3
McCahon	2	-	-	-	10						
C. Dromgool	2	-	-	-	10	***Totals***	***32***	***22***	***15***	***0***	***249***
Barnett	1	-	-	-	5						
Kopua	1	-	-	-	5	*Opposition scored*	*38*	*25*	*5*	*1*	*258*
Axtens	1	-	-	-	5						

THAMES VALLEY 2023

	Whanganui	Poverty Bay	West Coast	King Country	Mid Canterbury	South Canterbury	North Otago	Ngati Porou East Coast	Whanganui (sf)	**TOTALS**
Wood	15	-	15	15	15	15	-	15	15	**7**
E. Dromgool	s	11	-	14	14	-	14	-	14	**6**
Lafituanai	14	14	14	13	13	13	13	13	13	**9**
Morgan	11	15	11	11	11	11	15	11	-	**8**
Malielegaoi	s	s	s	-	-	s	s	-	-	**5**
Mulgrew	-	-	-	s	-	-	-	-	s	**2**
Kerr	-	-	-	-	-	14	11	14	11	**4**
Barnett	13	13	13	-	-	-	-	-	-	**3**
Mathew	-	-	-	s	s	-	-	-	s	**3**
McCahon (co-capt)	12	12	12	12	12	12	12	12	12	**9**
Beazley	10	10	10	10	10	10	10	10	10	**9**
Faapale	-	s	s	-	-	s	s	-	-	**4**
Neels	9	9	9	9	9	9	9	9	9	**9**
O'Connor	s	s	s	s	s	s	s	-	s	**8**
Tupaea	8	8	6	-	7	7	7	7	7	**8**
Axtens	-	-	8	-	-	-	-	-	-	**1**
Ropati	-	-	-	8	8	-	8	8	8	**5**
Davies	7	7	7	7	s	s	s	s	6	**9**
C. Dromgool (co-capt)	6	5	5	6	6	6	6	5	5	**9**
Halahuni	s	s	-	-	5	5	5	s	s	**7**
Dafel	-	6	-	-	-	-	-	-	-	**1**
Rosewarne	-	s	s	s	s	s	s	6	s	**8**
Barker	-	-	-	s	-	-	-	-	-	**1**
Pou	5	-	4	4	-	8	-	-	-	**4**
Erceg	4	4	s	5	4	4	4	4	4	**9**
Horne	s	-	-	-	-	-	-	-	-	**1**
Mafi	3	3	-	3	3	3	3	3	3	**8**
Paitai	1	1	3	1	s	1	-	-	-	**6**
Relph	s	s	1	s	-	-	-	-	-	**4**
Toia	s	2	-	-	1	s	1	1	1	**7**
Growe-Lolesi	-	s	s	s	s	s	-	s	s	**7**
Williams	-	-	s	-	-	-	s	s	-	**3**
Kopua	2	s	2	2	s	2	-	-	s	**7**
Janson	s	-	-	-	-	-	-	-	-	**1**
Dare-Johnson	-	-	s	s	2	s	-	-	s	**5**
Gilheany-Black	-	-	-	-	-	-	2	2	2	**3**

THAMES VALLEY TEAM RECORD 2023

Played 9 **Won 6** **Lost 3** **Points for 249** **Points against 258**

Date	Opponent	Location	Score	Tries	Con	PG	DG	Referee
August 12	Whanganui	Whanganui	36–33	Morgan (2), Neels, McCahon, Lafituanai	Morgan (4)	Morgan		Will Johnston
August 19	Poverty Bay	Te Aroha	24–17	Barnett, Neels, C. Dromgool	Morgan (3)	Morgan		Maggie Cogger-Orr
August 26	West Coast	Greymouth	30–22	Neels, Kopua, Axtens	Morgan (3)	Morgan (3)		Jackson Henshaw
September 2	King Country	Thames	27–21	Morgan, Lafituanai, Wood, C. Dromgool	Morgan (2)	Morgan		Andy Morton
September 9	Mid Canterbury	Ashburton	34–31	McCahon, Neels, Mafi, Davies, Tupaea	Morgan (3)	Morgan		Ben Alexander
September 16	South Canterbury	Whangamata	31–36	Morgan (2), Wood, Mafi, Lafituanai	Morgan (3)			Todd Petrie
September 23	North Otago	Maheno	33–34	Neels (2), Erceg, E. Dromgool	Morgan (2)	Morgan (3)		Josh Bamber
September 30	Ngati Porou East Coast	Waihi	31–26	Wood, Morgan, Mafi	Morgan (2)	Morgan (4)		Andy Morton
October 7	Whanganui (MC sf)	Whanganui	3–38			Beazley		Stu Catley

WAIKATO

2023 Status: Bunnings NPC
Founded 1909 as South Auckland.
Affiliated 1909. Name changed to Waikato 1921
President: A.R. (Allen) Grainger
Chairman: S.J. (Stephen) Shale
Chief executive officer: C.E. (Carl) Moon
Coach: R.A. (Ross) Filipo
Assistant coaches: A.J. (Adam) Thomson, M. (Mark) Roberts, D.W.H. (Dwayne) Sweeney
Main ground: FMG Stadium Waikato, Hamilton
Capacity: 27,000
Colours: Red, yellow and black

RECORDS

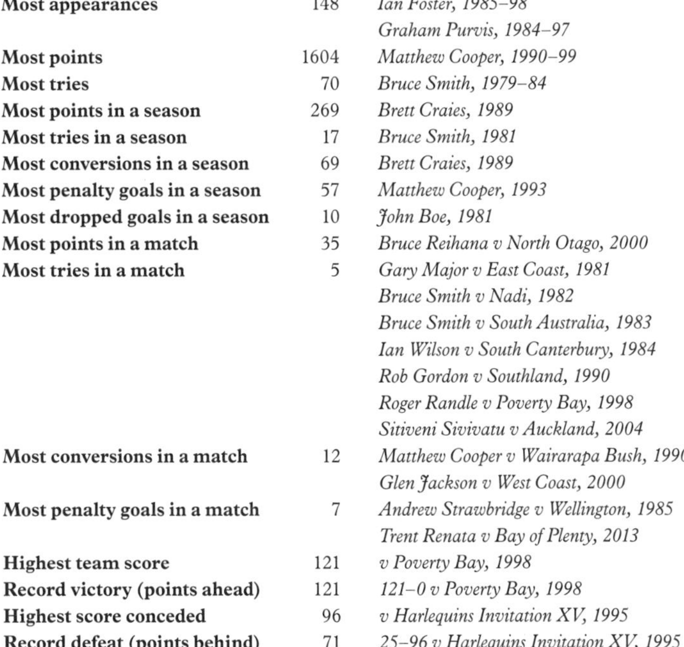

Most appearances	148	*Ian Foster, 1985–98*
		Graham Purvis, 1984–97
Most points	1604	*Matthew Cooper, 1990–99*
Most tries	70	*Bruce Smith, 1979–84*
Most points in a season	269	*Brett Craies, 1989*
Most tries in a season	17	*Bruce Smith, 1981*
Most conversions in a season	69	*Brett Craies, 1989*
Most penalty goals in a season	57	*Matthew Cooper, 1993*
Most dropped goals in a season	10	*John Boe, 1981*
Most points in a match	35	*Bruce Reihana v North Otago, 2000*
Most tries in a match	5	*Gary Major v East Coast, 1981*
		Bruce Smith v Nadi, 1982
		Bruce Smith v South Australia, 1983
		Ian Wilson v South Canterbury, 1984
		Rob Gordon v Southland, 1990
		Roger Randle v Poverty Bay, 1998
		Sitiveni Sivivatu v Auckland, 2004
Most conversions in a match	12	*Matthew Cooper v Wairarapa Bush, 1990*
		Glen Jackson v West Coast, 2000
Most penalty goals in a match	7	*Andrew Strawbridge v Wellington, 1985*
		Trent Renata v Bay of Plenty, 2013
Highest team score	121	*v Poverty Bay, 1998*
Record victory (points ahead)	121	*121–0 v Poverty Bay, 1998*
Highest score conceded	96	*v Harlequins Invitation XV, 1995*
Record defeat (points behind)	71	*25–96 v Harlequins Invitation XV, 1995*

Sporting a spotty 2–5 record with three games to play in the regular season, Waikato was staring down the barrel of having no playoffs rugby in October.

But the Mooloos rallied brilliantly to beat Auckland, Otago and Canterbury to edge into the quarter-final as the eighth qualifier. Facing the daunting task of the high-flying and unbeaten Wellington Lions on their home patch, Ross Filipo's charges made a stirring second stanza comeback to nearly steal the upset. But they will regret a sluggish start to the season and an horrendous injury toll. Co-captain Mitch Jacobson, for example, was injured in the first game and only returned in the last two weeks of the campaign.

Though competitive, Waikato had little to show for the vexed 'Storm' week and will lament a poor second half against Hawke's Bay, despite scoring five tries in that clash.

A confidence-boosting victory over the Steelers was followed by two decisive defeats to North Harbour and Wellington before the late season flourish.

There appeared to be a stable roster from 2022, and it seemed that Josh Ioane would be a good signing for Damian McKenzie, who was on All Blacks duty. Alas, injury ruled out Ioane after just one match.

Other losses in the off-season included Rob Cobb (Northland), Rhys Dickinson (retired), Sefo Kautai (Australia), Alapati Leiua (North Harbour) and James Thompson (Counties Manukau). The gains were several players back from injury, including midfielder Quinn Tupaea, who showed some decent form in between concussion issues, but too late to impress the All Blacks selectors.

Te Paea Cook-Savage was the Mr Fixit, wearing four jersey numbers in the backline, including first-five against Auckland, when he even landed a dropped goal. Wings Liam Coombes-Fabling and Daniel Sinkinson were also used at the back, an indicator of Waikato's attacking bent. Gideon Wrampling returned from long-term injury and ran with gusto and determination, his two tries including one of the team scores of the season against Canterbury. The promising Aki Tuivailala debuted before his 19th birthday.

Injury to Bailyn Sullivan meant he was never able to combine with Tupaea in midfield. But rookie Austin Anderson acquitted himself well and came up with some big plays.

Taha Kemara became the senior No 10 and had some good moments, but the SOS went out to the Waikato-domiciled Aaron Cruden, who made his Mooloos debut at 34 and showed he could still cut it at this level, giving a sterling display against Otago with 20 points.

Xavier Roe, who was top-notch against Auckland with a hat-trick, job-shared the halfback duties with Cortez Ratima. Between them, the duo scored eight tries.

Simon Parker shrugged off years of injury to cement the No 8 berth and be one of five Mooloos to appear in all 11 matches. Jack Lam missed the Manu Samoa RWC squad, so slotted back in but was not always available, while Bay of Plenty loaner Joe Johnston played with commitment at No 7.

The big movers, mostly on the blindside, were the talented Malachi Wrampling and Xavier Saifoloi. Samipeni Finau had just three outings after his All Blacks debut in August.

Hamilton Burr did some hard toil and assumed the captaincy when Ayden Johnstone was out. James Tucker was again the locking rock, though the lineout was not always smooth.

Tighthead George Dyer took more steps forwards and won the Aaron Hopa Memorial Trophy at the WRU awards night. Loosehead Ollie Norris, now with 51 caps under his belt, won the player of the year gong and kept Johnstone honest.

Injury to Rhys Marshall saw Pita Anae-Ah Sue and Sean Ralph share the hooking roles to good effect.

Higher honours went to:

New Zealand:	S. Finau, L. Jacobson, A. Lienert-Brown, D. McKenzie, S. Taukei'aho
New Zealand Sevens:	D. Collier, T. Mikkelson
All Blacks XV:	G. Dyer, O. Norris, B. Sullivan
New Zealand Under 20:	T. Kemara, W. Martin, G. Robinson, A. Tuivailala, M. Wrampling

WAIKATO REPRESENTATIVES 2023

Name	Club	Date of birth	Height	Weight	For Union Debut	Games	Points
P.A. (Pita) Anae-Ah Sue	Hautapu	16-12-92	1.88	115	2022	19	15
A.R.C. (Austin) Anderson	Te Awamutu Sports	18-11-03	1.86	94	2023	8	10
H.R. (Hamilton) Burr	Hautapu	19-06-96	1.95	109	2019	49	10
T.P.A. (Te Paea) Cook-Savage	Fraser Tech	02-08-01	1.73	83	2021	24	59
L.A. (Liam) Coombes-Fabling	Fraser Tech	07-07-98	1.8	83	2020	38	65
T.J. (Tai) Cribb	Te Awamutu Sports	09-02-04	1.95	106	2023	2	0
A.W. (Aaron) Cruden	Overseas	08-01-89	1.78	84	2023	4	22
G.E. (George) Dyer	Fraser Tech	22-10-99	1.88	118	2020	32	5
O.A. (Tolu) Fahamokoia	Greytown [1]	05-05-91	1.84	105	2020	4	0
S.U. (Samipeni) Finau	Hamilton Old Boys	10-05-99	1.96	115	2019	31	10
Z.P.K. (Zinzan) Hansen	University	30-01-03	2.02	113	2023	2	0
J.R. (Josh) Ioane	United Matamata Sports	11-07-95	1.76	85	2023	1	6
M.L. (Mitch) Jacobson	Hautapu	13-01-96	1.93	106	2015	75	30
C.A. (Ayden) Johnstone	Hautapu	24-10-96	1.84	123	2015	48	0
J.F.I. (Joe) Johnston	Te Puke Sports [2]	31-01-98	1.87	100	2023	7	0
T. (Taha) Kemara	Te Awamutu Sports	17-04-03	1.85	85	2022	13	52
J.T. (Jack) Lam	Hamilton Marist	18-11-87	1.86	103	2009	55	17
R.J.J. (Rhys) Marshall	University	12-10-92	1.84	107	2021	17	20
P.J. (Patrick) McCurran	Fraser Tech	05-06-98	1.92	110	2022	13	15
L.E. (Laghlan) McWhannell	Hautapu	20-10-98	1.98	117	2017	34	25
T.W. (Nui) Muriwai	University	16-05-02	1.79	83	2023	1	0
Q.H. (Quintony) Ngatai	Hautapu	26-09-00	1.78	85	2023	3	0
C.J. (Cody) Nordstrom	Te Awamutu Sports	07-04-03	1.8	86	2023	4	5
O.M. (Ollie) Norris	Hautapu	11-12-99	1.94	120	2019	51	25
S.C. (Simon) Parker	Hautapu	06-05-00	1.97	109	2019	22	15
S. (Sean) Ralph	Te Awamutu Sports	22-06-03	1.77	105	2023	10	10
C.P. (Cortez) Ratima	Otorohanga	22-03-01	1.79	87	2020	38	45
T.R. (Te Rama) Reuben	University	26-06-02	1.9	113	2021	9	0
X.O. (Xavier) Roe	Hamilton Old Boys	13-12-98	1.79	86	2020	36	50
X.E. (Xavier) Saifoloi	University	23-06-03	1.96	115	2023	6	0
D.P. (Daniel) Sinkinson	Melville	08-02-01	1.85	92	2021	22	57
B.W.M. (Bailyn) Sullivan	Hamilton Marist	03-09-98	1.88	98	2017	60	90
J.F. (James) Tucker	Hamilton Marist	05-08-94	1.97	112	2015	69	60
T. (Tana) Tuhakaraina	United Matamata Sports	07-07-97	1.9	95	2022	17	10
G.A.M. (Aki) Tuivailala	Hamilton Old Boys	24-09-04	1.86	98	2023	3	5
S.M. (Solomone) Tukuafu	Hamilton Old Boys	14-09-96	1.86	122	2022	14	0
M.T.T.O.P. (Mason) Tupaea	Hamilton Marist	16-10-02	1.84	118	2023	2	0
Q.P.C. (Quinn) Tupaea	Hamilton Old Boys	10-05-99	1.86	97	2018	38	100
G.T. (Gideon) Wrampling	Hamilton Old Boys	26-07-01	1.88	102	2020	25	15
M.I.R.T. (Malachi) Wrampling	Hamilton Old Boys	15-04-04	1.92	112	2023	9	15

1. Loaned by Wairarapa-Bush RFU *2. Loaned by Bay of Plenty RFU*

INDIVIDUAL SCORING

	Tries	Con	PG	DG	Points		Tries	Con	PG	DG	Points
Cook-Savage	3	11	3	1	49	Ioane	-	3	-	-	6
Roe	5	-	-	-	25	Dyer	1	-	-	-	5
Cruden	2	6	-	-	22	Finau	1	-	-	-	5
Sinkinson	4	1	-	-	22	Norris	1	-	-	-	5
Kemara	-	5	3	-	19	Parker	1	-	-	-	5
Anae-Ah Sue	3	-	-	-	15	Marshall	1	-	-	-	5
Ratima	3	-	-	-	15	McCurran	1	-	-	-	5
Tucker	3	-	-	-	15	Nordstrom	1	-	-	-	5
M. Wrampling	3	-	-	-	15	Tuhakaraina	1	-	-	-	5
Anderson	2	-	-	-	10	Tuivailala	1	-	-	-	5
Coombes-Fabling	2	-	-	-	10	Q. Tupaea	1	-	-	-	5
Ralph	2	-	-	-	10						
Sullivan	2	-	-	-	10	***Totals***	***47***	***26***	***6***	***1***	***310***
G. Wrampling	2	-	-	-	10						
Penalty try	1	-	-	-	7	*Opposition scored*	*41*	*28*	*8*	*0*	*285*

WAIKATO 2023	Southland	Bay of Plenty	Hawke's Bay	Taranaki	Counties Manukau	North Harbour	Wellington	Auckland	Otago	Canterbury	Wellington (QF)	**Totals**
Cook-Savage	15	15	s	s	15	14	15	10	14	14	14	**11**
Tuivailala	–	–	–	–	–	–	–	11	s	–	s	**3**
Tuhakaraina	s	s	11	–	s	s	13	13	13	13	13	**10**
Coombes-Fabling	–	14	15	15	14	15	s	–	–	–	–	**6**
Nordstrom	–	–	14	–	–	–	14	14	s	–	–	**4**
Sinkinson	11	11	–	11	11	11	11	15	15	15	15	**10**
Anderson	–	s	12	12	–	12	12	12	12	12	–	**8**
G. Wrampling	13	12	s	13	13	–	–	–	–	11	11	**7**
Sullivan	14	13	13	14	–	–	–	–	11	–	–	**5**
Q. Tupaea	12	–	–	s	12	13	–	–	–	s	12	**6**
Kemara	s	10	10	10	10	10	10	–	–	–	10	**8**
Cruden	–	–	–	–	s	s	–	–	10	10	–	**4**
Ioane	10	–	–	–	–	–	–	–	–	–	–	**1**
Muriwai	–	–	s	–	–	–	–	–	–	–	–	**1**
Roe	s	s	9	s	s	s	9	9	9	9	–	**10**
Ratima	9	9	–	9	9	9	s	–	–	–	9	**7**
Ngatai	–	–	–	–	–	–	–	s	s	s	–	**3**
Parker	8	8	s	8	8	8	8	8	8	8	8	**11**
Reuben	–	–	8	s	–	–	s	–	–	–	–	**3**
Lam	–	s	–	–	7	7	–	s	–	s	–	**5**
Johnston	–	–	–	–	s	s	7	7	7	7	7	**7**
M. Jacobson	7	–	–	–	–	–	–	–	–	s	s	**3**
McCurran	s	7	7	7	–	–	–	–	–	–	–	**4**
M. Wrampling	6	6	–	–	s	6	s	s	s	6	s	**9**
Saifoloi	–	–	6	6	–	s	6	s	–	s	–	**6**
Finau	–	–	–	–	–	–	–	6	6	–	6	**3**
Hansen	–	–	s	–	–	–	s	–	–	–	–	**2**
Cribb	s	–	4	–	–	–	–	–	–	–	–	**2**
McWhannell	–	–	–	5	5	–	–	s	s	–	–	**4**
Burr (co-capt)	5	5	5	s	6	5	5	5	5	5	5	**11**
Tucker	4	4	–	4	4	4	4	4	4	4	4	**10**
Tukuafu	s	s	3	s	s	s	s	s	s	s	s	**11**
Fahamokoia	–	–	s	–	–	–	–	–	–	–	–	**1**
Dyer	3	3	–	3	3	3	3	3	3	3	3	**10**
Norris	s	1	1	1	1	1	s	s	s	s	s	**11**
M. Tupaea	–	–	s	s	–	–	–	–	–	–	–	**2**
Johnstone (co-capt)	1	–	–	–	s	s	1	1	1	1	1	**8**
Anae-Ah Sue	2	2	–	2	2	2	s	s	2	2	2	**10**
Marshall	–	s	2	–	–	–	–	–	–	–	–	**2**
Ralph	s	–	s	s	s	s	2	2	s	s	s	**10**

WAIKATO TEAM RECORD 2023

Played 11 **Won 5** **Lost 6** **Points for 310** **Points against 285**

Date	*Opponent*	*Location*	*Score*	*Tries*	*Con*	*PG*	*DG*	*Referee*
August 6	Southland	Invercargill	29–21	Ratima (2), M. Wrampling, Anae-Ah Sue	Ioane (3)	Kemara		Fraser Hannon
August 12	Bay of Plenty	Tauranga	15-19	M. Wrampling, Sullivan	Kemara	Kemara		Brendon Pickerill
August 16	Hawke's Bay	Napier	32–35	Sullivan, Coombes-Fabling, Anderson, Marshall, Nordstrom	Kemara (2)	Kemara		Angus Mabey
August 20	Taranaki	Hamilton	17–29	Dyer, Sinkinson, McCurran	Cook-Savage			Dan Waenga
August 27	Counties Manukau	Hamilton	37–15	Sinkinson (2), Ratima, Q. Tupaea, penalty try	Cook-Savage (2)	Cook-Savage (2)		Angus Mabey
September 2	North Harbour	Albany	17–39	Coombes-Fabling, Norris, Ralph	Cruden			Nick Hogan
September 8	Wellington	Hamilton	24–41	Cook-Savage, Roe, Sinkinson, Tucker	Cook-Savage (2)			Nick Briant
September 16	Auckland	Auckland	27–12	Roe (3), Tuivailala	Cook-Savage (2)		Cook-Savage	Jono Bredin
September 24	Otago	Hamilton	47–7	Cruden (2), Anae-Ah Sue, Finau, Parker, Anderson, Cook-Savage	Cruden (5), Sinkinson			Angus Mabey
September 30	Canterbury	Hamilton	37–35	G. Wrampling (2), M. Wrampling, Cook-Savage, Roe, Tucker	Cook-Savage (2)	Cook-Savage		Cam Stone
October 7	Wellington (QF)	Wellington	28–32	Tucker, Anae-Ah Sue, Ralph, Tuhakaraina	Cook-Savage (2), Kemara (2)			Dan Waenga

WAIRARAPA BUSH

2023 Status: Heartland Championship
Founded: Wairarapa 1886 and original member 1892. Bush 1890 and affiliated 1893. Amalgamated 1971.
President: G.W. (Bunter) Anderson
Chairman: J.N. (Jason) Carruthers
Chief executive officer: A.R. (Tony) Hargood
Coach: R.A. (Reece) Robinson
Assistant coach: J.C. (James) Bruce, S.S. (Stan) Wright
Main ground: Memorial Park, Masterton
Capacity: 10,000
Colours: Green

RECORDS

Highest attendance	12,000	*Wairarapa-Bush v South Africa 1956, British Isles 1971, 1983*
Most appearances	132	*G.K. McGlashan, 1971–83*
Most points	561	*P. Harding-Rimene, 1999–2008*
Most tries	43	*M.T. Foster, 1984–92*
Most points in a season	166	*G.M. Walters, 2012*
Most tries in a season	14	*S.F. Simanu, 2005*
Most conversions in a season	28	*M.F.C. Benton, 1987*
Most penalty goals in a season	34	*G.M. Walters, 2012*
Most dropped goals in a season	7	*K.W. Carter, 1985*
Most points in a match	26	*M.J. Berry v South Canterbury, 1995*
Most tries in a match	5	*S. Malatai v Buller, 2018*
Most conversions in a match	11	*M.F.C. Benton v Horowhenua, 1987*
Most penalty goals in a match	6	*J.T. Te Huia v Buller, 2010* *G.M. Walters v South Canterbury, 2012*
Highest team score	82	*v Horowhenua, 1987*
Record victory (points ahead)	73	*82–9 v Horowhenua, 1987*
Highest score conceded	96	*v Canterbury, 2006*
Record defeat (points behind)	86	*10–96 v Canterbury, 2006*

With four wins and four losses, Wairarapa Bush finished sixth in the Heartland Championship to qualify for a home semi-final in the Lochore Cup. North Otago and Whanganui proved too strong but the loss to winless Horowhenua Kapiti was a disappointing one and new coach Reece Robinson made changes after that game.

Wairarapa Bush's best performance was the 33–28 win over Mid Canterbury in Ashburton in the final round robin match where they secured the required bonus point win to guarantee a home semi-final in the Lochore Cup. Poor starts were a feature of the season, which meant having to play catch up. This occurred again in the semi-final – a poor first half for a 3–28 halftime deficit but a much-improved second half in losing 27–33 to West Coast.

The team had one of the smaller packs in the Heartland Championship which meant an up-tempo attacking style of play. Nevertheless, the forwards still won an ample supply of possession for use.

Logan Wakefield and captain Sam Gammie were both hard-working locks who performed to a high standard. Wakefield was the premier lineout winner and Gammie's all-round game was to the fore. Props Tupou Lea'aemanu and Stan Wright were effective scrummagers, with Lea'aemanu also a very prominent ball carrier who was co-top try-scorer with four.

In the loose forwards, newcomer Isireli Biumaiwai improved steadily throughout the season at No. 8 and it was unfortunate injury prevented him from completing the season. Inia Katia reached the landmark of 100 first-class games for Wairarapa Bush against North Otago. He has had an interesting career, firstly as a long-standing halfback and then in recent years as a utility back. This year he was switched to flanker and the move paid off well.

Player of Origin Isaac Bracewell was an accomplished halfback who threw out accurate passes and was a dangerous runner with the ball. Andre Taylor, who was assisting the side off the field, played more than was probably intended but his experience was invaluable and he made a difference at first-five in the last three matches.

Impressive second-five Tafa Tafa defended well and created attacking opportunities and Aseri Waqa and Nikora Ewe stood out in the outside backs.

Thirty-seven players were used in the nine games with 14 being new. Of the newcomers, Andre Taylor had previously represented Manawatu/Taranaki/Hurricanes/NZ Maori, loan player Sase Va'a had represented Horowhenua Kapiti and, at the age of 42, Tana Isaac had represented Manawatu way back in 2001.

INDIVIDUAL SCORING

	Tries	*Con*	*PG*	*DG*	*Points*		*Tries*	*Con*	*PG*	*DG*	*Points*
Haira	1	9	5	-	38	Hunt	1	-	-	-	5
Taylor	1	3	6	-	29	Ale	1	-	-	-	5
Brooking-Jacobs	-	3	5	-	21	Waqa	1	-	-	-	5
Ewe	4	-	-	-	20	Bracewell	1	-	-	-	5
Lea'aemanu	4	-	-	-	20	Mataitai	1	-	-	-	5
Walton-Sexton	2	-	-	-	10	Campbell	1	-	-	-	5
I. Biumaiwai	2	-	-	-	10	Tameilau	-	2	-	-	4
Keelan	2	-	-	-	10						
Gammie	2	-	-	-	10	***Totals***	***27***	***17***	***16***	***0***	***217***
Katia	2	-	-	-	10						
Tekii	1	-	-	-	5	*Opposition scored*	*39*	*27*	*10*	*0*	*279*

WAIRARAPA BUSH REPRESENTATIVES 2023

		For Union		
Name	Club	Debut	Games	Points
M.A. (Marcus) Ale	Marist	2018	8	5
C.C. (Cyrus) Baker	Greytown	2010	21	10
I.L. (Isireli) Biumaiwai	Carterton	2023	6	10
M.K. (Malakia) Biumaiwai	Carterton	2023	2	0
I.D. (Isaac) Bracewell [1]	Oriental Rongotai [2]	2021	15	5
B.W. (Ben) Brooking-Jacobs	Carterton	2022	8	25
L.P. (Lewis) Bush	Greytown	2019	25	40
Tom Campbell	Marist	2023	6	5
H.J. (Hayden) Cooper	Marist	2023	2	0
F.W.H. (Frederick) Eschenbach	Gladstone	2023	1	0
H.P.W. (Harry) Eschenbach	Gladstone	2022	7	0
N.V. (Nikora) Ewe	Pioneer	2017	20	45
S.G. (Sam) Gammie	Eketahuna	2016	58	57
T.T. (Tipene) Haira	Martinborough	2011	62	156
J.A. (Jared) Hawkins	Martinborough	2007	34	20
N.S. (Nathan) Hunt	Martinborough	2012	33	45
T.C.A. (Tana) Isaac	Greytown	2023	2	0
I.S.T. (Inia) Katia	Carterton	2011	105	80
Jayden Keelan	College OB [3]	2023	2	10
T.E. (Tupou) Lea'aemanu	Carterton	2020	26	50
C.F. (Charles) Mataitai	Marist	2022	10	20
G.W.M. (George) Parke	East Coast	2023	5	0
M.W. (Matt) Perry	East Coast	2021	9	0
Epeli Rayaqayaqa	East Coast	2017	19	40
Tyne Stafford	Tuhirangi	2023	2	0
Tafa Tafa	Marist	2020	23	25
F.N. (Fiula) Tameilau	Carterton	2021	18	9
A.S. (Andre) Taylor	Greytown	2023	5	29
T.T.A. (Terongo) Tekii	Carterton	2019	12	5
Sase Va'a	Kia Toa [3]	2023	6	0
I.P. (Isaac) Vollebregt	Tuhirangi	2023	2	0
T.K. (Ty) Waight	Martinborough	2023	9	0
Logan Wakefield	Carterton	2022	16	0
S.D. (Sam) Walton-Sexton	Greytown	2022	16	15
A.N. (Aseri) Waqa	Carterton	2022	15	25
T.J.Z. (Tom) Woelders	Martinborough	2023	6	0
S.G. (Stan) Wright	Marist	2022	13	0

1. Player of Origin *2. Wellington RU* *3. Loaned by Manawatu RU*

WAIRARAPA-BUSH 2023	Ngati Porou East Coast	North Otago	Poverty Bay	Horowhenua Kapiti	King Country	Buller	Whanganui	Mid Canterbury	West Coast (sf)	TOTALS
Taylor	15	15	–	–	–	–	10	10	10	**5**
Ewe	14	14	14	14	–	14	–	–	–	**5**
Waqa	11	11	15	15	15	11	15	–	15	**8**
Hunt	s	s	–	11	–	–	–	–	–	**3**
Mataitai	–	–	11	13	11	–	–	11	11	**5**
F. Eschenbach	–	–	–	–	14	–	–	–	–	**1**
Keelan	–	–	–	–	s	15	–	–	–	**2**
Cooper	–	–	–	–	–	–	14	14	–	**2**
Vollebregt	–	–	–	–	–	s	11	–	–	**2**
Tameilau	13	13	13	12	13	–	13	13	13	**8**
Tafa	12	12	12	–	12	–	–	12	12	**6**
Baker	–	–	s	s	s	12	s	–	–	**5**
Brooking-Jacobs	10	10	10	10	–	–	–	s	14	**6**
H. Eschenbach	s	s	s	–	–	13	12	s	–	**6**
Haira	–	–	–	s	10	10	s	15	s	**6**
Walton-Sexton	9	s	s	s	s	s	s	s	s	**9**
Bracewell	s	9	9	9	9	9	9	9	9	**9**
I. Biumaiwai	8	8	8	8	8	8	–	–	–	**6**
Perry	–	–	–	–	–	s	s	s	–	**3**
Katia	7	7	7	7	–	–	7	7	7	**7**
Wakefield	6	5	5	5	6	6	5	5	5	**9**
Hawkins	s	s	s	6	s	7	6	6	6	**9**
Rayaqayaqa	–	s	s	s	7	–	–	–	–	**4**
Stafford	–	–	–	–	s	–	s	–	–	**2**
Isaac	–	–	–	–	–	–	–	s	s	**2**
Campbell	5	–	–	s	–	s	8	8	8	**6**
Gammie (capt.)	4	4	4	4	4	4	4	4	4	**9**
Ale	s	6	6	–	–	–	–	–	–	**3**
M. Biumaiwai	–	–	–	–	5	5	–	–	–	**2**
Wright	3	3	3	–	3	3	3	3	3	**8**
Lea'aemanu	1	1	1	1	1	1	1	1	1	**9**
Bush	s	s	s	3	s	s	s	s	s	**9**
Waight	s	s	s	s	s	s	s	s	s	**9**
Woelders	–	–	s	s	–	s	s	s	s	**6**
Tekii	2	2	–	–	–	–	–	–	–	**2**
Parke	s	s	2	2	s	–	–	–	–	**5**
Va'a	–	–	–	s	2	2	2	2	2	**6**

WAIRARAPA BUSH TEAM RECORD 2023

Played 9 **Won 4** **Lost 5** **Points for 217** **Points against 279**

Date	*Opponent*	*Location*	*Score*	*Tries*	*Con*	*PG*	*DG*	*Referee*
August 12	Ngati Porou East Coast	Masterton	32–31	Ewe, Walton-Sexton, Tekii, Hunt	Brooking-Jacobs (3)	Brooking-Jacobs (2)		Nick Hogan
August 19	North Otago	Oamaru	3–50			Brooking-Jacobs		Dan Moore
August 26	Poverty Bay	Masterton	30–24	Ale, Ewe, Waqa, I. Biumaiwai	Tameilau (2)	Brooking-Jacobs (2)		Jack Sargentina
September 2	Horowhenua Kapiti	Levin	19–24	Ewe, Bracewell, Haira	Haira (2)			Tipene Cottrell
September 9	King Country	Masterton	35–26	I. Biumaiwai, Mataitai, Lea'aemanu, Keelan	Haira (3)	Haira (3)		Stu Catley
September 16	Buller	Westport	20–27	Keelan, Gammie, Ewe	Haira	Haira		Ben Alexander
September 23	Whanganui (BSC)	Masterton	18–36	Taylor, Walton-Sexton	Taylor	Taylor (2)		Jack Sargentina
September 30	Mid Canterbury	Ashburton	33–28	Lea'aemanu (2), Katia, Gammie	Taylor (2)	Taylor (3)		Jackson Henshaw
October 7	West Coast (LC sf)	Masterton	27–33	Lea'aemanu, Campbell, Katia	Haira (3)	Taylor, Haira		Will Johnston

BSC Bruce Steel Cup

WELLINGTON

2023 Status: Bunnings NPC
Founded 1879. Original member 1892
President: M.P. (Murray) Blandford
Chairman: R. (Russell) Poole
Chief Executive Officer: M.G. (Matt) Evans
Coach: T.E. (Tamati) Ellison
Assistant coaches: G.A. (Greg) Halford, T.W.K. (Trent) Renata, A.T. (Alando) Soakai
Main ground: Sky Stadium, Wellington
Capacity: 34,500
Colours: Black

RECORDS

Most appearances	173	*Graham Williams, 1964–76*
Most points	893	*Allan Hewson, 1977–86*
Most tries	100	*Bernie Fraser, 1975–86*
Most points in a season	199	*John Gallagher, 1987*
Most tries in a season	24	*Bernie Fraser, 1981*
Most conversions in a season	47	*Jackson Garden-Bachop, 2017*
Most penalty goals in a season	38	*Jon Preston, 1994*
Most dropped goals in a season	7	*John Dougan, 1971*
Most points in a match	34	*David Holwell v Bay of Plenty, 2002*
Most tries in a match	7	*Nigel Geany v Whanganui, 1991*
Most conversions in a match	14	*Peter O'Shaughnessy v Horowhenua, 1988* *Simon Mannix v Rosario, 1995*
Most penalty goals in a match	7	*Jackson Garden-Bachop v North Harbour, 2016*
Highest team score	118	*v Rosario, 1995*
Record victory (points ahead)	101	*118–17 v Rosario, 1995*
Highest score conceded	82	*v Otago, 1998*
Record defeat (points behind)	72	*10–82 v Otago, 1998*

The Wellington Lions looked like the best team in the NPC right up until their nemesis, the Hawke's Bay Magpies, inflicted a second defeat in a fortnight on them in the semi-final.

New head coach Tamati Ellison, who moved on at the season's end, pulled all the right strings early doors, despite having to use 47 players in all, 17 of whom were wearing the jersey for the first time. He mixed some form club players with returning pros and it proved to be mostly a heady mix.

Two July Ranfurly Shield challenges, in Levin and Lower Hutt, were comfortably repelled and it enabled No 10 Aidan Morgan to regain confidence, which he took through the NPC, goalkicking at 74 percent and running the cutter with more aplomb.

By the playoffs, Wellington was top of the table and had just come off a 21-game win streak, including 19 in the NPC. The campaign built slowly and steadily, showing its defensive resilience by making 212 tackles in the 7–0 midweek Ranfurly Shield defence against the Tasman Mako at Hutt Rec. Four days later, the 36–31 win with a green squad over a stacked Canterbury in Christchurch, the middle match of the 'storm' week, was the most meritorious of the season.

Decisive wins over Counties Manukau, for the Shield and the Jonah Lomu Memorial Trophy,

Waikato, Bay of Plenty and North Harbour, saw the Lions in pole position until Hawke's Bay divested them of the Shield. The Lions then hung on in the quarter against Waikato after running up a big early lead and then nearly storming home in a pulsating semi-final against the Magpies.

Ruben Love bounced back from a chronic groin injury during Super Rugby to cement the fullback position and he made some telling assists and brilliant solo plays. TJ Clarke showed promise in behind.

Injury only allowed Julian Savea to play the last three games, but Losi Filipo seized his chance to be close to the best No 14 in the NPC, running in eight tries in all for the Lions. Injuries meant no player cemented the No 11 jersey.

Billy Proctor was again the star turn at centre, and his partnership with Peter Umaga-Jensen was a fruitful one, possibly the best in the NPC. The latter expanded his game, bringing in some deft grubbers. Riley Higgins offered very useful back-up.

First-five Morgan was the only player to appear in all 14 games and he played with consistency and growing maturity, making 18 offloads and seven try assists in the NPC.

Prolific tryscoring halfback at club level, Kyle Preston, made the early No 9 running, but was later overtaken by the smart and seasoned Kemara Hauiti-Parapara.

Peter Lakai played just eight games but there was no sign of second year syndrome. Captain Du'Plessis Kirifi's play was again of the highest quality, securing 21 turnovers to lead the NPC in that stat, and always playing with heart, passion and commitment. Rookie Dominic Ropeti offered good impact off the bench both with and without the ball.

Brad Shields didn't miss a beat after several seasons in the north, bringing his usual mix of high work-rate and good skills. That meant top lineout forward Caleb Delany, was mostly used at lock, where he formed a strong combination with Dominic Bird, who pulled down 40 lineouts.

Wellington used no less than nine props, the best of them again loosehead Xavier Numia, though NZ Under 20s tighthead Siale Lauaki made good strides.

At hooker, James O'Reilly stepped in for the injured Asafo Aumua and played some very good rugby. Aumua's five tries were bloated by his quartet against South Canterbury.

Higher honours went to:
New Zealand: D. Coles, A. Savea
All Blacks XV: D. Kirifi, R. Love, X. Numia, B. Proctor
New Zealand Under 20: P. Lakai, S. Lauaki

WELLINGTON REPRESENTATIVES 2023

Name	Club	Date of birth	Height	Weight	For Union Debut	Games	Points
U.H. (Ha'amea) Ahio	Johnsonville	25-10-92	1.83	115	2016	7	0
A.J. (Asafo) Aumua	Avalon	05-05-97	1.79	112	2016	62	155
D.J. (Dominic) Bird	Upper Hutt Rams	09-04-91	2.06	124	2021	30	0
S.M. (Sam) Clarke	Paremata-Plimmerton	23-07-99	1.83	92	2023	6	13
T. (Tjay) Clarke	Petone	20-08-02	1.8	89	2023	7	23
C. (Caleb) Delany	Old Boys-University	04-02-00	1.98	110	2020	36	5
J.D. (James) Douglas	Johnsonville	10-10-94	1.82	107	2023	1	0
C.D. (Chicago) Doyle	Marist-St Pat's	28-08-03	1.71	77	2023	4	0
J.A. (Joe) Faleafaga	Paremata-Plimmerton	10-12-99	1.8	90	2023	1	5
L.F. (Losi) Filipo	Petone	29-12-97	1.8	97	2017	22	50
C.C. (Connor) Garden-Bachop	Northern United	04-02-00	1.89	94	2019	24	30
J. (Joyner) Gaualofa	Tawa	17-10-02	1.8	110	2023	1	0
S.V.H.L.L. (Sione) Halalilo	Oriental-Rongotai	03-02-02	1.94	104	2022	8	25
K.M. (Kemara) Hauiti-Parapara	Tawa	05-03-97	1.93	90	2017	54	40
L.E. (Logan) Henry	Feilding[1]	02-09-96	1.71	84	2023	2	0
R.J. (Riley) Higgins	Petone	10-09-02	1.87	99	2022	19	40
S. (Sam) Howling	Poneke	19-03-03	1.77	83	2023	2	0
A.S. (Akira) Ieremia	Tawa	14-11-01	1.92	115	2023	6	0
D.P.A. (Du'Plessis) Kirifi	Northern United	03-03-97	1.81	103	2017	63	70
P.A. (Peter) Lakai	Petone	04-03-03	1.86	109	2021	22	20
S.G. (Siale) Lauaki	Tawa	30-05-03	1.87	115	2022	13	5
R. (Ruben) Love	Wainuiomata	28-04-01	1.83	91	2020	38	130
M.D. (Morgan) Mitchell	Eastern-Northern Barbarians[2]	20-07-93	1.8	122	2023	1	0
A. (Aidan) Morgan	Marist-St Pat's	07-06-01	1.75	82	2020	36	226
L. (Louis) Northcott	Paremata-Plimmerton	03-07-01	1.86	88	2023	1	5
X.S. (Xavier) Numia	Oriental-Rongotai	29-11-98	1.84	118	2018	60	40
J.P. (James) O'Reilly	Hutt Old Boys-Marist	12-11-94	1.83	102	2013	70	55
C.R. (Cameron) Orr	Western Suburbs	02-04-95	1.88	132	2023	12	0
P. (Pepesana) Patafilo	Tawa	29-05-96	1.8	94	2019	45	75
T.A.M. (Filo) Paulo	Hutt Old Boys-Marist	06-10-87	1.98	114	2023	5	0
A.J. (Anthony) Pettett	Johnsonville	26-06-96	2.01	126	2023	2	0
H.J. (Hugo) Plummer	Tawa	25-08-00	1.98	118	2022	13	10
P. (Penieli) Poasa	Oriental Rongotai	25-07-97	1.72	107	2023	8	10
K.R. (Kyle) Preston	Old Boys-University	13-09-99	1.77	75	2023	11	10
B.D. (Billy) Proctor	Marist-St Pat's	14-05-99	1.87	97	2017	59	57
D.P. (Dominic) Ropeti	Oriental Rongotai	04-02-03	1.93	106	2023	12	10
S.L. (Solomona) Sakalia	Northern United	02-02-91	1.9	120	2012	16	0
I. (Isi) Saumaki	Tawa	04-07-02	1.85	109	2023	5	25
S.J. (Julian) Savea	Oriental-Rongotai	07-08-90	1.92	106	2010	63	115
P.J. (PJ) Sheck	Tawa	10-03-00	1.93	122	2021	27	0
B.D.F. (Brad) Shields	Petone	02-04-91	1.93	111	2010	71	40
J.T. (Josh) Southall	Petone	23-06-00	1.8	103	2022	6	10
J. (Josiah) Tavita-Metcalfe	Northern United	02-04-99	1.84	119	2020	11	0
K. (Pasi) Uluilakepa	Petone	18-01-99	1.9	135	2018	19	15
P.I.J. (Peter) Umaga-Jensen	Wainuiomata	31-12-97	1.87	104	2016	56	75
E. (Ethan) Webster-Nonu	Paremata-Plimmerton	10-04-01	1.78	95	2023	1	0
K.T. (Keelan) Whitman	Marist-St Pat's	30-12-00	1.89	105	2021	29	10

1. Loaned by Manawatu RFU   *2. Loaned by Southland RFU*

INDIVIDUAL SCORING

	Tries	Con	PG	DG	Points		Tries	Con	PG	DG	Points
Morgan	1	37	17	–	130	Shields	2	–	–	–	10
Filipo	8	–	–	–	40	Southall	2	–	–	–	10
Aumua	5	–	–	–	25	Umaga-Jensen	2	–	–	–	10
Saumaki	5	–	–	–	25	Delany	1	–	–	–	5
Love	4	2	–	–	24	Faleafaga	1	–	–	–	5
T. Clarke	2	5	1	–	23	Garden-Bachop	1	–	–	–	5
Halalilo	3	–	–	–	15	Hauiti-Parapara	1	–	–	–	5
Higgins	3	–	–	–	15	Lakai	1	–	–	–	5
Kirifi	3	–	–	–	15	Lauaki	1	–	–	–	5
Proctor	3	–	–	–	15	Northcott	1	–	–	–	5
S. Clarke	1	4	–	–	13	Savea	1	–	–	–	5
Numia	2	–	–	–	10	Uluilakepa	1	–	–	–	5
O'Reilly	2	–	–	–	10	Whitman	1	–	–	–	5
Patafilo	2	–	–	–	10						
Plummer	2	–	–	–	10	***Totals***	***68***	***48***	***18***	***0***	***490***
Poasa	2	–	–	–	10						
Preston	2	–	–	–	10	*Opposition scored*	*33*	*20*	*8*	*0*	*229*
Ropeti	2	–	–	–	10						

WELLINGTON 2023	Horowhenua Kapiti (RS)	South Canterbury (RS)	Manawatu	Otago	Southland (RS)	Tasman (RS)	Canterbury	Counties Manukau (RS)	Waikato	Bay of Plenty	North Harbour (RS)	Hawke's Bay (RS)	Waikato (QF)	Hawke's Bay (SF)	**Totals**
T. Clarke	15	15	s	–	15	s	15	–	–	–	11	–	–	–	**7**
Love	–	–	15	15	10	15	–	15	15	–	15	15	15	15	**10**
Savea	–	–	–	–	–	–	–	–	–	–	–	s	14	14	**3**
Garden-Bachop	–	–	–	s	14	–	–	–	–	–	s	11	s	s	**6**
Doyle	–	s	s	–	–	–	11	–	–	15	–	–	–	–	**4**
Faleafaga	14	–	–	–	–	–	–	–	–	–	–	–	–	–	**1**
Filipo	–	13	14	14	s	14	14	14	14	14	14	14	–	–	**11**
Saumaki	11	14	–	–	–	–	s	11	11	–	–	–	–	–	**5**
Patafilo	–	11	11	11	11	11	–	–	–	11	–	–	–	–	**6**
Northcott	s	–	–	–	–	–	–	–	–	–	–	–	–	–	**1**
Webster-Nonu	13	–	–	–	–	–	–	–	–	–	–	–	–	–	**1**
Proctor	–	–	13	13	13	13	–	13	13	13	13	13	13	13	**11**
Umaga-Jensen	12	12	12	12	–	12	13	12	s	12	12	s	12	12	**13**
Higgins	–	–	–	s	12	s	12	s	12	s	s	12	11	11	**11**
S. Clarke	s	s	–	–	–	–	10	s	s	s	–	–	–	–	**6**
Morgan	10	10	10	10	s	10	s	10	10	10	10	10	10	10	**14**
Hauiti-Parapara	–	–	9	9	s	9	–	s	9	9	9	9	9	9	**11**
Preston	s	9	s	s	9	s	9	9	–	–	s	s	–	s	**11**
Howling	–	–	–	–	–	–	s	–	s	–	–	–	–	–	**2**
Henry	9	s	–	–	–	–	–	–	–	–	–	–	–	–	**2**
Whitman	8	8	8	–	8	–	–	8	6	–	–	–	s	s	**8**
Lakai	–	–	–	8	s	8	8	–	8	8	8	8	–	–	**8**
Ieremia	s	s	s	s	5	–	–	s	–	–	–	–	–	–	**6**
Halalilo	7	7	–	–	–	–	7	–	–	7	–	–	–	–	**4**
Kirifi (capt)	–	–	7	7	7	7	–	7	7	–	7	7	7	7	**10**
Ropeti	6	–	s	s	6	s	s	s	s	s	s	s	–	s	**12**
Shields	–	–	6	6	–	6	6	6	s	6	6	6	8	8	**11**
Delany	–	6	4	4	4	4	–	–	–	–	s	5	6	6	**9**
Plummer	5	5	5	5	–	s	4	5	5	s	5	–	s	s	**12**
Pettett	s	s	–	–	–	–	–	–	–	–	–	–	–	–	**2**
Paulo	–	–	–	–	s	–	s	–	–	5	–	–	5	5	**5**
Bird	4	4	–	–	–	5	5	4	4	4	4	4	4	4	**11**
Sheck	3	3	3	s	3	s	3	–	s	–	s	s	–	–	**10**
Tavita-Metcalfe	s	s	–	–	s	–	s	s	–	s	–	–	s	s	**8**
Mitchell	–	–	–	–	–	–	–	–	–	–	–	–	–	3	**1**
Lauaki	–	–	s	3	–	3	–	3	3	3	3	3	3	–	**9**
Sakalia	–	1	–	–	–	–	–	–	–	–	–	–	–	–	**1**
Uluilakepa	s	s	–	–	–	–	–	–	–	–	–	–	–	–	**2**
Ahio	1	–	–	–	–	–	–	–	–	s	–	–	–	–	**2**
Orr	–	–	s	s	1	s	s	s	1	1	s	s	s	s	**12**
Numia	–	–	1	1	s	1	1	1	s	–	1	1	1	1	**11**
Douglas	–	s	–	–	–	–	–	–	–	–	–	–	–	–	**1**
Aumua	2	2	–	–	–	–	–	–	–	–	–	–	–	s	**3**
O'Reilly	–	–	–	2	2	2	–	2	2	2	2	2	2	2	**10**
Southall	–	–	2	s	s	s	2	–	–	–	–	–	–	–	**5**
Gaualofa	s	–	–	–	–	–	–	–	–	–	–			–	**1**
Poasa	–	–	s	–	–	–	s	s	s	s	s	s	s	–	**8**

WELLINGTON TEAM RECORD 2023

Played 14 **Won 12** **Lost 2** **Points for 490** **Points against 229**

Date	*Opponent*	*Location*	*Score*	*Tries*	*Con*	*PG*	*DG*	*Referee*
July 12	Horowhenua Kapiti (RS)	Levin	68–7	Saumaki (2), Halalilo, Plummer, Northcott, Faleafaga, S. Clarke, T. Clarke, Uluilakepa, Aumua	Morgan (9)			Natarsha Ganley
July 19	South Canterbury (RS)	Lower Hutt	67–21	Aumua (4), Saumaki (2), Halalilo, Whitman, Filipo, T. Clarke, Patafilo	Morgan (5), T. Clarke			Dan Waenga
August 5	Manawatu	Palmerston North	22–6	Umaga-Jensen	Morgan	Morgan (5)		Nick Hogan
August 12	Otago	Dunedin	28–5	Lakai, Shields, Kirifi	Morgan (2)	Morgan (3)		Jackson Henshaw
August 19	Southland (RS)	Lower Hutt	39–17	Patafilo, Delany, Higgins, Ropeti, Garden-Bachop, Southall	T. Clarke (3)	T. Clarke		Ben O'Keeffe
August 23	Tasman (RS)	Wellington	7–0	O'Reilly	Morgan			James Doleman
August 27	Canterbury	Christchurch	36–31	Filipo (2), Southall, Umaga-Jensen, Halalilo, Preston	S. Clarke (2), T. Clarke			Jono Bredin
September 2	Counties Manukau (RS)	Wellington	56–25	Love (2), Preston, Proctor, Saumaki, Kirifi, Hauiti-Parapara	Morgan (4), S. Clarke (2)	Morgan (3)		Stu Curran
September 8	Waikato	Hamilton	41–24	Filipo (3), Love, Plummer, Numia	Morgan (4)	Morgan		Nick Briant
September 17	Bay of Plenty	Rotorua	26–14	Filipo, Lauaki, Shields, Poasa	Morgan (3)			Angus Mabey
September 24	North Harbour (RS)	Porirua	26–6	Filipo, Proctor, Morgan, Love	Morgan (3)			Dan Waenga
September 30	Hawke's Bay (RS)	Wellington	18–20	Numia, Poasa	Morgan	Morgan (2)		Nick Briant
October 7	Waikato (QF)	Wellington	32–28	Savea, Higgins, O'Reilly, Kirifi	Morgan (3)	Morgan (2)		Dan Waenga
October 14	Hawke's Bay (SF)	Wellington	24–25	Proctor, Ropeti, Higgins	Love (2), Morgan	Morgan		Cam Stone

WEST COAST

2023 Status: Heartland Championship
Founded 1890. Affiliated 1893
President: P.J. (Paddy) Kennedy
Chairman: M.J. (Mike) Meehan
Chief executive officer: Mike Connors
Coach: S.J. (Sean) Cuttance
Assistant coaches: J.V. (Jared) Mitchell, T.K. (Troy) Tauwhare
Main ground: John Sturgeon Park, Greymouth
Capacity: 8000
Colours: Red and white

RECORDS

Highest attendance	10,000	*West Coast–Buller v British Isles, 1959*
Most appearances	101	*M.T. Mudu, 2004–2019*
Most points	712	*M.A. Foster, 1992–2000*
Most tries	27	*K.J.J. Beams, 1965–78*
Most points in a season	176	*M.A. Foster, 1999*
Most tries in a season	9	*P.A. Teen, 1975*
Most conversions in a season	23	*L.J. Ross, 2023*
Most penalty goals in a season	38	*M.A. Foster, 1999*
Most dropped goals in a season	9	*A.P. O'Regan, 1987*
Most points in a match	24	*M.A. Foster v Horowhenua Kapiti, 1999*
Most tries in a match	4	*K. McNee v Buller, 1964*
		F.P. O'Donnell v Buller, 1970
		P.A. Teen v Nelson Bays, 1975
		R.J. Stanton v Ngati Porou East Coast, 2018
Most conversions in a match	6	*L.T. Martyn v Golden Bay-Motueka, 1933*
Most penalty goals in a match	6	*P.W. Hutchison v East Coast, 1991*
		C.N. Simpson v South Canterbury, 2007
Highest team score	62	*v Ngati Porou East Coast, 2018*
Record victory (points ahead)	42	*45–3 v Golden Bay-Motueka, 1933*
Highest score conceded	128	*v Canterbury, 1992*
Record defeat (points behind)	128	*0–128 v Canterbury, 1992*

It was a season to remember for West Coast as they won their first ever national trophy with their 23–20 win over Poverty Bay in the Lochore Cup final. With six wins in their 10 matches it was a tremendous improvement on last year when they finished bottom of the Heartland Championship without a win.

The Heartland Championship started well with two good wins against King Country and Horowhenua Kapiti, but the next three matches were all against the seemingly perennial top three teams Thames Valley, Whanganui and South Canterbury and losses ensued.

This dropped the team down to seventh and the final round robin game was a must-win match to retain their Lochore Cup playoff spot. Under this pressure, they responded with their best performance of the season to win 27–12 against their more fancied opponents North Otago. In both the semi-final and final West Coast established decent leads at halftime with their defence then being put to the test in the second halves.

West Coast fielded its usual strong pack which laid the foundations for the team's success, the rolling maul being put to great effect. Tyler Kearns, Troy Tauwhare and Daniel Davis formed a strong and experienced front row, capable of holding their own against most teams. Tauwhare scored five tries and finished the season on 99 first-class games for the union. Locks Josh Manning and Tumama Tu'ulua were good lineout forwards and worked hard in the rucks and mauls.

Steven Soper was one of the most consistent loose forwards in the Heartland Championship on both attack and defence and his leadership was an inspiration to his team. Number eight Amenatave Tukana gave his usual fine service until injury put him out of action halfway through the campaign.

At halfback, Cleveland Barrell had an outstanding debut season at first-class level. His quick, accurate passing was allied with a strong running and support game that netted him seven tries. The first-five position was eventually filled by 19-year-old Matthew Robbins who was player of origin.

In the midfield, the experience of Shayne Anderson and newcomer Nick Foxley combined well and Logan Ross was in excellent goal kicking form, setting a new record for conversions in a season, just falling short of 100 points for the season.

The Seddon Shield, won last year, was lost in the first defence. On July 30 at Murchison, West Coast led 21–0 early in the second half before Nelson Bays sub-union fought their way back to win 34–26.

Higher honours went to:
New Zealand Heartland: S. Anderson, T. Kearns

WEST COAST REPRESENTATIVES 2023

Name	Club	For Union Debut	Games	Points
S.W. (Shayne) Anderson	Grey Valley	2022	15	10
C.J.D. (Cleveland) Barrell	Grey Valley	2023	10	38
L.H. (Levi) Carew	Grey Valley	2023	8	0
D.J. (Daniel) Davis	Kiwi	2017	52	10
J.C. (Jarrod) Ferguson	Kiwi	2014	52	30
D.M. (Daniel) Foord	Kiwi	2016	47	20
N.J.H. (Nick) Foxley	Sydenham [2]	2023	10	15
T.W. (Tamati) Frost [1]	Burnside [3]	2023	3	0
J.A. (Jaime) Garland	Wests	2021	25	15
A.W. (Arnold) Gibbens	Wests	2022	12	0
S.K. (Sincere) Harraway	Marist	2023	1	0
J.K. (Jarel) Hemehema	Nelson Marist [4]	2023	6	5
Q.T.L. (Quinn) Johnsen	Kiwi	2023	1	0
T.J. (Tyler) Kearns	Grey Valley	2018	27	10
S.P. (Sione) Lonitenisi	Grey Valley	2023	6	5
J.P. (Jacob) Lowe	Marist	2021	14	38
J.S. (Jesse) MacRae	South Westland	2015	49	0
J.J. (Joshua) Manning	-	2013	41	20
S.R. (Sean) McClure	Kiwi	2011	83	167
K.G. (Kane) Parker	Kiwi	2023	2	0
J.C. (Jack) Rea	Kiwi	2023	1	0
T.M. (Matthew) Robbins [1]	Christchurch HSOB [3]	2023	7	0
L.J. (Logan) Ross	Wests	2022	18	113
C.S. (Cameron) Rutherford	-	2022	9	0
W.J.S. (William) Schmetz	Wests	2023	10	0
J.W. (Joseph) Scott	Grey Valley	2021	23	43
S.G. (Steven) Soper	Grey Valley	2017	44	75
M.R. (Mitchell) Tapp	South Westland	2022	2	0
T.K. (Troy) Tauwhare	Kiwi	2009	99	114
P.E. (Peter) Te Rakau	Kiwi	2014	28	25
J.P. (Joshua) Tomlinson	Wests	2017	37	35
T.M.L. (Tumama) Tu'ulua	Sydenham [2]	2018	24	10
A.V. (Amenatave) Tukana	Belfast [2]	2016	51	71
L.H.F. (Logan) Winter	Kiwi	2014	37	16

1. Player of Origin 2. Loaned by Canterbury RU 3. Canterbury RU 4. Loaned by Tasman RU

INDIVIDUAL SCORING

	Tries	Con	PG	DG	Points		Tries	Con	PG	DG	Points
Ross	3	23	12	-	97	Hemehema	1	-	-	-	5
Barrell	7	-	1	-	38	Foord	1	-	-	-	5
Tauwhare	5	-	-	-	25	Tomlinson	1	-	-	-	5
Foxley	3	-	-	-	15	Soper	1	-	-	-	5
McClure	3	-	-	-	15	Lonitenisi	1	-	-	-	5
Penalty Try	2	-	-	-	14	Garland	1	-	-	-	5
Kearns	2	-	-	-	10						
Manning	2	-	-	-	10	***Totals***	***37***	***23***	***13***	***0***	***274***
Tukana	2	-	-	-	10						
Scott	1	-	-	-	5	*Opposition scored*	*35*	*21*	*14*	*0*	*259*
Anderson	1	-	-	-	5						

WEST COAST 2023	King Country	Horowhenua Kapiti	Thames Valley	Whanganui	South Canterbury	Mid Canterbury	Buller	North Otago	Wairarapa Bush (sf)	Poverty Bay (f)	**TOTALS**
Garland	15	s	s	15	-	s	s	11	11	11	**9**
Te Rakau	-	-	-	-	s	-	-	-	-	-	**1**
Hemehema	-	-	-	10	-	15	15	15	15	15	**6**
Ross	14	14	14	14	14	14	14	14	14	14	**10**
Lowe	11	11	-	-	-	-	-	-	-	-	**2**
Harraway	s	-	-	-	-	-	-	-	-	-	**1**
Carew	-	s	11	11	11	-	s	s	s	s	**8**
Foxley	13	12	12	12	13	13	13	13	13	13	**10**
Anderson	-	13	13	13	12	12	-	12	12	12	**8**
McClure	12	15	15	-	-	s	12	s	s	s	**8**
Scott	10	10	10	s	15	11	11	-	-	-	**7**
Parker	s	-	-	-	s	-	-	-	-	-	**2**
Robbins	-	-	-	s	10	10	10	10	10	10	**7**
Barrell	9	9	9	9	9	s	9	9	9	9	**10**
Ferguson	s	s	-	s	s	9	s	s	-	-	**7**
Tukana	8	8	8	8	8	-	-	-	-	-	**5**
Winter	s	-	-	-	s	s	s	s	-	s	**6**
Soper (capt.)	7	7	7	7	7	7	8	8	8	8	**10**
Schmetz	6	6	6	s	s	s	6	6	6	6	**10**
Tomlinson	-	s	s	6	6	6	7	7	7	7	**9**
Manning	5	5	5	5	5	5	5	5	5	5	**10**
Tu'ulua	4	4	4	-	4	4	4	4	4	4	**9**
Gibbens	s	s	s	s	-	-	s	s	-	-	**6**
Rutherford	-	-	-	4	-	8	-	-	-	-	**2**
Rea	-	-	-	-	-	-	-	-	s	-	**1**
Kearns	3	3	1	1	1	1	1	1	1	1	**10**
Frost	1	1	s	-	-	-	-	-	-	-	**3**
Davis	s	s	3	3	3	3	3	3	3	3	**10**
MacRae	s	-	-	s	s	s	s	s	s	s	**8**
Tapp	-	s	-	-	-	-	-	-	-	-	**1**
Foord	-	-	s	s	s	s	s	s	s	s	**8**
Tauwhare	2	2	2	2	2	2	2	2	2	2	**10**
Lonitenisi	s	s	-	s	-	-	-	s	s	s	**6**
Johnsen	-	-	-	-	-	-	s	-	-	-	**1**

WEST COAST TEAM RECORD 2023

Played 10 **Won 6** **Lost 4** **Points for 274** **Points against 259**

Date	Opponent	Location	Score	Tries	Con	PG	DG	Referee
August 12	King Country	Greymouth	40–9	Tauwhare, Barrell, Kearns, Manning	Ross (4)	Ross (4)		Ben Alexander
August 19	Horowhenua Kapiti	Levin	48–28	Barrell (2), Foxley (2), McClure (2), Scott	Ross (5)	Ross		Stu Catley
August 26	Thames Valley	Greymouth	22–30	Tukana (2), Barrell	Ross (2)	Barrell		Jackson Henshaw
September 2	Whanganui	Whanganui	12–36	Tauwhare (2)	Ross			Ben Woolerton
September 9	South Canterbury	Fairlie	26–39	Anderson, Manning, Penalty Try, Tauwhare	Ross (2)			Dan Moore
September 16	Mid Canterbury	Greymouth	32–29 aet	Foxley, Hemahema, McClure, Foord	Ross (3)	Ross (2)		Josh Bamber
September 23	Buller	Christchurch	11–29	Ross		Ross (2)		Dan Moore
September 30	North Otago	Greymouth	27–12	Barrell (2), Tomlinson, Soper, Lonitenisi	Ross			George Haswell
October 7	Wairarapa Bush (LC sf)	Masterton	33–27	Ross (2), Tauwhare, Kearns, Garland	Ross (4)			Will Johnston
October 15	Poverty Bay (LC f)	Greymouth	23–20	Barrell, Penalty Try	Ross	Ross (3)		Jackson Henshaw

WHANGANUI

2023 Status: Heartland Championship
Founded 1888. Original member 1892;
name changed to Whanganui 2021
President: J.C. (Jeff) Slight
Chairman: J.M. (Jeff) Phillips
Chief executive officer: B.S. (Bridget) Belsham
Coach: J.P. (Jason) Hamlin
Assistant coaches: Kim McNaught,
P.G. (Peter) O'Shaughnessy
Selector: M.F. (Marty) McGrath (since 2014)
Main ground: Cooks Gardens
Capacity: 15,000
Colours: Royal blue, black and white

RECORDS

Highest attendance	6500	*Whanganui v Scotland, 1996*
Most appearances	146	*T.T.T. Olney, 1973–90*
Most points	980	*R.B. Barrell, 1963–77*
Most tries	48	*J.D. Hainsworth, 1984–95*
Most points in a season	184	*G.R.J. Lennox, 1994*
Most tries in a season	14	*H.S. Gordon, 1988*
	14	*P. Fetuia, 2006*
Most conversions in a season	44	*M.K. Davis, 2008*
Most penalty goals in a season	39	*R.B. Barrell, 1975*
Most dropped goals in a season	6	*L.T. Head, 1952*
Most points in a match	32	*K.H. Chase v East Coast, 1989*
Most tries in a match	6	*D.F. Philipson v Taranaki, 1919*
Most conversions in a match	10	*L.K. Harding v West Coast, 1993*
		G.R.J. Lennox v Buller, 1994
Most penalty goals in a match	6	*R.B. Barrell v Manawatu, 1971*
		R.B. Barrell v Taranaki, 1975
		M.K. Davis v East Coast, 2011
Highest team score	83	*v Buller, 2022*
Record victory (points ahead)	77	*80–3 v King Country, 2017*
Highest score conceded	88	*v Taranaki, 2000*
Record defeat (points behind)	84	*0–84 v Taranaki, 1995*

With two defeats in their first three games, Whanganui found themselves in the unaccustomed position of eighth on the points table. From there on they found their stride and reeled off six consecutive wins for a place in the Meads Cup final for the 13th time in the 17 years of the Heartland Championship.

The 38–3 demolition of Thames Valley in the semi-final was a very impressive performance and reversed the result of their encounter in the opening game. Whanganui and South Canterbury produced a hard-fought match in the final which ended in defeat for Whanganui, 30–40, a scoreline that was similar to last year's final between the two teams.

Coach Jason Hamlin had most of his 2022 regulars returning, although frontline players missing were Ezra Malo and Semi Vodosese (both Hawke's Bay) and Ethan Robinson and Ben Whale (both overseas). Kameli Kuruyabaki, Tyler Rogers-Holden and Jack Yarrall did not make the final selection which underlined the talent Hamlin had at his disposal.

Apolosi Tanoa and Peceli Malanicagi were the two outside backs who stood out. Newcomer Tanoa looked very promising and scored six tries, while Malanicagi gave some good displays at both wing and fullback.

Whanganui had strength in midfield where Timoci Seruwalu was a strong second-five both on attack and defence, but the star of the backline was flying centre Alekesio Vakarororogo. His ability to create openings, together with his powerful running, netted him 13 tries, just one short of the Heartland Championship season record. His five tries against Horowhenua Kapiti equalled the Heartland Championship for most tries in a game.

Halfback Lindsay Horrocks passed his century of games for Whanganui and again rendered excellent service. He has missed only two games since his debut in the opening match of the 2013 season. Captain Dane Whale was a very astute general at first-five and his excellent goalkicking was a big asset. He showed his class in the playoffs.

Loose forwards Samu Kubunavanua, Jamie Hughes and Doug Horrocks were a very effective trio, their play around the field was of a high order on both attack and defence. Lock Josh Lane won plenty of lineout ball and Peter-Travis Hay-Horton played some fine games in the second half of the season, coming back from a head knock stand down. Matthew Ashworth was a ready-made replacement for both.

Prop was well covered by Hadlee Hay-Horton, Gabriel Hakaraia, Keightley Watson, Raymond Salu and newcomer Konradd Newland. They all received good game time as injuries occurred. Roman Tutauha played his 100th game in the semi-final, and made his usual solid contribution at hooker.

WHANGANUI REPRESENTATIVES 2023

Name	Club	Debut	For Union Games	For Union Points
M.T. (Matthew) Ashworth	Kaierau	2020	24	0
Josaia Bogileka	Marist	2019	31	45
J.A. (Joshua) Brunger	Kaierau	2023	6	5
Eben Claassen	Kaierau	2023	10	5
G.T.E. (Gabriel) Hakaraia	Ruapehu	2016	46	20
Hadlee Hay-Horton	Taihape	2020	20	0
P.T.H. (Peter-Travis) Hay-Horton	Taihape	2018	27	5
Doug Horrocks	Kaierau	2013	19	20
L.D. (Lindsay) Horrocks	Border	2013	102	127
J.N. (Jamie) Hughes	Ruapehu	2016	70	58
S.N. (Samu) Kubunavanua	Marist	2014	56	101
Josh Lane	Kaierau	2017	39	15
Peceli Malanicagi	Kaierau	2021	17	25
Josefa Namosimalua	Border	2023	10	0
K.H.R. (Konradd) Newland [1]	Napier Pirates [2]	2023	9	5
Sheldon Pakinga	Kaierau	2023	5	9
Raymond Salu	Kaierau	2019	17	35
T.S. (Timoci) Seruwalu	College OB [3]	2017	41	110
A.T. (Apolosi) Tanoa	Kaierau	2023	10	30
Renato Tikoisolomone	Border	2015	29	11
A.W. (Alesana) Tofa	Marist	2023	10	15
R.B.K. (Roman) Tutauha	Ruapehu	2012	101	66
Alekesio Vakarorogo	Border	2020	32	150
S.F. (Silio) Waqalevu	Border	2023	6	0
K.L. (Keightley) Watson	Marist	2022	16	0
D.J. (Dane) Whale	Taihape	2014	78	267
L.P. (Luke) Whale	Taihape	2023	8	5
E.K.M. (Emmanuel) Wineera	Border	2023	2	0

1. Player of Origin   2. Hawke's Bay RU   3. Loaned by Manawatu RU

INDIVIDUAL SCORING

	Tries	Con	PG	DG	Points		Tries	Con	PG	DG	Points
D. Whale	1	25	10	1	88	Newland	1	-	-	-	5
Vakarorogo	13	-	-	-	65	Hughes	1	-	-	-	5
Tanoa	6	-	-	-	30	Brunger	1	-	-	-	5
Seruwalu	4	-	-	-	20	Lane	1	-	-	-	5
D. Horrocks	4	-	-	-	20	Claassen	1	-	-	-	5
Tofa	3	-	-	-	15	Tutauha	1	-	-	-	5
L. Horrocks	3	-	-	-	15	L. Whale	-	1	1	-	5
Malanicagi	3	-	-	-	15						
Kubunavanua	2	-	-	-	10	***Totals***	***47***	***29***	***12***	***1***	***332***
Salu	2	-	-	-	10						
Pakinga	-	3	1	-	9	*Opposition scored*	*26*	*18*	*11*	*0*	*199*

WHANGANUI 2023	Thames Valley	Buller	King Country	West Coast	North Otago	Ngati Porou East Coast	Wairarapa Bush	Horowhenua Kapiti	Thames Valley (sf)	South Canterbury (f)	**TOTALS**
Pakinga	15	15	15	15	15	-	-	-	-	-	**5**
Malanicagi	s	14	14	14	14	15	15	15	15	15	**10**
Vakarorogo	14	13	13	13	13	13	13	13	13	13	**10**
Bogileka	11	11	11	11	-	11	11	11	11	11	**9**
Brunger	-	-	-	-	s	s	s	s	s	s	**6**
Tanoa	s	s	s	s	11	14	14	14	14	14	**10**
Waqalevu	13	s	s	s	s	-	-	-	-	s	**6**
Seruwalu	12	12	12	12	12	12	12	12	12	12	**10**
D. Whale (capt.)	10	10	10	10	10	10	10	10	10	10	**10**
L. Horrocks	9	9	9	9	9	9	9	9	9	9	**10**
Claassen	s	s	s	s	s	s	s	s	s	s	**10**
Kubunavanua	8	8	8	6	6	s	6	6	-	-	**8**
Hughes	7	7	7	7	7	7	7	7	7	7	**10**
D. Horrocks	6	6	6	8	8	8	8	8	8	8	**10**
Namosimalua	s	s	s	s	s	6	s	s	6	6	**10**
L. Whale	-	s	s	-	s	s	s	s	s	s	**8**
Lane	5	5	5	5	5	5	5	5	5	5	**10**
P. Hay-Horton	4	-	-	4	-	s	4	4	4	4	**7**
Ashworth	s	4	4	s	4	4	s	s	s	s	**10**
Hakaraia	3	-	-	-	-	-	s	s	s	s	**5**
H. Hay-Horton	1	-	-	-	s	s	1	1	1	1	**7**
Tikoisolomone	s	-	-	s	-	-	-	-	s	-	**3**
Watson	s	3	3	s	s	s	-	-	-	-	**6**
Newland	-	1	1	1	1	1	s	s	s	s	**9**
Wineera	-	s	s	-	-	-	-	-	-	-	**2**
Salu	-	s	s	3	3	3	3	3	3	3	**9**
Tutauha	2	2	2	2	2	2	s	2	2	2	**10**
Tofa	s	s	s	s	s	s	2	s	s	s	**10**

WHANGANUI TEAM RECORD 2023

Played 10 **Won 7** **Lost 3** **Points for 332** **Points against 199**

Date	Opponent	Location	Score	Tries	Con	PG	DG	Referee
August 12	Thames Valley	Whanganui	33–36	Vakarorogo, Seruwalu, Kubunavanua, D. Horrocks, Tofa	Pakinga (2), D. Whale (2)			Will Johnston
August 19	Buller	Westport	13–5	D. Horrocks (2)		D. Whale		Ben Alexander
August 26	King Country	Taumarunui	17–23	Newland, Tanoa	Pakinga, L. Whale	Pakinga		Natarsha Ganley
September 2	West Coast	Whanganui	36–12	Vakarorogo (3), Seruwalu, Hughes	D. Whale (4)	D. Whale		Ben Woolerton
September 9	North Otago	Oamaru	34–19	Vakarorogo (2), Tanoa (2), Brunger	D. Whale (3)	D. Whale		Jackson Henshaw
September 16	Ngati Porou East Coast	Whanganui	40–24	L. Horrocks (2), Vakarorogo (2), Tofa	D. Whale (3)	D. Whale (3)		Stu Curran
September 23	Wairarapa Bush (BSC)	Masterton	36–18	Kubunavanua, Tofa, Lane, Malanicagi, Claassen	D. Whale (4)	D. Whale		Jack Sargentina
September 30	Horowhenua Kapiti (BSC)	Whanganui	55–19	Vakarorogo (5), L. Horrocks, Tanoa, D. Horrocks, Seruwalu	D. Whale (5)			Will Johnston
October 7	Thames Valley (MC sf)	Whanganui	38–3	Malanicagi (2), Tanoa, Tutauha, Salu	D. Whale (2)	D. Whale, L. Whale	D. Whale	Stu Catley
October 14	South Canterbury (MC f)	Temuka	30–40	Seruwalu, D. Whale, Salu, Tanoa	D. Whale (2)	D. Whale (2)		Fraser Hannon

(BSC) Bruce Steel Cup

RANFURLY SHIELD 2023

Wellington's 7–0 win over Tasman was the lowest scoring Shield match since Canterbury retained the Shield with a 3–3 draw against Wellington in 1970, and the lowest winning score since 1980 when Waikato defeated Auckland 7–3.

Having established 21 consecutive wins in first-class matches, a record for the province, Wellington lost the Ranfurly Shield in the final defence of the season. A 78th minute try under the posts, followed by the successful conversion, put Hawke's Bay 20–18 in front to win.

Results

Wellington

721	July 12	v Horowhenua Kapiti	Levin	won	68–7
722	July 19	v South Canterbury	Lower Hutt	won	67–21
723	August 19	v Southland	Lower Hutt	won	39–17
724	August 23	v Tasman	Wellington	won	7–0
725	September 2	v Counties Manukau	Wellington	won	56–25
726	September 24	v North Harbour	Porirua	won	26–6
727	September 30	v Hawke's Bay	Wellington	lost	18–20

First and most recent Ranfurly Shield match				*Drawn as*		*Points*	
	Played	*Won*	*Lost*	*holder*	*challenger*	*for*	*against*
Auckland (1904–2015)	203	158	39	5	1	5849	2220
Bay of Plenty (1920–2021)	25	2	23	–	–	361	691
Buller (1907–2001)	12	–	11	–	1	36	328
Bush (1927–1968)	7	–	7	–	–	41	285
Canterbury (1904–2020)	199	151	41	6	1	5835	2591
Counties Manukau (1958–2023)	35	7	26	–	2	623	961
Ngati Porou East Coast (1953–2021)	8	–	8	–	–	27	523
Golden Bay-Motueka (1958)	1	–	1	–	–	8	56
Hawke's Bay (1905–2023)	113	76	33	3	1	2795	1772
Horowhenua Kapiti (1914–2023)	11	–	11	–	–	99	631
King Country (1922–2016)	20	–	20	–	–	120	664
Manawatu (1914–2020)	40	14	25	–	1	543	812
Manawhenua (1927–1929)	6	3	3	–	–	84	110
Marlborough (1908–2005)	20	7	13	–	–	245	539
Mid Canterbury (1933–2017)	15	–	15	–	–	111	620
Nelson (1924–1959)	2	–	2	–	–	17	66
Nelson Bays (1973–2005)	6	–	6	–	–	46	334
North Harbour (1986–2023)	23	4	19	–	–	516	690
North Otago (1938–2021)	16	–	16	–	–	99	943
Northland (1935–2020)	49	17	31	1	–	732	1086
Otago (1904–2021)	93	44	46	1	2	1515	1402
Poverty Bay (1911-2022)	18	–	18	–	–	100	885
South Auckland (1911)	1	–	1	–	–	5	21
South Canterbury (1920–2023)	28	3	25	–	–	314	926
Southland (1906–2023)	76	30	43	–	3	1140	1547
Taranaki (1906–2020)	103	50	47	3	3	1703	1705
Tasman (2008–2023)	4	–	4	–	–	82	116
Thames Valley (1951–2019)	16	–	16	–	–	97	706
Waikato (1932–2022)	111	67	40	3	1	3193	1788
Wairarapa (1905–1969)	30	13	16	–	1	431	504
Wairarapa Bush (1973–2015)	9	–	9	–	–	67	491
Whanganui (1907–2018)	31	–	30	–	1	239	985
Wellington (1904–2023)	108	58	44	1	5	1897	1491
West Coast (1932–2000)	15	–	15	–	–	107	588

HIGHEST WINNING MARGIN BY A SHIELD HOLDER

134 points Auckland 139 North Otago 5 at Oamaru 1993

HIGHEST WINNING MARGIN BY A CHALLENGER

45 points Waikato 52 North Harbour 7 at Albany 2007

INDIVIDUAL PERFORMANCES

Most matches	57	*G.J. Fox, Auckland*
Most points	932	*G.J. Fox, Auckland*
Most tries	53	*T.J. Wright, Auckland*
Most conversions	233	*G.J. Fox, Auckland*
Most penalty goals	142	*G.J. Fox, Auckland*
Most dropped goals	14	*R.H. Brown, Taranaki; D. Trevathan, Otago*
Most goals from a mark	3	*J.H. Dufty, Auckland*
Most points in a match	40	*J.J. Kirwan, Auckland v North Otago, 1993*
Most tries in a match	8	*J.J. Kirwan, Auckland v North Otago, 1993*
Most conversions in a match	12	*B.M. Craies, Auckland v Horowhenua,1986; G.J. Fox, Auckland v Nelson Bays, 1991; G.W. Jackson, Waikato v West Coast, 2000; L.H. Munro, Auckland v North Otago, 2008*
Most penalty goals in a match	7	*R.M. Deans, Canterbury v Counties, 1984 C.J. McIntyre, Canterbury v Wellington, 2003*
Most dropped goals in a match	3	*R.H. Brown, Taranaki v Wanganui, 1964; R.H. Brown, Taranaki v North Auckland, 1964; G.P. Coffey, Canterbury v Auckland, 1990; A.P. Mehrtens, Canterbury v Southland, 1995*

WINNING CHALLENGES

Canterbury	16	Otago	7	Marlborough	1
Auckland	15[1]	Hawke's Bay	7	Manawatu	1
Waikato	11	Northland	4	Bay of Plenty	1
Wellington	11	Wairarapa	3	North Harbour	1
Southland	7	South Canterbury	2	Counties Manukau	1
Taranaki	7	Manawhenua	1		

[1] Auckland were also the first holders, presented the Shield in 1902 by the NZRFU for having the best record that year.

TENURES

Longest tenure	*Challenges resisted*	
Auckland	1985–93	61
Auckland	1960–63	25
Canterbury	1982–85	25
Hawke's Bay	1922–27	24
Auckland	1905–13	23
Canterbury	1953–56	23
Canterbury	2000–03	23
Hawke's Bay	1966–69	21
Waikato	1997–00	21

Shortest tenure		*Days*
Hawke's Bay	2013	6
Wellington	1963	7
Waikato	2007	7
Otago	2020	7
Taranaki	2020	8
Otago	2013	9
Auckland	1972	10
North Auckland	1960	11

North Auckland resisted one challenge; the other unions were defeated by the first challenger.

HAPPENINGS

The 2022 New Zealand Under 19 squad visited South Africa for four games, the tour assisting in the development of players ahead of the proposed Under 20 Rugby World Cup in July 2023.

Squad:
Ale Aho, Leo Gordon, Sam Hainsworth-Fa'aofo, Byron Smith, Essendon Tuitupou, Riley Williams *(Auckland)*; Taine Kolose, Toby Taylor *(Bay of Plenty)*; Tahlor Cahill, Isaac Hutchinson, Fiti Sa, Nic Shearer *(Canterbury)*; Keran van Staden *(Counties Manukau)*; Cooper Flanders *(Hawke's Bay)*; Hunter Morrison, Jordi Viljoen, Epeli Waqaicece *(Manawatu)*; Rory Woods *(Northland)*; Ajay Faleafaga, Finn Hurley, Will Stodart, Semisi Tupou Ta'eiloa *(Otago)*; Jack Taylor *(Southland)*; Dylan Irvine *(Tasman)*; Cody Nordstrom, Andrew Smith, Gabe Robinson *(Waikato)*; Bradley Crichton, Siale Lauaki, *(Wellington)*. Torian Barnes (Canterbury) was injured after selection and replaced by Fiti Sa. Mefi Poseti Tupou *(Hawke's Bay)* was another original selection who could not tour.
Director of Rugby: Matt Sexton
Head coach: Mark Hammett
Assistant coaches: PJ Williams, Ben Fisher, Sam Moore
Manager: Ross Everiss

Results:
September 19, v Western Province Under 19, at Paul Roos Stadium, Stellenbosch. Won 86–0.
Waqaicece (2), Gordon (2), Tuitupou (2), Williams (2), Nordstrom (2), J. Taylor, Woods, Hutchinson, Kolose tries; Faleafaga (7), B. Smith conversions.
September 24, v Sharks Under 19, at Durban High School, Durban. Won 54–13.
Morrison (2), Nordstrom (2), Kolose, Hutchinson, Waqaicece, van Staden tries; B. Smith (5), Faleafaga (2) conversions.
September 29, v Leopards Under 19, at Olen Park Stadium, Potchefstroom. Won 42–31.
Waqaicece (2), Irvine, Morrison, Ta'eiloa, Tuitupou tries; Faleafaga (5), B. Smith conversions.
October 4, v Lions Under 19, at Emirates Airline Park Stadium, Johannesburg. Won 42–10.
Tuitupou (3), Faleafaga, Kolose, Hainsworth-Fa'aofo tries; Faleafaga (4), B. Smith (2) conversions.
(The editors regret the tour record was omitted from 2023 edition)

• • •

During a senior game on March 25 at Easton Park, Foxton, the referee issued five red and ten yellow cards in a game between Foxton and Shannon clubs.

• • •

USA competition Major League Rugby (MLR) has proved to be an increasingly popular destination for NZ provincial players without a Super Rugby contract between NPC seasons. The 2023 Bunnings NPC contained 45 players who had played MLR this year, spread across 12 of the 14 unions:

Auckland (1), Bay of Plenty (2), Counties Manukau (1) , Hawke's Bay (6), Manawatu (12), North Harbour (6), Northland (3), Otago (3), Southland (2), Taranaki (7), Tasman (1), Waikato (1).

• • •

The Kiwi club on the West Coast has won 82 consecutive matches and eight championships, and the streak is still alive going into 2024. Twelve players have appeared in all eight winning finals:
Jarrod Ferguson, Daniel Foord, Joshua Kearns, Sean McClure, Nick Muir, Matthew Olson, Kyle Parker, James Stephens, Peter Te Rakau, Daniel Tauwhare, Troy Tauwhare and Logan Winter.

• • •

It's believed Mahia produced a run of 133 consecutive wins during the 1980's in the Wairoa sub-union championship. Timaru's Celtic club won 10 consecutive South Canterbury titles between 2009 and 2018, and Star of Invercargill managed a yet to be, and highly unlikely to be repeated, 14 club final victories on the trot between 1890 and 1903.

• • •

Notable winning streaks in metro unions are held by the Ponsonby Fillies (the premier women's team), who won eight consecutive championships and 86 straight games between 1986 and 1993; and the Ponsonby premier men won 10 out of 11 Gallaher Shields between 2001 and 2011, which included a run of 41 successive wins between 2008 and 2010. Their overall record in this period read: Played 211, won 189, drew 2, lost 20, points for 7975, against 2619. Marist St Pats in Wellington won 42 games in a row from 1978 to 1980 while Ian Upston engineered a glorious reign as Petone coach in the capital. He won 172 out of 192 matches, including eight Jubilee Cups in a decade in the 60s and 70s.

• • •

The Black Ferns won their 100th Test when they beat Canada 52–21 in the Pac4 Series, in their 117th Test, making New Zealand the quickest Tier I country to achieve 100 Test wins. England reached the landmark in 119 Tests in 2006. England's won their first Test in 1987 against Wales 22–4 in Pontypool. The Red Roses won their 100th Test match on March 1, 2006, when they beat France 28–0 at Stade Robert Bobin, Bondoufle. France took 184 Test matches to reach a century. They raised a ton on March 13, 2010, when they beat Italy 45–14 at Stade du Manoir, Montpellier. France won the first official women's international against the Netherlands (4–0) in 1982. The All Blacks won their 100th Test after 141 matches against Wales in Christchurch (19–0) in 1969.

• • •

On Saturday September 23 all six Crusaders region provincial teams played amongst themselves in derby matches at Apollo Projects Stadium in Christchurch in a triple-header. In the Bunnings NPC Canterbury was drawn to host Tasman, while in the Heartland Championship Buller was to host West Coast and South Canterbury was to host Mid Canterbury. The Bunnings NPC draw was released first and the Canterbury v Tasman fixture was down for September 23. The Unions asked NZR if the Heartland Championship draw could be aligned by the Buller v West Coast and South Canterbury v Mid Canterbury fixtures also being set for September 23, which was done. South Canterbury defeated Mid Canterbury 50–35 to retain the Hanan Shield in the 2.05pm match, Canterbury defeated Tasman 30–28 in the 4.35pm contest and Buller defeated West Coast 29–11 at 7.05pm to retain the Rundle Cup.
The six unions remain committed to trying it again in the future.

• • •

Tactical substitutions before halftime are a rarity and all eight substitutions coming on at the same time is something that no one can pinpoint as ever having previously occurred. But in just the 32nd minute of the Bunnings NPC match between Southland and Bay of Plenty at Invercargill, Southland emptied their entire eight-man bench in one go.

New Zealand domestic competitions allow for players subbed off tactically to return to the field as a replacement for injured players, and two of the players subbed off in the 32nd minute — Jack Sexton and Danny Drake — both returned to the field in the 72nd minute as injury replacements for Hunter Fahey and Shneil Singh.

• • •

Bay of Plenty lock Manaaki Selby-Rickit scored nine tries to top the try count for the NPC competition. This made him just the fourth forward to lead the NPC try scoring in a season:

1986 — Dale Atkins (Canterbury) — 7 tries*
1987 — Zinzan Brooke (Auckland) — 11 tries
1990 — John Mitchell (Waikato) — 11 tries
2023 — Manaaki Selby-Rickit (Bay of Plenty) — 9 tries
*shared with three other players.

• • •

Tamaiti Williams became the heaviest man to play for New Zealand (or perhaps the player who admitted to the largest weight) when he debuted against South Africa at Auckland on July 15:

140kg — Tamaiti Williams, 2023
136kg — Neemia Tialata, 2005–2010
135kg — Karl Tu'inukuafe, 2018–2022
130kg — Jamie Mackintosh, 2008
127kg — Charlie Faumuina, 2012–2017
127kg — Atu Moli, 2017–2019
127kg — Tyrel Lomax, 2018–2023

• • •

The All Blacks' 7–35 loss to South Africa at Twickenham on August 25 was the All Blacks' biggest ever Test defeat:

28 points — 7–35 v South Africa, Twickenham, 2023
21 points — 7–28 v Australia, Sydney, 1999
21 points — 26–47 v Australia, Perth, 2019
17 points — 0–17 v South Africa, Durban, 1928
17 points — 21–38 v England, Twickenham, 2012

The All Blacks' biggest Test defeat on home soil is:

15 points — 5–20 v Australia, Wellington, 1964

• • •

Rieko Ioane and Will Jordan both scored their 100th first-class try during the course of the year:

Rieko Ioane for Blues v Hurricanes, Auckland, May 27
Will Jordan for New Zealand v Argentina, World Cup semi-final, Paris, October 20
Jordan scored three tries v Argentina, the first of the three was his 100th first-class try.

• • •

When Sam Whitelock took the field for New Zealand v Italy on September 29 in the World Cup match at Lyon, it was his 149th Test, making him the most capped All Black of all time, going past the mark of 148 set by Richie McCaw in 2015.
Since Colin Meads played his 55th (and final) Test in 1971, the progression of the record has been:

58 — Gary Whetton, 1981–1991 (56th v Canada, October 20, 1991)
63 — John Kirwan, 1984–1994 (59th v France, Christchurch, June 26, 1994)
92 — Sean Fitzpatrick, 1986–1997 (64th v Ireland, Johannesburg, May 27, 1995)
98* — Richie McCaw, 2001–2011 (93rd v Ireland, Dublin, November 20, 2010)
98* — Mils Muliaina, 2003–2011 (93rd v Ireland, Dublin, November 20, 2010)
148 — Richie McCaw, 2001–2015 (99th v Tonga, Auckland, September 9, 2011)
153 — Sam Whitelock, 2010–2023 (149th v Italy, Lyon, September 29, 2023)
*McCaw and Muliaina played their 93rd to 98th Tests simultaneously in the same matches.

• • •

On October 6, at Navigation Homes Stadium, Pukekohe the New Zealand U18 Māori Ngā Māreikura Girls defeated the New Zealand Barbarians U18 Girls 31–7. It was the first time a girls' fixture between the two teams occurred, with a boys' equivalent established in 2018. The Māori tries were scored by Braxton Sorensen-McGee, Justine McGregor, Janelle Dheddadig, Anahera Hamahona, and Kesha Church with Kaea Nepia kicking three conversations. Barbarians halfback Abigail Paton scored a converted try.
Ngā Māreikura were led by Bay of Plenty's Jarvy Aoake as Head Coach supported by former Black Fern Stephanie Te Ohaere-Fox (Forwards Coach) and current Matatū player Te Rauoriwa Gapper as Backs Coach. The NZ Barbarians were led by Mark Hooper (Auckland) and Jimmy Sinclair (Canterbury), assisted by former Black Ferns Kendra Cocksedge and Aleisha Nelson.

• • •

High School Old Boys Light Bears from Christchurch won the fourth edition of the National Under 85kg Cup defeating North Harbour champions Takapuna Bombers 45–17 in a curtain raiser to the North Harbour v Northland NPC match on September 16. The Light Bears were an assortment of Colts and premier players in the absence of organised competition in Canterbury. On the way to the final, they defeated Prebbleton (Ellesmere & North Canterbury), 55–5, Waihora (Ellesmere & North Canterbury), 37–7, Southern Bush Pigs (Otago), 30–17, University Squids (Auckland), 26–19 and Grammar Tech (Auckland), 20–5. A New Zealand Barbarians squad of 31 players that didn't play a fixture, but reflected the growth of interest in the grade was selected.

• • •

Following the National Under 85kg Cup a New Zealand Barbarians Selection was picked:
Forwards: Liam Bernet (Tukapa Bantams), Lewis Craik (Morrinsville Majestic Pukekos), Jeandre Du Toit (Pakuranga Black Panthers), Luke Eyre (Massey Rock & Rumble), Jayden Ford (New Plymouth Old Boys Half Pints), Josh Gellert (Auckland University Slugs), Frazer Harrison (Auckland University Squids), Kasey Joe-McIndoe (Ponsonby Hustlers), Morgan Jones (Southern Bushpigs), Logan Kinnear (Pakuranga Black Panthers), Tyler Konning (Eden Lizards), Jordan Roylance (New Plymouth Half Pints), Shaan Waite (New Plymouth Old Boys Half Pints)
Backs: Campbell Busby (Auckland University RFC Squids), Taine Codell-Hull (High School Old Boys Light Bears), George Coull (High School Old Boys Light Bears), Jackson Ephraims (Takapuna Bombers), Matt Fowler (Old Boys University Scallywags), Freddie Gibson (High School Old Boys Light Bears), James Guthrie-Croft (Grammar Tech Old Boys), Macka Haugh (Southern Bushpigs), Kees Jansen (Old Boys University Scallywags), Ben Megson (Grammar Tech Old Boys), Jarred Percival (High School Old Boys Light Bears), Reece Plumtree (Old Boys University Scallywags), Tom Rance (Ponsonby Hustlers), Eamon Reily (Ponsonby Hustlers)

There were no fixtures played but there is a desire to tour Sri Lanka in the near future.

• • •

A second New Zealand University women's side was selected and played two matches in Wellington in September. On the 12th at the NZCIS-NZ Campus of Innovation and Sport in Trentham, NZU was beaten 17–10 by a Wellington Invitational XV. Two tries from Black Ferns XV openside Leah Miles wasn't enough to subdue a stubborn opponent. Four days later NZU cut loose and slayed the New Zealand Defence Force 75–19 at nearby Davis Field. NZU scored a dozen tries. Scorers were Victoria Makea (3), Nicole Purdom (2), Sarita de Gouw (2), Calista Ruruku (2) Emma Dermody, Mia Cochrane, and Te Amohaere Ngata-Aerengamate collecting the tries; Cochrane four conversions and a penalty, and Neave Rowland kicked two conversations. The coach was Dave Jensen, assisted by James Clabburn.
The full squad was:
Auckland University: Katrina Hall
Canterbury University: Charlotte Allen, Sarita de Gouw, Kelsyn McCook, Nicole Purdom, Jorja Simpson, Sammy Spence, Erana Te Moananui, Holly Wratt-Groewneweg
Lincoln University: Emma Dermody
Otago University: Sammie Bean, Lucy Blyde, Lucy Cahill, Mia Cochrane, Lucy Hall, Dallas McKnight, Leah Miles, Neave Rowland
Waikato University: Claudia Hobbs, Victoria Makea, Finau Mafi, Calista Ruruku, Te Amohaere Ngata-Aerengamate, Mia Robertson

• • •

There was much speculation over whether Super Rugby Aupiki would include offshore teams for the 2024 season, but on 10 October the answer was revealed as being 'No'. Despite the interest, no teams from the Pacific Islands or Australia were included, but the season was elongated to include a full home and away series followed by a final, the biggest yet. With a base of six matches — seven for the two finalists — increased contract values were also announced. The four teams were named on 28 November.

• • •

Within five weeks towards the end of the year, two centenarians of Antipodean rugby, Roy Roper (New Zealand) and Eric Tweedale (Australia), died. Each was the first former international from their respective countries to reach the age of 100, and naturally they were their nations' oldest living internationals.

Tweedale, the older of the pair, toured New Zealand in 1946 and Britain and France in 1947–48 with the Wallabies, but after winning ten caps he transferred to Parkes — close to the back of beyond in rugby terms in those days — and played little more rugby of note. Born on 5 May 1921, his 100th birthday was marked by the renaming of his old club's home ground at Parramatta as the Eric Tweedale Stadium.

Roper made his debut against Australia at home in 1949, while 30 players were touring South Africa. He wasn't the only one of the 'second string' to make his mark; a colleague was Tiny White, one of New Zealand's greatest locks. Roper played all four tests against the Lions in 1950 but a knee injury later that season ended his career in top rugby. He was born on 11 August 1923, so still had some of his beat years ahead when he was injured.

Both were Navy men during World War II — Tweedale had even played First Grade in Sydney before the War — and each had remained in good health apart from the encroaches of old age. Roy Roper died on 14 September 2023, and Eric Tweedale died on 17 October.

• • •

The New Zealand Rugby Players' Association announced its annual awards in December, the finalists and winners being voted by the players (winner in bold).

All Blacks Player of the Year — Jordie Barrett, Scott Barrett, Rieko Ioane, **Ardie Savea.**

All Blacks Sevens — **Leroy Carter**, Ngarohi McGarvey-Black, Akuila Rokolisoa, Joe Webber.

Maori All Blacks — Cullen Grace, Billy Harmon, Josh Ioane, **Shaun Stevenson.**

All Blacks XV — Luke Jacobson, Damian McKenzie, TJ Perenara, **Shaun Stevenson.**

Super Rugby Pacific — Jordie Barrett, Cullen Grace, Stephen Perofeta, **Pita Gus Sowakula.**

NPC — Billy Harmon, Du'Plessis Kirifi, Cam Roigard, **Mark Telea.**

Men's young player — George Bell, Riley Higgins, **Noah Hotham**, Peter Lakai.

Black Ferns — **Ruahei Demant**, Theresa Fitzpatrick, Maiakawanakaulani Roos, Ruby Tui.

Black Ferns Sevens — **Sarah Hirini**, Shiray Kaka, Risaleaana Pouri-Lane, Alena Saili.

Super Rugby Aupiki — Joanah Ngan-Woo, Kaipo Olsen-Baker, **Hazel Tubic**, Portia Woodman.

Farah Palmer Cup — **Liana Mikaele-Tu'u**, Joanah Ngan-Woo, Kendra Reynolds, Stephanie Te Ohaere-Fox.

Women's young player — **'Sylvia' Brunt**, Kerri Johnson, Jorja Miller, Santo Taumata.

• • •

The NZRU Awards were presented in December, with the nominees for various awards being (winners are in bold):

New Zealand Rugby Referee of the Year — Maggie Cogger-Orr , Angus Mabey , **Ben O'Keeffe**

Charles Monro Rugby Volunteer of the Year — Chris Fife (Northland), John Hume (Counties Manukau), Sharlene Wiseman (Canterbury), **Allen Grainger** (Waikato)

Bunnings Warehouse Rugby Club of the Year — Tamatea Rugby Sports Clubs (Hawke's Bay), **Auckland University Rugby Football Club** (Auckland), Beachlands Maraetai Rugby Club (Counties Manukau)

Te Hāpai New Zealand Rugby Community Impact Award — **Steven Li** (Asian Non-Contact Rugby Programme), Te Kahurangi Skelton (Otago Māori Rugby), Richard Perkins (Otago Rugby Football Union)

New Zealand Rugby Age Grade Player of the Year — **Harry Godfrey** (Hawke's Bay), Macca Springer (Tasman), Angelica Mekeke-Vahai (Auckland)

Ian Kirkpatrick Medal (Bunnings Warehouse Heartland Championship Player of the Year) — **Siu Kakala** (South Canterbury), Stuart Leach (Poverty Bay), Alekesio Vakarorogo (Whanganui)

Duane Monkley Medal (Bunnings Warehouse NPC Player of the Year) — **Etene Nanai-Seturo** (Counties Manukau), Adrian Choat (Auckland), Fergus Burke (Canterbury), Timoci Tavatavanawai (Tasman)

Fiao'o Faamausili Medal (FPC presented by Bunnings Warehouse Player of the Year) — **Krysten Cottrell** (Hawke's Bay), Laura Bayfield (Canterbury), Kaipo Olsen-Baker (Manawatu)

ASB National Men's Coach of the Year — Nigel Walsh (South Canterbury), **Neil Barnes** (Taranaki), Scott Robertson (Crusaders)

ASB National Women's Coach of the Year — **Rawinia Everitt** (Northland), Blair Baxter (Matatū), Willie Walker (Auckland)

ASB New Zealand Coach of the Year — **Cory Sweeney** (Black Ferns Sevens)

DHL Super Rugby Pacific Player of the Year — Mark Tele'a (Blues), **Scott Barrett** (Crusaders), Damian McKenzie (Chiefs)

Sky Super Rugby Aupiki Player of the Year — Renee Holmes (Matatū), **Lucy Jenkins** (Matatū), Luka Connor (Chiefs Manawa), Tanya Kalounivale (Chiefs Manawa)

Tom French Memorial Māori Player of the Year — **Aaron Smith** (Ngāti Kahungunu, Manawatu), Billy Harmon (Ngāi Tahu), Stacey Waaka (Ngāi Tūhoe), Arihiana Marino-Tauhinu (Nga

Puhi, Ngai Tahuhu)

Richard Crawshaw Memorial All Blacks Sevens Player of the Year — Leroy Carter, Akuila Rokolisoa, Dylan Collier

Black Ferns Sevens Player of the Year — Jorja Miller, Stacey Waaka, Risaleaana Pouri-Lane

Black Ferns Player of the Year — Maiakawanakaulani Roos, Liana Mikaele-Tu'u, Amy du Plessis

All Blacks Player of the Year — Jordie Barrett, Scott Barrett, *Ardie Savea*, Aaron Smith

adidas National Men's Team of the Year — Crusaders, Taranaki Bulls, South Canterbury

adidas National Women's Team of the Year — Auckland Storm, Northland Kauri, Matatū

adidas New Zealand Team of the Year — All Blacks Sevens

Steinlager Salver for an Outstanding Contribution to New Zealand Rugby — Rob Fisher

Kelvin R Tremain Memorial Trophy for the Player of the Year — Ardie Savea

2023 SEASON'S STATISTICS

LEADING SCORERS IN ALL FIRST-CLASS MATCHES IN NEW ZEALAND AND FOR NEW ZEALAND TEAMS OVERSEAS

(Record: 519, G.J. Fox, 1989 in 32 games, 2 Tries, 122 Con, 88 PG, 1 DG)

	Teams	*M*	*Tries*	*Con*	*PG*	*DG*	*Total*
R. Mo'unga	Crusaders/New Zealand	27	5	85	24	1	270
D.S. McKenzie	Chiefs/New Zealand	23	8	60	31	0	253
S.J. Gilbert	Highlanders/All Blacks XV/Otago	21	5	43	20	0	171
L.F. McClutchie	Moana Pasifika/Hawke's Bay	21	3	51	16	0	165
F.W. Burke	Crusaders/Canterbury	26	8	36	13	0	151
A. Morgan	Hurricanes/Wellington	25	3	38	17	0	142
J.M. Barrett	Hurricanes/New Zealand	22	4	37	14	0	136
Z. Sullivan	Blues/Auckland	23	9	27	10	0	129
B.J. Barrett	Blues/New Zealand	23	5	34	12	0	129
F.R. Morgan	Thames Valley/NZ Heartland	9	7	22	14	0	121
S. Perofeta	Blues/All Blacks XV/Taranaki	22	6	21	16	0	120

LEADING TRY-SCORERS

(Record: 36, J.J. Kirwan, 1987 in 32 games)

Tries	*Games*		*Teams*
18	18	L.O.K.W.P. Fainga'anuku	Crusaders/New Zealand
16	25	S.T. Stevenson	Chiefs/New Zealand/North Harbour
16	20	M.E. Telea	Blues/New Zealand
15	11	S.I.F. Kakala	South Canterbury
14	25	M.R. Springer	Crusaders/New Zealand Under 20/Tasman
13	23	C.J. Taylor	Crusaders/New Zealand
13	22	K.V. Naholo	Hurricanes/Taranaki
13	10	A. Vakarorogo	Whanganui
13	19	C.D. Roigard	Hurricanes/New Zealand
13	21	S.T.M. Rayasi	Hurricanes/Auckland
13	17	W.T. Jordan	Crusaders/New Zealand
12	24	E.W.P.S. Nanai-Seturo	Chiefs/All Blacks XV/Counties Manukau
12	23	A.S. Savea	Hurricanes/New Zealand
11	29	J.R. Riccitelli	Blues/All Blacks XV/Taranaki
11	23	T.T. Tavatavanawai	Moana Pasifika/Tasman
11	24	B.D. Proctor	Hurricanes/All Blacks XV/Wellington

THREE (or more) TRIES IN A MATCH

(Record: 8, T.R. Heeps, New Zealand v Northern NSW, 1962;
J.J. Kirwan, Auckland v North Otago, 1993)

5	A. Vakarorogo	Whanganui v Horowhenua Kapiti
4	M.E. Telea	Blues v Hurricanes, May 27
4	B.D. Proctor	All Blacks XV v Japan
4	A. Aumua	Wellington v South Canterbury
3	S.T. Stevenson	Chiefs v Moana Pasifika, March 4
3	L.O.K.W.P. Fainga'anuku	Crusaders v Blues, March 18
3	B.L. McAlister	Crusaders v Force
3	A.S. Savea	Hurricanes v Moana Pasifika, May 13
3	J.P.C. Asi	New Zealand Universities v Japan Under 20 (fc debut)
3	M.R. Springer	New Zealand Under 20 v Japan Under 20
3	P.P.I.N.H.V.F. Matakaiongo	South Canterbury v King Country
3	B.J. Murray	Canterbury v Wellington
3	A. Vakarorogo	Whanganui v West Coast
3	X.R. Tito-Harris	Auckland v Southland (fc debut)
3	N.R.F. Hotham	Tasman v Manawatu
3	L.F. Filipo	Wellington v Waikato, September 8
3	S.I.F. Kakala	South Canterbury v West Coast
3	G.J.L. Reeves	Buller v Horowhenua Kapiti
3	J.S.T. Gray	Counties Manukau v Southland
3	M.S.J. Manson	Southland v Counties Manukau
3	X.O. Roe	Waikato v Auckland
3	H.M. Tisdall	North Otago v Poverty Bay, September 16
3	M. Masoe	Horowhenua Kapiti v King Country
3	K.V. Leatigaga	South Canterbury v Mid Canterbury
3	A.L. Smith	New Zealand v Italy
3	L. Simote	South Canterbury v Poverty Bay
3	L.O.K.W.P. Fainga'anuku	New Zealand v Uruguay
3	C.J. Tiatia	Hawke's Bay v Wellington, October 14
3	W.T. Jordan	New Zealand v Argentina, October 20

21 (or more) POINTS IN A MATCH

(Record: 45, S.D. Culhane, New Zealand v Japan, 1995, 1 try, 20 conversions)

26	D.S. McKenzie	New Zealand v Namibia
25	B.J. Barrett	Blues v Highlanders, Feb 25
25	A. Vakarorogo	Whanganui v Horowhenua Kapiti
24	J.D. Jacomb	Taranaki v North Harbour
23	Z. Sullivan	Auckland v North Harbour
22	R. Mo'unga	Crusaders v Highlanders, March 3
22	R. Mo'unga	Crusaders v Blues, June 16
22	R. Patricio	Poverty Bay v Buller
21	J.M. Barrett	Hurricanes v Moana Pasifika, May 13
21	F.R. Morgan	Thames Valley v Whanganui, August 12 (fc debut)
21	F.R. Morgan	Thames Valley v Ngati Porou East Coast

SIX (or more) CONVERSIONS IN A MATCH

(Record: 20, J.P. Preston, Canterbury v West Coast, 1992; S.D. Culhane, New Zealand v Japan, 1995)

9	A. Morgan	Wellington v Horowhenua Kapiti
9	R. Mo'unga	New Zealand v Italy
8	J.M. Barrett	Hurricanes v Moana Pasifika, May 13
8	W.A. Wright	South Canterbury v Buller
8	D.S. McKenzie	New Zealand v Namibia
7	B.J. Barrett	Blues v Highlanders, Feb 25
7	R. Mo'unga	Crusaders v Highlanders, March 3
7	D.S. McKenzie	Chiefs v Highlanders, May 5
7	L.F. McClutchie	Hawke's Bay v Manawatu
7	J.D. Jacomb	Taranaki v North Harbour
6	B.J. Barrett	Blues v Waratahs, April 22
6	R. Mo'unga	Crusaders v Waratahs
6	R. Mo'unga	Crusaders v Fijian Drua, June 10
6	R. Patricio	Poverty Bay v Buller
6	F.W. Burke	Canterbury v Manawatu
6	B.E.C. Gatland	North Harbour v Northland

FOUR (or more) PENALTY GOALS IN A MATCH

(Record: 9, A.P. Mehrtens, New Zealand v Australia, at Auckland, 1999;
A.P. Mehrtens, New Zealand v France, at Paris, 2000;
B.J. Barrett, Taranaki v Bay of Plenty, 2011)

5	D.S. McKenzie	Chiefs v Crusaders, April 29
5	D.S. McKenzie	Chiefs v Reds, June 10
5	A. Morgan	Wellington v Manawatu
4	B.D. Cameron	Hurricanes v Brumbies, June 10
4	R. Mo'unga	Crusaders v Blues, June 16
4	D.S. McKenzie	Chiefs v Brumbies, June 17
4	F.W. Burke	Canterbury v Northland
4	L.J. Ross	West Coast v King Country
4	O.V.H. Koller	North Harbour v Canterbury
4	M. Banks	Southland v Northland
4	J.T. Tatu-Robertsson	Horowhenua Kapiti v Wairarapa Bush
4	S.J. Gilbert	Otago v Taranaki
4	F.R. Morgan	Thames Valley v Ngati Porou East Coast
4	J.D. Jacomb	Taranaki v Canterbury, October 13

DROPPED GOALS IN A MATCH

(Record: 5, M.K. Sisam, Hawke's Bay v East Coast, 1979)

1	R. Mo'unga	Crusaders v Chiefs, February 24
1	T. Kemara	NZ Under 20 v Australia Under 20
1	T.J. Reekie	Mid Canterbury v Poverty Bay
1	T.P.A. Cook-Savage	Waikato v Auckland
1	D.J. Whale	Whanganui v Thames Valley, October 7

SCORED IN ALL FOUR WAYS

No player scored all four ways in a match in 2023

CURRENT PLAYER STATISTICS

CAREER RECORDS OF PLAYERS APPEARING IN NEW ZEALAND FIRST-CLASS RUGBY 2023

125 GAMES OF FIRST-CLASS RUGBY

Player	Games
A.L. Smith	366
S.L. Whitelock	363
L.J. Messam	351
B.J. Barrett	315
O.T. Franks	312
D.S. Coles	308
T.T.R. Perenara	275
S.J. Savea	275
S.J. Cane	274
L. Romano	271
A.S. Savea	260
B. May	259
B.A. Retallick	254
C.J.D. Taylor	250
A.O.H.M. Tu'ungafasi	249
J.J.G. Bekhuis	246
B.M. Weber	244
M.D. Drummond	238
A.W.F. Ta'avao	238
I.F. Afoa	231
R. Mo'unga	227
J.P.T. Moody	219
N.E. Laulala	218
D.K. Havili	216
S.K. Barrett	209
A.R. Lienert-Brown	209
D.S. McKenzie	207
R.M.N. Ranger	204
A.L. Ioane	203
D.P. Lienert-Brown	195
R.E. Ioane	192
J.R. Riccitelli	190
Q.J. MacDonald	188
B.C.J. Funnell	186
P.T. Tuipulotu	183
M.J. Hunt	181
J.M. Barrett	177
S.T. Stevenson	176
D.J. Bird	168
R.J. Prinsep	167
T.T. Tahuriorangi	164
A.P. Nankivell	160
F.J. Levave	156
T.S. Lomax	155
S.F.S. Taukei'aho	153
A.T. Hodgman	152
S.T. Mafileo	151
S.J. Nock	150
E.J. Goodhue	146
A. Makalio	145
W.A. Heinz	144
A. Ross	144
J.M. Dickson	143
F.T. Christie	143
A.J. Aumua	141
S. Perofeta	141
S.M. Frizell	141
J.A.R. Lentjes	135
I.E.T. Walker-Leawere	134
D.R. Papali'i	132
B.T. Gibson	132
Q.J. Strange	132
P.G.N. Sowakula	131
J.R. Ioane	130
J.W.C. Emery	129
M. Banks	128
D.A. Kirifi	128
W.K. Harmon	127
L.B. Jacobsen	126
W.T. Jordan	125
B.D. Proctor	125
M.C. Renata	125
C.J. Tiatia	125

500 POINTS IN FIRST-CLASS RUGBY

B.J. Barrett	2397
R. Mo'unga	2107
D.S. McKenzie	1737
J.M. Barrett	1284
M. Banks	1158
M.J. Hunt	1022
B.E.C. Gatland	873
S. Perofeta	761
J.R. Ioane	746
S.J. Savea	695
H.R.J. Plummer	607
B.D. Cameron	597
R.E. Ioane	515
W.T. Jordan	510

50 TRIES IN FIRST-CLASS RUGBY

S.J. Savea	139
R.E. Ioane	103
W.T. Jordan	102
B.J. Barrett	95
S.L. Reece	91
A.L. Smith	77
B.M. Weber	76
C.J.D. Taylor	73
D.S. Coles	70
A.S. Savea	70
S.T. Stevenson	70
D.S. McKenzie	68
D.K. Havili	63
R. Mo'unga	62
J.M. Barrett	58
R.M.N. Ranger	53

100 GAMES FOR A TEAM

Aaron Smith	185	Highlanders
Samuel Whitelock	182	Crusaders
Owen Franks	153	Crusaders
Julian Savea	153	Hurricanes
Sam Whitelock	153	New Zealand
Sam Cane	150	Chiefs
TJ Perenara	150	Hurricanes
Dane Coles	141	Hurricanes
Luke Romano	136	Crusaders
Josh Bekhuis	134	Southland
Ofa Tuungafasi	134	Blues
Mitch Drummond	132	Crusaders
Ardie Savea	131	Hurricanes
Codie Taylor	129	Crusaders
Brodie Retallick	128	Chiefs
Beauden Barrett	125	Hurricanes
Aaron Smith	125	New Zealand
Beauden Barrett	124	New Zealand
Brad Weber	123	Chiefs
David Havili	119	Crusaders
Quentin MacDonald	118	Tasman
Rene Ranger	118	Northland
Joe Moody	116	Crusaders
Ryan Shelford	116	Horowhenua Kapiti
Daniel Lienert-Brown	113	Highlanders
Scott Barrett	112	Crusaders
Damian McKenzie	111	Chiefs
Richie Mo'unga	109	Crusaders
Brodie Retallick	109	New Zealand
Anton Lienert-Brown	106	Chiefs
Akira Ioane	105	Blues
Inia Katia	105	Wairarapa-Bush
Lindsay Horrocks	102	Whanganui
Roman Tutauha	101	Whanganui
Verdon Bartlett	101	Ngati Porou East Coast
Rieko Ioane	100	Blues

400 POINTS FOR A TEAM

Beauden Barrett	1238	Hurricanes	Richie Mo'unga	468	New Zealand
Richie Mo'unga	1230	Crusaders	William Wright	460	South Canterbury
Damian McKenzie	1070	Chiefs	Dan Hawkins	454	Northland
Beauden Barrett	740	New Zealand	Lincoln McClutchie	454	Hawke's Bay
Jordie Barrett	753	Hurricanes	Josh Ioane	427	Otago
Bryn Gatland	647	North Harbour	Damian McKenzie	423	Waikato
Marty Banks	628	Tasman	Fergus Burke	409	Canterbury
Mitch Hunt	562	Tasman			

25 TRIES FOR A TEAM

Julian Savea	62*	Hurricanes	Richie Mo'unga	32	Crusaders
TJ Perenara	58	Hurricanes	Ardie Savea	32	Hurricanes
Kalavini Leatigaga	54	South Canterbury	Asafo Aumua	31	Wellington
Rieko Ioane	50	Blues	Will Jordan	31	New Zealand
Sevu Reece	46	Crusaders	Leicester Fainga'anuku	30	Crusaders
Iliesa Tora	45	Buller	Jona Nareki	30	Otago
Beauden Barrett	43	New Zealand	Alekesio Vakarorogo	30	Whanganui
Codie Taylor	42	Crusaders	Aaron Smith	29	New Zealand
Salesi Rayasi	40	Auckland	Dane Coles	29	Hurricanes
David Havili	39	Crusaders	Shaun Stevenson	28	Chiefs
Will Jordan	38	Crusaders	Akira Ioane	27	Blues
Rieko Ioane	36	New Zealand	Brad Weber	27	Chiefs
Siu Kakala	36	South Canterbury	Paula Fifita	26	South Canterbury
Aaron Smith	35	Highlanders	Mark Telea	26	Blues
Beauden Barrett	34	Hurricanes	Braydon Ennor	25	Crusaders
Mitieli Kaloudigibeci	33	Buller	Sevu Reece	25	Waikato

* Includes two penalty tries

FIRST-CLASS STATISTICS

to January 1, 2024

250 GAMES OF FIRST-CLASS RUGBY

K.F. Mealamu	384	2000-15
W.W.V. Crockett	375	2005-19
A.L. Smith	366	2008-23
S.L. Whitelock	363	2008-23
C.E. Meads	361	1955-74
L.J. Messam	351	2003-22
S.B.T. Fitzpatrick	348	1983-97
M.A. Nonu	348	2002-21
K.J. Read	341	2005-20
R.H. McCaw	334	2000-15
T.D. Woodcock	330	2000-15
J.F. Umaga	329	1994-2011
A.M. Haden	328	1971-86
Q.J. Cowan	326	2000-16
R.W. Loe	321	1980-97
B.J. Barrett	315	2010-23
G.W. Whetton	314	1979-95
O.T. Franks	312	2007-23
Z.V. Brooke	311	1985-97
A.K. Hore	311	1999-2016
W.F. McCormick	310	1958-78
D.S. Coles	308	2007-23
C.S. Ralph	306	1996-2008
G.J. Fox	303	1982-95
A.D. Oliver	300	1993-2007
N.J. Hewitt	296	1988-2001
J. Kaino	296	2003-18
S.C. McDowell	294	1982-98
R.M. Brooke	292	1987-2001
C.R. Flynn	289	2001-17
D.W. Carter	287	2002-15
I.D. Jones	286	1988-2000
I.A. Kirkpatrick	286	1966-79
W.K. Little	285	1988-2000
J.W. Marshall	284	1992-2005
P.A.T. Weepu	284	2003-17
B.R. Smith	284	2007-19
A.P. Mehrtens	282	1993-2005
R.S. Crotty	279	2008-19
A.J. Wyllie	279	1964-80
C.J. Spencer	277	1992-2005
A.M. Stone	275	1980-94
J.A. Collins	275	1994-2010
T.T.R. Perenara	275	2010-22
S.J. Savea	275	2010-23
A.L. Dixon	274	2008-21
S.J. Cane	274	2010-23
L. Romano	271	2009-23
M.J.A. Cooper	270	1985-99
D.E. Holwell	270	1995–2010
J.M. Muliaina	270	1999-2014
B.G. Williams	269	1968-84
K.R. Tremain	268	1957-72
J.J. Kirwan	268	1983-94
A.M. Ellis	267	2004-16
L.R. MacDonald	266	1994-2009
C.G. Smith	266	2003-15
C.C. King	265	2002-18
G.L. Slater	263	1991-2005
R.D. Thorne	263	1996-2011
H.T.P. Elliot	261	2005-17
K.J. Crowley	260	1980-94
T.J. Blackadder	260	1990-2001
C.H. Hoeft	260	1993-2005
A.S. Savea	260	2012-23
I.A. Eliason	259	1964-82
C.S. Jane	259	2003-17
B. May	259	2004-22
E. Clarke	258	1990-2005
S.J. Bachop	257	1986-99
G.A. Knight	255	1972-86
G.M. Somerville	255	1997-2008
B.A. Retallick	254	2010-23
I.J. Clarke	252	1951-63
S.M. Going	252	1962-80
B.J. Robertson	250	1971-84
C.J.D. Taylor	250	2011-23

1000 POINTS IN FIRST-CLASS RUGBY

	Career	Games	Tries	Con	PG	DG/Mark	Points
G.J. Fox	1982–95	303	29	901	683	47	4112
D.W. Carter	2002–2015	287	78	649	646	19	3683
A.P. Mehrtens	1993–2005	282	40	556	571	55	3190
M.J.A. Cooper	1985–99	270	78	475	420	2	2573
B.J. Barrett	2010-23	315	95	496	304	6	2397
K.J. Crowley	1980–94	260	87	375	376	9	2265
G.J.L Cooper	1984–96	188	60	384	385	14	2210
D.E. Holwell	1995–2010	270	39	451	366	2	2201
W.B. Johnston	1986–2001	220	29	420	396	5	2177
R. Mo'unga	2013–23	227	62	564	220	3	2107
R.M. Deans	1979–90	187	45	390	370	1	2073
W.F. McCormick	1958–78	310	57	457	314	9	2065
T.E. Brown	1995–2011	211	29	345	373	14	1996
A.R. Cashmore	1992–2005	187	64	356	294	2	1920
C.J. Spencer	1992–2005	277	101	335	221	12	1872
D.B. Clarke	1951–64	226	22	366	320	28/3	1851
S.R. Donald	2001-19	243	68	337	274	2	1842
D.S. McKenzie	2014-23	207	68	343	235	2	1737
S.D. Culhane	1988–99	155	20	291	313	19	1672
J.B. Cunningham	1990–98	136	52	316	226	1	1569
B.A. Blair	1999–2006	149	59	302	221	–	1562
L.Z. Sopoaga	2010-18	171	26	295	265	5	1530
A.W. Cruden	2008–20	212	34	253	272	3	1501
G.W. Jackson	1996–2004	175	41	267	215	8	1408
D.W. Hill	1997–2006	177	30	279	230	1	1401
A.R. Hewson	1973–88	154	19	247	229	17	1308
J.M. Barrett	2016-23	177	58	281	144	-	1284
J.P. Preston	1987–98	175	21	244	230	–	1276
M. Williment	1958–68	121	17	296	188	16	1255
F.M. Botica	1985–2001	150	37	263	176	7	1224
L.W. Mains	1967–76	142	13	212	228	13	1194
E.J. Crossan	1987–96	91	29	191	219	–	1158
M. Banks	2012-23	128	17	226	205	2	1158
G.D. Rowlands	1969–82	179	42	198	185	15	1151
C.L. McAlister	2002–11	151	19	204	207	1	1127
I.T. West	2012–18	139	27	223	179	2	1124
J.W. Wilson	1992–2002	233	151	76	68	4	1123
W.J. Burton	1990–96	93	11	217	199	5	1099
J.A. Gopperth	2002–09	126	27	228	167	2	1098
J.A. Gallagher	1984–90	139	67	196	144	1	1095
B.J.W. Fairbrother	1981–92	118	20	132	183	61	1076
R.B. Barrell	1963–79	147	20	125	225	10	1030
D.P. Lilley	1993–2003	162	41	139	176	6	1029
M.J. Hunt	2015-23	181	28	243	131	1	1022
G.W. Anscombe	2010–14	83	27	163	182	1	1010

100 TRIES IN FIRST-CLASS RUGBY

	Games	Tries
J.J. Kirwan	268	199
T.J. Wright	217	177
D.C. Howlett	240	173
B.G. Fraser	200	171
C.M. Cullen	233	164
Z.V. Brooke	311	161
J.F. Umaga	329	156
J.W. Wilson	233	151
R.A. Jarden	134	145
R.Q. Randle	189	141
S.J. Savea	275	139
B.G. Williams	269	137
K.R. Tremain	268	136
P.J. Cooke	195	133
C.S. Ralph	306	133
J.T. Lomu	203	126
M. Clamp	139	123
M.A. Nonu	348	120
A.E. Cooke	131	119
S.W. Sivivatu	187	116

	Games	Tries
I.A. Kirkpatrick	286	114
N.R. Berryman	190	114
J. Vidiri	153	114
C.I. Green	162	111
J.T. Rokocoko	214	111
H.E. Gear	230	111
G.B. Batty	142	109
B.R. Ford	196	109
E. Clarke	258	109
J.K.R. Timu	182	108
R.L. Gear	198	108
T.W. Mitchell	155	106
S.S. Wilson	202	106
A.R. Sutherland	211	103
E.J. Rush	205	103
R.E. Ioane	192	103
R.M. Smith	152	102
B.W. Smith	147	102
W.T. Jordan	125	102
C.J. Spencer	277	101

MOST DROPPED GOALS IN FIRST-CLASS RUGBY

B.J.W. Fairbrother	61
A.P. Mehrtens	55
M.B. Roulston	50
G.J. Fox	47
M.A. Herewini	47
R.J. Preston	39
J.W. Boe	37
R.H. Brown	35
P.M. Martin	34
B.J. McKechnie	33
E.J. Dunn	31
D. Trevathan	31

MOST POINTS IN A FIRST-CLASS MATCH

	Match	Tries	Con	PG	DG	Total
S.D. Culhane	New Zealand v Japan, 1995	1	20	–	–	45
J.P. Preston	Canterbury v West Coast, 1992	1	20	–	–	44
R.M. Deans	New Zealand v South Australia, 1984	3	14	1	–	43
A.R. Cashmore	Auckland v Mid Canterbury, 1995	5	9	–	–	43
J.F. Karam	New Zealand v South Australia, 1974	2	15	1	–	41
J.J. Kirwan	Auckland v North Otago, 1993	8	–	–	–	40
P.W. Turner	Otago v East Coast, 1986	2	14	1	–	39
J.W. Wilson	New Zealand Colts v Thames Valley, 1993	4	5	3	–	39
D.J. Kellett	Western Samoa v Marlborough, 1993	3	12	–	–	39
R.A. Jarden	New Zealand v Central West (Aust), 1951	6	10	–	–	38
D.E. Holwell	Northland v Thames Valley, 1997	2	14	–	–	38
B.A. Blair	New Zealand v Ireland A, 2001	3	4	5	–	38
R.J. du Preez	Sharks v Blues 2018	1	6	7	–	38
J.L. Graham	Counties v East Coast, 1972	–	14	3	–	37
S.D. Culhane	Southland v Manawatu, 1994	1	1	8	2	37
J.B. Cunningham	Central Vikings v South Canterbury, 1997	3	11	–	–	37
B.A. Blair	Canterbury v Counties Manukau, 1999	3	11	–	–	37

100 GAMES FOR TWO TEAMS

Colin Meads	King Country 139	New Zealand 133	1955-74
Bruce Robertson	Counties 123	New Zealand 102	1971-84
Bryan Williams	Auckland 130	New Zealand 113	1968-84
Andy Haden	Auckland 157	New Zealand 117	1971-86
Gary Whetton	Auckland 178	New Zealand 101	1979-95
Zinzan Brooke	Auckland 140	New Zealand 100	1985-97
Sean Fitzpatrick	Auckland 153	New Zealand 128	1983-97
Tana Umaga	Wellington 100	Hurricanes 122	1994-2011
Dan Carter	Crusaders 141	New Zealand 112	2002-15
Keven Mealamu	Blues 164	New Zealand 133	2000-15
Richie McCaw	Crusaders 145	New Zealand 149	2000-15
Tony Woodcock	Blues 137	New Zealand 118	2000-15
Jimmy Cowan	Southland 111	Highlanders 108	2000-16
Owen Franks	Crusaders 153	New Zealand 108	2007-23
Ma'a Nonu	Hurricanes 126	New Zealand 104	2002-21
Kieran Read	Crusaders 157	New Zealand 128	2005-20
James Parsons	North Harbour 106	Blues 115	2007-20
Ash Dixon	Hawke's Bay 111	Highlanders 100	2008-21
Sam Whitelock	Crusaders 182	New Zealand 153	2010-23
Aaron Smith	Highlanders 185	New Zealand 125	2011-23
Beauden Barrett	Hurricanes 125	New Zealand 123	2011-23
Liam Messam	Waikato 104	Chiefs 183	2003-22
Brodie Retallick	Chiefs 128	New Zealand 109	2010-23

150 GAMES FOR A TEAM

I.A. Eliason	Taranaki	222	1964-81
W.F. McCormick	Canterbury	220	1959-75
W.W.V. Crockett	Crusaders	203	2006-18
A.J. Dawson	Counties	201	1976-89
K.J. Crowley	Taranaki	199	1980-94
H.L. White	Auckland	192	1950-63
G.J. Fox	Auckland	189	1982-93
A.J. Wyllie	Canterbury	187	1964-79
A.L. Smith	Highlanders	185	2011-23
L.J. Messam	Chiefs	183	2006-21
S.L. Whitelock	Crusaders	182	2010-23
A.W. Slater	Taranaki	180	1989-2001
J.N. Coe	Counties Manukau	179	1986-99
G.W. Whetton	Auckland	178	1980-92
R.S. Sutherland	Marlborough	177	1958-74
G.L. Slater	Taranaki	174	1991-2005
L.G. Brownlee	Buller	174	1999-2018
G.C. Williams	Wellington	173	1964-76
R.C. Ketels	Counties	171	1974-87
R.J. Knight	Otago	170	1982-92

K.E. Barrett	Taranaki	167	1986-99
L.J. Davis	Canterbury	166	1964-77
J.E. Morgan	North Auckland	165	1967-81
K.F. Mealamu	Blues	164	2000-15
D.E. Latta	Otago	162	1986-96
G.D. Rowlands	Bay of Plenty	161	1969-82
W.B. Johnston	North Auckland	161	1986-97
P.L. Phillips	Marlborough	160	1980-97
N.W. Thimbleby	Hawke's Bay	158	1959-71
J.C. Ross	Mid Canterbury	158	1970-87
A.M. Haden	Auckland	157	1971-86
K.J. Read	Crusaders	157	2007-19
D.R. Mohi	Bay of Plenty	156	1961-77
P.J. Beveridge	Buller	156	1993-2021
K.C. Bloxham	Otago	155	1974-86
T.J. Stuart	Buller	154	1984-99
A.M. Ellis	Crusaders	154	2006-16
J.E. Spiers	Counties	153	1970-82
S.B.T. Fitzpatrick	Auckland	153	1984-97
P.M. Hirini	Horowhenua	153	1986-2000
O.T. Franks	Crusaders	153	2009-19
B.R. Smith	Highlanders	153	2009-19
S.J. Savea	Hurricanes	153	2011-23
S.L. Whitelock	New Zealand	153	2012-23
L.J. Hughes	Counties	152	1968-81
R.J. Preston	Bay of Plenty	152	1980-91
G.C. Frew	Mid Canterbury	152	1979-94
F.W. Marfell	Marlborough	152	1982-95
S.J. Todd	South Canterbury	152	1986-2001
R.S. Crotty	Crusaders	152	2009-19
C.R. Flynn	Crusaders	151	2002-14
A.J. Whetton	Auckland	150	1981-92
E. Clarke	Auckland	150	1991-2002
S.T. Ngatu	Poverty Bay	150	2003-18
S.J. Cane	Chiefs	150	2011-23
T.T.R. Perenara	Hurricanes	150	2012-23

1000 POINTS FOR A TEAM

			Games	Tries	Con	PG	DG	Total
G.J. Fox	Auckland	1982-93	189	25	613	441	31	2746
K.J. Crowley	Taranaki	1980-94	199	64	291	286	5	1723
D.W. Carter	Crusaders	2003-15	141	36	287	307	11	1708
W.B. Johnston	North Auckland	1986-97	161	21	320	303	4	1656
R.M. Deans	Canterbury	1979-90	146	34	299	296	1	1625
M.J.A. Cooper	Waikato	1990-99	124	38	331	252	1	1604
D.W. Carter	New Zealand	2003-15	112	29	293	281	8	1598
G.J.L. Cooper	Otago	1984-96	121	36	261	280	3	1520
W.F. McCormick	Canterbury	1959-75	220	38	269	204	7	1294
B.J. Barrett	Hurricanes	2011-19	125	34	249	189	1	1238
R. Mo'unga	Crusaders	2016-23	109	32	319	141	3	1230
D.S. McKenzie	Chiefs	2015-23	111	33	214	158	1	1070
G.J. Fox	New Zealand	1984-93	78	2	225	192	1	1067
B.J.W. Fairbrother	South Canterbury	1981-92	115	20	130	180	60	1060
A.P. Mehrtens	Canterbury	1993-2005	108	15	204	163	28	1056
W.J. Burton	North Harbour	1990-96	88	11	210	188	5	1052
G.D. Rowlands	Bay of Plenty	1969-82	161	38	166	164	15	1008

70 TRIES FOR A TEAM

		Games	Tries	
T.J. Wright	Auckland	135	112	1984-93
J.J. Kirwan	Auckland	141	104	1983-94
B.G. Fraser	Wellington	121	100	1975-86
Z.V. Brooke	Auckland	140	94	1986-97
P. Bale	Canterbury	102	93	1989-96
R.M. Smith	Canterbury	134	92	1949-60
B.R. Ford	Marlborough	145	81	1972-83
B.A. Grenside	Hawke's Bay	87	73	1918-31
P.J. Cooke	Otago	107	73	1990-96
J.C. Stringfellow	Wairarapa	109	72	1925-35
M. Clamp	Wellington	87	72	1980-88
E. Clarke	Auckland	150	72	1991-2002
P.L. Phillips	Marlborough	160	71	1980-97
N.R. Berryman	Northland	107	71	1991-2003
R.A. Jarden	Wellington	61	70	1949-56
B.W. Smith	Waikato	83	70	1979-84
D.C. Laursen	Horowhenua	121	70	1980-92
P.M. Hirini	Horowhenua	153	70	1986-2000

REFEREES

by Chris Jansen

2023 NEW ZEALAND RUGBY NATIONAL REFEREES SQUAD

	Union	*Squad Debut*	*Tests*	*SR*	*P*	*HC*	*FPC*	*Sevens*	*Nat*[1]	*Prov*[2]	RS[3]	*Total*
B.A. Alexander	Tasman	2023	–	–	–	4	–	–	–	–	–	4
J.R. Bredin	Hawke's Bay	2019	–	–	21	7	4	–	2	–	1	34
N.P. Briant	Bay of Plenty	2009	8	58	83	11	2	27	14	2	16	205
S.C. Catley	Hawke's Bay	2021	–	–	3	16	4	2	1	1	–	27
T.M.T. Cottrell	Hawke's Bay	2017	–	–	9	22	2	1	–	1	–	35
Dr S.T.W. Curran	Manawatu	2019	–	–	15	11	1	–	2	–	2	29
J.J. Doleman	Otago	2014	8	28	39	18	2	30	8	1	4	134
F.I.L. Hannon	Otago	2021	–	–	6	15	3	–	1	–	–	25
G.W.J. Haswell	Canterbury	2019	–	–	–	15	4	1	–	–	–	20
J.G. Henshaw	South Canterbury	2021	–	–	3	14	3	–	–	2	–	22
N.E.R. Hogan	Hawke's Bay	2017	–	2	19	17	6	20	1	1	–	66
W.G. Johnston	Taranaki	2022	–	–	–	9	5	–	1	–	–	15
A.W.B. Mabey	Auckland	2014	–	4	46	22	1	–	13	–	2	86
D.M. Moore	Canterbury	2019	–	–	–	14	4	–	–	–	–	18
A. Morton	Bay of Plenty	2022	–	–	–	9	1	–	–	1	–	11
Dr B.D. O'Keeffe	Horowhenua Kapiti	2012	43	86	58	6	1	1	2	9	9	206
B.E. Pickerill	North Harbour	2012	10	57	58	8	1	3	12	2	6	151
M.E. Playle	Auckland	2019	–	–	10	5	3	–	1	–	1	19
J. Sargentina	Wellington	2022	–	–	–	2	2	–	–	–	–	4
C.J. Stone	Taranaki	2012	–	–	41	24	1	2	1	2	2	71
D.J. Waenga	Hawke's Bay	2018	–	3	29	3	2	1	7	1	3	46
P.M. Williams	Taranaki	2014	34	62	43	7	–	3	7	3	6	159
M.C.J. Winter	Waikato	2015	–	2	22	28	8	6	2	–	–	68
B.R. Woolerton	Waikato	2021	–	–	–	9	8	–	1	–	–	18

SR Super Rugby

P Bunnings National Provincial Championship (total includes former Mitre 10 and ITM Cup fixtures)

HC Heartland Championship

FPC Farah Palmer Cup

[1]NZR appointment — international tour, Ranfurly Shield (non-NPC), national trial, and women's international.

[2]interprovincial (non-NPC, non-Heartland Championship, non-Ranfurly Shield)

[3]Ranfurly Shield — also included within N1 or Nat (if a non-NPC match)

[4] Men refereeing FPC fixtures are credited with a first-class appointment.

REFEREE APPOINTMENTS 2023

Ben Alexander				
August	12	HC	West Coast v King Country	Greymouth
	19	HC	Buller v Whanganui	Westport
September	9	HC	Mid Canterbury v Thames Valley	Ashburton
	16	HC	Buller vs Wairarapa Bush	Westport
Josh Bamber (Canterbury)				
September	16	HC	West Coast v Mid Canterbury	Greymouth
	23	HC	North Otago v Thames Valley	Maheno
Jono Bredin				
May	3	PRC	Junior Japan v Fiji Warriors	Apia
	8	PRC	Samoa A v Fiji Warriors	Apia
August	13	P	Manawatu v Taranaki	Palmerston North
	27	P	Canterbury v Wellington	Christchurch
September	2	P	Bay of Plenty v Otago	Rotorua
	16	P	Auckland v Waikato	Pakuranga
	23	P	Counties Manukau v Manawatu	Pukekohe
October	1	P	Bay of Plenty v Tasman	Tauranga
Nick Briant				
August	13	P	North Harbour v Canterbury	Takapuna
	20	P	Hawke's Bay v Otago	Napier
September	2	P	Canterbury v Taranaki	Rangiora
	8	P	Waikato v Wellington	Hamilton
	23	P	Taranaki v Auckland	New Plymouth
	30	P/RS	Wellington v Hawke's Bay	Wellington
October	6	P qf	Canterbury v Auckland	Christchurch
Ben Brownlie (Waikato)				
August	19	FPC	North Harbour v Taranaki	Takapuna
Stu Catley				
August	19	HC	Horowhenua Kapiti v West Coast	Levin
September	2	HC	Poverty Bay v King Country	Gisborne
	9	HC	Wairarapa Bush v King Country	Masterton
October	1	P	Manawatu v Southland	Palmerston North
	7	MC sf	Whanganui v Thames Valley	Whanganui
November	10–12		Oceania Sevens	Brisbane
Dr Stu Curran				
August	5	P	Hawke's Bay v North Harbour	Napier
	12	P	Tasman v Auckland	Blenheim
	27	P	Taranaki v Bay of Plenty	New Plymouth
September	2	P/RS	Wellington v Counties Manukau	Wellington
	16	HC	Whanganui v East Coast	Whanganui
	23	P	Canterbury v Tasman	Christchurch
October	7	P qf	Taranaki v Tasman	New Plymouth
	13	P sf	Taranaki v Canterbury	New Plymouth

Tipene Cottrell				
August	19	BOT	East Coast v Mid Canterbury	Ruatoria
September	2	HC	Horowhenua Kapiti v Wairarapa Bush	Levin
	9	P	Manawatu v North Harbour	Palmerston North
	23	HC	East Coast v King Country	Ruatoria
	30	HC	Poverty Bay v South Canterbury	Patutahi
James Doleman				
January	28	URC	Edinburgh vs Cell C Sharks	Edinburgh
February	12	6N	England v Italy	London
	25	SR	Moana Pacifica v Fijian Drua	Auckland
March	3	SR	Rebels v Hurricanes	Melbourne
	11	SR	Brumbies vs Reds	Canberra
	18	SR	Blues v Crusaders	Auckland
April	1	SR	Fijian Drua v Rebels	Lautoka
	7	SR	Crusaders v Moana Pasifika	Christchurch
	28	SR	Hurricanes v Brumbies	Wellington
May	7	SR	Rebels v Brumbies	Melbourne
	20	SR	Chiefs v Hurricanes	Hamilton
	27	SR	Crusaders v Waratahs	Christchurch
August	15		Tonga v Canada	Nuku'alofa
	23	P/RS	Wellington v Tasman	Wellington
	27	P	Otago v Southland	Dunedin
Fraser Hannon				
August	6	P	Southland v Waikato	Invercargill
	19	P	Canterbury v Manawatu	Christchurch
	26	HC	Mid Canterbury v Horowhenua Kapiti	Ashburton
September	2	HC	North Otago v South Canterbury	Oamaru
	15	P	Hawke's Bay v Manawatu	Napier
	17	P	Canterbury v Southland	Christchurch
	27	P	Southland v Bay of Plenty	Invercargill
October	7	LC sf	North Otago v Poverty Bay	Oamaru
	14	MC f	South Canterbury v Whanganui	Temuka
November	4		NZ Heartland XV v NZ Barbarians	Oamaru
George Haswell				
July	15	FPC/ST	Canterbury v Wellington	Christchurch
August	12	HC	Mid Canterbury v North Otago	Ashburton
	26	HC	South Canterbury v Buller	Geraldine
September	23	HC	South Canterbury v Mid Canterbury	Christchurch
	30	HC	West Coast v North Otago	Greymouth
Jackson Henshaw				
August	12	P	Otago v Wellington	Dunedin
	26	HC	West Coast v Thames Valley	Greymouth
September	3	P	Southland v Auckland	Invercargill
	9	HC	North Otago v Whanganui	Oamaru
	17	P	Tasman v Counties Manukau	Blenheim
	30	HC	Mid Canterbury v Wairarapa Bush	Ashburton
October	15	LC f	West Coast v Poverty Bay	Greymouth
Nick Hogan				
January	21/22		New Zealand World Rugby Sevens	Hamilton

	27–29		Australia World Rugby Sevens	Sydney
February	25/26		USA World Rugby Sevens	Los Angeles
March	3–05		Canada World Rugby Sevens	Vancouver
	11	SRA	Hurricanes Poua v Blues	Wellington
	25	SRA f	Chiefs Manawa v Matatu	Hamilton
	31–02		Hong Kong World Rugby Sevens	Hong Kong
April	8/9		Singapore World Rugby Sevens	Singapore
May	12–14		France World Rugby Sevens	Toulouse
	20/21		England World Rugby Sevens	London
August	5	P	Manawatu v Wellington	Palmerston North
	12	HC	Wairarapa Bush v East Coast	Masterton
	30	P	Auckland v Manawatu	Auckland
September	2	P	North Harbour v Waikato	Albany
	13	P	Counties Manukau v Canterbury	Pukekohe
	23	HC	Horowhenua Kapiti v Poverty Bay	Levin
October	7	MC sf	South Canterbury v East Coast	Pleasant Point
November	10–12		Oceania Sevens	Brisbane
December	2/3		Dubai World Rugby Sevens	Dubai
	9/10		South Africa World Rugby Sevens	Cape Town
Will Johnston				
July	23	FPC	Wellington v Auckland	Lower Hutt
August	12	HC	Whanganui v Thames Valley	Whanganui
	26	FPC	Counties Manukau v Hawke's Bay	Pukekohe
September	2	FPC sf	Manawatu v Tasman	Palmerston North
	9	HC	Horowhenua Kapiti v Buller	Levin
	30	HC	Whanganui v Horowhenua Kapiti	Whanganui
October	7	LC sf	Wairarapa Bush v West Coast	Masterton
Angus Mabey				
February	3	6NU20	England U20 vs Scotland U20	London
	10	6NU20	Ireland U20 v France U20	Cork
March	19	SR	Highlanders v Force	Invercargill
April	29	SR	Moana Pasifika v Rebels	Auckland
June	29	JWC	Australia U20 v Ireland U20	Paarl
July	9	JWC sf	France U20 v England U20	Cape Town
	15	JWC	Wales U20 v Australia U20	Cape Town
August	4	P	Tasman v Otago	Nelson
	9	P	Northland v Taranaki	Whangarei
	16	P	Hawke's Bay v Waikato	Napier
	27	P	Waikato v Counties Manukau	Hamilton
September	10	P	Taranaki v Tasman	New Plymouth
	17	P	Bay of Plenty v Wellington	Rotorua
	24	P	Waikato v Otago	Hamilton
October	8	P qf	Bay of Plenty v Hawke's Bay	Tauranga
	21	P f	Taranaki v Hawke's Bay	New Plymouth
December	9	JTL	Toshiba v Shizuoka	Kanagawa
	16	JTL	Yokohama Canon v Toyota Verblitz	Kanagawa
Scott McKenzie (North Harbour)				
July	22	FPC	Waikato v Canterbury	Hamilton
August	11	FPC	Counties Manukau v Auckland	Pukekohe
	27	FPC	Waikato v Wellington	Hamilton
September	2	FPC sf	Northland v Otago	Whangarei

Daniel Moore				
July	29	FPC/ST	Canterbury v Bay of Plenty	Christchurch
August	12	HC	South Canterbury v Horowhenua Kapiti	Waimate
	19	HC	North Otago v Wairarapa Bush	Oamaru
September	2	HC	Buller v East Coast	Westport
	9	HC	South Canterbury v West Coast	Fairlie
	23	HC	Buller v West Coast	Christchurch
Andrew Morton				
August	26	BOT	East Coast v North Otago	Ruatoria
September	2	HC	Thames Valley v King Country	Thames
	16	HC	Poverty Bay v North Otago	Gisborne
	30	HC	Thames Valley v East Coast	Waihi
Ben O'Keeffe				
February	24	SR	Crusaders v Chiefs	Christchurch
March	5	SR	Blues v Brumbies	Melbourne
	11	6N	England v France	London
	26	SR	Blues v Force	Auckland
	31	SR	Moana Pasifika v Highlanders	Auckland
April	7	SR	Reds v Brumbies	Brisbane
	21	SR	Rebels v Crusaders	Melbourne
	29	SR	Fijian Drua v Blues	Suva
May	5	SR	Highlanders v Chiefs	Dunedin
	20	SR	Waratahs v Fijian Drua	Sydney
June	2	SR	Blues v Highlanders	Auckland
	9	SR qf	Blues v Waratahs	Auckland
	24	SR f	Chiefs v Crusaders	Hamilton
July	8	RC	South Africa v Australia	Pretoria
	29		Scotland v Italy	Edinburgh
August	5		Scotland v France	Edinburgh
	19	P/RS	Wellington v Southland	Lower Hutt
September	14	RWC	France v Uruguay	Lille
	23	RWC	South Africa v Ireland	Paris
October	8	RWC	Japan v Argentina	Nantes
	15	RWC qf	France v South Africa	Paris
	21	RWC sf	England v South Africa	Paris
Todd Petrie (Auckland)				
August	6	FPC	North Harbour v Manawatu	North Shore
	20	FPC	Bay of Plenty v Hawke's Bay	Whakatane
September	16	HC	Thames Valley v South Canterbury	Whangamata
Brendon Pickerill				
February	25	SRA	Matatu v Blues Women	Dunedin
March	11	SR	Fijian Drua v Crusaders	Lautoka
	17	SR	Hurricanes v Waratahs	Wellington
	24	SR	Crusaders v Brumbies	Christchurch
April	14	SR	Moana Pasifika v Reds	Auckland
	21	SR	Chiefs v Fijian Drua	Hamilton
May	6	SR	Crusaders v Force	Christchurch
	13	SR	Hurricanes v Moana Pasifika	Wellington

	26	SR	Highlanders v Reds	Dunedin
June	3	SR	Hurricanes v Crusaders	Wellington
	10	SR sf	Crusaders v Fijian Drua	Christchurch
August	12	P	Bay of Plenty v Waikato	Tauranga
	19	P	Northland v Tasman	Whangarei
December	9	JTL	Mitsubishi Dynaboars v Kintetsu	Kanagawa
	16	JTL	Suntory v Toshiba	Tokyo
Marcus Playle				
August	13	P	Southland v Northland	Invercargill
	18	P	Counties Manukau v Bay of Plenty	Pukekohe
September	3	P	Tasman v Manawatu	Nelson
	10	P	Otago v Northland	Dunedin
	23	P	Southland v Hawke's Bay	Invercargill
Brandon Roberts (Counties Manukau)				
August	5	FPC	Northland v Otago	Whangarei
	26	FPC	Auckland v Canterbury	Auckland
Jack Sargentina				
July	29	FPC	Manawatu v Northland	Palmerston North
August	26	HC	Wairarapa Bush v Poverty Bay	Masterton
September	23	HC	Wairarapa Bush v Whanganui	Masterton
Cameron Stone				
August	19	P	North Harbour v Auckland	Takapuna
	25	P	Manawatu v Northland	Palmerston North
September	9	P	Hawke's Bay v Bay of Plenty	Napier
	16	P	North Harbour v Northland	Albany
	30	P	Waikato v Canterbury	Hamilton
October	14	P sf	Wellington v Hawke's Bay	Wellington
Daniel Waenga				
March	18	SR	Chiefs v Rebels	Hamilton
May	26	SR	Rebels v Force	Melbourne
July	14		Tonga v Australia A	Nuku'alofa
	19	RS	Wellington v South Canterbury	Upper Hutt
August	6	P	Bay of Plenty v Auckland	Tauranga
	20	P	Waikato v Taranaki	Hamilton
	27	P	Tasman v North Harbour	Nelson
September	9	P	Auckland v Canterbury	Auckland
	16	P	Otago v Taranaki	Dunedin
	24	P/RS	Wellington v North Harbour	Porirua
	29	P	Auckland v Northland	Auckland
October	7	P qf	Wellington v Waikato	Wellington
December	9	JTL	NEC v Urayasu	Chiba
	16	JTL	Ricoh v Mitsubishi Dynaboars	Tokyo
Paul Williams				
January	28	URC	Connacht v Emirates Lions	Connacht
February	4	6N	England v Scotland	London
	25	SR	Highlanders v Blues	Dunedin

March	5	SR	Force v Reds	Melbourne
	10	SR	Chiefs v Highlanders	Hamilton
	25	SR	Highlanders v Fijian Drua	Dunedin
April	2	SR	Hurricanes v Force	Palmerston North
	22	SR	Blues v Waratahs	Auckland
May	12	SR	Chiefs v Reds	New Plymouth
	20	SR	Highlanders v Rebels	Dunedin
June	3	SR	Fijian Drua v Reds	Suva
July	22	PNC	Fiji v Tonga	Lautoka
August	4	P	Taranaki v Tasman	New Plymouth
	12		Portugal v USA	Algarve
	19		Ireland v England	Dublin
September	16	RWC	Samoa v Chile	Bordeaux
	23	RWC	Georgia v Portugal	Toulouse
	30	RWC	Argentina v Chile	Nantes
Michael Winter				
March	4	SRA	Matatu v Hurricanes Poua	Christchurch
	19	SRA sf	Matatu v Blues	Albany
August	11	P	Counties Manukau v Hawke's Bay	Pukekohe
	26	P	Auckland v Hawke's Bay	Auckland
September	6	P	North Harbour v Otago	Albany
	9	P	Counties Manukau v Southland	Pukekohe
	22	P	Northland v Bay of Plenty	Whangarei
	30	P	Taranaki v North Harbour	New Plymouth
Ben Woolerton				
July	23	FPC	Taranaki v Manawatu	New Plymouth
August	12	FPC	Hawke's Bay v Canterbury	Hastings
	19	HC	King Country v South Canterbury	Taupo
September	2	HC	Whanganui v West Coast	Whanganui
	9	BOT	East Coast v Poverty Bay	Ruatoria
	30	HC	King Country v Buller	Taupo

RWC	*Rugby World Cup*	*MC*	*Meads Cup*
RC	*Rugby Championship*	*LC*	*Lochore Cup*
JWC	*U20 Junior World Championship*	*BOT*	*Bill Osborne Trophy*
SR	*Super Rugby Pacific*	*URC*	*United Rugby Championship*
SRA	*Super Rugby Aupiki*	*FPC*	*Farah Palmer Cup*
JTL	*Japan Top League*	*ST*	*JJ Stewart Trophy*
RS	*Ranfurly Shield*		

One overseas referee controlled one Bunnings NPC fixture, and one Heartland Championship fixture: Katsuki Furuse (Japan) Aug 5 Northland v Canterbury; Aug 12 Poverty Bay v Buller.

INTERNATIONAL ASSISTANT REFEREES AND TELEVISION MATCH OFFICIALS

James Doleman					
July	15	RC	Australia v Argentina		Sydney
	22	PNC	Fiji v Tonga		Lautoka
	29	PNC	Samoa v Fiji		Apia
August	5	PNC	Japan v Fiji		Tokyo
September	9	RWC	Australia v Georgia		Paris
	14	RWC	France v Uruguay		Lille
	16	RWC	Samoa v Chile		Bordeaux
	23	RWC	South Africa v Ireland		Paris
	30	RWC	Scotland v Romania		Lille
October	7	RWC	Wales v Georgia		Nantes
	8	RWC	Japan v Argentina		Nantes
	15	RWC qf	France v South Africa		Paris
Dr Ben O'Keeffe					
February	4	6N	England v Scotland		London
March	18	6N	Ireland v England		Dublin
September	9	RWC	England v Argentina		Marseille
	28	RWC	Japan v Samoa		Toulouse
Aaron Paterson					
September	30		New Zealand v Australia	(TMO)	Hamilton
Brendon Pickerill					
February	4	6N	England v Scotland	(TMO)	London
	11	6N	Ireland v France	(TMO)	Dublin
July	8	RC	South Africa v Australia	(TMO)	Pretoria
August	5	PNC	Japan v Fiji	(TMO)	Tokyo
September	9	RWC	Ireland v Romania	(TMO)	Bordeaux
	23	RWC	South Africa v Ireland	(TMO)	Paris
	30	RWC	Scotland v Romania	(TMO)	Lille
October	7	RWC	Wales v Georgia	(TMO)	Nantes
	8	RWC	Japan v Argentina	(TMO)	Nantes
	15	RWC qf	France v South Africa		Paris
	21	RWC sf	England v South Africa		Paris
Marcus Playle					
July	14		Tonga v Australia A		Nuku'alofa
Paul Williams					
July	8	RC	South Africa v Australia		Pretoria
	15	RC	Australia v Argentina		Sydney
September	9	RWC	Italy v Namibia		St. Etienne
	14	RWC	France v Uruguay		Lille
October	8	RWC	Japan v Argentina		Nantes
	15	RWC qf	France v South Africa		Paris
	21	RWC sf	England v South Africa		Paris
Mike Winter					
July	14		Tonga v Australia A		Nuku'alofa
	22	PNC	Fiji v Tonga		Lautoka

(TMO) Television Match Official *(RWC) Rugby World Cup* *(RC) Rugby Championship* *(PNC) Pacific Nations Cup*

2023 INTERNATIONAL REFEREES

J.J. Doleman — 2021: Australia v France, Italy v Argentina, Georgia v Fiji, 2022: Australia v England, Argentina v South Africa, England v Japan, 2023: England v Italy, Tonga v Canada.

Dr B.D. O'Keeffe — 2016: Samoa v Georgia, Japan v Scotland, Scotland v Argentina; 2017: Italy v France, South Africa v France, South Africa v Australia, Ireland v South Africa, England v Australia; 2018: Wales v France, South Africa v England, South Africa v Argentina, Wales v Australia, Ireland v USA; 2019: Ireland v France, Australia v Argentina, Fiji v Tonga, England vs Italy, Australia v Fiji (RWC), France v USA (RWC), Japan v Scotland (RWC), 2020: Italy v Scotland, England v Wales, Australia v New Zealand, 2021: New Zealand v Tonga, Samoa v Tonga (RWCQ), Australia v France, South Africa v British & Irish Lions, France v Argentina; 2022: Scotland v England, 2022: Scotland v England, Fiji v Tonga, Argentina v Scotland, Australia v South Africa, Wales v Argentina, Ireland v Australia, 2023: England v France, South Africa v Australia, Scotland v Italy, Scotland v France, France v Uruguay (RWC), South Africa v Ireland (RWC), Japan v Argentina (RWC), Farnce v South Africa (RWC qf), England v South Africa (RWC sf).

P.M. Williams — 2016: Romania v USA; 2017: Italy v Scotland, Fiji v Italy, Samoa vs Fiji (RWCQ), Ireland v Fiji; 2018: Australia v Ireland, England v Japan, Scotland v Argentina; 2019: England v Scotland, South Africa v Australia, Australia v Samoa, England v Tonga (RWC), Georgia v Fiji (RWC), Argentina v USA (RWC), 2020: Scotland v France, New Zealand v Australia, Argentina v Australia, 2021: New Zealand v Fiji, Samoa v Tonga (RWCQ), New Zealand v Australia, Japan v Australia, Wales v South Africa, 2022: Australia v England, Australia v South Africa, Georgia v Uruguay, Spain v Namibia, USA v Portugal (RWCQ), 2023: England v Scotland, Fiji v Tonga, Portugal v USA, Ireland v England, Samoa v Chile (RWC), Georgia v Portugal (RWC), Argentina v Chile (RWC).

MOST INTERNATIONAL APPOINTMENTS BY REFEREES

to January 1, 2024

W. Barnes	England	2006-2023	111	D.A. Lewis	Ireland	1998-2010	45
N. Owens	Wales	2003-2020	100	W.D. Bevan	Wales	1985-2000	44
R. Poite	France	2006-2022	73	A.R. Gardner	Australia	2011-2023	44
J.I. Kaplan	South Africa	1996-2013	70	Dr. B.D. O'Keeffe	New Zealand	2016-2023	43
C.P. Joubert	South Africa	2003-2016	69	J J.M. Fleming	Scotland	1985–2001	41
J.D. Peyper	South Africa	2011-2023	67	A.J. Spreadbury	England	1990–2008	41
A.C.P. Rolland	Ireland	2001-2014	66	M.J. Carley	England	2015–2023	39
S.R. Walsh	New Zealand/			E.F. Morrison	England	1991–2001	38
	Australia	1998-2014	60	P.D. O'Brien	New Zealand	1994–2005	37
J. Garces	France	2010-2019	55	J. Jutge	France	1996–2007	35
P. Gauzere	France	2010-2021	52	P.M. Williams	New Zealand	2016–2023	34
C.R. White	England	1998-2009	51	N.J. Berry	Australia	2016–2023	33
L.W. Pearce	England	2013-2023	49	A.J. Cole	Australia	1997–2005	32
M.R.J. Raynal	France	2009-2023	48	G.W. Jackson	New Zealand	2012–2019	32
S.J. Dickinson	Australia	1997-2011	47	J.G.A. Lacey	Ireland	2010–2018	31
P.G. Honiss	New Zealand	1997-2008	46	A. Brace	Ireland	2017–2023	30
G.J. Clancy	Ireland	2006-2016	45	P.L. Marshall	Australia	1993–2003	30

INTERNATIONAL REFEREES

to January 1, 2024

Bishop, D.J. (Southland) 1986–95	26
Bray, L.E. (Wellington) 2001–08	9
Briant, N.P. (Bay of Plenty) 2014–2018	8
Brown, K.W. (Southland) 2008–11	8
Campbell, A. (Auckland) 1908	2
Dainty, C.J. (Wellington) 1982–86	2
Deaker, K.M. (Hawke's Bay) 2001–08	23
Doleman, J.J. (Otago) 2021–2023	8
Doocey, T.F. (Canterbury) 1976–83	3
Downes, A.D. (Otago) 1913	1
Duffy, B.W. (Taranaki) 1977	1
Duncan, J. (Otago) 1908	1
Evans, F.T. (Canterbury) 1904	1
Farquahar, A.B. (Auckland) 1961–64	6
Fleury, A.L. (Otago) 1959	1
Fong, A.S. (West Coast) 1946–50	2
Forsyth, R.A. (Taranaki) 1958	1
Francis, R.C. (Wairarapa Bush) 1984–86	10
Fraser, M.I. (Wellington) 2013–19	8
Fright, W.A. (Canterbury) 1956	2
Frood, J. (Otago) 1952	1
Garrard, W.G. (Canterbury) 1899	1
Gillies, C.R. (Waikato) 1958–59	4
Griffiths, A.A. (Waikato) 1952	1
Harrison, G.L. (Wellington) 1979–83	4
Hawke, C.J. (South Canterbury) 1990–2001	24
Hill, E.D. (Auckland) 1949	1
Hollander, S. (Canterbury) 1930–31	4
Honiss, P.G. (Canterbury & Waikato) 1997–2008	46
Jackson, G.W. (Bay of Plenty) 2012–2019	32
King, J.S. (Wellington) 1937	2
Lawrence, B.J. (Bay of Plenty) 2005–11	25
Lawrence, K.H. (Bay of Plenty) 1985–91	13
Macassey, L.E. (Otago) 1937	1
McAuley, C.J. (Otago) 1962	1
McDavitt, P.A. (Wellington) 1972–77	5
McKenzie, E. (Wairarapa) 1921	1
McKenzie, H.J. (Wairarapa) 1936	1
McLachlan, L.L. (Otago) 1989–94	7
McMullen, R.F. (Auckland) 1973	1
Matheson, A.M. (Taranaki) 1946	1
Millar, D.H. (Otago) 1965–78	8
Moffit, J. (Wellington) 1936	1
Munro, V.G. (Canterbury) 2009–10	2
Murphy, J.P. (North Auckland) 1959–69	13
Neilson, A.E. (Wellington) 1921	2
Nicholson, G.W. (Auckland) 1913	1
O'Brien, P.D. (Southland) 1994–2005	37
O'Keeffe, Dr B.D. (Wellington) 2016–2023	43
Parkinson, F.G.M. (Manawatu) 1955–56	3
Pickerill, B.E. (North Harbour) 2017–2022	10
Pollock, C.J. (Hawke's Bay) 2005–2015	22
Pring, J.P.G. (Auckland) 1966–72	8
Robson, C.F. (Waikato) 1963	1
Simpson, J.L. (Wellington) 1913	1
Skeen, B.D. (Auckland) 2008–09	2
Sullivan, G. (Taranaki) 1950	1
Sutherland, F.E. (Auckland) 1930	1

Taylor, A.R. (Canterbury) 1965–72	3	White, J.M (Auckland) 2013	2
Thompson, M.W. (Auckland) 1983	2	Williams, J. (Otago) 1905	1
Tindill, E.W.T. (Wellington) 1950–55	3	Williams, P.M. (Taranaki) 2016–2023	34
Wahlstrom, G.K. (Auckland) 1994–97	6	Williamson G.L. (Wellington) 2010–13	2
Walsh, L. (Canterbury) 1949	1	Wise, G.J. (Hawke's Bay) 2004	1
Walsh, S. (Wellington) 1994–97	5	Wolstenholme, B.H. (Poverty Bay) 1955	1
Walsh, S.R. (North Harbour) 1998–2008	33		

100 AND MORE FIRST-CLASS MATCHES

to January 1, 2024

P.D. O'Brien	1988–2005	230	B.E. Pickerill	2012–2023	151
P.G. Honiss	1992–2008	228	R.P. Kelly	2009–2020	147
S.R. Walsh	1994–2008	214	L.E. Bray	1991–2008	144
M.I. Fraser	2007–2022	208	J.J. Doleman	2014–2023	134
Dr. B.D. O'Keeffe	2012–2023	206	G.K. Wahlstrom	1985–2002	132
N.P. Briant	2009–2023	205	G.L. Williamson	2003–2014	117
B.J. Lawrence	1997–2012	205	Dr. J.M. White	2000–2013	116
C.J. Pollock	2000–2016	204	D.J. Bishop	1976–1995	114
G.W. Jackson	2010–2019	196	G.J. Wise	1996–2007	114
C.J. Hawke	1983–2001	183	K.W. Brown	1999–2012	112
K.M. Deaker	1996–2008	181	S. Walsh	1980–2000	103
P.M. Williams	2013–2023	159	K.H. Lawrence	1971–1992	100

WOMEN'S REFEREES

2023 NEW ZEALAND RUGBY NATIONAL REFEREE SQUAD

	Union	*Squad Debut*	*Tests*	*SR*	*P*	*HC*	*FPC*	*Sevens*	*Nat*[1]	*Prov*[2]	*RS*[3]	*Total*
T.A. Anderson	Bay of Plenty	2019	–	–	–	2	16	2	2	–	–	22
M.C. Cogger-Orr	Auckland	2017	15	5	2	3	39	5	–	–	–	69
E.L. Doherty	Otago	2022	–	–	–	–	4	–	–	–	–	4
N.M. Ganley	North Harbour	2013	3	4	–	1	28	4	1	–	1	41
G.E. Mason	Otago	2022	–	–	–	–	2	–	–	–	–	2
T.S. Uerata	Canterbury	2021	–	–	–	–	14	–	–	–	–	14
C.T. Watt	Southland	2021	–	–	–	–	14	–	–	–	–	14

SRA *Super Rugby Aupiki*
P *National Provincial Championship*
HC *Heartland Championship*
FPC *Farah Palmer Cup*
ST *JJ Stewart Trophy*
Nat1 *NZR appointment – international tour, Ranfurly Shield (non–NPC), national trial, and women's international*

REFEREE APPOINTMENTS 2023

Tiana Anderson (nee Ngawati)				
July	15	FPC	Hawke's Bay v Auckland	Hastings
	29	FPC	Hawke's Bay v Waikato	Hastings
August	4	FPC	Taranaki v Tasman	New Plymouth
	20	FPC	Auckland v Waikato	Auckland
September	2	FPC sf	Waikato v Auckland	Hamilton
	23		Black Ferns XV v Samoa	Pukekohe
November	10–12		Oceania Sevens	Brisbane
Maggie Cogger-Orr				
January	21/22		New Zealand World Rugby Sevens	Hamilton
February	25	SRA	Hurricanes Poua v Chiefs Manawa	Levin
March	11	SRA	Chiefs Manawa v Matatu	Hamilton
	26	W6N	Italy v France	Parma
April	1	W6N	Scotland v Wales	Edinburgh
May	20		Australia v Fiji	Sydney
July	15	FPC	Bay of Plenty v Waikato	Rotorua
	23	FPC	North Harbour v Northland	North Shore
August	5	FPC	Waikato v Counties Manukau	Hamilton
	12	FPC	Bay of Plenty v Wellington	Tauranga
	19	HC	Thames Valley v Poverty Bay	Te Aroha
	27	FPC q–f	Tasman v Taranaki	Nelson
September	1	P	Northland v Hawke's Bay	Whangarei
	10	FPC cf	Manawatu v Northland	Palmerston North
	16	HC	King Country v Horowhenua Kapiti	Te Kuiti
October	1	P	Otago v Counties Manukau	Dunedin
	27	WXV1	England v Canada	Dunedin
November	4	WXV 1	France v Canada	Auckland
December	2/3		Dubai World Rugby Sevens	Dubai
	9/10		South Africa World Rugby Sevens	Cape Town

Erin Doherty				
July	29	FPC	Tasman v North Harbour	Nelson
August	19	FPC	Tasman v Auckland	Blenheim
Natarsha Ganley				
March	4	SRA	Blues Women v Chiefs Manawa	Albany
	19	SRA sf	Chiefs Manawa v Hurricanes Poua	Albany
	25	SRA f	Blues v Hurricanes Poua	Hamilton
April	8	SR W	Rebels v Force	Melbourne
July	12	RS	Wellington v Horowhenua Kapiti	Levin
	22	FPC	Counties Manukau v Bay of Plenty	Pukekohe
August	5	FPC	Auckland v Bay of Plenty	Auckland
	12	FPC	Northland v Taranaki	Kaikohe
	19	FPC/ST	Canterbury v Counties Manukau	Christchurch
	26	HC	King Country v Whanganui	Taumarunui
September	9	FPC pf	Canterbury v Auckland	Christchurch
	16		Japan v Fiji	Tokyo
October	13	WXV 2	Scotland v South Africa	Cape Town
	28	WXV 2	USA v Italy	Cape Town
Georgia Mason				
August	13	FPC	Manawatu v Tasman	Palmerston North
Taneika Uerata				
July	22	FPC	Tasman v Otago	Nelson
	30	FPC	Wellington v Counties Manukau	Lower Hutt
August	19	FPC	Otago v Manawatu	Dunedin
Cassie Watt				
July	29	FPC	Otago v Taranaki	Oamaru
August	6	FPC	Wellington v Hawke's Bay	Lower Hutt
	12	FPC	Otago v North Harbour	Dunedin
	26	FPC q–f	Otago v North Harbour	Dunedin
September	3	FPC sf	Canterbury v Hawke's Bay	Christchurch

WXV1	*W.XV Tier 1*	*RS*	*Ranfurly Shield*
WXV2	*W.XV Teir 2*	*ST*	*JJ Stewart Trophy*
W6N	*Women's Six Nations*	*HC*	*Heartland Championship*
SRA	*Super Rugby Aupiki*	*P*	*Bunnings National Provincial Championship*
FPC	*Farah Palmer Cup*		

2023 INTERNATIONAL REFEREES

M.C. Cogger–Orr — 2022: Wales v France, Ireland v Scotland, Australia v Japan, USA v Australia, Japan v South Africa, New Zealand v Australia, New Zealand v Japan, South Africa v France (RWC), Japan v Italy (RWC), England v Australia (RWC), 2023: Italy v France, Scotland v Wales, Australia v Fiji, England v Canada, France v Canada.

N.M. Ganley — 2023: Japan v Fiji, Scotland v South Africa, USA v Italy

INTERNATIONAL ASSISTANT REFEREES

Tiana Anderson				
November	3	WXV 1	Australia v Wales	Auckland
	4	WXV 1	France v Canada	Auckland
Maggie Cogger–Orr				
September	23		Black Ferns XV v Samoa	Pukekohe
October	20	WXV 1	England v Australia	Wellington
	21	WXV 1	Canada v Wales	Wellington
Natarsha Ganley				
May	20		Australia v Fiji	Sydney
June	29	PAC4	Australia v New Zealand	Brisbane
September	23		Black Ferns XV v Samoa	Pukekohe
	30		New Zealand v Australia	Hamilton
October	20	WXV 2	USA v Scotland	Cape Town
	20	WXV 2	Japan v Samoa	Cape Town
Tanieka Uerata				
October	20	WXV 1	England v Australia	Wellington
	21	WXV 1	Canada v Wales	Wellington
Cassie Watt				
October	27	WXV 1	England v Canada	Dunedin
	28	WXV 1	France v Australia	Dunedin
Estelle Whaiapu				
September	23		Black Ferns XV v Samoa (TMO)	Pukekohe

WXV1 W.XV Tier 1
WXV2 W.XV Teir 2
PAC4 Pacific Four Series

INTERNATIONAL REFEREES

to January 1, 2024

Beard, J.D.L. (Counties Manukau) 2014–16	10
Cogger–Orr, M.C. (Auckland) 2022–23	15
Ganley, N.M. (North Harbour) 2023	3
Inwood, N.A. (Wanganui & Canterbury) 2002–14	32
Jenner, L.A. (Counties Manukau) 2022–22	7
Mahoney, R.M. (Wairarapa Bush) 2016–2020	9
Mellor, K.E. (North Harbour) 2006	1
Woolerton, L.J. (Waikato) 2022	3

TWENTY-FIVE AND MORE FIRST-CLASS MATCHES

to January 1, 2024

N.A. Inwood	2000–14	86	L. Jeffrey	2003–16	42
M.C. Cogger–Orr	2017–23	69	N.M. Ganley	2013–23	41
R.M. Mahoney	2015–20	60	C.F. Gurr	2011–16	37
J.D.L. Beard	2012–16	53	B.J. Andrew	2015–20	26
L.A. Jenner	2017–22	47			

MOST INTERNATIONAL APPOINTMENTS BY REFEREES

to November 4, 2023

A.P. Barrett-Theron	South Africa	2016–23	37	A. McLachlan	Australia	2018–23	18
S.L. Cox MBE	England	2014–23	36	D. Teagarden	United States	2006–12	16
C.L. Daniels	England	2005–13	34	M.C. Cogger-Orr	New Zealand	2022–23	15
S. Trumbull	Canada	2009–16	34	H. O'Reilly	Ireland	2013–17	15
N.A. Inwood	New Zealand	2002–14	32	P. Pazani	Zimbabwe	2019–23	15
H. Davidson	Scotland	2018–23	30	J. Henry	Canada	2006–12	14
C.A Hodnett	England	2011–17	29	S. Corrigan	Australia	2006–11	12
A. Groizeleau	France	2018–23	27	G. Lee Wing Yi	Hong Kong	2009–15	12
C. Munarini	Italy	2018–23	27	L.A. Jenner	New Zealand/Italy	2022–23	11
J.M. Neville	Ireland	2016–23	26	J.D.L. Beard	New Zealand	2014–16	10
A. Nievas	Spain	2014–18	22	C. Bigaran	France	2006–14	10
L. Berard	USA	2013–16	19	M. LeMatte	France	2015–18	10
A.E. Perrett	Australia	2014–19	19	K. Ljungdahl	Germany	2003–08	10

SEVENS RUGBY

NEW ZEALAND SEVENS SQUADS 2023

By winning five of the eleven tournaments, the All Blacks Sevens won the 2022/23 World Rugby HSBC Sevens series. Of the 22 who took part only five were debutants and veteran Tim Mikkelson made a welcome return and became the first player to appear in one hundred tournaments in the national team.

Rising stars Leroy Carter and Akuila Rokolisoa, along with Brady Rush, appeared in all ten events of the 2023 calendar year. Rokolisoa was top tryscorer with 35 and with his goalkicking contributed 335 points. In May, Tomasi Cama succeeded Clark Laidlaw as head coach. Injury prevented squad members Tone Ng Shiu, Andrew Knewstubb and Kitiona Vai from appearing. Jayden Keelan was a reserve at Dubai and Cape Town

		Date of					*Career*	
		Birth	*Height*	*Weight*	*Debut*	*Tournaments*	*Tries*	*Points*
L.B. (Leroy) Carter	Bay of Plenty	24-02-99	1.85	85	2022	17	45	225
C.P.J. (Che) Clark	Auckland	22-04-03	1.90	93	2022	10	11	55
D.J. (Dylan) Collier	Waikato	27-04-91	1.94	101	2015	57	77	385
T.A. (Tepaea) Cook-Savage	Waikato	08-02-01	1.73	84	2022	7	6	86
S.B. (Scott) Curry	Bay of Plenty	17-05-88	1.94	96	2010	66	142	736
S.N. (Sam) Dickson (capt)	Canterbury	28-10-89	1.90	99	2012	74	100	506
R.M. (Rhodes) Featherstone	Taranaki	06-02-97	1.92	93	2023	2	0	0
F.F. (Fehi) Fineanganofo	Bay of Plenty	31-08-02	1.86	105	2023	6	5	25
M.J. (Moses) Leo	North Harbour	11-08-97	1.88	95	2022	15	39	195
N.M. (Ngarohi) McGarvey-Black	Bay of Plenty	20-05-96	1.86	90	2018	28	64	570
T.J. (Tim) Mikkelson	Waikato	13-08-86	1.94	101	2007	103	253	1287
S.L.J. (Sione) Molia	Counties Manukau	05-09-93	1.89	92	2016	55	91	455
A.P. (Amanaki) Nicole	Southland	08-02-92	1.90	99	2018	23	22	110
L.H. (Lewis) Ormond	Taranaki	05-02-94	1.92	96	2015	21	30	152
A.T. (Akuila) Rokolisoa	Counties Manukau	26-07-95	1.78	82	2018	34	88	798
B.J.K. (Brady) Rush	Northland	24-04-99	1.88	98	2022	17	30	154
R.S. (Roderick) Solo	Bay of Plenty	07-07-01	1.83	80	2022	10	29	145
P.C. (Payton) Spencer	Auckland	23-04-04	1.90	91	2023	3	3	17
X.R. (Xavier) Tito-Harris	Auckland	05-01-05	1.78	91	2023	3	5	25
C.M. (Codemeru) Vai	Bay of Plenty	25-02-04	1.88	86	2023	4	8	40
R.E. (Regan) Ware	Bay of Plenty	07-08-94	1.88	89	2015	55	136	680
T.J. (Joe) Webber	Bay of Plenty	27-08-93	1.86	90	2011	54	108	639

Coach: Clark Laidlaw (Taranaki), to May 15 (France); Tomasi Cama (Manawatu) from May 15 (England)
Assistant coaches: Tomasi Cama, to May 15; Euan Mackintosh (Bay of Plenty), at 1st, 7th to 10th tournaments
Manager: David Ormrod (Taranaki)
Physiotherapist: Damian Banks (Bay of Plenty), at Hamilton only; Rachel Lambert
Analyst: Tom Martin (Wellington)
S & C coach: Travis McMaster (North Harbour)

Final points for 2022/23 World Rugby Sevens Series: New Zealand 201, Argentina 181, Fiji 157, France 152, Australia 135, Samoa 134, South Africa 125, Ireland 116, Great Britain 105, USA 103, Spain 60, Uruguay 54, Kenya 41, Canada 39, Japan 25, Tonga 12, Hong Kong China 5, Uganda 2, Chile 2. The series was held over 11 tournaments between November 2022 and May 2023.

Series winners: New Zealand 2000, 2001, 2002, 2003, 2004, 2005, 2007, 2008, 2011, 2012, 2013, 2014, 2020, 2023; Fiji 2006, 2015, 2016, 2019; South Africa 2009, 2017, 2018, 2021; Samoa 2010; Australia 2022.

World Rugby Sevens Series Cup championship titles (1999 to January 1, 2024): New Zealand 62, Fiji 44, South Africa 39, England 19, Samoa 12, Australia 10, Argentina 7, United States 3, Scotland 2, France 1, Kenya 1, Canada 1.

	New Zealand	Australia	USA	Canada	Hong Kong	Singapore	France	England	Dubai	South Africa	**TOTALS**		Tries	Conversions	**Points**
Leroy Carter	*	*	*	*	*	*	*	*	*	*	**10**	–	31	–	**155**
Che Clark	*	*	–	–	–	–	*	*	*	*	**6**	–	6	–	**30**
Dylan Collier	*	*	*	*	*	*	*	*	–	–	**8**	–	9	–	**45**
Tepaea Cook-Savage	–	–	–	–	*	*	*	*	*	*	**6**	–	5	25	**75**
Scott Curry	–	–	–	–	–	–	*	*	*	*	**4**	–	7	1	**37**
Sam Dickson (capt)	*	*	*	*	–	–	*	*	–	–	**6**	–	3	–	**15**
Rhodes Featherstone	–	–	–	–	*	*	–	–	–	–	**2**	–	–	–	**0**
Fehi Fineanganofo	–	–	*	*	*	*	–	–	*	*	**6**	–	5	–	**25**
Moses Leo	*	–	*	*	–	*	*	–	*	*	**7**	–	18	–	**90**
Ngarohi McGarvey-Black	*	*	*	*	*	–	–	–	*	*	**7**	–	16	41	**162**
Tim Mikkelson	–	–	–	–	–	–	*	*	*	*	**4**	–	1	–	**5**
Sione Molia	*	*	–	–	*	*	*	*	*	*	**8**	–	11	–	**55**
Amanaki Nicole	*	*	*	*	*	*	–	–	–	–	**6**	–	3	–	**15**
Lewis Ormond	–	*	*	*	*	*	–	–	–	–	**5**	–	5	–	**25**
Akuila Rokolisoa	*	*	*	*	*	*	*	*	*	*	**10**	–	35	80	**335**
Brady Rush	*	*	*	*	*	*	*	*	*	*	**10**	–	16	–	**80**
Roderick Solo	*	*	*	*	–	–	*	*	–	–	**6**	–	23	–	**115**
Payton Spencer	–	*	*	*	–	–	–	–	–	–	**3**	–	3	1	**17**
Xavier Tito-Harris	–	–	–	–	*	–	–	*	–	*	**3**	–	5	–	**25**
Codemeru Vai	–	–	–	–	*	*	–	–	*	*	**4**	–	8	–	**40**
Regan Ware	*	–	–	–	–	*	*	*	*	–	**5**	–	10	–	**50**
Joe Webber	*	*	*	*	–	–	–	–	–	–	**4**	–	12	–	**60**

Totals – 232 tries; 1 penalty try; 148 conversions; 1463 points. 646 points were conceded.

Collier and Molia were co-captains at Hong Kong and Singapore, Molia being captain at Dubai and Cape Town.

NEW ZEALAND AT NEW ZEALAND HSBC SEVENS

FMG Stadium, Hamilton — **January 21/22, 2023**

Date	Opponent	Result	Tries	Conversions
Jan 21	Tonga	won 45–0	McGarvey-Black (2), Leo, Ware, Webber, Solo, Rush	McGarvey-Black (3), Rokolisoa (2)
Jan 21	Australia	won 21–19	Webber, Rokolisoa, Solo	Rokolisoa (3)
Jan 21	Great Britain	won 19–12	Solo (2), Webber	McGarvey-Black (2)
Jan 22	Ireland (quarterfinal)	won 10–5	Dickson, Rush	
Jan 22	France (semifinal)	won 38–0	Carter (2), Rokolisoa (2), Ware, Solo	Rokolisoa (3), McGarvey-Black
Jan 22	Argentina (Cup final)	lost 12–14	Rokolisoa, Solo	Rokolisoa

NEW ZEALAND AT AUSTRALIA HSBC SEVENS

Allianz Stadium, Sydney — **January 27–29, 2023**

Date	Opponent	Result	Tries	Conversions
Jan 27	Uruguay	won 45–7	Spencer (2), Clark, Dickson, Carter, Rush, Rokolisoa	McGarvey-Black (4), Rokolisoa
Jan 28	Kenya	won 33–0	Rokolisoa, Molia, Collier, Solo, Ormond	Rokolisoa (2), McGarvey-Black (2)
Jan 28	South Africa	lost 14–17	Webber, Solo	Rokolisoa (2)
Jan 28	Samoa (quarterfinal)	won 12–0	Solo, McGarvey-Black	McGarvey-Black
Jan 29	France (semifinal)	won 36–5	Rokolisoa (3), Carter (2), Spencer	Rokolisoa (3)
Jan 29	South Africa (Cup final)	won 38–0	Solo, Rokolisoa, Webber, Dickson, Nicole, McGarvey-Black	Rokolisoa (2), McGarvey-Black, Spencer

NEW ZEALAND AT USA HSBC SEVENS

Dignity Health Sports Park, Carson, Los Angeles — **February 25/26, 2023**

Date	Opponent	Result	Tries	Conversions
Feb 25	Chile	won 26–7	Carter (2), Solo, Rush	McGarvey-Black (2), Rokolisoa
Feb 25	USA	won 36–15	Collier (2), Rush, Rokolisoa, Leo, Webber	Rokolisoa (2), McGarvey-Black
Feb 25	Samoa	lost 7–14	Carter	McGarvey-Black
Feb 26	Great Britain (quarterfinal)	won 24–12	Carter, Leo, Rokolisoa, Solo	Rokolisoa (2)
Feb 26	Australia (semifinal)	won 33–17	Carter (2), Rokolisoa, Solo, Ormond	Rokolisoa (3), McGarvey-Black
Feb 26	Argentina (Cup final)	won 22–12	Carter (2), Leo, Rush	Rokolisoa

NEW ZEALAND AT CANADA HSBC SEVENS

BC Place Stadium, Langford, Vancouver **March 3–5, 2023**

Date	Opponent	Result	Tries	Conversions
Mar 3	USA	won 52–0	McGarvey-Black (2), Carter (2), Nicole, Leo, Ormond, Rush	McGarvey-Black (5), Rokolisoa
Mar 3	Spain	won 17–7	Leo (2), Rokolisoa	McGarvey-Black
Mar 4	Samoa	won 40–5	Webber (3), McGarvey-Black, Rush, Rokolisoa	McGarvey-Black (5)
Mar 4	Australia (Cup quarterfinal)	lost 7–17	McGarvey-Black	McGarvey-Black
Mar 5	Great Britain (semifinal for 5th)	won 19–5	Solo (2), Rush	Rokolisoa (2)
Mar 5	USA (final for 5th)	won 50–7	Webber (3), Carter, McGarvey-Black, Fineanganofo, Solo, Leo	McGarvey-Black (3), Rokolisoa (2)

Argentina defeated France 33–21 in the Cup final

NEW ZEALAND AT HONG KONG HSBC SEVENS

Hong Kong Stadium, Hong Kong **March 31–April 2, 2023**

Date	Opponent	Result	Tries	Conversions
Mar 31	Kenya	won 29–5	Rokolisoa (2), Carter, Collier, Vai	McGarvey-Black, Rokolisoa
Apr 1	South Africa	won 12–7	Carter, Vai	Rokolisoa
Apr 1	Ireland	won 26–7	Rush, McGarvey-Black, Carter, Fineanganofo	Rokolisoa (3)
Apr 2	Argentina (quarterfinal)	won 24–10	Carter, Molia, Rokolisoa, Tito-Harris	Rokolisoa (2)
Apr 2	France (semifinal)	won 12–7	Ormond, McGarvey-Black	Cook-Savage
Apr 2	Fiji (Cup final)	won 24–17	Vai, Molia, Carter, McGarvey-Black	Rokolisoa (2)

NEW ZEALAND AT SINGAPORE HSBC SEVENS

National Stadium, Singapore **April 8/9, 2023**

Date	Opponent	Result	Tries	Conversions
Apr 8	Hong Kong China	won 47–0	Leo (2), Carter (2), Rokolisoa, Cook-Savage, Fineanganofo	Rokolisoa (3), Cook-Savage (3)
Apr 8	Australia	won 24–12	Molia (2), Leo, Ormond	Rokolisoa (2)
Apr 8	South Africa	won 12–7	Collier, Vai	Cook-Savage
Apr 9	Great Britain (quarterfinal)	won 22–10	Rokolisoa, Carter, Nicole, Ware	Rokolisoa
Apr 9	Fiji (semifinal)	won 19–10	penalty try, Leo, Ware	Rokolisoa
Apr 9	Argentina (Cup final)	won 19–17	Collier, Leo, Rush	Rokolisoa (2)

NEW ZEALAND AT FRANCE HSBC SEVENS

Stade Ernest-Wallon, Toulouse **May 12–14, 2023**

Date	Opponent	Result	Tries	Conversions
May 12	Canada	won 29–12	Collier, Rokolisoa, Ware, Molia, Solo	Rokolisoa, Cook-Savage
May 12	Kenya	won 31–5	Solo (2), Clark, Ware, Leo	Rokolisoa (2), Cook-Savage
May 13	Uruguay	won 14–12	Rush, Solo	Cook-Savage (2)
May 13	Ireland (quarterfinal)	won 35–0	Leo (2), Rokolisoa, Rush, Curry	Rokolisoa (4), Cook-Savage
May 14	France (semifinal)	won 19–14	Rokolisoa, Ware, Rush	Rokolisoa (2)
May 14	Argentina (Cup final)	won 24–19 aet	Solo (2), Ware, Rokolisoa	Rokolisoa (2)

NEW ZEALAND AT ENGLAND HSBC SEVENS

Twickenham, London **May 20/21, 2023**

Date	Opponent	Result	Tries	Conversions
May 20	USA	won 35–17	Carter (2), Solo, Molia, Tito-Harris	Rokolisoa (4), Cook-Savage
May 20	Great Britain	won 20–5	Collier, Ware, Rokolisoa, Molia	
May 20	South Africa	won 32–21	Rokolisoa (3), Tito-Harris (2), Clark	Cook-Savage
May 21	France (quarterfinal)	won 19–17	Rokolisoa, Curry, Mikkelson	Rokolisoa (2)
May 21	Fiji (semifinal)	lost 17–19	Rokolisoa, Collier, Ware	Rokolisoa
May 21	Samoa (for 3rd place)	lost 19–24	Tito-Harris, Rush, Clark	Cook-Savage (2)

Argentina defeated Fiji 35–14 in the Cup final

NEW ZEALAND AT DUBAI HSBC SVNS

The Sevens, Dubai **December 2/3, 2023**

Date	Opponent	Result	Tries	Conversions
Dec 2	Canada	won 26–21	Curry (2), Rokolisoa, Fineanganofo,	Cook-Savage (2), Rokolisoa
Dec 2	Samoa	won 14–12	Curry, Rush	Rokolisoa, Cook-Savage
Dec 2	South Africa	lost 19–21	Cook-Savage, McGarvey-Black, Leo	Cook-Savage (2)
Dec 3	USA (Cup quarterfinal)	won 40–0	Cook-Savage (2), Curry, Rokolisoa, Clark, Carter	Rokolisoa (5)
Dec 3	Argentina (semifinal)	lost 19–21	Clark, Carter, Rokolisoa	Rokolisoa (2)
Dec 3	Fiji (for 3rd place)	won 17–12	Rokolisoa, Vai, Fineanganofo	Rokolisoa

South Africa defeated Argentina 12–7 in the Cup final

NEW ZEALAND AT SOUTH AFRICA HSBC SVNS

DHL Stadium, Cape Town — **December 9–10, 2023**

Date	Opponent	Result	Tries	Conversions
Dec 9	Canada	lost 7–19	Molia	Cook-Savage
Dec 9	Australia	won 35–5	Carter (3), Leo, McGarvey-Black	McGarvey-Black (4), Curry
Dec 9	Samoa	lost 14–21	Molia, Curry	McGarvey-Black, Cook-Savage
Dec 10	Ireland (Cup quarter-final)	lost 21–36	Cook-Savage, Vai, McGarvey-Black	Cook-Savage (2), McGarvey-Black
Dec 10	South Africa (for 5th place)	won 31–7	Vai (2), McGarvey-Black, Molia, Rokolisoa	Cook-Savage (2), Rokolisoa
Argentina defeated Australia 45–12 in the Cup final				

NEW ZEALAND SELECTION AT OCEANIA RUGBY SEVENS CHAMPIONSHIP

In preparation for the commencement of the 2023/24 HSBC World Series a squad took part at the Oceania Sevens in Brisbane. Fifteen players travelled with 12 listed for each game. Because of the enlarged squad being rotated during the tournament the team was not accorded full All Blacks Sevens status. Regular international tournaments are limited to 13 players. Jayden Keelan was the only newcomer to the national squad. .

Squad: Che Clark, Dylan Collier, Tepaea Cook-Savage, Scott Curry, Sam Dickson, Fehi Fineanganofo, Jayden Keelan, Moses Leo, Ngarohi McGarvey-Black, Tim Mikkelson, Sione Molia, Akuila Rokolisoa, Payton Spencer, Codemeru Vai, Regan Ware. Collier was captain for games 1,2,4,5, Molia 3, and Dickson game 6.

Coach: Tomasi Cama
Assistant coach: Euan Mackintosh
Manager: David Ormrod
S & C: Travis McMaster
Physio: Rachel Lambert
Analyst: Tom Martin

NEW ZEALAND SELECTION AT OCEANIA RUGBY SEVENS CHAMPIONSHIP

Ballymore Stadium, Brisbane — **November 10–12, 2023**

Date	Opponent	Result	Tries	Conversions
Nov 10	Oceania Barbarians	won 54–0	McGarvey-Black, Ware, Vai, Cook-Savage, Clark, Collier, Mikkelson, Leo	Cook-Savage (5), Rokolisoa (2)
Nov 10	Fiji	lost 5–12	Leo	
Nov 11	Niue	won 56–0	Leo (2), Keelan (2), Spencer (2), Molia, Clark,	Cook-Savage (7), Rokolisoa
Nov 11	Australia	won 14–10	Rokolisoa, Ware	Rokolisoa (2)
Nov 12	Fiji	won 24–17	Clark (3), Leo	Rokolisoa (2)
Nov 12	Samoa (final)	won 24–19 aet	Rokolisoa (2), Fineanganofo, Cook-Savage	Rokolisoa, Cook-Savage

NEW ZEALAND INTERNATIONAL SEVENS

FMG Waikato Stadium, Hamilton **January 21/22, 2023**

POOL PLAY

A Fiji 26 France 10; Samoa 31 Kenya 5; Fiji 21 Kenya 7; France 21 Samoa 10; Fiji 22 Samoa 12; France 26 Kenya 21.

B New Zealand 45 Tonga 0; Australia 28 Great Britain 14; Tonga 26 Great Britain 21; New Zealand 21 Australia 19; Australia 36 Tonga 7; New Zealand 19 Great Britain 12.

C Ireland 14 Uruguay 12; USA 40 Japan 12; Japan 24 Uruguay 19; USA 14 Ireland 14; USA 28 Uruguay 12; Ireland 33 Japan 12.

D South Africa 34 Canada 5; Argentina 20 Spain 5; Argentina 29 Canada 14; South Africa 19 Spain 12; South Africa 17 Argentina 14; Canada 12 Spain 5.

Quarterfinals for 9th	Kenya 21, Canada 5; Samoa 24, Spain 21; Great Britain 24, Japan 12; Tonga 12, Uruguay 7.
Cup quarterfinals	France 22, South Africa 17; Argentina 19, Fiji 10; USA 28, Australia 14; New Zealand 10, Ireland 5.
Semifinals for 13th	Canada 21, Uruguay 17; Spain 21, Japan 17
Semifinals for 9th	Kenya 33, Tonga 19; Samoa 24, Great Britain 14
Semifinals for 5th	Ireland 21, South Africa 14; Australia 26, Fiji 19
Cup semifinals	New Zealand 38, France 0; Argentina 24, USA 14
Play-off for 13th	Spain 24, Canada 14
Play-off for 9th	Samoa 26, Kenya 5
Play-off for 5th	Australia 26, Ireland 17
Bronze final	USA 15, France 14
Cup final	Argentina 14, New Zealand 12

Tournament referees: Paulo Duarte (Portugal), Morne Ferreira (South Africa), Francisco Gonzalez (Uruguay), Nick Hogan (NZ), AJ Jacobs (South Africa), Reuben Keane (Australia), Adam Leal (England), Tevita Rokovereni (Fiji).

NEW ZEALAND INTERNATIONAL SEVENS TOURNAMENTS

	Cup final	*Plate winner*	*Bowl winner*	*Shield winner*
2000	Fiji 24, New Zealand 14	Canada	France	
2001	Australia19, Fiji 17	Samoa	South Africa	Japan
2002	South Africa 17, Samoa 14	Argentina	France	Cook Is
2003	New Zealand 38, England 26	Samoa	Canada	Tonga
2004	New Zealand 33, Fiji 15	Tonga	Argentina	USA
2005	New Zealand 31, Argentina 7	Australia	Kenya	Niue
2006	Fiji 27, South Africa 22	England	Scotland	Tonga
2007	Samoa 17, Fiji 14	England	Argentina	Portugal
2008	New Zealand 22, Samoa 7	South Africa	England	USA
2009	England 19, New Zealand 17	South Africa	Cook Is	Scotland
2010	Fiji 19, Samoa 14	Australia	Wales	USA
2011	New Zealand 29, England 14	Fiji	Kenya	USA
2012	New Zealand 24, Fiji 7	South Africa	Kenya	Scotland
2013	England 24, Kenya 19	Australia	Canada	Wales
2014	New Zealand 21, South Africa 0	Australia	Kenya	USA
2015	New Zealand 27, England 21	Fiji	France	Canada
2016	New Zealand 24, South Africa 21	Australia	Samoa	France

	Cup final	*Challenge Trophy winner*
2017	South Africa 26, Fiji 5	Kenya
2018	Fiji 24, South Africa 17	USA
2019	Fiji 38, USA 0	England
2020	New Zealand 27, France 5	
2023	France 14, New Zealand 12	

PLAYING RECORD OF NEW ZEALAND SEVENS TEAMS

	Tournaments			Games				Points	
	Attended	Won	Runner-up	Played	Won	Draw	Lost	For	Against
1973	1	–	–	3	2	–	1	58	50
1983	1	–	–	5	4	–	1	114	4
1984	1	–	1	5	4	–	1	74	40
1985	1	–	–	4	3	–	1	88	18
1986	3	3	–	16	15	–	1	414	72
1987	2	1	1	11	10	–	1	284	66
1988	2	1	1	11	10	–	1	274	37
1989	2	2	–	11	11	–	–	316	71
1990	1	–	1	5	4	–	1	134	44
1991	1	–	1	5	4	–	1	150	18
1992	1	–	1	5	4	–	1	130	34
1993	3	–	–	17	12	–	5	420	175
1994	2	1	–	10	9	–	1	361	89
1995	5	2	1	22	19	–	3	681	182
1996	5	3	2	29	27	–	2	1263	236
1997	4	1	1	21	18	–	3	670	287
1998	11	6	2	59	54	–	5	2134	473
1999	10	7	2	54	49	1	4	1574	426
2000	10	6	3	59	55	–	4	2048	354
2001	10	7	1	60	56	–	4	2042	330
2002	13	8	2	75	68	1	6	2377	565
2003	7	1	3	40	34	–	6	1285	411
2004	8	3	2	46	39	–	7	1396	395
2005	8	3	1	48	41	–	7	1509	441
2006	9	2	1	48	36	2	10	1380	551
2007	8	4	–	44	40	–	4	1391	355
2008	8	4	2	47	43	–	4	1350	367
2009	9	2	2	49	37	–	12	1262	514
2010	9	2	2	51	43	1	7	1531	541
2011	9	4	1	50	43	–	7	1479	519
2012	9	3	4	54	46	–	8	1375	556
2013	10	3	4	60	52	–	8	1651	584
2014	10	4	3	60	50	–	10	1645	511
2015	8	1	3	47	33	1	13	1039	692
2016	11	3	1	64	45	3	16	1357	860
2017	11	1	2	64	48	–	16	1396	802
2018	13	3	1	73	52	–	21	1746	887
2019	10	2	2	60	47	-	13	1594	730
2020	4	2	–	21	19	–	2	545	221
2021	1	–	1	6	5	–	1	161	75
2022	10	1	4	58	45	–	13	1498	724
2023	10	5	1	59	48	–	11	1463	646
TOTALS	***271***	***101***	***60***	***1536***	***1284***	***9***	***243***	***43659***	***14953***

SEVENS RECORDS

to January 1, 2024

BY NEW ZEALAND TEAMS

Most successive wins	47	2007–08
Most successive tournament wins	7	2007–08
Most successive appearances in finals	12	1986–92

Tournament records

Most points	463	Portugal, 1996
Most tries	69	Portugal, 1996
Most conversions	59	Portugal, 1996

Match records

Highest team score	94	v Moldova, Portugal, 1996
Record victory (*points ahead*)	94	94–0, v Moldova, 1996
Highest score conceded	61	v Fiji, Japan, 1996
Record defeat (*points behind*)	56	5–61, v Fiji, Japan, 1996
Most tries	14	v Moldova, Portugal, 1996
Most conversions	12	v Moldova, Portugal, 1996
		v Hungary, Portugal, 1996

BY THE PLAYERS

Career records

Attended most tournaments	103	T.J. Mikkelson
Most points	2122	T. Cama
Most tries	253	T.J. Mikkelson

Tournament records

Most points	136	C.M. Cullen, Hong Kong, 1996
Most tries	20	B.R.M. Fleming, Portugal, 1996
Most conversions	28	D.A. Smith, Portugal, 1996

Match records

Most points	37	C.M. Cullen, v Sri Lanka, Hong Kong, 1996
Most tries	7	C.M. Cullen, v Sri Lanka, Hong Kong, 1996
Most conversions	9	T.J. Wright, v Korea, Sydney, 1989
		M. Ashford, v Sri Lanka, Dubai, 2001

NEW ZEALAND SEVENS REPRESENTATIVES, 1973–2023

	Tournaments
Ahki, P.J. (*North Harbour*) 2013–14–16	7
Ai'i, O. (*Auckland*) 1999–00–01–02–04–05	25
Alley, G. (*North Harbour*) 1992–93	2
Andrews, L.S. (*Otago*) 1999	2
Anesi, S.R. (*Waikato*) 2004–06	7
Arnold, T.C. (*Bay of Plenty*) 2009–10–11–12	19
Ashford, M.R. (*Auckland*) 2001–05	10
Atiga, B.A.C. (*Auckland*) 2007	1
Austin, H.S.E. (*Taranaki*) 1999	1
Auva'a, O.J. (*Auckland*) 2006–09	5
Bachop, G.T.M. (*Canterbury*) 1990–91–92–94	5
Baker, K.T. (*Manawatu*) 2008–09–17–18–19 (*Taranaki*) 2010–12–13–14–16–20 (*Hawke's Bay*) 2021–22	53
Bale, P. (*Canterbury*) 1990–92–93	3
Barrett, B.J. (*Taranaki*) 2010	2
Batty, G.B. (*Wellington*) 1973	1
Baxter, C.N.O. (*Bay of Plenty*) 2003–06–07	9
Berryman, N.R. (*Northland*) 1997	1
Blackadder, T.J. (*Canterbury*) 1993	2
Blackie, J.M. (*Otago*) 2002–03–04–05–06	12
Blowers, A.F. (*Auckland*) 1995	3
Blythe, T.G. (*Waikato*) 1999 (*Bay of Plenty*) 2001	3
Booth, J.P. (*Manawatu*) 2017	2
Botica, F.M. (*North Harbour*) 1985–86–87–88	8
Bourke, C.R. (*Hawke's Bay*) 2004	3
Brooke, Z.V. (*Auckland*) 1986–87–88–89–90	10
Brooke-Cowden, M. (*Auckland*) 1986–87	5
Bruning, K.T. (*Waikato*) 1994 (*Nelson Bays*) 1995	3
Bryant, R.J. (*Taranaki*) 1997	1
Bunce, F.E. (*North Harbour*) 1993	2
Bunce; J.F. (*Manawatu*) 2015 (*Waikato*) 2018	4
Bunting, A.M. (*Bay of Plenty*) 2002–03	6
Cama, T. (*Manawatu*) 2005–07–08–09–10–11–12–13–14	63
Camburn, M. (*North Harbour*) 2005	3
Carter, L.B. (*Bay of Plenty*) 2022–23	17
Cashmore, A.R. (*Auckland*) 1995	4
Christie, S.A. (*Tasman*) 2011	2
Clamp, M. (*Wellington*) 1984–85–86	4
Clark, C.P.J. (*Auckland*) 2022–23	10
Clarke, C.D. (*Auckland*) 2018–20	5
Clarke, E. (*Auckland*) 1993	1
Clutterbuck, M.J. (*Bay of Plenty*) 2014	1
Cocker, E. (*Otago*) 2005–06–07 (*Auckland*) 2008–09	28
Collier, D.J. (*Waikato*) 2015–16–17–18–19–20–21–22–23	57
Colling, G.L. (*Otago*) 1973	1
Collins, N.I. (*Bay of Plenty*) 2001–02	6
Cook-Savage, T.A. (*Waikato*) 2022–23	7
Crowley, A.E. (*Taranaki*) 1987–88–89–91	6
Cullen, C.M. (*Manawatu*) 1995–96 (*Wellington*) 1998–00	7
Curry, S.B. (*Manawatu*) 2010–12–13 (*Bay of Plenty*) 2011–14–15–16–17–18–19–20–21–22–23	66
Curtis, A.A.D. (*Wellington*) 2013–14–15 (*Manawatu*) 2017	19
Dagg, I.J.A. (*Hawke's Bay*) 2007–08	6
Daniel, B.W. (*Bay of Plenty*) 1997	2
Dauwai, A. (*Thames Valley*) 2006	2
Dawson, A.J. (*Counties*) 1983–85	2
De Goldi, C.D. (*Bay of Plenty*) 1998–99–00 (*Auckland*) 2001–02–03–04	41
Dickson, S.N. (*Canterbury*) 2012–13–14–15–16–17–18–19–20–22–23	74
Donald, A.J. (*Wanganui*) 1983	1
Duggan, R.J.L. (*Waikato*) 1997	1
Ellis, M.C.G. (*Otago*) 1993	1
Ellison, T.E. (*Wellington*) 2005–06	5

	Tournaments
Ensor A.C. (*Otago*) 2014	1
Erenavula, L. (*Counties*) 1994	2
Evans, N.J. (*North Harbour*) 2002	8
Faddes, M.A. (*Otago*) 2013	3
Fainga'anuku, L.T. (*Tasman*) 2018	1
Farani, D. (*Wellington*) 1997	1
Featherstone, R.M. (*Taranaki*) 2023	2
Fineanganofo, F.F. (*Bay of Plenty*) 2023	6
Flavell, T.V. (*North Harbour*) 1998	2
Fleming, B.R.M. (*Bay of Plenty*) 1995 (*Canterbury*) 1996–97–98 (*Wellington*) 1998–99–00–01–02 (*Otago*) 2003–04	35
Foote, B.M. (*Waikato*) 1997 (*North Harbour*) 1998	3
Forbes, D.J. (*Auckland*) 2006–07 (*Counties Manukau*) 2008–09–10–11–12–13–14–15–16–17	94
Forster, S.T. (*Otago*) 1993	2
Fry, R.J. (*Auckland*) 1983–84	2
Fuatai, F. (*Otago*) 2017	2
Gallagher, J.A. (*Wellington*) 1989–90	3
Gear, R.L. (*Auckland*) 1998–99–01	9
Gear, H.E. (*North Harbour*) 2003 (*Wellington*) 2010–12	4
Going, S.J. (*Northland*) 1999–00–01–02–03	29
Goodhue, E.J. (*Northland*) 2015	2
Granger, K.W. (*Manawatu*) 1983	1
Grant, P.W. (*Otago*) 2008–09–10	15
Green, C.I. (*Canterbury*) 1986	2
Gregory, S.J. (*Northland*) 2018–19	8
Grice, R.J.L. (*Waikato*) 2011	3
Guildford, Z.R. (*Hawke's Bay*) 2010	1
Haami, B.D. (*Taranaki*) 2000	2
Halai, F. (*Waikato*) 2010–11–12	15
Hales, D.A. (*Canterbury*) 1973	1
Hamilton, L.G. (*North Harbour*) 2009	1
Hamilton, A.R. (*Hawke's Bay*) 1994–95–96	5
Haugh, T.C. (*Otago*) 2018	2
Heem, B.I. (*Auckland*) 2010–11–12 (*Tasman*) 2013–14	22

	Tournaments
Hoeata, J.M.R.A. (*Taranaki*) 2006	2
Holmes, B. (*North Auckland*) 1973	1
Hona, J. (*Bay of Plenty*) 2005	4
Houston, J.D.W. (*Canterbury*) 2017	1
Howarth, S.P. (*Auckland*) 1991	1
Hudson, C. (*Canterbury*) 1999–00	6
Hunt, N. (*Wellington*) 2005–06–07–08 (*Bay of Plenty*) 2009	28
Ieremia, A. (*Wellington*) 1997	1
Ioane, A. (*Counties Manukau*) 1997	2
Ioane, A.L. (*Auckland*) 2014–16	11
Ioane, R.E. (*Auckland*) 2015–16	11
Ioasa, T.S.J. (*Hawke's Bay*) 2001–04–05–06–07–08 (*Wellington*) 2002–03	48
Iopu, I.P. (*Auckland*) 2012 (*Taranaki*) 2016–17	9
Izatt, C.S. (*Manawatu*) 1999	2
Jackman, M.B. (*HB/Cant*) 2012–13–14	10
Jane, C.S. (*Wellington*) 2006	5
Joass, T.J. (*Tasman*) 2017–22 (*Tas/BOP*) 2018–19	19
John, O.W. (*Counties Manukau*) 1996	2
Jones, M.T. (*Bay of Plenty*) 1993–94–95–96–97	11
Kaino, J. (*Auckland*) 2005	2
Kaka, G.G. (*Hawke's Bay*) 2013–14–15–16	33
Kamana, T.J.K.J. (*Waikato*) 2007	2
Karauna, D.T. (*Waikato*) 1996–97–98–00–01–02–03	35
Kepu, S.K.M. (*Auckland*) 2001	1
Keresoma, M.M. (*Auckland*) 2012–13	3
Khan, R.N. (*Auckland*) 2013–16–17–18	12
King, P.S.V. (*Bay of Plenty*) 2006–07–08–09–10 (*North Harbour*) 2011–12	33
Kinikinilau, R.U. (*Wellington*) 2002–03–04–05–06 (*Waikato*) 2007	13
Kiri Kiri, A.I. (*Manawatu*) 2015–16	4
Kirk, D.E. (*Otago*) 1984 (*Auckland*) 1985–86	5
Kirwan, J.J. (*Auckland*) 1984–85–86–88	5

Tournaments

Knewstubb, A.S. (*Tasman*) 2017 (*Tas/Horo Kap*) 2018 (*Horowhenua Kapiti*) 2019–20–22 (*Canterbury*) 2021 — 31
Koloto, E.T. (*Manawatu*) 1987 — 2
Konia, G.N. (*Hawke's Bay*) 1997 — 1
Koonwaiyou, A. (*Auckland*) 2002 — 1
Koroi, V.T. (*Otago*) 2017–18–19–20 — 23

Lahmert, W.H. (*Taranaki*) 2012–13 — 5
Lam, M.B. (*Auckland*) 2012–13–14–16 — 15
Lam, P.R. (*Auckland*) 1989–90–91–92–93 — 7
Latimer, T.D. (*Bay of Plenty*) 2004–05–06 — 15
Lawrence, Z.W. (*North Harbour*) 2005–06–07 (*Bay of Plenty*) 2008–09–10 — 35
Lee, F.A. (*Counties Manukau*) 2010 — 4
Leo, M.J. (*North Harbour*) 2022–23 — 15
Leo'o, J.J. (*Canterbury*) 2000–01 — 8
Lewis, A.J. (*Otago*) 1984 — 1
Lindsay, A.C. (*Canterbury*) 1983–84 — 2
Llewellyn, R.A.M. (*Canterbury*) 2012 — 1
Lomu, J.T. (*Counties Manukau*) 1994–95–96–98–99 (*Wellington*) 2000–01 — 13
Lynn, K.G. (*Southland*) 2008 — 2

McMaster, A. (*Manawatu*) 1987 — 2
McPhee, J.B. (*North Harbour*) 2010 — 2
McQuoid, G.A. (*Bay of Plenty*) 2004 — 3
MacDonald, L.T.J. (*Bay of Plenty*) 2005–09 — 3
McGarvey-Black, N.M. (*Bay of Plenty*) 2018–19–20–21–22–23 — 28
McKenzie, M.R. (*Southland*) 2014 — 2
Mafi, L.O. (*Manawatu*) 2003 (*Taranaki*) 2004–05 — 8
Maher, J.T. (*Counties Manukau*) 2006 — 2
Maidens, T.K. (*Hawke's Bay*) 1995 — 1
Malo, J.R. (*Waikato*) 2012 — 1
Marshall, J.R. (*Tasman*) 2011 — 2
Martin, E.M. (*Waikato*) 1996 — 1
Martin, R.E. (*Bay of Plenty*) 2001–02 — 11
Martine, H.R.I. (*King Country*) 2000 — 1

Tournaments

Masirewa, L.R. (*Waikato*) 2012–13 (*Bay of Plenty*) 2018 — 12
Masirewa, W. (*Counties Manukau*) 1996–97–98 — 10
Masoe, M.C. (*Taranaki*) 2001–02–04 — 22
Messam, L.J. (*Bay of Plenty*) 2002 (*Waikato*) 2003–04–05–06–10–16 — 26
Mikkelson, T.J. (*Waikato*) 2007–08–09–10–11–12–13–14–15–16–17–18–19–20–21–23 — 103
Miller, A.J. (*Bay of Plenty*) 1997 — 1
Mills, J.G. (*Auckland*) 1984 — 1
Milne, B.W.T. (*Southland*) 2002 — 2
Molia, S.L.J. (*Counties Manukau*) 2016–17–18–19–20–21–22–23 — 55
Monaghan, A.C. (*Northland*) 1998–00 — 18
Muliaina, J.M. (*Auckland*) 1999–00–01–02 — 11
Munro, L.H. (*Auckland*) 2006 — 4
Murray, C.D. (*Counties*) 1994 — 1

Naholo, W.R. (*Taranaki*) 2012–13–14 — 8
Nanai-Seturo, E.W.P.S. (*Counties Manukau*) 2018–20–21 — 13
Nanai-Williams, T.T. (*Counties Manukau*) 2008–09 — 7
Naoupu, G.E. (*Canterbury*) 2005 — 3
Nareki, J.M. (*Otago*) 2018–19 — 14
Nepia, D.S.M. (*Bay of Plenty*) 2000–01 — 5
Newby, C.A. (*Bay of Plenty*) 1999 (*North Harbour*) 1999–00–01–02 — 13
Ng Shiu, I.J.S. (*Tasman*) 2017–18–19–20 (*Auckland*) 2021–22 — 38
Ngaluafe, N.S.J. (*Southland*) 2016 — 1
Nicole, A.P. (*Canterbury*) 2018–19–20–21 (*Southland*) 2022–23 — 23
Nonoa, S.I. (*Waikato*) 1998 — 1
Nonu, M.A. (*Wellington*) 2004 — 2
Nowell, B.C. (*Canterbury*) 2008 — 2

O'Donnell, D.P.T. (*Waikato*) 2010–11–14–15 — 12
O'Donnell, K.F.T. (*Taranaki*) 2011–12 — 5
Ormsby, K.M.T. (*Counties Manukau*) 2000 — 1
Ormond, J.T. (*Taranaki*) 2010–11 — 3

Tournaments

Ormond, L.H. (*Taranaki*) 2015–16–17–22–23 21
Osborne, G.M. (*Nth Harbour*) 1992–93–94–96–97 6

Paramore, J. (*Counties*) 1993 2
Parkinson, D.T. (*Auckland*) 1998–99 (*Otago*) 2001 (*North Harbour*) 2003 15
Parkinson, M.T. (*North Harbour*) 1999–2003–04 (*Bay of Plenty*) 2005 14
Peacocke, G.M. (*North Harbour*) 1996–97 3
Pearson, M.B. (*Wellington*) 2015 1
Pedersen, H.L. (*Otago*) 2005 2
Pelenise, A. (*Canterbury*) 2005–06–07 13
Phillips, C.M. (*North Auckland*) 1986 3
Philpott, S. (*Canterbury*) 1988 2
Pierce, M.S.L. (*North Harbour*) 1989–91–92–93–95 6
Piutau, S.T. (*Auckland*) 2011–12 8
Popoali'i, B. (*Wellington*) 2009 (*Otago*) 2011 8
Puletua, J.R. (*Auckland*) 2009 1
Pulu, A.W. (*Counties Manukau*) 2015–16 7
Putt, K.B. (*Waikato*) 1987–89 2

Qio, J. (*NZ Fijians*)[1] 1999 1

Raikabula, L. (*Wellington*) 2006–11–12–13–14–15 (*Hawke's Bay*) 2007 (*Manawatu*) 2008–09–10 70
Raikuna, D.A. (*Counties Manukau*) 2011 (*North Harbour*) 2013–14 12
Raki, L.E. (*Counties Manukau*) 1985–87 3
Ralph, C.S. (*Bay of Plenty*) 1996–97–98 (*Canterbury*) 2000 7
Ranby, R.M. (*Waikato*) 2005 2
Randle, R.Q. (*Hawke's Bay*) 1995–96–97–98 (*Waikato*) 2000–01–02 10

Tournaments

Ranger, R.M.N. (*Northland*) 2006–07–08 8
Ravouvou, J. (*Auckland*) 2017–18–19 (*Bay of Plenty*) 2020 24
Rayasi, P. (*Wellington*) 1993 1
Rayasi, S.T.M. (*Auckland*) 2018–19–20 7
Reid, H.B. (*Otago*) 2001 (*North Harbour*) 2002–03–04 (*Bay of Plenty*) 2005–06 28
Reid, H.R. (*Bay of Plenty*) 1983 1
Reihana, B.T. (*Waikato*) 1998–02 2
Rich, G.J.W. (*Auckland*) 1983–84–85 3
Rickards, W.T.C. (*Southland*) 2006–07–08–09 8
Robertson, G.A. (*Waikato*) 2011 3
Rokocoko, J.T. (*Auckland*) 2002–05 8
Rokolisoa, A.T. (*Counties Manukau*) 2018–19–20–22-23 34

Ropiha, B.J. (*Hawke's Bay*) 2016 1
Ruddell, N.K. (*North Auckland*) 1986 1
Ruru, J.L. (*Otago*) 2016 2
Rush, B.J.K. (*Northland*) 2022–23 17
Rush, E.J. (*Auckland*) 1988–89–90–91 (*North Harbour*) 1992–93–94–95–96–97–98–99–00–01–02–03–04 62

Samuels, T.D.G. (*Hawke's Bay*) 2017 1
Savea, A.S. (*Wellington*) 2012–16 8
Savea, S.J. (*Wellington*) 2008–09 7
Savou, T.H. (*Manawatu*) 1998 1
Schmidt-Uili, P.T. (*Manawatu*) 1998 2
Schrijvers, D.J. (*Wellington*) 2018 1
Schuster, N.J. (*Wellington*) 1986–88–89–90 6
Scown, A.I. (*Taranaki*) 1973 1
Scrimgeour, O.J. (*Bay of Plenty*) 1995–96 (*Waikato*) 1995–96–97–98–99 22
Senio, K. (*Auckland*) 2001 2
Seymour, D.J. (*Canterbury*) 1988–89–90–91–92–93–99–00–02 (*Hawke's Bay*) 1994–95–96 (*Wellington*) 1997–98–99 35
Shelford, W.T. (*North Harbour*) 1985–86–87 5

Tournaments

Simonsson, B.G. (*Bay of Plenty*) 2017–18 3
Skudder, G.R. (*Waikato*) 1973 1
Smith, B.R. (*Otago*) 2010 1
Smith, B.W. (*Waikato*) 1983 1
Smith, David (*Auckland*) 2008 1
Smith, D.A. (*Canterbury*) 1996 3
Smith, W.R. (*Canterbury*) 1984–85–86 4
Smylie, C.B. (*North Harbour*) 2002 2
Soakai, A. (*Otago*) 2006–07 9
Solo, R.S. (*Bay of Plenty*) 2022–23 10
So'oialo, R. (*Wellington*) 2000–01–02 6
Souness, B.J. (*Taranaki*) 2009–10–11 17
Spencer, P.C. (*Auckland*) 2023 3
Spooner-Neera, T.A. (*Hawke's Bay*) 2013 4
Stanaway, T.Z.B.P. (*Bay of Plenty*) 2015–16–17–18 9
Stanley, J.T. (*Auckland*) 1983 1
Steinmetz, P.C. (*Wellington*) 1999 3
Stephens, T.P.O.T.R. (*Tasman*) 2019 1
Stevens, I.N. (*Wellington*) 1973 1
Stowers, S.L. (*Auckland*) 2004 (*Counties Manukau*) 2009–10–12–13–14–15–16–17 42
Sutherland, A.R. (*Marlborough*) 1973 1
Sweeney, D.W.H. (*Waikato*) 2006 6

Tagaloa, T.D.L. (*Wellington*) 1991 1
Tairea, F.T. (*Auckland*) 2009 1
Tamani, G.B. (*Japan*)[1] 1997 1
Tangatau, C.L. (*Auckland*) 2022 9
Tanivula, I. (*Auckland*) 2002 2
Taramai, M.V.U. (*Wellington*) 2014–15 4
Taufahema, T. (*Auckland*) 1998 5
Tauiwi, J.J. (*Bay of Plenty*) 1994–95–96–97 14
Te Aute, I.N. (*Bay of Plenty*) 2016 1
Te Nana, K.S. (*Wellington*) 1996–97–98–99 (*North Harbour*) 1999–00–01–02–03 42
Te Tamaki, I.R. (*Waikato*) 2015–16–17–18 15
Thomas, J.T. (*Waikato*) 1998 1
Thomson, A.J. (*Otago*) 2007 4
Thomson, N.J. (*Canterbury*) 2006–07 6

Tournaments

Thorpe, A.J. (*Canterbury*) 1984 1
Tiatia, J.A. (*Canterbury*) 2000–01–02–03–04 21
Tietjens, G.F. (*Waikato*) 1983 1
Tilsley, G. (*Wellington*) 2011 (*Manawatu*) 2014 6
Timu, J.K.R. (*Otago*) 1993 2
Tipoki, T.R. (*Auckland*) 1997–98 (*North Harbour*) 1998–99–02 10
Tito-Harris, X.R. (*Auckland*) 2023 3
Toeava, I. (*Auckland*) 2005 3
Tokula, S. (*Waikato*) 2009–10 12
Tololima-Auva'a, O.J. *see* **Auva'a, O.J.** (*Auckland*) 2006
Tuatagaloa, B. (*Wellington*) 2012 (*Canterbury*) 2013 9
Tuhakaraina, M. (*Bay of Plenty*) 1999–00 2
Tui'avii, D. (*Wellington*) 1993 1
Tuilevu, A. (*Waikato*) 1997–98 5
Tuitavake, A.S. (*North Harbour*) 2002–03–04 20
Tuitavake, N.H. (*North Harbour*) 2008–09–10 12
Tulou, A. (*Wellington*) 2008 1
Tuoro, C.K. (*Counties Manukau*) 2008–09 10
Tupuola, T. (*Wellington*) 2010 2
Umaga-Marshall, T.P. (*Wellington*) 2006–09 4

Vai, C.M. (*Bay of Plenty*) 2023 4
Vai, K.D. (*Bay of Plenty*) 2022 4
Vaka, S.T. (*Counties Manukau*) 2014–15 4
Valence, A. (*Auckland*) 1998–99–00–01–02–05–06 (*Hawke's Bay*) 2003–04 67
van Lieshout, J.J.A. (*Counties Manukau*) 2016 2
Verran, J.A. (*Canterbury*) 2012 1
Vidiri, J. (*Counties Manukau*) 1995–96–98 (*Auckland*) 2000 6
Visinia, L. (*Auckland*) 2012 2
Vito, V.V.J. (*Wellington*) 2007–08–09 8

[1]Tournament reserve players called upon when injuries prevented New Zealand from having fit reserves for the final.

Waaka, B.R.T. (*Taranaki*)
2015–16–17 14
Waldrom, S.L. (*Wellington*) 2002
(*Taranaki*) 2007–10 5
Walker, N.A.
(*Bay of Plenty*) 2002–03–04 15
Waqaseduadua, V.M.
(*North Harbour*) 2005–09 4
Warbrick, W.J.P. (*Bay of Plenty*)
2019–20–21 4
Ware, R.E. (*Waikato*) 2015–16
(*Bay of Plenty*) 2017–18–19–21–22–23 55
Webb, G.A. (*Otago*) 2003 1
Webber, T.J. (*Waikato*) 2011–12–
13–14–15–16–17
(*Bay of Plenty*) 18–19–20–21–22–23 54
Whitelock, A.J. (*Canterbury*) 2014 2
Williams, S.
(*Counties Manukau*) 2016 7
Williams-Spiers, G.D.
(*Auckland*) 2012 1
Wilson, B.A. (*North Harbour*) 2005 1
Wilson, J.C. (*Bay of Plenty*) 1999–00
(*Auckland*) 2001–02
(*Wellington*) 2003–04–05 32
Wilson, J.H. (*Bay of Plenty*) 2012 3
Wolfe, T.W.N. (*Taranaki*) 1993 1
Woods, P.G.A. (*Bay of Plenty*) 1993
(*Nth Harbour*) 1994–95–96–97–98 15
Wotherspoon, K.J.
(*Hawke's Bay*) 1996 1
Wright, T.J.
(*Auckland*) 1986–87–88–89–90–
91–92 11
Wulf, R.N.
(*North Harbour*) 2004–05–06 7
Wyllie, A.J. (*Canterbury*) 1973 1

Yates, S.P. (*Canterbury*) 2007–08 12

2023 SENIOR CLUB COMPETITIONS

With club rugby having been affected by Covid-19 to varying degrees over the past three years, the club season for the first time since 2019 was able to be played uninterrupted. The Southland competition was the first to start on March 18 and the Hawke's Bay, Horowhenua Kapiti, Northland, the two Otago country regions and Thames Valley competitions started seven days later. April 1 proved to be the most popular start date with 12 unions commencing on that date.

Auckland — Gallaher Shield:

July 22: Manukau Rovers 20, University 14

Down 5–14 after 44 minutes, Manukau Rovers scored a converted try and a penalty goal in the last ten minutes to complete a perfect season of 13 wins from 13 games and consecutive titles.

Bay of Plenty — Farmlands Baywide Premier Trophy

July 8: Te Puna 23, Mount Maunganui 14

Repeat finalists. Halftime 18–0. Played in the rain and on a sodden, muddy field. Te Puna led 23–0 before Mt Maunganui scored two converted tries

Buller — Senior Shield:

July 8: White Star 28, Westport 18

Leading 15–13 at halftime, White Star came from 15–18 down to win the title in their 125th Jubilee year.

Canterbury

Metropolitan — Bascik Transport Premier Trophy

July 30: Marist Albion 31, High School OB 26

Halftime 21–11. HSOB scored a try in the final minute to reduce the gap to five points.

Ellesmere-Mid Canterbury-North Canterbury — Luisetti Combined Country Cup:

June 17: Celtic (Mid Canterbury) 19, Prebbleton (Ellesmere) 7

Halftime 7–0. In the rain, Celtic scored three tries to one.

Ellesmere sub union — Coleman Shield:

July 29: Prebbleton 37, Waihora 3

Waihora scored first with a penalty goal in the 5th minute, then all the remaining scoring was done by Prebbleton for their first title since 1974.

North Canterbury sub union — Hunnibel Memorial Trophy:

July 29 : Glenmark Cheviot 30, Kaiapoi 19

Halftime 27–0. Kaiapoi dominated the second half and closed the gap to 27–19 but Glenmark Cheviot scored a penalty goal just before fulltime.

Counties Manukau — McNamara Cup:

July 15: Manurewa 25, Karaka 24

Halftime 10–14. Larenz Thomsen scored a last minute try, and converted it, for Manurewa to win.

Ngati Porou East Coast — Rangiora Keelan Memorial Shield:

July 15: Hicks Bay 13, Tihirau Victory Club 7

With TVC leading 7–6, the game stopped after 63 minutes when a Hicks Bay player suffered a broken leg. After 25 minutes delay and no ambulance arrived yet, the referee indicated he would call the game off if not restarted within another 15 minutes. With assistance, the player crawled off the field to allow the game to proceed. In the 74th minute, Hicks Bay scored a converted try to retake the lead. The match ended with TVC in possession a metre short of the Hicks Bay goal-line and conceded a penalty. Hicks Bay's first ever title.

Hawke's Bay — Maddison Trophy Cup:

July 15: Tech OB 36, Taradale 34

Repeat finalists. Tech OB led 24–8 after 45 minutes, but required a converted try in the final minute to win the title for the first time since 2013.

Horowhenua Kapiti — Ramsbotham Cup:

July 29: Rahui 23, Shannon 22

Halftime 11–9. Shannon scored a converted try in the 78th minute to lead 22–20. In the 80th minute Rahui's Alazay Roache kicked his sixth penalty goal for a 23–22 win and a perfect season of 14 wins from 14 games. Both teams scored one try each.

King Country — Meads Shield:

July 15: Taupo RS 42, Tongariro United 35

Halftime 24–14. Needing a converted try to force extra time, a Tongariro United attack ended in the Taupo RS 22 with a forward pass, to finish the game. Both teams scored five tries.

Manawatu — Hankins Shield:

July 15: Massey University 34 College OB 33

From 12–33 down after 43 minutes, Massey University scored four tries, the last one in the final minute, to win. The missed conversion did not matter. College OB had won both previous matches in 2023.

Mid Canterbury — Watters Cup:

July 22: Celtic 30, Methven 22

Halftime 20–19. A penalty goal with six minutes left took Celtic two scores clear. Brothers Jonetani and Raitube Vasurakuta scored all four tries between them for Celtic — two each.

For the Ellesmere-Mid Canterbury-North Canterbury competition, see Canterbury.

Northland — Joe Morgan Memorial Trophy:

July 22: Mid Northern 26, Kamo 12

Halftime 13–5. Kamo scored the last points with a converted try five minutes from fulltime to reduce the gap.

Bay of Islands sub union — Championship Shield:

July 8: Taiamai Ohaewai 65, Kaeo 5

Halftime 29–0. Taiamai Ohaewai were also runners-up in the Northland North Zone Championship.

Mangonui sub union — Bell Shield:
July 8: Eastern United 28, Te Rarawa 19
Halftime 21–12. No scoring in the final 15 minutes. Eastern United also won the Northland North Zone Championship

North Harbour — A.S.B. Cup:
July 15: North Shore 26, Takapuna 10
Halftime 6–3. North Shore scored three tries to one in the second half to win the title in their 150th Jubilee year.

North Otago — Citizens Shield:
July 15: Valley 26, Excelsior 23
Halftime 19–13. Valley scored a last minute converted try to win 26–23 and complete a perfect season of 11 wins from 11 games.

Otago
Metropolitan — Speight's Championship Shield:
July 29: Southern 30, Dunedin 20
Southern led 17–0 after 24 minutes and 17–15 at halftime.

Central Region — Super Liquor Trophy:
July 15: Alexandra 32, Upper Clutha 24
Down 11–24 after 46 minutes, Alexandra ran in three converted tries for their first title since 2015. It was Upper Clutha's only defeat of the season..

Southern Region — Speight's Cup:
July 8: West Taieri 28, Clutha 23
Halftime 10–8. A West Taieri penalty goal with six minutes left completed the scoring. Both teams scored three tries.

Otago Country — Countrywide Shield
July 22: West Taieri (Southern) 46, Alexandra (Central) 36
Halftime 32–17. Eight tries to six.

Poverty Bay — Lee Brothers Shield:
July 8: YMP 15, Waikohu 0
Halftime 5–0. YMP played the last 57 minutes with 14 men and completed a perfect season winning all 11 games to retain the title.

Southland — Galbraith Shield:
July 8: Pirates Old Boys 37, ENC Barbarians 10
Halftime 20–10. Pirates Old Boys first title since 2006.

South Canterbury — Hamersley Cup:
July 29: Temuka 38, Waimate 31
Halftime 13–24. Temuka scored 25 unanswered points in the second half until Waimate scored a converted try just before fulltime.

Taranaki — McMasters Shield:
July 15: New Plymouth OB 26 aet, Stratford Eltham 12 aet
Halftime 12–12. 80 minutes 12–12. A converted try in each half of extra time gave New Plymouth OB a perfect season of 16 wins from 16 games.

Tasman — Tasman Trophy
July 15: Central 20, Marist 16
Halftime 14–16. Two penalty goals by Central was the only scoring in the second half, the second one in the 79th minute, for back-to-back titles.

Marlborough sub union — Champion of Champions Trophy
April 29: Central 38, Waitohi 5
Halftime 12–0. Six tries to one.

Nelson Bays sub union — Centennial Cup:
April 8-May 6: 1st Marist 17 pts; 2nd Kahurangi 13 pts
The last round of the round robin competition was cancelled due to forecast heavy rain. Marist and Kahurangi, scheduled to play each other, received two points each.

Thames Valley — McClinchy Cup:
July 15: Whangamata 33, Hauraki North 20
0–17 down after 30 minutes, Whangamata scored three second half tries to win. Hauraki North had won 52–5 earlier in the competition.

Waikato — Breweries Shield:
July 15: Hautapu 41, Marist 33
Halftime 26–12. Seven tries to five.

Wairarapa Bush — Chris "Moose" Kapene Memorial Cup:
July 15: Carterton 29, Greytown 26
Halftime 16–16. A Ben Brooking penalty goal with the last kick of the game gave Carterton back-to-back titles.

Wellington — Jubilee Cup:
July 22: Oriental-Rongotai 34, Paremata-Plimmerton 21
Down 13–14 after 25 minutes, Oriental-Rongotai scored three converted tries to lead 34–14 after 60 minutes for their first title since 2011. Paremata-Plimmerton's first final since 1959.

West Coast — Taylorville Wallsend Trophy:
July 8: Kiwi 35, Wests 30
Kiwi led 35–13 during the second half and withstood a fightback to win their 8th consecutive title and have now won their last 82 games. Same finalists for fourth consecutive year.

Whanganui — President's Rosebowl:
July 8: Border 24, Taihape 23
Border led 17–6 at halftime but required a converted try after 78 minutes to nose 24–23 ahead for a Whanganui record fourth consecutive title.

Most consecutive championships:

14 Star (Southland) 1890-1903

10 Athletic (North Otago) 1906-1915; Celtic (South Canterbury) 2009-2018

8 Star (Southland) 1919-1926; Carterton (Wairarapa) 1946–1953; Westport (Buller) 1963-1970; Invercargill (Southland) 1987-1994; Ponsonby (Auckland) 2004-2011; Kiwi (West Coast) 2016–2023.

Most consecutive Sub Union championships:

13 Mahia (Wairoa) 1981-1993

11 Dannevirke O.B. (Dannevirke) 1946-1955, (Central HB-Dannevirke) 1956

SECONDARY SCHOOLS RUGBY

by Adam Julian

The NZ Schools regained the trans-Tasman Shield, which they lost from Australia in 2019, with two resounding victories at Viking Park in Canberra.

New Zealand achieved its largest margin of victory since 1995 after a sluggish start in the first Test. Four days later, New Zealand passed 50 points for the first time in 39 meetings, stretching back to 1978, against Australia.

The New Zealand team had plenty of size, skill, and athleticism in the forwards. Openside and captain Oli Mathis won the coveted Rugby News/Jerry Collins Bronze Boot as the best Kiwi player in the series as voted by the opposition.

Rico Simpson was a backline general of real quality. New Zealand had a settled midfield combination and excitement machine Tevita Naufahu on the wing.

A total of 26 players were used in the first two matches with 25 employed for the final Test.

New Plymouth Boys' High School mourned the loss of Max Carroll (QSM) aged 91 on November 21.

Carroll was closely associated with New Plymouth BHS for 65 years, as a student, teacher, master, sports coach, old boys' organiser and author. He wrote five books documenting the history of cricket, rugby, boarding and military cadet service at the school. For 15 years (1965-79) Carroll fashioned a formidable record as coach of the First XV. In 85 inter-school games, there were 58 wins and six draws, 12 defences of the Moascar Cup (Ranfurly Shield of schools rugby), an unbeaten 1973 season under the captaincy of Bruce Middleton, and a period beginning in 1967 which went seven seasons when only two of 38 games were lost. Three All Blacks emerged – flanker Graham Mourie, who also captained the All Blacks, halfback Mark Donaldson and loose forward Geoff Old. The John George-Max Carroll Trophy is competed for annually in the match between New Plymouth BHS and Francis Douglas Memorial College.

NEW ZEALAND SCHOOLS 2023

	School	Date of Birth	Height	Weight
Mosese Bason	Feilding HS	5/9/05	1.88	94
Marshall Blakely	Christchurch BHS	14/11/05	1.93	103
James Cameron	Westlake BHS	15/10/05	1.85	82
Micah Fale	St John's (Hamilton)	9/2/06	1.83	98
Robson Faleafa	St Peter's (Auckland)	19/11/05	1.83	124
Kiseki Fifita	Southland BHS	1/4/06	1.86	85
Jake Frost	Christchurch BHS	24/2/06	1.96	100
Tayne Harvey	Palmerston North BHS	30/5/05	1.85	93
Tonga Helu	Sacred Heart College	24/12/05	1.82	108
Quinten Holland	King's HS	8/9/05	1.97	102
Shaun Kempton	Rolleston Coll/Selwyn Comb	20/10/05	1.85	96
Manumaua Letiu	Christchurch BHS	25/9/05	1.80	105
Rangiwai Lunjevich	Hamilton BHS	28/4/05	1.86	84
Sione Mafi	Nelson College	19/5/05	1.85	120
Oli Mathis (capt)	Hamilton BHS	12/9/05	1.84	91
Isaac Murray-McGregor	Westlake BHS	17/10/05	1.87	74
Tevita Naufahu	St Kentigern College	7/11/05	1.83	85
Raharuhi Palmer	Hamilton BHS	31/1/06	1.75	96
Dylan Pledger	King's HS	5/6/05	1.70	70
Caelys-Paul Putoko	Hamilton BHS	12/7/05	1.83	93
Rico Simpson	Sacred Heart College	24/12/05	1.93	85
Charlie Sinton	Tauranga BC	24/11/06	1.71	77
Josh Tengblad	Sacred Heart College	19/10/05	2.01	109
Frank Vaenuku	De La Salle College	7/9/05	1.79	92
Aisake Vakasiuola	Tauranga BC	5/5/05	1.97	125
Logan Wallace	Palmerston North BHS	1/9/05	1.83	108

NB. Pledger and Putoko were also in the 2022 squad.

Manager: Nick Reid (*Awatapu College*)
Head coach: Kane Jury (*Highlanders*)
Assistant coaches: James Hantz (*Auckland Grammar*), Ngatai Walker (*Puketapu School*)
Strength & conditioning coach: Peter Shaw (*Counties Manukau*)
Physiotherapist: Bede Christey (*Crusaders*)
Video analyst: Doug Neilson (*Taranaki*)
Campaign manager: Ben Fisher (*NZ Rugby*)
Campaign support: Ezra Iupeli (*NZ Rugby*)

INDIVIDUAL SCORING

	Tries	Con	PG	DG	Points
Simpson	–	17	4	–	46
Mathis	5	–	–	–	25
Bason	2	–	–	–	10
Kempton	2	–	–	–	10
Naufahu	2	–	–	–	10
Tengbald	2	–	–	–	10
Wallace	2	–	–	–	10
Cameron	1	–	–	–	5
Fifita	1	–	–	–	5
Harvey	1	–	–	–	5
Pledger	1	–	–	–	5
Vakasioula	1	–	–	–	5
Totals	***20***	***17***	***4***	***0***	***146***
Opposition scored	*9*	*5*	*2*	*0*	*61*

NEW ZEALAND SCHOOLS 2023

	NZ Barbarians	Australia (1)	Australia (2)	**TOTALS**
Murray-McGregor	15	15	–	**2**
Lunjevich	s	s	15	**3**
Blakely	s	s	s	**3**
Naufahu	14	14	14	**3**
Fifita	11	11	s	**3**
Vaenuku	s	s	11	**3**
Cameron	13	13	13	**3**
Putoko	12	12	12	**3**
Simpson	10	10	10	**3**
Pledger	9	9	9	**3**
Sinton	s	s	s	**3**
Harvey	s	s	s	**3**
Bason	8	8	8	**3**
Mathis	7	7	7	**3**
Holland	6	6	s	**3**
Fale	s	s	6	**3**
Frost	s	s	s	**3**
Vakasioula	5	5	5	**3**
Tengblad	4	4	4	**3**
Faleafa	s	s	s	**3**
Wallace	3	3	s	**3**
Mafi	s	s	3	**3**
Helu	1	1	s	**3**
Palmer	s	s	1	**3**
Letiu	2	2	2	**3**
Kempton	s	s	s	**3**

NEW ZEALAND SCHOOLS 2023

Played 3 ***Won 3*** ***Points for 146*** ***Points against 61***

Date	*Opponent*	*Location*	*Score*	*Tries*	*Con*	*PG*	*DG*	*Referee*
September 23	NZ Barbarians Under 18	Hamilton	57–22	Mathis (2), Bason (2), Pledger, Tengblad, Harvey, Kempton	Simpson (7)	Simpson		Will Johnston
September 28	Australian Under 18	Canberra	34–3	Wallace, Mathis, Tengblad, Vakasioula	Simpson (4)	Simpson (2)		George Myers (AUS)
October 2	Australian Under 18	Canberra	55–36	Naufahu (2), Mathis (2), Cameron, Fifita, Kempton, Wallace	Simpson (6)	Simpson		Will Pugsley (AUS)

NEW ZEALAND BARBARIANS UNDER 18s

Results:
September 23 v **NZ Schools at St Paul's Collegiate**, Hamilton; Lost 22–57
Tries: Rangitutia (*2*), Salmon, Tapara tries; Con: Robinson

September 29 v **NZ Māori Ngā Mareikura** U18s at St Paul's Collegiate; Won 41–5
Tries: Salmon (*4*), Oudenryn, Roberts, O'Connor; Cons: O'Connor (*2*), Robinson

Backs: Josh Augustine (*Napier BHS*), Halen King (*St John's College, Hamilton*), Riley Lucas (*Green Island RFC*), Cohen Norrie (*Sacred Heart College*), Liam O'Connor (*Palmerston North BHS*), Kyan Rangitutia (*Dunedin RFC*), Cooper Roberts (*University of Canterbury RFC*), Hugh Robinson (*Marlborough BC*), Joel Russell (*Napier BHS*), Nathan Salmon (*Old Boys-Marist RFC, Northland*), Jai Tamati (*Rotorua BHS*)
Forwards: Tamiano Ahloo (*Sacred Heart College*), JJ Fisher (*Southland BHS*), Harry Irving (*Scots College*), Lenz Itunu-Morunga (*Manurewa RFC*), Fa'auma Kupita (*Tauranga BC*), Shaun McNaughten (*Hastings BHS*), Brooke Mitchell (*Whakarewarewa RFC*), Samiuela Moimoi (*Nelson College*), Eli Oudenryn (*Palmerston North BHS*), Radford Powell (*St Andrew's College*), Jack Ruske (*St Paul's Collegiate*), Saumaki Saumaki (*Nelson College*), Kaleb Tapara (*St Peter's School, Cambridge*), Joey Taumateine (*Wesley College*)

Head Coach: Dave Dillon (*Highlanders*)
Assistant Coaches: Matt MacDougall (*Crusaders*), Rocky Khan (*Mt Albert Grammar School*)
Physiotherapist: Shane Derry (*Hamilton Marist*)
Manager: James Kumate (*Howick College*)
Analyst: Stephlin Hanekam (*Christchurch BHS*)
Strength & Conditioning coach: Jayden Pinfold (*Hawke's Bay*)
Campaign Support: Ezra Iupeli (*New Zealand Rugby*)

NEW ZEALAND MĀORI NGA MAREIKURA UNDER 18s

Results:
September 23 v **Northland Under 19s** at St Paul's Collegiate, Hamilton; Won 62–0
Tries: Hana (*3*), Cole (*2*), Waitai-Haenga (*2*), Nikora-Wilson, Mathieson, Pender; Cons: Mathieson (*4*), Lidgard (*2*)

September 28 v **NZ Barbarians Under 18s** at St Paul's Collegiate; Lost 5–41
Try: Eti

Backs: Kurtis Hana (*Hamilton BHS*), Maiti Leef (*Hastings BHS*), Blake Lidgard (*Westlake BHS*), Hone Mathison (*Te Kuiti HS*), Joe Parkinson (*Otago BHS*), Jimmy Pender (*Greerton Marist RFC*), Mac Russ (*Hamilton BHS*), Reimana Saunderson-Rurawhe (*Westlake BHS*), Stanley Solomon (*Petone RFC*), Quinn Sturmey (*Palmerston North BHS*), Hiraka Waitai-Haenga (*Hamilton BHS*)
Forwards: Liam Anderson (*Fraser Tech RFC*), Taiora Cameron (*Francis Douglas Memorial College*), Hōhepa Chandler (*Tauranga BC*), Will Cole (*Rathkeale College*), Ryan Dunn (*Tauranga BC*), Dylan Eti (*St Peter's School, Cambridge*), Christian MacEwan (*Hamilton BHS*), Jack McCarthy (*Whanganui Collegiate*), Amaziah Mitchell (*Southland BHS*), Liam Strum (*Hamilton BHS*), Phoenix Tapatu (*Otago BHS*), Lucas Te Rangi (*St Andrew's College, Christchurch*), Oscar Ritchie (*Hastings BHS*), Hoani Nikora-Wilson (*Southland BHS*)

Head coach: Kahu Carey (*Canterbury*)
Assistant coaches: Willie Brown (*Canterbury*), Jackson Willison (*Waikato*), Scott Palmer (*Auckland*)
Physiotherapist: Kara Thomas (*Waikato*)
Managers: Simon Craggs (*Counties Manukau*), Duncan Cameron (*Manawatū*)
Head of tikanga: Kahurangi Falaoa (*Poverty Bay*)
Tikanga support: Mati Morrison (*Canterbury*), Joseph Tyro (*Canterbury*)

NEW ZEALAND BARBARIANS AREA SCHOOLS

Results:
September 20 v **Te Awamutu College First XV** at Te Awamutu RFC; Won 34–7

September 23 v **King Country Under 18s** at Te Awamutu RFC; Won 22–17

Squad: Lukas Barlow (*TKKM o Kaikohe, Northland*), Cullen Bevan (*Mercury Bay Area School, Thames Valley*), Maitland Bevan (*Mercury Bay Area School*), Earl Cacho (*Oxford Area School, North Canterbury*), Luke Chisnall (*Hurunui College, North Canterbury*), Haydon Danford (*Onewhero Area School, Counties Manukau*), Mitchell du Toit (*South West Area School*), Sam Edgecombe (*Kaitaia Abundant Life, Northland*), Eru Harawira (*Te Wharekura O Ruatoki, Bay of Plenty*), Toby Harrex (*Lawrence Area School, Otago*), Honour Ingle (*TKKM o Horouta Wananga, Poverty Bay*), Te Ao Marama Bennett (*TKMM o Te Koutu, Bay of Plenty*), John McGregor (*Mercury Bay Area School*), Leon Melde (*Mercury Bay Area School*), Joshua Mitt (*TKKM o Hokianga, Northland*), Flynn Morgan (*Tapawera Area School, Tasman*), Ben Rillstone (*Collingwood Area School, Tasman*), Kyle Searle (*Hurunui College*), Ziah Senior (*Te Wharekura o Te Kaokaoroa o Patetere*), Caden Swindlehurst (*Mercury Bay Area School*), Tino Enosi Tuipulotu (*Akaroa Area School, Ellesmere*), Khalon Walters (*Opononi Area School, Northland*), Clayton Wikaira (*TKKM o Hokianga*)

Manager: Stephen Beck (*Hurunui College*)
Head coach: Justin Marsh (*Tongariro AS, King Country*)
Assistant coach: Hone Manuel (*Te Wharekura o Manaia, Thames Valley*), Ratu Mataira (*Raglan, Waikato*)
Trainer: Ilai Arona (*Northland*)
Kaumātua: Mike Smith (*Thames Valley*)
Resource coach: Kingi Matenga (*Manawatū*)

SCHOOLS RUGBY REVIEW

NATIONAL TOP FOUR

In a genuine fairytale, Southland Boys' HS became the first South Island school since Christchurch Boys' High School in 2006 to win the National Top 4 title, upsetting prolific scoring Blues champion Westlake BHS 32–29 in the final at Central Energy Arena in Palmerston North.

In nine previous trips to the Top 4, Southland had only made the final once, when it was smashed 25–7 by St Peter's College (Auckland) in 1987.

Excluding the four occasions when two South Island schools have attended the National Top 4 and played each other, South Island schools have only won 15 of their 72 matches at the tournament since its inception in 1982. Indeed, before the weekend South Island entrants hadn't won a single Top 4 match since 2013. The last time Southland competed in 2017, it suffered a record 49–0 whitewash against Hamilton BHS, which converted just two of its nine tries.

Southland was hindered by having five of its starting lineup out with injury for the final, including captain Gregor Rutledge, as well as its best 10-12-13 combo. Flanker Lachie Riley spent 69 minutes on the wing in the 20–19 semi-final win against Palmerston North BHS on the Friday.

The Sunday final proved to be a thriller, with Southand rallying from 19–5 down to prevail. A 45-metre dropped goal to Year 11 fullback Jimmy Taylor with less than 10 minutes remaining when the score was 29–24 will long live in Invercargill folklore. Southland No 8 Justin Shaw was a tower of strength. He embarked on a 50-metre weaving run early in the second half and then crashed over for a try several phases later. Southland centre Kiseki Fifita was a powerhouse and scored a try.

Westlake certainly contributed to an outstanding spectacle with centre James Cameron scoring twice and fullback Isaac Murray-Macgregor scoring a try and setting up two for winger Reimana Saunderson-Rurawhe.

Southland was beaten twice by Otago BHS in the Otago Schools competition before winning the final 22–10. Southand then eliminated Christchurch BHS 29–28 in the South Island final, with Taylor nailing the winning sideline conversion. In the semifinal against Palmerston North, Southland only had a third of possession.

A unique feature of Southland's success was the close ties the players and coaches enjoyed with old boys of the school and the Southland rugby community. Southand's assistant coach was Peter Skelt (along with Chris McIlwrick, Jason Rutledge, and head coach Jason Dermody). Skelt played in the 1972 and 1973 First XVs that won 38 out of 40 games, including all 20 in 1973 and later coached the First XV from 1991 to 2010, making the National Top 4 in 1993, 1995, 1997, 2001 and 2003. Skelt coached both Rutledge and Dermody in the First XV.

Meanwhile, the Dermody family is something of a Southland rugby dynasty. Dad Fergus Dermody played 62 games for Southland at lock between 1974 and 1983. His brother and fellow lock Gerald was capped 128 times and another brother Stuart also represented Southland.

Jason's cousins Grant, Sean and Malcom played for Southland, and his brother Clarke Dermody (Highlanders coach) was an All Blacks prop in three Tests in 2006. Jason's great-great-grandfather was 1893 All Black Graham Shannon. Female cousins Emma and Jessica Dermody have played in the Farah Palmer Cup. Gregory Rutledge is the son of a Southland centurion, Jason, whose grandfather Leicester Rutledge was an All Black.

Jimmy Taylor's brothers Jack and Harry played for Otago and Southland in the NPC respectively. Fa Muliaina is All Black Mils' brother and the father of the two Muliaina boys in the team, Mika, and Rico Muliaina. Rico survived a cancer scare last year to play.

Invercargill Mayor Nobby Clark commissioned a ticker-tape parade which was cancelled due to foul weather, so he hosted the team at council offices instead.

Semifinals: Southland BHS 20–19 Palmerston North BHS,
Westlake BHS 43–40 Tauranga Boys' College

3 v 4: Palmerston North BHS 31–24 Tauranga BC

Final: Southland BHS 32–29 Westlake BHS

GIRLS' HINE POUNAMU TROPHY

Manukura won the Hine Pounamu Trophy with a resounding 31–0 thrashing of four-time previous winner Hamilton GHS in the final.

Based in Palmerston North, Manukura shared the title with Christchurch Girls' High School last year and is undoubtedly a slick outfit. Coached by former Black Ferns halfback Kristina Sue and Black Ferns Sevens representative Rhiarna Ferris, they come equipped with a mental skills advisor (Pounamu Wharehinga) and video analyst (India O'Connell) too.

Manukura scored five tries and led 17–0 at halftime in a lopsided decider.

The most eye-catching tries were to halfback Maia Davis, who strode gracefully from halfway and hooker Lashaye Blake who resembled a steamroller in her 30 metre charge.

The handling and creativity of the Manukura backs were excellent. Second five Manaia Blake scored twice in the semis and her brute force was ideal beside the guile of centre Mia Sutherland.

The Manukura forwards were direct and abrasive with No 8 Te Maia Sweetman an imposing force.

Tragically, Manukura only played four official fixtures in 2023 and a couple of tournaments under varying rules. Moves are afoot to develop a New Zealand Secondary Schoolgirls team. Who they will play remains a mystery.

Semifinals: Manukura 36–12 Christchurch GHS;
Hamilton GHS 28–5 Mount Albert Grammar

3 v 4: Christchurch GHS 15–5 Mt Albert

Final: Manukura 31–0 Hamilton GHS

MOASCAR CUP

Hamilton BHS started the 2023 season with the Moascar Cup and looked like favourite for the national title when it successfully resisted challenges from New Plymouth BHS (64–14), Rotorua BHS (40–7), St John's College, Hamilton (43–14), Hastings BHS (30–15), Gisborne BHS (25–7) and Wesley College (52–5).

However, Hamilton came unstuck in the Chiefs regional final against Tauranga BC (33–26). Tauranga surrendered the Moascar to Westlake BHS (43–40) in the semifinal of the Top 4, Westlake reclaiming the Moascar for the first time since 1989. Two days later, Southland won it off Westlake (32–29) in the final.

OTHER HIGHLIGHTS

*Feilding High School successfully defended the Taine Randell Cup as Central North Island champion, defeating St John's College, Hamilton, 24–17 in the final.

*The ludicrous 1A First XV media ban was applied but hypocrisy was glaring with King's College employing a former New Zealand Herald journalist as a media assistant and a production company run by Sacred Heart College old boys recording the historic 1A final win against St Kentigern College. New Zealand Herald journalist Bruce Holloway did an honourable job with his weekly column covering the scene.

*St Kent's won all 11 matches in the round-robin of the Auckland 1A competition but was overturned in the final by Sacred Heart (39–29) in front of an estimated 8000 people at Waitemata Rugby Club in west Auckland. Sacred Heart No 10 Rico Simpson was man of the match with 19 points. Prop Tonga Helu and halfback Sione Finau each scored two tries. It was Sacred Heart's seventh 1A title but first since 1965.

*Scots College won its fourth Wellington Premiership (undefeated) in five years with a 29–27 victory over St Patrick's College Silverstream in the final. Since 2012, Silverstream has won 93 Premiership games, Scots 92. Following a 43–35 win over Feilding HS in the Hurricanes regional semifinal, Scots defaulted the final for a place at the National Top 4 against Palmerston North BHS due to safety concerns owing to a shortage of front rowers. This an unprecedented and frankly unsatisfactory event.

*Westlake BHS won the 20th North Harbour title, thrashing Rosmini College 42–8 in the final. Westlake has now won 29 games competition games in a row.

*Christchurch BHS won the UC Championship, ending the two-year reign of Nelson College as title holder with a 30–26 win in the final in Nelson. Christchurch scored two of its four tries from lineout drives. Nelson halfback Oliver Gibbons scored three tries.

*Marlborough BC holds the Trustbank Cup, the Ranfurly Shield of South Island secondary schools rugby, after a 24–22 win over Christchurch BHS. It's the first time since 2021 that MBC has held the trophy.

*Hamilton BHS won the Super 8 for the 15th time since 2006, crushing Napier BHS by a record score of 56–22 in the final. Napier had beaten Hamilton 17–15 in the round-robin.
Under Nigel Hotham and Greg Kirkham (2003–23), Hamilton BHS has won five National Top 4 and 15 Super 8 titles, producing 51 NZ Schools players. In 404 matches, Hamilton has recorded 345 wins, scored 13,390 points, and conceded 4242 for an average score of 33–11. In December 2022 and April 2023, Hamilton won two World Schools titles in Thailand and Japan.

* In the final, Rotorua Boys' High School won its second Condor Sevens title with a 19–12 victory over Feilding High School. It was the first time since 2015 that Hamilton BHS didn't win the title. In the semis, Hamilton was conquered 17–12 by Rotorua. Manukura successfully defended the girls' title with a 33-19 win over Howick College in the final.

WOMEN'S RUGBY

THE ALMANACK NEW ZEALAND XV

Renee Holmes
Waikato

Katelyn Vahaakolo
Auckland

Amy du Plessis
Canterbury

Mererangi Paul
Counties Manukau

Sylvia Brunt
Auckland

Ruahei Demant (co-capt)
Auckland

Arihiana Marino-Tauhinu
Counties Manukau

Liana Mikaele-Tu'u
Auckland

Kennedy Simon (co-capt) *Waikato*

Chelsea Bremner
Canterbury

Maia Roos
Auckland

Alana Bremner
Canterbury

Amy Rule
Canterbury

Georgia Ponsonby
Canterbury

Krystal Murray
Northland

Reserves –

Luka Connor (*Bay of Plenty*), Kate Henwood (*Bay of Plenty*), Sophie Fisher (*Auckland*), Charmaine Smith (*Northland*), Lucy Jenkins (*Canterbury*), Iritana Hohaia (*Taranaki*), Rosie Kelly (*Canterbury*), Angelica Mekemeke Vahai (*Auckland*).

PLAYER OF THE YEAR

Liana Elizabeth Tomzena Mikaele-Tu'u (*Auckland*) was one of only three players to start in each of the Black Ferns seven tests of 2023, the strong running and hard-tackling number eight impressed with her high work-rate and ball skills. The 21-year-old has developed well since making her test debut in 2021 and we see her tally of 18 tests being extended in future years. In November, she was nominated, for the second time, for the Black Ferns Player of the Year, her first nomination being in 2021.

Liana Mikaele-Tu'u made her Farah Palmer Cup debut for Hawke's Bay in 2019 as a 17-year-old schoolgirl, as a substitute, in the Bay's second game. Having impressed the coach, she was in the starting lineup, mainly at lock, for the remaining five games. The Almanack noted that she was a player 'to look out for in the future.' Moving to Auckland in 2020 she joined College Rifles club and became a regular loose forward in the Storm FPC team.

The 2021 season commenced with an appearance in the Blues game against the Chiefs, then three games for Auckland in a season interrupted by the pandemic. Late in the year the 19-year-old was selected for the four-test tour of England and France. The Black Ferns lost all four tests but Mikaele-Tu'u made an impression with her performances in each test, so much so that she was one of three nominations for Black Ferns Player of the Year.

The Black Ferns had a heavy schedule of 12 tests in 2022 with Mikaele-Tu'u sharing the number eight position with Kaipo Olsen-Baker and later the experienced Charmaine McMenamin. However, for the World Cup later in the year Mikaele-Tu'u became the preferred player but injury in the semifinal, against France, prevented her from appearing in the final. Although she played only three FPC games she was voted the Farah Palmer Cup Player of the Year by the NZ Rugby Players' Association, the award being voted on by the players. She was also nominated for the Super Rugby Aupiki Player of the Year award at the NZR annual awards.

Liana Mikaele-Tu'u was born in Wellington on March 2, 2002, the family moving to Hastings in 2007 where Liana attended Hastings Central School and Hastings Intermediate before moving on to Hastings Girls' High School in 2015. Being keen on sport she represented New Zealand Under 14 at netball in 2015. Liana played her first rugby in 2017 when former Black Fern Emma Jensen arrived at the school and encouraged the girls to form a First XV. Two years later, her final year at high school, she was included in the Hawke's Bay Tui squad. In 2020 she moved north to study for a Bachelor of Health Science (Physiotherapy) degree at the Auckland University of Technology.

Liana grew up with two older brothers, twins Marino and Antonio, who were equally talented at rugby. Marino, a loose forward, appearing for Hawke's Bay since 2016, playing for the Highlanders and Moana Pasifika and has appeared for the All Blacks XV. In 2021 Liana and Marino became the first brother-sister combination to play Super Rugby. Antonio played for North Harbour (2020) and represented NZ Universities in 2018. Their father Tamiano played for Samoa 1990-93.

PROMISING PLAYER OF THE YEAR

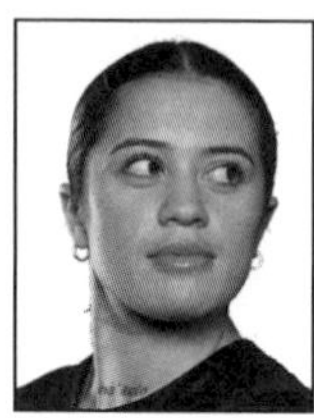

Katelyn Saloni Cherith Vahaakolo (*Auckland*) is among many dual internationals to stand out at both rugby and league, the fleet-footed wing performing with distinction during 2023 for the Blues, Auckland Storm and the Black Ferns. The 23-year-old impressed in her six tests for the Black Ferns, scoring two tries against Australia at Hamilton followed by a try in each of the three WXV tests against France, Wales and England. Such was her fine form in her first year of international rugby, World Rugby awarded her the Women's XV Breakthrough Player of the Year trophy for 2023 and she is destined to feature in the game for many years.

Born in Auckland on April 18, 2000 Katelyn Vahaakolo attended St Dominic's College, Rutherford College and Epsom Girls' Grammar and during 2020-21 studied at Te Wananga Takiura.

Katelyn played league with Te Atatu Roosters in 2020 before crossing the Tasman to play with Newcastle Knights in the NSW league. Back in Auckland in 2022, she appeared for the Pt Chevalier Pirates, often playing on Sundays after playing union for Marist club on Saturdays. Her first taste of rugby union was with Ardmore Marist club in 2021 and she moved to Auckland Marist in 2023.

An Auckland touch representative, she made her first-class rugby union debut for Auckland Storm in 2022, appearing in all eight Farah Palmer Cup games scoring six tries. In November, she joined the Kiwi Ferns league team for the Rugby League World Cup in Britain. Returning to union in 2023, she played in all five of the Blues games and was a regular on the wing for Auckland during a campaign which climaxed with the winning of the Farah Palmer Cup.

Older brother Freedom has played for Otago and the Highlanders in recent seasons.

SEASON IN REVIEW

In November NZR announced that 29,448 women and girls were active players during 2023, an increase of 20 per cent from 2022. There were 4,515 playing senior club rugby, 28 per cent more than 2022 and 40 per cent more than 2019. At junior club level there were 11,540 players, 14 per cent more than 2022 and 36 per cent more than in 2019. The figures show that playing numbers have significantly increased post-pandemic and following the Black Ferns World Cup success.

The season commenced during late February-March with the Sky Super Rugby Aupiki competition which was won by Matatu in a close final with Chiefs Manawa. The competition started and finished while the rugby public were still largely in summer-mode, but we expect the 2024 competition will attract greater public interest with the series being lengthened to two full rounds, home and away.

The Black Ferns took part in the Pacific Four Series mid-season, defeating Australia in Brisbane before heading to Canada to meet Canada and USA. The Black Ferns comfortably won all three games to win the tournament. In September, the Black Ferns met the Wallaroos again, at Hamilton, for the second O'Reilly Cup test. The Ferns totally dominated the first half but allowed their standards to slip during the second until finishing with two late tries. The O'Reilly Cup test was a buildup for the World Rugby WXV competition held at home in October-November.

The Black Ferns suffered a one-point loss to RWC semi-final opponents France, defeated Wales, then lost to England 33–12 at Eden Park, England gaining revenge for their RWC final loss to the Ferns the previous November. New Zealand finished fourth, behind England, Canada and Australia. The Ferns did not play Canada or Australia, two teams that caused upsets, both defeating France.

One of the oddities of the WXV tournament was that each of the six nations played only three games, not five as in a usual round-robin event. The same occurred in the Tier 2 event in South Africa (won by Scotland) and Tier 3 in Dubai (won by Ireland), each with six nations playing three games.

The Farah Palmer Cup Premiership division was won by Auckland and the Championship division by Northland, neither team having finished top of the points ladder after the round-robin. Auckland were third after Waikato and Canterbury but produced outstanding form in the semi-final and final. Manawatu, unbeaten in the round-robin, looked favourites for the Championship but were defeated by Northland in a hard-fought final. Members of the Black Ferns squad participating in the Pacific Four Series in Canada missed the first two weeks of the provincial competition.

The Black Ferns Sevens dominated the 2022/23 HSBC World Rugby Sevens Series by winning six of the seven tournaments. During the series the team played 42 games for 41 wins, the solitary loss being to Australia in the Cup final at the first event, at Dubai, in December 2022. The Black Ferns Sevens were certainly the most successful of our national teams in 2023.

Women's rugby continues to grow and as NZR offers more contracts to players, many are able to give up their regular employment to concentrate on rugby. During spells in the domestic programme some have taken advantage of crossing the Tasman to play rugby or league in Australia, while some go to Japan or USA to play fifteens or sevens. In the sporting world, women have not generally attracted the large spectator interest of men's sports and for many years to come women's rugby will be heavily reliant on the power of the All Blacks brand for income.

NEW ZEALAND BLACK FERNS

BLACK FERNS APPEARANCES, 2023

	Union	*Date of Birth*	*Debut*	*Tests at 1/1/24*
A.J. (Ariana) Bayler	Waikato	14-12-96	2021	8
A.J. (Alana) Bremner	Canterbury	10-02-97	2021	19
C.J. (Chelsea) Bremner	Canterbury	11-04-95	2020	18
G.E (Grace) Brooker	Canterbury	20-06-99	2019	4
S.L.L. (Sylvia) Brunt	Auckland	01-01-04	2022	13
L.H.J. (Luka) Connor	Bay of Plenty	24-09-96	2019	20
D.R. (Ruahei) Demant (co-capt)	Auckland	21-04-95	2018	33
A. (Amy) du Plessis	Canterbury	07-07-99	2020	14
E.E. (Esther) Faiaoga-Tilo	Waikato	26-09-94	2023	1
S.R. (Sophie) Fisher	Auckland	25-11-98	2023	2
G.L.F. (Grace) Gago	Counties Manukau	05-05-98	2023	1
K.K. (Kate) Henwood	Bay of Plenty	28-01-89	2023	4
I. (Iritana) Hohaia	Taranaki	01-03-00	2023	6
R.M.M. (Renee) Holmes	Waikato	21-12-99	2020	16
L.V.M. (Lucy) Jenkins	Canterbury	30-11-00	2023	6
J.M.E. (Tanya) Kalounivale	Waikato	20-01-99	2022	11
R.C. (Rosie) Kelly	Canterbury	16-01-00	2023	4
P.E.A. (Phillipa) Love	Canterbury	08-04-90	2014	27
P. (Patricia) Maliepo	Auckland	13-03-03	2021	7
A.A.H. (Arihiana) Marino-Tauhinu	Counties Manukau	29-03-92	2019	19
M.M.S. (Martha) Mataele	Canterbury	19-07-99	2023	2
L.E.T. (Liana) Mikaele-Tu'u	Auckland	02-03-02	2021	18
K.R. (Krystal) Murray	Northland	16-06-93	2021	14
J.M.P. (Joanah) Ngan-Woo	Wellington	15-12-95	2019	19
M.K. (Mererangi) Paul	Counties Manukau	29-10-98	2023	5
G.R.A. (Georgia) Ponsonby	Canterbury	14-12-99	2021	20
K.L. (Kendra) Reynolds	Bay of Plenty	25-01-93	2020	12
M.C.T. (Maia) Roos	Auckland	27-07-01	2021	21
A.M. (Amy) Rule	Canterbury	15-07-00	2021	19
L.Y.J. (Layla) Sae	Manawatu	22-10-00	2023	3
K.W. (Kennedy) Simon (co-capt)	Waikato	01-10-96	2019	20
C.B. (Charmaine) Smith	Northland	15-11-90	2015	29
G.L. (Grace) Steinmetz	Canterbury	16-01-98	2020	2
K.J. (Kelsey) Teneti	Waikato	12-05-03	2022	3
R.M. (Ruby) Tui	Counties Manukau	13-12-91	2022	13
K.S.C. (Katelyn) Vahaakolo	Auckland	18-04-00	2023	6
C.Z.F. (Chryss) Viliko	Auckland	25-12-00	2023	2
T.R. (Tenika) Willison	Waikato	07-12-97	2023	2

Director of rugby: Allan Bunting
Assistant coaches: Tony Christie, Mike Delany, Steve Jackson
Resource coach: Dan Cron
Manager: Jenelle Strickland
Physiotherapist: Kara Fowke
Assistant physiotherapist: Jen Ardagh
Doctor: Dr Alyse Cameron
Strength & conditioning coach: Craig Twentyman
Assistant strength & conditioning coach: Ashleigh Parrott, Tasmyn Jackson
Mental skills coach: Ian Saunders
Analyst: Ryan Runciman
Videographer: Rachael Whareaitu, Arizona Leger
Nutritionist: Loagan Posthumous
Team liaison: Jonathan Chappell
Media manager: Amanda Meade
Commercial manager: James King

	Tries	Con	PG	DG	Points
Holmes	1	20	2	–	51
Paul	7	–	–	–	35
Vahaakolo	5	–	–	–	25
Demant	3	4	–	–	23
du Plessis	4	–	–	–	20
Tui	4	–	–	–	20
Brunt	3	–	–	–	15
Jenkins	3	–	–	–	15
Mikaele-Tu'u	2	–	–	–	10
A. Bremner	1	–	–	–	5
C. Bremner	1	–	–	–	5
Connor	1	–	–	–	5
Gago	1	–	–	–	5
Hohaia	1	–	–	–	5
Kalounivale	1	–	–	–	5
Love	1	–	–	–	5
Maliepo	1	–	–	–	5
Marino-Tauhinu	1	–	–	–	5
Mataele	1	–	–	–	5
Murray	1	–	–	–	5
Simon	1	–	–	–	5
Teneti	1	–	–	–	5
Kelly	–	1	–	–	2
Willison	–	1	–	–	2
Totals	***45***	***26***	***2***	***0***	***283***
Opposition scored	*13*	*11*	*4*	*0*	*99*

BLACK FERNS, 2023	Australia	Canada	USA	Australia	France	Wales	England	**TOTALS**
Holmes	15*	15	s	–	15*	15	15*	**6**
Willison	s	–	15*	–	–	–	–	**2**
Maliepo	–	–	–	15*	s	s	s	**4**
Mataele	–	–	–	s	s	–	–	**2**
Paul	14	14	–	14	–	11	11*	**5**
Teneti	–	s	14	–	–	–	–	**2**
Tui	–	–	–	–	14	14*	14	**3**
Vahaakolo	11	11*	–	11	11	s	s	**6**
Steinmetz	–	–	11	–	–	–	–	**1**
du Plessis	13	13	13	13	13	13	13	**7**
Brunt	12*	12*	–	12*	12*	12*	12	**6**
Brooker	–	–	12*	–	–	–	–	**1**
Demant	10	10	s	10	10	10	10	**7**
Kelly	s	s	10	s	–	–	–	**4**
Marino-Tauhinu	9*	9*	s	9*	9*	9*	9	**7**
Hohaia	s	s	9*	s	–	s	s	**6**
Bayler	–	–	–	–	s	–	–	**1**
Mikaele-Tu'u	8	8*	8	8	8	8*	8	**7**
Simon	7*	7	s	7*	7	7	7*	**7**
Reynolds	s	s	7*	–	–	–	–	**3**
A. Bremner	6	6	–	6*	6*	s	6*	**6**
Jenkins	–	s	6	s	s	s	s	**6**
Sae	–	–	–	s	–	6*	s	**3**
C. Bremner	5*	5	s	–	s	5	5	**6**
Roos	4	4	5	4	4	4	4	**7**
Ngan-Woo	s	–	4*	–	–	–	–	**2**
Smith	–	–	–	5	5*	–	–	**2**
Kalounivale	3*	s	s	s	s	–	–	**5**
Rule	s	3*	3*	3*	3*	3*	3*	**7**
Fisher	–	–	–	–	–	s	s	**2**
Henwood	1*	s	–	–	–	1*	1*	**4**
Murray	s	–	–	1*	1*	s	s	**5**
Love	–	1*	s	–	–	–	–	**2**
Faiaoga-Tilo	–	–	1*	–	–	–	–	**1**
Viliko	–	–	–	s	s	–	–	**2**
Ponsonby	2*	s	s	2*	2*	2*	2*	**7**
Connor	s	2*	–	s	s	s	s	**6**
Gago	–	–	2*	–	–	–	–	**1**

BLACK FERNS IN 2023

Played 7 ***Won 5*** ***LOST 2*** ***Points for 283*** ***Points against 99***

Date	Opponent	Location	Score	Tries	Con	PG	DG	Referee
June 29	Australia (PFS)	Brisbane	50–0	Brunt (2), Paul (2), Kalounivale, C. Bremner, A. Bremner, Hohaia	Holmes (4), Willison			Amy Barrett-Theron (SA)
July 8	Canada (PFS)	Ottawa	52–21	Paul (2), du Plessis (2), Connor, Demant, Holmes, Teneti	Holmes (6)			Sara Cox (ENG)
July 14	USA (PFS)	Ottawa	39–17	Gago, Marino-Tauhinu, Love, Mikaele-Tu'u, Demant, du Plessis	Holmes (3)	Holmes		Julianne Zussman (CAN)
September 30	Australia	Hamilton	43–3	Vahaakolo (2), Murray, Maliepo, Brunt, Jenkins, Mataele	Demant (3), Kelly			Kat Roche (USA)
October 21	France (WXV)	Wellington	17–18	Mikaele-Tu'u, Vahaakolo	Holmes, Demant	Holmes		Hollie Davidson (SCO)
October 28	Wales (WXV)	Dunedin	70–7	Tui (4), Paul (3), Jenkins (2), du Plessis, Vahaakolo, Demant	Holmes (5)			Amber McLachlan (AUS)
November 4	England (WXV)	Auckland	12–33	Simon, Vahaakolo	Holmes			Amy Barrett-Theron (SA)

PACIFIC FOUR SERIES

The World Rugby Pacific Four Series commenced in April with Canada meeting USA in Spain, the second fixture being Australia v New Zealand at Brisbane. In July the four nations assembled in Ottawa, Canada, where each team played a further two games. New Zealand, being unbeaten, were the tournament winners.

Results:

April 1	Canada 50 USA 17, at Madrid
June 29	New Zealand 50 Australia 0, at Brisbane
July 8	Australia 58 USA 17; New Zealand 52 Canada 21
July 14	Canada 45 Australia 7; New Zealand 39 USA 17

Final standings

Team	*P*	*W*	*D*	*L*	*PF*	*PA*	*BP*	*Points*
New Zealand	3	3	–	–	141	38	3	15
Canada	3	2	–	1	116	76	2	10
Australia	3	1	–	2	65	112	1	5
USA	3	–	–	3	51	147	0	0

WORLD RUGBY WXV COMPETITION

World Rugby introduced an 18-team international event, WXV, involving 18 nations divided into three divisions. The Tier 1 nations tournament was held in New Zealand, Tier 2 in South Africa and Tier 3 in Dubai. England, unbeaten in 10 internationals since losing to New Zealand in the World Cup final, were too strong for all opponents and were deserving winners.

W.XV Tier 1 Results:

October 20	England 42 Australia 7, at Wellington
October 21	Canada 42 Wales 22; France 18 New Zealand 17, at Wellington
October 27	England 45 Canada 12, at Dunedin
October 28	New Zealand 70 Wales 7; Australia 29 France 20, at Dunedin
November 3	Australia 25 Wales 19, at Auckland
November 4	Canada 29 France 22; England 33 New Zealand 12, at Auckland

Final standings

Team	*P*	*W*	*D*	*L*	*PF*	*PA*	*BP*	*Points*
England	3	3	–	–	120	31	3	15
Canada	3	2	–	1	83	87	2	10
Australia	3	2	–	1	61	81	2	10
New Zealand	3	1	–	2	99	58	2	6
France	3	1	–	2	58	75	0	4
Wales	3	–	–	3	48	137	1	1

NEW ZEALAND v AUSTRALIA

Pacific Four Series/O'Reilly Cup

Test # 116 | Kayo Stadium, Brisbane | June 29, 2023

New Zealand won 50–0

NEW ZEALAND		AUSTRALIA
Renee Holmes	15	Faitala Moleka
Mererangi Paul	14	Maya Stewart
Amy du Plessis	13	Georgina Friedrichs
Sylvia Blunt	12	Cecilia Smith
Katelyn Vahaakolo	11	Ivania Wong
Ruahei Demant (co-capt)	10	Carys Dallinger
Arihiana Marino-Tauhinu	9	Layne Morgan
Liana Mikaele-Tu'u	8	Grace Hamilton
Kennedy Simon (co-capt)	7	Ashley Marsters
Alana Bremner	6	Kaitlan Leaney
Chelsea Bremner	5	Annabelle Codey
Maiakawanakaulani Roos	4	Michaela Leonard (capt)
Tanya Kalounivale	3	Eva Karpani
Georgia Ponsonby	2	Tania Naden
Kate Henwood	1	Bree-Anna Cheatham
Luka Connor (rep 2, 45m)	16	Madison Schuck (rep 2, 67m)
Krystal Murray (rep 1, 45m)	17	Emily Robinson (rep 1, 51m)
Amy Rule (rep 3, 45m)	18	Bridie O'Gorman (rep 3, 55m)
Joanah Ngan-Woo (rep 5, 55m)	19	Sera Naiqama (rep 5, 51m)
Kendra Reynolds (rep 7, 58m)	20	Emily Chancellor (rep 6, 51m)
Iritana Hohaia (rep 9, 51m)	21	Jasmin Huriwai (rep 9, 67m)
Rosie Kelly (rep 12, 51m)	22	Arabella McKenzie (rep 10, 48m)
Tenika Willison (rep 15, 56m)	23	Alana Elisaia (rep 14, 60m)
Brunt (2), Paul (2), Kalounivale, C. Bremner, A. Bremner, Hohaia	Tries	
Holmes (4), Willison	Cons	

Kickoff: 7.00pm ***Attendance:*** 7,055 ***Conditions:*** Fine, ground firm

Referee: Amy Barrett-Theron (South Africa)
Assistant referees: Amber McLachlan (Australia), Natarsha Ganley (New Zealand)
TMO: Cholm Johnson (Australia)

Scoring:
First half: 11m Kalounivale try, Holmes conversion 7–0, 23m Brunt try, Holmes conversion 14–0, 33m Brunt try, Holmes conversion 21–0, 36m Paul try 26–0
Second half: 41m Paul try 31–0, 54m C. Bremner try, Holmes conversion 38–0, 74m A. Bremner try, Willison conversion 45–0, 80m Hohaia try 50–0.

Black Ferns Test debuts: Henwood (No 245), Paul (246), Vahaakolo (247), Hohaia (248), Kelly (249), and Willison (250).

NEW ZEALAND v CANADA

Pacific Four Series

Test # 117 | **TD Place Stadium, Ottawa, Canada** | **July 8, 2023**

New Zealand won 52–21

NEW ZEALAND		***CANADA***
Renee Holmes	15	Sabina Poulin
Mererangi Paul	14	Florence Symonds
Amy du Plessis	13	Fancy Bermudez
Sylvia Blunt	12	Sara Kaljuvee
Katelyn Vahaakolo	11	Paige Farries
Ruahei Demant (co-capt)	10	Julia Schell
Arihiana Marino-Tauhinu	9	Justine Pelletier
Liana Mikaele-Tu'u	8	Sophie de Goede (capt)
Kennedy Simon (co-capt)	7	Fabiola Forteza
Alana Bremner	6	Gabrielle Senft
Chelsea Bremner	5	Courtney Holtkamp
Maiakawanakaulani Roos	4	Tyson Beukeboom
Amy Rule	3	DaLeaka Menin
Luka Connor	2	Emily Tuttosi
Phillipa Love	1	Olivia De Merchant
Georgia Ponsonby (rep 2, 37m)	16	Gillian Boag (rep 2, 70m)
Kate Henwood (rep 1, 45m)	17	McKinley Hunt (rep 1, 65m)
Tanya Kalounivale (rep 3, 45m)	18	Alexandria Ellis (rep 3, 59m)
Lucy Jenkins (rep 6, 50m)	19	Emma Taylor (rep 4, 66m)
Kendra Reynolds (rep 8, 65m)	20	Sara Svoboda (rep 6, 49m)
Iritana Hohaia (rep 9, 55m)	21	Olivia Apps (rep 9, 70m)
Rosie Kelly (rep 12, 70m)	22	Claire Gallagher (rep 10, 51m)
Kelsey Teneti (rep 11, 50m)	23	Shoshanah Seumanutafa (rep 12, 63m)
Paul (2), du Plessis (2), Connor, Demant, Holmes, Teneti	Tries	de Goede, Forteza, De Merchant
Holmes (6)	Cons	de Goede (3)

Kickoff: 7.00pm ***Attendance:*** 10,092 ***Conditions:*** Fine, ground firm

Referee: Sara Cox (England)
Assistant referees: Amelia Luciano (USA), Jenny Lui (USA)
TMO: Andrew McMenemy (Scotland)

Scoring:
First half: 1m Connor try, Holmes conversion 7–0, 14m Demant try, Holmes conversion 14–0, 18m Paul try, Holmes conversion 21–0, 33m de Goede try and conversion 21–7, 37m Fortez try, de Goede conversion 21–14.
Second half: 44m du Plessis try, Holmes conversion 28–14, 52m DeMerchant try, de Goede conversion 28–21, 56m Paul try 33–21, 61m Holmes try and conversion 40–21, 73m du Plessis try, Holmes conversion 47–21, 78m Teneti try 52–21.

Black Ferns Test debuts: Jenkins (No 251)

Yellow cards: de Goede 76m

NEW ZEALAND v USA

Pacific Four Series

Test # 118 — **TD Place Stadium, Ottawa, Canada** — **July 14, 2023**

New Zealand won 39–17

NEW ZEALAND		*USA*
Tenika Willison	15	Tess Feury
Kelsey Teneti	14	Jennine Detiveaux
Amy du Plessis	13	Kate Zachary (capt)
Grace Brooker	12	Eti Haungatau
Grace Steinmetz	11	Summer Harris-Jones
Rosie Kelly	10	McKenzie Hawkins
Iritana Hohaia	9	Taina Tukuafu
Liana Mikaele-Tu'u	8	Rachel Johnson
Kendra Reynolds	7	Georgie Perris-Redding
Lucy Jenkins	6	Freda Tafuna
Maia Roos (capt)	5	Hallie Taufo'ou
Joanah Ngan-Woo	4	Rachel Ehrecke
Amy Rule	3	Charli Jacoby
Grace Gago	2	Kathryn Treder
Esther Faiaoga-Tilo	1	Catherine Benson
Georgia Ponsonby (rep 2, 40m)	16	Tahlia Brody (rep 7, 74m)
Phillipa Love (rep 1, 44m)	17	Monalisa Tupou (temp 47-59m, rep 1, 74m)
Tanya Kalounivale (rep 3, 44m)	18	Tiara A'au (rep 3, 62m)
Chelsea Bremner (rep 4, 40m)	19	Evi Ashenbrucker (rep 6, 56m)
Kennedy Simon (rep 7, 48m)	20	Erica Jarrell (rep 4, 69m)
Arihiana Marino-Tauhinu (rep 11, 40m)	21	Olivia Ortiz (rep 9, 62m)
Ruahei Demant (rep 12, 30m)	22	Joanne Fa'avesi (rep 12, 51m)
Renee Holmes (rep 15, 40m)	23	Meya Bizer (rep 11, 73m)
Gago, Marino-Tauhinu, Love, Mikaele-Tu'u, Demant, du Plessis	Tries	Tafuna, Johnson
Holmes (3)	Cons	Hawkins (2)
Holmes	PG	Hawkins

Kickoff: 7.00pm ***Attendance:*** 1000 ***Conditions:*** Fine, ground firm

Referee: Julianne Zussman (Canada)
Assistant referees: Shanda Assmus (Canada), Kristine Lovatt (Canada)
TMO: Chris Assmus (Canada)

Scoring:
First half: Tafuna try, Hawkins conversion 7–0, 8m Gago try 7–5, 23m Johnson try, Hawkins conversion 14–5, 38m Hawkins penalty 17–5
Second half: 46m Marino-Tauhinu try, Holmes conversion 17–12, 49m Holmes penalty 17–15, 58m Love try, Holmes conversion 17–22, 67m Mikaele-Tu'u try, Holmes conversion 17–29, 72m Demant try 17–34, 79m du Plessis try 17–39.

Black Ferns Test debuts: Faiaoga-Tilo (No 252), Gago (253)

Yellow cards: Perris-Redding 7m, Mikaele-Tu'u 38m
Red cards: Hohaia 2m

NEW ZEALAND v AUSTRALIA

O'Reilly Cup

Test # 119 | FMG Stadium Waikato, Hamilton | September 30, 2023

New Zealand won 43–3

NEW ZEALAND		AUSTRALIA
Patricia Maliepo	15	Lori Cramer
Mererangi Paul	14	Maya Stewart
Amy du Plessis	13	Georgina Friedrichs
Sylvia Brunt	12	Trilleen Pomare
Katelyn Vahaakolo	11	Ivania Wong
Ruahei Demant (co-capt)	10	Carys Dallinger
Arihiana Marino-Tauhinu	9	Layne Morgan
Liana Mikaele-Tu'u (rep 19, 63m)	8	Ashley Marsters
Kennedy Simon (co-capt)	7	Emily Chancellor
Alana Bremner	6	Kaitlin Leaney
Charmaine Smith	5	Michaela Leonard (capt)
Maia Roos	4	Sera Naiqama
Amy Rule	3	Eva Karpani (rep 7, 73m)
Georgia Ponsonby	2	Adiana Talakai
Krystal Murray	1	Bree-Anna Cheatham
Luka Connor (rep 2, 60m)	16	Tania Naden (rep 2, 57m)
Chryss Viliko (rep 1, 48m)	17	Emily Robinson (rep 1, 57m)
Tanya Kalounivale (rep 3, 48m)	18	Bridie O'Gorman (rep 3, 57m)
Lucy Jenkins (temp 8, 51m, rep 7, 62m)	19	Leilani Nathan (rep 4, 60m)
Layla Sae (rep 6, 60m)	20	Tabua Tuinakauvadra (rep 8, 65m)
Iritana Hohaia (rep 9, 60m)	21	Jasmin Huriwai (rep 9, 65m)
Rosie Kelly (rep 12, 63m)	22	Cecilia Smith (rep 12, 60m)
Martha Mataele (rep 15, 57m)	23	Faitala Moleka (rep 15, 26m)
Vahaakolo (2), Murray, Maliepo, Brunt, Jenkins, Mataele	Tries	
Demant (3), Kelly	Cons	
	PG	Dallinger

Kickoff: 4.35pm ***Attendance:*** 10,700 ***Conditions:*** fine, ground firm

Referee: Kat Roche (USA)
Assistant referees: Natarsha Ganley (New Zealand), Jessica Ling (Australia)
TMO: Aaron Patterson (New Zealand)

Scoring:
First half: 11m Murray try, Demant conversion 7–0, 19m Maliepo try, Demant conversion 14–0, 29m Vahaakolo try 19–0, 33m Vahaakolo try 24–0, 39m Brunt try, Demant conversion 31–0
Second half: 42m Dallinger penalty 31–3, 76m Jenkins try, Demant conversion 38–3, 81m Mataele try 43–3.

Black Ferns Test debuts: Viliko (No 254), Mataele (255), Sae (256)

Red cards: O'Gorman 68m

NEW ZEALAND v FRANCE

WXV

Test # 120 | **Sky Stadium, Wellington** | **October 21, 2023**

France won 18–17

NEW ZEALAND		*FRANCE*
Renee Holmes	15	Morgana Bourgeois
Ruby Tui	14	Cyrielle Banet
Amy du Plessis	13	Marine Menager
Sylvia Brunt	12	Gabrielle Vernier
Katelyn Vahaakolo	11	Emilie Boulard
Ruahei Demant (co-capt)	10	Lina Queyroi
Arihiana Marino-Tauhinu	9	Alexandra Chambon
Liana Mikaele-Tu'u	8	Charlotte Escudero
Kennedy Simon (co-capt)	7	Gaelle Hermet
Alana Bremner	6	Axelle Berthoumieu
Charmaine Smith	5	Madoussou Fall
Maia Roos	4	Manae Feleu (capt)
Amy Rule	3	Clara Joyeux
Georgina Ponsonby	2	Elisa Riffonneau
Krystal Murray	1	Ambre Mwayembe
Luka Connor (rep 2, 59m)	16	Laure Touye (rep 2, 66m)
Chryss Viliko (rep 1, 45m)	17	Coco Lindelauf (rep 1, 41m)
Tanya Kalounivale (rep 3, 62m)	18	Assia Khalfaoui (rep 3, 62m)
Chelsea Bremner (rep 5, 45m)	19	Audrey Forlani (temp 5, 55m, rep 4, 66m)
Lucy Jenkins (rep 6, 59m)	20	Lea Champon (rep 20, 62m)
Ariana Bayler (rep 9, 55m)	21	Emeline Gros (rep 14, 62m)
Patricia Maliepo (temp 13, 40m)	22	Pauline Bourdon Sansus (rep 9, 59m)
Martha Mataele (temp 11, 40m, rep 15, 64m)	23	Nassira Konde (rep 13, 52m)
Mikaele-Tu'u, Vaha'akolo	Tries	Boulard, Banet
Holmes, Demant	Cons	Bourgeois
Holmes	PG	Bourgeois (2)

Kickoff: 7.00pm ***Attendance:*** 6,977 ***Conditions:*** fine, ground firm

Referee: Hollie Davidson (Scotland)
Assistant referees: Amy Barrett-Theron (South Africa), Amber McLachlan (Australia)
TMO: Ian Tempest (England)

Scoring:
First half: 5m Boulard try, Bourgeois conversion 7–0, 10m Mikaele-Tu'u try, Holmes conversion 7–7, 16m Banet try 12–7, 34m Bourgeois penalty 15–7.
Second half: 43m Bourgeois penalty 18–7, 53m Holmes penalty 18–10, 70m Vahaakolo try, Demant conversion 18–17.

Red cards: Viliko 62m.

* Black Ferns wore white shirts

NEW ZEALAND v WALES

WXV

Test # 121 | Forsyth Barr Stadium, Dunedin | October 28, 2023

New Zealand won 70–7

NEW ZEALAND		***WALES***
Renee Holmes	15	Mel Metcalfe
Ruby Tui	14	Jasmine Joyce (retired 78m, not replaced)
Amy du Plessis	13	Hannah Jones (capt)
Sylvia Brunt	12	Hannah Bluck
Mererangi Paul	11	Carys Williams-Morris
Ruahei Demant (co-capt)	10	Lleucu George
Arihiana Marino-Tauhinu	9	Keira Bevan
Liana Mikaele-Tu'u	8	Sioned Harries
Kennedy Simon (co-capt)	7	Alex Callender
Layla Sae	6	Alisha Butchers
Chelsea Bremner	5	Kate Williams
Maia Roos	4	Abbie Fleming
Amy Rule	3	Donna Rose
Georgina Ponsonby	2	Kelsey Jones
Kate Henwood	1	Gwenllian Pyrs
Luka Connor (rep 2, 48m)	16	Kat Evans (rep 2, 62m)
Krystal Murray (rep 1, 43m)	17	Abbey Constable (rep 1, 62m)
Sophie Fisher (rep 3, 57m)	18	Sisilia Tuipulotu (rep 3, 40m)
Alana Bremner (rep 6, 62m)	19	Bryonie King (rep 19, 47m)
Lucy Jenkins (rep 8, 62m)	20	Bethan Lewis (rep 7, 70m)
Iritana Hohaia (rep 9, 48m)	21	Megan Davies (rep 9, 47m)
Patricia Maliepo (rep 12, 66m)	22	Robyn Wilkins (rep 10, 54m)
Katelyn Vahaakolo (rep 14, 59m)	23	Megan Webb (rep 11, 54m)
Tui (4), Paul (3), Jenkins (2), du Plessis, Vahaakolo, Demant	Tries	Fleming
Holmes (5)	Cons	Wilkins

Kickoff: 4.00pm ***Attendance:*** 6,470 ***Conditions:*** fine, ground firm

Referee: Amber McLachlan (Australia)
Assistant referees: Hollie Davidson (Scotland), Sara Cox (England)
TMO: Rachel Horton (Australia)

Scoring:
First half: 12m Paul try 5–0, 14m Tui try, Holmes conversion 12–0, 19m Tui try 17–0, 24m Tui try 22–0, 27m Tui try 27–0.
Second half: 46m du Plessis try, Holmes conversion 34–0, 52m Paul try, Holmes conversion 41–0, 56m Fleming try, Wilkins conversion 41–7, 61m Vahaakolo try 46–7, 69m Demant try, Holmes conversion 53–7, 72m Jenkins try 58–7, 76m Jenkins try, Holmes conversion 65–7, 79m Paul try 70–7.

Black Ferns Test debuts: Fisher (No 257)

Yellow cards: Metcalfe 15m.

NEW ZEALAND v ENGLAND

WXV

Test # 122 | Mount Smart Stadium, Auckland | November 4, 2023

England won 33–12

NEW ZEALAND		ENGLAND
Renee Holmes	15	Ellie Kildunne
Ruby Tui	14	Abby Dow
Amy du Plessis	13	Helena Rowland
Sylvia Brunt	12	Tatyana Heard
Mererangi Paul	11	Claudia MacDonald
Ruahei Demant (co-capt)	10	Holly Aitchison
Arihiana Marino-Tauhinu	9	Natasha Hunt
Liana Mikaele-Tu'u	8	Alex Matthews
Kennedy Simon (co-capt)	7	Marlie Packer (capt)
Alana Bremner	6	Morwenna Talling
Chelsea Bremner	5	Rosie Galligan
Maia Roos	4	Zoe Aldcroft
Amy Rule	3	Sarah Bern
Georgina Ponsonby	2	Lark Atkin-Davies
Kate Henwood	1	Mackenzie Carson
Luka Connor (rep 2, 45m)	16	Connie Powell (rep 2, 72m)
Krystal Murray (rep 1, 45m)	17	Hannah Botterman (rep 1, 46m)
Sophie Fisher (rep 3, 71m)	18	Maud Muir (rep 3, 71m)
Layla Sae (rep 6, 45m)	19	Sarah Beckett (rep 5, 72m)
Lucy Jenkins (rep 7, 65m)	20	Maisy Allen (temp 6, 18m, rep 6, 71m)
Iritana Hohaia (rep 9, 48m)	21	Ella Wyrwas (rep 9, 61m)
Patricia Maliepo (temp 15, 53m, rep 13, 71m)	22	Megan Jones (temp 12, 51m, rep 13, 67m)
Katelyn Vahaakolo (rep 11, 40m)	23	Jess Breach (rep 11, 71m)
Simon, Vahaakolo	Tries	Matthews, Atkin-Davies, Bern, Talling, Aldcroft
Holmes	Cons	Aitchison (4)

Kickoff: 7.00pm ***Attendance:*** 7,065 ***Conditions:*** fine, ground firm

Referee: Aimee Barrett-Theron (South Africa)
Assistant referees: Hollie Davidson (Scotland), Amber McLachlan (Australia)
TMO: Andrew McMenemy (Scotland)

Scoring:
First half: 4m Matthews try, Aitchison conversion 7-0,12m Atkin–Davies try, Aitchison conversion 14–0, 22m Bern try 19–0, 38m Simon try, Holmes conversion 19–7
Second half: 48m Vahaakolo try 19–12, 54m Talling try, Aitchison conversion 26–12, 68m Aldcroft try, Aitchison conversion 33–12.

NEW ZEALAND REPRESENTATIVES 2023

Of the 38 players used during the seven tests of 2023 13 were making their debuts.

The first-class record of the 13 new Black Ferns are:

Kate Kahurangi Henwood *born Opotiki, January 28, 1989*
Black Ferns # 245
Bay of Plenty 2015(6)-16(6)-17-18(7)-22(6)-23(2); Chiefs Manawa 2023(5); New Zealand 2023(4).

Mererangi Karen Paul *born Whakatane, October 29, 1998*
Black Ferns # 246
Bay of Plenty 2020(5)-21(5); Counties Manukau 2022(6)-23(4); Chiefs Manawa 2023(5); New Zealand 2023(5).

Katelyn Saloni Cherith Vahaakolo *born Auckland, April 18, 2000*
Black Ferns # 247
Auckland 2022(8)-23(7); Blues 2023(5); New Zealand 2023(6).

Iritana Hohaia *born New Plymouth, March 1, 2000*
Black Ferns # 248
Taranaki 2019(6)-20(3)-21-23(3); Chiefs 2021; Hurricanes Poua 2022(2)-23(4); New Zealand Barbarians 2022(2); New Zealand 2023(6).

Rosie Clare Kelly *born Greymouth, January 16, 2000*
Black Ferns # 249
Canterbury 2017(4)-21(8)-22(8)-23(5); Otago 2018(8)-19(7)-20(5); Matatu 2022(3)-23(5); New Zealand Development 2019(2); New Zealand Barbarians 2020(2); New Zealand 2023(4).

Tenika Rangikopeka Willison *born Hamilton, December 7, 1997*
Black Ferns # 250
Waikato 2015(5)-16(5)-20(8)-21(2); Chiefs Manawa 2023(5); New Zealand 2023(2).

Lucy Victoria Margaret Jenkins *born Christchurch, November 30, 2000*
Black Ferns # 251
Canterbury 2017(8)-18(8)-19(8)-20(6)-21(7)-22(8)-23(6); Matatu 2022(3)-23(5); New Zealand 2023(6).

Esther Eseta Faiaoga-Tilo *born Hamilton, September 26, 1994*
Black Ferns # 252
Waikato 2018(5)-19(4)-20(7)-21(6)-22(7)-23(5); Hurricanes Poua 2022(2); Blues 2023(2); Black Ferns XV 2023; New Zealand 2023.

Grace Leaso Florence Gago *born Auckland, May 5, 1998*
Black Ferns # 253
Counties Manukau 2017(6)-18(6)-19(7)-20(6)-21-22(6)-23(6); Blues 2023(5); New Zealand 2023.

Chryss Zhonn Fakahoa Viliko *born Otahuhu, December 25,2000*
Black Ferns # 254
Auckland 2019(8)-20(6)-22(8)-23(8); Blues 2022-23(5); New Zealand 2023(2).

Mayalin Martha Siulolovao Mataele *born Auckland, July 19, 1999*
Black Ferns # 255
Canterbury 2019(4)-20(7)-21(3)-22(8)-23(7); Matatu 2022(3)-23(4); New Zealand Development 2019(3); New Zealand Barbarians 2020; New Zealand 2023(2).

Layla Yvonne Jacoba Sae *born Palmerston North, October 22, 2000*
Black Ferns # 256
Manawatu 2019(4)-20(5)-21(5)-22(6)-23(7); Hurricanes Poua 2022(2)-23(5); New Zealand 2023(3).

Sophie Rose Fisher *born North Shore, November 25, 1998*
Black Ferns # 257
North Harbour 2017(7)-18(7)-19(4)-20(4); Auckland 2021(4)-22(8)-23(8); Blues 2023(5); New Zealand 2023(2).

NEW ZEALAND WOMEN'S REPRESENTATIVES, 1989–2023

Name	*B&D*	*Representative Team*	*Games*	*Tests*
Aiatu, Muteremoana S.	1981–	(Wellington) 2011	1	1
Anderson, Lucy E.	1991–	(Canterbury) 2022	1	1
Andrew, Shannon R.	1972–	(Auckland) 1996	2	2
Aniseko, Fa'anati	1989–	(Auckland) 2007	2	2
Apiata, Jacquileen W.	1966–	(Canterbury) 1989–90–91–92–93–94–95	15	5
Atkins, Leanne T.	1976–	(Northland) 1994	1	–
Baker, Lise U.	1967–	(Wellington) 1990	3	–
Baker, Miriama	1962–	(Auckland) 1989–91	2	–
Baker, Shakira J.	1992–	(Wellington) 2011; (Manawatu) 2012–14	13	13
Ballinger, Shona H.	1970–	(Wellington) 1990–91	3	–
Barclay, F.J. see King, F.J.				
Bayler, Ariana J.	1996–	(Waikato) 2021–22–23	8	8
Berry, Zoey P.	1987–	(Canterbury) 2012	1	1
Blackledge, V.E. see Grant, V.E.				
Blackwell, Eloise S.	1990–	(Auckland) 2011–12–13–14–15–16–17–18–19–20–21	48	46
Blyde, Cherrie D.	1966–	(Taranaki) 1992	1	–
Borthwick, Nicole M.	1980–	(Auckland) 2005	2	2
Bosman (nee Ngatai), Melodie M.	1976–	(Auckland) 2004; (Waikato) 2005; (Hawke's Bay) 2006–11; (Canterbury) 2010–13	17	17
Brazier, Kelly A.	1989–	(Otago) 2009–10–12–13–14–16; (Canterbury) 2011; (Bay of Plenty) 2017–19–21	43	42
Bremner, Alana J.	1997–	(Canterbury) 2021–22–23	19	19
Bremner, Chelsea J.	1995–	(Canterbury) 2020–22–23	20	18
Brett, Lesley P.	1968–	(Canterbury) 1990–91	8	3
Brooker, Grace E.	1999–	(Canterbury) 2019–20–21–23	5	4
Broughton, Florence	1962–	(Wellington) 1990	1	–
Brunt, Sylvia L.L.	2004–	(Auckland) 2022–23	13	13
Burkin, Forne K.	1998–	(Canterbury) 2019	2	2
Canterbury, Marina R.	1984–	(Hawke's Bay) 2005	5	5
Chase, Debbie P.M.	1966–	(Canterbury) 1990–91–93	9	3
Chittock, Barbara J.	1985–	(Canterbury) 2009	1	–
Coady, Olivia R.	1990–	(Canterbury) 2008–09	5	4
Cobley, Rhonda J.	1971–	(Canterbury) 1992–94	2	–
Cocksedge, Kendra M.	1988–	(Canterbury) 2007–08–09–10–11–12–13–14–15–16–17–18–19–20–21–22	71	68
Codling, Monalisa M.	1977–	(Otago) 1998; (Auckland) 1999–02–03–04–05–06–07–08–10	30	30
Connor, Luka H.J.	1996–	(Bay of Plenty) 2019–20–22–23	22	20
Cootes, Vanessa	1969–	(Waikato) 1995–96–97–98–00–01–02	16	16
Cottrell, Krysten J.	1992–	(Hawke's Bay) 2018–19	8	8

Name	B&D	Representative Team	Games	Tests
Crossman, Lydia J.	1986–	(Hawke's Bay) 2011; (Auckland) 2012	5	5
Cunningham, Vicky G.	1961–	(Auckland) 1997	1	1
Davie, Mary	1961–	(Canterbury) 1992–93	2	2
Dawson, Susan M.	1971–	(Northland) 1999–00–02	4	4
de Jong, Catherine L.	1984–	(Otago) 2005	1	1
Delamere, Natalie M.	1996–	(Bay of Plenty) 2022	3	3
Demant, D. Ruahei	1995–	(Auckland) 2018–19–20–21–22–23	35	33
Demant, Kiritapu W.	1996–	(Auckland) 2015	2	2
du Plessis, Amy	1999–	(Otago) 2020 (Canterbury) 2022–23	16	14
Edwards, B.N. Tangaloa		(Auckland) 1989	1	–
Edwards (nee Shelford), Exia T.	1975–	(Bay of Plenty) 1998–99–00–01–02–03–04–05–06	27	27
Edwards, Maree D.	1975–	(Otago) 1998–00; (Canterbury) 2003	4	4
Elder (nee Ketu), Lesley T.	1987–	(Waikato) 2015–17; (Bay of Plenty) 2018–19–21	22	22
Ellis, Judith M.	1966–	(Canterbury) 1993–94–95	3	1
Engebretsen, Lauren J.	1983–	(Waikato) 2004	3	3
Epiha, Eva A.	1974–	(Auckland) 1994	1	–
Everitt, Rawinia P.	1986–	(Auckland) 2011–12; (Counties Manukau) 2013–14–16–17	21	21
Ewe, Donna	1964–	(Auckland) 1990–91	8	3
Fa'amausili, Fiao'o	1980–	(Auckland) 2002–03–05–06–07–08–09–10–11–12–13–14–15–16–17–18	57	57
Fa'aope, Lili	1964–	(Canterbury) 1989–90	3	–
Faiaoga-Tilo, Esther E.	1994–	(Waikato) 2023	1	1
Faleafaga, Dhys S.	2000–	(Wellington) 2021	2	2
Faneva, Karli J.K.	1998–	(Bay of Plenty) 2019	2	2
Farr, Amy M.	1982–	(Wellington) 2007	1	1
Fereti, J.S. see Patea-Fereti, J.S.				
Fisher, Sophie R.	1998–	(Auckland) 2023	2	2
Fitzgibbon, Maree	1966–	(Canterbury) 1989–90–91	9	3
Fitzpatrick, Theresa M.	1995–	(Auckland) 2017–18–19–22	18	18
Fluhler (nee Waaka), Stacey J.A.K.	1995–	(Waikato) 2015–17–18–21–22	25	25
Ford, Amanda J.	1970–	(Canterbury) 1989–90–91	6	1
Ford, Deborah	1965–	(Canterbury) 1989–90–91	4	–
Frost, Seuga M.	1966–	(Canterbury) 1990–91	3	–
Gago, Grace L.F.	1998–	(Counties Manukau) 2023	1	1
Garden, Susan C.	1961–2008	(Canterbury) 1989–90–91; (Otago) 1992	7	
Gavet, Sandra A.	1961–	(Auckland) 1990–92	4	–
Grant (nee Blackledge), Victoria E.	1982–	(Auckland) 2006–07–08–09–10–11; (Waikato) 2013	18	17
Gray, Isabella I.	1974–	(Wellington) 1999–02–05	5	5
Gubb (nee Halapua), Charlene P.T.	1988–	(Auckland) 2015–16–17	9	9

Name	B&D	Representative Team	Games	Tests
Halapua, C.P.T. see Gubb, C.P.T.				
Harrison, Sarah A.		(Wellington) 1999	2	2
Hayes, Carol E.	1970–	(Southland) 1989–91–92–93	5	–
Heenan, Janet M.	1969–	(Northland) 1996–98	5	5
Heighway, Victoria L	1980–	(Auckland) 2000–01–02–03–04–05–06–07–08–09–10	32	32
Henwood, Kate K.	1989–	(Bay of Plenty) 2023	4	4
Hiemer, Riki G.		(Wellington) 1997	2	2
Hina, Trisha R.	1977–	(Auckland) 2010	4	4
Hireme, A. Honey	1981–	(Waikato) 2014–15–16–17	18	18
Hirini (nee Goss), Sarah L.	1992–	(Manawatu) 2016 –17–22	17	17
Hirovanaa, Monique J.	1966–	(Auckland) 1994–95–96–97–98–99–00–01–02	26	24
Hohaia, Iritana	2000–	(Taranaki) 2023	6	6
Hohepa, Carla G.T.O.	1985–	(Otago) 2007–08–09–10; (Waikato) 2016–17–19–21	29	28
Holmes, Renee M.M.	1999–	(Waikato) 2020–21–22–23	17	16
Hopkins, Anna M.	1970–2014	(Wellington) 1991	1	–
Houpapa-Barrett, Grace P.	1995–	(Waikato) 2021	3	3
Hull, R.M. see Mahoney, R.M.				
Huxford, Sarah A.	1972–	(Wellington) 1993	1	–
Inwood, Nicola A.	1970–	(Canterbury) 1989–90–91	9	3
Itunu, Aldora T.	1991–	(Auckland) 2015–16–17–18–20–21	26	24
Itunu, Linda F.	1984–	(Auckland) 2003–04–06–07–08–09–10–14–15–17–18	40	39
Jenkins, Lucy V.M.	2000–	(Canterbury) 2023	6	6
Jensen, Emma M.	1977–	(Waikato) 2002–03–04; (Auckland) 2005–06–07–08–09–10–11–12–13–14–15	50	49
John, Chris K.A.	1960–	(Canterbury) 1990	2	–
Johnson, Fiona C.	1970–	(Wellington) 1990	1	–
Kahura, Dianne M.T.	1969–	(Auckland) 1998–99–00–02	12	12
Kalounivale, Tanya M.E.	1999–	(Waikato) 2022–23	11	11
Kay, Rhonda L.	1976–	(Waikato) 2000	1	1
Kelly, Rosie C.	2000–	(Canterbury) 2023	4	4
Ketu, L.T. see Elder, L.T.				
King (nee Barclay), Fiona J.	1972–	(Otago) 1996–97–98–99–00–01–02	18	18
Kingi, Mere A.	1974–	(Auckland) 2003–04	5	5
Kiwi, Kellie H.	1972–	(Bay of Plenty) 1996–97–98	8	8
Knight, Neroli J.	1974–	(Wellington) 1990–91–99–00–01	6	4
Konui, Toni R.H.	1966–	(Auckland) 1998	3	3
Kupa, Mel N.	1974–	(Hawke's Bay) 1997	2	2
Lafaele, Tafito P.	2001–	(Auckland) 2022	3	3
Lavea, Justine	1984–	(Auckland) 2004–05–07–09–10–11–12–13–14; (Counties Manukau) 2015	35	34
Lavea, Vaniya N.H.	1981–	(Auckland) 2003–04–07	5	5
Leiataua, Onjeurlina F.	1995–	(Auckland) 2013	1	1
Lemon, Tracey M.	1970–2012	(Auckland) 1991–94–95	5	2
Lene, Stacey O.	1980–	(Canterbury) 2003–04–05	7	7

Name	*B&D*	*Representative Team*	*Games*	*Tests*
Leti-I'iga, Ayesha A.	1999–	(Wellington) 2018–19–21–22	21	21
Levave, Sanita D.	1988–	(Wellington) 2014	5	5
Lili'i, Adrienne P.	1970–	(Auckland) 1999–02–03–04; (Waikato) 2000	12	12
Littleworth, Helen M.	1966–	(Canterbury) 1989–90–91–92–93–94; (Otago) 1995–96	18	8
Liua'ana, Rebecca K.	1970–	(Wellington) 1999–00–01–02	10	10
Lotui'iga, L. Brigitta	1968–	(Auckland) 1998	5	5
Love, Phillipa E.A.	1990–	(Otago) 2014; (Canterbury) 2017–18–19–20–21–22–23	28	27
McKay, K. Ruth	1986–	(Manawatu) 2007–08–09–10–12–13–14	25	25
McKenzie, Margaret J.	1970–	(Otago) 2000–05	5	5
McMenamin, Charmaine J.	1990–	(Auckland) 2013–16–17–18–19–20–22	33	31
Mahon, Helen L.	1968–	(Canterbury) 1989; (Wellington) 1991; (Waikato) 1992	7	3
Mahoney (nee Hull), Rebecca M.	1983–	(Manawatu) 2004–08; (Hawke's Bay) 2006; (Wellington) 2009–10–11	16	16
Makata, Rachel J.	1974–	(Auckland) 2006	2	2
Maliepo, Patricia	2003–	(Auckland) 2021–23	7	7
Maliukaetau, F. Diane L.	1986–	(Auckland) 2005–06	6	6
Mallard, Beth L.	1981–	(Otago) 2006–07–08–09	9	8
Manuel, Huriana R.	1986–	(Auckland) 2005–06–07–08–09–10–14	26	25
Marino-Tauhinu, Arihiana A.H.	1992–	(Counties Manukau) 2019–20–22–23	21	19
Marsh, A. see Rule, A.				
Martin, Rochelle L.	1973–	(Wellington) 1994–95; (Auckland) 1996–97–98–99–00–02–04–05–06	34	32
Mataele, M. Martha	1999–	(Canterbury) 2023	2	2
Matapo, P.E.A. 'Kelani'	1983–	(Auckland) 2011	1	1
Mata'u, Aotearoa K.	1997–	(Counties Manukau) 2016–17	8	8
Mihinui, M.T. Eliza	1960–	(Auckland) 1994	1	–
Mikaele-Tu'u, Liana E.T.	2002–	(Auckland) 2021–22–23	18	18
Moata'ane, Kilisitina	1997–	(Otago) 2019	1	1
Moore, Aroha	1978–	(Auckland) 2004	3	3
Moors, D.B. 'Natahlia'	1995–	(Auckland) 2018–19–20	3	2
Mortimer, Stephanie A.	1981–	(Canterbury) 2003–04–05–06	11	11
Mulipola, Tala	1981–	(Auckland) 2000–01–03	7	7
Mulu, Angel J.	1999–	(Bay of Plenty) 2022	2	2
Murphy, Amanda J.	1985–	(Canterbury) 2009–11	3	2
Murray, Krystal R.	1993–	(Northland) 2021–22–23	14	14
Myers, H.J. see Porter, H.J.				
Nathan-Wong, Tyla B.	1994–	(Northland) 2022	1	1
Natua Toka I.	1991–	(Waikato) 2015–16–17–19–20	24	22
Nelson, Aleisha P.	1990–	(Auckland) 2012–14–15–16–17–18–19–20–21	41	39
Nemaia, Ana H.		(Auckland) 1989	1	–
Nesbit, Joanne L.		(Canterbury) 1989	1	–
Ngan-Woo, Joanah M.F.	1995–	(Wellington) 2019–21–22–23	19	19
Ngata-Aerengamate, Te Kura R.	1991–	(Counties Manukau) 2014–15–16–17–18–19–21 (Northland) 2020	34	32

Name	B&D	Representative Team	Games	Tests
Ngatai, M.M. see Bosman, M.M.				
Nielsen, Jacinta	1972–	(Otago) 1997–98–00	7	7
O'Leary, Pauline M.	1966–	(Wanganui) 1993	1	–
O'Reilly, Lauren M.	1967–	(Canterbury) 1992–93–94	4	1
Olsen-Baker, Kaipo T.	2002–	(Manawatu) 2022	2	2
Paasi, Poinisitia T.	1970–2018	(Wellington) 2001–07	4	4
Paitai, Elsie	1963–	(Auckland) 1990–91	4	–
Palmer, Farah R.	1972–	(Otago) 1996–98–99–00; (Waikato) 1997; (Manawatu) 2001–02–03–04–05–06	35	35
Papalii, Christine	1962–	(Auckland) 1989–90–92	6	–
Parkes, Marcelle J.	1997–	(Wellington) 2018–19	5	5
Patea-Fereti, Jackie S.	1986–	(Wellington) 2012–13–14–16–18–19	18	18
Paul, Geraldine N.	1965–	(Bay of Plenty) 1989–91–97; (Taranaki) 1994	8	4
Paul, Mererangi K.	1998–	(Counties Manukau) 2023	5	5
Paul, Tamaku M.E.	1979–	(Bay of Plenty) 2001	1	1
Penetito, K.E. see Stowers, K.E.				
Perese, Leilani L.R.	1993–	(Counties Manukau) 2018–19–22	12	12
Piho, Mata	1972–	(Otago) 1998–00	3	3
Ponsonby, Georgia R.A.	1999–	(Canterbury) 2021–22–23	20	20
Porter (nee Myers), Hannah J.	1979–	(Otago) 2000–02; (Auckland) 2003–04–05–06–08	22	22
Reader, Heidi C.	1971–	(Otago) 1993; (Waikato) 1994–96; (Bay of Plenty) 1995	5	3
Rees, Vivian L.	1971–	(Wellington) 1993–94–95	5	2
Rere (Ratu), Ericka R.	1963–	(Wellington) 1990–91–92; (Bay of Plenty) 1993	9	3
Reynolds, Julie	1966–	(Canterbury) 1993–94	2	–
Reynolds, Kendra L.	1993–	(Bay of Plenty) 2020–21–22–23	13	12
Richards, Anna M.	1964–	(Auckland) 1990–91–92–93–94–96–97–98–99–00–01–02–03–04–05–06–07–08–10	58	49
Richards, Fiona C.	1970–	(Canterbury) 1993–94–95–96; (Auckland) 1997–98–99	17	14
Richardson, Claire	1984–	(Otago) 2003–04–05–06–07–12; (Auckland) 2013–14	23	23
Rikihana-Broughton, Judy J.	1963–	(Wellington) 1990	1	–
Robertson, Casey J.	1981–	(Canterbury) 2002–03–04–05–06–09–10–11–12–13–14	38	38
Robins-Reti, Cheyelle R.A.	1997–	(Waikato) 2020–21–22	6	5
Robinson, Melodie C.	1973–	(Wellington) 1996–97–98–99; (Auckland) 2001–02	18	18
Robinson, Vita J.	1982–	(Auckland) 2007–09–10–11–13	15	14
Rodd, Christine A.	1959–	(Canterbury) 1990–91	7	2
Roos, Maiakawanakaulani C.T.	2001–	(Auckland) 2021–22–23	21	21
Ross, L. Christine	1964–	(Mid C'bury) 1989–92–96; (Canterbury) 1990–91	12	5
Rowat, Claire L.	1983–	(Wellington) 2009	1	–

Name	B&D	Representative Team	Games	Tests
Rule (nee Marsh), Amiria	1983–	(Canterbury) 2000–01–02–03–5–06–09–11–13–14	35	34
Rule, Amy M.	2000–	(Canterbury) 2021–22–23	19	19
Ruscoe, Melissa J.	1976–	(Canterbury) 2004–05–06–07–08–10	22	22
Rush, Annaleah M.	1976–	(Otago) 1996–97–98–99; (Auckland) 2000–01–02	20	20
Rush, Erin L.	1970–	(Wellington) 2003	2	2
Sae, Layla Y.J.	2000–	(Manawatu) 2023	3	3
Saili, Alena F.	1998–	(Southland) 2018–19	5	5
Savage, Aroha	1990–	(Auckland) 2010–11–12; (Counties Manukau) 2013–14–16–17–18 (Northland) 2020	35	33
Semple (nee Alley), Chelsea H.	1992–	(Waikato) 2013–14–17–18–19–20–21–22; (North Harbour) 2015–16	31	29
Sheck, Regina	1969–	(Auckland) 1994–96–97–98; (Waikato) 1999–00–01–02–03–04	26	25
Shelford, E.T. see Edwards, E.T.				
Shortland, Suzanne	1974–	(Auckland) 1997–98–99–00–01–02	18	18
Simon, Kennedy W.	1996–	(Waikato) 2019–20–21–22–23	22	20
Simpson-Brown, Lenadeen H.	1964–	(Canterbury) 1994; (Waikato) 1995–96–97	9	8
Sio, Nina	1963–	(Auckland) 1989–91–92; (Waikato) 1994	9	4
Sione, Joan L.	1986–	(Auckland) 2005–10	6	6
Sisifa, Angelene A.F.	1989–	(Otago) 2015–16	7	7
Smith, Charmaine B.	1990–	(North Harbour) 2015–16–17; (Auckland) 2018–19 (Northland) 2023	29	29
Smith, Kimberly M.	1985–	(Canterbury) 2005–06–07–08–09	12	11
Solomon, Pikihuia P.	1983–	(Otago) 2005	2	2
Steinmetz, Grace L.	1998–	(Canterbury) 2020–22–23	3	2
Stowers (nee Penetito), Karina E.	1986–	(Auckland) 2005–09–10–11–12–13	19	18
Su'a, S.M.A. 'Nara'	1969–	(Auckland) 1996	2	2
Suasua-White, D. see White, D.M.				
Subritzky-Nafatali, Victoria S.	1991–	(Otago) 2012–14; (Counties Manukau) 2015–16–17	19	19
Sue, Kristina J.	1987–	(Manawatu) 2016–17–18	15	15
Sutorius, Aimee E.	1979–	Wellington) 2007–08–09	4	3
Tagoai, Monica F.	1998–	(Wellington) 2018	3	3
Tahu, Bella M.	1970–	(Auckland) 1996	3	3
Talawadua, Sosoli J.	1989–	(Waikato) 2016–17	8	8
Tamihana, Florence N.	1960–	(Wellington) 1995	1	1
Tangen-Wainohu, Awhina K.	1997–	(Waikato) 2022	4	4
Tapsell, Pia H.	1998–	(North Harbour) 2019 (Bay of Plenty) 2020	7	6
Taufateau, Doris J.T.	1987–	(Auckland) 2008–10–11	5	5
Taumata, Santo	2003–	(Bay of Plenty) 2022	7	7
Taylor, Karen	1968–	(Bay of Plenty) 1996	2	2
Teddy, Waimania L.	1979–	(Auckland) 2005–06–07	6	6
Te Tamaki, Teresa K.	1981–	(Auckland) 2007–08–11; (Waikato) 2012–15	10	10
Tekeu, No'o	1960–2011	(Wellington) 1990	1	–

Name	*B&D*	*Representative Team*	*Games*	*Tests*
Te Ohaere-Fox,Stephanie A.	1985–	(Canterbury) 2008–09–10–12–13–14; (Wasps) 2011	25	24
Teneti, Kelsey J.	2003–	(Waikato) 2022–23	3	3
Thomas, Emma H.	1958–	(Bay of Plenty) 1996–97–98	9	9
Tiplady, Anika M.	1980–	(Manawatu) 2007; (Canterbury) 2009	3	2
Tiplady-Hurring, Halie A.	1986–	(Canterbury) 2008–10–14; (Otago) 2012	13	13
Tiriamai, Kimi	1964–	(Auckland) 1990–91	5	2
Tofa, L. Cristo. S.	1987–	(North Harbour) 2018 (Auckland) 2020	3	2
Tubic, Hazel S.	1990–	(Auckland) 2011–12; (Counties Manukau) 2016–17–20–22	24	22
Tui, Ruby M.	1991–	(Counties Manukau) 2022–23	13	13
Va'aga, Helen	1977–	(Auckland) 2002–03–05–06	10	10
Vaeteru, Teina R.	1964–	(Auckland) 1990	2	–
Vaha'akolo, Katelyn S.C.	2000–	(Auckland) 2023	6	6
Vaughan, Janna M.	1988–	(Manawatu) 2015–16	6	6
Veainu, Lanulangi L.	1993–	(Counties Manukau) 2020	2	–
Viliko, Chryss Z.F.	2000–	(Auckland) 2023	2	2
Waaka, Cheryl M.	1970–	(Auckland) 1997–98–00–01–02–03–04; (Northland) 1999	20	20
Waaka, S.J.A.K. see Fluhler, S.J.A.K.				
Wall, Louisa H.	1972–	(Waikato) 1994; (Auckland) 1995–96–97–98–99	16	15
Ward-Duin, Olivia Y.	1993–	(North Harbour) 2019	2	2
Waters, Tracey J.R.	1973–	(Canterbury) 1995–96–98	10	10
Wharton, Julie		(Auckland) 1990	1	–
Whata-Simpkins, Katarina R.	1990–	(Wellington) 2011	1	1
White, Davida M.	1967–	(Auckland) 1993–94–95–96–98–00	15	13
Wickliffe, Renee W.M.	1987–	(Auckland) 2009–10–11; (Counties Manukau) 2013–14–15–16–17; (Bay of Plenty) 2018–19–21–22	48	47
Wihongi, Kamila T.	1982–	(Otago) 2005	1	1
Williams, Amy L.	1986–	(Hawke's Bay) 2005–06	6	6
Williams, Tasha A.	1973–	(Manawatu) 1994	2	1
Willison, Tenika R.	1997–	(Waikato) 2023	2	2
Willoughby, Shannon M.	1982–	(Otago) 2005–06	8	8
Wills, Kelsie P.	1993–	(Bay of Plenty) 2020–21	4	2
Wilson, Tammi	1973–	(Auckland) 1998–99–00–01–02	16	16
Wilton, Kathleen A.	1984–	(Otago) 2007–11–12–13–14	18	18
Winiata, Selica C.	1986–	(Manawatu) 2008–12–13–14–15–16–17–18–19–20	41	40
Wong, Natasha A.	1967–	(Canterbury) 1990–91–92–93–94	10	3
Wood, Rebecca J.	1987–	(North Harbour) 2017	7	7
Woodman, Portia L.	1991–	(Auckland) 2013; (Counties Manukau) 2016–17; (Northland) 2021–22	25	25
Woodman, Sharnita K.	1986–	(Counties Manukau) 2016	2	2
Yates, Sandy	1979–	(Counties Manukau) 2001	1	1

BLACK FERNS INTERNATIONAL RECORDS

NEW ZEALAND INTERNATIONAL CAPTAINS

Fiao'o Faamausili	2012–18	35
Farah Palmer	1997–2006	30
Ruahei Demant	2022–23	17
Leslie Elder	2019–21	9
Melissa Ruscoe	2007–10	8
Lenadeen Simpson-Brown	1994–96	6
Kennedy Simon	2023	6
Helen Littleworth	1991	3
Victoria Grant	2010–11	3
Rochelle Martin	2005–06	2
Victoria Heighway	2009	2
Davida White	1998	1
Anna Richards	2005	1
Casey Robertson	2011	1
Amiria Rule	2014	1
Kendra Cocksedge	2019	1
Arihiana Marino-Tauhinu	2022	1
Maia Roos	2023	1

Demant and Simon were co-captains in 6 tests 2023

MOST APPEARANCES IN INTERNATIONALS

K.M. Cocksedge	2007 –22	68	K.A. Brazier	2009 –21	42
F.M. Faamausili	2002 –18	57	S.C. Winiata	2008 –19	40
A.M. Richards	1991 –10	49	A.P. Nelson	2012 –21	39
E.M. Jensen	2002 –15	49	C.J. Robertson	2002 –14	38
R.W.M. Wickliffe	2009 –22	47	L.F. Itunu	2003 –18	38
E.S. Blackwell	2011 –21	46	F.R. Palmer	1996 –06	35

MOST SUCCESSIVE INTERNATIONALS

K.M. Cocksedge	2011 –22	53

MOST POINTS IN INTERNATIONALS

	Tries	*Con*	*PG*	*DG*	*Total*		*Tries*	*Con*	*PG*	*DG*	*Total*
K.M. Cocksedge	19	97	33	–	388	K.A. Brazier	11	45	15	–	190
V. Cootes	43	–	–	–	215	H.J. Porter	5	42	20	–	169
T. Wilson	21	29	11	–	196	P.L. Woodman	38	–	–	–	190
S.C. Winiata	39	–	–	–	195	A.M. Rush	14	34	6	–	156

MOST POINTS IN AN INTERNATIONAL

V. Cootes	v France, 1996	45	(9 tries)
P.L. Woodman	v Hong Kong, 2017	40	(8 tries)
T. Wilson	v USA, 1999	36	(6 tries, 3 conversions)
P.L. Woodman	v Japan 2022	35	(7 tries)
L.C. Ross	v France, 1996	34	(2 tries, 12 conversions)
K.M. Cocksedge	v Hong Kong, 2017	31	(1 try, 13 conversions)
T. Wilson	v Germany, 1998	30	(4 tries, 5 conversions)

MOST TRIES IN AN INTERNATIONAL

V. Cootes	v France, 1996	9	V. Cootes	v USA, 1996	5
P.L. Woodman	v Hong Kong, 2017	8	V. Cootes	v USA, 1998	5
P.L. Woodman	v Japan 2022	7	V. Cootes	v Germany, 2002	5
T. Wilson	v USA, 1999	6	S.C. Winiata	v Samoa, 2014	5

MOST PENALTY GOALS IN AN INTERNATIONAL

K.A. Brazier	v England, 2013	4	K.M. Cocksedge	v England, 2015	4

MOST CONVERSIONS IN AN INTERNATIONAL

K.M. Cocksedge	v Hong Kong, 2017	13	L.C. Ross	v Canada, 1996	9
L.C. Ross	v France, 1996	12	H.C. Reader	v USA, 1996	8

INTERNATIONAL MATCH RECORD

1991	v	Canada[1]	Glamorgan	won	24	8
	v	Wales[1]	Llanharen	won	24	6
	v	USA[1] (semi-final)	Cardiff	lost	0	7
1994	v	Australia	Sydney	won	37	0
1995	v	Australia	Auckland	won	64	0
1996	v	Australia	Sydney	won	28	5
	v	Canada	St Albert	won	88	3
	v	USA	Edmonton	won	86	8
	v	France	Edmonton	won	109	0
1997	v	England	Burnham	won	67	0
	v	Australia	Dunedin	won	40	0
1998	v	Germany[1]	Amsterdam	won	134	6
	v	Scotland[1]	Amsterdam	won	76	0
	v	Spain[1] (quarter-final)	Amsterdam	won	46	3
	v	England[1] (semi-final)	Amsterdam	won	44	11
	v	USA[1] (final)	Amsterdam	won	44	12
	v	Australia	Sydney	won	27	3
1999	v	Canada	Palmerston North	won	73	0
	v	USA	Palmerston North	won	65	5
2000	v	Canada	Winnipeg	won	41	0
	v	USA	Winnipeg	won	45	0
	v	England	Winnipeg	won	32	13
2001	v	England	Rotorua	won	15	10
	v	England	Albany	lost	17	22
2002	v	Germany[1]	Barcelona	won	117	0

	v	Australia[1]	Barcelona	won	36	3
	v	France[1] (semi-final)	Barcelona	won	30	0
	v	England[1] (final)	Barcelona	won	19	9
2003	v	World XV	Auckland	won	37	0
	v	World XV	Whangarei	won	38	19
2004	v	Canada	Vancouver	won	32	5
	v	USA	Calgary	won	35	0
	v	England	Edmonton	won	38	0
2005	v	Scotland	Ottawa	won	30	9
	v	Canada	Ottawa	won	43	3
	v	Canada	Ottawa	won	32	5
	v	England	Auckland	won	33	8
	v	England	Hamilton	won	24	15
2006	v	Canada[1]	Edmonton	won	66	7
	v	Samoa[1]	Edmonton	won	50	0
	v	Scotland[1]	Edmonton	won	21	0
	v	France[1] (semi-final)	Edmonton	won	40	10
	v	England[1] (final)	Edmonton	won	25	17
2007	v	Australia	Wanganui	won	21	11
	v	Australia	Wellington	won	29	12
2008	v	Australia	Canberra	won	37	3
	v	Australia	Canberra	won	22	16
2009	v	England	London	won	16	3
	v	England	London	lost	3	10
2010	v	South Africa[1]	London	won	55	3
	v	Australia[1]	London	won	32	5
	v	Wales[1]	London	won	41	8
	v	France[1] (semi-final)	London	won	45	7
	v	England[1] (final)	London	won	13	10
2011	v	England	London	lost	0	10
	v	England	London	lost	7	21
	v	England	London	draw	8	8
2012	v	England	Esher	lost	13	16
	v	England	Aldershot	lost	8	17
	v	England	London	lost	23	32
2013	v	England	Auckland	won	29	10
	v	England	Hamilton	won	14	9
	v	England	Pukekohe	won	29	8
2014	v	Australia	Rotorua	won	38	3
	v	Samoa	Auckland	won	90	12
	v	Canada	Tauranga	won	16	8
	v	Canada	Whakatane	won	33	21
	v	Kazakhstan[1]	Marcoussis	won	79	5
	v	Ireland[1]	Marcoussis	lost	14	17
	v	USA[1]	Marcoussis	won	34	3
	v	Wales[1]	Paris	won	63	7
	v	USA[1]	Paris	won	55	5
2015	v	Canada	Calgary	won	40	22
	v	England	Red Deer	won	26	7
	v	USA	Edmonton	won	49	14
2016	v	Australia	Auckland	won	67	3
	v	Australia	Albany	won	29	3
	v	England	London	won	25	20

	v	Canada	Dublin	won	20	10
	v	Ireland	Dublin	won	38	8
2017	v	Canada	Wellington	won	28	16
	v	Australia	Christchurch	won	44	17
	v	England	Rotorua	lost	21	29
	v	Wales[1]	Dublin	won	44	12
	v	Hong Kong[1]	Dublin	won	121	0
	v	Canada[1]	Dublin	won	48	5
	v	USA[1] (semi-final)	Belfast	won	45	12
	v	England[1] (final)	Belfast	won	41	32
2018	v	Australia	Sydney	won	31	11
	v	Australia	Auckland	won	45	17
	v	USA	Chicago	won	67	6
	v	France	Toulon	won	14	0
	v	France	Grenoble	lost	27	30
2019	v	Canada	San Diego	won	35	20
	v	USA	San Diego	won	33	0
	v	France	San Diego	lost	16	25
	v	England	San Diego	won	28	13
	v	Australia	Perth	won	47	10
	v	Australia	Auckland	won	37	8
2021	v	England	Exeter	lost	12	43
	v	England	Northampton	lost	15	56
	v	France	Pau	lost	13	38
	v	France	Castres	lost	7	29
2022	v	Australia	Tauranga	won	23	10
	v	Canada	Auckland	won	28	0
	v	USA	Whangarei	won	50	6
	v	Australia	Christchurch	won	52	5
	v	Australia	Adelaide	won	22	14
	v	Japan	Auckland	won	95	12
	v	Australia[1]	Auckland	won	41	17
	v	Wales[1]	Auckland	won	56	12
	v	Scotland[1]	Whangarei	won	57	0
	v	Wales[1] (quarter-final)	Whangarei	won	55	3
	v	France[1] (semi-final)	Auckland	won	25	24
	v	England[1] (final)	Auckland	won	34	31
2023	v	Australia	Brisbane	won	50	0
	v	Canada	Ottawa	won	52	21
	v	USA	Ottawa	won	39	17
	v	Australia	Hamilton	won	43	3
	v	France	Wellington	lost	17	18
	v	Wales	Dunedin	won	70	7
	v	England	Auckland	lost	12	33

[1]World Cup

SUMMARY OF INTERNATIONALS

Played:	122	Drawn:	1
Won:	103	Points for:	4773
Lost:	18	Points against:	1287

BLACK FERNS XV

The Black Ferns XV squad consisted largely of younger players who had impressed during the Farah Palmer Cup competition. The game was also a warmup for the Samoan team prior to their participation in the WXV2 competition in South Africa.

BLACK FERNS XV v MANUSINA

Navigation Homes Stadium, Pukekohe **September 23, 2023**

Black Ferns XV won 38–12

BLACK FERNS XV		***MANUSINA***
Tara Turner (Northland)	15	Hasting Leiataua
Angelica Mekemeke Vahai (Auckland)	14	Linda Fiafia
Cheyenne Cunningham (Otago)	13	Allison Futialo
Grace Brooker (capt, Canterbury)	12	Bella Milo
Harmony Kautai (Wellington)	11	Michelle Curry
Maia Joseph (Otago)	10	Cassie Siataga
Di Hiini (Canterbury)	9	Fa'alua Tugaga
Elizabeth Moimoi (Auckland)	8	Nina Foaese
Leah Miles (Otago)	7	Sui Pauaraisa (capt)
Holly Wratt-Groeneweg (Canterbury)	6	Sinead Ryder
Laura Bayfield (Canterbury)	5	Ana-Lise Sio
Maama Vaipulu (Auckland)	4	Easter Savelio
Moomooga Palu (Hawke's Bay)	3	Glory Aiono
Atlanta Lolohea (Canterbury)	2	Lulu Leuta
Eilis Doyle (Otago)	1	Ana Mamea
Vici-Rose Green (Waikato) rep 2, 50m	16	Avau Filimaua (rep 3, 60m)
Maddi Robinson (Canterbury) rep 1, 70m	17	Maletina Brown (rep 2, 63m)
Esther Faiaoga-Tilo (Waikato) rep 3, 45m	18	Teuila Aukusitino (rep 1, 73m)
Emma Dermody (Canterbury) rep 19, 50m	19	Olalini Tafoulua (rep 5, 52m)
Mia Anderson (Waikato) rep 8, 65m	20	Utumalama Atonio (rep 8, 54m)
Kahlia Awa (Hawke's Bay) rep 9, 60m	21	Saelua Leaula (rep 9, 40m)
Rangimarie Sturmey (Manawatu) rep 10, 40m	22	Perise Tumutumu (rep 13, 63m)
Justine McGregor (Wellington) rep 11, 50m	23	Lutia Col Aumua (rep 11)
Mekemeke Vahai (2), Palu, Brooker, Bayfield, Faiaoga-Tilo	Tries	Fiafia (2)
Joseph (3), Cunningham	Cons	Siataga

Referee: Tiana Anderson
Coach: Whitney Hansen
Assistant coaches: Linda Itunu, Peter Breen
Manager: Arizona Leger
Assistant manager: Lauren Cournane

Reserve forward Marcelle Parkes (*Canterbury*) was injured during the warmup and replaced by Robinson. Grace Gago (*Counties Manukau*), Samantha Taylor (*Manawatu*) and Lela Ieremia (*Waikato*) were squad members not required for the game.

SKY SUPER RUGBY AUPIKI 2023

The Sky Super Rugby Aupiki competition provided entertaining high-scoring games with many close results. Defending champions Chiefs Manawa comfortably cruised through the round-robin but were upset in the final by a committed Matatū that had fought its way back into the game after trailing 19–0 after 20 minutes. After 80 minutes Matatū held a narrow 33–31 lead when Chiefs were awarded a penalty but Tenika Willison's attempt at goal failed and the southerners, winless in 2022, took the title.

The competition was all too brief. No sooner had the four teams completed their three round-robin games they were into the semifinals. Being held early season during February-March the five-week competition was too short to capture the attention of the rugby public. It is pleasing that the 2024 competition is extended to six round-robin games (home and away).

SUPER RUGBY PACIFIC FINAL STANDINGS

Team	*P*	*W*	*D*	*L*	*F*	*A*	*TF*	*TA*	*+/-*	*BP*	*Pts*
Chiefs Manawa	*3*	*3*	–	–	*149*	*92*	*23*	*14*	*71*	*1*	*13*
Matatū	*3*	*1*	–	*2*	*95*	*102*	*15*	*16*	*-7*	*1*	*5*
Blues	*3*	*1*	–	*2*	*95*	*105*	*15*	*15*	*-10*	*1*	*5*
Hurricanes Poua	*3*	*1*	–	*2*	*68*	*108*	*10*	*18*	*-40*		*4*
TOTALS		**6**	**–**	**6**	**407**	**407**	**63**	**63**			

Semifinals: Matatū 26 Blues 23; Chiefs Manawa 43 Hurricanes Poua 21
Playoff for third: Hurricanes Poua 29 Blues 24
Final: Matatū 33 Chiefs Manawa 31

BLUES

Postal address: 32 Campbell Crescent,
Auckland 1051
Telephone: (09) 846 5425
Email: info@blues.rugby
Colours: Blue
Coach: Willie Walker
Assistant coaches: Linda Itunu, Carlos Spencer
Manager: Georgia Ramatalei
Home ground: North Harbour Stadium

	Club	Date of Birth	Height	Weight	Blues debut	Blues games	Blues points
A.J. (Ariana) Bayler	Waikato	14-12-96	1.65	74	2023	5	0
E.S. (Eloise) Blackwell	Auckland	28-12-90	1.80	98	2021	7	0
D. (Danjian) Brown	Auckland	10-02-03	1.78	80	-	0	0
S.L.L. (Sylvia) Brunt	Auckland	01-01-04	1.66	82	2021	6	5
K.J. (Krystal) Cottrell	Hawke's Bay	17-02-92	1.62	68	2022	6	25
D.R. (Ruahei) Demant	Auckland	21-04-95	1.70	82	2021	8	19
K.W. (Kiri) Demant	Auckland	08-10-96	1.71	78	2023	3	0
E.E. (Esther) Faiaoga-Tilo	Waikato	26-09-94	1.79	100	2023	2	0
S.R. (Sophie) Fisher	Auckland	25-11-98	1.82	108	2023	5	5
G.L.F. (Grace) Gago	Counties Manukau	05-05-98	1.62	85	2023	5	10
H.S. (Hayley) Hutana	North Harbour	21-11-95	1.71	66	2021	2	0
J. (Jaymie) Kolose	Counties Manukau	06-07-01	1.68	63	2023	5	25
T.P. (Tafito) Lafaele	Auckland	17-02-01	1.80	95	2022	7	5
L.F.L. (Letelemalanuola) Lavea	North Harbour	22-07-02	1.75	100	2023	1	0
S.L. (Shannon) Leota	Auckland	13-03-95	1.74	85	2021	6	5
C.J. (Charmaine) McMenamin	Auckland	13-05-90	1.73	97	2021	6	0
P. (Patricia) Maliepo	Auckland	13-03-03	1.75	79	2021	8	26
L.E.T. (Liana) Mikaele-Tu'u	Auckland	02-03-02	1.77	88	2021	8	5
T.I. (Toka) Natua	Waikato	22-11-91	1.65	121	2023	4	0
A. (Alakoka) Po'oi	Auckland	04-06-99	1.67	100	2023	2	0
M.C. (Melanie) Puckett	Auckland	07-06-99	1.60	63	2022	7	0
M.C.T. (Maia) Roos	Auckland	27-07-01	1.79	85	2021	3	0
C. (Cheyenne) Tuli-Fale	Auckland	27-11-99	1.76	119	–	0	0
T.L. (Tara) Turner	Northland	22-12-03	1.57	60	2023	3	0
K.S.C. (Katelyn) Vaha'akolo	Auckland	18-04-00	1.67	75	2023	5	15
M. (Maama) Vaipulu	Auckland	26-11-02	1.80	86	2023	5	10
C.Z.F. (Chryss) Viliko	Auckland	25-12-00	1.68	102	2022	6	0
H.S. (Holly) Williams	North Harbour	21-06-04	1.68	75	2023	1	5

Joanna Fanene Lolo (Auckland) was an original selection but did not take part in Aupiki due to injury.

INDIVIDUAL SCORING

	Tries	Con	PG	DG	Points
Kolose	5	–	–	–	25
Cottrell	1	6	2	–	23
R. Demant	1	7	–	–	19
Maliepo	3	–	–	–	15
Vaha'akolo	3	–	–	–	15
Gago	2	–	–	–	10
Vaipulu	2	–	–	–	10
Fisher	1	–	–	–	5
Lafaele	1	–	–	–	5
Mikaele-Tu'u	1	–	–	–	5
Roos	1	–	–	–	5
Williams	1	–	–	–	5
Totals	***22***	***13***	***2***	***0***	***142***
Opposition scored	*23*	*18*	*3*	*0*	*160*

BLUES 2023

	Matatū	Chiefs Manawa	Hurricanes Poua	Matatū	Hurricanes Poua	**TOTALS**
K. Demant	15	15	15	–	–	**3**
Turner	s	s	s	–	–	**3**
Kolose	14	14	14	14	14	**5**
Vaha'akolo	11	11	11	11	11	**5**
Williams	–	–	–	–	s	**1**
Brunt	13	13	13	13	13	**5**
Hutana	12	–	–	–	–	**1**
Maliepo	s	12	12	15	15	**5**
R. Demant (capt)	10	10	10	12	12	**5**
Cottrell	–	s	s	10	10	**4**
Bayler	9	9	9	s	s	**5**
Puckett	s	s	s	9	9	**5**
Mikaele-Tuu	8	8	8	8	8	**5**
Lafaele	7	s	7	7	7	**5**
Leota	s	7	–	s	s	**4**
McMenamin	6	6	6	6	6	**5**
Roos	5	5	5	5	5	**5**
Blackwell	4	s	s	4	4	**5**
Vaipulu	s	4	4	s	s	**5**
Faiaoga-Tilo	3	3	–	–	–	**2**
Fisher	s	s	3	3	3	**5**
Lavea	–	–	–	–	s	**1**
Viliko	1	1	1	1	1	**5**
Natua	s	s	–	s	s	**4**
Gago	2	2	2	2	2	**5**
Po'oi	s	s	–	–	–	**2**

BLUES TEAM RECORD 2023

Played 5 Won 1 Lost 4 Points for 142 Points against 160

Date	*Opponent*	*Location*	*Score*	*Tries*	*Con*	*PG*	*DG*	*Referee*
February 25	Matatū	Dunedin	31–33	Kolose (2), Gago, Vaha'akolo, Fisher	R. Demant (3)			Brendon Pickerill
March 4	Chiefs Manawa	Albany	33–50	Vaipulu (2), Kolose (2), Roos	R. Demant (3), Cottrell			Natarsha Ganley
March 11	Hurricanes Poua	Wellington	31–22	Maliepo (2), Vaha'akolo, R. Demant, Cottrell	Cottrell (2), R. Demant			Nick Hogan
March 19	Matatū (semifinal)	Albany	23–26	Vaha'akolo, Maliepo, Mikaele-Tu'u	Cottrell	Cottrell (2)		Michael Winter
March 25	Hurricanes Poua (for 3rd)	Hamilton	24–29	Kolose, Gago, Lafaele, Williams	Cottrell (2)			Natarsha Ganley

CHIEFS MANAWA

Postal address: Box 4292, Hamilton East 3247
Telephone: (07) 853 0231
Email: info@chiefs.co.nz
Colours: Pink and Black
Coach: Crystal Kaua
Assistant coaches: Brent Kaua, Greg Smith, Darryl Suasua
Manager: Gareth Duncan
Home ground: FMG Stadium Waikato

	Club	Date of Birth	Height	Chiefs debut	Chiefs games	Chiefs points
C.J. (Chelsea) Bremner	Canterbury	11-04-95	1.81	2023	5	5
L.H.J. (Luka) Connor	Bay of Plenty	24-09-96	1.71	2021	9	50
G.L. (Georgia) Daals	Wellington	13-09-93	1.63	2022	7	25
D.S. (Dhys) Faleafaga	Wellington	17-10-00	1.75	2023	5	5
T.A. (Tynealle) Fitzgerald	Bay of Plenty	06-01-00	1.69	2022	8	5
V. (Vici-Rose) Green	Waikato	08-04-02	1.68	2023	1	0
V. (Violet) Hapi-Wise	Waikato	13-12-98	1.60	2023	3	0
K.K. (Kate) Henwood	Bay of Plenty	28-01-89	1.77	2023	5	0
C.G.T.O. (Carla) Hohepa	Waikato	27-07-85	1.75	2022	8	5
C.H.M.P. (Chyna) Hohepa	Waikato	15-12-89	1.72	2021	2	0
G.P. (Grace) Houpapa-Barrett	Waikato	25-07-95	1.68	2021	6	10
J.M.E. (Tanya) Kalounivale	Waikato	20-01-99	1.78	2021	9	10
A.A.M. (Azalleyah) Maaka	Bay of Plenty	05-06-00	1.73	2023	5	0
T.R.T. (Te Urupounamu) McGarvey	Bay of Plenty	28-12-02	1.62	2023	4	0
V.R. (Victoria) Makea	Waikato	14-08-90	1.62	2022	8	0
A.A.H. (Arihiana) Marino-Tauhinu	Counties Manukau	29-03-92	1.61	2021	9	5
A.J. (Angel) Mulu	Wellington	21-11-99	1.63	2021	5	5
A. (Apii) Nicholls	Auckland	26-02-93	1.65	2023	4	0
M.K. (Mererangi) Paul	Counties Manukau	29-10-98	1.71	2023	5	30
A.A. (Amanda) Rasch	Wellington	09-08-93	1.74	–	0	0
A.S. (Abigail) Roach	Auckland	12-09-00	1.62	2023	4	0
K.W. (Kennedy) Simon	Waikato	01-10-96	1.72	2021	9	20
C.B. (Charmaine) Smith	Northland	15-11-90	1.83	2023	5	5
A.K. (Awhina) Tangen-Wainohu	Waikato	16-12-97	1.69	2021	4	0
S. (Santo) Taumata	Bay of Plenty	05-02-03	1.78	2022	3	0
H. (Harono) Te Iringa	Counties Manukau	01-05-96	1.83	2021	7	0
K.P. (Kelsie) Thwaites (nee Wills)	Bay of Plenty	08-01-93	1.84	2021	6	0
H.S. (Hazel) Tubic	Counties Manukau	31-12-90	1.65	2021	9	53
L.L. (Langi) Veainu	Counties Manukau	03-11-93	1.67	2021	4	10
O.A. (Olive) Watherston	Bay of Plenty	17-05-04	1.68	–	0	0
T.R. (Tanika) Willison	Waikato	07-12-97	1.69	2023	5	39

Original selections Merania Paraone (Waikato), Chelsea Semple (Waikato), Pia Tapsell (Bay of Plenty) and Renee Wickliffe (Bay of Plenty) withdrew from the squad for various reasons.

Squad members Chyna Hohepa, Rasch, Tangen-Wainohu, Taumata and Veainu, for various reasons, were not chosen in any playing 23. Watherston was on the bench for the final.

Nicholls (Gold Coast Titans) and Roach (Richmond Roses) were NZ League representatives in 2022.

INDIVIDUAL SCORING

	Tries	Con	PG	DG	Points
Willison	3	12	–	–	39
Connor	7	–	–	–	35
Paul	6	–	–	–	30
Tubic	–	10	3	–	29
Daals	5	–	–	–	25
Simon	3	–	–	–	15
Houpapa-Barrett	2	–	–	–	10
Kalounivale	2	–	–	–	10
Bremner	1	–	–	–	5
Faleafaga	1	–	–	–	5
Fitzgerald	1	–	–	–	5
Hohepa	1	–	–	–	5
Marino-Tauhinu	1	–	–	–	5
Smith	1	–	–	–	5
Totals	***34***	***22***	***3***	***0***	***223***
Opposition scored	*21*	*16*	*3*	*0*	*146*

CHIEFS MANAWA 2023

	Hurricanes Poua	Blues	Matatū	Hurricanes Poua	Matatū	TOTALS
Willison	15	15	15	15	15	**5**
Paul	14	14	14	14	14	**5**
Daals	11	11	11	11	11	**5**
Nicholls	s	s	s	s	–	**4**
Carla Hohepa	13	13	13	13	13	**5**
Roach	s	s	s	s	–	**4**
Maaka	12	12	12	12	12	**5**
Tubic	10	10	10	10	10	**5**
Marino-Tauhinu	9	9	9	9	9	**5**
Hapi-Wise	s	–	s	s	–	**3**
Simon (capt)	8	8	8	8	8	**5**
Faleafaga	s	s	s	s	s	**5**
Fitzgerald	7	7	7	7	7	**5**
Smith	6	6	6	6	6	**5**
Makea	s	s	s	s	s	**5**
Bremner	5	5	5	5	5	**5**
Thwaites	4	4	4	4	4	**5**
Kalounivale	3	3	3	3	3	**5**
Mulu	–	s	–	–	–	**1**
Henwood	1	1	1	1	1	**5**
McGarvey	s	–	s	s	s	**4**
Green	s	–	–	–	–	**1**
Te Iringa	–	s	s	s	–	**3**
Connor	2	2	2	2	2	**5**
Houpapa-Barrett	s	s	s	s	–	**4**

CHIEFS MANAWA TEAM RECORD 2023

Played 5 ***Won 4*** ***Lost 1*** ***Points for 223*** ***Points against 146***

Date	*Opponent*	*Location*	*Score*	*Tries*	*Con*	*PG*	*DG*	*Referee*
February 25	Hurricanes Poua	Levin	53–21	Connor (3), Kalounivale, Simon, Bremner, Daals, Smith, Faleafaga	Willison (3), Tubic			Maggie Cogger-Orr
March 4	Blues	Albany	50–33	Paul (3), Daals (2), Connor, Houpapa-Barrett	Tubic (6)	Tubic		Natarsha Ganley
March 11	Matatū	Hamilton	46–38	Daals (2), Paul, Connor, Simon, Fitzgerald, Houpapa-Barrett	Tubic (3), Willison	Tubic		Maggie Cogger-Orr
March 19	Hurricanes Poua (semifinal)	Albany	43–21	Willison (2), Hohepa, Connor, Simon, Paul	Willison (5)	Tubic		Natarsha Ganley
March 25	Matatū (final)	Hamilton	31–33	Kalounivale, Marino-Tauhinu, Willison, Paul, Connor	Willison (3)			Nick Hogan

HURRICANES POUA

Postal address: Box 7201, Wellington
Telephone: (04) 389 0020
Email: mail@hurricanes.co.nz
Colours: Yellow and Black
Coach: Victoria Grant
Assistant coaches: Fusi Feaunati, Travis Church
Manager: Emma Paisley
Home grounds: Levin Domain; Sky Stadium

	Club	Date of Birth	Height	Weight	Hurricanes debut	Hurricanes games	Hurricanes points
S.C.R. (Saphire) Abraham	Auckland	03-07-01	1.68	89	2023	4	0
K.M. (Kahlia) Awa	Hawke's Bay	30-05-04	1.56	68	2023	1	0
S.J. (Shakira) Baker		04-01-92	1.72	92	2023	5	0
C.N. (Carys) Dallinger	Manawatu	03-04-00	1.64	70	2022	7	23
M.R. (Maddie) Feaunati	Wellington	18-05-02	1.75	83	2023	4	0
T.N.W. (Teilah) Ferguson	Hawke's Bay	30-12-99	1.63	75	2022	3	0
R.R. (Rhiarna) Ferris	Manawatu	27-06-92	1.78	80	2022	7	5
I. (Iritana) Hohaia	Taranaki	01-03-00	1.64	64	2022	6	0
B.L. (Baye) Jacob	Bay of Plenty	15-11-91	1.72	93	2023	1	0
A.A. (Ayesha) Leti-I'iga	Wellington	03-01-99	1.65	86	2022	6	20
M.M. (Milly) Mackey	Wellington	23-02-02	1.65	61	2023	4	0
C.A.M. (Crystal) Mayes	Manawatu	28-05-94	1.68	72	2022	7	0
K.R. (Krystal) Murray	Northland	16-06-93	1.72	97	2023	5	0
J.M.P. (Joanah) Ngan-Woo	Wellington	15-12-95	1.81	93	2022	7	15
Te K.R. (Te Kura) Ngata-Aerengamate	Wellington	21-10-91	1.64	96	2022	7	10
K.T. (Kaipo) Olsen-Baker	Manawatu	07-05-02	1.75	82	2022	7	5
J.S. (Jackie) Patea-Fereti	Wellington	30-09-86	1.80	85	2022	2	0
C (Cilia-Marie) Po'e-Tofaeono	Auckland	05-05-02	1.71	130	2023	5	0
R.E. (Rachael) Rakatau	Manawatu	07-10-90	1.72	80	2022	7	0
M.B.J. (Bernadette) Robertson	Wellington	04-06-93	1.70	80	2023	2	0
L.Y.J. (Layla) Sae	Manawatu	22-10-00	1.72	80	2022	7	5
A. (Aroha) Savage	Northland	11-03-90	1.78	87	2023	3	0
A. (Autumn-Rain) Stephens-Daly		06-08-96	1.64	69	2023	4	25
K.J. (Kahurangi) Sturmey	Manawatu	27-04-99	1.79	84	2022	3	0
V.S. (Victoria) Subritzky-Nafatali	Otago	02-12-91	1.72	99	2023	5	0
M.F. (Monica) Tagoai	Wellington	17-10-98	1.68	87	2022	6	10
S.J. (Sosoli) Talawadua	Manawatu	30-01-89	1.62	95	2023	5	0
L.C.S. (Cristo) Tofa	Auckland	11-12-87	1.69	105	2023	5	0
I.C. (Isabella) Waterman	Canterbury	12-05-00	1.82	81	2023	5	26

Stephens-Daly (Newcastle Knights) represented NZ League 2022.
Patea-Fereti was captain in first game.

INDIVIDUAL SCORING

	Tries	Con	PG	DG	Points
Waterman	1	6	3	–	26
Stephens-Daly	5	–	–	–	25
Dallinger	–	6	–	–	12
Leti-I'iga	2	–	–	–	10
Ngan-Woo	2	–	–	–	10
Ngata-Aerengamate	2	–	–	–	10
Tagoai	2	–	–	–	10
Ferris	1	–	–	–	5
Olsen-Baker	1	–	–	–	5
Sae	1	–	–	–	5
Totals	***17***	***12***	***3***	***0***	***118***
Opposition scored	*28*	*16*	*1*	*0*	*175*

HURRICANES POUA 2023

	Chiefs Manawa	Matatū	Blues	Chiefs Manawa	Blues	TOTALS
Waterman	15	15	s	15	15	**5**
Mayes	s	s	15	s	11	**5**
Robertson	14	–	–	11	–	**2**
Stephens-Daly	–	14	14	14	14	**4**
Ferguson	–	–	–	–	s	**1**
Leti-I'iga	11	11	11	13	–	**4**
Baker	13	13	13	12	13	**5**
Tagoai	12	s	s	–	12	**4**
Subritzky-Nafatali	s	12	12	10	10	**5**
Dallinger	10	10	10	s	s	**5**
Hohaia	9	9	9	–	9	**4**
Mackey	s	s	–	9	s	**4**
Awa	–	–	–	s	–	**1**
Olsen-Baker	s	8	8	8	s	**5**
Feaunati	–	s	s	s	s	**4**
Savage	–	–	s	s	8	**3**
Ferris	7	7	7	7	7	**5**
Sae	8	6	6	6	6	**5**
Sturmey	6	s	–	–	–	**2**
Palea-Fereti	5	–	–	–	–	**1**
Rakatau (capt)	s	5	5	5	5	**5**
Ngan-Woo	4	4	4	4	4	**5**
Tofa	3	s	s	s	s	**5**
Po'e-Tofaeono	s	3	3	3	3	**5**
Talawadua	s	s	s	s	s	**5**
Murray	1	1	1	1	1	**5**
Jacob	–	–	–	s	–	**1**
Ngata-Aerengamate	2	2	2	2	2	**5**
Abraham	s	s	s	–	s	**4**

HURRICANES POUA TEAM RECORD 2023

Played 5 Won 2 Lost 3 Points for 118 Points against 175

Date	*Opponent*	*Location*	*Score*	*Tries*	*Con*	*PG*	*DG*	*Referee*
February 25	Chiefs Manawa	Levin	21–53	Ngata-Aerengamate, Leti-I'iga, Ferris	Dallinger (3)			Maggie Cogger-Orr
March 4	Matatū	Christchurch	25–24	Stephens-Daly (2), Leti-I'iga, Ngan-Woo	Dallinger	Waterman		Michael Winter
March 11	Blues	Wellington	22–31	Stephens-Daly (2), Ngan-Woo	Dallinger (2)	Waterman		Nick Hogan
March 19	Chiefs Manawa (semifinal)	Albany	21–43	Ngata-Aerengamate, Olsen-Baker, Sae	Waterman (3)			Natarsha Ganley
March 25	Blues (for 3rd)	Hamilton	29–24	Tagoai (2), Stephens-Daly, Waterman	Waterman (3)	Waterman		Natarsha Ganley

MATATŪ

Postal address: Box 755, Christchurch
Telephone: (03) 379 8300
Email: info@crfu.co.nz
Colours: Teal and Blue
Coach: Blair Baxter
Assistant coaches: Whitney Hansen, Tony Christie, Dan Cron
Manager: Rebecca Archibald
Home ground: Nga Puna Wai Sports Hub

	Club	*Date of Birth*	*Height*	*Weight*	*Matatū debut*	*Matatū games*	*Matatū points*
A.J. (Alana) Bremner	Canterbury	10-02-97	1.78	83	2022	8	5
G.E. (Grace) Brooker	Canterbury	20-06-99	1.73	80	2023	5	10
G.R.R. (Georgia) Cormick	Otago	12-10-95	1.57	60	2023	4	0
C.B. (Cheyenne) Cunningham	Otago	09-11-99	1.71	73	–	0	0
N.M. (Natalie) Delamere	Bay of Plenty	09-11-96	1.71	85	2022	7	5
E.K. (Emma) Dermody	Canterbury	08-05-01	1.79	85	2023	4	0
E.O. (Ellis) Doyle	Otago	21-03-97	1.77	94	2023	1	0
A. (Amy) du Plessis	Canterbury	07-07-99	1.70	74	2022	8	0
Te R. (Te Rauoriwa) Gapper	Canterbury	01-02-92	1.64	67	2022	3	0
D.J.M. (Dianne) Hiini	Canterbury	15-09-92	1.63	68	2022	7	5
R.M.M. (Renee) Holmes	Waikato	21-12-99	1.70	76	2022	8	59
L.V.M. (Lucy) Jenkins	Canterbury	30-11-00	1.68	73	2022	8	10
R.C. (Rosie) Kelly	Canterbury	16-01-00	1.60	62	2022	8	5
A.G.N. (Atlanta) Lolohea	Canterbury	16-04-03	1.64	85	2023	2	0
P.E.A. (Phillipa) Love	Canterbury	08-04-90	1.73	100	2022	7	5
M.M. (Martha) Mataele	Canterbury	09-07-99	1.65	88	2022	7	15
L.J. (Leah) Miles	Otago	08-11-01	1.56	70	2023	1	0
S. (Sera) Naiqama	New South Wales	26-07-95	1.82	82	2023	3	0
C.L. (Cindy) Nelles	Canterbury	19-08-93	1.81	88	2023	5	0
M.A. Moomooga (Ashley) Palu	Canterbury	23-09-01	1.88	150	2022	7	0
M.J. (Marcelle) Parkes	Canterbury	09-09-97	1.77	86	2022	6	0
C.E. (Charntay) Poko	Canterbury	10-11-95	1.74	100	2023	4	0
G.R.A. (Georgia) Ponsonby	Canterbury	14-12-99	1.73	87	2022	8	0
K.L. (Kendra) Reynolds	Bay of Plenty	25-01-93	1.63	77	2022	7	15
C.R.A. (Cheyelle) Robins-Reti	Waikato	09-03-97	1.62	66	2023	5	20
A.M. (Amy) Rule	Canterbury	15-07-00	1.69	99	2022	8	10
G.L. (Grace) Steinmetz	Canterbury	16-01-98	1.68	73	2022	6	10
S.A. (Stephanie) Te Ohaere-Fox	Canterbury	06-04-85	1.65	105	2022	6	0

INDIVIDUAL SCORING

	Tries	Con	PG	DG	Points
Holmes	4	15	3	–	59
Robins-Reti	4	–	–	–	20
Reynolds	3	–	–	–	15
Brooker	2	–	–	–	10
Jenkins	2	–	–	–	10
Mataele	2	–	–	–	10
Bremner	1	–	–	–	5
Delamere	1	–	–	–	5
Hiini	1	–	–	–	5
Kelly	1	–	–	–	5
Rule	1	–	–	–	5
Steinmetz	1	–	–	–	5
Totals	***23***	***15***	***3***	***0***	***154***
Opposition scored	*24*	*12*	*4*	*0*	*156*

MATATŪ 2023

	Blues	Hurricanes Poua	Chiefs Manawa	Blues	Chiefs Manawa	TOTALS
Holmes	15	15	15	15	15	**5**
Robins-Reti	14	14	14	14	14	**5**
Mataele	11	11	–	11	11	**4**
Steinmetz	s	s	11	–	–	**3**
du Plessis	13	13	13	13	13	**5**
Poko	s	–	s	s	s	**4**
Brooker	12	12	12	12	12	**5**
Kelly	10	10	10	10	10	**5**
Hiini	9	9	9	9	9	**5**
Cormick	s	s	s	s	–	**4**
Parkes	8	8	8	s	s	**5**
Lolohea	–	–	s	–	s	**2**
Reynolds	7	7	7	7	7	**5**
Miles	s	–	–	–	–	**1**
Jenkins	6	6	6	6	6	**5**
Nelles	5	5	5	5	5	**5**
Bremner (capt)	4	4	4	8	8	**5**
Naiqama	s	s	–	s	–	**3**
Dermody	–	s	s	4	4	**4**
Rule	3	3	3	3	3	**5**
Palu	s	s	s	s	s	**5**
Love	1	1	1	1	1	**5**
Doyle	s	–	–	–	–	**1**
Te Ohaere-Fox	–	s	s	s	s	**4**
Ponsonby	2	2	2	2	2	**5**
Delamere	s	s	s	s	s	**5**

HURRICANES POUA TEAM RECORD 2023

Played 5 Won 3 Lost 2 Points for 154 Points against 156

Date	*Opponent*	*Location*	*Score*	*Tries*	*Con*	*PG*	*DG*	*Referee*
February 25	Blues	Dunedin	33–31	Reynolds, Bremner, Mataele, Hiini, Jenkins	Holmes (4)			Brendon Pickerill
March 4	Hurricanes Poua	Christchurch	24–25	Holmes (2), Reynolds, Brooker	Holmes (2)			Michael Winter
March 11	Chiefs Manawa	Hamilton	38–46	Robins-Reti, Kelly, Steinmetz, Delamere, Jenkins, Brooker	Holmes (4)			Maggie Cogger-Orr
March 19	Blues (semifinal)	Albany	26–23	Robins-Reti (3), Reynolds	Holmes (3)			Michael Winter
March 25	Chiefs Manawa (final)	Hamilton	33–31	Holmes (2), Rule, Mataele	Holmes (2)	Holmes (3)		Nick Hogan

RESULTS FROM 2023 FIRST-CLASS SEASON IN NEW ZEALAND

AND TEAMS OF NEW ZEALANDERS OVERSEAS

Key:	SRA	Super Rugby Aupiki
	PFS	Pacific Four Series
	WXV	Women's XV international competition (Tier 1)
	OC	O'Reilly Cup
	P	Farah Palmer Cup Premiership
	C	Farah Palmer Cup Championship
	qf	quarter-final
	sf	semi-final
	f	final
	ST	J.J. Stewart Trophy
	*	non first-class

January							
Sat/Sun	21/22	*	New Zealand HSBC Sevens				Hamilton
Fri-Sun	27-29	*	Australia HSBC Sevens				Sydney
February							
Sat	21	SRA	Chiefs Manawa	53	Hurricanes Poua	21	Levin
		SRA	Matatu	33	Blues	31	Dunedin
March							
Fri-Sun	3-5	*	Canada HSBC Sevens				Vancouver
Sat	4	SRA	Chiefs Manawa	50	Blues	33	Albany
		SRA	Hurricanes Poua	25	Matatu	24	Christchurch
Sat	11	SRA	Chiefs Manawa	46	Matatu	38	Hamilton
		SRA	Blues	31	Hurricanes Poua	22	Wellington
Sun	19	SRA sf	Matatu	26	Blues	23	Albany
		SRA sf	Chiefs Manawa	43	Hurricanes Poua	21	Albany
Sat	25	SRA 3/4	Hurricanes Poua	29	Blues	24	Hamilton
		SRA f	Matatu	33	Chiefs Manawa	31	Hamilton
Fri-Sun	31-2	*	Hong Kong HSBC Sevens				Hong Kong
May							
Fri-Sun	12-14	*	France HSBC Sevens				Toulouse
June							
Thu	29	PFS	New Zealand	50	Australia	0	Brisbane
July							
Sat	8	PFS	New Zealand	52	Canada	21	Ottawa
Fri	14	PFS	New Zealand	39	USA	17	Ottawa
Sat	15	P/ST	Canterbury	58	Wellington	29	Christchurch
		P	Hawke's Bay	32	Auckland	31	Hastings
		P	Waikato	50	Bay of Plenty	0	Rotorua
Sat	22	P	Waikato	27	Canterbury	24	Hamilton
		P	Counties Manukau	51	Bay of Plenty	5	Pukekohe

		C	Otago	34	Tasman	28	Nelson
Sun	25	P	Auckland	17	Wellington	15	Lower Hutt
		C	Manawatu	84	Taranaki	0	New Plymouth
		C	Northland	24	North Harbour	7	Takapuna
Sat	29	P/ST	Canterbury	42	Bay of Plenty	12	Christchurch
		P	Waikato	14	Hawke's Bay	10	Hastings
		C	Tasman	26	North Harbour	21	Nelson
		C	Otago	41	Taranaki	0	Oamaru
		C	Manawatu	34	Northland	28	Palmerston North
Sun	30	P	Counties Manukau	53	Wellington	20	Lower Hutt
August							
Fri	4	C	Tasman	61	Taranaki	10	New Plymouth
Sat	5	P	Auckland	61	Bay of Plenty	19	Auckland
		P	Waikato	13	Counties Manukau	5	Hamilton
		P	Northland	42	Otago	20	Whangarei
Sun	6	P	Hawke's Bay	33	Wellington	22	Lower Hutt
		C	Manawatu	57	North Harbour	9	Silverdale
Fri	11	P	Auckland	37	Counties Manukau	10	Pukekohe
Sat	12	P	Bay of Plenty	37	Wellington	7	Tauranga
		P	Canterbury	84	Hawke's Bay	14	Hastings
		C	Northland	67	Taranaki	0	Kaikohe
		C	Otago	37	North Harbour	12	Dunedin
Sun	13	C	Manawatu	46	Tasman	14	Palmerston North
Sat	19	P/ST	Canterbury	33	Counties Manukau	17	Christchurch
		C	Taranaki	31	North Harbour	19	Takapuna
		C	Northland	31	Tasman	6	Blenheim
		C	Manawatu	31	Otago	27	Dunedin
Sun	20	P	Hawke's Bay	35	Bay of Plenty	28	Whakatane
		P	Auckland	25	Waikato	15	Auckland
Sat	26	P	Canterbury	27	Auckland	24	Auckland
		P	Counties Manukau	63	Hawke's Bay	26	Pukekohe
		C qf	Otago	39	North Harbour	13	Dunedin
Sun	27	P	Waikato	31	Wellington	29	Hamilton
		C qf	Tasman	45	Taranaki	20	Nelson
September							
Sat	2	P sf	Auckland	29	Waikato	22	Hamilton
		C sf	Manawatu	73	Tasman	10	Palmerston North
		C sf	Northland	29	Otago	19	Whangarei
Sun	3	P sf	Canterbury	59	Hawke's Bay	29	Christchurch
Sat	9	P f	Auckland	39	Canterbury	27	Christchurch
Sun	10	C f	Northland	32	Manawatu	29	Palmerston North
Sat	23		Black Ferns XV	38	Manusina	12	Pukekohe
Sat	30	OC	New Zealand	43	Australia	3	Hamilton
October							
Fri	20	WXV	England	42	Australia	7	Wellington
Sat	21	WXV	Canada	42	Wales	22	Wellington
		WXV	France	18	New Zealand	17	Wellington
Fri	27	WXV	England	45	Canada	12	Dunedin
Sat	28	WXV	New Zealand	70	Wales	7	Dunedin

		WXV	Australia	29	France	20	Dunedin
November							
Fri	3	WXV	Australia	25	Wales	19	Auckland
Sat	4	WXV	Canada	29	France	22	Auckland
		WXV	England	33	New Zealand	12	Auckland
Fri-Sun	10-12	*	Oceania Sevens				Brisbane
December							
Sat/Sun	2/3	*	Dubai HSBC SVNS				Dubai
Sat/Sun	9/10	*	South Africa HSBC SVNS				Cape Town

WOMEN'S CLUB FINALS

Results of the 2023 senior club finals. Counties Manukau and North Harbour clubs participated in the Auckland competition.

Union	*Winner*		*Runner-up*	
Auckland	Ponsonby	27	College Rifles	22
Bay of Plenty	Mount Maunganui	17	Rangataua	10
Canterbury	Canterbury Univ	19	Christchurch	14
East Coast	Hikurangi	14	Tihirau Victory	7
Hawke's Bay	Tech OB	33	Clive	17
Manawatu	Kia Toa	27	OB Marist	20
Northland	Te Rarawa	44	OB Marist	36
Otago	Alhambra Union	29	Dunedin	24
Southland	Marist	43	Midlands	10
Taranaki	Southern	15	Clifton	12
Tasman	Marist[1]	38	Kahurangi	5
Waikato	Hamilton OB[2]	43	Melville	22
Wellington	Marist St Pat's	34	Petone	32
Whanganui	Marist	20	Kaierau	17

[1] also won in 2022 [2] also won in 2021 and 2022

FARAH PALMER CUP

Auckland won its first Premiership title since 2015 after determined efforts over Waikato in a semi-final and then defeating Canterbury in the final. There was little between Auckland, Waikato and Canterbury, the latter having scored 41 tries through the round-robin. Hawke's Bay impressed and justified promotion from the Championship division. Bay of Plenty, lacking an accurate goalkicker, and Wellington both had disappointing results.

Manawatu, having been relegated from the Premiership, was unbeaten in the round-robin and met Northland in the Championship final which was expected to be a grand contest. However, when Manawatu captain Selica Winiata was red-carded in the eighth minute her side missed her leadership and Northland took advantage and won 32–29.

Final standings after round robin:

								FOR					AGAINST				
	P	*W*	*D*	*L*	*B⁴*	*B⁷*	*Pts*	*T*	*C*	*PG*	*DG*	*Total*	*T*	*C*	*PG*	*DG*	*Total*
PREMIERSHIP																	
Canterbury	6	5	–	1	6	1	**27**	41	24	5	–	268	19	11	2	–	123
Waikato	6	5	–	1	3	–	**23**	21	12	7	–	150	14	7	3	–	93
Auckland	6	4	–	2	3	2	**21**	30	18	3	–	195	18	8	4	–	118
Hawke's Bay	6	3	–	3	4	1	**17**	21	18	3	–	150	39	19	3	–	242
Counties Manukau	6	3	–	3	3	–	**15**	34	13	1	–	199	20	8	6	–	134
Bay of Plenty	6	1	–	5	2	1	**7**	16	6	3	–	101	37	26	3	–	246
Wellington	6	–	–	6	2	2	**4**	20	8	2	–	122	36	20	3	–	229
TOTALS								***183***	***99***	***24***	***0***	***1185***	***183***	***99***	***24***	***0***	***1185***
CHAMPIONSHIP																	
Manawatu	5	5	–	–	5	0	**25**	39	24	3	–	252	11	4	5	–	78
Northland	5	4	–	1	5	1	**22**	30	18	2	–	192	8	6	5	–	67
Otago	5	3	–	2	4	1	**17**	26	10	3	–	159	17	11	2	–	113
Tasman	5	2	–	3	3	1	**12**	21	9	4	–	135	21	14	3	–	142
Taranaki	5	1	–	4	1	–	**5**	6	4	1	–	41	46	21	–	–	272
North Harbour	5	–	–	5	0	1	**1**	9	7	3	–	68	28	16	1	–	175
TOTALS								***131***	***72***	***16***	***0***	***847***	***131***	***72***	***16***	***0***	***847***

B⁴ bonus points for four or more tries in a match. *B⁷ bonus points for loss by seven or fewer points.*

PREMIERSHIP

Semi-finals:	Auckland 29, Waikato 22, at Hamilton;
	Canterbury 59, Hawke's Bay 29, at Christchurch.
Final:	Auckland 39, Canterbury 27, at Christchurch.

CHAMPIONSHIP

Quarter-finals:	Otago 39, North Harbour 13, at Dunedin;
	Tasman 45, Taranaki 20, at Nelson.
Semi-finals:	Manawatu 73, Tasman 10, at Palmerston North;
	Northland 29, Otago 19, at Whangarei.
Final:	Northland 32, Manawatu 29, at Palmerston North.

LEADING POINTS-SCORERS

Selica Winiata	Manawatu	86
Ruahei Demant	Auckland	68
Rosie Kelly	Canterbury	67
Krystal Murray	Northland	65
Angelica Mekemeke Vahai	Auckland	60

LEADING TRY-SCORERS

Angelica Mekemeke Vahai	Auckland	12
Jamie Church	Otago	11
Karla Wright-Akeli	Canterbury	9
Martha Mataele	Canterbury	8
Fiaali'i Solomona	Tasman	8

CAREER CHAMPIONSHIP RECORDS

Points

1085	Kendra Cocksedge (Canterbury)
629	Selica Winiata (Manawatu)
572	Emma Jensen (Waik/Auck/HB)
456	Chelsea Alley (Auck/Waik/NH)

Tries

78	Selica Winiata (Manawatu)
68	Kendra Cocksedge (Canterbury)
56	Ayesha Leti-I'iga (Wellington)
46	Fiao'o Faamausili (Auckland)

Games

139	Emma Jensen (Waik/Auck/HB)
117	Stephanie Te Ohaere-Fox (Canterbury)
114	Justine Lavea (Auckland/Counties Manukau)
106	Fiao'o Faamausili (Auckland)
101	Selica Winiata (Manawatu)
100	Kendra Cocksedge (Canterbury)

GRAND FINAL RESULTS

	Division I	Division II
1999	Auckland	
2000	Auckland	
2001	Auckland	
2002	Auckland	Auckland B
2003	Auckland	Hawke's Bay
2004	Auckland	Bay of Plenty
2005	Auckland	Manawatu
2006	Wellington	
2007	Auckland	
2008	Auckland	
2009	Auckland	
2011	Auckland	
2012	Auckland	
2013	Auckland	
2014	Auckland	
2015	Auckland	
2016	Counties Manukau	

	Premiership	Championship
2017	Canterbury	Bay of Plenty
2018	Canterbury	Wellington
2019	Canterbury	Otago
2020	Canterbury	
2021	Waikato	Manawatu
2022	Canterbury	Hawke's Bay
2023	Auckland	Northland

CHAMPIONSHIP RECORDS

BY THE TEAMS

	BEST PERFORMANCE 2023		RECORD	
Season Totals				
Most points	354	by Canterbury and Manawatu	449	by Wellington, 2018
Most tries	55	by Manawatu	69	by Wellington, 2018
Most conversions	35	by Manawatu	49	by Wellington, 2018
Most penalty goals	8	by Waikato	14	by Otago, 2013
Most dropped goals	0		2	by Manawatu, 2002; Auckland, 2012
Match Records				
Most points	84	by Canterbury v Hawke's Bay; by Manawatu v Taranaki	118	by Wellington v Taranaki, 2018
Most tries	14	by Manawatu v Taranaki	18	by Auckland v North Harbour, 1999; by Wellington v Taranaki, 2018
Most conversions	9	by Manawatu v Tasman (s-f)	14	by Wellington v Taranaki, 2018
Most penalty goals	3	on three occasions by three teams	6	by Auckland v Wellington, 2001
Most dropped goals	0		1	on 10 occasions
Biggest winning margin	84	by Manawatu v Taranaki (84–0)	118	by Wellington v Taranaki (118–0), 2018

BY THE PLAYERS

	BEST PERFORMANCE 2023		RECORD	
Season Totals				
Most points	86	Selica Winiata (Manawatu)	118	Amanda Rasch (Wellington), 2018
Most tries	12	Angelica Mekemeke Vahai	16	Mele Hufanga (Auckland), 2015
Most conversions	31	Selica Winiata (Manawatu)	46	Amanda Rasch (Wellington), 2018
Most penalty goals	6	Rosie Kelly (Canterbury)	12	Chelsea Alley (Waikato), 2013
Most dropped goals	0		2	Rebecca Hull (Manawatu), 2002; Bella Milo (Auckland), 2012
Match Totals				
Most points	23	Selica Winiata (Manawatu) v Tasman (s-f)	45	Kelly Brazier (Otago) v Hawke's Bay, 2012
Most tries	4	Te Whetumarama Nuku (Manawatu) v Taranaki	8	Annaleah Rush (Otago) v Hanan Shield Dist), 1999
Most conversions	9	Selica Winiata (Manawatu) v Tasman (s-f)	14	Amanda Rasch (Wellington) v Taranaki, 2018
Most penalty goals	3	by three players	6	Annaleah Rush (Auckland) v Wellington, 2001
Most dropped goals	0		1	by 8 players on 10 occasions

AUCKLAND STORM

2023 Status: Premiership
NPC participation: 1999–
Manager: Amy Courtney
Coach: Willie Walker
Assistant coaches: Mark Hooper, Anna Richards
Home ground: Colin Maiden Park; Eden Park (v Canterbury))
Colours: Blue and white

RECORDS

Most appearances	106	*Fiao'o Fa'amausili,* 1999–2018
Most points	452	*Emma Jensen, 2004–17*
Most tries	46	*Fiao'o Fa'amausili, 1999–2018*
Most points in a season	101	*Tammi Wilson, 1999;*
Most tries in a season	16	*Mele Hufanga, 2015*
Most conversions in a season	27	*Bella Milo, 2012* *Patricia Maliepo, 2019*
Most penalty goals in a season	9	*Emma Jensen, 2014*
Most dropped goals in a season	2	*Bella Milo, 2012*
Most points in a match	31	*Tammi Wilson v North Harbour, 1999*
Most tries in a match	4	*Louisa Wall v North Harbour, 1999;* *v Northland, 1999;* *Victoria Grant v Otago, 2008;* *Jade Le Pesq v Manawatu, 2012* *Mele Hufanga v Wellington, 2014;* *v Hawke's Bay, 2014;* *v Canterbury 2015;* *Natahlia Moors v Bay of Plenty, 2015*
Most conversions in a match	13	*Tammi Wilson v North Harbour, 1999*
Most penalty goals in a match	6	*Annaleah Rush v Wellington, 2001*
Highest team score	116	*v North Harbour, 1999*
Record victory (points ahead)	116	*116–0 v North Harbour, 1999*
Highest score conceded	45	*14–45 v Waikato, 2018;* *12–45 v Canterbury, 2019*
Record defeat (points behind)	36	5–41 v Waikato 2022

Auckland looked anything but champions at a freezing Hutt Recreation Ground with ten minutes remaining in their second-round fixture against Wellington. Down two players for yellow cards, and 15–10 on the scoreboard, somehow, they found a way to rally and win. Veteran lock Eloise Blackwell — back from her spell in the bin — rumbled over for the winning try. The try was converted by prop Sophie Fisher who'd missed a kick the previous week to win the game against Hawke's Bay.

It appeared the losses of Mele Hufanga (NRLW, Broncos), Tafito Lafaele (NRLW, Broncos), Jade Bowen (overseas), Saphire Abraham (North Harbour) Abby Lockhart (Police College), and Shannon Leota (overseas) would prove telling.

After the Wellington predicament, however, Auckland soared. They played an eye-catching brand of attacking, abrasive, and expansive rugby with youth flourishing around key Black Ferns.

Blackwell was in top form, much of her industry wasn't glamorous but her leadership was hugely influential. Her display in the final, with two tries, was world-class. She topped the tackle count throughout the season with 73.

Ruahei Demant added real authority and flair when she returned while Sylvia Brunt has more appearances for the Black Ferns than she has for Auckland. Black Ferns No.8 Liana Mikaele-Tu'u was suspended on August 20 for two weeks. She played the final like a caged animal set loose.

Maia Roos switched from lock to blindside in the decider to accommodate Maama Vaipulu whose size and athleticism were an undeniable asset.

The growing confidence of youth was the tale of Auckland's season. Chryss Viliko was named player of the year. The loosehead prop completely outplayed Black Ferns regular Pip Love in the final and usurped the 33-year-old into the end-of-year Tests. Fellow prop Sophie Fisher played 22 games for North Harbour, but most of them were at lock. Under the tutelage of Manu Samoa legend Census Johnston (60 tests), Fisher gained selection to the Blacks Ferns squad.

It was in the backs where Auckland's youth truly flourished: Angelica Mekemeke-Vahai scored a dozen tries and topped the team in metres run (844), defenders beaten (59), and clean breaks (15). It's scarcely believable that fullback Braxton Sorensen-McGee is only 16. She was named Auckland's most promising player.

Japanese international Nijiho Nagata, Jessica Dermody (Players' player of the year), and loosies Muizuho Kataoka and Elizabeth Moimoi (62 tackles) were unsung heroes. Halfback Melanie Puckett delivered a competition-leading 506 passes. She had been part of four FPC-winning Premierships with Canterbury.

After two defeats to Canterbury in finals, Anna Richards finally reached the FPC summit as a coach.

Higher honours went to:

New Zealand:	S. Brunt, R. Demant, S. Fisher, P. Maliepo, L. Mikaele-Tu'u, M. Roos, K. Vaha'akolo, C. Viliko
New Zealand Sevens:	T.M. Fitzpatrick, N.L.V. Guthrie, T.R. Ikenasio

AUCKLAND REPRESENTATIVES 2023

	Club	Date of Birth	Height	Debut for Union	Games for Union	Points for Union
E.S. (Eloise) Blackwell	Ponsonby	28-12-90	1.82	2009	82	90
F.T. (France) Bloomfield	College Rifles	17-07-98	1.65	2023	8	2
S.L. (Sylvia) Brunt	Ponsonby	01-01-04	1.68	2020	16	30
S.G.B. (Sam) Curtis	College Rifles	06-05-96	1.69	2021	10	10
D.R. (Ruahei) Demant	College Rifles	21-04-95	1.70	2013	59	304
A.P. (Princess) Elliot	College Rifles	04-09-01	1.67	2019	21	50
G. (Gillian) Fa'aumu	College Rifles	25-08-05	1.64	2023	7	0
D. (Danny-Elle) Fesolai	Ponsonby	06-10-06	1.66	2023	6	0
S.R. (Sophie) Fisher	Ponsonby	25-11-98	1.82	2021	20	21
S. (Sulieti) Halafihi	Ponsonby	24-06-98	1.67	2022	10	0
M. (Milahn) Ieremia	Ponsonby	01-05-06	1.63	2022	4	0
A.T. (Aldora) Itunu	Ponsonby	28-06-91	1.57	2012	57	75
M. (Mikaya) Kaipo	Ponsonby	09-02-06	1.75	2023	2	0
S. (Samaria) Kaipo	Ponsonby	25-03-04	1.70	2023	1	0
M. (Mizuho) Kataoka	Ponsonby	11-10-94	1.59	2023	8	5
P. (Patricia) Maliepo	Marist	13-03-03	1.75	2019	26	174
A. (Angelica) Mekemeke Vahai	Ponsonby	17-03-05	1.70	2022	11	65
L.E.T. (Liana) Mikaele-Tu'u	College Rifles	02-03-02	1.77	2020	16	15
E. (Elizabeth) Moimoi	College Rifles	13-10-02	1.66	2022	10	0
D.B. (Natahlia) Moors	Ponsonby	07-12-95	1.63	2015	35	95
N. (Nijiho) Nagata	Ponsonby	06-12-00	1.62	2023	6	5
D.L. (Daynah) Nankivell	Ponsonby	28-05-01	1.75	2019	26	20
Z. (Zahnia) Papalii	Ponsonby	05-04-05	1.65	2023	1	0
A. (Alakoka) Po'oi	Ponsonby	04-06-99	1.63	2018	20	0
M.C. (Mel) Puckett	College Rifles	07-06-99	1.60	2022	16	15
M.C.T. (Maia) Roos	College Rifles	27-07-01	1.79	2019	28	20
B. (Braxton) Sorensen-McGee	Auckland Girls' Grammar	26-10-06	1.70	2023	7	15
L.C.S. (Cristo) Tofa	Ponsonby	11-12-87	1.70	2015	30	25
C. (Cheyenne) Tuli-Fale	Ponsonby	27-11-99	1.77	2022	13	5
M. (Mataele) Vaea	Ponsonby	18-06-05	1.67	2023	2	0
K.S.C (Katelyn) Vaha'akolo	Ardmore Marist	18-04-00	1.63	2022	15	45
M. (Maama) Vaipulu	College Rifles	26-11-02	1.80	2021	18	10
C.Z.F. (Chryss) Viliko	Marist	25-12-00	1.68	2019	30	15

INDIVIDUAL SCORING

	Tries	Con	PG	DG	Points
Demant	3	19	5	–	68
Mekemeke Vahai	12	–	–	–	60
Blackwell	4	–	–	–	20
Puckett	3	–	–	–	15
Sorensen-McGee	3	–	–	–	15
Vaha'akolo	3	–	–	–	15
Brunt	2	–	–	–	10
Vaipulu	2	–	–	–	10
Viliko	2	–	–	–	10
Fisher	–	3	–	–	6
Elliot	1	–	–	–	5
Kataoka	1	–	–	–	5
Mikaele-Tu'u	1	–	–	–	5
Nagata	1	–	–	–	5
Roos	1	–	–	–	5
Tuli-Fale	1	–	–	–	5
Bloomfield	–	1	–	–	2
Maliepo	–	1	–	–	2
Totals	***40***	***24***	***5***	***0***	***263***
Opposition scored	*24*	*13*	*7*	*0*	*167*

AUCKLAND 2023

	Hawke's Bay	Wellington	Bay of Plenty	Counties Manukau	Waikato	Canterbury	Waikato	Canterbury	**TOTALS**
Elliot	15	s	s	–	–	–	–	–	**3**
Sorensen-McGee	–	s	15	15	15	15	15	15	**7**
Curtis	14	–	–	–	–	–	–	–	**1**
Vaha'akolo	–	14	14	14	14	14	14	14	**7**
Mekemeke Vahai	11	11	11	11	11	11	11	11	**8**
Ieremia	s	–	–	–	s	–	–	–	**2**
Papalii	–	s	–	–	–	–	–	–	**1**
Moors	13	15	–	s	13	–	–	–	**4**
Nankivell	s	13	s	13	12	13	13	s	**8**
Brunt	–	–	13	12	–	12	12	13	**5**
Bloomfield	12	12	12	s	s	s	s	s	**8**
Maliepo	–	–	–	–	–	–	s	12	**2**
Fa'aumu	10	10	s	s	s	–	s	s	**7**
Demant	–	–	10	10	10	10	10	10	**6**
Puckett	9	9	9	9	9	9	9	9	**8**
Moimoi	8	8	6	6	6	8	8	s	**8**
Mikaele-Tu'u	–	–	8	8	8	–	–	8	**4**
Kataoka	7	7	7	7	7	7	7	7	**8**
Vaea	6	6	–	–	–	–	–	–	**2**
Fesolai	s	s	s	s	s	s	–	–	**6**
Halafihi	–	–	s	–	–	s	s	s	**4**
S. Kaipo	–	–	–	–	–	–	s	–	**1**
Vaipulu	5	5	–	s	s	6	5	5	**7**
Roos	–	–	5	5	5	5	6	6	**6**
Blackwell (captain)	4	4	4	4	4	4	4	4	**8**
M. Kaipo	s	s	–	–	–	–	–	–	**2**
Itunu	3	3	s	s	s	s	s	s	**8**
Fisher	s	s	3	3	3	3	3	3	**8**
Viliko	1	1	1	1	1	1	1	1	**8**
Tuli-Fale	s	s	s	s	s	s	s	s	**8**
Tofa	2	–	–	–	–	–	s	s	**3**
Nagata	s	2	2	2	2	2	–	–	**6**
Po'oi	–	s	s	s	s	s	2	2	**7**

AUCKLAND TEAM RECORD 2023

Played 8 ***Won 6*** ***Lost 2*** ***Points for 263*** ***Points against 167***

Date	*Opponent*	*Location*	*Score*	*Tries*	*Con*	*PG*	*DG*	*Referee*
July 15	Hawke's Bay	Hastings	31–32	Puckett, Elliot, Mekemeke Vahai, Kataoka, Tuli-Fale	Fisher (2), Bloomfield			Tiana Anderson
July 23	Wellington	Lower Hutt	17–15	Vaha'akolo, Mekemeke Vahai, Blackwell	Fisher			Will Johnston
August 5	Bay of Plenty	Auckland	61–19	Mekemeke Vahai (3), Vaha'akolo, Sorensen-McGee, Puckett, Brunt, Blackwell, Demant	Demant (8)			Natarsha Ganley
August11	Counties Manukau	Pukekohe	37–10	Mekemeke Vahai (3), Nagata, Puckett, Vaha'akolo, Sorensen-McGee	Demant			Scott McKenzie
August 20	Waikato	Auckland	25–15	Sorensen-McGee, Mekemeke Vahai, Mikaele-Tu'u	Demant (2)	Demant (2)		Tiana Anderson
August 26	Canterbury	Auckland	24–27	Viliko (2), Brunt	Demant (3)	Demant		Brandon Roberts
September 2	Waikato (semifinal)	Hamilton	29–22	Vaipulu (2), Mekemeke Vahai, Demant	Demant (2), Maliepo	Demant		Tiana Anderson
September 9	Canterbury (final)	Christchurch	39–27	Mekemeke Vahai (2), Blackwell (2), Roos, Demant	Demant (3)	Demant		Natarsha Ganley

BAY OF PLENTY VOLCANIX

2023 Status: Premiership
NPC participation: 1999–2005, 2014–
Manager: Susan Karl
Coach: Kyle McLean
Assistant coaches: Jarvy Aoake, Brendon Phillips, Renee Woodman-Wickliffe
Home ground: Stadium, Rotorua; Domain, Tauranga; Rugby Park, Whakatane
Colours: Blue and gold

RECORDS

Most appearances	51	*Luka Connor, 2014–23*
		Kendra Reynolds, 2014–23
Most points	112	*Sapphire Williams 2016–23*
Most tries	21	*Luka Connor 2014–23*
Most points in a season	55	*Tamaku Paul, 1999*
Most tries in a season	11	*Tamaku Paul, 1999*
Most conversions in a season	12	*Puawai Hohepa, 2004*
Most penalty goals in a season	4	*Renee Wickliffe, 2018*
Most dropped goals in a season	1	*Puawai Hohepa, 2000*
Most points in a match	20	*Tamaku Paul v Counties Manukau, 1999*
		Mahina Paul v North Harbour 2021
Most tries in a match	4	*Tamaku Paul v Counties Manukau, 1999*
		Mahina Paul v North Harbour 2021
Most conversions in a match	7	*Kelly Brazier v North Harbour 2021*
Most penalty goals in a match	2	*Heidi Reader v Northland, 1999;*
		Puawai Hohepa v Waikato, 2000
		Kymbillie Raynes v North Harbour, 2016
		Renee Wickliffe v Auckland 2018
Highest team score	73	*v Taranaki, 2018*
		v Taranaki 2020
Record victory (points ahead)	73	*73–0 v Taranaki, 2018*
Highest score conceded	101	*v Auckland, 2015*
Record defeat (points behind)	101	*0–101 v Auckland, 2015*

Bay of Plenty avoided relegation with a resounding victory against Wellington but will otherwise reflect upon 2023 with some disappointment. They led four times against Hawke's Bay only to fade in the last ten minutes. Against Canterbury, the Volcanix only trailed 14–7 at halftime. It should be noted a third of the entire squad debuted this year and coach Renee Woodman-Wickliffe was forced out of retirement to cover in two matches.

Unquestionably the highlight was Black Ferns Kendra Reynolds and Luka Connor both celebrating their 50th cap in the Wellington victory. Both players have been involved with the Volcanix since their rebirth in 2014 and have done much to grow the game in the Bay of Plenty. Reynolds' influence on Bay of Plenty was so profound she was awarded player of the year. Fellow Black Ferns Kelsie Thwaites and Natalie Delamere can't have been far behind. Thwaites topped the tackle count with 66. Delamere often retreated from hooker to eight and performed with gusto.

There is real promise about Te Urupounamu McGarvey. Her carries are frequent and penetrating and her scrummaging, despite frequent rotation on the tighthead side, was solid. She was named forward of the year. Tighthead Kate Henwood only made two appearances but when the accountant and mother of two was picked for the Black Ferns she joked she was a "golden child." Her brother is former Chiefs, Hurricanes and Māori All Blacks loose forward Sam Henwood. Payton Takimoana was named club player of the year. She offered flair, stability, and utility to the Volcanix backline. A vital member of the successful Mount Maunganui club, Olive Watherston played every game. First five-eighth Sapphire Williams and halfback Kanyon Paul were sound inside backs, unfortunately, both missed the last game due to concussion after their heads clashed in a tackle against Wellington. Bay of Plenty struggled for size and continuity in midfield and again lacked a reliable goalkicker.

New Zealand Māori U18 halfback Kesha Church is brave and skilful and has a bright future.

Higher honours went to:

New Zealand:	L. Connor, K. Henwood, K. Reynolds
New Zealand Sevens:	M.G. Blyde, K.A. Brazier, M.A. Paul, R.I.R. Pouri-Lane, A.F. Saili, S.J.A.K. Waaka

BAY OF PLENTY REPRESENTATIVES 2023

	Club	Date of Birth	Height	Weight	Debut for Union	Games for Union	Points for Union
J.M. (Jayde) August	Ruatoki	13-11-91	1.78	125	2022	3	0
R.C. (Regan) Casey	Mt Maunganui	17-07-01	1.70	75	2023	5	0
H. (Hayley) Church	Poroporo	15-10-03	1.62	75	2023	1	0
K.J. (Kesha) Church	Poroporo	05-05-05	1.60	74	2023	3	5
L.H.J. (Luka) Connor	Opotiki	24-09-96	1.71	95	2014	51	105
N.M. (Natalie) Delamere	Mt Maunganui	09-11-96	1.71	82	2014	35	10
T.A. (Tynealle) Fitzgerald	Mt Maunganui	06-01-00	1.68	76	2018	31	5
H.A.N. (Hope) Garner	Rangataua	03-02-01	160	64	2020	2	0
K.K. (Kate) Henwood	Opotiki	28-01-89	1.75	110	2015	28	10
I.T.M.R. (Ihimana) Herewini	Poroporo	02-04-88	1.75	77	2023	2	0
S. (Sakura) Horike	Mt Maunganui	15-01-00	1.60	63	2023	6	0
B.L. (Baye) Jacob	Rangataua	15-11-91	1.75	95	2014	35	10
G.N. (Grace) Kahle	Rangataua	19-05-05	1.77	82	2023	1	0
A.A.M. (Azalleyah) Maaka	Rangataua	05-06-00	1.71	78	2019	20	5
T.R.T. (Te Urupounamu) McGarvey	Ruatoki	28-12-02	1.65	109	2021	14	25
E.P. (Emily) Magee	Mt Maunganui	11-03-90	1.72	68	2018	7	10
F.M. (Fredom) Marou	Poroporo	18-10-93	1.65	86	2023	3	0
M. (Moe) Nagaoka	Rangataua	07-06-99	1.63	67	2023	6	0
K.W. (Kiri) Ngawati	Rangataua	11-05-01	1.80	72	2022	7	5
G.T. (Grace) Parata-Stewart	Mt Maunganui	07-03-00	1.66	70	2021	15	10
K.T. (Kanyon) Paul	Rangataua	05-10-97	1.56	65	2021	11	7
A.A. (Alisi) Qalo-Wilson	Rangataua	14-09-90	1.67	95	2023	6	0
T.N. (Tania-Rose) Raharuhi	Rangataua	30-04-92	1.65	71	2017	24	5
K.R. (Kokako) Raki	Poroporo	25-07-05	1.64	80	2023	1	0
K.L. (Kendra) Reynolds	Poroporo	25-01-93	1.63	75	2014	51	20
K.S. ('Kiki') Tahere	Rangataua	30-10-00	1.71	70	2020	16	24
P.D. (Payton) Takimoana	Mt Maunganui	10-09-03	1.75	70	2021	14	25
R.E. (Ruby) Tawa	Rangataua	18-06-03	1.69	85	2020	6	0
K.P. (Kelsie) Thwaites (nee Wills)	Mt Maunganui	08-01-93	1.84	81	2019	27	10
O.A. (Olivia) Warlow	Mt Maunganui	11-04-99	1.76	94	2023	4	5
O.A. (Olive) Watherston	Mt Maunganui	17-05-04	1.68	69	2022	9	5
J.C. (Jessie) Wharekura	Waikite	29-12-99	1.84	92	2021	13	0
S.N.K. (Sapphire) Williams	Ruatoki	25-02-98	1.60	65	2016	37	96
A.K. (Amanda) Wilshier	Poroporo	17-12-92	1.80	118	2023	2	0
E.G. (Ella) Wisnewski	Mt Maunganui	14-11-03	1.62	61	2023	4	0
R.W.M. (Renee) Woodman-Wickliffe (nee Wickliffe)	Rangataua	30-05-87	1.63	68	2018	20	70

INDIVIDUAL SCORING

	Tries	Con	PG	DG	Points		Tries	Con	PG	DG	Points
McGarvey	4	–	–	–	20	Raharuhi	1	–	–	–	5
Williams	1	4	1	–	16	Parata-Stewart	1	–	–	–	5
Connor	3	–	–	–	15	Warlow	1	–	–	–	5
Takimoana	2	–	–	–	10	Tahere	–	–	1	–	3
Woodman-Wickliffe	–	2	1	–	7						
K. Church	1	–	–	–	5	***Totals***	***16***	***6***	***3***	***0***	***101***
Henwood	1	–	–	–	5						
Paul	1	–	–	–	5	*Opposition scored*	*37*	*26*	*3*	*0*	*246*

BAY OF PLENTY 2023	Waikato	Counties Manukau	Canterbury	Auckland	Wellington	Hawke's Bay	**TOTALS**
Takimoana	15	15	15	14	14	15	**6**
Woodman-Wickliffe	–	–	–	s	15	–	**2**
Watherston	14	14	s	11	11	11	**6**
Parata-Stewart	11	11	14	s	s	14	**6**
K. Church	s	–	11	–	–	s	**3**
Magee	s	s	–	–	–	–	**2**
Horike	12	13	13	13	s	s	**6**
Ngawati	–	s	s	s	13	13	**5**
Maaka	13	12	12	–	12	12	**5**
Williams	10	10	10	15	10	–	**5**
Tahere	–	–	–	10	–	10	**2**
Paul	9	9	9	9	9	–	**5**
Garner	s	–	–	–	–	–	**1**
Raki	–	s	–	–	–	–	**1**
Raharuhi	–	–	s	12	s	9	**4**
H. Church	–	–	–	–	–	s	**1**
Delamere	2	2	8	8	8	8	**6**
Fitzgerald	8	7	6	6	–	–	**4**
Reynolds (co-capt)	–	8	7	7	7	7	**5**
Nagaoka	7	6	s	s	6	6	**6**
Casey	6	5	s	s	s	–	**5**
Wisnewski	s	s	–	–	s	s	**4**
Tawa	–	s	–	–	s	s	**3**
Thwaites	5	–	5	5	5	5	**5**
Wharekura	4	4	4	4	4	4	**6**
Herewini	s	–	–	–	–	s	**2**
Kahle	–	–	s	–	–	–	**1**
Jacob	3	3	–	–	–	–	**2**
Qalo-Wilson	s	s	s	s	s	3	**6**
Henwood	–	–	3	–	3	–	**2**
Wilshier	–	–	–	3	s	–	**2**
McGarvey	1	1	1	1	1	1	**6**
Warlow	s	s	s	–	–	s	**4**
August	–	–	–	s	–	s	**2**
Connor (co-capt)	–	–	2	2	2	2	**4**
Marou	s	s	–	s	–	–	**3**

Thwaites was co-capt for game 1;
Delamere co-capt for games 1 and 2.

BAY OF PLENTY TEAM RECORD 2023

Played 6 **Won 1** **Lost 5** **Points for 101** **Points against 246**

Date	*Opponent*	*Location*	*Score*	*Tries*	*Con*	*PG*	*DG*	*Referee*
July 15	Waikato	Rotorua	0–50					Maggie Cogger-Orr
July 22	Counties Manukau	Pukekohe	5–51	Williams				Natarsha Ganley
July 29	Canterbury (ST)	Christchurch	12–42	McGarvey, Warlow	Williams			Dan Moore
August 5	Auckland	Auckland	19–61	Connor, McGarvey, Takimoana	Williams (2)			Natarsha Ganley
August 12	Wellington	Tauranga	37–7	Takimoana, Paul, Henwood, McGarvey, Raharuhi	Woodman-Wickliffe (2), Williams	Williams, Woodman-Wickliffe		Maggie Cogger-Orr
August 20	Hawke's Bay	Whakatane	28–35	Connor (2), McGarvey, Parata-Stewart, K. Church		Tahere		Todd Petrie

ST Stewart Trophy

CANTERBURY

2023 Status: Premiership
NPC participation: 1999–
Managers: Donna Gardiner, Heather Algar
Coach: Jimmy Sinclair
Assistant coaches: Solomona Paraki, Sidney Tauamiti
Home grounds: Rugby Park; Orangetheory Stadium (v Counties Manukau
Colours: Red and black

RECORDS

Most appearances	113	*Stephanie Te Ohaere-Fox, 2004–22*
Most points	1085	*Kendra Cocksedge, 2007–22*
Most tries	68	*Kendra Cocksedge, 2007–22*
Most points in a season	116	*Kendra Cocksedge, 2018*
Most tries in a season	10	*Kendra Cocksedge, 2018*
Most conversions in a season	27	*Kendra Cocksedge, 2018* *Kendra Cocksedge, 2019*
Most penalty goals in a season	11	*Kendra Cocksedge, 2014*
Most dropped goals in a season	1	*Charntay Poko, 2017;* *Kendra Cocksedge, 2019*
Most points in a match	30	*Kendra Cocksedge, v Taranaki, 2013* *v North Harbour, 2016*
Most tries in a match	4	*Stephanie Mortimer v Waikato, 2004;* *Kendra Cocksedge, v Taranaki, 2013* *v Auckland, 2018* *Martha Lolohea v Tasman 2020*
Most conversions in a match	8	*Kendra Cocksedge v Hawke's Bay, 2012*
Most penalty goals in a match	5	*Kendra Cocksedge v Auckland, 2009* *v Waikato, 2016*
Highest team score	92	*v Taranaki, 2013*
Record victory (points ahead)	84	*84–0 v Tasman, 2020*
Highest score conceded	70	*v Auckland, 2015*
Record defeat (points behind)	62	*8–70 v Auckland, 2015*

Canterbury looked odds on to repeat their 2022 Premiership success scoring more points and tries in 2023. Their only blemish in the round-robin, absent of several Black Ferns, was to Waikato in extra time in Hamilton. Canterbury hosted the final in picturesque conditions at Rugby Park and came unstuck against a more committed and vibrant Auckland. Down 27–13, shortly after halftime, centre Amy du Plessis cut loose to help tie the scores with 19 minutes remaining. The visitors finished strongest. Chelsea Bremner suffered defeat for the first time in 43 matches for Canterbury and conceded, "They played to their strengths and were very physical. There were momentum shifts, but they wanted it more which is not to say we didn't, but they were the better team on the day."

Tellingly veteran loosehead Pip Love was omitted from the Black Ferns for the end-of-year tests at the expense of Auckland's Chryss Viliko. Di Hiini is a capable halfback, but Canterbury missed the leadership, guile, and prodigious boot of Kendra Cocksedge when it most counted. Perhaps Canterbury's preparation for the final suffered after two straightforward victories in a month against Hawke's Bay. By contrast, Auckland had two arm wrestles against Waikato to reach the decider.

Canterbury fielded ten debutants two of whom cracked the Black Ferns XV. Flanker Holly Wratt-Groeneweg was spectacular scoring a hat-trick in a dozen minutes in the semi-final against Hawke's Bay and bursting 40 metres in a memorable solo effort against Counties Manukau a fortnight earlier.

Lock Laura Bayfield is a New Zealand Army captain at just 24. At the age of 20, she led a team of military engineers to build one of the longest Bailey bridges in New Zealand — across the Waiho River on the West Coast — after raging floodwaters washed away the lifeline between two key tourism communities. Accompanied by Lisa Dermody she was at the heart of a Canterbury pack that bettered most and boasted the best rolling maul in the competition. Karla Wright-Akeli is a youngster worth tracking, she scoring nine tries and often sought work, proving elusive. She represented Manusina.

The promotion of winger Martha Mataele to the Black Ferns was a rich reward for two outstanding seasons. Mataele has scored at least a single try in 12 of her last 15 appearances for Canterbury. She topped the following statistical categories for her team: Carries (96) metres gained (718), defenders beaten (42), clean breaks (17), and offloads (19). The versatile Hayley Hutana was a welcome addition from North Harbour. She covered three positions and occasionally kicked goals. Tireless openside Lucy Jenkins topped the tackle count with 83.

Canterbury retained the JJ Stewart Trophy. They've held the Ranfurly Shield of women's rugby for 19 successive defences stretching back to 2017. In the same span, they have won 52 out of 56 games.

Higher honours went to:

New Zealand:	A. Bremner, C. Bremner, G. Brooker, A. du Plessis, L. Jenkins, R. Kelly, P. Love, M. Mataele, G. Ponsonby, A. Rule, G. Steinmetz
New Zealand Sevens:	J.R. Miller

CANTERBURY REPRESENTATIVES 2023

	Club	Date of Birth	Height	Weight	Debut for Union	Games for Union	Points for Union
L.K. (Laura) Bayfield	Linwood	05-03-99	1.77	80	2023	8	5
A.J. (Alana) Bremner	Lincoln Univ	10-02-97	1.78	77	2014	64	85
C.J. (Chelsea) Bremner	Lincoln Univ	11-04-95	1.82	88	2016	44	20
G.E. (Grace) Brooker	HSOB	20-06-99	1.73	82	2017	41	130
R.M.E. (Rosanna) Buchanan-Brown	HSOB	17-05-00	1.70	73	2023	6	0
E.K. (Emma) Dermody	Lincoln Univ	08-05-01	1.79	85	2021	20	0
A. (Amy) du Plessis	Christchurch	07-07-99	1.69	74	2021	18	40
D.J.M. (Dianne) Hiini	Canterbury Univ	15-09-92	1.63	68	2012	45	20
S.M. (Sally-James) Houlahan	HSOB	17-12-03	1.76	86	2023	1	0
H.S. (Haley) Hutana	Lincoln Univ	21-11-95	1.71	66	2023	7	18
L.V.M. (Lucy) Jenkins	Christchurch	30-11-00	1.68	74	2017	51	45
R.C. (Rosie) Kelly	Christchurch	16-01-00	1.59	63	2017	25	125
H.C.R. (Hannah) King	Lincoln Univ	13-01-04	1.69	69	2022	10	15
A.G.N. (Atlanta) Lolohea	Christchurch	16-04-03	1.64	85	2022	13	10
P.E.A. (Phillipa) Love	Christchurch	08-04-90	1.73	100	2015	55	85
K.A. (Kelsyn) McCook	Canterbury Univ	23-05-03	1.65	65	2022	5	5
M.M. (Martha) Mataele	Christchurch	19-07-99	1.64	88	2021	29	145
A.F. (Amy) Milnes	HSOB	19-09-00	1.73	90	2020	18	0
S. (Stacey) Niao	Canterbury Univ	28-10-92	1.78	78	2021	21	5
W.G. (Winnie) Palamo	HSOB	01-03-04	1.75	70	2023	1	5
M.J. (Marcelle) Parkes	Canterbury Univ	09-09-97	1.77	86	2021	21	20
G.R.A. (Georgia) Ponsonby	Lincoln Univ	14-12-99	1.73	87	2018	39	45
N.J. (Nicole) Purdom	Canterbury Univ	20-08-96	1.65	87	2015	25	20
M.M. (Maddison) Robinson	Lincoln Univ	03-06-01	1.73	85	2023	8	0
A.M. (Amy) Rule	Lincoln Univ	15-07-00	1.69	96	2019	30	20
K.D. (Keighley) Simpson	Canterbury Univ	15-02-05	1.67	65	2023	2	5
T.C. (Tayla) Simpson	Canterbury Univ	16-10-00	1.68	79	2020	12	5
S.J. (Samantha) Spence	Canterbury Univ	30-08-00	1.76	71	2022	5	0
G.L. (Grace) Steinmetz	HSOB	16-01-98	1.68	74	2018	25	80
K.L.S. (Kalesi) Taga	Christchurch	12-06-93	1.76	85	2019	8	0
E.R. (Erana) Te Moananui	Canterbury Univ	29-07-99	1.67	110	2023	2	0
J.L. (Jamee) Te Moananui	Canterbury Univ	29-07-99	1.65	85	2023	2	0
I.C. (Isabella) Waterman	Christchurch	12-05-00	1.80	83	2020	23	70
H.J. (Holly) Wratt-Groeneweg	Canterbury Univ	19-08-03	1.73	74	2023	7	25
K. (Karla) Wright-Akeli	Lincoln Univ	15-09-01	1.65	57	2022	14	45

INDIVIDUAL SCORING

	Tries	*Con*	*PG*	*DG*	*Points*		*Tries*	*Con*	*PG*	*DG*	*Points*
Kelly	1	22	6	–	67	Lolohea	2	–	–	–	10
Wright-Akeli	9	–	–	–	45	Love	2	–	–	–	10
Mataele	8	–	–	–	40	Bayfield	1	–	–	–	5
Ponsonby	5	–	–	–	25	McCook	1	–	–	–	5
Wratt-Groeneweg	5	–	–	–	25	Palamo	1	–	–	–	5
Steinmetz	4	–	–	–	20	Rule	1	–	–	–	5
Hutana	2	4	–	–	18	K. Simpson	1	–	–	–	5
Brooker	3	–	–	–	15	Waterman	–	2	–	–	4
Parkes	3	–	–	–	15						
King	–	6	1	–	15	***Totals***	***53***	***34***	***7***	***0***	***354***
du Plessis	2	–	–	–	10						
Jenkins	2	–	–	–	10	*Opposition scored*	*30*	*16*	*3*	*0*	*191*

CANTERBURY 2023	Wellington	Waikato	Bay of Plenty	Hawke's Bay	Counties Manukau	Auckland	Hawke's Bay	Auckland	**TOTALS**
Hutana	15	15	s	s	14	11	15	–	**7**
Wright-Akeli	11	11	15	15	15	15	–	15	**7**
Palamo	14	–	–	–	–	–	–	–	**1**
Mataele	–	14	14	14	13	14	14	14	**7**
Steinmetz	–	–	11	11	11	–	11	11	**5**
McCook	13	–	–	s	–	–	–	s	**3**
du Plessis	–	–	13	13	–	13	13	13	**5**
Waterman	12	12	–	–	–	s	s	s	**5**
Brooker	–	13	12	12	12	–	12	12	**6**
T. Simpson	s	s	–	–	s	12	–	–	**4**
King	10	10	s	s	s	10	s	–	**7**
K. Simpson	s	s	–	–	–	–	–	–	**2**
Kelly	–	–	10	10	10	–	10	10	**5**
Hiini	9	9	9	9	9	9	–	9	**7**
Buchanan-Brown	s	s	s	–	s	s	9	–	**6**
Parkes	8	8	8	8	8	–	–	s	**6**
Spence	s	s	–	–	–	–	–	–	**2**
A. Bremner (captain)	–	–	6	6	6	8	8	8	**6**
Wratt-Groeneweg	7	7	–	s	s	7	7	7	**7**
Jenkins	–	–	7	7	7	6	6	6	**6**
Taga	6	6	–	s	–	–	–	–	**3**
Houlahan	s	–	–	–	–	–	–	–	**1**
Dermody	5	5	4	5	5	5	5	s	**8**
Niao	–	s	s	–	s	s	s	–	**5**
C. Bremner	–	–	5	–	–	–	s	5	**3**
Bayfield	4	4	s	4	4	4	4	4	**8**
Milnes	3	3	s	s	1	s	s	s	**8**
E. Te Moananui	s	–	–	–	s	–	–	–	**2**
Rule	–	–	3	3	3	3	3	3	**6**
Robinson	1	1	s	s	s	s	s	s	**8**
J. Te Moananui	s	s	–	–	–	–	–	–	**2**
Love	–	–	1	1	–	1	1	1	**5**
Lolohea	2	2	s	s	2	–	–	s	**6**
Purdom	s	–	–	–	–	–	s	–	**2**
Ponsonby	–	–	2	2	s	2	2	2	**6**

Parkes was captain in Bremner's absence.

CANTERBURY TEAM RECORD 2023

Played 8 Won 6 Lost 2 Points for 354 Points against 191

Date	*Opponent*	*Location*	*Score*	*Tries*	*Con*	*PG*	*DG*	*Referee*
July 15	Wellington (ST)	Christchurch	58–29	Parkes (2), Wright-Akeli (2), Lolohea (2), Palamo, Mataele, Hutana, K. Simpson	Hutana (4)			George Haswell
July 22	Waikato	Hamilton	24–27	Wright-Akeli (2), Bayfield, Mataele	Waterman (2)			Scott McKenzie
July 29	Bay of Plenty (ST)	Christchurch	42–12	Brooker (2), Wright-Akeli (2), Parkes, Hutana	Kelly (6)			Dan Moore
August 12	Hawke's Bay	Hastings	84–14	Steinmetz (3), Jenkins (2), Mataele (2), Ponsonby, Love, Wright-Akeli, McCook, Kelly, Brooker	Kelly (5), King (3)	Kelly		Ben Woolerton
August 19	Counties Manukau (ST)	Christchurch	33–17	Wratt-Groeneweg (2), Wright-Akeli, Ponsonby	Kelly (2)	Kelly (3)		Natarsha Ganley
August 26	Auckland	Auckland	27–24	Mataele (2), Ponsonby (2)	King (2)	King		Brandon Roberts
September 3	Hawke's Bay (semifinal)	Christchurch	59–29	Wratt-Groeneweg (3), Mataele (2), Love, Steinmetz, du Plessis, Rule	Kelly (6), King			Cassie Watt
September 9	Auckland (final)	Christchurch	27–39	Wright-Akeli, du Plessis, Ponsonby	Kelly (3)	Kelly (2)		Natarsha Ganley

ST Stewart Trophy

COUNTIES MANUKAU HEAT

2023 Status: Premiership
NPC participation: 1999–2005, 2013–
Manager: Letticia Jones
Coach: Saua Leaupepetele
Assistant coaches: Sione Sione, Davida Suasua
Home ground: Navigation Homes Stadium, Pukekohe
Colours: Red, white and black

RECORDS

Most appearances	62	*Arihiana Marino-Tauhinu, 2013–23*
Most points	397	*Hazel Tubic, 2005–23*
Most tries	27	*Te Kura Ngata-Aerengamate, 2013–21*
Most points in a season	78	*Hazel Tubic, 2017*
Most tries in a season	10	*Renee Wickliffe, 2015*
Most conversions in a season	28	*Hazel Tubic, 2017*
Most penalty goals in a season	8	*Hazel Tubic, 2013*
Most dropped goals in a season	0	
Most points in a match	27	*Hazel Tubic v Taranaki, 2013*
Most tries in a match	4	*Renee Wickliffe v Otago, 2015* *Portia Woodman v Wellington 2016* *Waikohika Flesher v North Harbour 2020*
Most conversions in a match	11	*Hazel Tubic v Taranaki, 2020*
Most penalty goals in a match	4	*Hazel Tubic v Auckland, 2013*
Highest team score	107	*v Taranaki 2020*
Record victory (points ahead)	104	*107–3 v Taranaki 2020*
Highest score conceded	65	*v Auckland B, 2005*
Record defeat (points behind)	65	*0–65 v Auckland B, 2005*

Counties Manukau were frustratingly inconsistent. They cracked a half-century against the two sides beneath them and demolished semi-final-bound Hawke's Bay in the last round. At their best, they were able to bully opponents with an imperious scrum and lineout. Mercurial first five-eighth Victoria Subritzky-Nafatali was mesmerising at times and there was an abundance of quality on the wings.

The diminutive Jaymie Kolose continued her strong Super Rugby Aupiki form. Mererangi Paul has grown enormously since becoming a Black Fern and there was great fanfare when Ruby Tui returned after a sabbatical in USA.

A lack of discipline, however, would prove to be a major Achilles heel. Auckland was the only opponent to clearly outplay the Heat. The worst of Counties ill-discipline occurred in Christchurch against Canterbury. In the opening quarter, Tui and Paul went within a whisker of scoring tries as Counties caused serious consternation. A dozen penalties in a row let Canterbury off the hook. Even in the 53–20 destruction of Wellington Vinita Teutau was unnecessarily sin-binned late in proceedings.

Subritzky-Nafatali was sumptuous in the Hawke's Bay thrashing. In addition to a try-saving tackle she directly created four tries with four precise kick-passes. It was a masterclass of superior skill as the kicks were short, long, high, and low. A third of all kicks she made during the season were regained by the Heat.

Black Ferns Arihiana Marino-Tauhinu and Hazel Tubic returned for the final game, their poise would have been helpful from the outset. There was a lot to like about the Counties forwards. Captain and hooker Grace Gago displayed the consistency that earned her a Black Ferns test cap. Harano Te Iringa converted from lock to tighthead with success and started every game. Rebecca Burch and Teutau weren't displaced at lock and loose forward Stacey Brown remains one of the most brutal tacklers in the competition.

Glory Aiono, Utumalalama Atonio, Ana Mamea, Cathy Leuta and Ti Taiasosi are Manusina internationals.

Higher honours went to:
New Zealand: G. Gago, A. Marino-Tauhinu, M. Paul, R. Tui

COUNTIES MANUKAU REPRESENTATIVES 2023

	Club	Date of Birth	Height	Weight	Debut for Union	Games for Union	Points for Union
N. (Ngatokotoru) Arakua	Manurewa	13-05-97	1.62	80	2020	10	10
U. (Utumalama) Atonio	Pukekohe	07-11-99	1.70	81	2017	19	15
S.J. (Stacey) Brown	Papakura	24-07-87	1.58	76	2014	54	10
R.M. (Rebecca) Burch	Pukekohe	22-10-95	1.78	80	2019	27	0
K. (Kataraina) Enosa-Taifau	Pukekohe	23-10-93	1.62	70	2021	12	15
J. (Joanna) Fanene Lolo	Manurewa	11-11-98	1.80	92	2022	10	5
W. (Waikohika) Flesher	Manurewa	09-11-95	1.58	65	2018	25	50
G.L.F. (Grace) Gago	Manurewa	05-05-98	1.65	80	2017	38	45
M. (Mau) Gautusa	Pukekohe	27-01-02	1.62	90	2023	1	0
A. (Alana) Grace	Manurewa	24-02-03	1.70	75	2023	1	0
E.F. (Emily) Kitson	Pukekohe	17-07-00	1.67	80	2017	37	57
J. (Jaymie) Kolose	Pukekohe	06-07-01	1.65	65	2022	12	45
C. (Cathy) Leuta	Manurewa	27-07-01	1.63	90	2020	13	10
A. (Anastasia) Mamea	Manurewa	23-11-01	1.77	93	2018	21	25
M. (Margaret) Manase	Pukekohe	24-12-04	1.80	88	2022	6	0
A.A.H. (Arihiana) Marino-Tauhinu	Manurewa	29-03-92	1.61	70	2013	62	240
P. (Paris) Mataroa	Manurewa	12-01-03	1.80	80	2022	12	0
M.K. (Mererangi) Paul	Pukekohe	29-10-98	1.71	77	2022	10	41
L. (Lana) Samuelu	Manurewa	17-09-99	1.80	100	2022	10	10
L. (Lauryn) Steed	Pukekohe	10-12-98	1.70	100	2016	26	25
V.S. (Victoria) Subritzky-Nafatali	Pukekohe	02-12-91	1.70	90	2015	22	67
T. (Ti) Tauasosi	Pukekohe	06-11-87	1.73	80	2021	14	10
H. (Harono) Te Iringa	Manurewa	01-05-96	1.83	100	2017	35	35
V.N. (Vinita) Teutau	Manurewa	08-07-01	1.80	83	2023	6	0
S. (Shyanne) Thompson	Pukekohe	12-11-97	1.72	75	2018	27	20
S. (Shonte) To'a	Pukekohe	03-02-99	1.74	75	2018	17	27
H.S. (Hazel) Tubic	Manurewa	31-12-90	1.65	70	2005	52	397
R.M. (Ruby) Tui	Pukekohe	13-12-91	1.70	69	2020	12	80
J. (Joy) Vaaga	Manurewa	24-09-05	1.80	100	2023	2	0
L. (Leititia) Vaka	Manurewa	01-08-03	1.56	80	2019	27	14
A.O.R.T.M. (Azania) Watene	Pukekohe	20-03-85	1.60	70	2014	34	20

INDIVIDUAL SCORING

	Tries	Con	PG	DG	Points		Tries	Con	PG	DG	Points
Kolose	6	–	–	–	30	Arakua	1	–	–	–	5
Paul	5	1	–	–	27	Atonio	1	–	–	–	5
To'a	2	6	1	–	25	Fanene-Lolo	1	–	–	–	5
Tui	4	–	–	–	20	Mamea	1	–	–	–	5
Enosa-Taifau	2	–	–	–	10	Tauasosi	1	–	–	–	5
Gago	2	–	–	–	10	Thompson	1	–	–	–	5
Kitson	2	–	–	–	10						
Leuta	2	–	–	–	10	***Totals***	***34***	***13***	***1***	***0***	***199***
Samuelu	2	–	–	–	10						
Vaka	1	2	–	–	9	*Opposition scored*	*20*	*8*	*6*	*0*	*134*
Tubic	–	4	–	–	8						

COUNTIES MANUKAU 2023

	Bay of Plenty	Wellington	Waikato	Auckland	Canterbury	Hawke's Bay	**TOTALS**
Paul	–	–	15	15	15	13	**4**
Tubic	–	–	–	–	–	15	**1**
Kolose	15	15	11	11	11	11	**6**
Flesher	14	11	–	–	–	–	**2**
Enosa-Taifau	s	14	–	–	s	–	**3**
Kitson	s	s	14	s	–	–	**4**
Tui	–	–	–	14	14	14	**3**
Grace	11	–	–	–	–	–	**1**
Thompson	13	13	13	13	13	s	**6**
To'a	12	12	12	12	s	s	**6**
Arakua	s	s	s	s	12	12	**6**
Subritzky-Nafatali	10	10	10	10	10	10	**6**
Vaka	9	9	9	9	9	s	**6**
Watene	s	s	–	s	s	–	**4**
Marino-Tauhinu	–	–	–	–	–	9	**1**
Fanene Lolo	8	–	8	8	8	8	**5**
Brown	7	7	7	7	7	–	**5**
Atonio	6	8	s	6	6	6	**6**
Manase	s	s	s	–	–	s	**4**
Mataroa	5	6	6	s	s	7	**6**
Tauasosi	–	s	–	s	s	s	**4**
Teutau	s	5	5	5	5	5	**6**
Burch	4	4	4	4	4	4	**6**
Te Iringa	3	3	3	3	3	3	**6**
Vaaga	–	s	–	–	–	s	**s**
Mamea	1	s	s	1	1	–	**5**
Samuelu	s	1	1	–	s	s	**5**
Steed	–	–	–	–	s	1	**2**
Leuta	2	2	–	s	s	–	**4**
Gago (captain)	s	s	2	2	2	2	**6**
Gautusa	–	–	–	–	–	s	**1**

Thompson was captain for games 1 and 2.

COUNTIES MANUKAU TEAM RECORD 2023

Played 6 **Won 3** **Lost 3** **Points for 199** **Points against 134**

Date	*Opponent*	*Location*	*Score*	*Tries*	*Con*	*PG*	*DG*	*Referee*
July 22	Bay of Plenty	Pukekohe	51–5	Kolose (3), To'a (2), Leuta (2), Enosa-Taifau, Samuelu	To'a (3)			Natarsha Ganley
July 30	Wellington	Lower Hutt	53–20	Kitson (2), Samuelu, Enosa-Taifau, Vaka, Gago, Mamea, Thompson	To'a (3), Vaka (2)	To'a		Taneika Uerata
August 5	Waikato	Hamilton	5–13	Kolose				Maggie Cogger-Orr
August 11	Auckland	Pukekohe	10–37	Kolose, Paul				Scott McKenzie
August 19	Canterbury (ST)	Christchurch	17–33	Tui (2), Paul	Paul			Natarsha Ganley
August 26	Hawke's Bay	Pukekohe	63–26	Paul (3), Tui (2), Fanene-Lolo, Gago, Kolose, Atonio, Arakua, Tauasosi	Tubic (4)			Will Johnston

ST Stewart Trophy

HAWKE'S BAY TUI

2023 Status: Premiership
NPC participation: 1999–2012, 2014–2015, 2017–
Manager: Sharlena Maui
Coaches: Sione Cherrington-Kite
Assistant coaches: Vaine Maui
Home ground: Hawke's Bay Regional Sports Park, Hastings
Colours: Black and white

RECORDS

Most appearances	75	*Chanel Atkin, 2001–19*
Most points	301	*Krysten Cottrell, 2015–23*
Most tries	21	*Deidre Hakopa, 1999–2009*
Most points in a season	82	*Krysten Cottrell, 2015–21*
Most tries in a season	9	*Deidre Hakopa, 2003*
Most conversions in a season	24	*Krysten Cottrell, 2015–21*
Most penalty goals in a season	8	*Nerina Hawkins, 2003;*
Most dropped goals in a season	0	
Most points in a match	30	*Krysten Cottrell v Tasman, 2021*
Most tries in a match	5	*Deidre Hakopa v Southland, 2003*
Most conversions in a match	10	*Krysten Cottrell v Tasman, 2021*
Most penalty goals in a match	5	*Kaitlin Bates v Otago, 2020*
Highest team score	100	*v Southland, 2003*
Record victory (points ahead)	95	*100–5 v Southland, 2003*
Highest score conceded	93	*v Auckland, 2014*
Record defeat (points behind)	93	*0–93 v Auckland, 2014*

Promoted to the Premiership, the Hawke's Bay Tui finished the season with their best FPC placing since 2006 when they reached the then single division semi-final. They defeated Auckland, Wellington and Bay of Plenty to confirm a semi-final berth with a game to spare and had led Waikato until conceding a late try with 14 players on the field after a yellow card. In the semi-final Canterbury, with their many Black Ferns, proved too good, but the Tui showed their character by winning the second half.

Missing from last year were Emma Jensen (retired), Amelia Pasikala (Sydney Roosters in the NRLW competition) and Harmony Kautai (Wellington).

In her second season, 19-year-old Kahlia Awa looks on-course to make the national team. The halfback, also a talented netballer, received the player of the year award. At first five-eighth the captain Krysten Cottrell was a key player with her decision making and excellent goalkicking, and passed 50 games for the Tui.

In the midfield Leilani Hakiwai was always aware of her support and a good distributor while Teilah Ferguson scored three tries against Wellington. Julie Ferguson appeared three times on the wing, being outside her daughter Teilah in two of those appearances.

Kathleen Brown was a very good loose forward and Gemma Woods, who is in sight of becoming the most capped Tui, was always in the thick of things. The scrum struggled at times, but always went better when tighthead prop Moomooga (Ashley) Palu played, and she was also hard to stop with ball in hand. Hooker Tamia Edwards played every minute of the campaign and scored three tries.

HAWKE'S BAY REPRESENTATIVES 2023

	Club	Date of Birth	Height	Weight	Debut for Union	Games for Union	Points for Union
N.A. (Nicolette) Adamson	Central HB	29-03-95	1.75	78	2019	19	55
D. (Denise) Aiolupotea	MAC	01-10-88	1.71	109	2020	10	10
T. (Tee) Aiolupotea	MAC	04-12-95	1.76	83	2023	6	10
K.M. (Kahlia) Awa	MAC	30-05-04	1.64	65	2022	10	20
M.S.D. (Michaela) Baker	Napier Tech OB	03-10-94	1.68	71	2019	30	65
R. (Raedeen) Blake	Clive	06-01-05	1.66	66	2023	6	5
K.M.T. (Kathleen) Brown	Napier Tech OB	22-04-93	1.68	86	2015	35	55
K.J. (Krysten) Cottrell	Napier Tech OB	17-02-92	1.66	68	2007	55	301
T.T. (Tamia) Edwards	MAC	14-05-98	1.65	83	2014	27	30
T.N. (Tuia) Edwards	Hastings RS	23-09-02	1.64	70	2021	12	5
J.M. (Julie) Ferguson	Napier Tech OB	31-07-77	1.67	67	2000	41	80
T.N.W. (Teilah) Ferguson	Napier Tech OB	30-12-99	1.67	84	2017	7	20
L.M. (Leilani) Hakiwai	Clive	25-10-04	1.66	68	2021	12	10
H.L. (Hope) Hakopa	Clive	20-05-94	1.68	70	2015	18	0
S. (Sharn) Heenan	Hastings RS	27-05-91	1.64	70	2023	3	0
T.P.L.A. (Tori) Iosefo	Hastings RS	23-08-95	1.76	115	2018	20	65
L.S. (Lara) Kendrick	MAC	20-02-97	1.70	85	2018	13	0
O.V. (Olioli) Mua	Hastings RS	19-10-02	1.70	93	2022	11	0
J.E.M.L. (Journey) Otene	MAC	03-06-99	1.89	102	2021	10	0
M.A. (Moomooga) Palu	Hastings RS	23-09-01	1.75	135	2019	19	45
L. (Laura) Parsons	Clive	10-10-97	1.76	110	2023	2	0
P.E.J. (Phoenix) Reid-Stowers	Hastings RS	10-01-06	1.66	81	2022	3	0
J.M. (Jaimee) Robin	Clive	14-09-87	1.68	96	2006	35	45
L. (Leykin) Rowlands	Clive	09-05-95	1.76	115	2023	6	0
L. (Luatola) Semisi	Hastings RS	26-10-04	1.69	84	2023	3	0
J. (Jade) Tangaere-Tuhua	Clive	26-02-89	1.63	71	2023	6	5
L.R.D. (Leah) Tuhi	Napier Tech OB	29-12-98	1.69	82	2021	20	10
K. (Kaya) Whaitiri-Dee	Clive	25-07-05	1.71	90	2023	1	0
T. (Tali) Wilson-Munday	Napier Tech OB	23-08-05	1.66	94	2023	5	0
G.L. (Gemma) Woods	Napier Tech OB	23-08-88	1.71	82	2005	72	80

INDIVIDUAL SCORING

	Tries	Con	PG	DG	Points		Tries	Con	PG	DG	Points
Cottrell	–	20	3	–	49	Blake	1	–	–	–	5
Adamson	4	–	–	–	20	Brown	1	–	–	–	5
T. Ferguson	4	–	–	–	20	Iosefo	1	–	–	–	5
Awa	3	–	–	–	15	Tangaere-Tuhua	1	–	–	–	5
Tamia Edwards	3	–	–	–	15	Tuhi	1	–	–	–	
D. Aiolupotea	2	–	–	–	10						
T. Aiolupotea	2	–	–	–	10	***Totals***	***26***	***20***	***3***	***0***	***179***
Robin	2	–	–	–	10						
Baker	1	–	–	–	5	*Opposition scored*	*48*	*26*	*3*	*0*	*301*

HAWKE'S BAY 2023	Auckland	Waikato	Wellington	Canterbury	Bay of Plenty	Counties Manukau	Canterbury	**TOTALS**
Baker	15	15	15	11	15	15	15	**7**
Heenan	s	–	s	15	–	–	–	**3**
T. Aiolupotea	14	14	–	14	11	11	11	**6**
Semisi	s	–	14	–	–	s	–	**3**
J. Ferguson	–	s	–	–	s	–	14	**3**
Adamson	11	11	11	s	14	14	s	**7**
T. Ferguson	13	13	13	13	–	–	13	**5**
Hakiwai	12	12	12	12	13	13	12	**7**
Robin	–	–	s	s	12	12	s	**5**
Cottrell (co-capt)	10	10	10	10	10	10	10	**7**
Awa	9	9	–	–	9	9	9	**5**
Blake	–	s	9	9	s	s	s	**6**
Brown	8	8	8	–	8	3	8	**6**
Hakopa	7	s	s	6	s	7	6	**7**
Tuhi	s	7	7	4	6	s	7	**7**
Rowlands	s	s	s	s	–	s	s	**6**
Woods	6	6	6	8	7	8	–	**6**
Wilson-Munday	–	–	s	s	s	s	s	**5**
Mua	5	5	5	5	5	6	5	**7**
Otene	4	4	4	s	4	4	s	**7**
Kendrick	–	–	–	s	s	5	4	**4**
Whaitiri-Dee	–	–	–	–	–	s	–	**1**
D. Aiolupotea (co-capt)	3	1	1	3	3	–	1	**6**
Iosefo	s	s	s	1	1	1	s	**7**
Tangaere-Tuhua	s	–	s	s	s	s	s	**6**
Palu	–	3	3	–	–	–	3	**3**
Parsons	1	–	–	s	–	–	–	**2**
Tamia Edwards	2	2	2	7	2	2	2	**7**
Tuia Edwards	s	s	s	2	–	–	–	**4**
Reid-Stowers	–	–	–	–	–	s	–	**1**

HAWKE'S BAY TEAM RECORD 2023

Played 7 Won 3 Lost 4 Points for 179 Points against 301

Date	Opponent	Location	Score	Tries	Con	PG	DG	Referee
July 15	Auckland	Hastings	32–31	Awa, T. Aiolupotea, T. Ferguson, Tuhi	Cottrell (3)	Cottrell (2)		Tiana Anderson
July 29	Waikato	Hastings	10–14	Brown	Cottrell	Cottrell		Tiana Anderson
August 6	Wellington	Lower Hutt	33–22	T. Ferguson (3), Blake, Robin	Cottrell (4)			Cassie Watt
August 12	Canterbury	Hastings	14–84	Adamson, Baker	Cottrell (2)			Ben Woolerton
August 20	Bay of Plenty	Whakatane	35–28	D. Aiolupotea (2), Awa, Iosefo, Tamia Edwards	Cottrell (5)			Todd Petrie
August 26	Counties Manukau	Pukekohe	26–63	Tamia Edwards, Adamson, Robin, Awa	Cottrell (3)			Will Johnston
September 3	Canterbury (semifinal)	Christchurch	29–59	Adamson (2), T. Aiolupotea, Tamia Edwards, Tangaere-Tuhua	Cottrell (2)			Cassie Watt

MANAWATU CYCLONES

2023 Status: Championship
NPC participation: 1999–
Manager: Chris Day
Coach: Chris Wilton
Assistant coach: Bryce Grant
Home ground: Central Energy Trust Arena
Colours: Green and white

RECORDS

Most appearances	102	*Selica Winiata, 2001–23*
Most points	629	*Selica Winiata, 2001–23*
Most tries	78	*Selica Winiata, 2001–23*
Most points in a season	110	*Selica Winiata, 2012*
Most tries in a season	14	*Selica Winiata, 2012*
Most conversions in a season	31	*Selica Winiata, 2023*
Most penalty goals in a season	11	*Carys Dallinger, 2022*
Most dropped goals in a season	2	*Rebecca Hull, 2002*
Most points in a match	38	*Selica Winiata v Waikato, 2012*
Most tries in a match	4	*Catherine Doyle v Poverty Bay-East Coast, 2002*
		Selica Winiata v Waikato, 2012
		Selica Winiata v Wellington, 2012
		Te Whetumarama Nuku v Taranaki 2023
Most conversions in a match	9	*Elizabeth Goulden v Hawke's Bay, 2017*
		Selica Winiata v Tasman, 2020
		Selica Winiata v Tasman (sf) 2023
Most penalty goals in a match	4	*Anika Tiplady v Bay of Plenty, 2004*
		Carys Dallinger v Waikato, 2022
Highest team score	88	*v Tasman, 2020*
Record victory (points ahead)	88	88–0 *v Tasman 2020*
Highest score conceded	70	*v Auckland, 2011*
Record defeat (points behind)	65	*5–70 v Auckland, 2011*

Relegated down to the Championship division the Cyclones enjoyed some big wins through the round-robin and only tested by Northland and Otago. At Dunedin the home team held a commanding 27–19 lead well into the second half and looked to be deserving winners but the Cyclones rallied to score two tries in the final three minutes to snatch a 31–27 victory. Hollyrae Mete's length of the field game-winning try was one of the best seen in the FPC. The game was Selica Winiata's 100th in the Cyclones shirt.

After demolishing Tasman in a semi-final Manawatu met Northland at Palmerston North in a game which was to be the last for veteran Selica Winiata, a career which had spanned 23 years. Her farewell appearance was to be, sadly, short-lived. The crowd were stunned when she was red-carded in the eighth minute for an accidental head clash. Her sudden departure appeared to take the sting out of the Cyclones performance and Northland dominated much of the play to lead 26–19 at halftime. In the later stages Manawatu appeared to be getting the better of a tiring Northland forward pack, Ruci Malanicagi scored in the 73rd minute, closing the gap to 32–29 with time remaining. Moments later the lights went out and the game delayed for 25 minutes. The momentum Manawatu had been gaining was lost as, during the long break, Northland recovered their energy and managed to hold on to win the Championship title. It was a disappointing finale for the Cyclones season who could have made a deserved return to the Premiership division for 2024. However, Northland could not be denied their win, Manawatu's loss was affected by the red card (should have been yellow) and lighting failure.

Former Horowhenua Kapiti Heartland coach Chris Wilton replaced Fusi Feaunati as head coach. Winiata captained the side, as she had done in 12 of her 21 years in the team and was the top points-scorer in the FPC with 86. Carys Dallinger had been the playmaker and goalkicker in recent years but, after the Aupiki Super series, she crossed the Tasman to play in Australia. Once the Wallaroos selectors learned of Dallinger's father being born in Australia they snapped her up and she played in the tests against the Black Ferns, the team she had been disappointed not to have been chosen for.

Midfielders Rangimarie Sturmey, Mete and wings Jashana Te Uawiri and Te Whetumarama Nuku were a dangerous backline unit on attack while the loose forward trio of Kaipo Olsen-Baker, Rhiarna Ferris and Layla Sae were very effective.

Sae gained selection in the Black Ferns squad while Rangimarie Sturmey and lock Sam Taylor were included in the Black Ferns XV squad. Olsen-Baker was a powerful number eight enjoying her busiest season and topped the FPC charts for most carries (113), most defenders beaten (69) and most offloads (26), proving to be the most damaging loose forward ball-carrier in the competition.

Higher honours went to:

New Zealand:	L. Sae
New Zealand Sevens:	S.L. Hirini

MANAWATU REPRESENTATIVES 2023

	Club	Date of Birth	Height	Weight	Debut for Union	Games for Union	Points for Union
M.T.H. (Mele) Bason	Kia Toa	21-08-06	1.68	75	2023	2	5
C. (Caitlin) Burt-Poloai	Kia Toa	01-11-98	1.68	98	2023	7	5
M. (Maia) Davis	Feilding OB Oroua	02-04-06	1.70	71	2023	6	9
R.R. (Rhiarna) Ferris	Feilding OB Oroua	27-06-92	1.78	74	2016	33	35
E.P.M.R. (Elinor-Plum) King	Feilding OB Oroua	06-01-04	1.72	71	2021	19	15
M. (Marilyn) Live	Kia Toa	13-01-95	1.61	112	2015	37	45
P. Te A.E. (Paige) Lush	Freyberg OB	28-07-99	1.61	60	2020	21	25
T.O. (Tra'est-Brelua) Mafile'o	Old Boys Marist	05-01-05	1.69	108	2023	6	0
R.L. (Ruci) Malanicagi	Kia Toa	25-07-96	1.67	67	2017	8	35
J. (Jayda) Maniapoto	Freyberg OB	21-06-06	1.64	67	2023	1	0
M.T.H. (Mia) Maraku	Feilding OB Oroua	02-10-04	1.68	78	2022	9	2
L.W. (Leiana) Marshall-Barton	Freyberg OB	03-07-04	1.65	62	2022	7	0
H.M. (Hollyrae) Mete	Kia Toa	24-12-03	1.72	82	2021	16	30
R.E. (Ruby-May) Ngaruhe	Bush	20-06-02	1.78	98	2022	8	0
T.M. (Te Whetumarama) Nuku	Freyberg OB	09-11-00	1.62	72	2023	5	30
K.T. (Kaipo) Olsen-Baker	Freyberg OB	07-05-02	1.76	93	2019	19	30
T.S. (Te Uarangi) Olsen-Baker	Freyberg OB	26-05-98	1.72	80	2023	7	5
R.E. (Rachael) Rakatau	Feilding OB Oroua	07-10-90	1.70	80	2018	31	10
L.Y.J. (Layla) Sae	Old Boys Marist	22-10-00	1.72	80	2019	27	40
K.J. (Kahurangi) Sturmey	Old Boys Marist	27-04-99	1.80	88	2019	28	25
R.T. (Rangimarie) Sturmey	Old Boys Marist	11-05-01	1.64	72	2019	25	60
S.J. (Sosoli) Talawadua	Whanganui Marist	30-01-89	1.64	108	2019	23	15
M. (Ngano) Tavake	Old Boys Marist	10-07-01	1.72	100	2019	25	0
S. (Samantha) Taylor	Freyberg OB	29-12-02	1.78	84	2023	6	0
J. (Jashana) Te Uawiri	Freyberg OB	24-06-02	1.72	80	2023	7	35
S.J. (Samantha) Tipene	Bush	20-03-91	1.65	77	2014	50	35
R.C. (Rebekah) Tufuga	Kia Toa	02-05-96	1.68	85	2014	26	15
B.C. (Brianna) Wallace	OB Marist	01-10-03	1.78	75	2023	1	0
C.M. (Corrineke) Windle	Bush	30-11-96	1.64	65	2015	30	20
S.C. (Selica) Winiata	Kia Toa	14-11-86	1.63	53	2001	102	629

INDIVIDUAL SCORING

	Tries	Con	PG	DG	Points		Tries	Con	PG	DG	Points
Winiata	3	31	3	–	86	Bason	1	–	–	–	5
Te Uawiri	7	–	–	–	35	Burt-Poloai	1	–	–	–	5
Nuku	6	–	–	–	30	King	1	–	–	–	5
Live	5	–	–	–	25	T. Olsen-Baker	1	–	–	–	5
K. Olsen-Baker	5	–	–	–	25	Rakatau	1	–	–	–	5
Mete	4	–	–	–	20	K. Sturmey	1	–	–	–	5
Sae	4	–	–	–	20	Talawadua	1	–	–	–	5
R. Sturmey	4	–	–	–	20	Maraku	–	1	–	–	2
Lush	3	–	–	–	15						
Malanicagi	3	–	–	–	15	***Totals***	***55***	***35***	***3***	***0***	***354***
Ferris	2	–	–	–	10						
Davis	1	2	–	–	9	*Opposition scored*	*16*	*8*	*8*	*0*	*120*
Windle	1	1	–	–	7						

MANAWATU 2023	Taranaki	Northland	North Harbour	Tasman	Otago	Tasman	Northland	**TOTALS**
Winiata (captain)	15	15	15	15	15	15	15	**7**
Nuku	14	14	14	–	–	14	14	**5**
Malanicagi	–	–	–	14	14	s	s	**4**
Te Uawiri	11	11	11	11	11	11	11	**7**
Marshall-Barton	s	s	s	–	–	s	–	**4**
Mete	13	13	s	13	13	13	13	**7**
Maniapoto	s	–	–	–	–	–	–	**1**
Tufuga	–	s	13	s	s	s	s	**6**
R. Sturmey	12	12	12	12	12	12	12	**7**
Maraku	10	10	10	s	10	–	–	**5**
Windle	s	–	–	10	–	10	10	**4**
Davis	9	s	s	s	s	–	s	**6**
Lush	–	9	9	9	9	9	9	**6**
K. Olsen-Baker	8	8	8	8	8	8	8	**7**
Ferris	7	7	7	7	7	–	–	**5**
King	s	s	s	–	s	7	7	**6**
Sae	6	6	6	6	6	6	6	**7**
Tipene	–	s	–	–	–	–	–	**1**
Bason	–	–	–	s	–	s	–	**2**
Rakatau	5	5	5	5	5	5	5	**7**
K. Sturmey	4	4	4	4	4	s	s	**7**
Taylor	s	s	s	–	s	4	4	**6**
Wallace	–	–	–	s	–	–	–	**1**
Ngaruhe	s	3	s	–	–	s	s	**5**
Burt-Poloai	s	s	3	s	s	s	s	**7**
Live	–	–	s	3	3	3	3	**5**
Mafileó	3	1	1	1	1	–	1	**6**
Tavake	1	2	–	s	s	s	–	**5**
Talawadua	2	–	s	2	2	1	2	**6**
T. Olsen-Baker	s	s	2	s	s	2	s	**7**

MANAWATU TEAM RECORD 2023 — **Played 7** **Won 6** **Lost 1** **Points for 354** **Points against 120**

Date	*Opponent*	*Location*	*Score*	*Tries*	*Con*	*PG*	*DG*	*Referee*
July 23	Taranaki	New Plymouth	84–0	Nuku (4), K. Olsen-Baker (3), Ferris (2), Mete (2), Te Uawiri (2), Sae	Winiata (6), Maraku			Ben Woolerton
July 29	Northland	Palmerston North	34–28	R. Sturmey, Te Uawiri, K. Olsen-Baker, King	Winiata (4)	Winiata (2)		Jack Sargentina
August 6	North Harbour	Silverdale	57–9	Sae (2), R. Sturmey, Te Uawiri, Rakatau, T. Olsen-Baker, K. Olsen-Baker, K. Sturmey, Winiata	Winiata (5), Davis			Todd Petrie
August 13	Tasman	Palmerston North	46–14	Lush (2), Malanicagi (2), Winiata, Live, Windle	Winiata (4)	Winiata		Georgia Mason
August 19	Otago	Dunedin	31–27	Mete (2), Te Uawiri, Live, Davis	Winiata (3)			Taneika Uerata
September 2	Tasman (semifinal)	Palmerston North	73–10	Te Uawiri (2), R. Sturmey (2), Live, Sae, Winiata, Talawadua, Bason, Burt-Poloai, Lush	Winiata (9)			Will Johnston
September 10	Northland (final)	Palmerston North	29–32	Nuku (2), Live (2), Malanicagi	Windle, Davis			Maggie Cogger-Orr

NORTH HARBOUR HIBISCUS

2023 Status: Championship
NPC participation: 1999–2005, 2016–
Manager: Rebecca Stanaway
Coach: Bill Wigglesworth
Assistant coach: Lewis McClintock, Dean Watkins
Home ground: Onewa Domain, Takapuna; War Memorial Park, Silverdale
Colours: White, black and cardinal

RECORDS

Most appearances	31	*Olivia Ward-Duin 2016–21*
Most points	101	*Hayley Hutana, 2020–22*
Most tries	10	*Pia Tapsell, 2016–20*
Most points in a season	64	*Hayley Hutana, 2022*
Most tries in a season	5	*Caitlyn Cox, 2017* *Simone Small, 2019*
Most conversions in a season	14	*Sophie Fisher, 2018*
Most penalty goals in a season	9	*Hayley Hutana, 2022*
Most dropped goals in a season	0	
Most points in a match	24	*Sophie Fisher v Taranaki, 2018*
Most tries in a match	3	*Simone Small v Taranaki, 2019*
Most conversions in a match	7	*Sophie Fisher v Taranaki, 2018*
Most penalty goals in a match	4	*Hayley Hutana v Tasman, 2022*
Highest team score	59	*v Taranaki, 2018*
Record victory (points ahead)	59	*59–0 v Taranaki, 2018*
Highest score conceded	116	*v Auckland, 1999*
Record defeat (points behind)	116	*0–116 v Auckland, 1999*

North Harbour suffered a winless season for the first time since 2020. In Nelson, against Tasman, however, the Hibiscus looked certain to secure a victory. Lucia Bolton snatched an intercept and dashed 65 metres just before halftime to make it 21–0. The match turned in the 47th minute when centre Moana Courtney was yellow carded for a high tackle. Tasman lifted their intensity and scored two tries to close the gap to 21–12. The momentum had shifted permanently, and the Hibiscus conceded a try with the last play of the game to lose.

North Harbour should have had Taranaki's measure but by that point of the season, it wasn't a happy camp. Moana Courtney scored a third of North Harbour's tries, the centre featuring in every game and her try against Otago bumping off two defenders was a real beauty.

Olivia Waldron (27 games for Otago), Grace Freeman (one game for Auckland) and Bolton (Hong Kong sevens & netball) were mainstays of a backline that was settled but struggled collectively to prise open opposition defence. Freeman (67 carries and 27 defenders beaten) and Bolton (5 clean breaks) were statistically the most effective players.

The loose forward trio was hard-working and unchanged for every fixture. Danielle Mellow topped the tackle count with 79. Tenaija Fletcher was industrious and added an option in the lineout.

North Harbour struggled in the lineout and prop was a revolving door. Hooker Katelyn Hilton did last all six games. Mary Auvele and Olalini Tafoulua were picked for Manusina.

NORTH HARBOUR REPRESENTATIVES 2023

	Club	Date of Birth	Height	Weight	Debut for Union	Games for Union	Points for Union
M.S. (Mary) Auvele	Silverdale	28-11-99	1.74	97	2022	13	0
H.D. (Hailey) Beale	North Shore	30-03-02	1.60	59	2019	25	5
L.M.P. (Lucia) Bolton	Silverdale	04-06-01	1.70	68	2022	13	5
M.G.M (Moana) Courtenay	Silverdale	03-03-00	1.72	70	2021	8	15
J.C.M. (Jessie) Courtenay-Malupo	Silverdale	24-05-94	1.74	68	2021	10	10
S.G.B. (Sam) Curtis		06-05-96	1.68	65	2023	4	0
T.V. (Tenaija) Fletcher	North Shore	24-06-02	1.78	75	2019	29	5
G.A. (Grace) Freeman	Glenfield	11-12-00	1.73	72	2023	6	46
C. (Claudia) Hanham	North Shore	03-03-94	1.70	66	2023	1	0
K.A. (Katelyn) Hilton	Silverdale	25-04-99	1.65	87	2018	28	10
M.K.H. (Manutala'aho) Huni-Po'ese	North Shore	20-06-93	1.79	97	2020	13	5
A.M. (Ava-Lee) Jericevich	North Shore	19-04-04	1.61	70	2021	11	10
A. (Armani) Lam	North Shore	17-12-00	1.79	97	2023	2	0
L.F.L. (Letelemalanuola) Lavea	North Shore	22-07-02	1.76	98	2022	12	0
M.J. (Madisson) Mata'afa	Silverdale	19-11-03	1.76	86	2021	14	0
A. (Ashlee) Matapo	Glenfield	20-09-06	1.74	82	2023	4	0
D.B. (Danielle) Mellow	North Shore	01-08-01	1.67	72	2020	21	5
C.M. (Ciara) O'Connor	North Shore	16-12-88	1.64	107	2021	13	15
F. (Fa'asua) Pepe	North Shore	26-02-04	1.70	90	2023	2	0
L.L. (Lovely) Pulotu	Silverdale	08-09-01	1.63	68	2022	13	0
A. (Avalon) Strang	North Shore	07-10-04	1.70	76	2023	2	0
O.M. (Olalini) Tafoulua	Silverdale	08-08-95	1.57	74	2023	3	0
M. (Meriana) Te Nana	North Shore	24-04-91	1.68	98	2023	4	0
A.C.J. (Alanis) Toia-Tigafua	Glenfield	15-10-97	1.76	80	2023	5	0
L.M. (Latisha) Trigwell-Achmad	North Shore	23-05-02	1.70	72	2020	7	0
C. (Clementine) Varea	Glenfield	24-03-90	1.76	115	2020	10	20
O.N. (Olivia) Waldron	North Shore	11-05-95	1.67	71	2020	19	0
H.S. (Holly) Williams	North Shore	21-06-04	1.68	74	2022	7	0
M.U.N. (Melita) Williams	Silverdale	11-02-94	1.73	116	2021	15	5
J.C. (Jade) Wong	North Shore	09-07-99	1.83	81	2021	15	15
M.J.M. (Margaret) Wye	North Shore	12-08-95	1.78	75	2022	10	0

INDIVIDUAL SCORING

	Tries	Con	PG	DG	Points
Freeman	3	8	5	–	46
Courtenay	3	–	–	–	15
Bolton	1	–	–	–	5
Mellow	1	–	–	–	5
Varea	1	–	–	–	5
Wong	1	–	–	–	5
Totals	***10***	***8***	***5***	***0***	***81***
Opposition scored	*35*	*18*	*1*	*0*	*214*

NORTH HARBOUR 2023	Northland	Tasman	Manawatu	Otago	Taranaki	Otago	**TOTALS**
Waldron (co-capt)	15	15	15	12	15	12	**6**
Curtis	–	s	14	15	–	15	**4**
Jericevich	–	14	s	14	14	14	**5**
Bolton	11	11	11	11	11	11	**6**
Trigwell-Achmad	s	–	–	–	s	s	**3**
Courtenay	14	13	s	s	13	13	**6**
Courtenay-Malupo	s	s	13	13	12	s	**6**
H. Williams	13	12	12	–	–	–	**3**
Pepe	12	–	–	s	–	–	**2**
Freeman	10	10	10	10	10	10	**6**
Beale	9	9	s	–	–	–	**3**
Pulotu	s	s	9	9	9	9	**6**
Hanham	–	–	–	s	–	–	**1**
Fletcher (co-capt)	8	8	8	8	8	8	**6**
Matapo	–	s	s	s	–	s	**4**
Mellow	7	7	7	7	7	7	**6**
Strang	–	–	s	–	–	s	**2**
Mataafa	s	6	6	6	6	6	**6**
Tafoulua	–	s	s	–	s	–	**3**
Toia-Tigafua	5	5	5	4	–	4	**5**
Wong	4	4	–	5	5	5	**5**
Wye	6	–	4	s	4	–	**4**
Huni-Po'ese	s	–	–	–	s	–	**2**
Lam	–	s	–	–	–	s	**2**
Te Nana	3	3	–	–	1	1	**4**
Varea	s	1	3	3	–	s	**5**
O'Connor	–	–	–	s	3	3	**3**
Lavea	1	–	1	1	s	s	**5**
M. Williams	s	s	s	s	s	–	**5**
Hilton	2	2	2	2	2	2	**6**
Auvele	s	s	s	s	s	s	**6**

NORTH HARBOUR TEAM RECORD 2023

Played 6 **Won 0** **Lost 6** **Points for 81** **Points against 214**

Date	Opponent	Location	Score	Tries	Con	PG	DG	Referee
July 23	Northland	Takapuna	7–24	Wong	Freeman			Maggie Cogger-Orr
July 29	Tasman	Nelson	21–26	Varea, Mellow, Bolton	Freeman (3)			Erin Doherty
August 6	Manawatu	Silverdale	9–57			Freeman (3)		Todd Petrie
August 12	Otago	Dunedin	12–37	Freeman (2)	Freeman			Cassie Watt
August 19	Taranaki	Takapuna	19–31	Courtenay (2), Freeman	Freeman (2)			Ben Brownlie
August 26	Otago (quarterfinal)	Dunedin	13–39	Courtenay	Freeman	Freeman (2)		Cassie Watt

NORTHLAND KAURI

2023 Status: Championship
NPC participation: 1999–2005, 2019–
Manager: Hannah Shalders
Coach: Rawinia Everitt
Assistant coach: Marcelle Kaipo
Home ground: Semenoff Stadium, Whangarei; Kaikohe RFC, Kaikohe
Colours: Cambridge blue

RECORDS

Most appearances	29	*Krystal Murray 2019–23*
		Tyler Nankivell 2019–23
Most points	216	*Krystal Murray, 2019–23*
Most tries	19	*Krystal Murray, 2019–23*
Most points in a season	65	*Krystal Murray, 2023*
Most tries in a season	9	*Portia Woodman, 2020*
Most conversions in a season	14	*Krystal Murray, 2019*
Most penalty goals in a season	5	*Krystal Murray, 2019*
Most dropped goals in a season	0	
Most points in a match	30	*Portia Woodman v Taranaki, 2020*
Most tries in a match	6	*Portia Woodman v Taranaki, 2020*
Most conversions in a match	6	*Pohutukawa Kakara v Otago 2023*
Most penalty goals in a match	2	*by six players*
Highest team score	77	*v Taranaki, 2020*
Record victory (points ahead)	74	*77–3 v Taranaki, 2020*
Highest score conceded	65	*v Auckland, 2000*
Record defeat (points behind)	58	*7–65 v Auckland, 2000*

It's not unusual for some Northland players to commute two hours in one direction for training. With that in mind, it was a phenomenal achievement for the Kauri to win their maiden Championship. An enterprising approach, where it was sometimes difficult to distinguish the difference between backs and forwards, made their success all the sweeter.

In June 2020 lock Charmaine Smith was forced to retire with an unusual neck (disc) injury which, left unattended, could have caused her permanent pain. She was in outstanding form and the police sergeant was recalled to the Black Ferns after a four-year hiatus.

Back of the year, Aroha Savage is typically a loose forward who appeared in five positions. Her cross-kick to set up the first try of the final against Manawatū was as good as any Beauden Barrett did for the All Blacks. Savage ran 512 metres, made 10 clean breaks, beat 48 defenders, and topped the tackle count with 87. Black Ferns prop Krystal Murray and player of the year Te Kura Ngata-Aerengamate perhaps best illustrated why Northland was such a threat. Between them, they scored a dozen tries and delivered 40 offloads. Northland had the size to bully and maul opponents and that coupled with improving fitness was a toxic recipe. No.8 Hikitia Wikaira was a trojan with an immense 111 carries, second only to Manawatu's Kaipo Olsen-Baker (113). Lock Corina Blair was acknowledged as the most improved player. Her unassuming toil was the ideal foil for the flair of her forward colleagues.

The backline took time to take shape but by the end of the season they had a more than competent appearance. Halfback Holli O'Sullivan cleared promptly and Harmony Covacich-Baanders was the glue in midfield. The back three of Ocean Tierney, Kerri Johnson and Tara Turner took some stopping.

In the Championship final at Palmerston North, Northland were leading 32–29 and hanging on grimly against determined Manawatu attacks. Suddenly, in the 74th minute, the lights failed, plunging the ground into darkness. The lengthy 25-minute break gave Northland the time to re-energise and hold out Manawatu's desperate efforts to score during the final six minutes of play.

Higher honours went to:

New Zealand:	K. Murray, C. Smith
New Zealand Sevens:	T.B. Nathan-Wong, P.L. Woodman-Wickliffe

NORTHLAND REPRESENTATIVES 2023

	Club	Date of Birth	Height	Debut for Union	Games for Union	Points for Union
C.K. (Corina) Blair	Te Rarawa	06-12-04	1.72	2022	8	5
K. (Kredence) Brown	Te Rarawa	23-11-95	1.68	2021	8	0
R. (Ruihana) Clarke	Hora Hora	21-12-92	1.73	2023	2	5
L.R. (Lara) Cooper	Kaikohe	05-11-89	1.75	2021	16	20
H.K. (Harmony) Covacich-Baanders	Hora Hora	05-10-04	1.63	2022	14	15
I. (Ilaise) Fale	Kaikohe	24-09-91	1.70	2023	1	0
S.F. (Steffi) Hooson	Hora Hora	17-05-97	1.59	2022	11	5
A. (Ari) Ihaka	Te Rarawa	11-10-94	1.69	2023	1	0
K.J. (Kerri) Johnson	Kaikohe	26-03-03	1.72	2022	11	40
P. (Pohutukawa) Kakara	Hora Hora	07-05-04	1.70	2023	4	29
J. (Justice) Karena	Te Rarawa	12-03-95	1.64	2019	28	0
N. (Nora) Maaka	Te Rarawa	23-02-88	1.69	2023	5	5
T.M. (Tui) McGeorge	Hora Hora	26-02-92	1.76	2019	28	10
C. (Cydney) McNally	Kaikohe	25-08-97	1.55	2023	1	0
J. (Jane) Matthews	Hokianga	11-06-89	1.65	2023	1	0
K.R. (Krystal) Murray	Te Rarawa	16-06-93	1.71	2019	29	216
S.R. (Serai) Murray-Wihongi	Hora Hora	27-05-99	1.64	2022	7	5
T.B. (Tyler) Nankivell	Moerewa	03-07-97	1.75	2019	29	81
T.R. (Te Kura) Ngata-Aerengamate	Te Rarawa	21-10-91	1.65	2019	19	80
H. (Holli) O'Sullivan	Hora Hora	28-11-97	1.64	2020	13	10
A.A.H. (Alisha) Proctor	Kaikohe	25-02-89	1.58	2019	21	5
W. (Wikitoria) Rogers	OB Marist	10-12-05	1.75	2023	5	0
A. (Aroha) Savage	OB Marist	11-03-90	1.72	2020	13	15
E. (Elizabeth) Shelford	Moerewa	13-12-94	1.69	2023	2	0
K.W. (Kahurangi) Shelford	Moerewa	04-12-84	1.55	2019	21	0
C.B. (Charmaine) Smith	OB Marist	15-11-90	1.83	2022	13	20
T.E. (Tuira) Stowers	Kaikohe	15-05-93	1.71	2021	11	0
N. (Nicky-Lee) Tapurau	Kaikohe	05-08-06	1.63	2023	1	0
O. (Ocean) Tierney	OB Marist	16-05-01	1.68	2023	7	20
T. (Tara) Turner	Hora Hora	22-12-03	1.57	2022	7	20
P.A. (Patricia) Vaka	Kaikohe	17-05-86	1.70	2019	24	10
C. (Carly) Whaikawa	OB Marist	09-10-96	1.73	2020	10	0
H.M. (Hikitia) Wikaira	Kaikohe	03-07-93	1.78	2020	22	30

Note: weights not supplied by this union

INDIVIDUAL SCORING

	Tries	Con	PG	DG	Points		Tries	Con	PG	DG	Points
Murray	6	13	3	–	65	Clarke	1	–	–	–	5
Ngata-Aerengamate	6	–	–	–	30	Maaka	1	–	–	–	5
Kakara	1	9	2	–	29	Murray-Wihongi	1	–	–	–	5
Johnson	5	–	–	–	25	Savage	1	–	–	–	5
Tierney	4	–	–	–	20	Vaka	1	–	–	–	5
Cooper	3	–	–	–	15	Nankivell	–	2	–	–	4
Smith	3	–	–	–	15						
Turner	2	–	–	–	10	***Totals***	***38***	***24***	***5***	***0***	***253***
Wikaira	2	–	–	–	10						
Blair	1	–	–	–	5	*Opposition scored*	*16*	*10*	*5*	*0*	*115*

NORTHLAND 2023

	North Harbour	Manawatu	Otago	Taranaki	Tasman	Otago	Manawatu	TOTALS
Turner	15	15	–	–	–	15	15	**4**
Johnson	14	11	14	14	14	14	–	**6**
Murray-Wihongi	–	–	s	s	15	s	14	**5**
Cooper	11	14	–	15	s	s	s	**6**
Tierney	13	13	11	11	11	11	11	**7**
E. Shelford	s	–	13	–	–	–	–	**2**
McNally	–	–	s	–	–	–	–	**1**
Covacich-Baanders	12	s	s	13	13	s	12	**7**
Proctor	s	–	–	12	12	13	13	**5**
Ihaka	–	–	–	–	s	–	–	**1**
Savage	7	12	12	6	10	12	10	**7**
Nankivell	10	s	15	s	–	–	–	**4**
Kakara	–	10	10	10	–	10	–	**4**
Whaikawa	9	9	9	–	s	–	s	**5**
O'Sullivan	s	–	s	9	9	9	9	**6**
Hooson	–	s	–	s	–	s	s	**4**
Wikaira (co-capt)	8	8	8	8	8	8	8	**7**
Stowers	–	s	s	s	s	s	–	**5**
Mathews	–	–	–	s	–	–	–	**1**
Maaka	s	7	7	7	7	–	–	**5**
Tapurau	–	–	–	s	–	–	–	**1**
Karena	6	6	–	–	6	6	6	**5**
McGeorge	5	5	6	–	s	7	7	**6**
Blair	4	s	5	5	5	5	5	**7**
Smith	–	4	4	4	4	4	4	**6**
Fale	s	–	–	–	–	–	–	**1**
K. Shelford	3	3	3	3	–	3	s	**6**
Clarke	s	–	–	s	–	–	–	**2**
Brown	–	–	s	–	3	s	3	**4**
Murray (co-capt)	1	1	1	1	1	1	1	**7**
Rogers	s	–	s	s	s	s	–	**5**
Vaka	2	s	s	2	s	s	–	**6**
Ngata-Aerengamate	s	2	2	–	2	2	2	**6**

NORTHLAND TEAM RECORD 2023

Played 7 ***Won 6*** ***Lost 1*** ***Points for 253*** ***Points against 115***

Date	*Opponent*	*Location*	*Score*	*Tries*	*Con*	*PG*	*DG*	*Referee*
July 23	North Harbour	Takapuna	24–7	Johnson (2), Turner, Cooper	Murray (2)			Maggie Cogger-Orr
July 29	Manawatu	Palmerston North	28–34	Ngata-Aerengamate, Cooper, Maaka, Murray	Kakara	Kakara (2)		Jack Sargentina
August 5	Otago	Whangarei	42–20	Murray (3), Smith (2), Tierney	Kakara (6)			Brandon Roberts
August 12	Taranaki	Kaikohe	67–0	Johnson (3), Murray (2), Kakara, Smith, Tierney, Cooper, Clarke, Murray-Wihongi	Murray (4), Nankivell (2)			Natarsha Ganley
August 19	Tasman	Blenheim	31–6	Ngata-Aerengamate, Tierney, Blair, Savage, Vaka	Murray (3)			Erin Doherty
September 2	Otago (semifinal)	Whangarei	29–19	Ngata-Aerengamate (2), Wikaira, Tierney	Kakara (2), Murray	Murray		Scott McKenzie
September10	Manawatu (final)	Palmerston North	32–29	Ngata-Aerengamate (2), Wikaira, Turner	Murray (3)	Murray (2)		Maggie Cogger-Orr

OTAGO SPIRIT

2023 Status: Championship
NPC participation: 1999–
Manager: Roddy Scoles
Coach: Craig Sneddon
Assistant coaches: Matt Direen, Rodney Stringer
Home grounds: Forsyth Barr Stadium; Logan Park, Dunedin (v Manawatu); Whitestone Stadium, Oamaru
Colours: Dark blue

RECORDS

Most appearances	66	*Greer Muir, 2011–21*
Most points	221	*Claire Richardson, 2002–12*
Most tries	29	*Greer Muir, 2011–21*
Most points in a season	107	*Rosie Kelly, 2019*
Most tries in a season	11	*Annaleah Rush, 1999* *Jamie Church 2023*
Most conversions in a season	32	*Rosie Kelly, 2019*
Most penalty goals in a season	12	*Hannah Myers, 2000*
Most dropped goals in a season	0	
Most points in a match	45	*Kelly Brazier v Hawke's Bay, 2012*
Most tries in a match	8	*Annaleah Rush v Mid/South Canterbury, 1999*
Most conversions in a match	10	*Kelly Brazier v Hawke's Bay, 2012* *Rosie Kelly v North Harbour, 2019*
Most penalty goals in a match	5	*Anika Tiplady v Auckland, 2013*
Highest team score	90	*v North Harbour, 2019*
Record victory (points ahead)	90	*90–0 v North Harbour, 2019*
Highest score conceded	86	*v Auckland, 2011*
Record defeat (points behind)	81	*5–86 v Auckland, 2011*

Otago was clearly the third-best team in the Championship and should have beaten round-robin winners Manawatū. In the 77th minute at Logan Park, the Spirit led 27–19 before conceding two long-range tries to lose the game in heartbreaking circumstances. In the Championship semi-final, Otago was living off scraps against a comparatively larger Northland in Whangarei but refused to surrender meekly, forcing the Kauri into a sustained period of defence late in proceedings.

It was a real compliment to the Otago work ethic that four of the top five individual tacklers in the FPC were Spirit players. Leah Miles topped the count with 130 and was awarded player of the year. Spirit Players' player of the year Bella Rewiri-Wharerau was next with 114. Zoe Whatarau (108) and veteran hooker Tegan Hollows (100) also featured in the top five, but the fact Otago was doing so much defending tells another story. The Spirit were unable to gain sufficient possession to really contend for the championship.

When they had the ball Otago was eye-catching and efficient. Centre Cheyenne Cunningham was named back of the year. She has scored at least a single try in 10 of her past 13 games. The Kurow shepherd was selected for the Black Ferns XV and has formed a fine midfield pairing with Keely Hill. Her dad Alan Hill spent many years on the wing for Otago Country, while her brother, Josh Hill, plays lock for Otago and the Melbourne Rebels.

Left wing Jamie Church joined her sister Paige on the roster for the first time since 2020. Jamie made a huge impression equalling the Otago record of Annaleah Rush for most tries in a season. Church ranked in the top five of the FPC for clean breaks (13) and metres run (719). Fellow wing Oceana Campbell had some good moments, especially in the first round against Tasman when she scored a try in the final minute for a 34–28 victory. It was a wild match with four yellow cards and eight lead changes.

It was a relief that 2022 Fiao'o Fa'amausili medallist Maia Joseph avoided the injuries that plagued her at the end of that season. It appears Joseph has settled at first five-eighth, having played mainly at halfback.

Otago fielded five debutants with Tongan international Pesalini Lave-Heehau a welcome addition at loosehead prop. Outside back Charlotte Va'afusaga is the daughter of Erik Va'afusaga who played 269 games for Taieri and Green Island. Erik coaches the successful St Hilda's Collegiate First XV. Lock Julia Gorinski was again a highly respected captain.

OTAGO REPRESENTATIVES 2023

	Club	Date of Birth	Height	Weight	Debut for Union	Games for Union	Points for Union
S.A. (Sammie) Bean	University	29-08-03	1.78	78	2023	5	0
O.M. (Oceana) Campbell	Dunedin	21-10-03	1.67	79	2021	14	35
Te A.K.J. (Te Atawhai) Campbell	Dunedin	27-12-05	1.65	85	2022	8	15
J.P. (Jamie) Church	Alhambra Union	14-11-02	1.55	64	2020	10	55
P.L.L. (Paige) Church	Alhambra Union	25-09-96	1.58	86	2013	36	10
M.A. (Mia) Cochrane	University	16-02-04	1.74	74	2022	4	5
G.R.R. (Georgia) Cormick	Alhambra Union	12-10-95	1.57	56	2022	14	90
C.B. (Cheyenne) Cunningham	Waitaki	09-11-99	1.71	72	2017	42	125
E.O. (Eilis) Doyle	Alhambra Union	21-03-97	1.77	95	2015	44	5
E.P. (Ella) Gomez	Dunedin	20-01-04	1.74	84	2021	18	0
J.F. (Julia) Gorinski	University	24-06-94	1.74	84	2014	58	20
L.E. (Lucy) Hall	University	17-12-03	1.76	68	2022	3	0
G.R. (Grace) Hastie	Alhambra Union	23-04-05	1.76	78	2022	6	0
K.A. (Keely) Hill	University	12-06-03	1.77	75	2021	19	40
T.J. (Tegan) Hollows	Big River Country	14-05-97	1.65	78	2015	58	65
A.R. (Atawhai) Hotene	Dunedin	19-10-98	1.73	70	2022	12	10
S.J. (Sheree) Hume	Dunedin	14-06-91	1.63	70	2009	63	147
K.E. (Kayley) Johnson	Big River Country	18-06-01	1.70	74	2022	11	0
M.R. (Maia) Joseph	Dunedin	20-05-02	1.69	64	2020	21	24
P. (Pesalini) Lave-Heehau	Waitaki	19-03-89	1.80	98	2023	6	5
H.J. (Hannah) Lithgow	Kaikorai	06-02-06	1.64	64	2023	6	0
L.J. (Leah) Miles	University	08-11-01	1.57	68	2020	24	30
R.J. (Rawinia) Ngamoki-Moana	Dunedin	03-03-04	1.73	78	2023	1	0
A.A. (Abigail) Paton	Dunedin	20-05-05	1.57	58	2023	4	0
I.R. (Isla) Pringle	Big River Country	18-05-99	1.65	85	2017	41	10
B. (Bella) Rewiri-Wharerau	Alhambra Union	23-02-02	1.65	78	2023	7	5
C.M. (Charlotte) Va'afusaga	St Hilda's Collegiate	12-12-06	1.70	68	2023	5	10
R.L. (Rebekah) Wairau	Dunedin	12-07-99	1.81	93	2019	16	0
Z.J.T. (Zoe) Whatarau	Alhambra Union	29-06-94	1.65	73	2014	49	10

Joseph was captain v Manawatu

INDIVIDUAL SCORING

	Tries	Con	PG	DG	Points		Tries	Con	PG	DG	Points
J. Church	11	–	–	–	55	Joseph	1	1	–	–	7
Cormick	–	12	3	–	33	T. Campbell	1	–	–	–	5
Cunningham	5	–	–	–	25	Lave-Heehau	1	–	–	–	5
Hill	4	–	–	–	20	Rewiri-Wharerau	1	–	–	–	5
Hume	3	1	–	–	17						
Hollows	3	–	–	–	15	***Totals***	***36***	***14***	***3***	***0***	***217***
O. Campbell	2	–	–	–	10						
Miles	2	–	–	–	10	*Opposition scored*	*22*	*15*	*5*	*0*	*155*
Va'afusaga	2	–	–	–	10						

OTAGO 2023	Tasman	Taranaki	Northland	North Harbour	Manawatu	North Harbour	Northland	**TOTALS**
Hume	15	10	15	15	15	15	–	**6**
Va'afusaga	–	15	s	14	–	14	15	**5**
Hotene	14	14	s	–	–	s	14	**5**
O. Campbell	s	s	14	s	s	–	12	**6**
T. Campbell	s	–	s	s	14	s	–	**5**
Cochrane	–	s	–	–	–	–	–	**1**
Hall	–	–	–	–	–	–	1	**1**
J. Church	11	11	11	11	11	11	11	**7**
Cunningham	13	13	13	13	13	13	13	**7**
Hill	12	12	12	12	12	12	–	**6**
Ngamoki-Moana	–	–	–	–	–	–	s	**1**
Joseph	10	–	10	10	10	10	10	**6**
Cormick	9	9	9	9	9	9	9	**7**
Paton	–	s	–	s	–	s	s	**4**
Rewiri-Wharerau	8	8	8	8	8	8	8	**7**
Miles	7	7	7	7	7	7	7	**7**
Whatarau	6	6	6	6	6	6	6	**7**
Lithgow	–	s	s	s	s	s	s	**6**
Hastie	–	–	–	s	–	s	s	**3**
Gorinski (captain)	5	5	5	5	–	5	5	**6**
Bean	4	4	4	s	5	–	–	**5**
Johnson	s	s	s	4	4	4	s	**7**
Gomez	–	s	s	–	s	s	4	**5**
P. Church	3	3	3	s	s	s	s	**7**
Wairau	–	s	s	3	3	–	–	**4**
Doyle	1	1	1	1	1	3	3	**7**
Lave-Heehau	s	s	s	–	s	1	1	**6**
Pringle	–	–	–	s	s	s	s	**4**
Hollows	2	2	2	2	2	2	2	**7**

OTAGO TEAM RECORD 2023

Played 7 **Won 4** **Lost 3** **Points for 217** **Points against 155**

Date	Opponent	Location	Score	Tries	Con	PG	DG	Referee
July 22	Tasman	Nelson	34–28	J. Church (2), Hollows, Lave-Heehau, O. Campbell	Cormick (3)	Cormick		Taneika Uerata
July 29	Taranaki	Oamaru	41–0	Cunningham (2), Hollows, Rewiri-Wharerau, Hill, J. Church, Va'afusaga	Cormick (3)			Cassie Watt
August 5	Northland	Whangarei	20–42	J. Church, Hill, T. Campbell	Cormick	Cormick		Brandon Roberts
August 12	North Harbour	Dunedin	37–12	Miles, Hollows, J. Church, Hume, Va'afusaga, Cunningham	Cormick, Hume	Cormick		Cassie Watt
August 19	Manawatu	Dunedin	27–31	Hill (2), J. Church (2), Cunningham	Cormick			Taneika Uerata
August 26	North Harbour (quarterfinal)	Dunedin	39–13	J. Church (3), Hume (2), Cunningham, Miles	Cormick (2)			Cassie Watt
September 2	Northland (semifinal)	Whangarei	19–29	O. Campbell, Joseph, J. Church	Cormick, Joseph			Scott McKenzie

TARANAKI WHIO

2023 Status: Championship
NPC participation: 2000–01, 2013, 2018–
Manager: Peita Kensington
Coach: Maifea Maifea
Assistant coach: Kerry Eynon, Lance White
Home ground: Yarrow Stadium, New Plymouth
Colours: Amber and black

RECORDS

Most appearances	34	*Leah Barnard 2013–23*
Most points	34	*Chelsea Fowler, 2019–21*
Most tries	6	*Iritana Hohaia, 2019–23; Paige Neilson, 2020–22*
Most points in a season	29	*Chelsea Fowler, 2019*
Most tries in a season	4	*Michaela Blyde, 2013 Aroha Nuku, 2021*
Most conversions in a season	7	*Chelsea Fowler, 2019*
Most penalty goals in a season	2	*Kate Broadmore, 2013 Laura Claridge 2023*
Most dropped goals in a season	0	
Most points in a match	12	*Gayle Broughton v North Harbour 2020*
Most tries in a match	2	Seven times by five players
Most conversions in a match	3	*Chelsea Fowler v North Harbour, 2019 Laura Claridge v North Harbour 2023*
Most penalty goals in a match	1	*Six times by four players*
Highest team score	34	*v Tasman 2021*
Record victory (points ahead)	22	*34–12 v Tasman 2021*
Highest score conceded	118	*v Wellington, 2018*
Record defeat (points behind)	118	*0–118 v Wellington, 2018*

After 14 consecutive losses, half of those conceding 40-plus points, Taranaki won their first FPC game since 2021, at Onewa Domain against North Harbour. A blistering start had the Whio ahead 21–0 in as many minutes. It had taken them 172 minutes to score a solitary point. North Harbour regrouped and rallied bravely to be in touch at halftime but when centre Louise Blyde sizzled clear and sprinted 65 metres the Hibiscus was always chasing. Louise is the cousin of Black Ferns Sevens star Michaela Blyde. The Blyde family has been playing positive rugby for years. Michaela's mother Cherry Blyde was a Black Fern and her two sons Cole and Liam have played for Taranaki. Louise's older sisters Lucy and Tara played for Taranaki in 2022. Louise started playing when she was five.

Taranaki's rare victory was a triumph in perseverance for ten players who featured in every match. An opening round 84–0 loss to Manawatū suggested it would be a struggle. They missed 47 tackles against Otago but only conceded half the number of points. Against Tasman, they conceded two yellow cards, 18 penalties, and 13 turnovers.

However, after the North Harbour win, Taranaki gave an honest account of themselves in a second meeting with Tasman. After being bullied in the first half the Whio only lost the second half 17–19. Second five-eighth Hohaia Kahu was rigorous and openside Hayley Gabriel became the first player to make more than 100 tackles in the season. Her high in a single game was 23 against North Harbour.

Halfback Iritana Hohaia showed her energetic flair. She set up two tries, one with a 75-metre run. After a year off to train at the Police College in 2022, Hohaia was selected for the Black

Ferns. She is a product of the Southern club, winner of the club championship.

Fellow halfback Luciana Haami is one to keep an eye on. She captained the Taranaki U18s and played for the New Zealand U18 Māori and Inglewood seniors. A leader in Kapa Haka she was named the 2022 sportswoman of the year (an honour she also received in 2020) at Taranaki Diocesan School. Flanker Elle Johns is a respected leader and defensively defiant. She averaged 13 tackles a game.Loosehead Angel Lindsay was durable and tighthead Ashley Rupapera added impact with ball in hand. Laura Claridge (ex-Manawatu) and Danielle Muggeridge are mainstays of the backline, and both are under 24.

Higher honours went to:
New Zealand: I. Hohaia

TARANAKI REPRESENTATIVES 2023

	Club	Date of Birth	Debut for Union	Games for Union	Points for Union
M.I. (Mereana) Anderson	Clifton	20-04-99	2023	6	0
V. (Victoria) Arnold	Southern		2023	1	0
L. (Leah) Barnard	Coastal	31-07-88	2013	34	5
L.C. (Louise) Blyde	Clifton	17-06-06	2023	6	15
A.V. (Aleasha) Brider	Inglewood	29-07-88	2023	3	0
S.E. (Sharee) Brown	Southern	06-09-90	2018	18	0
C.J. (Catherine) Butler	Clifton	18-05-04	2022	9	0
L.I. (Laura) Claridge	Old Boys Marist[1]	03-10-01	2023	6	14
B.A.R. (Beth) Cook	Coastal	11-11-05	2023	5	0
M.L. (Maree) Dallinger-Phipps	Clifton	24-11-87	2018	20	0
J.J. (Janelle) Dhedadig	Clifton	19-05-06	2022	9	5
F.S. (Freedom) Edmonds	Clifton	11-12-92	2018	11	0
S.B. (Sarah) Farmer	Southern	04-09-02	2023	3	0
H.M. (Hayley) Gabriel	Kaierau[2]	28-06-05	2023	6	0
G.A. (Gemma) Gardner-Harrison	Clifton	11-06-03	2022	9	0
B.A.W. (Bronte) Gorham	Southern	08-05-01	2020	3	0
L. (Luciana) Haami	Inglewood	20-10-05	2022	5	0
I. (Iritana) Hohaia	Southern	01-03-00	2019	13	30
R. (Rongo) Hohaia	Waikato Univ[3]		2023	1	0
E. (Elle) Johns	Inglewood	21-12-00	2018	22	5
P.S.R. (Pearl) Kahui	Southern	12-12-05	2023	4	0
A.R. (Angel) Lindsay	Inglewood	24-06-97	2021	10	0
H.A. (Hannah) McLean	Southern	09-06-01	2021	11	10
E.S. (Eva) Martin	Clifton	03-01-07	2023	5	10
J.A. (Jenna) Moratti	Inglewood	13-05-88	2023	3	0
D.G. (Danielle) Muggeridge	Inglewood	07-10-03	2020	16	21
B.E. (Brooke) Neilson	Inglewood	24-09-00	2019	21	20
J.A. (Jaymi) Ngaia	Coastal	12-06-93	2020	15	5
P.M. (Pareake) O'Brien	Okaiawa	06-09-88	2021	13	0
A.J. (Ashley) Rupapera	Coastal	19-08-92	2023	6	0
L. (Lyn) Smith	Southern	29-11-91	2013	5	0
K.V. (Kate) Thomson	Southern	17-01-97	2018	8	0
A.J. (Abby) Thornley	Clifton	03-07-01	2023	4	0

1 Manawatu RU *2Whanganui RU* *3Waikato RU*

NOTE: No heights or weights were supplied by this union

INDIVIDUAL SCORING

	Tries	Con	PG	DG	Points		Tries	Con	PG	DG	Points
Blyde	3	–	–	–	15	Neilson	1	–	–	–	5
Claridge	–	4	2	–	14						
Martin	2	–	–	–	10	***Totals***	***9***	***5***	***2***	***0***	***61***
Muggeridge	1	1	–	–	7						
Dhedadig	1	–	–	–	5	*Opposition scored*	*53*	*26*	*0*	*0*	*317*
McLean	1	–	–	–	5						

TARANAKI 2023	Manawatu	Otago	Tasman	Northland	North Harbour	Tasman	**TOTALS**
Muggeridge	15	15	15	15	15	15	**6**
R. Hohaia	s	–	–	–	–	–	**1**
Smith	s	–	–	–	–	–	**1**
Arnold	–	–	–	–	–	s	**1**
Martin	14	14	s	14	14	–	**5**
McLean	11	11	s	s	s	11	**6**
Farmer	–	–	14	11	11	–	**3**
Blyde	13	13	13	13	13	13	**6**
Kahui	12	–	11	–	12	12	**4**
Brider	–	12	12	12	–	–	**3**
Claridge	10	10	10	10	10	10	**6**
Haami	9	–	9	s	–	s	**4**
Cook	s	9	s	s	–	14	**5**
I. Hohaia	–	–	–	9	9	9	**3**
Neilson	8	s	s	8	8	8	**6**
Edmonds	–	8	8	–	–	–	**2**
Gabriel	7	7	7	7	7	7	**6**
Johns (captain)	6	6	6	–	6	6	**5**
Dhedadig	s	–	–	s	s	s	**4**
Moratti	s	–	–	s	–	s	**3**
Brown	5	–	–	–	–	–	**1**
Ngaia	–	5	–	–	–	–	**1**
Butler	4	4	5	5	4	4	**6**
Gardner-Harrison	–	s	s	4	–	s	**4**
Thornley	–	–	4	6	5	5	**5**
Rupapera	3	s	s	3	s	s	**6**
Barnard	s	3	–	s	2	s	**5**
Anderson	s	s	3	s	s	s	**6**
Thomson	–	–	s	s	3	3	**4**
Lindsay	1	1	1	1	1	1	**6**
O'Brien	2	–	–	–	s	2	**3**
Dallinger-Phipps	s	2	s	2	–	–	**4**
Gorham	–	s	2	–	–	–	**2**

Brown was co-capt with Johns game 1; Hohaia was captain game 4 and co-capt with Johns game 5

TARANAKI TEAM RECORD 2023

Played 6 ***Won 1*** ***Lost 5*** ***Points for 61*** ***Points against 317***

Date	*Opponent*	*Location*	*Score*	*Tries*	*Con*	*PG*	*DG*	*Referee*
July 23	Manawatu	New Plymouth	0–84					Ben Woolerton
July 29	Otago	Oamaru	0–41					Cassie Watt
August 4	Tasman	New Plymouth	10–61	Muggeridge	Muggeridge	Claridge		Tiana Anderson
August 12	Northland	Kaikohe	0–67					Natarsha Ganley
August 19	North Harbour	Takapuna	31–19	Blyde (2), Martin (2), Neilson	Claridge (3)			Ben Brownlie
August 27	Tasman (quarterfinal)	Nelson	20–45	McLean, Dhedadig, Blyde	Claridge	Claridge		Maggie Cogger-Orr

TASMAN MAKO

tasman rugbyunion

2023 Status: Championship
NPC participation: 2017–
Manager: Helen Leota
Coach: Mel Bosman
Assistant coach: La Toya Mason
Home grounds: Trafalgar Park, Nelson; Lansdowne Park, Blenheim
Colours: Navy blue and red

RECORDS

Most appearances	40	*Tamara Silcock, 2017–23*
Most points	87	*Cassie Siataga 2022–23*
Most tries	8	*Fiaali'i Solomona 2021–2023*
Most points in a season	50	*Cassie Siataga 2023*
Most tries in a season	8	*Fiaali'i Solomona 2023*
Most conversions in a season	15	*Cassie Siataga 2023*
Most penalty goals in a season	6	*Cassie Siataga 2022*
Most dropped goals in a season	0	
Most points in a match	15	*Amelia Hammett v Taranaki, 2018*
Most tries in a match	3	*Amelia Hammett v Taranaki, 2018* *Precious Auimatagi v Taranaki 2023;* *Iva Sauira v Taranaki 2023;* *Fiaali'i Solomona v Taranaki 2023*
Most conversions in a match	5	*Hayley Hutana v Taranaki, 2018* *Cassie Siataga v Taranaki 2023*
Most penalty goals in a match	2	*by two players on five occasions*
Highest team score	65	*v Taranaki, 2018*
Record victory (points ahead)	53	*65–12 v Taranaki, 2018*
Highest score conceded	88	*v Wellington, 2018* *v Manawatu 2020*
Record defeat (points behind)	88	*0–88 v Manawatu 2020*

Tasman won two consecutive games for just the third time in their history and achieved their second-largest victory at Yarrow Stadium, New Plymouth when they overpowered Taranaki. In the first round, they let slip a royal chance to defeat Otago. In a wild match with four yellow cards and eight lead changes, Tasman had an edge in the set-piece but conceded a try in the last minute of regulation time which they couldn't erase despite attacking until the 83rd minute.

At the heart of the Makos improvement was a heavier and more accomplished pack. Former Black Ferns prop Mel Bosman is maturing into a fine coach and was rewarded when she was appointed to assist the USA. However, there was great sadness in May when assistant coach Billy Guyton died.

A more nurturing culture clearly aided the pack. From a league background, Peleoaiga Loto was consistently robust on the loosehead side and lock Tanita Garnet, who overcame leukaemia in her youth, didn't miss a game. Hooker Precious Auimatagi had another impressive campaign, and the loose forward trio was settled and combative.

Blindside flanker Neve Anglesey was named player of the year. The leadership and courage of

Sui Pauaraisa (83 tackles) was acknowledged when she was named Tasman woman of the year. She shared the captaincy with Tamara Silcock.

Tasman scored 14 tries in 2022. Between them, Fiaali'i Solomona and rookie of the year Iva Sauira scored 13 in 2023. Sauira was rewarded with Fijian selection. Solomona, from a netball background, should attract Super Rugby Aupiki interest. In addition to scoring a Tasman record eight tries she was in the top five in the FPC for metres run (704) and clean breaks (13).

Cassie Siataga is a playmaker of genuine quality. She's better now than when she helped Canterbury win four Premierships. Tasman benefited greatly from a more stable midfield partnership. Lesieli Taufa only missed the Manawatū match. Young utility back Sarah Jones was picked for the New Zealand Barbarians U18s.

TASMAN REPRESENTATIVES 2023

	Club	Date of Birth	Height	Weight	Debut for Union	Games for Union	Points for Union
N.K. (Neve) Anglesey	Waimea OB	21-04-04	1.63	72	2021	16	10
P.S. (Precious) Auimatagi	Marist	13-09-00	1.65	96	2022	11	15
L.S.H. (Lucy) Brown	Kahurangi	16-11-00	1.60	57	2023	6	0
S.H. (Shevaun) Collier	Marist	18-09-94	1.79	99	2022	5	0
C.E. (Chloe) Dixon	Kahurangi	13-12-04	1.75	78	2022	12	10
M. (Marama) Elkington	Marist	17-04-98	1.68	98	2022	6	0
A.V. (Avau) Filimaua	Lincoln Univ[1]	04-08-03	1.65	105	2023	7	5
E.G.S. (Eve) Findlay	Waimea OB	26-07-01	1.65	75	2020	14	23
T.J. (Tanita) Garnet	Kahurangi	12-11-02	1.73	78	2020	17	0
G. (Grace) Guyton	Waimea OB	08-02-04	1.77	72	2023	6	0
A. (Amelia) Hammett	Marist	06-03-99	1.62	57	2018	10	15
J.M. (Jessica) Harvie	Waimea OB	06-11-02	1.74	80	2019	18	0
S. (Sarah) Jones	Kahurangi	24-10-06	1.76	85	2023	7	10
S. (Shelby) Lin	Marist	27-05-92	1.58	62	2023	2	0
B.K. (Brooklyn) Logan	Waimea OB	23-09-03	1.74	85	2022	10	10
P. (Peleoaiga) Loto	Linwood[1]	24-01-01	1.73	97	2023	7	0
B. (Bethan) Manners	Waimea OB	12-02-98	1.74	68	2019	21	21
M. (Mili) Mills	Marist	07-01-95	1.70	73	2023	4	0
M.T. (Sui) Pauaraisa	Linwood[1]	30-10-87	1.65	73	2021	17	25
P. (Philomena) Petaia	Linwood[1]	25-03-95	1.82	117	2023	2	0
K. (Keeley) Ridley	Waimea OB	27-03-04	1.65	70	2021	10	0
R. (Raumati) Rogers	Wairau	05-11-02	1.73	125	2021	12	0
A. (Alicia) San Martin Alonso	Waimea OB	24-08-94	1.65	70	2023	5	0
I. (Iva) Sauira	Marist	30-08-01	1.65	74	2023	7	25
C.M.T. (Cassie) Siataga	Linwood[1]	27-11-95	1.74	82	2022	12	87
T.L. (Tamara) Silcock	Marist	10-02-96	1.73	73	2017	40	15
F. (Fiaali'i) Solomona	Moutere	01-06-04	1.76	90	2021	11	40
L. (Luisa) Tafia	Kahurangi	30-04-04	1.68	87	2023	3	0
L. (Lesieli) Taufa	Marist	27-10-04	1.72	90	2021	12	10
A.M. (Ashley) Ulutupu	Marist	16-10-93	1.75	109	2017	14	10
A. (Ashleigh) Wood	Kahurangi	22-03-05	1.62	56	2023	1	0

1. Canterbury RU

INDIVIDUAL SCORING

	Tries	Con	PG	DG	Points		Tries	Con	PG	DG	Points
Siataga	1	15	5	–	50	Filimaua	1	–	–	–	5
Solomona	8	–	–	–	40	Pauaraisa	1	–	–	–	5
Sauira	5	–	–	–	25	Silcock	1	–	–	–	5
Auimatagi	3	–	–	–	15	Ulutupu	1	–	–	–	5
Anglesey	2	–	–	–	10						
Dixon	2	–	–	–	10	***Totals***	***29***	***15***	***5***	***0***	***190***
Jones	2	–	–	–	10						
Taufa	2	–	–	–	10	*Opposition scored*	*35*	*24*	*4*	*0*	*235*

TASMAN 2023	Otago	North Harbour	Taranaki	Manawatu	Northland	Taranaki	Manawatu	**TOTALS**
Hammett	15	15	–	s	–	s	–	**4**
Jones	s	s	15	13	15	15	15	**7**
Manners	–	–	s	15	–	–	s	**3**
Sauira	14	14	14	14	14	14	14	**7**
Solomona	11	11	11	11	11	11	11	**7**
Taufa	13	13	13	–	13	13	13	**6**
Findlay	–	–	–	s	s	s	s	**4**
Dixon	12	12	12	12	12	12	12	**7**
Siataga	10	10	10	10	10	10	10	**7**
Wood	–	–	s	–	–	–	–	**1**
Brown	9	9	–	9	9	9	9	**6**
Lin	s	–	s	–	–	–	–	**2**
Ridley	–	s	9	s	s	s	s	**6**
Silcock	8	8	–	6	s	6	6	**6**
Harvie	s	s	8	–	–	–	–	**3**
Anglesey	6	6	6	8	8	8	8	**7**
Pauaraisa	7	7	7	7	7	7	7	**7**
Mills	–	–	s	s	6	s	–	**4**
Tafia	–	–	–	s	–	s	s	**3**
Garnett	5	5	5	5	5	5	5	**7**
Logan	4	4	4	4	4	–	s	**6**
Guyton	s	s	s	–	s	4	4	**6**
Ulutupu	3	3	–	3	s	3	–	**5**
Elkington	s	s	3	–	–	–	–	**3**
Petaia	–	–	–	s	–	–	3	**2**
Loto	1	1	1	1	1	1	1	**7**
Rogers	–	–	s	–	–	s	s	**3**
Collier	–	–	–	–	s	s	s	**3**
Auimatagi	2	2	2	2	2	s	s	**7**
Filimaua	s	s	s	s	3	2	2	**7**
San Martin Alonso	s	s	s	s	s	–	–	**5**

Silcock was captain games 1 and 2, co-capt game 4; Pauaraisa was captain games 3,5,6,7 and co-capt game 4.

TASMAN TEAM RECORD 2023

Played 7 ***Won 3*** ***Lost 4*** ***Points for 190*** ***Points against 235***

Date	Opponent	Location	Score	Tries	Con	PG	DG	Referee
July 22	Otago	Nelson	28–34	Ulutupu, Dixon, Solomona, Pauaraisa	Siataga	Siataga (2)		Taneika Uerata
July 29	North Harbour	Nelson	26–21	Dixon, Jones, Solomona, Taufa	Siataga (3)			Erin Doherty
August 4	Taranaki	New Plymouth	61–10	Auimatagi (3), Sauira (3), Solomona (3), Anglesey, Jones	Siataga (3)			Tiana Anderson
August 13	Manawatu	Palmerston North	14–46	Solomona (2)	Siataga (2)			Georgia Mason
August 19	Northland	Blenheim	6–31			Siataga (2)		Erin Doherty
August 27	Taranaki (quarterfinal)	Nelson	45–20	Sauira (2), Solomona, Anglesey, Silcock, Taufa, Filimaua	Siataga (5)			Maggie Cogger-Orr
September 2	Manawatu (semifinal)	Palmerston North	10–73	Siataga	Siataga	Siataga		Will Johnston

WAIKATO

2023 Status: Premiership
NPC participation: 1999–2005, 2012–
Manager: David Fox
Coach: Greg Smith
Assistant coaches: Sam Christie, Daniel Teka
Home ground: St Paul's Collegiate;
FMG Stadium Waikato (v Wellington)
Colours: Red, yellow and black

RECORDS

Most appearances	62	*Victoria Makea, 2012–23*
Most points	407	*Chelsea Semple, 2012–22*
Most tries	31	*Stacey Fluhler 2014–20*
Most points in a season	81	*Chelsea Alley, 2014*
Most tries in a season	11	*Stacey Waaka, 2014*
Most conversions in a season	21	*Chelsea Alley, 2014, 2018*
Most penalty goals in a season	12	*Chelsea Alley, 2013*
Most dropped goals in a season	1	*Emma Jensen, 2000*
		Chelsea Alley, 2019
Most points in a match	20	*Chelsea Alley v Taranaki, 2020*
Most tries in a match	3	*Jordon Webber v Manawatu, 2012*
		Honey Hireme v Manawatu, 2014
		Stacey Waaka v Canterbury, 2014
		v Bay of Plenty, 2015
		v North Harbour, 2020
Most conversions in a match	5	*Chelsea Alley v Manawatu, 2014*
		v Bay of Plenty, 2014
		v Auckland, 2018
		v Taranaki, 2020
		Tenika Willison v North Harbour, 2020
Most penalty goals in a match	4	*Emma Jensen v Northland, 2000*
		Tenika Willison v North Harbour, 2016
Highest team score	76	*v Taranaki 2020*
Record victory (points ahead)	62	*76–14 v Taranaki 2020*
		62–0 v North Harbour 2020
Highest score conceded	78	*v Auckland, 2002*
Record defeat (points behind)	78	*0–78 v Auckland, 2002*

When Waikato rallied to upset Canterbury in the first match, decided in golden-point extra time, it looked like they were serious Premiership contenders. In a wild climax, turnovers by Rina Paraone and Kaea Nepia were the catalysts for a long sequence of attacks that started on the right flank and worked towards centre field. Blindside flanker Victoria Makea was typically inspirational and drove over beside the posts giving Samantha Wood a routine chance to tie the scores with the last play in regulation time. In extra time Waikato was able to earn favourable territory and then employed their rolling maul to extract a penalty advantage. Wood kept her cool to secure a memorable victory.

Strangely, Waikato regressed thereafter, outclassed twice by Auckland, and scraping their way to unconvincing victories against Hawke's Bay, Counties Manukau, and Wellington. Waikato started the semi-final against the Storm like a freight train leading 12–0 after five minutes but faded as Auckland eventually matched the hosts' physicality. Injuries didn't help Waikato. Joint with Canterbury they used the most players in the Premiership with 35.

The forwards packed a punch with Black Ferns front rowers Grace Houpapa-Barrett and Tanya Kalounivale regularly coming off the bench. Toka Natua and Esther Faiaoga-Tilo started a handful of games each. Faiaoga-Tilo was at a crossroads when she was dumped from the Blues Super Rugby Aupiki squad only to attend an open training session and regain her place mid-season.

Waikato mauled strongly but their lineout wasn't always reliable. Sesilia Sakalia and Te Amohaere Ngata-Aerengamate were partners at lock in the first two matches. Otherwise, Waikato underwent constant change with even Makea covering that position.

As a collective Waikato's backs were disappointing. Yes, halfback Ariana Bayler did enough to retain her Black Ferns place, timeless talent Carla Hohepa won Waikato player of the year and first five-eighth Kiriana Nolan showed promise. However, the backs only scored 10 tries in seven games, half of those in the first-round thumping of Bay of Plenty.

Captain Chyna Hohepa took home the Māori player of the year award. The excellence of Black Ferns skipper, Kennedy Simon saw her acknowledged as female club player of the year for her involvement with champions Hamilton Old Boys and also awarded the Gallagher Sportsperson of the Year and Ian Clarke Trophy. The Ian Clarke Trophy is awarded to a Waikato person who has achieved the highest level whilst upholding Waikato Rugby core values over the past 12 months. Simon became the second female player after Stacey Waaka in 2021 to win the Ian Clarke honour.

Higher honours went to:

New Zealand:	E. Faiaoga-Tilo, R. Holmes, T. Kalounivale, K. Simon, K. Teneti, T. Willison
New Zealand Sevens:	J. Felix-Hotham., S. Kaka, M. Nuku, T. Te Tamaki, K. Teneti, T. Willison

INDIVIDUAL SCORING

	Tries	Con	PG	DG	Points		Tries	Con	PG	DG	Points
Wood	–	4	4	–	20	Houpapa-Barrett	1	–	–	–	5
Bayler	–	6	2	–	18	Konui	1	–	–	–	5
Makea	3	–	–	–	15	Natua	1	–	–	–	5
Wilson-Jenkins	3	–	–	–	15	Puni-Lio	1	–	–	–	5
Holmes	–	3	2	–	12	Sakalia	1	–	–	–	5
Gaby-Sutherland	2	–	–	–	10	Simon	1	–	–	–	5
Carla Hohepa	2	–	–	–	10	Nolan	–	1	–	–	2
Chyna Hohepa	2	–	–	–	10						
Ieremia	2	–	–	–	10	***Totals***	**24**	**14**	**8**	**0**	**172**
M. Paraone	2	–	–	–	10						
M. Anderson	1	–	–	–	5	*Opposition scored*	*18*	*10*	*4*	*0*	*122*
Crozier	1	–	–	–	5						

WAIKATO REPRESENTATIVES 2023

	Club	Date of Birth	Height	Weight	Debut for Union	Games for Union	Points for Union
M.T. (Mia) Anderson	University	04-03-02	1.70	94	2020	19	30
R.R. (Reese) Anderson	Hamilton OB	12-04-03	1.68	70	2021	12	0
A.J. (Ariana) Bayler	Hamilton OB	14-12-96	1.65	73	2013	51	99
C. (Caitlin) Crozier	University	09-07-02	1.67	90	2023	6	5
R. (Roelien) du Plessis	Hamilton OB	12-06-00	1.68	75	2023	2	0
E.E. (Esther) Faiaoga-Tilo	Hamilton OB	26-09-94	1.75	105	2018	34	20
T. (Tafiau) Fetalaiga	Hamilton OB	23-03-01	1.58	102	2020	9	0
A.J. (Ashlee) Gaby-Sutherland	Melville	13-06-89	1.66	82	2012	41	30
V. (Vici-Rose) Green	Hamilton OB	08-04-02	1.75	88	2022	14	0
E-L. (Emma-Lee) Heta	Kihikihi	30-06-91	1.63	73	2016	45	10
C.M. (Claudia) Hobbs	University	27-11-96	1.67	105	2021	14	0
C.G.T.O. (Carla) Hohepa	Kihikihi	27-07-85	1.70	70	2012	21	30
C.H.M.P. (Chyna) Hohepa	Kihikihi	15-12-89	1.72	70	2012	40	25
R.M.M. (Renee) Holmes	Hamilton OB	21-12-99	1.73	76	2019	24	92
G.P. (Grace) Houpapa-Barrett	Otorohanga	25-07-95	1.67	98	2014	44	65
L. (Lela) Ieremia	Melville	11-09-02	1.63	73	2022	7	10
J.M.E. (Tanya) Kalounivale	Hamilton OB	20-01-99	1.78	128	2017	33	35
L. (Leomie) Kloppers	Hamilton OB	10-03-98	1.79	95	2017	35	0
A (Aaliyah) Konui	Hamilton OB	03-09-04	1.71	63	2023	2	5
V.R. (Victoria) Makea	University	14-08-90	1.69	82	2012	62	40
B. (Baylee) Maniapoto	Hamilton OB	13-04-99	1.68	91	2023	1	0
A. (Ana) Marsters	Hamilton OB	12-08-96	1.74	91	2013	18	36
T.I.T. (Toka) Natua	University	22-11-91	1.65	120	2014	44	30
K. (Kaea) Nepia	Hamilton OB	09-09-05	1.72	80	2023	7	0
L. (Lonita) Ngalu-Lavemai	Hamilton OB	25-02-01	1.72	103	2018	16	40
T.E. (Te Amohaere) Ngata-Aerengamate	University	07-01-95	1.75	97	2023	3	0
K.L.A. (Kiriana) Nolan	Kihikihi	26-04-02	1.67	81	2019	13	7
M.M.K. (Merania) Paraone	Kihikihi	21-05-01	1.63	73	2020	21	30
R.W. (Rina) Paraone	Kihikihi	27-01-99	1.75	85	2017	36	20
L. (Leota) Puni Lio	Hamilton OB	05-01-03	1.70	83	2022	10	10
S. (Sesilia) Sakalia	Melville	22-03-97	1.72	75	2023	4	5
E.I.A. (Easter) Savelio	Kihikihi	04-04-99	1.75	80	2023	1	0
K.W. (Kennedy) Simon	Hamilton OB	01-10-96	1.72	80	2013	37	35
C. (Chantae) Wilson-Jenkins	Southern United	14-04-98	1.64	75	2022	9	15
S. (Samantha) Wood	Melville	17-07-04	1.66	79	2023	7	20

WAIKATO 2023	Bay of Plenty	Canterbury	Hawke's Bay	Counties Manukau	Auckland	Wellington	Auckland	TOTALS
Ieremia	15	15	11	–	15	15	15	**6**
Holmes	–	–	15	15	–	–	–	**2**
Wilson-Jenkins	14	14	–	14	14	14	14	**6**
Paraone	11	11	–	11	–	–	–	**3**
R. Anderson	–	–	14	–	11	11	11	**4**
Konui	–	–	s	–	s	–	–	**2**
Paraone	13	13	13	13	–	–	–	**4**
Marsters	12	12	–	s	13	13	–	**5**
Carla Hohepa	s	s	–	12	12	12	12	**6**
Nolan	10	10	12	10	10	10	10	**7**
Nepia	s	s	10	s	s	s	13	**7**
Wood	9	s	s	9	s	s	s	**7**
Bayler	s	9	9	s	9	9	9	**7**
Chyna Hohepa	8	8	–	–	8	8	8	**5**
Heta	7	7	–	7	–	s	7	**5**
Simon	–	s	–	8	7	7	–	**4**
du Plessis	–	–	7	–	–	–	s	**2**
Gaby-Sutherland	s	–	8	6	6	6	6	**6**
Puni-Lio	s	–	6	s	s	s	4	**6**
M. Anderson	–	s	s	s	s	s	s	**6**
Sakalia	–	5	5	5	–	–	s	**4**
Makea	6	6	–	4	5	–	5	**5**
Ngata-Aerengamate	4	4	–	–	–	5	–	**3**
Kloppers	5	–	4	–	4	4	s	**5**
Ngalu-Lavemai	–	–	s	–	–	–	–	**1**
Savelio	–	–	s	–	–	–	–	**1**
Hobbs	3	3	3	s	–	s	s	**6**
Fetalaiga	s	s	–	–	–	–	–	**2**
Faiaoga-Tilo	–	–	s	3	3	3	s	**5**
Kalounivale	–	–	–	–	s	s	3	**3**
Crozier	1	s	s	s	s	1	–	**6**
Maniapoto	s	–	–	–	–	–	–	**1**
Natua	–	1	1	1	1	–	1	**5**
Green	2	s	2	s	2	2	2	**7**
Houpapa-Barrett	s	2	s	2	s	s	s	**7**

Chyna was captain games 1,2,5,7; Holmes and Gaby-Sutherland co-captains game 3,4; Hohepa and Simon co-captains game 6.

WAIKATO TEAM RECORD 2023

Played 7 **Won 5** **Lost 2** **Points for 172** **Points against 122**

Date	Opponent	Location	Score	Tries	Con	PG	DG	Referee
July 15	Bay of Plenty	Rotorua	50–0	M. Paraone (2), Wilson-Jenkins (2), Chyna Hohepa, Houpapa-Barrett, Ieremia	Bayler (2), Wood	Wood (3)		Maggie Cogger-Orr
July 22	Canterbury	Hamilton	27–24	Makea (2), Wilson-Jenkins, M. Anderson	Bayler, Wood	Wood		Scott McKenzie
July 29	Hawke's Bay	Hastings	14–10	Sakalia, Crozier	Holmes (2)			Tiana Anderson
August 5	Counties Manukau	Hamilton	13–5	Natua	Holmes	Holmes (2)		Maggie Cogger-Orr
August 20	Auckland	Auckland	15–25	Chyna Hohepa, Konui	Wood	Bayler		Tiana Anderson
August 27	Wellington	Hamilton	31–29	Gaby-Sutherland, Carla Hohepa, Ieremia, Simon, Puni-Lio	Bayler (2), Wood			Scott McKenzie
September 2	Auckland (semifinal)	Auckland	22–29	Carla Hohepa, Makea, Gaby-Sutherland	Bayler Nolan	Bayler		Tiana Anderson

WELLINGTON PRIDE

2023 Status: Premiership
NPC participation: 1999–
Manager: Emma Paisley
Coach: Fusi Feaunati
Assistant coaches: Serena Curtis, Ryan Setefano, Aimee Sutorius
Home ground: Hutt Recreation Ground, Lower Hutt
Colours: Black

RECORDS

Most appearances	79	*Jackie Patea-Fereti, 2006–23*
Most points	280	*Ayesha Leti-I'iga, 2015–22*
Most tries	56	*Ayesha Leti-I'iga 2015–22*
Most points in a season	118	*Amanda Rasch, 2018*
Most tries in a season	12	*Ayesha Leti-I'iga, 2019*
Most conversions in a season	46	*Amanda Rasch, 2018*
Most penalty goals in a season	11	*Elizabeth Goulden, 2014*
Most dropped goals in a season	0	
Most points in a match	43	*Amanda Rasch v Taranaki, 2018*
Most tries in a match	5	*Ayesha Leti-I'iga v Manawatu, 2019*
Most conversions in a match	14	*Amanda Rasch v Taranaki, 2018*
Most penalty goals in a match	5	*Elizabeth Goulden v Taranaki, 2013*
Highest team score	118	*v Taranaki, 2018*
Record victory (points ahead)	118	*118–0 v Taranaki, 2018*
Highest score conceded	65	*v Auckland, 2012*
Record defeat (points behind)	65	*0–65 v Auckland, 2012*

For the first time since its inception in 1999, Wellington failed to win a single game in a season and is on a record eight-game losing streak and demoted to the Championship for the first time since 2017. The Pride were well off the pace against Canterbury, Bay of Plenty, and Counties Manukau but could have beaten Waikato, Hawke's Bay, and should have tamed Auckland.

Against Auckland, the Pride were ahead 15–10 with a two-player advantage and turned down a straightforward penalty shot to extend their advantage beyond a converted try. Their scrum then imploded, and discipline wavered as Auckland scored a converted try with the last play. Against Hawke's Bay, Harmony Kautai had a try disallowed in the 78th minute when Wellington was down 22-26. A minute later, Hawke's Bay scored at the opposite end and the Pride came away with nothing.

Wellington's young backs outclassed Waikato in Hamilton but two tries from lineout drives was enough to sink the Pride again. Wellington lacked killer instinct and their set-piece struggled too often. The Pride also failed to settle upon an authoritative 9–10 combination, though former New Zealand Tae Kwon Do representative Tamara Ruaporo undoubtedly improved.

The Pride fielded nine debutants. Undoubtedly one of the success stories of 2023 was the emergence of 17-year-old threequarter Justine McGregor who won the Erin Rush medal as the best and fairest player in Wellington club rugby. She scored six tries, including an exceptional hat-trick against Canterbury with two tries scored by herself from past halfway. In midfield Monica Tagoai made several fine breaks and was acknowledged as player of the year.

Angelica Schwencke featured for the Western Force in Super Rugby W in Australia and showed the benefit of that experience by starting every match at loosehead prop. Petone tighthead

Lavinia Lea was a success, her barnstorming and 'big hits' made her a crowd favourite. Lock Jackie Patea-Fereti reached 100 first-class games and topped the tackle count with 70. Black Ferns lock Joanah Ngan-Woo often played at No.8 to cover injuries.

Manusina honours went to Nina Foaese, Schwencke, Fa'alua Tugaga and Sinead Ryder.

New Zealand: J. Ngan-Woo.

WELLINGTON REPRESENTATIVES 2023

	Club	Date of Birth	Height	Weight	Debut for Union	Games for Union	Points for Union
H.A. (Hosanna) Aumua	Avalon	04-05-02	1.70	96	2021	14	5
T. (Tawny) Burgess	Paremata-Plimmerton	19-01-95	1.63	73	2017	7	0
L. (Leah) Conley	Northern United	16-04-94	1.69	87	2023	2	0
D.T. (Drenna) Falaniko	Marist St Pats	30-01-04	1.72	65	2023	5	5
L. (Lyric) Faleafaga	Marist St Pats	13-10-99	1.80	90	2019	16	25
M.R. (Maddie) Feaunati	Marist St Pats	18-05-02	1.73	83	2022	11	0
S.L. (Siaiga) Filipo	Avalon	24-05-00	1.77	70	2023	2	5
N.M. (Nina) Foaese	Northern United	24-10-88	1.65	92	2018	30	15
P.H. (Petrina) Foaese	Marist St Pats	03-07-95	1.62	105	2023	5	0
S.A. (Sophie) Irving	Poneke	06-11-02	1.71	68	2023	4	0
H.M.E. (Harmony) Kautai	Petone	08-05-04	1.72	82	2023	6	20
A.M. (Arene) Landon-Lane	Northern United	21-08-04	1.71	70	2022	6	4
K. (Kelly) Laumalili-Tuiatua	Marist St Pats	15-09-91	1.78	120	2012	8	0
L.V.T.N. (Lavinia) Lea	Petone	12-02-01	1.70	115	2023	4	10
J.L. (Justine) McGregor	Petone	11-04-06	1.68	70	2022	7	30
M.M. (Milly) Mackey	Petone	23-02-02	1.64	61	2021	14	0
O.T. (Octavia) Nanai-lafeta	Marist St Pats	10-03-96	1.65	105	2023	3	0
J.M.P. (Joanah) Ngan-Woo	Oriental Rongotai	15-12-95	1.81	83	2013	67	90
J.S. (Jackie) Patea-Fereti	Petone	30-09-86	1.80	85	2006	79	95
A.S. (Ashlyn) Pescini	Marist St Pats	26-10-01	1.77	80	2023	6	0
T.T.H. (Tamara) Ruaporo	Marist St Pats	15-11-03	1.68	70	2022	9	18
S.V. (Sinead) Ryder	Oriental Rongotai	19-12-91	1.65	84	2017	33	30
I.I.J. (Ivana) Samani	Oriental Rongotai	19-12-01	1.72	74	2022	7	5
A.S.V. (Angelica) Schwencke (formerly Uila)	Petone	18-01-96	1.70	119	2016	38	55
M.F. (Monica) Tagoai	Marist St Pats	17-10-98	1.68	82	2016	40	60
B. (Barbra) Taumoli	Oriental Rongotai	07-09-94	1.70	114	2019	18	0
C.J. (Chloe) Te Moananui	Petone	29-07-99	1.70	113	2021	6	0
S.J. (Jaydah) Timu	Marist St Pats	11-12-96	1.70	94	2022	3	0
F.I. (Fa'alua) Tugaga	Marist St Pats	22-12-01	1.65	63	2023	6	0
V.M.K. (Valini) Vaka	Marist St Pats	30-04-03	1.68	85	2021	7	0
S.L. (Sydnee) Wilkins	Marist St Pats	14-06-99	1.68	72	2022	6	0

INDIVIDUAL SCORING

	Tries	Con	PG	DG	Points		Tries	Con	PG	DG	Points
McGregor	6	–	–	–	30	Patea-Fereti	1	–	–	–	5
Kautai	4	–	–	–	20	Schwencke	1	–	–	–	5
Ruaporo	–	6	2	–	18	Tagoai	1	–	–	–	5
Lea	2	–	–	–	10	Landon-Lane	–	2	–	–	4
Falaniko	1	–	–	–	5						
Faleafaga	1	–	–	–	5	***Totals***	***20***	***8***	***2***	***0***	***122***
Filipo	1	–	–	–	5						
N. Foaese	1	–	–	–	5	*Opposition scored*	*36*	*20*	*3*	*0*	*229*
Ngan-Woo	1	–	–	–	5						

WELLINGTON 2023

	Canterbury	Auckland	Counties Manukau	Hawke's Bay	Bay of Plenty	Waikato	TOTALS
Wilkins	15	15	–	s	–	s	**4**
Samani	14	–	s	15	15	s	**5**
Kautai	s	14	14	14	11	14	**6**
Falaniko	s	s	13	–	14	15	**5**
McGregor	11	11	s	13	13	13	**6**
Tagoai	13	13	12	–	12	12	**5**
Faleafaga	12	12	11	11	s	11	**6**
Burgess	–	–	–	12	s	–	**2**
Landon-Lane	10	10	15	–	–	–	**3**
Ruaporo	s	–	10	10	10	10	**5**
Tugaga	9	9	9	s	9	s	**6**
Mackey	s	s	s	9	s	9	**6**
Aumua	8	s	–	–	–	s	**3**
N. Foaese	–	8	8	8	8	s	**5**
Conley	–	–	–	s	s	–	**2**
Irving	7	7	7	–	s	–	**4**
Feaunati	–	–	6	7	7	6	**4**
Ryder	–	–	s	–	–	7	**2**
Filipo	6	6	–	–	–	–	**2**
Timu	s	–	–	6	–	–	**2**
Patea-Fereti (capt)	5	5	4	4	5	5	**6**
Ngan-Woo	–	–	5	5	6	8	**4**
Pescini	4	4	s	s	4	4	**6**
Te Moananui	3	s	–	–	3	–	**3**
Nanai-Iafeta	s	–	s	–	–	s	**3**
Lea	–	3	3	3	–	3	**4**
Schwencke	1	1	1	1	1	1	**6**
Taumoli	s	–	s	s	s	s	**5**
Laumalili-Tuiatua	–	s	–	s	s	–	**3**
Vaka	2	2	2	2	2	2	**6**
P. Foaese	s	s	s	–	s	s	**5**

WELLINGTON TEAM RECORD 2023

Played 6 ***Lost 6*** ***Points for 122*** ***Points against 229***

Date	*Opponent*	*Location*	*Score*	*Tries*	*Con*	*PG*	*DG*	*Referee*
July 15	Canterbury (ST)	Christchurch	29–58	McGregor (3), Filipo, Schwencke	Landon-Lane (2)			George Haswell
July 23	Auckland	Lower Hutt	15–17	Faleafaga, McGregor, N. Foaese				Will Johnston
July 30	Counties Manukau	Lower Hutt	20–53	Lea, Falaniko, McGregor	Ruaporo	Ruaporo		Taneika Uerata
August 6	Hawke's Bay	Lower Hutt	22–33	Patea-Fereti, Kautai, Ngan-Woo	Ruaporo (2)	Ruaporo		Cassie Watt
August 12	Bay of Plenty	Tauranga	7–37	McGregor	Ruaporo			Maggie Cogger-Orr
August 27	Waikato	Hamilton	29–31	Kautai (3), Lea, Tagoai	Ruaporo (2)			Scott McKenzie

ST Stewart Trophy

2023 WOMEN'S SEASON'S STATISTICS

LEADING SCORERS IN ALL FIRST-CLASS MATCHES IN NEW ZEALAND AND FOR NEW ZEALAND TEAMS OVERSEAS

(Record: 173, Kendra Cocksedge, 2018 in 13 games, 13 tries, 45 conversions, 6 penalty goals)

	Teams	*M*	*Tries*	*Con*	*PG*	*DG*	*Total*
Renee Holmes	Waikato/Chiefs/New Zealand	13	5	38	7	–	122
Ruahei Demant	Auckland/Blues/New Zealand	18	7	30	5	–	110
Mererangi Paul	Counties Manukau/Chiefs/New Zealand	14	18	1	–	–	92
Selica Winiata	Manawatu	7	3	31	3	–	86
Rosie Kelly	Canterbury/Matatu/New Zealand	14	2	23	6	–	74
Krysten Cottrell	Hawke's Bay/Blues	11	1	26	5	–	72
Angelica Mekemeke Vahai	Auckland/Black Ferns XV	9	14	–	–	–	70
Krystal Murray	Northland/Hurricanes/New Zealand	17	7	13	3	–	70

THREE (or more) TRIES IN A MATCH

(Record: 9, Vanessa Cootes, New Zealand v France, 1996)

4	Te Whetumarama Nuku	Manawatu v Taranaki
4	Ruby Tui	New Zealand v Wales
3	Precious Auimatagi	Tasman v Taranaki
3	Jamie Church	Otago v North Harbour (sf)
3	Luka Connor	Chiefs Manawa v Hurricanes Poua
3	Kerri Johnson	Northland v Taranaki
3	Harmony Kautai	Wellington v Waikato
3	Jaymie Kolose	Counties Manukau v Bay of Plenty
3	Justine McGregor	Wellington v Canterbury
3	Angelica Mekemeke Vahai	Auckland v Bay of Plenty
3	Angelica Mekemeke Vahai	Auckland v Counties Manukau
3	Krystal Murray	Northland v Otago
3	Mererangi Paul	Chiefs Manawa v Blues
3	Mererangi Paul	Counties Manukau v Hawke's Bay
3	Mererangi Paul	New Zealand v Wales
3	Cheyelle Robins-Reti	Matatu v Blues (sf)
3	Iva Sauira	Tasman v Taranaki
3	Fiaali'i Solomona	Tasman v Taranaki
3	Grace Steinmetz	Canterbury v Hawke's Bay
3	Holly Wratt-Groeneweg	Canterbury v Hawke's Bay (sf)

LEADING TRY-SCORERS

(Record: 19, Dianne Kahura, 2002, in 11 games)

Tries	Games		Teams
18	14	Mererangi Paul	Counties Manukau/Chiefs/New Zealand
14	9	Angelica Mekemeke Vahai	Auckland/Black Ferns XV
11	7	Jamie Church	Otago
11	15	Luka Connor	Bay of Plenty/Chiefs/New Zealand
11	11	Jaymie Kolose	Counties Manukau/Blues
11	13	Martha Mataele	Canterbury/Matatu/New Zealand
11	18	Liana Vaha'akolo	Auckland/Blues/New Zealand

18 (or more) POINTS IN A MATCH

(Record: Record: 45, Vanessa Cootes, New Zealand v France, 1996, 9 tries; Kelly Brazier, Otago v Hawke's Bay, 2012, 5 tries, 10 conversions)

23	Selica Winiata	Manawatu v Tasman (sf), 1t, 9c
21	Ruahei Demant	Auckland v Bay of Plenty, 1t, 8c
20	Te Whetumarama Nuku	Manawatu v Taranaki, 4t
20	Ruby Tui	New Zealand v Wales, 4t
18	Krystal Murray	Northland v Taranaki, 2t, 4c

SIX (OR MORE) CONVERSIONS IN A MATCH

(Record: 14, Amanda Rasch, Wellington v Taranaki, 2018)

9	Selica Winiata	Manawatu v Tasman (sf)
8	Ruahei Demant	Auckland v Bay of Plenty
6	Renee Holmes	New Zealand v Canada
6	Pohutukawa Kakara	Northland v Otago
6	Rosie Kelly	Canterbury v Bay of Plenty
6	Rosie Kelly	Canterbury v Hawke's Bay (sf)
6	Selica Winiata	Manawatu v Taranaki

THREE (or more) PENALTY GOALS IN A MATCH

(Record: 6, Annaleah Rush, Auckland v Wellington, 2001)

3	Grace Freeman	North Harbour v Manawatu
3	Renee Holmes	Matatu v Chiefs Manawa (final)
3	Rosie Kelly	Canterbury v Counties Manukau
3	Samantha Wood	Waikato v Bay of Plenty

WOMEN'S FIRST-CLASS STATISTICS

to January 1, 2024

100 GAMES IN FIRST-CLASS RUGBY

	Career	Games		Career	Games
Emma Jensen	1999–2022	189	Casey Robertson	1999–2014	118
Kendra Cocksedge	2007–22	172	Te Kura Ngata-Aerengamate	2012–23	118
Fiao'o Faamausili	1999–2018	164	Aleisha Nelson	2008–21	117
Justine Lavea	2001–20	152	Charmaine McMenamin	2009–23	107
Stephanie Te Ohaere-Fox	2003–23	150	Hazel Tubic	2005–23	105
Selica Winiata	2001–23	144	Ruahei Demant	2013–23	103
Eloise Blackwell	2009–23	138	Arihiana Marino-Tauhinu	2011–23	103
Anna Richards	1990–2011	125	Linda Itunu	2003–19	101
Phillipa Love	2009–23	119	Jackie Patea-Fereti	2006–23	100

100 GAMES FOR A TEAM

Stephanie Te Ohaere-Fox	Canterbury	2004–22	113
Fiao'o Faamausili	Auckland	1999–2018	106
Selica Winiata	Manawatu	2001–2023	102
Kendra Cocksedge	Canterbury	2007–22	100

300 POINTS IN FIRST-CLASS RUGBY

	Career	Games	Tries	Con	PG	DG	Points
Kendra Cocksedge	2007–22	172	89	357	111	1	1495
Selica Winiata	2001–23	144	117	94	17	–	824
Emma Jensen	1999–22	189	13	154	82	1	622
Hazel Tubic	2005–23	105	25	165	43	–	584
Hannah Porter	1999–2008	59	20	115	61	–	513
Chelsea Semple	2011–22	95	31	99	44	1	488
Kelly Brazier	2005–22	82	35	97	31	–	462
Tammi Wilson	1998–2001	45	40	92	24	1	459
Krysten Cottrell	2013–23	96	19	123	35	–	446
Ruahei Demant	2013–23	103	40	85	14	–	412
Rosie Kelly	2017–23	61	23	97	10	–	339
Claire Richardson	2001–14	79	36	33	25	–	321
Renee Woodman-Wickliffe	2009-23	97	57	10	5	–	320
Fiao'o Faamausili	1999–2018	164	63	–	–	–	315

50 TRIES IN FIRST-CLASS RUGBY

	Tries	Games		Tries	Games
Selica Winiata	117	144	Vanessa Cootes	54	50
Kendra Cocksedge	89	172	Portia Woodman	54	38
Ayesha Leti-I'iga	73	76	Dianne Kahura	53	36
Fiao'o Faamausili	63	164	Carla Hohepa	53	79
Renee Woodman-Wickliffe	57	97	Victoria Grant	51	69

MOST DROPPED GOALS IN FIRST-CLASS RUGBY

	DG	Games
Rebecca Mahoney (*nee* Hull)	4	69

WOMEN'S SEVENS RUGBY

The Black Ferns Sevens had a vintage 2022/23 HSBC Sevens series. After taking silver at the opening event, at Dubai in December 2022, the squad won the Cup final in each of the remaining six tournaments. There were no newcomers in 2023, the squad being a fine blend of experience and talented youngsters who had been introduced during the previous couple of years. The experienced regular flyers Michaela Blyde, Portia Woodman-Wickliffe and Stacey Waaka each scored 30 tries or more, so often benefitting from the skills of experienced campaigners Kelly Brazier, Theresa Fitzpatrick, Shiray Kaka, Niall Guthrie, Alena Saili and the elusive Tyla Nathan-Wong. Ruby Tui was having a year's break from sevens.

In the brief 14-minute games success is gained by quick-thinkers who in a split second capitalise on an opportunity or quickly react, without hesitation, to a referee's call. Inspirational captain Sarah Hirini was again responsible for igniting breaks which resulted, many times, in game-winning tries. Her severe injury on the opening day at Dubai in December appeared to affect the team's performances in the opening two rounds of the 2023/24 series.

The younger brigade is making an increasing impact and taking on more responsibility. One could be excused for thinking strong-running 19-year-old Jorja Miller had been in the game for many years, so effective was she in creating breaks. Jazmin Felix-Hotham, Manaia Nuku and Mahina Paul are becoming more prominent, and Risi Pouri-Lane took over kicking duties from Nathan-Wong and captained the side during Hirini's absence late in the year

		Date of				Career		
		Birth	Height	Weight	Debut	Tournaments	Tries	Points
M.G. (Michaela) Blyde	Bay of Plenty	29-12-95	1.65	65	2013	46	258	1290
K.A. (Kelly) Brazier	Bay of Plenty	28-10-89	1.73	68	2013	48	119	697
J.A-M.R. (Jazmin) Felix-Hotham	Waikato	02-07-00	1.72	67	2020	14	30	150
T.M. (Theresa) Fitzpatrick	Auckland	25-02-95	1.68	74	2016	32	23	115
N.L.V. (Niall) Guthrie (nee Williams)	Auckland	21-04-88	1.74	76	2015	38	49	245
S.L. (Sarah) Hirini	Manawatu	09-12-92	1.77	76	2012	58	117	585
T.R. (Tysha) Ikenasio	Auckland	13-09-97	1.65	70	2022	5	1	5
S.T. (Shiray) Kaka	Waikato	26-03-95	1.68	68	2013	28	69	345
J.R. (Jorja) Miller	Canterbury	08-02-04	1.67	71	2022	10	25	125
T.B. (Tyla) Nathan-Wong	Northland	01-07-94	1.65	59	2012	54	61	1591
M.C. (Manaia) Nuku	Waikato	03-09-02	1.69	68	2022	5	1	15
M.A. (Mahina) Paul	Bay of Plenty	19-04-01	1.69	74	2019	6	14	70
R.I.R. (Risaleaana) Pouri-Lane	Bay of Plenty	28-05-00	1.64	63	2018	19	28	326
A.F. (Alena) Saili	Bay of Plenty	13-12-98	1.71	70	2017	29	46	230
S.J.A.K. (Stacey) Waaka	Bay of Plenty	03-11-95	1.73	73	2016	31	108	540
T.R. (Tenika) Willison	Waikato	07-12-97	1.67	69	2016	23	10	150
P.L. (Portia) Woodman-Wickliffe	Northland	12-07-91	1.72	75	2012	47	289	1445

Coach: Cory Sweeney
Manager: Jess Jones
Video analyst: Jessica Chittenden

Assistant coaches: Stu Ross, Edwin Cocker
Physiotherapist: Kate Niederer
S & C coach: Amanda Murphy

Final points for 2022/23 World Rugby Sevens Series: New Zealand 138, Australia 118, USA 108, France 92, Ireland 74, Fiji 68, Great Britain 68, Japan 40, Canada 39, Spain 28, Brazil 16, Poland 2, Papua New Guinea 2, China 2, Hong Kong China 1, Colombia 1, South Africa 1. The series was held over seven tournaments between November 2022 and May 2023.

Series winners: New Zealand 2013, 2014, 2015, 2017, 2019, 2020, 2023; Australia 2016, 2018, 2022. Series was not held during 2021 due to the pandemic.

World Rugby Sevens Series Cup championship titles (1999 to January 1, 2024): New Zealand 33, Australia 15, Canada 4, England 2, USA 3.

	New Zealand	Australia	Canada	Hong Kong	France	Dubai	South Africa	**TOTALS**		Tries	Conversions	**Points**
Michaela Blyde	*	*	*	*	–	*	*	6	–	35	–	**175**
Kelly Brazier	–	–	*	*	*	*	*	5	–	5	–	**25**
Jazmin Felix-Hotham	*	*	*	*	*	*	*	7	–	20	–	**100**
Theresa Fitzpatrick	*	*	*	–	–	–	–	3	–	1	–	**5**
Niall Guthrie	*	*	–	–	*	–	–	3	–	–	–	**0**
Sarah Hirini (capt)	*	*	*	*	*	*	–	6	–	17	–	**85**
Tysha Ikenasio	–	*	*	–	–	–	*	3	–	–	–	**0**
Shiray Kaka	*	*	*	*	*	*	*	7	–	17	–	**85**
Jorja Miller	*	*	*	*	*	*	*	7	–	23	–	**115**
Tyla Nathan-Wong	*	*	*	*	*	–	–	5	–	7	70	**175**
Manaia Nuku	–	–	–	*	–	*	*	3	–	–	3	**6**
Mahina Paul	–	–	–	–	*	*	*	3	–	9	–	**45**
Risaleaana Pouri-Lane	*	*	*	*	*	*	*	7	–	12	37	**134**
Alena Saili	*	–	–	*	*	*	*	5	–	7	–	**35**
Stacey Waaka	*	*	*	*	*	*	*	7	–	37	–	**185**
Tenika Willison	*	*	–	–	–	*	*	4	–	5	8	**41**
Portia Woodman-Wickliffe	*	*	*	*	*	*	*	7	–	30	–	**150**

Totals – 225 tries; 1 penalty try; 118 conversions; 1368 points. 322 points were conceded.

Pouri-Lane was captain at Cape Town

NEW ZEALAND AT NEW ZEALAND HSBC SEVENS

FMG Stadium, Hamilton **January 21/22, 2023**

Date	Opponent	Result	Tries	Conversions
Jan 21	Papua New Guinea	won 58–0	Waaka (3), Blyde (2), Hirini (2), Kaka, Saili, Miller	Nathan-Wong (3), Pouri-Lane
Jan 21	Fiji	won 27–0	Pouri-Lane, Blyde, Felix-Hotham, Waaka, Hirini	Nathan-Wong
Jan 21	Great Britain	won 20–0	Blyde (2), Waaka, Woodman-Wickliffe	
Jan 22	Japan (quarterfinal)	won 43–12	Kaka (3), Pouri-Lane (2), Miller, Woodman-Wickliffe	Nathan-Wong (2), Pouri-Lane (2)
Jan 22	Ireland (semifinal)	won 32–0	Miller (2), Blyde (2), Waaka, Woodman-Wickliffe	Nathan-Wong
Jan 22	USA (Cup final)	won 33–7	Blyde (3), Felix-Hotham, Woodman-Wickliffe	Nathan-Wong (3), Pouri-Lane

NEW ZEALAND AT AUSTRALIA HSBC SEVENS

Allianz Stadium, Sydney **January 27–29, 2023**

Date	Opponent	Result	Tries	Conversions
Jan 27	Papua New Guinea	won 48-0	Nathan-Wong (2), Fitzpatrick, Felix-Hotham, Miller, Kaka, Woodman-Wickliffe, Blyde	Nathan-Wong (4)
Jan 27	France	won 29-14	Waaka (2), Felix-Hotham, Miller, Woodman-Wickliffe	Pouri-Lane (2)
Jan 28	Japan	won 27-12	Blyde (3), Waaka, Kaka	Nathan-Wong
Jan 28	Japanl (quarterfinal)	won 33-0	Miller (2), Blyde, Waaka, Woodman-Wickliffe	Nathan-Wong (4)
Jan 29	Ireland (semifinal)	won 41–0	Kaka (3), Hirini (2), Waaka, Felix-Hotham	Nathan-Wong (2), Pouri-Lane
Jan 29	France (Cup final)	won 35–0	Felix-Hotham (2), Willison (2), Woodman-Wickliffe	Nathan-Wong (4), Pouri-Lane

NEW ZEALAND AT CANADA HSBC SEVENS

BC Place Stadium, Langford, Vancouver **March 3–5, 2023**

Date	Opponent	Result	Tries	Conversions
Mar 3	Colombia	won 60–0	Blyde (3), Woodman-Wickliffe (2), Felix-Hotham (2), Nathan-Wong, Waaka, Hirini	Nathan-Wong (5)
Mar 3	Great Britain	won 43–7	Waaka (2), Hirini (2), Miller, Kaka, Nathan-Wong	Nathan-Wong (4)
Mar 4	Fiji	won 24–7	Blyde (2), Hirini, Felix-Hotham	Pouri-Lane (2)
Mar 4	Canada (quarterfinal)	won 10–5	Woodman-Wickliffe, Blyde	
Mar 5	France (semifinal)	won 36–7	Waaka (2), Hirini, Nathan-Wong, Blyde, Felix-Hotham	Nathan-Wong (3)
Mar 5	Australia (Cup final)	won 19–12	Hirini, Waaka, Miller	Nathan-Wong (2)

NEW ZEALAND AT HONG KONG HSBC SEVENS

Hong Kong Stadium, Hong Kong **March 31–April 2, 2023**

Date	Opponent	Result	Tries	Conversions
Mar 31	Hong Kong China	won 50–0	Waaka (3), Woodman-Wickliffe (2), Brazier, Hirini, Felix-Hotham	Pouri-Lane (3), Nathan-Wong (2)
Mar 31	Great Britain	won 43–0	Kaka (2), Pouri-Lane (2), Felix-Hotham, Waaka, Blyde	Nathan-Wong (4)
Apr 1	Canada	won 46–0	Kaka (2), Woodman-Wickliffe (2), Blyde, Brazier, Saili, Waaka	Nathan-Wong (3)
Apr 1	Canada (quarterfinal)	won 45–14	Miller (2), Pouri-Lane (2), Blyde, Brazier, Saili	Nathan-Wong (5)
Apr 2	Fiji (semifinal)	won 31–5	Woodman-Wickliffe (2), Blyde, Waaka, Miller	Nathan-Wong (2), Pouri-Lane
Apr 2	Australia (Cup final)	won 26–17	Waaka (2), penalty try, Blyde	Nathan-Wong (2)

NEW ZEALAND AT FRANCE HSBC SEVENS

Stade Ernest-Wallon, Toulouse **May 12–14, 2023**

Date	Opponent	Result	Tries	Conversions
May 12	Poland	won 50–0	Hirini (2), Woodman-Wickliffe (2), Paul (2), Kaka, Saili	Pouri-Lane (3), Nathan-Wong (2)
May 12	USA	won 31–12	Woodman-Wickliffe (2), Waaka, Miller, Nathan-Wong	Nathan-Wong (3)
May 13	Canada	won 28–7	Miller (2), Waaka, Hirini	Nathan-Wong (3), Pouri-Lane
May 13	Japan (quarterfinal)	won 29–7	Pouri-Lane (2), Woodman-Wickliffe, Nathan-Wong, Waaka	Nathan-Wong (2)
May 14	France (semifinal)	won 31–7	Woodman-Wickliffe (2), Hirini, Kaka, Paul	Pouri-Lane (2), Nathan-Wong
May 14	USA (Cup final)	won 19–14	Waaka (2), Felix-Hotham	Nathan-Wong (2)

NEW ZEALAND AT DUBAI HSBC SVNS

The Sevens, Dubai **December 2/3, 2023**

Date	Opponent	Result	Tries	Conversions
Dec 2	South Africa	won 19–14	Paul, Felix-Hotham, Hirini	Pouri-Lane (2)
Dec 2	Great Britain	won 43–7	Blyde (2), Woodman-Wickliffe, Waaka, Saili, Miller, Paul	Pouri-Lane (2), Willison (2)
Dec 2	Fiji	won 29–21	Waaka (2), Felix-Hotham, Saili, Paul	Pouri-Lane (2)
Dec 3	Brazil (Cup quarterfinal)	won 26–14	Woodman-Wickliffe, Willison, Paul, Brazier	Pouri-Lane (2), Nuku
Dec 3	Canada (semifinal)	won 21–19	Pouri-Lane, Blyde, Miller	Pouri-Lane, Willison, Nuku
Dec 3	Australia (Cup final)	lost 19–26	Miller (3)	Pouri-Lane, Willison

NEW ZEALAND AT SOUTH AFRICA HSBC SVNS

DHL Stadium, Cape Town **December 9–10, 2023**

Date	Opponent	Result	Tries	Conversions
Dec 9	Great Britain	won 37–5	Woodman-Wickliffe (2), Blyde (2), Felix-Hotham, Waaka, Kaka	Willison
Dec 9	Brazil	won 22–12	Pouri-Lane, Saili, Felix-Hotham, Waaka	Pouri-Lane
Dec 9	Ireland	won 33–7	Miller, Felix-Hotham, Waaka, Willison, Paul	Willison (2), Pouri-Lane, Nuku
Dec 10	Canada (Cup quarterfinal)	won 41–0	Woodman-Wickliffe, Felix-Hotham, Blyde, Brazier, Willison, Paul, Waaka	Pouri-Lane (2), Willison
Dec 10	France (semifinal)	lost 12–24	Blyde, Woodman-Wickliffe	Pouri-Lane
Dec 10	USA (for 3rd place)	won 19–7	Miller, Blyde, Pouri-Lane	Pouri-Lane (2)
Australia defeated France 29-26 in the Cup final				

NEW ZEALAND DEVELOPMENT AT OCEANIA RUGBY SEVENS CHAMPIONSHIP

In preparation for the commencement of the 2023/24 HSBC World Series, a Development squad took part at the Oceania Sevens in Brisbane. Six of the twelve players were current Black Ferns Sevens players, Te Tamaki and Teneti had appeared in 2022 and Faleafaga in 2019. Anderson (Waikato), Watherston (Bay of Plenty) and Steinmetz (Canterbury) were making their first appearance in a national sevens squad.

Squad: Tenika Willison (co-capt), Theresa Fitzpatrick (co-capt), Reese Anderson, Dhys Faleafaga, Tysha Ikenasio, Shiray Kaka, Jorja Miller, Manaia Nuku, Grace Steinmetz, Terina Te Tamaki, Kelsey Teneti, Olive Watherston.

Coach: Ed Cocker
Assistant coach: Dan Goodwin
Manager: Lisa Appert
S & C coach: Albert Chang
Physiotherapist: Peter Hughes

NEW ZEALAND DEVELOPMENT AT OCEANIA RUGBY SEVENS CHAMPIONSHIP

Ballymore Stadium, Brisbane **November 10–12, 2023**

Date	Opponent	Result	Tries	Conversions
Nov 10	Australia	lost 19–21	Ikenasio, Miller, Kaka	Willison (2)
Nov 10	Australia	drew 21–21	Willison, Ikenasio, Kaka	Willison (2), Fitzpatrick
Nov 11	Australia	lost 12–26	Miller, Kaka	Willison
Nov 11	Australia	lost 12–40	Nuku, Kaka	Willison
Nov 12	Australia (semifinal)	lost 10–20	Kaka, Steinmetz	
Nov 12	Papua New Guinea (for 3rd)	won 20–0	Ikenasio (3), Steinmetz	
Nov 12	Samoa (final)	won 24–19 aet	Rokolisoa (2), Fineanganofo, Cook-Savage	Rokolisoa, Cook-Savage
Australia defeated France 29-26 in the Cup final				

NEW ZEALAND INTERNATIONAL SEVENS

FMG Waikato Stadium, Hamilton **January 21/22, 2023**

POOL PLAY

A Fiji 19, Great Britain 14; New Zealand 58, Papua New Guinea 0; Great Britain 36, Papua New Guinea 0; New Zealand 27, Fiji 0; Fiji 50, Papua New Guinea 0; New Zealand 20, Great Britain 0.

B France 12, Canada 12; Australia 26, Japan 14; France 26, Japan 12; Australia 33, Canada 7; Japan 17, Canada 7; Australia 43, France 0.

C USA 31, Spain 12; Ireland 28, Brazil 5; Ireland 31, Spain 5; USA 41, Brazil 0; Brazil 36, Spain 17; USA 15, Ireland 7.

Cup quarterfinals	Australia 38, Great Britain 0; USA 27, Fiji 7; Ireland 24, France 7; New Zealand 43, Japan 12.
Semifinals for 9th	Brazil 41, Papua New Guinea 7; Spain 7, Canada 0
Semifinals for 5th	Great Britain 12, Fiji 0; Japan 19, France 12
Cup semifinals	USA 10, Australia 7; New Zealand 32, Ireland 0
Play-off for 11th	Canada 44, Papua New Guinea 5
Play-off for 9th	Spain 17, Brazil 12
Play-off for 7th	France 34, Fiji 5
Play-off for 5th	Great Britain 14, Japan 10
Bronze final	Australia 33, Ireland 17
Cup final	New Zealand, 33 USA 7

Tournament referees: Finlay Brown (Scotland), Craig Chan (Hong Kong), Talal Chaudry (Canada), Maggie Cogger-Orr (NZ), Paulo Duarte (Portugal), Nick Hogan (NZ), AJ Jacobs (South Africa), Francisco Lopez (USA), Kat Roche (USA).

PLAYING RECORD OF NEW ZEALAND SEVENS TEAMS

	Tournaments			Games				Points	
	Attended	Won	Runner-up	Played	Won	Draw	Lost	For	Against
2000	1	1	–	7	7	–	–	293	20
2001	3	3	–	15	15	–	–	661	17
2008	1	–	1	6	4	–	2	174	57
2009	1	–	1	6	5	–	1	177	37
2012	2	2	–	12	10	2	–	378	69
2013	6	3	1	36	30	–	6	958	279
2014	6	5	1	37	36	–	1	1102	262
2015	6	3	–	36	30	–	6	1011	402
2016	6	1	3	36	30	–	6	915	279
2017	7	5	–	41	39	–	2	1018	251
2018	8	7	1	45	44	–	1	1432	307
2019	8	5	1	46	40	1	5	1254	430
2020	2	2	–	10	10	–	–	294	87
2021	1	1	–	6	6	–	–	172	57
2022	6	2	3	33	28	1	4	979	275
2023	7	5	1	42	40	–	2	1368	322
TOTALS	***71***	***45***	***13***	***414***	***374***	***4***	***36***	***11271***	***3151***

TOURNAMENT CAPTAINS

Sarah Hirini	2013–23	47
Huriana Manuel	2012-14	11
Tyla Nathan-Wong	2017, 19, 22	6
Anna Richards	2000-01	4
Melissa Ruscoe	2008	1
Hannah Porter	2009	1
Risi Pouri-Lane	2023	1

SEVENS RECORDS

to January 1, 2024

BY NEW ZEALAND TEAMS

Most successive wins	50	2018-19
Most successive tournament wins	9	2018-19
Most successive appearances in finals	10	2013–15, 2018-19

Tournament records

Most points	293	Hong Kong, 2000
Most tries	47	Hong Kong, 2000
Most conversions	30	New Zealand 2001

Match records

Highest team score	83	v International Selection, Japan 2001
Record victory (points ahead)	83	83–0 v International Selection, Japan 2001
Highest score conceded	35	v Australia (final), Dubai 2013
Record defeat (points behind)	31	0–31 v Australia, Sydney 2018
Most tries	13	v International Selection, Japan 2001
Most conversions	10	v Tahiti, Fiji 2017

BY THE PLAYERS

Career records

Attended most tournaments	58	S.L. Hirini
Most points	1591	T.B. Nathan-Wong
Most tries	289	P.L. Woodman
Most conversions	643	T.B. Nathan-Wong

Tournament records

Most points	70	P.L. Woodman, USA 2015
Most tries	14	P.L. Woodman, USA 2015
Most conversions	29	A.M. Richards, New Zealand 2001

Match records

Most points	30	M. Blyde, v Sri Lanka, Commonwealth Games 2022
Most tries	6	M. Blyde, v Sri Lanka, Commonwealth Games 2022
Most conversions	10	T.R. Willison v Tahiti, Fiji 2017

NEW ZEALAND SEVENS REPRESENTATIVES, 2000–23

Tournaments

Alley, C.H. (*Waikato*) 2014 1
Aniseko, F. (*Auckland*) 2008 1
Baker, S.J. (*Wellington*) 2012 (*Manawatu*) 2013 (*Waikato*) 2016–17–18–19 21
Bird, O.M. (*Canterbury*) 2013 1
Blyde, M.G. (*Taranaki*) 2013–14–15–16 (*Bay of Plenty*) 2017–18–19–20–21–22–23 46
Brazier, K.A. (*Otago*) 2013–14 (*Bay of Plenty*) 2015–16–17–18–19–20–21–22–23 48
Broughton, G.P. (*Taranaki*) 2014–15–16–17–18–19–20–21 29
Burgess, L.A. (*Taranaki*) 2012–13 2
Cocksedge, K.M. (*Canterbury*) 2008–12–13 3
Cootes, V. (*Waikato*) 2001 3
Drummond, J.A. (*Tasman*) 2017 2
Davis, M.F. (*Counties Manukau*) 2012 1
Faleafaga, D.S. (*Wellington*) 2019 3
Felix-Hotham, J.A-M.R. (*Waikato*) 2020–22–23 14
Ferguson, J. (*Hawke's Bay*) 2009 1
Ferris, R.R. (*Manawatu*) 2019 2
Fitzpatrick, T.M. (*Auckland*) 2016–17–18–19–20–21–22–23 32
Forbes, M.H. (*Tasman*) 2012 1
Gould, L. (*Canterbury*) 2000 (*Wellington*) 2001 (*Bay of Plenty*) 2012 4
Grant, K.M. (*Canterbury*) 2014 1
Grant, V.E. (*Auckland*) 2008–09 2
Greig, V.A.P. (*Manawatu*) 2013 2
Guthrie, N.L.V. (Auckland) 2015–16–17–18–19–20–22–23 38
Halapua, C. (*Auckland*) 2012 1
Hansen, S. (*Wanganui*) 2000 1
Harding, H.R. (*Waikato*) 2018–19 3
Hira-Herangi, A.P. (*Waikato*) 2014 1
Hireme, A.H. (*Waikato*) 2013–14–15 11
Hirini, S.L. (*nee Goss*) (*Manawatu*) 2012–13–14–15–16–17–18–19–20–21–22–23 58
Hohepa, C.G. (*Otago*) 2009 (*Waikato*) 2012–13–14–15 10
Hohepa, C.H. (*Waikato*) 2012 1
Holden, S.E. (*Manawatu*) 2000 (*Wellington*) 2001 2
Hotham, J.A-M.R. (*Waikato*) 2020 1
Hurring, H.A. (*Otago*) 2013 2
Hutana, H.S. (*Manawatu*) 2013 2
Ikenasio, T.R. (*Auckland*) 2022–23 5
Itunu, L.F. (*Auckland*) 2009–12–13–14 11
Kahura, D.M.T. (*Auckland*) 2000–01 4
Kaka, S.T. (*nee Tane*) (*Waikato*) 2013–14–15–16–18–19–20–21–22–23 28
Karanga, P. (*Manawatu*) 2001 1
Kurei, N. (*Bay of Plenty*) 2000 1
Lavea, J. (*Auckland*) 2009 1
Lavea, V.N.H. (*Auckland*) 2008 1
McAlister, K.M. (*Auckland*) 2012–13–14–15–16–17 20
McGregor, A. (*Auckland*) 2008–09 2
Manuel, H.R. (*Auckland*) 2008–09–12–13–14–16 16
Mayes, C.A.M. (*Manawatu*) 2013–17 3
Miller, J.R. (*Canterbury*) 2022–23 10
Morrow, M.L. (*Bay of Plenty*) 2014–15 3
Naoupo, T. (*Auckland*) 2001 3
Nathan-Wong, T.B. (*Auckland*) 2012–13–14–15–16–17–18–19–20 (*Northland*) 2021–22–23 54
Ngawati, T.A. (*Auckland*) 2012 1
Nuku, M.C. (*Waikato*) 2022–23 5
Paul, M.A. (*Bay of Plenty*) 2019–20–22–23 6
Paul, T. (*Bay of Plenty*) 2001 3
Porter, H.J. (*nee Myers*) (*Otago*) 2000–01 (*Auckland*) 2008–09 6
Pouri-Lane, R.I.R. (*Tasman*) 2018–19–20 (*Bay of Plenty*) 2021–22–23 19
Reti, T.C. (*Manawatu*) 2017 1
Richards, A.M. (*Auckland*) 2000–01 4
Robins-Reti, C.R.A. (*Waikato*) 2017–19 6
Ruscoe, M.J. (*Canterbury*) 2008 1

Rush, A.M. (*Auckland*) 2000–01 3

Saili, A.F. (*Southland*) 2017–18–19–20–21 (*Bay of Plenty*) 2022–23 29

Scanlan, C.R. (*Auckland*) 2014–15 3

Shelford, E.T. (*Bay of Plenty*) 2001 3

Shortland, S. (*Auckland*) 2000–01 4

Sue, K.J. (*Manawatu*) 2013 2

Sutorius, A.E. (*Wellington*) 2008 1

Tane, S.T. (*Waikato*) 2013–14–15–16 10

Tairakena, M.G.T. (*Waikato*) 2019 1

Tapsell, A.N.O. (*Canterbury*) 2013 (*Bay of Plenty*) 2015 5

Te Tamaki, T.K. (*Auckland*) 2008–09 2

Te Tamaki, T.L.R. (*Waikato*) 2016–17–18–19–22 21

Teneti, K.J. (*Waikato*) 2022 2

Townsend, M.A. (*Manawatu*) 2008 1

Tubic, H.S. (*Counties Manukau*) 2012–13–14–15–16 15

Tufuga, R. (*Manawatu*) 2016–17 3

Tui, R.M. (*Canterbury*) 2012–13–14–15–16–17–18–19 (*Bay of Plenty*) 2020 (*Counties Manukau*) 2021 40

Vaughan, J.M. (*Manawatu*) 2016 1

Waaka, S.J.A.K. (*Waikato*) 2016–17–18–19–20–21 (*Bay of Plenty*) 2022–23 31

Webber, J.B.M. (*Waikato*) 2014–15–16 10

Whata-Simpkins, K.R. (*Wellington*) 2014–15–16–17–18–19 20

Wickliffe, R.W.M. (*Counties Manukau*) 2009–13–16–17 7

Wikeepa, R. (*Waikato*) 2009 1

Williams, N.L.V. (*Auckland*) 2015–16–17–18–19–20–22 35

Willison, T.R. (*Waikato*) 2016–17–18–19–20–21–22–23 23

Wilson, T. (*Auckland*) 2000 1

Winiata, S.C. (*Manawatu*) 2008–09–13–14–15–16 15

Woodman-Wickliffe, P.L. (*Auckland*) 2012–13–14–15 (*Counties Manukau*) 2016–17–18 (*Northland*) 2021–22–23 47

CHRONICLE OF EVENTS

JANUARY 2023

11 Finalists for the Halberg Awards are named: The Black Ferns (team of the year); Ruahei Demant (sports woman of the year); Wayne Smith (coach of the year) . . . The leading clubs in the North Harbour, Auckland and Counties Manukau unions will play a combined three-weeks knockout competition as a prelude to their individual club competitions.

23 The Highlanders sign former England fly-half Freddie Burns as an injury replacement for prop Luca Inch who will miss the season with injury.

27 World Rugby confirm the return of the Under 20 Championship which will be held in South Africa in 2023 and 2024. It was not held 2020–2022 due to Covid-19.

30 Campbell Johnstone comes out as the first openly gay All Black on TVNZ news programme Seven Sharp.

FEBRUARY

1 World Rugby announce the match official's appointments for the Women's Six Nations. Maggie Cogger-Orr and Lauren Jenner receive two refereeing appointments each with Jenner also receiving an assistant referee appointment.

7 NZR release the All Blacks' test schedule for 2023 with home tests against South Africa (Mt Smart, Auckland) and Australia (Dunedin). Eden Park is unavailable due to its use in the Women's football World Cup being hosted by New Zealand and Australia. The Rugby Championship will be played over just one round . . . Aaron Smith and Beauden Barrett have both signed for Japanese club Toyota Verblitz after the World Cup. Smith's signing is for three years and Barrett for one.

8 Brodie Retallick announces he has signed with Japanese club Kobelco after this year's World Cup.

9 Dane Coles announces he will retire from rugby at the end of this year.

10 Alan Bunting is the new Black Ferns Director of Rugby, replacing Wayne Smith who stepped down after last year's World Cup. He is appointed through to the 2025 Women's World Cup.

14 Super Rugby Pacific will trial new law innovations this season, which have the support of World Rugby. (1) The referee will put a stopwatch on goalkickers who will have 90 seconds to complete the conversion from the time the try is awarded and 60 seconds to complete a penalty goal once the referee signals a shot for goal, (2) Match officials will expect lineouts and scrums to be formed within 30 seconds of the respective marks being set, (3) The TMO will only interrupt play to investigate serious and clear and obvious dangerous play missed by the match officials, (4) If a player receive a yellow card, while he is off the field the TMO will have 8 minutes to uphold the 10-minute yellow card decision or increase it to a 20-minute red card, (5) Referees can issue a full red card for deliberate foul play in which case the player concerned will not be able to return to the field after 20 minutes or be replaced.

15 At the Halberg Awards: The Black Ferns win Team of the Year; Wayne Smith wins Coach of the Year.

20 Canterbury a loss of $35,867 for 2022.

24 The All Blacks XV will play two matches in Japan in July, one of them against the Japan national team . . . At an auction house in Wales, the Barbarians jersey worn by Gareth Edwards in 1973 against the All Blacks sells for a world record £240,000 (NZ$456,000).

27 A total of $250,000 is raised for the NZ Red Cross Disaster Fund and Cyclone Gabrielle relief from the opening round of Super Rugby Pacific and Super Rugby Aupiki. NZR and Sky TV pledged $500 for every point scored in the six matches involving NZ teams, then added a further $55,500 to bring the final total up to $250,000.

28 Hawke's Bay a profit of $1,078,178 . . . World Rugby confirms a new format for the third edition of the Pacific Four Series. It will take place over three windows (instead of one) and the top three nations will qualify for the top tier (six nations) of the new Women's XV tournament later this year.

MARCH

1 NZR announce the appointment of the All Blacks head coach for next year will be made in four to six weeks, instead of after this year's World Cup as it has traditionally been . . . Current All Blacks head coach Ian Foster responds that he will not re-apply.

3 The third edition of the NZ Super Rugby U20 tournament will be expanded to eight teams with the addition of Moana Pasifika and Fijian Drua squads. For the first time it will be structured for a tournament winner.

5 Black Ferns Sevens win the Vancouver leg of the HSBC World Rugby Women's Sevens Series. The 20 points earned for winning the final guarantees them a top four finish in the 2022–2023 Series final standings (with two tournaments still to play) and automatic qualification for the 2024 Paris Olympics.

7 Ardie Savea receives a one-week suspension following the Hurricanes match with the Melbourne Rebels. He received a yellow card after a melee and then made a throat-slitting gesture to an opponent as he walked away. After the match the match Citing Commissioner ruled Savea's gesture to be a contravention of Law 9.27: against the spirit of good sportsmanship and the equivalent of another yellow card. Two yellow cards means facing the SANZAAR Judiciary. The Judiciary ruled the combination of the two was worth a one-week suspension.

11 Current All Black assistant coach/selector Joe Schmidt announces he will not be applying for any All Blacks coaching role after this year's World Cup.

13 Wellington announce their two Ranfurly Shield defences against Heartland Unions will be against Horowhenua Kapiti (in Levin) and South Canterbury.

15 NZR announce that International Career Management recruitment firm Robert Walters have partnered with NZR for three years. This will allow NZR access to global talent information, recruitment advice and support.

17 The draw for the Heartland Championship is released.

18 All Blacks Mental Skills Coach Gilbert Enoka will leave the All Blacks set up after the World Cup. He has been in the role since 2000.

21 Scott Robertson is announced as the new All Blacks coach from 2024–2027. NZR decline to confirm any other interviewees but say it was a contested process, and Robertson's appointment was a unanimous decision by the Board. (see August 10)

22 The draw for the Bunnings NPC is released and there is a change in format for the competition. The two pools structure in use last year is scrapped and a return is made to a single points table for all 14 teams with the top eight qualifying for the quarter-finals . . . North Harbour a profit of $1,390,505.

23 Bay of Plenty a loss of $71,367.

26 Counties Manukau a profit of $1,299,980.

27 NZR grants dispensation to the Crusaders and Blues for Scott Barrett, Hoskins Sotutu and Stephen Perofeta to play a sixth consecutive game this weekend due to the injury toll in both squads. They were all members of last year's All Blacks end of year tour and as such are only allowed to play a maximum five consecutive games and then must have a week off . . . Hurricanes announce the re-signing of Brad Shields for 2024 from French club Perpignan. He played 103 games for the Hurricanes before leaving in 2018 to go to English club Wasps, and played nine Tests for England.

28 Former All Blacks Sevens coach Clark Laidlaw is confirmed as New Zealand Under 20's coach . . . Northland a profit of $736,182.

29 Manawatu a loss of $337,977 . . . Otago a profit of $956,712.

30 NZR have renewed their partnership with apparel supplier adidas to supply all the national teams with playing kit, apparel, boots and footwear.

APRIL

1 NZR launch All Blacks Performance Labs to provide executives and their organisations with the framework and tools needed to accelerate performance. ABPL, in conjunction with Propel Performance Group, will share the skills and knowledge of the Teams in Black and wider organisations management, coaching and playing group through executive coaching journeys for senior leaders, three-day in-camp experiences, high performing teams' workshops, half-day virtual sessions and keynote speaking events.

5 NZR launch Systems Strategy to transform women's rugby over the next ten years 2023–2033 with a $21.7 million action plan this year which includes the establishment of six new dedicated women's rugby roles across community rugby, high performance rugby and commercial. Provincial Unions and clubs will use the Strategy to develop action plans across the five key areas of culture, system, participation, performance and transition.

6 After the final tournament in the Womens Sevens Series at Toulouse next month, Sarah Hirini will take a sabbatical from the Black Ferns Sevens to play for Japanese club Mie Pearls. She will return in 2024 to play for the Black Ferns Sevens at the Paris Olympics.

9 All Blacks Sevens win the Singapore Sevens and qualify for the 2024 Olympics. With two tournaments left they lead the standings and confirmed themselves a top four finish for the qualification.

13 Tony Christie, Steve Jackson and Mike Delany are confirmed as Black Ferns assistant coaches to Allan Bunting.

17 The 34 players contracted to the Black Ferns this year are named. The players will train in regionalised hubs at Auckland, Hamilton, Tauranga, Wellington and Christchurch . . . Rugby Southland a profit of $1,077,364.

18 Farah Palmer Cup draw is released.

20 Roger Tuivasa-Sheck announces he will return to rugby league next year and has re-signed with the NZ Warriors.

26 Leon MacDonald, Jason Holland and Scott Hansen are confirmed as assistant coaches to All Blacks coach Scott Robertson next year. Current assistant coach Jason Ryan will continue as well . . . Northland announce head coach Marty Veale has resigned due to personal circumstances. He was appointed in December last year . . . Tasman a profit of $748,139.

27 NZR AGM. A loss of $47.4 million is announced for 2022. Record revenue of $270.8

million was received and reserves now stand at $95 million. Catherine Savage is an Appointed member to the Board replacing Bart Campbell who did not seek re-election, and Stu Mather wins a vote against Shaun Nixon for the Elected position vacated by Bailey Mackey who moved to the Nominated position replacing Stewart Mitchell who has completed the maximum terms. Former All Black and past NZR Board member Graham Mourie is elected a Life Member.

30 Ruby Tui, Iritana Hohaia and Kate Henwood have been added to the Black Ferns squad for 2023.

MAY

5 World Rugby announces New Zealand will host the inaugural WXV tournament in October for women's top six nations. The Black Ferns schedule is announced with a home and away series against Australia before participating in the Pacific Four Series in Canada (see Feb 28) . . . World Health Organisation announces that Covid-19 is now an established and ongoing health issue which no longer constitutes a public health emergency of international concern.

10 NZR and the Japan RFU have signed a Memorandum of Understanding, through to end of 2027, to explore strategic and commercial opportunities, including more regular matches between the two countries various national teams . . . Refereeing appointments for the World Cup are announced by World Rugby. Ben O'Keeffe and Paul Williams will be referees, James Doleman will be an assistant referee, and Brendon Pickerill will be a TMO.

11 World Rugby Council unanimously approves an opt-in global trial of a lower tackle height in community rugby to below the base of the sternum (stomach or belly). This should reduce the number of head-on-head contacts and concussion. New Zealand Rugby is already trialling this in community rugby this year.

14 At the completion of the 2022–2023 World Rugby Women's Sevens Series, Black Ferns Sevens players Sarah Hirini, Tyla Nathan-Wong, Stacey Waaka and Michaela Blyde are selected in the tournament's Dream Team. Jorja Miller is selected as Rookie of the Year.

17 World Rugby announce the trial use of a Gilbert iNNOVO Smart ball at the U20 World Championship next month. It will be tracked in 3D and real time with beacons around the field determining the exact position of the ball up to 20 times a second. This will assist with determining a forward pass, when the ball goes into touch, a partial charge down, ball on or over the line for a try, if a lineout throw is crooked. The TMO will receive a direct feed and provide such information to the referee. A TMO Bunker will also be trialled

19 Brad Weber confirms he will join French club Stade Francais at the end of the year.

21 At the completion of the 2022–2023 World Rugby Men's Sevens Series, All Blacks Sevens players Leroy Carter and Akuila Rokolisoa are selected in the tournament's Dream Team.

22 Aaron Mauger announces his resignation as Moana Pasifika head coach at the end of this campaign, even though he still has one year to go on his contract.

24 Tyla Nathan-Wong has been a granted a release from her Black Ferns Sevens contract to play for rugby league club St George Illawarra Dragons in the upcoming NRLW season. She will return at the end of the competition to compete for a place in the Black Ferns Sevens for the Olympic Games next year . . . Taranaki a profit of $1,000,395.

26 Wayne Smith is appointed to a new role of Performance Coach to the Black Ferns and

All Blacks. It will include mentoring and supporting their respective head coaches.

27 Crusaders announce the short-term signing of former All Black John Afoa, who has returned to NZ from overseas, due to the number of injured players they have at present. He will be ineligible for the playoffs.

30 Clark Laidlaw is appointed Hurricanes head coach for 2024.

JUNE

1 Sam Whitelock announces his signing with French club Pau after the World Cup . . . Darren Shand will finish as All Black's manager at the end of the World Cup. He has been in the role since 2004.

5 King's Birthday Honours: Wayne Smith is made a Knights Companion of the NZOM (KNZM); former All Black Andy Leslie is an Officer of the NZOM (ONZM); Black Ferns Ruahei Demant and Kennedy Simon are Members of the NZOM (MNZM).

6 Rob Penney is appointed Crusaders head coach for the next two years . . . NZ Under 20 team for the World Championship is named.

7 Black Ferns named . . . A Burnham Dunsandel Irwell player in the combined Canterbury Country–Mid Canterbury division two competition receives a 36-weeks ban for an attack on a Southbridge player in a match on May 27.

8 Leicester Fainga'anuku has signed for French club Toulon after the World Cup . . . Kaikohe senior women's team is banned from their semi-final this weekend by the Northland RU for "repeated and serious" breaches of the union's code of conduct during the season.

17 Ardie Savea turns out for his club Oriental Rongotai against Poneke.

18 All Blacks 36-man squad for The Rugby Championship and the 30-man All Blacks XV squad for Japan are named.

22 Nepo Laulala has signed for French club Toulouse after the World Cup.

26 NZR CEO Mark Robinson comes out in support of Ben O'Keeffe, who refereed the Super Rugby final, in response to unhappy Chiefs supporters who vented on social media.

27 Bunnings NZ announce applications are open to the rugby clubs of New Zealand for Bunnings Rugby Assist 2023 where 10 clubs will receive $30,000 worth of Bunnings products and materials for the upgrading of their facilities.

28 The All Blacks playing strip for the World Cup is unveiled . . . Orangetheory Stadium will have a name change to Apollo Projects Stadium from August 1. Apollo Projects are a design and construction company.

29 Crusaders announce a pre-season tour next year where they will play Munster and Bristol.

30 Jack Goodhue confirms a two-year deal with French club Castres.

JULY

1 SANZAAR and Six Nations Rugby announce they are working in partnership to establish a new international competition starting in 2026. The new competition will take place in the existing July and November international windows every second year, incorporating a final, and comprise the four SANZAAR nations, all of the Six Nations unions and two invited unions. SANZAAR and Six Nations Rugby will own and operate the competition. World Rugby will create a second-tier competition to facilitate promotion and relegation from 2030.

3 Vern Cotter is announced as Blues head coach for next two years.

9 Moana Pasifika announce Tana Umaga as their newly appointed coach for the next three years.

12 The five NZ Super Rugby clubs have signed a collective five-year agreement with Australasian apparel brand Classic.

18 As outlined in November 2022, World Rugby launch their revamped Sevens circuit with the announcement of the cities hosting the events. Now called SVNS, it will be played across seven rounds from December to May and contain 12 teams at each venue for both the men's and women's competitions – Dubai, Cape Town, Perth, Vancouver, Los Angeles, Hong Kong and Singapore. In June Madrid will host the grand final for the top eight men's and women's teams. Madrid will also host a promotion-relegation playoff for the teams ranked 9th–12th along with the top four teams from the Challenger series to determine which four of these teams will join the following SVNS series alongside the top eight.

19 The itinerary for the British and Irish Lions tour of Australia in 2025 is released. It includes a fixture against an Invitational Australia-New Zealand XV on July 12 at Brisbane. The All Blacks will be involved in a home test series against France at the same time.

20 SANZAAR announce an annual Under 20 Rugby Championship starting next year for the four partners. It will be held prior to the World Championship.

25 The All Blacks gift a special wooden bench to each of the 26 provincial unions as a thank you to the communities. All 26 benches have the words Me eke mai. Our bench is your bench. Thanks for all your support alongside the All Blacks logo and a special design that portrays a bird . . . 18 days before their opening game in the Heartland Championship, King Country part ways with head coach Crag Jeffries by mutual consent. Assistant coach Aarin Dunster takes over.

26 Former All Black Ryan Crotty has returned from playing in Japan and has been included in Canterbury's NPC squad.

31 The All Blacks move past France into second place in the world rankings following their win over Australia in Melbourne.

AUGUST

7 All Blacks' World Cup squad of 33 is announced. Four players named in the Rugby Championship squad miss out – Braydon Ennor, Samipeni Finau, Josh Lord and Dallas McLeod. One player not in the Rugby Championship squad but selected in the World Cup squad is David Havili.

10 Highlanders announce Jamie Joseph has been appointed for four years to a newly created position of Head of Rugby, which will oversee the club's entire rugby programme. Clark Dermody remains as head coach . . . Joseph confirms he did interview for the All Blacks' coaching job back in March.

11 All Black #515 – Roy Roper – becomes the first All Black to reach 100 years of age. He played five Tests 1949–50 from Taranaki . . . Tomasi Cama is the new All Blacks Sevens head coach through to the Paris Olympics in July next year.

14 Government announces the last remaining Covid-19 requirements will be removed. As of 12.01am tomorrow, the seven-day mandatory isolation period, and the wearing of face masks to healthcare facilities, will end. These final two requirements have been in place since September 12 last year.

15 The ten rugby clubs to each receive $30,000 worth of Bunnings products and materials in the Bunnings Rugby Assist 2023 to upgrade their facilities are: Bombay (Counties

Manukau), Bluff (Southland), Eskview (Hawke's Bay), Massey (North Harbour), Moerewa (Northland), Taieri (Otago), Timaru OB (South Canterbury), Waimea OB (Tasman), Wairarapa Wahine Toa (Wairarapa Bush) and Whangamata (Thames Valley). There were applications from 164 clubs. (see June 27).

17 The streaming platform NZR+ begins. For a free sign-up, it will provide exclusive content of documentaries, podcasts, short films and more . . . A "new" Ranfurly Shield is handed over to Wellington. The old Ranfurly Shield has been decommissioned as the wood had started to degrade. New wood of English oak has been sourced and 28 new badges have been added to it. The original wood and the 28 badges on it (which were new in 2012) remain with NZR.

18 NZR announce a new national team – the Black Ferns XV. The team will provide an opportunity for emerging talent and a fixture will be played against Samoa on September 23. Whitney Hansen has appointed head coach of the Black Ferns XV.

22 The result of the Hurricanes Schools first XV semi-final between Scots College and Feilding HS played on Saturday is overturned on protest. Scots won 43–35 but Feilding appealed to the Hurricanes Youth Rugby Council who ruled in favour of Feilding. Teams are supposed to have two front row reserves on a bench of seven, or one front row reserve on a bench of six, or if no front row reserves then only a bench of five. The game went to uncontested scrums after 13 minutes with an injury to the Scots College tighthead. Feilding HS protested that Scots had a bench of six while Scot's maintained they had a bench of five, which is why the match went to uncontested scrums.

24 On appeal from Scots College, the NZ Secondary Schools RU reinstate Scot's College as the winner of the semi-final, and Scots College will play Palmerston North BHS in the Hurricanes Final.

25 Scots College withdraw from tomorrow's final due to a number of injuries from the semi-final. Palmerston North BHS are declared winners of the Hurricanes final and will go through to the National Top Four 1st XV Championship.

28 All Blacks drop from second to fourth in the World Rankings after their record defeat to South Africa at Twickenham.

31 NZR receive the independent review of its constitution and governance review which had been commissioned in December. The Review finds that the current constitution and governance structure is not fit for purpose — it does not ensure the appointment of the very best possible Board members with the required range of competencies to govern the organisation. The Review recommends: (1) The creation of an independent process for the appointment of a fully independent Board. (a) The Board size to remain at nine, with a maximum three terms of three years. Three terms to expire each year. Terms may be extended beyond nine years in exceptional circumstances; (b) an Appointments Panel to replace the current Appointments and Remunerations Committee. The Panel to have five members — two independent members appointed by NZ Institute of Directors, one independent member appointed by NZR Board (who is not a current Board member) and two members appointed by the stakeholder Council (do not have to be independent); (c) The Panel to engage an external recruitment company to provide the Panel with a shortlist; (d) The Panel to select a group of candidates to interview; (e) Candidates matching the number of vacancies to be forwarded by the Panel to the NZR Board who will then recommend to the NZR AGM; (f) The vote at the AGM to be either yes or no for each candidate; (g) If a no vote, then the Panel must resubmit another option to a further General Meeting, (h) Independence at all stages from (a) to (e) is defined as four years out of the game or out of positions of influence within the game; (2) The creation of a stakeholder Council — minimum 11 members, maximum 15 members — comprising Provincial Unions (3 elected at NZR AGM),

NZRPA (1 nominated), NZ Maori Rugby Board (1 nominated), NZR Pasifika Advisory group (1 nominated), Super Rugby clubs (1 nominated), NZ Secondary Schools RU (1 nominated), NZ Rugby Foundation (1 nominated), Women in Rugby Aotearoa (1 nominated), Local Government NZ (grounds, facilities, venues etc) (1 nominated), Sport NZ (1 nominated). Members to have no restriction on holding office in rugby or related activities. The Council is to be a consultative body, not a decision-making body, and have an independent Chair with an honorarium. The full Council to meet at least twice a year and at least one of those meetings should be directly with the Board.

SEPTEMBER

6 Nigel Walsh has been reappointed NZ Heartland XV coach and the team will play two matches this year.

8 The New Zealand Schools, New Zealand Barbarian U18 and New Zealand Maori U18 teams are named.

11 The 30-strong Black Ferns squad for their end of year tests against Australia and the inaugural WXV tournament is named. There are four uncapped players – Chryss Viliko, Sophie Fisher, Layla Sae and Martha Mataele. Ayesha Leti-I'iga, Awhina Tangen Wainohu, Charmaine McMenamin and Santo Taumata are unavailable due to injury . . . The inaugural Black Ferns XV 27-player squad is named.

OCTOBER

1 A video on social media emerges which shows the Ranfurly Shield, won by Hawke's Bay off Wellington yesterday, broken into two pieces this morning. Hawke's Bay RU investigate and determine it was a genuine accident with the Shield having been dropped onto a concrete floor at a player's flat. Up to a dozen people were at the flat including non-players. NZR announce they will initiate an investigation through an independent investigator. Media determines that a scattering of something on the Shield looks like an illegal white powder.

2 The Ranfurly Shield is returned to NZR.

3 James Dwan, who has been repairing the Shield over the last eight years, reckons the what looks like white powder is actually plaster he put behind the centrepiece to strengthen it previously.

4 In Auckland District Court Roger Tuivasa-Sheck pleads guilty to a drink-driving charge. He is fined $600 and disqualified from driving for six months.

10 A new format is confirmed for the 2024 and 2025 Super Rugby Aupiki competitions. There is a full home and away programme of six matches for each team plus a final. There will also be a longer pre-season of four weeks that will include two matches. Each club will contract 30 players (up from this year's 28). Non-Black Ferns will receive payment of a minimum $17,000 for the season.

12 NZ Rugby World monthly magazine announces it has merged with rival monthly NZ Rugby News and been incorporated into NZ Rugby News. Rugby World's final issue was its combined August–September issue (issue 274).

16 After their World Cup quarter-final win over Ireland, the All Blacks jump to second in the world rankings, behind South Africa. Ireland and France, first and second before their quarter-final defeats, drop to third and fourth respectively.

18 NZR announce their findings into the broken Ranfurly Shield. They accept the break was an accident. The only positive identification made from the "white powder" was fabric of plaster . . . The New Zealand Heartland XV squad of 23 is named for their two matches. There are 11 players new to the jersey.

24 World Rugby announce: Expansion to 24 teams (from 20) at 2027 men's World Cup; Launch of a new biennial men's international competition from 2026 comprising a top division of 12 countries (Six Nations Unions, SANZAAR Unions plus two more unions to be selected via a process run by SANZAAR) and a second division run by World Rugby of 12 countries. Promotion/relegation will occur from 2030 onwards. The competition will be played in the July and November international release windows; First ever dedicated international release windows for the women's game.

29 World Rugby Awards announced in Paris: Ardie Savea is named Men's 15s Player of the year; Tyla Nathan-Wong is Women's 7's Player of the year, Mark Telea is Men's 15's Breakthrough Player of the year. Four All Blacks Scott Barrett, Ardie Savea, Richie Mo'unga and Will Jordan are named in the Men's 15's Dream Team of the year. Tamaiti Williams was also a finalist for the Men's 15's Breakthrough player of the year and Ian Foster was a finalist for Coach of the year.

30 All Blacks drop from second to third in the world rankings after their loss to South Africa in the World Cup final.

NOVEMBER

3 All Blacks captain Sam Cane will take up a sabbatical option in his NZR contract to play for Japan club Suntory next year instead of playing Super Rugby for the Chiefs.

4 World Rugby Awards announced in Auckland: Black Fern Katelyn Vahaakolo is named as Women's 15's Breakthrough Player of the year. Team mate Mererangi Paul was also a finalist for the award. Six Black Ferns are named in the Women's 15's Dream Team of the year – Krystal Murray, Maiakawanakaulani Roos, Liana Mikaele-Tu'u, Ruahei Demant, Amy Du Plessis and Ruby Tui. Ruahei Demant was also a finalist for Women's 15's Player of the year.

6 A head impact study on community rugby — The ORCHID Community Study — is published in a joint project between World Rugby, NZR, Otago RU, University of Otago and Prevent Biometrics. Using Prevent Biometrics mouthguards on 328 male community players from Under 13s to Premier club players to measure the g-force on their heads in trainings and games, it was found that (a) 86 per cent of forces measured are the same or less than those experienced in other forms of exercise such as running, jumping, skipping, (b) 94 per cent of forces are lower than those previously measured on people jumping on a trampoline, (c) Most events resulting in the highest measured forces were caused by poor technique in the tackle and at the breakdown.

9 All Super Rugby squads for 2024 are announced. Crusaders have signed Welsh international Leigh Halfpenny and the Highlanders have signed Welsh international Rhys Patchell. Codie Taylor will exercise a non-playing sabbatical option in his NZR contract next year, returning to the Crusaders two or three weeks before the playoffs.

14 NZR announce: the Community rugby tackle height trial introduced this year will continue for two more years. (First tackler must tackle below the sternum and target the belly area, the second tackler can tackle below the shoulders in accordance with current rugby law.) Match analysis showed there were more offloads made and the majority of participants thought the game was made safer. 147,434 players were registered this year, a 7 per cent rise on last year. This is mainly due to a 20 per cent rise in womens/girls numbers while junior boys numbers decreased 2 per cent. Community coach registrations increased 4 per cent and referees increased 8 per cent.

15 Finalists are announced for this year's ASB NZ Rugby Awards.

22 The new playing strips for our five Super Rugby squads for next year are revealed. (see July 12.)

24 NZR release their Pasifika Strategy 2024-2029. It aims to create more opportunities for Pasifika peoples at all levels of the game and will act as a guide for all provincial unions, Super Rugby clubs and provincial clubs for a greater diversity and inclusion.

28 The Super Rugby Aupiki squads are announced.

DECEMBER

4 Beauden Barrett, who left for Japanese club Toyota Verblitz after the World Cup, has re-signed with NZR through to the next World Cup. He will be immediately available for the All Blacks when he returns in June.

5 The Super Rugby Aupiki 2024 draw is released . . . World Rugby confirm the refereeing appointments for the 2024 Six Nations Championship. NZ refs appointed are – Paul Williams (1 Ref); Ben O'Keeffe (1 Ref, 1 AR); James Doleman (1 Ref, 1 AR); Angus Mabey (1 AR); Brendon Pickerill (2 TMO).

11 An Auckland City Council working group receives submissions on the best future option for a main stadium in the city. Four options that were presented were: a redevelopment of Eden Park; downtown at Bledisloe Wharf; at Quay Park near Spark Arena; at Tank Farm near Wynyard Point. NZR CEO Mark Robinson was part of the presentation for Quay Park.

12 Former All Black and Waikato coach Jono Gibbes is named as head coach of the New Zealand Under 20 team.

14 ASB NZ Rugby Awards: Ardie Savea wins the Kelvin R Tremain Memorial Trophy as Player of the Year; NZR Life Member and former Chairman Rob Fisher is awarded the Steinlager Salver for outstanding contribution to rugby.

21 NZR confirms the 2024 All Blacks management group. Paul McLaughlan is the new All Blacks team manager, having previously managed the Highlanders and the Wallabies.

22 NZR announce that the second (and final) part of their deal with Silver Lake has been concluded. This second part allowed for $100 million to be subscribed to by local institutions and Silver Lake who could underwrite a minimum $62.5 million. There was no subscription taken up by local investors and the $62.5 million from Silver Lake has been accepted. Silver Lake's interest in NZ Commercial Co increases from 5.71 per cent to 7.5 per cent. A $60 million legacy fund will be created from which annual grants will be made to community rugby initiatives.

30 New Year Honours List: Long standing sports journalist Phil Gifford is made on Officer of the NZOM (ONZM); Kevin Pivac, instrumental in the founding of the NZ Deaf Rugby Union, and a life member, is also an Officer of the NZOM (ONZM).

INTERNATIONAL RESULTS 2023

SIX NATIONS CHAMPIONSHIP

Date	*Home*		*Away*		*Location*	*Referee*
Feb 04	Ireland	34	Wales	10	Cardiff	K Dickson (England)
Feb 04	Scotland	29	England	23	London	P Williams (NZ)
Feb 05	France	29	Italy	24	Rome	M Carley (England)
Feb 11	Ireland	32	France	19	Dublin	W Barnes (England)
Feb 11	Scotland	35	Wales	7	Edinburgh	A Brace (Ireland)
Feb 12	England	31	Italy	14	London	J Doleman (NZ)
Feb 25	Ireland	34	Italy	20	Rome	M Adamson (Scotland)
Feb 25	England	20	Wales	10	Cardiff	M Raynal (France)
Feb 26	France	32	Scotland	21	Paris	N Amashukeli (Georgia)
Mar 11	France	53	England	10	London	B O'Keeffe (NZ)
Mar 11	Wales	29	Italy	17	Rome	D Murphy (Australia)
Mar 12	Ireland	22	Scotland	7	Edinburgh	L Pearce (England)
Mar 18	Scotland	26	Italy	14	Edinburgh	A Gardner (Australia)
Mar 18	France	41	Wales	28	Paris	N Berry (Australia)
Mar 18	Ireland	29	England	16	Dublin	J Peyper (SA)

FINAL TABLE

	P	*W*	*D*	*L*	*For*	*Against*	*BP*	*Pts*
Ireland	5	5	0	0	151	72	7	27
France	5	4	0	1	174	115	4	20
Scotland	5	3	0	2	118	98	3	15
England	5	2	0	3	100	135	2	10
Wales	5	1	0	4	84	147	2	6
Italy	5	0	0	5	89	149	1	1

RUGBY WORLD CUP 2023

Date	Home		Away		Location	Referee
Sep 08	France	27	New Zealand	13	Paris	J Peyper (SA)
Sep 09	Italy	52	Namibia	8	Paris	A Brace (Ireland)
Sep 09	Ireland	82	Romania	8	Bordeaux	N Amashukeli (Georgia)
Sep 09	Australia	35	Georgia	15	Paris	L Pearce (England)
Sep 09	England	27	Argentina	10	Marseille	M Raynal (France)
Sep 10	South Africa	18	Scotland	3	Marseille	A Gardner (Australia)
Sep 10	Wales	32	Fiji	26	Bordeaux	M Carley (England)
Sep 10	Japan	42	Chile	12	Toulouse	N Berry (Australia)
Sep 14	France	27	Uruguay	12	Lille	B O'Keeffe (NZ)
Sep 15	New Zealand	71	Namibia	3	Toulouse	L Pearce (England)
Sep 16	Ireland	59	Tonga	16	Nantes	W Barnes (England)
Sep 16	Wales	28	Portugal	8	Nice	K Dickson (England)
Sep 16	Samoa	43	Chile	10	Bordeaux	P Williams (NZ)
Sep 17	South Africa	76	Romania	0	Bordeaux	M Raynal (France)
Sep 17	Fiji	22	Australia	15	Paris	A Brace (Ireland)
Sep 17	England	34	Japan	12	Nice	N Amashukeli (Georgia)
Sep 20	Italy	38	Uruguay	17	Nice	A Gardner (Australia)
Sep 21	France	96	Namibia	0	Marseille	M Carley (England)
Sep 22	Argentina	19	Samoa	10	Paris	N Berry (Australia)
Sep 23	Ireland	13	South Africa	8	Paris	B O'Keeffe (NZ)
Sep 23	Georgia	18	Portugal	18	Toulouse	P Williams (NZ)
Sep 23	England	71	Chile	0	Lille	J Peyper (SA)
Sep 24	Scotland	45	Tonga	17	Nice	K Dickson (England)
Sep 24	Wales	40	Australia	6	Lyon	W Barnes (England)
Sep 27	Uruguay	36	Namibia	26	Lyon	M Raynal (France)
Sep 28	Japan	28	Samoa	22	Toulouse	J Peyper (SA)
Sep 29	New Zealand	96	Italy	17	Lyon	M Carley (England)
Sep 30	Scotland	84	Romania	0	Lille	W Barnes (England)
Sep 30	Fiji	17	Georgia	12	Bordeaux	K Dickson (England)
Sep 30	Argentina	59	Chile	5	Nantes	P Williams (NZ)
Oct 01	South Africa	49	Tonga	18	Marseille	L Pearce (England)
Oct 01	Australia	34	Portugal	14	Paris	N Amashukeli (Georgia)
Oct 05	New Zealand	73	Uruguay	0	Lyon	W Barnes (England)
Oct 06	France	60	Italy	7	Lyon	K Dickson (England)

Oct 07	Ireland	36	Scotland	14	Paris	N Berry (Australia)
Oct 07	Wales	43	Georgia	19	Nantes	M Raynal (France)
Oct 07	England	18	Samoa	17	Lille	A Brace (Ireland)
Oct 08	Tonga	45	Romania	24	Lille	A Gardner (Australia)
Oct 08	Portugal	24	Fiji	23	Toulouse	L Pearce (England)
Oct 08	Argentina	39	Japan	27	Nantes	B O'Keeffe (NZ)
Quarter-Finals						
Oct 14	Argentina	29	Wales	17	Paris	J Peyper (SA)
Oct 14	New Zealand	28	Ireland	24	Paris	W Barnes (England)
Oct 15	England	30	Fiji	24	Marseille	M Raynal (France)
Oct 15	South Africa	29	France	28	Paris	B O'Keeffe (NZ)
Semi-Finals						
Oct 20	New Zealand	44	Argentina	6	Paris	A Gardner (Australia)
Oct 21	South Africa	16	England	15	Paris	B O'Keeffe (NZ)
Bronze Final						
Oct 27	England	26	Argentina	23	Paris	N Berry (Australia)
Final						
Oct 28	South Africa	12	New Zealand	11	Paris	W Barnes (England)

OTHER INTERNATIONALS

Date	Home		Away		Location	Referee
Feb 04	Romania	67	Poland	27	Bucharest	S Abulashvili (Georgia)
Feb 04	Portugal	54	Belgium	17	Lisbon	H Davidson (Scotland)
Feb 05	Spain	28	Netherlands	20	Madrid	P Duarte (Portugal)
Feb 05	Georgia	75	Germany	12	Tbilisi	C Serban (Romania)
Feb 11	Georgia	40	Netherlands	8	Amsterdam	L Cayre (France)
Feb 11	Romania	56	Belgium	5	Brussels	M English (Wales)
Feb 11	Portugal	65	Poland	3	Gdynia	A Cole (Ireland)
Feb 12	Spain	32	Germany	14	Heidelberg	C Munarini (Italy)
Feb 18	Poland	21	Belgium	15	Gdynia	I Atorrasagasti (Spain)
Feb 18	Netherlands	33	Germany	29	Neckarsulm	A Ionescu (Romania)
Feb 18	Georgia	41	Spain	3	Torrelavega	E Cross (Ireland)
Feb 19	Portugal	38	Romania	20	Lisbon	N Amashukeli (Georgia)
Mar 05	Netherlands	31	Belgium	19	Amsterdam	M Todd (Scotland)
Mar 05	Germany	23	Poland	18	Gdynia	G Visser (Netherlands)
Mar 05	Portugal	27	Spain	10	Lisbon	T Charabas (France)
Mar 05	Georgia	31	Romania	7	Tbilisi	F Vedovelli (Italy)
Mar 18	Georgia	38	Portugal	11	Badajoz	LCayre (France)
Mar 19	Belgium	18	Poland	17	Amsterdam	C Serban (Romania)
Mar 19	Netherlands	50	Germany	28	Amsterdam	S Tevzadze (Georgia)
Mar 19	Romania	31	Spain	25	Badajoz	C Busby (Ireland)
Jun 03	South Korea	27	Malaysia	3	Kuala Lumpur	M Rodden (Hong Kong)
Jun 10	Hong Kong	88	Malaysia	9	Hong Kong	S Barr (Singapore)
Jun 17	Hong Kong	30	South Korea	10	Hong Kong	K Furuse (Japan)
Jul 08	New Zealand	41	Argentina	12	Mendoza	A Gardner (Australia)
Jul 08	South Africa	43	Australia	12	Pretoria	B O'Keeffe (NZ)
Jul 15	New Zealand	35	South Africa	20	Auckland	M Raynal (France)
Jul 15	Argentina	34	Australia	31	Sydney	J Peyper (SA)
Jul 22	Fiji	36	Tonga	20	Lautoka	P Williams (NZ)
Jul 22	Samoa	24	Japan	22	Sapporo	M Raynal (France)
Jul 29	South Africa	22	Argentina	21	Johannesburg	A Brace (Ireland)
Jul 29	New Zealand	38	Australia	7	Melbourne	W Barnes (England)
Jul 29	Fiji	33	Samoa	19	Apia	A Gardner (Australia)
Jul 29	Scotland	25	Italy	13	Edinburgh	B O'Keeffe (NZ)
Jul 29	Uruguay	26	Chile	25	Montevideo	L Pearce (England)

Date	Home		Away		Location	Referee
Jul 29	Japan	21	Tonga	16	Osaka	M Carley (England)
Aug 05	New Zealand	23	Australia	20	Dunedin	K Dickson (England)
Aug 05	Samoa	34	Tonga	9	Apia	A Gardner (Australia)
Aug 05	Fiji	35	Japan	12	Tokyo	M Carley (England)
Aug 05	United States	31	Romania	17	Bucharest	S Grove-White (Scotland)
Aug 05	South Africa	24	Argentina	13	Buenos Aires	N Amashukeli (Georgia)
Aug 05	Wales	20	England	9	Cardiff	N Berry (Australia)
Aug 05	Ireland	33	Italy	17	Dublin	M Raynal (France)
Aug 05	Uruguay	26	Namibia	18	Montevideo	L Pearce (England)
Aug 05	Scotland	25	France	21	Edinburgh	B O'Keeffe (NZ)
Aug 10	Tonga	28	Canada	3	Nuku'alofa	J Way (Australia)
Aug 12	Portugal	46	United States	20	Algarve	P Williams (NZ)
Aug 12	France	30	Scotland	27	Saint Etienne	N Berry (Australia)
Aug 12	Georgia	56	Romania	6	Tbilisi	W Barnes (England)
Aug 12	England	19	Wales	17	London	N Amashukeli (Georgia)
Aug 13	Namibia	28	Chile	26	Temuco	C Evans (Wales)
Aug 15	Tonga	36	Canada	12	Nuku'alofa	J Doleman (NZ)
Aug 19	South Africa	52	Wales	16	Cardiff	A Brace (Ireland)
Aug 19	Ireland	29	England	10	Dublin	P Williams (NZ)
Aug 19	France	34	Fiji	17	Nantes	N Amashukeli (Georgia)
Aug 19	Italy	57	Romania	7	San Benedetto	L Pearce (England)
Aug 20	Georgia	22	United States	7	Tbilisi	J Peyper (SA)
Aug 25	South Africa	35	New Zealand	7	London	M Carley (England)
Aug 26	Ireland	17	Samoa	13	Bayonne	W Barnes (England)
Aug 26	Argentina	62	Spain	3	Madrid	A Brace (Ireland)
Aug 26	Scotland	33	Georgia	6	Edinburgh	C Ridley (England)
Aug 26	Italy	42	Japan	21	Treviso	K Dickson (England)
Aug 26	Fiji	30	England	22	London	J Peyper (SA)
Aug 27	France	41	Australia	17	Paris	L Pearce (England)
Nov 12	United States	48	Brazil	3	Villajoyosa	A Jones (Wales)
Nov 12	Spain	42	Canada	20	Villajoyosa	D Schneider (Argentina)
Nov 14	Hong Kong	29	Germany	16	Hong Kong	S Barr (Singapore)
Nov 18	Hong Kong	46	Germany	10	Hong Kong	T Namekawa (Japan)
Nov 19	United States	42	Spain	12	Villajoyosa	A Jones (Wales)
Nov 19	Canada	40	Brazil	15	Villajoyosa	D Schneider (Argentina)

THE FOREIGN LEGION

by John Lea

These New Zealand origin players were either contracted with professional overseas clubs for play in 2023/24, or commenced and completed an overseas contract during 2023 (denoted by *). Those no longer eligible for New Zealand have their country of allegiance shown in brackets.

AUSTRALIA

Super Rugby

ACT Brumbies:	Austin Anderson, Jahrome Brown, Sefo Kautai, Noah Lolesio (Australia), Ollie Sapsford (Australia), Tamati Tua
Fijian Drua:	Isaiah Armstrong-Ravula, Te Ahiwaru Cirikidaveta, Mesulame Dolokoto (Fiji), Haereiti Hetet (Fiji), Caleb Muntz (Fiji), Waqa Nalaga, Leone Nawai*, Selestino Ravutaumada (Fiji), Zuriel Togiatama (Fiji), Etonia Waqa*
Melbourne Rebels:	Vaiolini Ekuasi, Josh Hill, Stacey Ili (Samoa)*, Matt Proctor, Anaru Rangi*, Lukhan Salakaia-Loto (Australia), Taniela Tupou (Australia), Tuaina Tualima, Jordan Uelese (Australia)
NSW Waratahs:	Tetera Faulkner (Australia)*, Lalakai Foketi (Australia), Mahe Vailanu
Queensland Reds:	Sef Fa'agase, Alex Hodgman, Phransis Sula-Siaosi, Jeff To'omaga-Allen (Samoa)
Western Force:	Nikolai Foliaki, Felix Kalapu, Manasa Mataele (Fiji)*, Atu Moli, Jacob Norris, Campbell Parata, Jeremy Thrush*, Chase Tiatia

ENGLAND

Aviva Premiership

Bath:	Hame Faiva (Italy)
Bristol Bears:	Jake Heenan, Steven Luatua, Viremi Vakatawa (France), Chris Vui (Samoa)
Exeter Chiefs:	Tom Hendrickson, Josh Iosefa-Scott, Ethan Roots
Harlequins:	Lewis Gjaltema, Viliami Taulani (Tonga)*
Leicester Tigers:	Solomone Kata (Tonga)
Newcastle Falcons:	Connor Collett*
Northampton Saints:	Temo Mayanavanua (Fiji), Brandon Nansen (Samoa)
Sale Sharks:	Telusa Veianu (Tonga), Jason Woodward (England)
Saracens:	Sean Maitland (Scotland), Mako Vunipola (England)

RFU Championship

Ampthill:	James Johnston
Cornish Pirates:	Marlen Walker
Doncaster Knights:	Harrison Courtney
Ealing Trailfinders:	James Little, Jimmy Roots
Nottingham:	Iosefo Maloney-Fiola, Javiah Pohe

EUROPE

Rugby Europe Super Cup

Castille Y Leon Iberians:	Nathan de Thierry (Hong Kong), Siosiua Moala
Netherlands/The Delta:	Te Hauora Campbell (Netherlands)
Romanian Wolves:	Nikau Murray, Jason Tomane (Romania)

FRANCE

Top 14

Bayonne:	Adam Coleman (Australia), Geoff Cridge, Mateaki Kafatolu (Tonga), Apisoloma Ratuniyarawa (Fiji), Michael Ruru, Peter Samu (Australia), Isaia Toeava
Bordeaux Begles:	Ben Tameifuna (Tonga)
Castres:	Ben Botica, Jack Goodhue, Filipo Nakosi (Fiji), Paul Ngauamo (Tonga), Abraham Papali'i (Samoa)
Clermont:	Fritz Lee (Samoa), George Moala (Tonga), Irae Simone (Australia), Pita-Gus Sowakula, Caleb Timu
La Rochelle:	Uini Atonio (France), Tawera Kerr-Barlow, Motu Matu'u (Samoa), Will Skelton (Australia), Ihiah West
Lyon:	Liam Allen, Toby Arnold, Liam Coltman, Montana Ioane (Italy), Josiah Maraku, Fletcher Smith, Jordan Taufua (Samoa)
Montpellier:	George Bridge, Ben Lam, Brandon Paenga-Amosa (Australia), Karl Tu'inukuafe
Oyonnax:	Tony Ensor, Leva Fifita (Tonga), Rory Grice, Manu Leiataua (Samoa), Jo Ravouvou, Jamie Ruru, Gavin Stark
Pau:	Ziegfried Fisi'ihoi (Tonga), Tumua Manu (Samoa), Siate Tokolahi (Tonga), Luke Whitelock, Sam Whitelock
Perpignan:	Shahn Eru (Cook Islands), So'otalo Fa'aso'o (Samoa), Hugh Roach, Brad Shields (England)*
Racing 92:	Veikoso Poloniati (Tonga), Francis Saili, Ben Volavola (Fiji)
Stade Francais:	Paul Alo-Emile (Samoa), Sione Anga'aelangi (Tonga), Brad Weber
Toulon:	Brian Alainu'uese (Samoa), Leicester Fainga'anuku, Duncan Paia'aua (Samoa)
Toulouse:	Piua Fa'asalele (Samoa), Charlie Faumuina (Samoa), Owen Franks*, Nepo Laulala

Second Division

Agen:	Tomasi Fineanganofo, Fotu Lokotui (Tonga), Mike Sosene-Feagai (USA), Sonatane Takalua (Tonga), George Tilsley
Aurillac:	Elijah Niko, Adrian Smith
Beziers:	Tim Nanai-Williams (Samoa), Jarrod Poi, Taleta Tupuola
Biarritz:	Elliot Dixon, Johnny Dyer (Fiji), Guy Millar, Henry Speight (Australia,), Luteru Tolai (Samoa)
Brive:	Jackson Garden-Bachop, Wesley Tapueluelu, Tietie Tuimauga (Samoa)
Colomiers:	Hika Elliot, Marco Fepuleai (Samoa), Ray Nu'u, Jack Whetton
Dax:	Nephi Leatigaga (Samoa), Matt Luamanu (Samoa), Genesis Mamea-Lemalu (Samoa)
Grenoble:	Siua Halonukanuka (Tonga), Terrence Hepetema, Brandon Nansen (Samoa)

Montauban:	Wharenui Hawera, Maselino Paulino (Samoa), Taleta Tupuola
Nevers:	Aviata Silago
Provence:	Peter Betham (Australia), Inga Finau, Jimmy Gopperth, Teimana Harrison (England), Josh Tyrell (Samoa)
Rouen-Normandie:	Alex Luatua, Valentino Mapapalangi (Tonga), Ope Peleseuma (Samoa), Belgium Tuatagaloa (Samoa), Daniel Waite*
Soyaux-Angouleme:	Jacob Botica, Motu Matu'u (Samoa)
Stade Montois:	Ambrose Curtis, Michael Faleafa (Samoa)
Valence Romans:	Isaac Te Temaki
Vannes:	John Afoa, Rodney Ah You (Ireland), Joe Edwards, Dan Hollinshead, Pat Leafa, Nelesoni Malaulau

IRELAND

United Rugby Championship

Connacht:	Bundee Aki (Ireland), Jarrad Butler, Leva Fifita (Tonga), Shamus Hurley-Langton, Dominic Robertson-McCoy
Leinster:	Michael Ala'alatoa (Samoa), Jamison Gibson-Park (Ireland), James Lowe (Ireland), Charlie Ngatai
Munster:	Joey Carberry (Ireland)
Ulster:	Sean Reidy (Ireland)*, Jeff To-omaga-Allen (Samoa)

ITALY

United Rugby Championship

Benetton Treviso:	Malakai Fekitoa (Tonga), Toa Halafihi (Italy), Siua Maile (Tonga), Onisi Ratave, Iliesa Ratuva Tavuyara (Italy), Scott Scrafton, Henry Time-Stowers (Samoa), Jacob Umaga (England)
Zebre:	Taina Fox-Matamatua, Scott Gregory, Junior Laloifi, Fetuil Paea (Tonga), Jimmy Tuivaiti (Italy)

JAPAN

Rugby League One

Hanazano Kintetsu Liners:	James Blackwell, Jed Brown, Sam Caird, Quade Cooper (Australia), Andrew Makalio, Semi Masirewa (Japan), Weimana Reidlinger-Kapa*, Sanaila Waqa (Japan)
Kobelco Kobe Steelers:	Gerard Cowley-Tuioti, Bryn Gatland, Tali Ioasa, Tim Lafaele (Japan), Michael Little, Ngani Laumape, Ata'ata Moeakiola (Japan), Brodie Retallick, Ardie Savea
Kubota Spears Funabashi:	Dane Coles, Ryan Crotty*
Mie Honda Heat:	Mitchell Hunt, Tevita Li, Tetuhi Roberts, Connor Wihongi
Mitsubishi Dynaboars:	Roland Alaia'sa*, Heiden Bedwell-Curtis*, Jackson Hemopo, Brackin Karauria-Henry (Australia), Marino Mikaele-Tu'u, Ben Paltridge, Curtis Rona (Australia), Jack Stratton, Matt Vaega, To'o Vaega
Ricoh Black Rams Tokyo:	Josh Goodhue, Nathan Hughes (England), Brodi McCurran, Matt McGahan, Hadleigh Parkes (Wales), Jacob Skeen
Saitama Wild Knights:	Mark Abbott, Asaeli Ai Valu (Japan), Vince Aso, Lachlan Boshier, Craig Millar (Japan), Liam Mitchell, Daniel Perez

Shizuoka Blue Revs:	Johnny Fa'auli (Japan), Keagen Faria, Bryn Hall, Charles Piutau (Tonga), Malo Tuitama
Tokyo Sun-Goliath:	Gareth Anscombe (Wales), Sam Cane, Aaron Cruden, Joe Kamana (Japan), Isaiah Punivai, Tom Sanders*, Hendrik Tui (Japan)
Toshiba Brave Lupus:	Michael Collins, Warner Dearns (Japan), Shannon Frizell, Michael Leitch (Japan), Richie Mo'unga, Nicholas McCurran, Jacob Pierce, Jack Stratton*, Seta Tamanivalu (Fiji), Tom Taylor, Rob Thompson, Matt Todd
Toyota Verblitz:	Beauden Barrett*, Josh Dickson, Tiaan Falcon, Charlie Lawrence, Isaiah Mapusua, Tom Robinson, Male Sa'u (Japan)*, Aaron Smith, Dick Wilson
Yokohama Canon Eagles:	Mitch Brown, Luteru Laulala, Liaki Moli

League Two

Green Rockets Tokatsu:	Ash Dixon, Whetu Douglas*, Lomani Lemeki (Japan), Tom Marshall, Maritino Nemani
Hino Red Dolphins:	Simon Hickey, Augustine Pulu (Tonga), Noah Tovio
Kamaishi Seawaves:	Cameron Bailey, Hamish Dalzell, Jamie Henry (Japan), Sam Henwood*, Setariki Koroitamana, Ben Nee Nee (Samoa), Dallas Tatana (Japan), Flynn Yates
NTT Docomo Hurricanes:	Michael Allardice, Blake Gibson, Liam Squire*
Toyota Industries Shuttles:	Chris Gabriel*, Taina Kapene, Ieremia Mataena, Chance Peni-Ataera, Taleni Seu (Samoa), Talifolofola Tangipa
Urayasu D-Rocks:	Otere Black, Hayden Cripps (Japan), Sekonaia Pole, Luke Thompson (Japan)*, Jimmy Tupou*

League Three

Kurita Water Gush:	Damon Leasuasu, Antonio Mikaele-Tu'u
Kyuden Voltex:	Phil Burleigh (Scotland), Tom Rowe, Ray Tatafu, Sam Vaka (Tonga)
Mazda Skyactivs Hiroshima:	Tevin Ferris, Isileli Manu, Beaudein Waaka
Shimizu Koto Blue Sharks:	Sam Chongkit, Kayne Hammington, Orbyn Leger, Lima Sopoaga (Samoa), Murphy Taramai

NORTH AMERICA

Major League Rugby

Chicago Hounds	Charlie Abel
Houston Sabercats:	AJ Alatimu (Samoa), Rob Cobb, Morgan Mitchell*, Vereniko Tikoisolomone*, Drew Wild
Miami Sharks:	Nick Grigg (Scotland), Stan Van den Hoven

New England Free Jacks: Seta Baker, Paula Balekana, Taniela Filimone*, Sam Fischlii*, Malakai Hala-Ngatai, Joel Hintz*, Mitch Jacobson, Alex Johnston, Kianu Kereru-Symes, Josh Larsen (Canada), Reece MacDonald, Kieran McClea*, Slade McDowall, Danyon Morgan-Puterangi, Semisi Paea (Tonga)*, Jesse Parete*, Terrell Peita, Jayson Potroz, Sean Ralph, Millenium Sanerivi*, Tevita Sole

New Orleans Gold: Jarred Adams (Samoa), Luke Campbell, Tom Florence*, Liam Hallam-Eames, Jonah Mau'u, Sean Paranihi, Isaac Salmon, Jordan Trainor

Old Glory DC: Kurt Baker*, Jamason Fa'anana-Schultz (USA), Niko Jones, Jason Robertson, Junior Sa'u*

Rugby Atlanta: Rewita Biddle*, Ben Strang*, Martini Talapusi*, Te Rangatira Waitokia*

Rugby United New York: Sam Davies, Jason Emery, Charlie Faumuina (Samoa), Ed Fidow (Samoa), Fa'asiu Fuatai, Jack Heighton, Tevita Langi, Nick Mayhew, Brendan O'Connor*, Albert O'Shannessy, Kara Pryor, Brad Tucker, Tei Walden

San Diego Legion: Tupou Afungia, Tomas Aoake, Richard Judd*, Shilo Klein*, Lincoln McClutchie, Isaac Ross

Seattle Seawolves: Charles Elton, Setefano Funaki (Tonga)*, Sam Matenga, Mahonri Ngakuru, Toni Pulu (Niue)

Toronto Arrows (Canada): Lolani Faleiva*, Will Grant*, Sam Malcolm*, Dennon Robinson-Bartlett*,Gene Symington*, Micaiah Torrance-Read*, Uete Tufuga*

Utah Warriors: Henry Bell, Liam Crowley, Zion Going*, Jamie Lane, Frank Lochore, Caleb Makene*, Michael Manson, Connor McLeod, Dylan Nel, Nick Souchon

SCOTLAND

United Rugby Championship

Edinburgh: Wes Goosen, Angus Williams

Glasgow: Simon Berghan (Scotland), Walter Fifita (Tonga), Cole Forbes*, Nick Grigg (Scotland)*, Tom Jordan, Josh McKay

WALES

United Rugby Championship

Cardiff Blues: Willis Halaholo (Wales), Rey Lee-Lo (Samoa)

Dragons: Aki Seuli, Sio Tomkinson

Llanelli Scarlets: Vaea Fifita (Tonga), Sam Lousi (Tonga), Johnny McNicholl (Wales), Taine Plumtree (Wales), Blade Thomson (Scotland)

OVERSEAS PLAYERS IN NEW ZEALAND FIRST-CLASS RUGBY 2023

Compiled by John Lea

For previously capped players the most recent year and level of selection are shown. Some players have since, or soon will, also become eligible for New Zealand.

Player	Country	Year	NZ Team in 2023
Bo Abra	Australia Schoolboys	2019	Hawke's Bay
Jermaine Ainsley	Australia	2018	Otago
Austin Anderson	Australia Under 20	2022	Waikato
Feleti Kaitu'u	Australia	2022	Tasman
Tyrel Lomax	Australia Under 20	2016	Hurricanes
Cameron Orr	Australia Under 20	2015	Wellington
Kalani Thomas	Australia	Uncapped	Auckland
Jordan Olsen	Canada A	2019	Northland
Tuakana Paitai	Cook Islands	2021	Thames Valley
Hayden Jurlina	Croatia	2022	Northland
Willi Heinz	England	2019	Canterbury
Brad Shields	England	2019	Wellington
Andrew Turner	England Under 20	2022	Crusaders
Paula Balekana	Fiji	Uncapped	Hawke's Bay
Mosese Dawai	Fiji	Uncapped	Highlanders
Alex Hodgman	Fiji Under 20	2012	Blues
Mitieli Kaloudigebeci	Fiji	Uncapped	Buller
Manasa Mataele	Fiji	2022	Canterbury
Tevita Nabura	Fiji Sevens	2017	East Coast
Waisake Naholo	Fiji	Uncapped	Otago
Tua Ravula	Fiji Sevens	2019	North Otago
Sevu Reece	Fiji	Uncapped	Crusaders
Pita-Gus Sowakula	Fiji	Uncapped	Taranaki
Timoci Tavatavanawai	Fiji Under 20	2016	Tasman
Vereniki Tikoisolomone	Fiji	Uncapped	Taranaki
Etonia Waqa	Fiji Under 20	2019	Bay of Plenty
Anton Segner	Germany Under 16	2016	Tasman
Michael Bent	Ireland	2022	Taranaki
Colm Hogan	Ireland	Uncapped	Tasman
Oliver Jager	Ireland Under 18	2013	Canterbury
John Poland	Ireland Under 20	2016	Manawatu
Sean Reidy	Ireland	2017	Counties-Manukau
Shun Miyake	Japan	Uncapped	Tasman
Funahashi Ryosuke	Japan Juniors	2016	Bay of Plenty
Hisamitsu Shimada	Japan	Uncapped	Hawke's Bay
Kaisei Timura	Japan	Uncapped	Southland
Fabian Holland	Netherlands	Uncapped	Otago
Stan Van Den Hoven	Netherlands	Uncapped	Manawatu
Toni Pulu	Niue Sevens	2011	Counties-Manukau
Jarred Adams	Samoa Under 20	2016	Northland
AJ Alatimu	Samoa	2022	Counties-Manukau
Tomasi Alosio	Samoa	2022	Tasman

Player	*Country*	*Year*	*NZ Team in 2023*
Donald Brighouse	Samoa	2022	Taranaki
Losi Filipo	Samoa	2021	Wellington
Kahn Fotuali'i	Samoa	2017	Horowhenua-Kapiti
Josh Ioane	Samoa Under 20	2015	Otago
Leif Keil-Schwenke	Samoa Under 20	2014	Manawatu
Alapati Leuia	Samoa	2017	North Harbour
Ezekiel Lindenmuth	Samoa	2022	Counties-Manukau
Melani Nanai	Samoa Under 20	2013	Bay of Plenty
Pepesana Patafilo	Samoa Under 20	2015	Wellington
Filo Paulo	Samoa	2021	Wellington
Savelio Ropati	Samoa 7s	2018	Thames Valley
Henry Taefu	Samoa	2022	Auckland
Tanielu Tele'a	Samoa Under 20	2017	Auckland
Chase Tiatia	Samoa Under 20	2015	Hawke's Bay
Ahsee Tuala	Samoa	2021	Counties-Manukau
Lolagi Visinia	Samoa	2022	Hawke's Bay
Hamilton Burr	Scotland Under 20	2016	Waikato
Nick Grigg	Scotland	2019	Hawke's Bay
Eric Annandale	South Africa	Uncapped	Auckland
Johan Momsen	South Africa	Uncapped	Manawatu
Dylan Nel	South Africa	Uncapped	
Jordi Viljoen	South Africa	Uncapped	Manawatu
Tolu Fahamakioa	Tonga	2018	Waikato
Tima Fainga'anuku	Tonga	2022	Manawatu
Folau Fakatava	Tonga	Uncapped	Hawke's Bay
Viliami Fine	Tonga	2021	Southland
Shannon Frizzell	Tonga Under 20	2014	Highlanders
Aisea Halo	Tonga	2022	North Harbour
Lotu Inisi	Tonga	2021	North Harbour
Samisoni Taukei'aho	Tonga Under 15	2013	Chiefs
Viliami Taulani	Tonga	2021	Counties-Manukau
Ma'ama Vaipulu	Tonga	2021	Counties-Manukau

NEW ZEALAND ORIGIN AND FIRST-CLASS PLAYERS CAPPED OVERSEAS 2023

Provincial Union and Year indicate most recent first-class play when applicable.

Player	Country	Last Representation	Year
Martin Bogado	Argentina	Highlanders	2023
Pablo Matera	Argentina	Crusaders	2022
Quade Cooper	Australia	Waikato	-
Lalakai Foketi	Australia	Bay of Plenty	2017
Ben Grant	Australia	North Harbour	2023
Andrew Kellaway	Australia	Counties Manukau	2019
Matthew Phillip	Australia	Southland	2016
Peter Samu	Australia	Crusaders	2018
Ollie Sapsford	Australia A	Hawke's Bay	2023
Will Skelton	Australia	Auckland	-
Taniela Tupou	Australia	Auckland	-
Josh Turner	Australia Sevens	Thames Valley	2014
Joey Walton	Australia A	Bay of Plenty	2022
Ben Donald	Brazil	Bay of Plenty	-
Wilton Rebolo	Brazil	Northland	2023
Spencer Jones	Canada	Waikato	-
Cole Keith	Canada	Manawatu	2023
Andrew Quattrin	Canada	Manawatu	2023
Djustice Sears-Duru	Canada	North Otago	2014
James Kora	Cook Islands Sevens	Northland	-
Haba Tamarua	Cook Islands Sevens	South Canterbury	-
Leandro Vakatini	Cook Islands Sevens	Auckland	-
Hayden Jurlina	Croatia	Auckland	-
Daniel Mau'u	Croatia	Auckland	-
Joe Marchant	England	Blues	2020
Mako Vunipola	England	Auckland	-
Te Ahiwaru Cirikidaveta	Fiji	Tasman	2022
Temo Mayanavanua	Fiji	Northland	2020
Caleb Muntz	Fiji	Waikato	-
Isoa Nasilasila	Fiji	North Harbour	2022
Peni Ravai	Fiji	Southland	2016
Samu Tawake	Fiji	Manawatu	2019
Zuriel Togiatama	Fiji	Counties Manukau	2022
Ben Volavola	Fiji	North Harbour	2017
Uini Atonio	France	Counties Manukau	2011
Nathan de Thierry	Hong Kong	Counties Manukau	2016
Bundee Aki	Ireland	Counties Manukau	2014
Jamison Gibson-Park	Ireland	Taranaki	2015
James Lowe	Ireland	Tasman	2017
Ephalahame Faiva	Italy	Hurricanes	2023
Toa Halafihi	Italy	Taranaki	2018
Monty Ioane	Italy	Bay of Plenty	2017
Asaeli Ai Valu	Japan	Otago	-

Player	Country	Last Representation	Year
Warner Dearns	Japan	Hawke's Bay	-
Kazuki Himeno	Japan	Highlanders	2021
Shota Horie	Japan	Otago	2012
Michael Leitch	Japan	Chiefs	2017
Lomano Lemeki	Japan	Auckland	-
Semisi Masirewa	Japan	Manawatu	2015
Craig Millar	Japan	Otago	2017
Willie Ambaka	Kenya Sevens	Manawatu	2018
Te Hauora Campbell	Netherlands	Marlborough	-
Chris Raymond	Netherlands	Wairarapa Bush	2018
Leroy Van Dam	Netherlands	Otago	2017
Jordan Bunce	Niue Sevens	Waikato	2018
Jason Tomane	Romania	Manawatu	-
Hinckley Vaovasa	Romania	Wellington	-
Nigel Ah Wong	Samoa	Bay of Plenty	2022
Michael Ala'alatoa	Samoa	Crusaders	2021
AJ Alatimu	Samoa	Counties Manukau	2022
Paul Alo-Emile	Samoa	Waikato	2013
Michael Curry	Samoa	Tasman	2023
Ene Enari	Samoa	Hawke's Bay	2022
Charlie Faumuina	Samoa	Blues	2017
Ed Fidow	Samoa	Manawatu	2022
Neria Fomai	Samoa	Hawke's Bay	2021
Stacy Ili	Samoa	Hawke's Bay	2023
Ben Lam	Samoa	Wellington	2019
Jack Lam	Samoa	Waikato	2023
James Lay	Samoa	Auckland	2023
Jordan Lay	Samoa	Blues	2023
Christian Leali'ifano	Samoa	Moana Pasifika	2023
Fritz Lee	Samoa	Counties Manukau	2013
Genesis Mamea Lemalu	Samoa	Wellington	2013
D'Angelo Leuila	Samoa	Waikato	2022
Steven Luatua	Samoa	Auckland	2017
Tumua Manu	Samoa	Auckland	2020
Meli Matavao	Samoa	Otago	2018
Alamanda Motuga	Samoa	Moana Pasifika	2022
Tim Nanai-Williams	Samoa	Chiefs	2018
Ray Niuia	Samoa	North Harbour	2022
Duncan Paia'aua	Samoa	Wellington	-
Paul Scanlan	Samoa Sevens	Auckland	-
Taleni Seu	Samoa	Chiefs	2019
Sam Slade	Samoa	Counties Manukau	2021
Lima Spopaga	Samoa	Highlanders	2018
Jordan Taufua	Samoa	Tasman	2019
Jonathan Taumateine	Samoa	Counties Manukau	2021
Danny Toala	Samoa	Hawke's Bay	2022
Luteru Tolai	Samoa	North Harbour	2022
Jeff To'omaga-Allen	Samoa	Hurricanes	2019
Tietie Tuimauga	Samoa	Manawatu	2021
Chris Vui	Samoa	North Harbour	2016
Simon Berghan	Scotland	Canterbury	-
James Dobie	Scotland	Bay of Plenty	2022
Pita Ahki	Tonga	Waikato	2017

Player	Country	Last Representation	Year
Sione Anga'aelangi	Tonga	Counties Manukau	2016
Joe Apikotoa	Tonga	Hawke's Bay	2022
Malakai Fekitoa	Tonga	Auckland	2017
Leva Fifita	Tonga	Waikato	2017
Vaea Fifita	Tonga	Hurricanes	2021
Penitoa Finau	Tonga	Bay of Plenty	2023
Ziegfried Fisi'ihoi	Tonga	Chiefs	2017
Samson Fualalo	Tonga Sevens	North Harbour	-
Solomone Funaki	Tonga	Hawke's Bay	2021
Sila Havili Talitui	Tonga	Crusaders	2023
William Havili	Tonga	Moana Pasifika	2023
William Helu	Tonga Sevens	Auckland	-
Sione Ika	Tonga Sevens	Hawke's Bay	2019
Fine Inisi	Tonga	Moana Pasifika	2023
Solomone Kata	Tonga	Moana Pasifika	2022
Tau Koloamatangi	Tonga	Otago	2022
Paula Latu	Tonga	Southland	2022
Sam Lousi	Tonga	Wellington	2019
Siua Maile	Tonga	Manawatu	2022
Otumaka Mausia	Tonga	Auckland	2017
George Moala	Tonga	Blues	2018
Samiuela Moli	Tonga	Tasman	2021
Paul Ngauamo	Tonga	Canterbury	2011
Manu Paea	Tonga	Auckland	2022
Semisi Paea	Tonga	Bay of Plenty	2023
Atieli Pakalani	Tonga Sevens	Auckland	2010
Salesi Piutau	Tonga	Auckland	2015
Augustine Pulu	Tonga	Blues	2019
Sonatane Takulua	Tonga	Northland	2014
Ben Tameifuna	Tonga	Waikato	2015
John Tapueluelu	Tonga Sevens	Otago	2023
Siate Tokolahi	Tonga	Highlanders	2021
Anzelo Tuitavuki	Tonga	Hawke's Bay	2023
Lucas Lacamp	United States Sevens	Canterbury	-
Mike Sosene-Feagai	United States	Auckland	2019
Toare Reuben	Vanuatu Sevens	Auckland	-
Gareth Anscombe	Wales	Auckland	2014
Taine Plumtree	Wales	Blues	2023

ALL BLACKS TEST MATCH RECORD

to January 1, 2024

Opponents	*Played*	*Won*	*Lost*	*Drawn*	*For*	*Against*
Argentina	37	34	2	1	1434	506
Australia	177	124	45	8	3928	2563
British Isles	41	30	7	4	700	399
Canada	6	6	–	–	376	54
England	43	33	8	2	1017	619
Fiji	7	7	–	–	481	86
France	63	48	14	1	1634	868
Georgia	1	1	–	–	43	10
Ireland	37	31	5	1	1041	516
Italy	16	16	–	–	963	157
Japan	5	5	–	–	389	92
Namibia	3	3	–	–	200	26
Pacific Islands	1	1	–	–	41	26
Portugal	1	1	–	–	108	13
Romania	2	2	–	–	99	14
Samoa	7	7	–	–	411	72
Scotland	32	30	–	2	953	372
South Africa	106	62	40	4	2196	1741
Tonga	7	7	–	–	520	42
United States	4	4	–	–	275	29
Uruguay	1	1	–	–	73	0
Wales	37	34	3	–	1219	430
World XV	3	2	1	–	94	69
	637	***489***	***125***	***23***	***18,195***	***8,704***

ALL BLACKS STATISTICS

to January 1, 2024

LEADING ALL BLACKS APPEARANCES IN ALL MATCHES

S.L. Whitelock	153	S.M. Going	86	R.M. Brooke	69
R.H. McCaw	149	K.R. Tremain	86	O.M. Brown	69
C.E. Meads	133	S.S. Wilson	85	F.E. Bunce	69
K.F. Mealamu	133	B.R. Smith	85	J.T. Rokocoko	69
S.B.T. Fitzpatrick	128	C.J.D. Taylor	85	M.W. Shaw	69
K.J. Read	128	I.J. Clarke	83	B.J. Lochore	68
A.L. Smith	125	A.K. Hore	83	C.W. Dowd	67
B.J. Barrett	124	J. Kaino	83	C.R. Jack	67
T.D. Woodcock	118	A.S. Savea	83	A.D. Oliver	67
A.M. Haden	117	S.C. McDowall	81	G.M. Somerville	67
I.A. Kirkpatrick	113	T.T.R. Perenara	81	I.J.A. Dagg	66
B.G. Williams	113	J.F. Umaga	79	G.A. Knight	66
D.W. Carter	112	G.J. Fox	78	A.J. Whetton	65
B.A. Retallick	109	R.W. Loe	78	A.R. Sutherland	64
O.T. Franks	108	A.J. Williams	78	T.J. Wright	64
I.D. Jones	105	W.J. Whineray	77	D.C. Howlett	63
M.A. Nonu	104	W.K. Little	75	K.L. Skinner	63
J.M. Muliaina	102	M.N. Jones	74	R. So'oialo	63
B.J. Robertson	102	J.T. Lomu	73	M.R. Brewer	61
G.W. Whetton	101	P.A.T. Weepu	73	M.J. Brownlie	61
Z.V. Brooke	100	W.W.V. Crockett	72	G.N.K. Mourie	61
S.J. Cane	96	A.P. Mehrtens	72	R.W. Norton	61
J.J. Kirwan	96	M.G. Mexted	72	T.C. Randell	61
C.G. Smith	94	S.K. Barrett	71	D. Young	61
D.S. Coles	90	A.R. Lienert-Brown	71	C.M. Cullen	60
D.B. Clarke	89	J.W. Wilson	71	B.C. Thorn	60
J.W. Marshall	88	R.E. Ioane	69		

LEADING POINTS-SCORERS IN ALL MATCHES FOR NEW ZEALAND

		Matches	Points
D.W. Carter	2003–15	112	1598
G.J. Fox	1985–93	78	1067
A.P. Mehrtens	1995–2004	72	994
D.B. Clarke	1956–64	89	781
B.J. Barrett	2012–23	124	740
R. Mo'unga	2017-23	57	468
W.F. McCormick	1965–71	44	453
B.G. Williams	1970–78	113	401*
C.J. Spencer	1995–2004	44	383
W.J. Wallace	1903–08	51	379
A.R. Hewson	1979–84	34	357
J.F. Karam	1972–75	42	345
A.W. Cruden	2010–17	50	322
K.J. Crowley	1983–91	35	316
J.W. Wilson	1993–2001	71	299
J.M. Barrett	2017-23	57	292
M.F. Nicholls	1921–30	51	284
J.J. Kirwan	1984–94	96	275
R.G. Wilson	1976–80	25	272
C.M. Cullen	1996–2002	60	266
R.M. Deans	1983–85	19	252
J.A. Gallagher	1986–89	41	251

** Includes one penalty try at three points*

LEADING TRY-SCORERS IN ALL MATCHES

		Matches	Tries
J.J. Kirwan	1984–94	96	67
B.G. Williams	1970–78	113	66*
C.M. Cullen	1996–2002	60	52
I.A. Kirkpatrick	1967–77	113	50
J.W. Wilson	1993–2001	71	50
S.S. Wilson	1976–83	85	50
D.C. Howlett	2000–07	63	49
T.J. Wright	1986–92	64	49*
J. Hunter	1905–08	36	48
J.T. Rokocoko	2003–10	69	47
B.G. Fraser	1979–84	55	46
S.J. Savea	2012–17	54	46
B.J. Barrett	2012-23	124	43
G.B. Batty	1972–77	56	45
J.T. Lomu	1994–2002	73	43
Z.V. Brooke	1987–97	100	42
M.J. Dick	1963–70	55	42

* Includes one penalty try

MOST APPEARANCES IN INTERNATIONALS

S.L. Whitelock	2010–23	153
R.H. McCaw	2001–15	148
K.F. Mealamu	2002–15	132
K.J. Read	2008–19	127
A.L. Smith	2012–23	125
B.J. Barrett	2012–23	123
T.D. Woodcock	2002–15	118
D.W. Carter	2003–15	112
B.A. Retallick	2012–23	109
O.T. Franks	2009–19	108
M.A. Nonu	2003–15	103
J.M. Muliaina	2003–11	100
S.J. Cane	2012–23	95
C.G. Smith	2004–15	94
S.B.T. Fitzpatrick	1986–97	92
D.S. Coles	2012–23	90
C.J.D. Taylor	2015-23	85
B.R. Smith	2009–19	84
A.K. Hore	2002–13	83
J. Kaino	2004–17	81
J.W. Marshall	1995–2005	81
A.S. Savea	2016-23	81
T.T.R. Perenara	2014–22	80
I.D. Jones	1990–99	79
A.J. Williams	2002–12	77
J.F. Umaga	1997–2005	74
W.W.V. Crockett	2009–17	71
P.A.T. Weepu	2004–13	71
A.R. Lienert-Brown	2016-23	70
A.P. Mehrtens	1995–2004	70
S.K. Barrett	2016-23	69
R.E. Ioane	2016-23	69
J.T. Rokocoko	2003–10	68
C.R. Jack	2001–07	67
I.J.A. Dagg	2010–17	66
G.M. Somerville	2000–08	66
J.J. Kirwan	1984–94	63
J.T. Lomu	1994–2002	63
R.M. Brooke	1992–99	62
D.C. Howlett	2000–07	62
R. So'oialo	2002–09	62
C.W. Dowd	1993–2000	60
J.W. Wilson	1993–2001	60
A.D. Oliver	1997–2007	59
B.C. Thorn	2003–11	59
Z.V. Brooke	1987–97	58
G.W. Whetton	1981–91	58
C.M. Cullen	1996–2002	58
S. Williams	2010–19	58
J.M. Barrett	2017-23	57
B.T. Kelleher	1999–2007	57
J.P.T. Moody	2014-21	57
A.O.H.M. Tuungafasi	2016-23	57
O.M. Brown	1992–98	56
L.R. MacDonald	2000–08	56
R. Mo'unga	2017-23	56
F.E. Bunce	1992–97	55
M.N. Jones	1987–98	55
C.E. Meads	1957–71	55
J.A. Kronfeld	1995–2000	54
S.J. Savea	2012–17	54
C.S. Jane	2008–14	53
N.E. Laulala	2015-23	53
Q.J. Cowan	2004–11	51
T.C. Randell	1997–2002	51
W.K. Little	1990–98	50
R.D. Thorne	1999–2007	50

MOST POINTS FOR NEW ZEALAND IN INTERNATIONALS

	Matches	Tries	Con	PG	DG	Mark	Points
D.W. Carter	112	29	293	281	8	–	1598
A.P. Mehrtens	70	7	169	188	10	–	967
B.J. Barrett	123	43	168	58	3	–	734
G.J. Fox	46	1	118	128	7	–	645
R. Mo'unga	56	11	144	41	-	-	466
A.W. Cruden	50	5	63	56	1	–	322
J.M. Barrett	57	24	47	26	-	-	292
C.J. Spencer	35	14	49	41	–	–	291
D.C. Howlett	62	49	–	–	–	–	245
C.M. Cullen	58	46	3	–	–	–	236
J.W. Wilson	60	44	1	3	1	–	234
J.T. Rokocoko	68	46	–	–	–	–	230
S.J. Savea	54	46	–	–	–	–	230
D.B. Clarke	31	2	33	38	5	2	207
A.R. Hewson	19	4	22	43	4	–	201
B.R. Smith	84	39	–	–	–	–	195
J.T. Lomu	63	37	–	–	–	–	185
J.F. Umaga	74	37*	–	–	–	–	185
R.E. Ioane	69	36	–	–	–	–	180
T.E. Brown	18	5	43	20	–	–	171
J.M. Muliaina	100	34	–	–	–	–	170
D.S. McKenzie	47	20	30	2	-	-	166
W.T. Jordan	31	31	-	-	-	-	155
M.A. Nonu	103	31	–	–	–	–	155
C.L. McAlister	30	7	26	22	–	–	153
A.L. Smith	125	29	1	-	-	-	147
L.R. MacDonald	56	15*	25	7	–	–	146
S.W. Sivivatu	45	29	–	–	–	–	145
J.J. Kirwan	63	35†	–	–	–	–	143
R.H. McCaw	148	28*	–	–	–	–	140
I.J.A. Dagg	66	26	1	2	–	–	138
C.G. Smith	94	26	–	–	–	–	130
K.J. Read	127	26	–	–	–	–	130
W.F. McCormick	16	–	23	24	1	–	121
J.W. Marshall	81	24	–	–	–	–	120
A.S. Savea	81	24	-	-	-	-	120
D.S. Coles	90	23	-	-	-	-	115
S.D. Culhane	6	1	32	15	–	–	114
K.J. Crowley	19	5	5	23	2	–	105
N.J. Evans	16	5	30	6	–	–	103
P.A.T. Weepu	71	7	10	16	–	–	103
C.J.D. Taylor	85	20	-	-	-	-	100

† includes three tries at five points   ** includes penalty try*

MOST STARTS IN EACH POSITION FOR NEW ZEALAND IN INTERNATIONALS

Fullback	J.M. Muliaina	2003–11	83	No 8	K.J. Read	2009–19	118
Wing	J.T. Rokocoko	2003–10	66	Flanker	R.H. McCaw	2001–15	139
Centre	C.G. Smith	2004–15	90	Lock	S.L. Whitelock	2010–23	127
2nd five-eighth	M.A. Nonu	2003–15	81	Prop	T.D. Woodcock	2002–15	105
1st five-eighth	D.W. Carter	2004–15	94	Hooker	S.B.T. Fitzpatrick	1986–97	91
Halfback	A.L. Smith	2012–23	114	Substitute	TJ Perenara	2014-22	58

The player must have started the match in that position. Appearances as replacements are not included except in this case Perenara.

MOST TRIES FOR NEW ZEALAND IN INTERNATIONALS

	Matches	Tries		Matches	Tries
D.C. Howlett	62	49	D.W. Carter	112	29
C.M. Cullen	58	46	S.W. Sivivatu	45	29
J.T. Rokocoko	68	46	A.L. Smith	125	29
S.J. Savea	54	46	R.H. McCaw	148	28*
J.W. Wilson	60	44	C.G. Smith	94	26
B.J. Barrett	123	43	I.J.A. Dagg	66	26
B.R. Smith	85	39	K.J. Read	127	26
J.T. Lomu	63	37	J.M. Barrett	57	24
J.F. Umaga	74	37*	J.W. Marshall	81	24
R.E. Ioane	69	36	A.S. Savea	81	24
J.J. Kirwan	63	35	D.S. Coles	90	23
J.M. Muliaina	100	34	F.E. Bunce	55	20
W.T. Jordan	31	31	D.S. McKenzie	47	20
M.A. Nonu	103	31	C.J.D. Taylor	85	20

** Includes one penalty try*

MOST TRIES IN AN INTERNATIONAL

M.C.G. Ellis	v Japan, 1995	6	J.W. Wilson	v Samoa, 1999	4
J.W. Wilson	v Fiji, 1997	5	J.M. Muliaina	v Canada, 2003	4
W.T. Jordan	v Tonga, 2021	5	S.W. Sivivatu	v Fiji, 2005	4
D. McGregor	v England, 1905	4	Z.R. Guildford	v Canada, 2011	4
C.I. Green	v Fiji, 1987	4	B.J. Barrett	v Australia, 2018	4
J.A. Gallagher	v Fiji, 1987	4	J.M. Barrett	v Italy, 2018	4
J.J. Kirwan	v Wales, 1988	4	G.C. Bridge	v Tonga, 2019	4
J.T. Lomu	v England, 1995	4	D.S. Coles	v Fiji, 2021	4
C.M. Cullen	v Scotland, 1996	4			

MOST PENALTY GOALS IN AN INTERNATIONAL

A.P. Mehrtens	v Australia, 1999	9	D.W. Carter	v Australia, 2007	7
A.P. Mehrtens	v France, 2000	9	P.A.T. Weepu	v Argentina, 2011	7
G.J. Fox	v W Samoa, 1993	7	B.J. Barrett	v BI Lions, 2017	7
A.P. Mehrtens	v South Africa, 1999	7			

MOST CONVERSIONS IN AN INTERNATIONAL

S.D. Culhane	v Japan, 1995	20	C.R. Slade	v Japan, 2011	9
N.J. Evans	v Portugal, 2007	14	R. Mo'unga	v USA, 2021	9
T.E. Brown	v Tonga, 2000	12	R. Mo'unga	v Italy, 2023	9
L.R. MacDonald	v Tonga, 2003	12	G.J. Fox	v Italy, 1987	8
T.E. Brown	v Italy, 1999	11	G.J. Fox	v Wales, 1988	8
G.J. Fox	v Fiji, 1987	10	A.P. Mehrtens	v Italy, 2002	8
C.J. Spencer	v Argentina, 1997	10	R. Mo'unga	v Canada, 2019	8
D.W. Carter	v Canada, 2003	9	J.M. Barrett	v Namibia, 2019	8

HIGHEST POINTS-SCORERS IN AN INTERNATIONAL

	Opponent	Tries	Con	PG	DG	Points
S.D. Culhane	Japan, 1995[1]	1	20	–	–	45
T.E. Brown	Italy, 1999	1	11	3	–	36
D.W. Carter	Lions, 2005	2	4	5	–	33
C.J. Spencer	Argentina, 1997[1]	2	10	1	–	33
A.P. Mehrtens	Ireland, 1997	1	5	6	–	33
N.J. Evans	Portugal, 2007	1	14	–	–	33
T.E. Brown	Tonga, 2000	1	12	1	–	32
M.C.G. Ellis	Japan, 1995	6	–	–	–	30
B.J. Barrett	Australia, 2018	4	5	–	–	30
T.E. Brown	Samoa, 2001	3	3	3	–	30
A.P. Mehrtens	Australia, 1999	–	1	9	–	29
A.P. Mehrtens	France, 2000	–	1	9	–	29
L.R. MacDonald	Tonga, 2003	1	12	–	–	29
D.W. Carter	Canada, 2007	3	7	–	–	29
A.P. Mehrtens	Canada, 1995[1]	1	7	3	–	28
D.W. Carter	Wales, 2010	2	4	3	–	27
A.R. Hewson	Australia, 1982	1	2	5	1	26
G.J. Fox	Fiji, 1987	–	10	2	–	26
D.W. Carter	Wales, 2005	2	5	2	–	26
D.W. Carter	England, 2006	1	3	5	–	26
T.E. Brown	Samoa, 1999[1]	–	7	4	–	26
B.J. Barrett	Wales, 2016	2	5	2	–	26
D.W. Carter	South Africa, 2006	–	2	7	–	25
G.J. Fox	Western Samoa, 1993	–	2	7	–	25
J.W. Wilson	Fiji, 1997	5	–	–	–	25
C.J. Spencer	South Africa, 1997	1	4	4	–	25
D.W. Carter	France, 2004	1	4	4	–	25
W.T. Jordan	Tonga, 2021	5	-	-	-	25
W.F. McCormick	Wales, 1969	–	3	5	1	24
B.J. Barrett	Samoa, 2017	2	7	–	–	24
D.S. McKenzie	France, 2018	2	7	–	–	24
D.S. McKenzie	Namibia, 2023	2	7	-	-	24

[1]*international debut*

NEW ZEALAND INTERNATIONAL CAPTAINS

R.H. McCaw	2004–15	110	J. Collins	2006–07	3
K.J. Read	2012–19	52	R.R. King	1937	3
S.B.T. Fitzpatrick	1992–97	51	D.J. Graham	1964	3
W.J. Whineray	1958–65	30	D.S. Loveridge	1980	3
S.J. Cane	2015–22	27	K.F. Mealamu	2008–11	3
R.D. Thorne	2002–07	23	J.M. Muliaina	2009	3
T.C. Randell	1998–2002	22	F.J. Oliver	1978	3
J.F. Umaga	2004–05	21	J. Richardson	1924	3
G.N.K. Mourie	1977–82	19	F. Roberts	1910	3
B.J. Lochore	1966–70	18	R.W. Roberts	1914	3
S.L. Whitelock	2017–22	18	G.G. Aitken	1921	2
A.G. Dalton	1981–85	17	R.H. Duff	1956	2
G.W. Whetton	1990–91	15	J.L. Griffiths	1936	2
W.T. Shelford	1988–90	14	A. McDonald	1913	2
D.E. Kirk	1986–87	11	N.A. Mitchell	1938	2
T.J. Blackadder	2000	10	M.J. O'Leary	1913	2
A.R. Leslie	1974–76	10	A.R. Reid	1957	2
A.D. Oliver	2001	10	K.L. Skinner	1952	2
I.A. Kirkpatrick	1972–73	9	J.B. Smith	1949	2
A.S. Savea	2021-23	8	P.B. Vincent	1956	2
C.G. Porter	1925–30	7	S.S. Wilson	1983	2
F.R. Allen	1946–49	6	J. Duncan	1903	1
R.R. Elvidge	1949–50	5	P.W. Henderson	1995	1
R. So'oialo	2008–09	5	A.K. Hore	2011	1
R.C. Stuart	1953–54	5	C.R. Laidlaw	1968	1
M.J. Brownlie	1928	4	H.T. Lilburne	1929	1
D. Gallaher	1905–06	4	R.M. McKenzie	1938	1
M.J.B. Hobbs	1985–86	4	J.R. Page	1934	1
J. Hunter	1907–08	4	B.A. Retallick	2021	1
P. Johnstone	1950–51	4	E.J. Roberts	1921	1
F.D. Kilby	1932–34	4	A.L. Smith	2021	1
J.E. Manchester	1935–36	4	B.R. Smith	2017	1
J.W. Marshall	1997	4	J.C. Spencer	1905	1
C.E. Meads	1971	4	W.A. Strang	1931	1
R.W. Norton	1977	4	K.R. Tremain	1968	1
J.W. Stead	1904–08	4	L.C. Whitelock	2018	1
I.J. Clarke	1955	3			

HIGHEST SCORES IN TEST MATCHES

Opponent	Home		Away		Opponent	Home		Away	
Argentina	93–8	(1997)	54–18	(2012)	Namibia	–	–	71-3	(2023)
Australia	57–22	(2021)	54–34	(2017)	Pacific Islands	41–26	(2004)	–	
British Isles	48–18	(2005)	–		Portugal	–	–	108–13	(2007)
Canada	79–15	(2011)	68–8	(2003)	Romania	–	–	85–8	(2007)
England	64–22	(1998)	45–29	(1995)	Samoa	101–14	(2008)	25–16	(2015)
Fiji	91–0	(2005)	–		Scotland	69–20	(2000)	51–15 51–22	(1993) (2012)
France	61–10	(2007)	62–13	(2015)	South Africa	57–0	(2017)	57-15	(2016)
Georgia	–	–	43–10	(2015)	Tonga	102–0	(2000, 2021)	91–7	(2003)
Ireland	66–28	(2010)	63–15	(1997)	USA	–	–	104–14	(2021)
Italy	70–6	(1987)	101–3	(1999)	Uruguay	–	–	73-0	(2023)
Japan	83–7	(2011)	145–17	(1995)	Wales	55–3	(2003)	54–16	(2021)

MOST POINTS BY AN ALL BLACK AGAINST AN OPPONENT

Opponent	In an International			In a Career	
Argentina	33	C.J. Spencer	1997	103	G.J. Fox
Australia	30	B.J. Barrett	2018	366	D.W. Carter
British Isles	33	D.W. Carter	2005	46	A.R. Hewson
Canada	29	D.W. Carter	2007	47	D.W. Carter
England	26	D.W. Carter	2006	178	D.W. Carter
Fiji	26	G.J. Fox	1987	29	C.M. Cullen
France	29	A.P. Mehrtens	2000	146	D.W. Carter
Georgia	15	S.J. Savea	2015	15	S.J. Savea
Ireland	33	A.P. Mehrtens	1997	81	A.P. Mehrtens
Italy	36	T.E. Brown	1999	53	D.W. Carter
Japan	45	S.D. Culhane	1995	45	S.D. Culhane
Namibia	24	D.S. McKenzie	2023	24	D.S. McKenzie
Pacific Islands	11	D.W. Carter	2004	11	D.W. Carter
Portugal	33	N.J. Evans	2007	33	N.J. Evans
Romania	17	N.J. Evans	2007	17	N.J. Evans
Samoa	30	T.E. Brown	2001	56	T.E. Brown
Scotland	23	A.P. Mehrtens	1995	108	A.P. Mehrtens
South Africa	25	C.J. Spencer	1997	255	D.W. Carter
	25	D.W. Carter	2006		
Tonga	32	T.E. Brown	2000	32	T.E. Brown
USA	23	R. Mo'unga	2021	23	R. Mo'unga
Uruguay	15	L.O.K.W.P. Fainga'anuku	2023	15	L.O.K.W.P. Fainga'anuku
	15	R. Mo'unga	2023	15	R. Mo'unga
Wales	27	D.W. Carter	2010	162	D.W. Carter

PLAYING RECORDS OF NEW ZEALAND TEAMS

1884–2023

		Played	Won	Lost	Drawn	Points for	Points against
1884	in **New South Wales** and **New Zealand**	9	9	–	–	176	17
1893	in **New Zealand, New South Wales** and **Queensland**	11	10	1	–	171	48
1894	**New South Wales** in **New Zealand**	1	–	1	–	6	8
1896	**Queensland** in **New Zealand**	1	1	–	–	9	0
1897	in **New Zealand, New South Wales** and **Queensland**	11	9	2	–	238	83
1901	**New South Wales** in **New Zealand**	2	2	–	–	44	8
1903	in **Australia** and **New Zealand**	11	10	1	–	281	27
1904	**Great Britain** in **New Zealand**	1	1	–	–	9	3
1905	in **Australia** and **New Zealand**	7	4	1	2	89	30
	Australia in **New Zealand**	1	1	–	–	14	3
1905/06	in **the British Isles, France** and **North America**	35	34	1	–	976	59
1907	in **Australia**	8	6	1	1	115	53
1908	**Anglo-Welsh** in **New Zealand**	3	2	–	1	64	8
1910	in **Australia** and **New Zealand**	8	7	1	–	138	78
1913	**Australia** in **New Zealand**	4	3	1	–	79	52
	in **North America**	16	16	–	–	610	6
1914	in **Australia** and **New Zealand**	11	10	1	–	260	69
1920	in **Australia** and **New Zealand**	10	9	–	1	352	91
1921	**South Africa** and **New South Wales** in **New Zealand**	4	1	2	1	18	31
1922	in **Australia** and **New Zealand**	8	6	2	–	198	102
1923	**New South Wales** in **New Zealand**	3	3	–	–	91	26
1924/25	in **Australia, New Zealand, the British Isles, France** and **Canada**	38	36	2	–	981	180
1925	in **Australia** and **New Zealand**	8	6	2	–	132	67
	New South Wales in **New Zealand**	1	1	–	–	36	10
1926	in **Australia** and **New Zealand**	8	6	2	–	187	109
1928	in **South Africa** and **Australia**	23	17	5	1	397	153
	New South Wales in **New Zealand**	4	3	1	–	79	40
1929	in **Australia**	10	6	3	1	186	80
1930	**Great Britain** in **New Zealand**	5	4	1	–	87	40
1931	**Australia** in **New Zealand**	1	1	–	–	20	13
1932	in **Australia** and **New Zealand**	11	9	2	–	331	135
1934	in **Australia** and **New Zealand**	9	7	1	1	201	107
1935/36	in **the British Isles** and **Canada**	30	26	3	1	490	183
1936	**Australia** in **New Zealand**	3	3	–	–	65	32
1937	**South Africa** in **New Zealand**	3	1	2	–	25	37
1938	in **Australia**	9	9	–	–	279	73
1946	**Australia** in **New Zealand**	2	2	–	–	45	18

		Played	Won	Lost	Drawn	Points for	Points against
1947	in Australia and New Zealand	10	8	2	–	263	113
1949	in South Africa	24	14	7	3	230	146
	Australia in New Zealand	2	–	2	–	15	27
1950	British Isles in New Zealand	4	3	–	1	34	20
1951	in Australia and New Zealand	13	13	–	–	375	86
1952	Australia in New Zealand	2	1	1	–	24	22
1953/54	in the British Isles, France and North America	36	30	4	2	598	152
1955	Australia in New Zealand	3	2	1	–	27	16
1956	South Africa in New Zealand	4	3	1	–	41	29
1957	in Australia and New Zealand	14	13	1	–	472	94
1958	Australia in New Zealand	3	2	1	–	45	17
1959	British Isles in New Zealand	4	3	1	–	57	42
1960	in Australia and South Africa	32	26	4	2	645	187
1961	France in New Zealand	3	3	–	–	50	12
1962	in Australia	10	9	1	–	426	49
	Australia in New Zealand	3	2	–	1	28	17
1963	England in New Zealand	2	2	–	–	30	17
1963/64	in the British Isles, France and Canada	36	34	1	1	613	159
1964	Australia in New Zealand	3	2	1	–	37	32
1965	South Africa in New Zealand	4	3	1	–	55	25
1966	British Isles in New Zealand	4	4	–	–	79	32
1967	Australia in New Zealand	1	1	–	–	29	9
	in the British Isles, France and Canada	17	16	–	1	370	135
1968	in Australia and Fiji	12	12	–	–	460	66
	France in New Zealand	3	3	–	–	40	24
1969	Wales in New Zealand	2	2	–	–	52	12
1970	in Australia and South Africa	26	23	3	–	789	234
1971	British Isles in New Zealand	4	1	2	1	42	48
1972	Internal Tour	9	9	–	–	355	88
	Australia in New Zealand	3	3	–	–	97	26
1972/73	in the British Isles, France and North America	32	25	5	2	640	266
1973	Internal Tour and England in New Zealand	5	2	3	–	88	83
1974	in Australia and Fiji	13	12	–	1	446	73
	in Ireland, Wales and England	8	7	–	1	127	50
1975	Scotland in New Zealand	1	1	–	–	24	–
1976	Ireland in New Zealand	1	1	–	–	11	3
	in South Africa	24	18	6	–	610	291
	in Argentina and Uruguay	9	9	–	–	321	72
1977	British Isles in New Zealand	4	3	1	–	54	41
	in France and Italy	9	8	1	–	216	86
1978	Australia in New Zealand	3	2	1	–	51	48
	in the British Isles	18	17	1	–	364	147
1979	France in New Zealand	2	1	1	–	42	33
	in Australia	2	1	1	–	41	15
	Argentina in New Zealand	2	2	–	–	33	15

		Played	Won	Lost	Drawn	Points for	Points against
1979	in **England** and **Scotland**	11	10	1	–	192	95
1980	in **Australia** and **Fiji**	16	12	3	1	507	126
	Fiji in **New Zealand**	1	1	–	–	33	–
	in **North America** and **Wales**	7	7	–	–	197	41
1981	**Scotland** in **New Zealand**	2	2	–	–	51	19
	South Africa in **New Zealand**	3	2	1	–	51	55
	in **Romania** and **France**	10	8	1	1	170	108
1982	**Australia** in **New Zealand**	3	2	1	–	72	53
1983	**British Isles** in **New Zealand**	4	4	–	–	78	26
	in **Australia**	1	1	–	–	18	8
	in **Scotland** and **England**	8	5	2	1	162	116
1984	**France** in **New Zealand**	2	2	–	–	41	27
	in **Australia**	14	13	1	–	600	117
	in **Fiji**	4	4	–	–	174	10
1985	**England** in **New Zealand**	2	2	–	–	60	28
	Australia in **New Zealand**	1	1	–	–	10	9
	in **Argentina**	7	6	–	1	263	87
1986	**France** in **New Zealand**	1	1	–	–	18	9
	Australia in **New Zealand**	3	1	2	–	34	47
	in **France**	8	7	1	–	218	87
1987	**World Cup**	6	6	–	–	298	52
	in **Australia**	1	1	–	–	30	16
	in **Japan**	5	5	–	–	408	16
1988	**Wales** in **New Zealand**	2	2	–	–	106	12
	in **Australia**	13	12	–	1	476	96
1989	**France** in **New Zealand**	2	2	–	–	59	37
	Argentina in **New Zealand**	2	2	–	–	109	21
	Australia in **New Zealand**	1	1	–	–	24	12
	in **Canada, Wales** and **Ireland**	14	14	–	–	454	122
1990	**Scotland** in **New Zealand**	2	2	–	–	52	34
	Australia in **New Zealand**	3	2	1	–	57	44
	in **France**	8	6	2	–	175	110
1991	in **Argentina**	9	9	–	–	358	80
	in **Australia**	1	–	1	–	12	21
	Australia in **New Zealand**	1	1	–	–	6	3
	World Cup	6	5	1	–	143	74
1992	**Centenary matches** in **New Zealand**	3	2	1	–	94	69
	Ireland in **New Zealand**	2	2	–	–	83	27
	in **Australia** and **South Africa**	16	13	3	–	567	252
1993	**British Isles** in **New Zealand**	3	2	1	–	57	51
	Australia in **New Zealand**	1	1	–	–	25	10
	Western Samoa in **New Zealand**	1	1	–	–	35	13
	in **England** and **Scotland**	13	12	1	–	386	156
1994	**France** in **New Zealand**	2	–	2	–	28	45
	South Africa in **New Zealand**	3	2	–	1	53	41

		Played	Won	Lost	Drawn	Points for	Points against
	in **Australia**	1	–	1	–	16	20
1995	**Canada** in **New Zealand**	1	1	–	–	73	7
	World Cup	6	5	1	–	327	119
	Australia in **New Zealand**	1	1	–	–	28	16
	in **Australia**	1	1	–	–	34	23
	in **Italy** and **France**	8	7	1	–	339	126
1996	**Western Samoa, Scotland** in **NZ**	3	3	–	–	149	53
	Tri Nations	4	4	–	–	119	60
	in **South Africa1**	7	5	1	1	190	139
1997	**Fiji, Argentina, Australia1** in **NZ**	4	4	–	–	256	36
	Tri Nations	4	4	–	–	159	109
	in **British Isles**	9	8	–	1	395	119
1998	**England** in **New Zealand**	2	2	–	–	104	32
	Tri Nations	4	–	4	–	65	88
	in **Australia1**	1	–	1	–	14	19
1999	**Internal, Samoa, France** in **NZ**	3	3	–	–	147	31
	Tri Nations	4	3	1	–	103	61
	World Cup	6	4	2	–	255	111
2000	**Tonga, Scotland** in **New Zealand**	3	3	–	–	219	34
	Tri Nations	4	2	2	–	127	117
	in **France** and **Italy**	3	2	1	–	128	87
2001	**Samoa, Argentina, France** in **NZ**	3	3	–	–	154	37
	Tri Nations	4	2	2	–	79	70
	in **Ireland, Scotland** and **Argentina**	5	5	–	–	179	98
2002	**Italy, Ireland, Fiji** in **New Zealand**	4	4	–	–	187	42
	Tri Nations	4	3	1	–	97	65
	in **England, France** and **Wales**	3	1	1	1	91	68
2003	**England, Wales, France** in **New Zealand**	3	2	1	–	99	41
	Tri Nations	4	4	–	–	142	65
	World Cup	7	6	1	–	361	101
2004	**England, Argentina, Pacific Islands** in **New Zealand**	4	4	–	–	154	48
	Tri Nations	4	2	2	–	83	91
	in **Europe**	4	4	–	–	177	60
2005	**Fiji, Lions** in **New Zealand**	4	4	–	–	198	40
	Tri Nations	4	3	1	–	111	86
	in **Europe**	4	4	–	–	138	39
2006	**Ireland** in **New Zealand**	2	2	–	–	61	40
	New Zealand in **Argentina**	1	1	–	–	25	19
	Tri Nations	6	5	1	–	179	112
	in **Europe**	4	4	–	–	156	44
2007	**France, Canada** in **New Zealand**	3	3	–	–	167	34
	Tri Nations	4	3	1	–	100	59
	World Cup	5	4	1	–	327	55
2008	**Ireland, England, Samoa** in **New Zealand**	4	4	–	–	203	57

		Played	Won	Lost	Drawn	Points for	Points against
	Tri Nations	6	4	2	–	152	106
	in **Hong Kong, United Kingdom** and **Ireland**	6	6	–	–	152	54
2009	**France, Italy** in **New Zealand**	3	2	1	–	63	43
	Tri Nations	6	3	3	–	141	131
	in **Japan** and **Europe**	6	5	1	–	147	80
2010	**Ireland, Wales** in **New Zealand**	3	3	–	–	137	47
	Tri Nations	6	6	–	–	184	111
	in **Hong Kong, United Kingdom** and **Ireland**	5	4	1	–	174	88
2011	**Fiji** in **New Zealand**	1	1	–	–	60	14
	Tri Nations	4	2	2	–	95	64
	World Cup	7	7	–	–	301	72
2012	**Ireland** in **New Zealand**	3	3	–	–	124	29
	Rugby Championship and **Bledisloe Cup**	7	6	–	1	195	84
	In **Europe**	4	3	1	–	147	80
2013	**France** in **New Zealand**	3	3	–	–	77	22
	Rugby Championship and **Bledisloe Cup**	7	7	–	–	243	148
	In **Japan** and **Europe**	4	4	–	–	134	69
2014	**England** in **New Zealand**	3	3	–	–	84	55
	Rugby Championship and **Bledisloe Cup**	7	5	1	1	193	119
	In **USA** and **United Kingdom**	4	4	–	–	156	59
2015	In **Samoa**, **Rugby Championship** and **Bledisloe Cup**	5	4	1	–	151	94
	World Cup	7	7	–	–	290	97
2016	**Wales** in **New Zealand**	3	3	–	–	121	49
	Rugby Championship and **Bledisloe Cup**	7	7	–	–	299	94
	In **USA**, **Italy**, **Ireland** and **France**	4	3	1	–	142	78
2017	**Samoa, Lions** in **New Zealand**	4	2	1	1	144	54
	Rugby Championship and **Bledisloe Cup**	7	6	1	–	264	142
	In **England, France, Scotland** and **Wales**	5	5	–	–	152	98
2018	**France** in **New Zealand**	3	3	–	–	127	38
	Rugby Championship and **Bledisloe Cup**	7	6	1	–	262	152
	In **Japan, England, Ireland** and **Italy**	4	3	1	–	160	65
2019	**Tonga** in New Zealand	1	1	–	–	92	7
	Rugby Championship and **Bledisloe Cup**	4	2	1	1	98	79
	World Cup	6	5	1	–	250	72
2020	**Tri-Nations and Bledisloe Cup**	6	3	2	1	161	77
2021	**Tonga, Fiji** in New Zealand	3	3	–	–	219	36
	Rugby Championship and **Bledisloe Cup**	7	6	1	–	251	129
	In **USA, Wales, Italy, Ireland** and **France**	5	3	2	–	250	108
2022	**Ireland** in **New Zealand**	3	1	2	–	76	74
	Rugby Championship and **Bledisloe Cup**	6	4	2	–	195	128
	in **Japan, Wales, Scotland** and **England**	4	3	–	1	149	102
2023	**Rugby Championship** and **Bledisloe Cup**	4	4	-	-	137	59
	World Cup Warm-up	1	-	1	-	7	35
	World Cup	7	5	2	-	336	89
	TOTALS	***1,361***	***1,142***	***178***	***41***	***37,976***	***13,929***

[1]non Tri Nations

SURVIVING NEW ZEALAND REPRESENTATIVES

(over the age of 70 years as at December 31, 2023)

	Born	*Represented New Zealand*
W.A. McCaw	August 26, 1927	1951-53-54
M.S. Cockerill	December 8, 1928	1951
L.B. Steele	January 19, 1929	1951
E.S. Diack	July 22, 1930	1959
S.G. Bremner	August 2, 1930	1952-56-60
D.L. Ashby	February 15, 1931	1958
D.N. McIntosh	April 1, 1931	1956-57
W.S.S. Freebairn	January 12, 1932	1953-54
I.N. MacEwan	May 1, 1934	1956-57-58-59-60-61-62
W.D. Gillespie	August 6, 1934	1957-58-60
K.F. Laidlaw	August 9, 1934	1960
D.M. Connor	September 9, 1935	1961-62-63-64
S.R. Nesbit	February 13, 1936	1960
J.F. McCullough	August 8, 1936	1959
R.W. Caulton	January 10, 1937	1959-60-61-63-64
D.W. McKay	August 7, 1937	1961-62-63
A.H. Clarke	February 23, 1938	1958-59-60
S.T. Meads	July 12, 1938	1961-62-63-64-65-66
D.H. Cameron	November 17, 1938	1960
K.A. Nelson	November 26, 1938	1962-63-64
N.W. Thimbleby	June 19, 1939	1970
W.M. Birtwistle	July 4, 1939	1965-67
E.W. Kirton	December 29, 1939	1963-64-67-68-69-70
D.W. Clark	February 22, 1940	1964
A.G.T. Jennings	June 15, 1940	1967
J. Major	August 8, 1940	1963-64-67
A.J. Stewart	October 11, 1940	1963-64
M.J. Dick	January 3, 1941	1963-64-65-66-67-69-70
D.A. Arnold	January 10, 1941	1963-64
J.F. Burns	February 17, 1941	1970
R.A. Guy	April 6, 1941	1971-72
M.C. Wills	October 11, 1941	1967
T.N. Wolfe	October 20, 1941	1961-62-63-68
T.J. Morris	January 3, 1942	1972-73
P.H. Clarke	January 23, 1942	1967
A.E. Smith	December 10, 1942	1967-69-70
W.L. Davis	December 15, 1942	1963-64-67-68-69-70
I.R. MacRae	April 6, 1943	1963-64-66-67-68-69-70
S.M. Going	August 19, 1943	1967-68-69-70-71-72-73-74-75-76-77
C.R. Laidlaw	November 16, 1943	1963-64-65-66-67-68-70
R.A. Urlich	February 8, 1944	1970-72-73
P.A. Johns	March 16, 1944	1968
L.A. Clark	May 1, 1944	1972-73

A.J. Wyllie	August 31, 1944	1970-71-72-73
A.R. Leslie	November 10, 1944	1974-75-76
R.J. Barber	January 14, 1945	1974
B.D.M. Furlong	March 10, 1945	1970
K.J. Tanner	April 25, 1945	1974-75-76
M.O. Knight	May 20, 1945	1968
G.F. Kember	November 15, 1945	1967-70
G.M. Crossman	November 30, 1945	1974-76
L.W. Mains	February 16, 1946	1971-76
G.S. Thorne	February 25, 1946	1967-68-69-70
B. Holmes	April 7, 1946	1970-72-73
M.W. O'Callaghan	April 27, 1946	1968
I.A. Kirkpatrick	May 24, 1946	1967-68-69-70-71-72-73-74-75-76-77
G.J. Whiting	June 4, 1946	1972-73
S.E.G. Cron	July 7, 1946	1976
P.J. Whiting	August 6, 1946	1971-72-73-74-76
O.G. Stephens	January 9, 1947	1968
H.H. Macdonald	January 11, 1947	1972-73-74-75-76
D.J. Robertson	February 6, 1947	1974-75-76-77
M. Sayers	May 1, 1947	1972-73
O.D. Bruce	May 23, 1947	1974-76-77-78
A.M. McNaughton	July 5, 1947	1971-72
J.E. Spiers	August 4, 1947	1976-79-80-81
M.G. Duncan	August 8, 1947	1971
K.A. Eveleigh	November 8, 1947	1974-76-77
D.A. Hales	November 22, 1947	1972-73
R.L. Stuart	January 9, 1948	1977
R.N. Lendrum	March 22, 1948	1973
J.D. Matheson	March 30, 1948	1972
I.N. Stevens	April 13, 1948	1972-73-74-76
P.H. Sloane	September 10, 1948	1973-76-79
A.I. Scown	October 21, 1948	1972-73
V.E. Stewart	October 28, 1948	1976-79
M.W.R. Jaffray	January 18, 1949	1976
W.K.Te P. Bush	January 24, 1949	1974-75-76-77-78-79
R.E. Burgess	March 26, 1949	1971-72-73
J.C. Ross	April 24, 1949	1981
J.S. McLachlan	June 23, 1949	1974
H.T. Joseph	August 25, 1949	1971
J.C. Ashworth	September 15, 1949	1977-78-79-80-81-82-83-84-85
L.G. Knight	September 24, 1949	1974-76-77
B.G. Ashworth	September 29, 1949	1978
K.M. Greene	December 31, 1949	1976-77
J.L. Jaffray	April 17, 1950	1972-75-76-77-78
B.McL. Gemmell	May 12, 1950	1974
J.A. Callesen	May 24, 1950	1974-75-76
E.J.T. Stokes	June 26, 1950	1976
R.G. Myers	July 6, 1950	1977-78
B.R. Johnstone	July 30, 1950	1976-77-78-79-80
K.R. Carrington	September 3, 1950	1971-72

T.W. Mitchell	September 11, 1950	1974-76
B.A. Hunter	September 16, 1950	1970-71
B.G. Williams	October 3, 1950	1970-71-72-73-74-75-76-77-78
N.M. Taylor	January 11, 1951	1976-77-78-82
H.A. Rickit	February 19, 1951	1981
K.W. Granger	March 20, 1951	1976
J.M. Hendrie	June 12, 1951	1970
G.S. Sims	June 25, 1951	1972
B.R. Ford	July 10, 1951	1977-78-79
J.E. Black	July 25, 1951	1976-77-78-79-80
G.A. Knight	August 26, 1951	1977-78-79-80-81-82-83-84-85-86
I.A. Hurst	August 27, 1951	1972-73-74
G.B. Batty	August 31, 1951	1972-73-74-75-76-77
A.G. Dalton	November 16, 1951	1977-78-79-80-81-82-83-84-85
J.F. Karam	November 21, 1951	1972-73-74-75
K.K. Lambert	March 23, 1952	1972-73-74-76-77
L.M. Rutledge	April 12, 1952	1978-79-80
D.S. Loveridge	April 22, 1952	1978-79-80-81-82-83-85
T.M. Twigden	May 14, 1952	1979-80
L.J. Brake	July 3, 1952	1976
G.N.K. Mourie	September 8, 1952	1976-77-78-79-80-81-82
B.L. Morrissey	September 14, 1952	1981
G.N. Kane	October 12, 1952	1974
K.W. Stewart	January 3, 1953	1972-73-74-75-76-79-81
K.J. Keane	February 9, 1953	1979
S.B. Conn	March 11, 1953	1976-80
J.K. Fleming	May 2, 1953	1978-79-80
R.G. Wilson	May 19, 1953	1976-78-79-80
R.G. Perry	May 26, 1953	1980
A.C.R. Jefferd	June 13, 1953	1980-81
B.G. Fraser	July 21, 1953	1979-80-81-82-83-84
A.A. McGregor	September 3, 1953	1978
M.G. Mexted	September 5, 1953	1979-80-81-82-83-84-85
B.J. McKechnie	November 6, 1953	1977-78-79-81

NEW ZEALAND REPRESENTATIVES

1884–2023

Union affiliations are shown in parentheses, preceded by date of birth and, where applicable, date of death. War casualties are denoted by an asterisk. The numbers that follow each entry show the number of games played for New Zealand. These are followed in parentheses by the number of appearances in test matches, which are included in the total. Franchise team rather than Provincial teams have been used from 2013.

Name	*B&D*	*Representative Team*	*Games*	*Tests*
Abbott H.L.	1882–1971	(Taranaki) 1905–06	11	(1)
Adkins G.T.A.	1910–1976	(South Canterbury) 1935–36	10	(–)
Afeaki B.T.P.	1988–	(Chiefs) 2013	1	(1)
Afoa I.F.	1983–	(Auckland) 2005–06–08–09–10–11	38	(36)
Aitken G.G.	1898–1952	(Wellington) 1921	2	(2)
Alatini P.F.	1976–	(Otago) 1999–2001	20	(17)
Algar B.	1894–1989	(Wellington) 1920–21	6	(–)
Allan J.	1860–1934	(Otago) 1884	8	(–)
Allen F.R.	1920–2012	(Auckland) 1946–47–49	21	(6)
Allen L.	1870–1932	(Taranaki) 1896–97–1901	13	(–)
Allen M.R.	1967–	(Taranaki) 1993–95–96; (Manawatu) 1997	27	(8)
Allen N.H.	1958–1984	(Counties) 1980	9	(2)
Alley G.T.	1903–1986	(Southland) 1926; (Canterbury) 1928	19	(3)
Anderson A.	1961–	(Canterbury) 1983–84–85–87–88	25	(6)
Anderson B.L.	1960–	(Wairarapa Bush) 1986–87	3	(1)
Anderson E.J.	1931–2014	(Bay of Plenty) 1960	10	(–)
Anesi S.R.	1981–	(Waikato) 2005	1	(1)
Archer J.A.	1900–1979	(Southland) 1925	2	(–)
Archer W.R.	1930–2018	(Otago) 1955; (Southland) 1956–57	13	(4)
Argus W.G.	1921–2016	(Canterbury) 1946–47	10	(4)
Armit A.M.	1874–1899	(Otago) 1897	9	(–)
Armstrong A.L.	1878–1959	(Wairarapa) 1903	5	(–)
Arnold D.A.	1941–	(Canterbury) 1963–64	15	(4)
Arnold K.D.	1920–2006	(Waikato) 1947	8	(2)
Ashby D.L.	1931–	(Southland) 1958	1	(1)
Asher A.A.	1879–1965	(Auckland) 1903	11	(1)
Ashworth B.G.	1949–	(Auckland) 1978	7	(2)
Ashworth J.C.	1949–	(Canterbury) 1977–78–79–80–81–82–83–84; (Hawke's Bay) 1985	52	(24)
Atiga B.A.C.	1983–	(Auckland) 2003	1	(1)
Atkinson H.J.	1888–1949	(West Coast) 1913	10	(1)
Aumua A.J.	1997–	(Wellington) 2017-20-21	8	(6)
Avery H.E.	1885–1961	(Wellington) 1910	6	(3)
Bachop G.T.M.	1967–	(Canterbury) 1987–88–89–90–91–92–94–95	54	(31)
Bachop S.J.	1966–	(Otago) 1992–93–94	18	(5)
Badeley C.E.O.	1896–1986	(Auckland) 1920–21–24	15	(2)
Badeley V.I.R.	1898–1971	(Auckland) 1922	5	(–)
Bagley K.P.	1931–1999	(Manawatu) 1953–54	20	(–)

Name	B&D	Representative Team	Games	Tests
Baird D.L.	1894–1943	(Southland) 1920	9	(–)
Baird J.A.S.*	1893–1917	(Otago) 1913	1	(1)
Balch W.	1871–1949	(Canterbury) 1894	1	(–)
Ball N.	1908–1986	(Wellington) 1931–32–35–36	22	(5)
Barber R.J.	1945–	(Southland) 1974	6	(–)
Barrell C.K.	1967–	(Canterbury) 1996–97	4	(–)
Barrett B.J.	1991–	(Taranaki) 2012; (Hurricanes) 2013–14–15–16–17–18-19; (Blues) 2020-21-22-23	124	(123)
Barrett J.	1888–1971	(Auckland) 1913–14	3	(2)
Barrett J.M.	1997	(Hurricanes) 2017–18-19-20-21-22-23	57	(57)
Barrett S.K.	1993–	(Crusaders) 2016–17–18-19-20-21-22-23	71	(69)
Barry E.F.	1905–1993	(Wellington) 1932–34	10	(1)
Barry K.E.	1936–2014	(Thames Valley) 1962–63–64	23	(–)
Barry L.J.	1971–	(North Harbour) 1993–95	10	(1)
Bates S.P.	1980–	(Waikato) 2004	2	(1)
Batty G.B.	1951–	(Wellington) 1972–73–74–75; (Bay of Plenty) 1976–77	56	(15)
Batty W.	1905–1979	(Auckland) 1928–30–31	6	(4)
Bayly A.	1866–1907	(Taranaki) 1893–94–97	20	(–)
Bayly W.	1869–1950	(Taranaki) 1894	1	(–)
Beatty G.E.	1925–2004	(Taranaki) 1950	1	(1)
Bell J.R.	1900–1963	(Southland) 1923	1	(–)
Bell R.C.	1893–1960	(Otago) 1922	8	(–)
Bell R.H.	1925–2016	(Otago) 1951–52	9	(3)
Belliss E.A.	1894–1974	(Wanganui) 1920–21–22–23	20	(3)
Bennet R.	1879–1962	(Otago) 1905	1	(1)
Berghan T.	1914–1998	(Otago) 1938	6	(3)
Berry M.J.	1966–	(Wairarapa Bush) 1986; (Wellington) 1993	10	(1)
Berryman N.R.	1973–2015	(Northland) 1998	1	(1)
Best J.J.	1914–1994	(Marlborough) 1935–36	6	(–)
Bevan V.D.	1921–1996	(Wellington) 1947–49–50–53–54	25	(6)
Bird D.J.	1991–	(Crusaders) 2013–14; (Chiefs) 2017	3	(2)
Birtwistle W.M.	1939–	(Canterbury) 1965; (Waikato) 1967	12	(7)
Black J.E.	1951–	(Canterbury) 1976–77–78–79–80	26	(3)
Black N.W.	1925–2016	(Auckland) 1949	11	(1)
Black R.S.*	1893–1916	(Otago) 1914	6	(1)
Blackadder E.J.	1995-	(Crusaders) 2021-23	10	(10)
Blackadder T.J.	1971–	(Canterbury) 1995–96–97–98–99–2000	25	(12)
Blair B.A.	1979–	(Canterbury) 2001–02	6	(4)
Blair J.A.	1872–1911	(Wanganui) 1897	9	(–)
Blake A.W.	1922–2010	(Wairarapa) 1949	1	(1)
Blake J.M.	1902–1988	(Hawke's Bay) 1925–26	13	(–)
Bligh S.	1887–1955	(West Coast) 1910	5	(–)
Blowers A.F.	1975–	(Auckland) 1996–97–99	18	(11)
Bloxham K.C.	1954–2000	(Otago) 1980	2	(–)
Boe J.W.	1955–	(Waikato) 1981	2	(–)
Boggs E.G.	1922–2004	(Auckland) 1946–49	9	(2)
Bond J.G.P.	1920–1999	(Canterbury) 1949	1	(1)
Boon R.J.	1935–2023	(Taranaki) 1960	6	(–)
Booth E.E.	1876–1935	(Otago) 1905–06–07	24	(3)

Name	B&D	Representative Team	Games	Tests
Boric A.F.	1983–	(North Harbour) 2008–09–10–11	25	(24)
Boroevich K.G.	1960–	(King Country) 1983–84; (Wellington) 1986; (North Harbour) 1988	26	(3)
Botica F.M.	1963–	(North Harbour) 1986–87–88–89	27	(7)
Botting I.J.	1922–1980	(Otago) 1949	9	(–)
Bowden N.J.G.	1926–2009	(Taranaki) 1952	1	(1)
Bower G.G.	1992-	(Crusaders) 2021-22	22	(22)
Bowers R.G.	1932–2000	(Wellington) 1953–54	15	(2)
Bowman A.W.	1915–1992	(Hawke's Bay) 1938	6	(3)
Bradanovich N.M.	1907–1961	(Otago) 1928	2	(–)
Braddon H.Y.	1863–1955	(Otago) 1884	7	(–)
Braid D.J.	1981–	(Auckland) 2002–03–08–10	6	(6)
Braid G.J.	1960–	(Bay of Plenty) 1983–84	13	(2)
Brake L.J.	1952–	(Bay of Plenty) 1976	5	(–)
Bremner S.G.	1930–	(Auckland) 1952; (Canterbury) 1956–60	18	(2)
Brewer M.R.	1964–	(Otago) 1986–87–88–89–90–91–92; (Canterbury) 1993–94–95	61	(32)
Bridge G.C.	1995–	(Crusaders) 2018-19-20-21	19	(19)
Briscoe K.C.	1936–2009	(Taranaki) 1959–60–62–63–64	43	(9)
Broadhurst J.P.	1987–	(Hurricanes) 2015	1	(1)
Brooke R.M.	1966–	(Auckland) 1992–93–94–95–96–97–98–99	69	(62)
Brooke Z.V.	1965–	(Auckland) 1987–88–89–90–91–92–93–94–95–96–97	100	(58)
Brooke-Cowden M.	1963–	(Auckland) 1986–87	6	(3)
Brooker F.J.	1875–1939	(Canterbury) 1897	4	(–)
Broomhall S.R.	1976–	(Canterbury) 2002	4	(4)
Brown C.	1887–1966	(Taranaki) 1913–20	11	(2)
Brown H.M.	1910–1965	(Auckland) 1935–36	8	(–)
Brown H.W.	1904–1973	(Taranaki) 1924–25–26	20	(–)
Brown O.M.	1967–	(Auckland) 1990–92–93–94–95–96–97–98	69	(56)
Brown R.H.	1934–2014	(Taranaki) 1955–56–57–58–59–61–62	25	(16)
Brown T.E.	1975–	(Otago) 1999–2000–01	19	(18)
Brownlie C.J.	1895–1954	(Hawke's Bay) 1924–25–26–28	31	(3)
Brownlie J.L.	1899–1972	(Hawke's Bay) 1921	1	(–)
Brownlie M.J.	1896–1957	(Hawke's Bay) 1922–23–24–25–26–28	61	(8)
Bruce J.A.	1887–1970	(Auckland) 1913–14	10	(2)
Bruce O.D.	1947–	(Canterbury) 1974–76–77–78	41	(14)
Bryers R.F.	1919–1987	(King Country) 1949	1	(1)
Buchan J.A.S.	1961–	(Canterbury) 1987	2	(–)
Budd A.	1880–1962	(South Canterbury) 1910	3	(–)
Budd T.A.	1922–1989	(Southland) 1946–49	2	(2)
Bullock-Douglas G.A.H.	1911–1958	(Wanganui) 1932–34	15	(5)
Bunce F.E.	1962–	(North Harbour) 1992–93–94–95–96–97	69	(55)
Burgess G.A.J.	1954–	(Auckland) 1980–81	2	(1)
Burgess G.F.	1876–1961	(Southland) 1905	1	(1)
Burgess R.E.	1949–	(Manawatu) 1971–72–73	30	(7)
Burgoyne M.M.	1951–2016	(North Auckland) 1979	6	(–)
Burke P.S.	1927–2017	(Taranaki) 1951–55–57	12	(3)
Burns J.F.	1941–	(Canterbury)1970	9	(–)
Burns P.J.	1881–1943	(Canterbury) 1908–10–13	9	(5)
Burrows J.T.	1904–1991	(Canterbury) 1928	9	(–)
Burry H.C.	1930–2013	(Canterbury) 1960	11	(–)
Burt J.R.	1874–1933	(Otago) 1901	1	(–)

Name	B&D	Representative Team	Games	Tests
Bush R.G.	1909–96	(Otago) 1931	1	(1)
Bush W.K. TeP.	1949–	(Canterbury) 1974–75–76–77–78–79	37	(12)
Butland H.	1872–1956	(West Coast) 1893–94	9	(–)
Butler V.C.	1907–1971	(Auckland) 1928	1	(–)
Buxton J.B.	1933–2007	(Canterbury) 1955–56	2	(2)
Cabot P.S. deQ.	1900–1998	(Otago) 1921	1	(–)
Cain M.J.	1885–1951	(Taranaki) 1913–14	24	(4)
Calcinai U.P.	1892–1963	(Wellington) 1922	5	(–)
Callesen J.A.	1950–	(Manawatu) 1974–75–76	18	(4)
Calnan J.J.	1876–1947	(Wellington) 1897	9	(–)
Cameron B.D.	1996	(Crusaders) 2018	1	(1)
Cameron D.	1887–1947	(Taranaki) 1908	3	(3)
Cameron D.H.	1938–	(Mid Canterbury) 1960	8	(–)
Cameron L.M.	1959–	(Manawatu) 1979–80–81	17	(5)
Cane S.J.	1992–	(Bay of Plenty) 2012; (Chiefs) 2013–14–15–16–17–18-19-20-21-22-23	96	(95)
Carleton S.R.	1904–1973	(Canterbury) 1928–29	21	(6)
Carrington K.R.	1950–	(Auckland) 1971–72	9	(3)
Carroll A.J.	1895–1974	(Manawatu) 1920–21	8	(–)
Carson W.N.*	1916–1944	(Auckland) 1938	3	(–)
Carter D.W.	1982–	(Canterbury) 2003–04–05–06–07–08–09–10–11–12; (Crusaders) 2013–14–15	112	(112)
Carter G.	1854–1922	(Auckland) 1884	7	(–)
Carter M.P.	1968–	(Auckland) 1991–97–98	10	(7)
Cartwright S.C.	1954–	(Canterbury) 1976	7	(–)
Casey S.T.	1882–1960	(Otago) 1905–06–07–08	38	(8)
Cashmore A.R.	1973	(Auckland) 1996–97	2	(2)
Catley E.H.	1915–1975	(Waikato) 1946–47–49	21	(7)
Caughey T.H.C.	1911–1993	(Auckland) 1932–34–35–36–37	39	(9)
Caulton R.W.	1937–	(Wellington) 1959–60–61–63–64	50	(16)
Cherrington N.P.	1924–1979	(North Auckland) 1950–51	7	(1)
Christian D.L.	1923–1977	(Auckland) 1949	11	(1)
Christie F.T.	1995-	(Blues) 2021-22-23	21	(21)
Clamp M.	1961–	(Wellington) 1984–85	15	(2)
Clark D.W.	1940–	(Otago) 1964	2	(2)
Clark F.L.	1902–1972	(Canterbury) 1928	4	(–)
Clark L.A.	1944–	(Otago) 1972–73	7	(–)
Clark W.H.	1929–2010	(Wellington) 1953–54–55–56	24	(9)
Clarke A.H.	1938–	(Auckland) 1958–59–60	14	(3)
Clarke, C.D.	1999-	(Blues) 2020-22-23	20	(20)
Clarke D.B.	1933–2002	(Waikato) 1956–57–58–59–60–61–62–63–64	89	(31)
Clarke E.	1968–	(Auckland) 1992–93–98	24	(10)
Clarke I.J.	1931–1997	(Waikato) 1953–54–55–56–57–58–59–60–61–62–63–64	83	(24)
Clarke P.H.	1942–	(Marlborough) 1967	4	(–)
Clarke R.L.	1909–1972	(Taranaki) 1932	9	(2)
Cobden D.G.*	1914–1940	(Canterbury) 1937	1	(1)
Cockerill M.S.	1928–	(Taranaki) 1951	11	(3)
Cockroft E.A.P.	1890–1973	(South Canterbury) 1913–14	7	(3)
Cockroft S.G.	1864–1955	(Manawatu) 1893; (Hawke's Bay) 1894	12	(–)
Codlin B.W.	1956–	(Counties) 1980	13	(3)
Coffin P.H.	1964–	(King Country) 1996	3	(–)

Name	B&D	Representative Team	Games	Tests
Coles D.S.	1986–	(Wellington) 2012; (Hurricanes) 2013–14–15–16–17–18-19-20-21-22-23	90	(90)
Colling G.L.	1946–2003	(Otago) 1972–73	21	(–)
Collins A.H.	1906–1988	(Taranaki) 1932–34	15	(3)
Collins J.	1980–2015	(Wellington) 2001–03–04–05–06–07	50	(48)
Collins J.L.	1939–2007	(Poverty Bay) 1964–65	3	(3)
Collins W.R.	1910–1993	(Hawke's Bay) 1935	7	(–)
Colman J.T.H.	1887–1965	(Taranaki) 1907–08	6	(4)
Coltman L.J.	1990–	(Highlanders) 2016–18-19	8	(8)
Conn S.B.	1953–	(Auckland) 1976–80	6	(–)
Connolly L.S.	1921–2005	(Southland) 1947	5	(–)
Connor D.M.	1935–	(Auckland) 1961–62–63–64	15	(12)
Conrad W.J.M.	1925–1972	(Waikato) 1949	10	(–)
Conway R.J.	1935–2022	(Otago) 1959–60; (Bay of Plenty) 1965	25	(10)
Cooke A.E.	1901–1977	(Auckland) 1924–25; (Hawke's Bay) 1926; (Wairarapa) 1928; (Wellington) 1930	44	(8)
Cooke A.E.	1870–1900	(Canterbury) 1894	1	(–)
Cooke R.J.	1880–1940	(Canterbury) 1903	10	(1)
Cooksley M.S.B.	1971–	(Counties) 1992–93; (Waikato) 1994–95–97–2001	23	(11)
Cooper G.J.L.	1965–	(Auckland) 1986; (Otago) 1992	7	(7)
Cooper M.J.A.	1966–	(Hawke's Bay) 1987; (Waikato) 1992–93–94–96	26	(8)
Corbett J.	1880–1945	(West Coast) 1905	16	(–)
Corkill T.G.	1901–1966	(Hawke's Bay) 1925	4	(–)
Corner M.M.N.	1908–1992	(Auckland) 1930–31–32–34–35–36	25	(6)
Cossey R.R.	1935–1986	(Counties) 1958	1	(1)
Cottrell A.I.	1907–1988	(Canterbury) 1929–30–31–32	22	(11)
Cottrell W.D.	1943–2013	(Canterbury) 1967–68–70–71	37	(9)
Couch M.B.R.	1925–1996	(Wairarapa) 1947–49	7	(3)
Coughlan T.D.	1934–2017	(South Canterbury) 1958	1	(1)
Cowan Q.J.	1982–	(Southland) 2004–05–06–08–09–10–11	53	(51)
Creighton J.N.	1937–2022	(Canterbury) 1962	6	(1)
Cribb R.T.	1976–	(North Harbour) 2000–01	15	(15)
Crichton S.	1954–	(Wellington) 1983–84–85	7	(2)
Crockett W.W.V.	1983–	(Canterbury) 2009–11–12; (Crusaders) 2013–14–15–16–17	72	(71)
Cron S.E.G.	1946–	(Canterbury) 1976	6	(–)
Cross T.	1876–1930	(Canterbury) 1901; (Wellington) 1904–05	3	(2)
Crossman G.M.	1945–	(Bay of Plenty) 1974–76	19	(–)
Crotty R.J.	1988–	(Crusaders) 2013–14–15–16–18-19	48	(48)
Crowley K.J.	1961–	(Taranaki) 1983–84–85–86–87–90–91	35	(19)
Crowley P.J.B.	1923–1981	(Auckland) 1949–50	21	(6)
Cruden A.W.	1989–	(Manawatu) 2010–11–12; (Chiefs) 2013–14–16–17	50	(50)
Culhane S.D.	1968–	(Southland) 1995–96	9	(6)
Cullen C.M.	1976–	(Manawatu) 1996–97; (Wellington) 1998–99–2000–01–02	60	(58)
Cummings W.	1889–1955	(Canterbury) 1913–21	3	(2)

Name	*B&D*	*Representative Team*	*Games*	*Tests*
Cundy R.T.	1901–1955	(Wairarapa) 1929	6	(1)
Cunningham G.R.	1955–	(Auckland) 1979–80	17	(5)
Cunningham W.	1874–1927	(Auckland) 1901–05–06–07–08	39	(9)
Cupples L.F.	1898–1972	(Bay of Plenty) 1922–23–24–25	29	(2)
Currey W.D.R.	1944–2023	(Taranaki) 1968	7	(–)
Currie C.J.	1955–	(Canterbury) 1978	4	(2)
Cuthill J.E.	1892–1970	(Otago) 1913	16	(2)
Dagg I.J.A.	1988–	(Hawke's Bay) 2010–11–12; (Crusaders) 2013–14–15–16–17	66	(66)
Dalley W.C.	1901–1989	(Canterbury) 1924–25–26–28–29	35	(5)
Dalton A.G.	1951–	(Counties) 1977–78–79–80–81–82–83–84–85	58	(35)
Dalton D.	1913–1995	(Hawke's Bay) 1935–36–37–38	21	(9)
Dalton R.A.	1919–1997	(Wellington) 1947; (Otago) 1949	20	(2)
Dalzell G.N.	1921–1989	(Canterbury) 1953–54	22	(5)
D'Arcy A.E.	1870–1919	(Wairarapa) 1893–94	7	(–)
Davie M.G.	1955–	(Canterbury) 1983	5	(1)
Davies W.A.	1939–2008	(Auckland) 1960; (Otago) 1962	17	(3)
Davis C.S.	1975–	(Manawatu) 1996	2	(–)
Davis K.	1930–2019	(Auckland) 1952–53–54–55–58	25	(10)
Davis L.J.	1943–2008	(Canterbury) 1976–77	16	(3)
Davis W.L.	1942–	(Hawke's Bay) 1963–64–67–68–69–70	53	(11)
Davy E.	1850–1935	(Wellington) 1884	3	(–)
Deans I.B.	1960–2019	(Canterbury) 1987–88–89	23	(10)
Deans R.G.	1884–1908	(Canterbury) 1905–06–08	24	(5)
Deans R.M.	1959–	(Canterbury) 1983–84–85	19	(5)
Delamore G.W.	1920–2008	(Wellington) 1949	9	(1)
Delany M.P.	1982–	(Bay of Plenty) 2009	2	(1)
de Groot E.L.	1998-	(Highlanders) 2021-22-23	22	(22)
de Malmanche A.P.	1984–	(Waikato) 2009–10	5	(5)
Dermody C.	1980–	(Southland) 2006	3	(3)
Devine S.J.	1976–	(Auckland) 2002–03	10	(10)
Dewar H.*	1883–1915	(Taranaki) 1913	16	(2)
Diack E.S.	1930–	(Otago) 1959	1	(1)
Dick J.	1912–2002	(Auckland) 1937–38	5	(3)
Dick M.J.	1941–	(Auckland) 1963–64–65–66–67–69–70	55	(15)
Dickinson G.R.	1903–1978	(Otago) 1922	5	(–)
Dickson D.McK.	1900–1978	(Otago) 1925	7	(–)
Dixon E.C.	1989–	(Highlanders) 2016	3	(3)
Dixon M.J.	1929–2004	(Canterbury) 1953–54–56–57	28	(10)
Dobson R.L.	1923–1994	(Auckland) 1949	1	(1)
Dodd E.H.*	1880–1918	(Wellington) 1901–05	3	(1)
Donald A.J.	1957–	(Wanganui) 1981–83–84	20	(7)
Donald J.G.	1898–1981	(Wairarapa) 1920–21–22–25	22	(2)
Donald Q.	1900–1965	(Wairarapa) 1923–24–25	23	(4)
Donald S.R.	1983–	(Waikato) 2008–09–10–11	25	(23)
Donaldson M.W.	1955–	(Manawatu) 1977–78–79–80–81	35	(13)
Donnelly T.J.S.	1981–	(Otago) 2009–10	15	(15)
Dougan J.P.	1946–2006	(Wellington) 1972–73	12	(2)
Douglas J.B.	1890–1964	(Otago) 1913	9	(–)
Dowd C.W.	1969–	(Auckland) 1993–94–95–96–97–98–99–2000	67	(60)
Dowd G.W.	1963–	(North Harbour) 1992	8	(1)

Name	B&D	Representative Team	Games	Tests
Downing A.J.*	1886–1915	(Auckland) 1913–14	26	(5)
Drake J.A.	1959–2008	(Auckland) 1985–86–87	12	(8)
Drake W.A.	1879–1941	(Canterbury) 1901	1	(–)
Drummond M.D.	1994–	(Crusaders) 2017–18	2	(1)
Duff R.H.	1925–2006	(Canterbury) 1951–52–55–56	18	(11)
Duffie M.D.	1990	(Blues) 2017	2	(–)
Duggan R.J.L.	1972–	(Waikato) 1999	1	(1)
Dumbell J.T.	1859–1936	(Wellington) 1884	5	(–)
Duncan J.	1869–1953	(Otago) 1897–1901–03	10	(1)
Duncan M.G.	1947–	(Hawke's Bay) 1971	2	(2)
Duncan W.D.	1892–1961	(Otago) 1920–21	11	(3)
Dunn E.J.	1955–	(North Auckland) 1978–79–81	20	(2)
Dunn I.T.W.	1960–	(North Auckland) 1983–84	13	(3)
Dunn J.M.	1918–2003	(Auckland) 1946	1	(1)
Earl A.T.	1961–	(Canterbury) 1986–87–88–89–91–92	45	(14)
Eastgate B.P.	1927–2007	(Canterbury) 1952–53–54	17	(3)
Eaton J.J.	1982–	(Taranaki) 2005–06–08–09	17	(15)
Eckhold A.G.	1885–1931	(Otago) 1907	3	(–)
Eliason I.M.	1945–2019	(Taranaki) 1972–73	19	(–)
Elliot H.T.P.	1986–	(Hawke's Bay) 2008–10,12; (Chiefs) 2015	5	(4)
Elliott K.G.	1922–2006	(Wellington) 1946	2	(2)
Ellis A.M.	1984–	(Canterbury) 2006–07–08–09–10–11; (Crusaders) 2015	28	(28)
Ellis M.C.G.	1971–	(Otago) 1992–93–95	21	(8)
Ellison T.E.	1983–	(Wellington) 2009; (Otago) 2012	5	(4)
Ellison T.R.	1867–1904	(Wellington) 1893	7	(–)
Elsom A.E.G.	1925–2010	(Canterbury) 1952–53–54–55	22	(6)
Elvidge R.R.	1923–2019	(Otago) 1946–49–50	19	(9)
Elvy W.L.	1901–1977	(Canterbury) 1925–26	12	(–)
Ennor, B.M.	1997-	(Crusaders) 2019-21-22-23	9	(9)
Erceg C.P.	1928–2019	(Auckland) 1951–52	9	(4)
Evans B.R.	1984–	(Hawke's Bay) 2009	2	(2)
Evans C.E.	1896–1975	(Canterbury) 1921	1	(–)
Evans D.A.	1886–1940	(Hawke's Bay) 1910	4	(1)
Evans G.O.	1991–	(Hurricanes) 2018	1	(1)
Evans N.J.	1980–	(North Harbour) 2004; (Otago) 2005–06–07	16	(16)
Eveleigh K.A.	1947–	(Manawatu) 1974–76–77	30	(4)
Fainga'anuku L.O.K.W.T.	1999-	(Crusaders) 2022-23	7	(7)
Fakatava F.M.L.N.	1999-	(Highlanders) 2022	2	(2)
Fanning A.H.N.	1890–1963	(Canterbury) 1913	1	(1)
Fanning B.J.	1874–1946	(Canterbury) 1903–04	9	(2)
Farrell C.P.	1956–	(Auckland) 1977	2	(2)
Faumuina C.C.	1986–	(Auckland) 2012; (Blues) 2013–14–15–16–17	50	(50)
Fawcett C.L.	1954–	(Auckland) 1976	13	(2)
Fea W.R.	1898–1988	(Otago) 1921	1	(1)
Feek G.E.	1975–	(Canterbury) 1999–2000–01	10	(10)
Fekitoa M.F.	1992–	(Highlanders) 2014–15–16–17	24	(24)

Name	B&D	Representative Team	Games	Tests
Fifita V.T.L.	1992–	(Hurricanes) 2017–18-19	12	(11)
Filipo R.A.	1979–	(Wellington) 2007–08	5	(4)
Finau, S.U.	1999-	(Chiefs) 2023	1	(1)
Finlay B.E.L.	1927–1982	(Manawatu) 1959	1	(1)
Finlay J.	1916–2001	(Manawatu) 1946	1	(1)
Finlay M.C.	1963–	(Manawatu) 1984	2	(–)
Finlayson I.	1899–1980	(North Auckland) 1925–26–28–30	36	(6)
Fisher T.	1891–1968	(Buller) 1914	5	(–)
Fitzgerald C.J.	1899–1961	(Marlborough) 1922	5	(–)
Fitzgerald J.T.	1928–1993	(Wellington) 1952–53–54	17	(1)
Fitzpatrick B.B.J.	1931–2006	(Poverty Bay) 1951; (Wellington) 1953–54	22	(3)
Fitzpatrick S.B.T.	1963–	(Auckland) 1986–87–88–89–90–91–92–93–94–95–96–97	128	(92)
Flavell T.V.	1976–	(North Harbour) 2000–01; (Auckland) 2006–07	22	(22)
Fleming J.K.	1953–	(Wellington) 1978–79–80	35	(5)
Fletcher C.J.C.	1894–1973	(North Auckland) 1921	2	(1)
Flynn C.R.	1981–	(Canterbury) 2003–04–08–09–10–11	17	(15)
Fogarty R.	1891–1980	(Taranaki) 1921	2	(2)
Ford B.R.	1951–	(Marlborough) 1977–78–79	20	(4)
Ford W.A.	1895–1959	(Canterbury) 1921–22–23	9	(–)
Forster S.T.	1969–	(Otago) 1993–94–95	12	(6)
Fox G.J.	1962–	(Auckland) 1984–85–86–87–88–89–90–91–92–93	78	(46)
Francis A.R.H.	1882–1957	(Auckland) 1905–07–08–10	18	(10)
Francis W.C.	1894–1981	(Wellington) 1913–14	12	(5)
Franks B.J.	1984–	(Tasman) 2008–10–11–12; (Hurricanes) 2013–14–15	48	(47)
Franks O.T.	1987–	(Canterbury) 2009–10–11–12; (Crusaders) 2013–14–15–16–17–18-19	108	(108)
Fraser B.G.	1953–	(Wellington) 1979–80–81–82–83–84	55	(23)
Frazer H.F.	1915–2003	(Hawke's Bay) 1946–47–49	15	(5)
Freebairn W.S.S.	1932–	(Manawatu) 1953–54	14	(–)
Freitas D.F.E.	1901–1968	(West Coast) 1928	4	(–)
Frizell S.M.	1994–	(Highlanders) 2018-19-20-21-22-23	33	(33)
Fromont R.T.	1969–	(Auckland) 1993–95	10	(–)
Frost H.	1869–1954	(Canterbury) 1896	1	(–)
Fryer F.C.	1886–1958	(Canterbury) 1907–08	9	(4)
Fuller W.B.	1883–1957	(Canterbury) 1910	6	(2)
Furlong B.D.M.	1945–	(Hawke's Bay) 1970	11	(1)
Gage D.R.	1868–1916	(Wellington) 1893–96	8	(–)
Gallagher J.A.	1964–	(Wellington) 1986–87–88–89	41	(18)
Gallaher D.*	1873–1917	(Auckland) 1903–04–05–06	36	(6)
Gard P.C.	1947–1990	(North Otago) 1971–72	7	(1)
Gardiner A.J.	1946–2021	(Taranaki) 1974	11	(1)
Gardner J.H.	1870–1909	(South Canterbury) 1893	4	(–)
Gatland W.D.	1963–	(Waikato) 1988–89–90–91	17	(–)
Gear H.E.	1984–	(Wellington) 2008–10–11–12	15	(14)
Gear R.L.	1978–	(North Harbour) 2004; (Nelson Bays) 2005; (Tasman) 2006; (Canterbury) 2007	20	(19)
Geddes J.H.	1907–1990	(Southland) 1929	6	(1)

Name	B&D	Representative Team	Games	Tests
Geddes W.McK.	1893–1950	(Auckland) 1913	1	(1)
Gemmell B.McL.	1950–	(Auckland) 1974	6	(2)
Gemmell S.W.	1896–1970	(Hawke's Bay) 1923	1	(–)
George V.L.	1908–1996	(Southland) 1938	7	(3)
Gibbes J.B.	1977–	(Waikato) 2004–05	8	(8)
Gibson D.P.E.	1975–	(Canterbury) 1999–2000–02	19	(19)
Gilbert G.D.M.	1911–2002	(West Coast) 1935–36	27	(4)
Gillespie C.T.	1883–1964	(Wellington) 1913	1	(1)
Gillespie W.D.	1934–	(Otago) 1957–58–60	23	(1)
Gillett G.A.	1877–1956	(Canterbury) 1905–06; (Auckland) 1907–08	38	(8)
Gillies C.C.	1912–1996	(Otago) 1936	2	(1)
Gilray C.M.	1885–1974	(Otago) 1905	1	(1)
Given F.J.	1876–1921	(Otago) 1903	9	(–)
Glasgow F.T.	1880–1939	(Taranaki) 1905–06; (Southland) 1908	35	(6)
Glenn W.S.	1877–1953	(Taranaki) 1904–05–06	19	(2)
Glennie E.	1870–1908	(Canterbury) 1897	6	(–)
Goddard J.W.	1920–1996	(South Canterbury) 1949	8	(–)
Goddard M.P.	1921–1974	(South Canterbury) 1946–47–49	20	(5)
Going K.T.	1942–2008	(North Auckland) 1974	3	(–)
Going S.M.	1943–	(North Auckland) 1967–68–69–70–71–72–73–74–75–76–77	86	(29)
Goldsmith J.A.	1969–	(Waikato) 1988	8	(–)
Good A.	1867–1938	(Taranaki) 1893	4	(–)
Good H.M.	1871–1941	(Taranaki) 1894	1	(–)
Goodhue E.J.	1995–	(Crusaders) 2017–18-19-20	19	(18)
Gordon S.B.	1967–	(Waikato) 1989–90–91–93	19	(2)
Gordon W.R.	1965–	(Waikato) 1990	3	(–)
Grace, C.J.	1999-	(Crusaders) 2020	1	(1)
Graham D.J.	1935–2017	(Canterbury) 1958–60–61–62–63–64	53	(22)
Graham J.B.	1884–1941	(Otago) 1913–14	19	(3)
Graham M.G.	1931–2015	(New South Wales) 1960	1	(–)
Graham W.G.	1957–	(Otago) 1978–79	8	(1)
Granger K.W.	1951–	(Manawatu) 1976	6	(–)
Grant L.A.	1923–2002	(South Canterbury) 1947–49–51	23	(4)
Gray G.D.	1880–1961	(Canterbury) 1908–13	14	(3)
Gray K.F.	1938–1992	(Wellington) 1963–64–65–66–67–68–69	50	(24)
Gray R.	1870–1951	(Wairarapa) 1893	2	(–)
Gray W.N.	1932–1993	(Bay of Plenty) 1955–56–57	11	(6)
Green C.I.	1961–	(Canterbury) 1983–84–85–86–87	39	(20)
Greene K.M.	1949–	(Waikato) 1976–77	8	(–)
Grenside B.A.	1899–1989	(Hawke's Bay) 1928–29	21	(6)
Griffiths J.L.	1912–2001	(Wellington) 1934–35–36–38	30	(7)
Gudsell K.E.	1924–2007	(Wanganui) 1949	6	(–)
Guildford Z.R.	1989–	(Hawke's Bay) 2009–10–11–12	10	(10)
Guy R.A.	1941–	(North Auckland) 1971–72	9	(4)
Haden A.M.	1950–2020	(Auckland) 1972–73–76–77–78–79–80–81–82–83–84–85	117	(41)
Hadley S.	1904–1970	(Auckland) 1928	11	(4)
Hadley W.E.	1910–1992	(Auckland) 1934–35–36	25	(8)
Haig J.S.	1924–1996	(Otago) 1946	2	(2)
Haig L.S.	1922–1992	(Otago) 1950–51–53–54	29	(9)

Name	*B&D*	*Representative Team*	*Games*	*Tests*
Halai F.	1988–	(Blues) 2013	1	(1)
Hales D.A.	1947–	(Canterbury) 1972–73	27	(4)
Hames K.S.	1988–	(Chiefs) 2016–17	10	(9)
Hamilton D.C.	1883–1925	(Southland) 1908	1	(1)
Hamilton S.E.	1980–	(Canterbury) 2006	2	(2)
Hammett M.G.	1972–	(Canterbury) 1999–2000–01–02–03	30	(29)
Hammond I.A.	1925–1998	(Marlborough) 1951–52	8	(1)
Handcock R.A.	1874–1956	(Auckland) 1897	8	(–)
Hardcastle W.R.	1874–1944	(Wellington) 1897	7	(–)
Harding S.	1980–	(Otago) 2002	1	(1)
Harper E.T.*	1877–1918	(Canterbury) 1904–05–06	11	(2)
Harper G.	1867–1937	(Nelson) 1893	3	(–)
Harris J.H.*	1903–1944	(Canterbury) 1925	8	(–)
Harris N.P.	1992–	(Chiefs) 2014–16–17–18	22	(20)
Harris P.C.	1946–2021	(Manawatu) 1976	4	(1)
Harris W.A.	1876–1950	(Otago) 1897	9	(–)
Hart A.H.	1897–1965	(Taranaki) 1924–25	17	(1)
Hart G.F.*	1909–1944	(Canterbury) 1930–31–32–34–35–36	35	(11)
Harvey B.A.	1959–	(Wairarapa Bush) 1986	1	(1)
Harvey I.H.	1903–1966	(Wairarapa) 1924–25–26–28	18	(1)
Harvey L.R.	1919–1993	(Otago) 1949–50	22	(8)
Harvey P.	1880–1949	(Canterbury) 1904	1	(1)
Hasell E.W.	1889–1966	(Canterbury) 1913–20	7	(2)
Havili D.K.	1994–	(Crusaders) 2017-21-22-23	29	(27)
Hay-MacKenzie W.E.	1874–1946	(Auckland) 1901	2	(–)
Hayman C.J.	1979–	(Otago) 2001–02–04–05–06–07	46	(45)
Hayward H.O.	1883–1970	(Auckland) 1908	1	(1)
Hazlett E.J.	1938–2014	(Southland) 1966–67	12	(6)
Hazlett W.E.	1905–1978	(Southland) 1926–28–30	26	(8)
Heeps T.R.	1938–2002	(Wellington) 1962	10	(5)
Heke W.R. (played as W. Rika)	1894–1989	(North Auckland) 1929	6	(3)
Helmore G.H.N.	1862–1922	(Canterbury) 1884	7	(–)
Hemara B.S.	1957–	(Manawatu) 1985	3	(–)
Hemi R.C.	1933–2000	(Waikato) 1953–54–55–56–57–59–60	46	(16)
Hemopo J.N.	1993–	(Highlanders) 2018-19	5	(5)
Henderson P.	1926–2014	(Wanganui) 1949–50	19	(7)
Henderson P.W.	1964–	(Otago) 1989–90–91; (Southland) 1992–93–95	25	(7)
Hendrie J.M.	1951–	(Western Australia) 1970	1	(–)
Herewini M.A.	1940–2014	(Auckland) 1962–63–64–65–66–67	32	(10)
Herrold M.	1869–1949	(Auckland) 1893	2	(–)
Hewett D.N.	1971–	(Canterbury) 2001–02–03	24	(22)
Hewett J.A.	1968–	(Auckland) 1991	1	(1)
Hewitt N.J.	1968–	(Hawke's Bay) 1993; (Southland) 1995–96–97–98	23	(9)
Hewson A.R.	1954–	(Wellington) 1979–81–82–83–84	34	(19)
Hickey P.H.	1899–1942	(Taranaki) 1922	2	(–)
Higginson G.	1954–	(Canterbury) 1980–81; (Hawke's Bay) 1982–83	20	(6)
Hill D.W.	1978–	(Waikato) 2001–06	3	(1)
Hill S.F.	1927–2019	(Canterbury) 1955–56–57–58–59	19	(11)
Hines G.R.	1960–	(Waikato) 1980	12	(1)

Name	B&D	Representative Team	Games	Tests
Hobbs F.G.	1920–1985	(Canterbury) 1947	6	(–)
Hobbs M.J.B.	1960–2012	(Canterbury) 1983–84–85–86	39	(21)
Hodgman, A.T.O.A.	1993-	(Blues) 2020	4	(4)
Hoeata J.M.R.A.	1982–	(Taranaki) 2011	3	(3)
Hoeft C.H.	1974–	(Otago) 1998–99–2000–01–03	31	(30)
Hogan J.	1881–1945	(Wanganui) 1907	2	(–)
Holah M.R.	1976–	(Waikato) 2001–02–03–04–05–06	39	(36)
Holden A.W.	1907–1970	(Otago) 1928	3	(–)
Holder E.C.	1908–1974	(Buller) 1932–34	10	(1)
Holmes B.	1946–	(North Auckland) 1970–72–73	31	(–)
Hook L.S.	1905–1979	(Auckland) 1928–29	12	(3)
Hooper J.A.	1913–1976	(Canterbury) 1937–38	7	(3)
Hopa A.R.	1971–1998	(Waikato) 1997	4	(–)
Hopkinson A.E.	1941–1999	(Canterbury) 1967–68–69–70	35	(9)
Hore A.K.	1978–	(Taranaki) 2002–04–05–06–07–08–09–10–11–12; (Highlanders) 2013	83	(83)
Hore J.	1907–1979	(Otago) 1928–30–32–34–35–36	45	(10)
Horsley R.H.	1932–2007	(Wellington) 1960; (Manawatu) 1963	31	(3)
Hotop J.	1929–2015	(Canterbury) 1952–55	3	(3)
Howarth S.P.	1968–	(Auckland) 1993–94	10	(4)
Howden J.	1900–1978	(Southland) 1928	1	(–)
Howlett D.C.	1978–	(Auckland) 2000–01–02–03–04–05–06–07	63	(62)
Hughes A.M.	1924–2005	(Auckland) 1947–49–50	7	(6)
Hughes D.J.	1869–1951	(Taranaki) 1894	1	(–)
Hughes E.	1881–1928	(Southland) 1907–08; (Wellington) 1921	9	(6)
Hullena L.C.	1965–	(Wellington) 1990–91	9	(–)
Humphreys G.W.	1870–1933	(Canterbury) 1894	1	(–)
Humphries A.L.	1874–1953	(Taranaki) 1897–1901–03	15	(–)
Hunt D.	1995-	(Highlanders) 2017-18	2	(1)
Hunter B.A.	1950–	(Otago) 1970–71	10	(3)
Hunter J.	1879–1962	(Taranaki) 1905–06–07–08	36	(11)
Hurst I.A.	1951–	(Canterbury) 1972–73–74	32	(5)
Ieremia A.	1970–	(Wellington) 1994–95–96–97–99–2000	40	(30)
Ifwersen K.D.	1893–1967	(Auckland) 1921	1	(1)
Innes C.R.	1969–	(Auckland) 1989–90–91	30	(17)
Innes G.D.	1910–1992	(Canterbury) 1932	7	(1)
Ioane A.L.	1995–	(Blues) 2017-20-21-22	22	(21)
Ioane, J.	1995-	(Highlanders) 2019	1	(1)
Ioane R.E.	1997–	(Blues) 2016–17–18-19-20-21-22-23	69	(69)
Irvine I.B.	1929–2013	(North Auckland) 1952	1	(1)
Irvine J.G.	1888–1939	(Otago) 1914	10	(3)
Irvine W.R.	1898–1952	(Hawke's Bay) 1923–24–25–26; (Wairarapa) 1930	41	(5)
Irwin M.W.	1935–2018	(Otago) 1955–56–58–59–60	25	(7)
Ivimey F.E.B.	1880–1961	(Otago) 1910	1	(–)
Jack C.R.	1978–	(Canterbury) 2001–02–03–04–05; (Tasman) 2006–07	68	(67)
Jackson E.S.	1914–1975	(Hawke's Bay) 1936–37–38	11	(6)
Jacob H.	1894–1955	(Horowhenua) 1920	8	(–)
Jacob J.P. LeG.	1877–1909	(Southland) 1901	2	(–)

Name	B&D	Representative Team	Games	Tests
Jacobson, L.B.	1997-	(Chiefs) 2019-21-23	18	(18)
Jaffray J.L.	1950–	(Otago) 1972–75–76–77–78; (South Canterbury) 1979	23	(7)
Jaffray M.W.R.	1949–	(Otago) 1976	4	(–)
Jane C.S.	1983–	(Wellington) 2008–09–10–11–12; (Hurricanes) 2013–14	55	(53)
Jarden R.A.	1929–1977	(Wellington) 1951–52–53–54–55–56	37	(16)
Jefferd A.C.R.	1953–	(East Coast) 1980–81	5	(3)
Jennings A.G.T.	1940–	(Bay of Plenty) 1967	6	(–)
Jervis F.M.	1870–1952	(Auckland) 1893	10	(–)
Jessep E.M.	1904–1983	(Wellington) 1931–32	8	(2)
Johns P.A.	1944–	(Wanganui) 1968	6	(–)
Johnson L.M.	1897–1983	(Wellington) 1925–28–30	25	(4)
Johnston D.	1903–1938	(Taranaki) 1925	2	(–)
Johnston W.	1881–1951	(Otago) 1905–07	27	(3)
Johnstone B.R.	1950–	(Auckland) 1976–77–78–79–80	45	(13)
Johnstone C.R.	1980–	(Canterbury) 2005	3	(3)
Johnstone P.	1922–1997	(Otago) 1949–50–51	26	(9)
Jones I.D.	1967–	(North Auckland) 1989–90–91–92–93; (North Harbour) 1994–95–96–97–98–99	105	(79)
Jones M.G.	1942–1975	(North Auckland) 1973	5	(1)
Jones M.N.	1965–	(Auckland) 1987–88–89–90–91–92–93–94–95–96–97–98	74	(55)
Jones P.F.H.	1932–1994	(North Auckland) 1953–54–55–56–58–59–60	37	(11)
Jordan, W.T.	1998-	(Crusaders) 2020-21-22-23	31	(31)
Joseph H.T.	1949–	(Canterbury) 1971	2	(2)
Joseph J.W.	1969–	(Otago) 1992–93–94–95	30	(20)
Kahui R.D.	1985–	(Waikato) 2008–10–11	18	(17)
Kaino J.	1983–	(Auckland) 2004–06–08–09–10–11; (Blues) 2014–15–16–17	83	(81)
Kane G.N.	1952–	(Waikato) 1974	7	(–)
Karam J.F.	1951–	(Wellington) 1972–73–74; (Horowhenua) 1975	42	(10)
Katene T.	1929–1992	(Wellington) 1955	1	(1)
Keane K.J.	1953–	(Canterbury) 1979	6	(–)
Kearney J.C.	1920–1998	(Otago) 1947–49	22	(4)
Kelleher B.T.	1976–	(Otago) 1999–2000–01–02–03–04; (Waikato) 2004–05–06–07	58	(57)
Kelly J.W.	1926–2002	(Auckland) 1949–53–54	16	(2)
Kember G.F.	1945–	(Wellington) 1967–70	19	(1)
Kenny D.J.	1961–	(Otago) 1986	3	(–)
Kerr A.	1871–1936	(Canterbury) 1896	1	(–)
Kerr-Barlow T.N.J.	1990–	(Waikato) 2012; (Chiefs) 2013–14–15–16–17	29	(27)
Ketels R.C.	1954–	(Counties) 1979–80–81	16	(5)
Kiernan H.A.D.	1876–1947	(Auckland) 1903	8	(1)
Kilby F.D.	1906–1985	(Wellington) 1928–32–34	18	(4)
Killeen B.A.	1911–1993	(Auckland) 1936	2	(1)
King R.M.	1980–	(Waikato) 2002	1	(1)
King R.R.	1909–1988	(West Coast) 1934–35–36–37–38	42	(13)
Kingstone C.N.	1895–1960	(Taranaki) 1921	3	(3)
Kirk D.E.	1961–	(Otago) 1983–84; (Auckland) 1985–86–87	34	(17)

Name	B&D	Representative Team	Games	Tests
Kirkpatrick A.	1898–1971	(Hawke's Bay) 1925–26	12	(–)
Kirkpatrick I.A.	1946–	(Canterbury) 1967–68–69; (Poverty Bay) 1970–71–72–73–74–75–76–77	113	(39)
Kirton E.W.	1939–	(Otago) 1963–64–67–68–69–70	49	(13)
Kirwan J.J.	1964–	(Auckland) 1984–85–86–87–88–89–90–91–92–93–94	96	(63)
Kivell A.L.	1897–1988	(Taranaki) 1929	5	(2)
Knight A.	1906–1990	(Auckland) 1926–28–34	14	(1)
Knight G.A.	1951–	(Manawatu) 1977–78–79–80–81–82–83–84–85–86	66	(36)
Knight L.A.G.	1901–1973	(Auckland) 1925	5	(–)
Knight L.G.	1949–	(Auckland) 1974; (Poverty Bay) 1976–77	35	(6)
Knight M.O.	1945–	(Counties) 1968	8	(–)
Koteka T.T.	1956–	(Waikato) 1981–82	6	(2)
Kreft A.J.	1945–2023	(Otago) 1968	4	(1)
Kronfeld J.A.	1971–	(Otago) 1995–96–97–98–99–2000	56	(54)
Kururangi R.	1957–	(Counties) 1978	8	(–)
Laidlaw C.R.	1943–	(Otago) 1963–64–65–66–67; (Canterbury) 1968; (Otago) 1970	57	(20)
Laidlaw K.F.	1934–	(Southland) 1960	17	(3)
Lam P.R.	1968–	(Auckland) 1992	1	(–)
Lambert K.K.	1952–	(Manawatu) 1972–73–74–76–77	40	(11)
Lambie J.T.	1870–1905	(Taranaki) 1893–94	12	(–)
Lambourn A.	1910–1999	(Wellington) 1934–35–36–37–38	40	(10)
Larsen B.P.	1969–	(North Harbour) 1992–93–94–95–96	40	(17)
Latimer T.D.	1986–	(Bay of Plenty) 2009	6	(5)
Laulala C.D.E.	1982–	(Canterbury) 2004–06	3	(2)
Laulala N.E.	1991–	(Crusaders) 2015–17–18; (Chiefs) 2019-20; (Blues) 2021-22-23	53	(53)
Laumape K.H.	1993–	(Hurricanes) 2017–18-19-20	17	(15)
Lauaki S.T.	1981–2017	(Waikato) 2005–07–08	17	(17)
Law A.D.	1904–1961	(Manawatu) 1925	4	(–)
Lawson G.P.	1899–1985	(South Canterbury) 1925	2	(–)
Lecky J.G.	1863–1917	(Auckland) 1884	7	(–)
Lee D.D.	1976–	(Otago) 2002	2	(2)
Leeson J.	1909–1960	(Waikato) 1934	5	(–)
LeLievre J.M.	1933–2016	(Canterbury) 1962–63–64	25	(1)
Lendrum R.N.	1948–	(Counties) 1973	3	(1)
Leonard B.G.	1985–	(Waikato) 2007–09	14	(13)
Leslie A.R.	1944–	(Wellington) 1974–75–76	34	(10)
Levien H.J.	1935–2008	(Otago) 1957	8	(–)
Leys E.T.	1907–1989	(Wellington) 1929	5	(1)
Lienert-Brown A.R.	1995–	(Chiefs) 2016–17–18-19-20-21-22-23	71	(70)
Lilburne H.T.	1908–1976	(Canterbury) 1928–29–30; (Wellington) 1931–32–34	40	(10)
Lindsay D.F.	1906–1978	(Otago) 1928	14	(3)
Lindsay W.G.	1879–1965	(Southland) 1914	4	(–)
Lineen T.R.	1936–2020	(Auckland) 1957–58–59–60	35	(12)
Lister T.N.	1943–2017	(South Canterbury) 1968–69–70–71	26	(8)
Little P.F.	1934–1993	(Auckland) 1961–62–63–64	29	(10)
Little W.K.	1969–	(North Harbour) 1989–90–91–92–93–94–95–96–97–98	75	(50)

Name	B&D	Representative Team	Games	Tests
Loader C.J.	1931–2021	(Wellington) 1953–54	16	(4)
Lochore B.J.	1940–2019	(Wairarapa) 1963–64–65–66–67–68–69–70; (Wairarapa Bush) 1971	68	(25)
Lockington T.M.	1913–2001	(Auckland) 1936	1	(–)
Loe R.W.	1960–	(Waikato) 1986–87–88–89–90–91–92; (Canterbury) 1994–95	78	(49)
Lomas A.R.	1894–1975	(Auckland) 1925–26	15	(–)
Lomax T.S.	1996–	(Highlanders) 2018; (Hurricanes) 2020-21-22-23	32	(32)
Lomu J.T.	1975–2015	(Counties Manukau) 1994–95–96–97–98–99; (Wellington) 2000–01–02	73	(63)
Long A.T.	1879–1960	(Auckland) 1903	10	(1)
Lord J.M.J.	2001-	(Chiefs) 2021-23	4	(4)
Loveday J.K.	1949–2023	(Manawatu) 1978	7	(–)
Loveridge D.S.	1952–	(Taranaki) 1978–79–80–81–82–83–85	54	(24)
Loveridge G.	1890–1970	(Taranaki) 1913–14	11	(–)
Lowen K.R.	1976–	(Waikato) 2002	1	(1)
Luatua D.S.	1991	(Blues) 2013–14–16	15	(15)
Lucas F.W.	1902–1957	(Auckland) 1923–24–25–28–30	41	(7)
Lunn W.A.	1926–1996	(Otago) 1949	2	(2)
Lynch T.W.	1892–1950	(South Canterbury) 1913–14	23	(4)
Lynch T.W.	1927–2006	(Canterbury) 1951	10	(3)
Maber G.	1869–1894	(Wellington) 1894	1	(–)
McAlister C.L.	1983–	(North Harbour) 2005–06–07–09	31	(30)
McAtamney F.S.	1934–2022	(Otago) 1956–57	9	(1)
McCahill B.J.	1964–	(Auckland) 1987–88–89–90–91	32	(10)
McCarthy P.	1893–1976	(Canterbury) 1923	1	(–)
McCashin T.M.	1944–2017	(Wellington) 1968	7	(–)
McCaw R.H.	1980–	(Canterbury) 2001–02–03–04–05–06–07–08–09–10–11–12; (Crusaders) 2013–14–15	149	(148)
McCaw W.A.	1927–	(Southland) 1951–53–54	32	(5)
McCleary B.V.	1897–1978	(Canterbury) 1924–25	12	(–)
McClymont W.G.	1905–1970	(Otago) 1928	3	(–)
McCool M.J.	1951–2020	(Wairarapa Bush) 1979	2	(1)
McCormick A.G.	1899–1969	(Canterbury) 1925	1	(–)
McCormick J.	1923–2006	(Hawke's Bay) 1947	3	(–)
McCormick W.F.	1939–2018	(Canterbury) 1965–67–68–69–70–71	44	(16)
McCullough J.F.	1936–	(Taranaki) 1959	3	(3)
McDonald A.	1883–1967	(Otago) 1905–06–07–08–13	41	(8)
Macdonald A.J.	1981–	(Auckland) 2005	2	(2)
Macdonald H.H.	1947–	(Canterbury) 1972–73–74; (North Auckland) 1975–76	48	(12)
MacDonald L.R.	1977–	(Canterbury) 2000–01–02–03–05–06–07–08	56	(56)
McDonnell P.	1874–1950	(Wanganui) 1896	1	(–)
McDonnell J.M.	1973–	(Otago) 2002	8	(8)
McDowall S.C.	1961–	(Auckland) 1985–86–87–88; (Bay of Plenty) 1989; (Auckland) 1989–90–91–92	81	(46)
McEldowney J.T.	1947–2012	(Taranaki) 1976–77	10	(2)
MacEwan I.N.	1934–	(Wellington) 1956–57–58–59–60–61–62	52	(20)
McGahan P.W.	1964–	(North Harbour) 1990–91	6	(–)
McGrattan B.	1959–	(Wellington) 1983–84–85–86	23	(6)

Name	B&D	Representative Team	Games	Tests
McGregor A.A.	1953–	(Southland) 1978	3	(–)
McGregor A.J.	1889–1963	(Auckland) 1913	11	(2)
McGregor D.	1881–1947	(Canterbury) 1903; (Wellington) 1904–05–06	31	(4)
McGregor N.P.	1901–1973	(Canterbury) 1924–25–28	27	(2)
McGregor R.W.	1874–1925	(Auckland) 1901–03–04	10	(2)
McHugh M.J.	1917–2010	(Auckland) 1946–49	14	(3)
MacIntosh C.N.	1869–1918	(South Canterbury) 1893	4	(–)
McIntosh D.N.	1931–	(Wellington) 1956–57	13	(4)
McKay D.W.	1937–	(Auckland) 1961–62–63	12	(5)
Mackay J.D.	1905–1985	(Wellington) 1928	2	(–)
McKechnie B.J.	1953–	(Southland) 1977–78–79–81	26	(10)
McKellar G.F.	1884–1960	(Wellington) 1910	5	(3)
McKenzie D.S.	1995–	(Chiefs) 2016–17–18-20-21-23	47	(47)
MacKenzie R.H.	1869–1940	(Auckland) 1893	2	(–)
MacKenzie R.H.C.	1904–1993	(Wellington) 1928	2	(–)
McKenzie R.J.	1892–1968	(Wellington) 1913; (Auckland) 1914	20	(4)
MacKenzie R.M.	1909–2000	(Manawatu) 1934–35–36–37–38	35	(9)
McKenzie W.	1871–1943	(Wairarapa) 1893; (Wellington) 1894–96–97	20	(–)
Mackintosh J.L.	1985–	(Southland) 2008	2	(1)
Mackrell W.H.C.	1881–1917	(Auckland) 1905–06	7	(1)
Macky J.V.	1887–1951	(Auckland) 1913	1	(1)
McLachlan J.S.	1949–	(Auckland) 1974	8	(1)
McLaren H.C.	1926–1992	(Waikato) 1952	1	(1)
McLean A.L.	1898–1964	(Bay of Plenty) 1921–23	3	(2)
McLean C.	1892–1965	(Buller) 1920	5	(–)
McLean H.F.	1907–1997	(Wellington) 1930–32; (Auckland) 1934–35–36	29	(9)
McLean J.K.	1923–2005	(King Country) 1947; (Auckland) 1949	5	(2)
McLean R.J.	1960–	(Wairarapa Bush) 1987	2	(–)
McLeod B.E.	1940–1996	(Counties) 1964–65–66–67–68–69–70	46	(24)
McLeod, D.A.M.	1999-	(Crusaders) 2023	1	(1)
McLeod S.J.	1973–	(Waikato) 1996–97–98	17	(10)
McMeeking D.T.M.	1896–1976	(Otago) 1923	2	(–)
McMinn A.F.	1880–1919	(Wairarapa) 1903; (Manawatu) 1905	10	(2)
McMinn F.A.	1874–1947	(Manawatu) 1904	1	(1)
McMullen R.F.	1933–2004	(Auckland) 1957–58–59–60	29	(11)
McNab J.A.	1895–1979	(Hawke's Bay) 1925	1	(–)
McNab J.R.	1924–2009	(Otago) 1949–50	17	(6)
McNaughton A.M.	1947–	(Bay of Plenty) 1971–72	9	(3)
McNeece J.*	1885–1917	(Southland) 1913–14	11	(5)
McNicol A.L.R.	1944–2017	(Wanganui) 1973	5	(–)
McPhail B.E.	1937–2020	(Canterbury) 1959	2	(2)
MacPherson D.G.	1882–1956	(Otago) 1905	1	(1)
Macpherson G.	1962–	(Otago) 1986	1	(1)
MacRae I.R.	1943–	(Hawke's Bay) 1963–64–66–67–68–69–70	45	(17)
McRae J.A.	1914–1977	(Southland) 1946	2	(2)
McRobie N.	1873–1929	(Southland) 1896	1	(–)
McWilliams R.G.	1901–1984	(Auckland) 1928–29–30	27	(10)
Maguire J.R.	1886–1966	(Auckland) 1910	6	(3)

Name	B&D	Representative Team	Games	Tests
Mahoney A.	1908–1979	(Bush) 1929–34–35–36	26	(4)
Mains L.W.	1946–	(Otago) 1971–76	15	(4)
Major J.	1940–	(Taranaki) 1963–64–67	24	(1)
Maka I.	1975–	(Otago) 1998	4	(4)
Maling T.S.	1975–	(Otago) 2001–02–04	13	(11)
Manchester J.E.	1908–1983	(Canterbury) 1932–34–35–36	36	(9)
Mannix S.J.	1971–	(Wellington) 1990–91–94	9	(1)
Markham P.F.	1891–1953	(Wellington) 1921	1	(–)
Marshall J.W.	1973–	(Canterbury) 1995–96–97–98–99–2000–01–02–03–04–05	88	(81)
Masaga L.T.C.	1986–	(Counties Manukau) 2009	1	(1)
Masoe M.C.	1979–	(Taranaki) 2005; (Wellington) 2006–07	20	(20)
Mason D.F.	1923–1981	(Wellington) 1947	6	(1)
Masters F.H.	1893–1980	(Taranaki) 1922	4	(–)
Masters R.R.	1900–1967	(Canterbury) 1923–24–25	31	(4)
Mataira H.K.	1910–1979	(Hawke's Bay) 1934	5	(1)
Matheson J.D.	1948–	(Otago) 1972	13	(5)
Mathewson A.S.	1985–	(Wellington) 2008–10	5	(4)
Mathieson R.G.	1899–1966	(Otago) 1922	4	(–)
Matson J.T.F.	1973	(Canterbury) 1995–96	5	(–)
Mattson H.A.	1900–1980	(Auckland) 1925	6	(–)
Mauger A.J.D.	1980–	(Canterbury) 2001–02–03–04–05–06–07	46	(45)
Mauger N.K.	1978–	(Canterbury) 2001	2	(–)
Max D.S.	1906–1972	(Nelson) 1931–32–34	8	(3)
Maxwell N.M.C.	1976–	(Canterbury) 1999–2000–01–02–04	36	(36)
Mayerhofler M.A.	1972–	(Canterbury) 1998	6	(6)
Meads C.E.	1936–2017	(King Country) 1957–58–59–60–61–62–63–64–65–66–67–68–69–70–71	133	(55)
Meads S.T.	1938–	(King Country) 1961–62–63–64–65–66	30	(15)
Mealamu K.F.	1979–	(Auckland) 2002–03–04–05–06–07–08–09–10–11–12; (Blues) 2013–14–15	133	(132)
Meates K.F.	1930–2022	(Canterbury) 1952	2	(2)
Meates W.A.	1923–2003	(Otago) 1949–50	20	(7)
Meeuws K.J.	1974–	(Otago) 1998–99–2000–01–02–04; (Auckland) 2003	45	(42)
Mehrtens A.P.	1973–	(Canterbury) 1995–96–97–98–99–2000–01–02–04	72	(70)
Mehrtens G.M.	1907–1954	(Canterbury) 1928	3	(–)
Messam L.J.	1984–	(Waikato) 2008–09–10–11–12; (Chiefs) 2013–14–15	45	(43)
Metcalfe T.C.	1909–1969	(Southland) 1931–32	7	(2)
Mexted G.G.	1927–2009	(Wellington) 1950–51	5	(1)
Mexted M.G.	1953–	(Wellington) 1979–80–81–82–83–84–85	72	(34)
Mika B.M.	1981–	(Auckland) 2002	3	(3)
Mika D.G.	1972–2018	(Auckland) 1999	8	(7)
Mill J.J.	1899–1950	(Hawke's Bay) 1923–24–25–26; (Wairarapa) 1930	33	(4)
Miller P.C.	1975–	(Otago) 2001	2	(–)
Miller T.J.	1974–	(Waikato) 1997	4	(–)
Milliken H.M.	1914–1993	(Canterbury) 1938	7	(3)
Mills H.P.	1873–1905	(Taranaki) 1897	8	(–)
Mills J.G.	1960–	(Auckland) 1984	2	(–)
Millton E.B.	1861–1942	(Canterbury) 1884	7	(–)
Millton W.V.	1858–1887	(Canterbury) 1884	8	(–)

Name	B&D	Representative Team	Games	Tests
Milner H.P.	1946–1996	(Wanganui) 1970	16	(1)
Milner-Skudder N.R.	1990–	(Hurricanes) 2015,17–18	13	(13)
Mitchell J.E.P.	1964–	(Waikato) 1993	6	(–)
Mitchell N.A.	1913–1981	(Southland) 1935–36–37; (Otago) 1938	32	(8)
Mitchell T.W.	1950–	(Canterbury) 1974–76	17	(1)
Mitchell W.J.	1890–1959	(Canterbury) 1910	5	(2)
Mitchinson F.E.	1884–1978	(Wellington) 1907–08–10–13	31	(11)
Moala G.	1990	(Blues) 2015–16	4	(4)
Moffitt J.E.	1889–1964	(Wellington) 1920–21	12	(3)
Moli A.	1995-	(Chiefs) 2017-19	5	(4)
Molloy B.P.J.	1931–2022	(Canterbury) 1957	5	(–)
Moody J.P.T.	1988–	(Crusaders) 2014–15–16–17–18-19-20-21	57	(57)
Moore G.J.T.	1923–1991	(Otago) 1949	1	(1)
Moreton R.C.	1942–2016	(Canterbury) 1962–64–65	12	(7)
Morgan H.D.	1902–1969	(Otago) 1923	1	(–)
Morgan J.E.	1945–2002	(North Auckland) 1974–76	22	(5)
Morris T.J.	1942–	(Nelson Bays) 1972–73	23	(3)
Morrison T.C.	1913–1985	(South Canterbury) 1938	5	(3)
Morrison T.G.	1951–2021	(Otago) 1973	5	(1)
Morrissey B.L.	1952–	(Waikato) 1981	3	(–)
Morrissey P.J.	1939–2013	(Canterbury) 1962	3	(3)
Mourie G.N.K.	1952–	(Taranaki) 1976–77–78–79–80–81–82	61	(21)
Mo'unga R.	1994–	(Crusaders) 2017–18-19-20-21-22-23	57	(56)
Mowlem J.	1870–1951	(Manawatu) 1893	4	(–)
Muliaina J.M.	1980–	(Auckland) 2003–04–05; (Waikato) 2006–07–08–09–10–11	102	(100)
Muller B.L.	1942–2019	(Taranaki) 1967–68–69–70–71	35	(14)
Mumm W.J.	1922–1993	(Buller) 1949	1	(1)
Munro H.G.	1896–1974	(Otago) 1924–25	9	(–)
Murdoch K.	1943–2018	(Otago) 1970–72	27	(3)
Murdoch P.H.	1941–1995	(Auckland) 1964–65	5	(5)
Murray F.S.M.	1871–1952	(Auckland) 1893–97	20	(–)
Murray H.V.	1888–1971	(Canterbury) 1913–14	22	(4)
Murray P.C.	1884–1968	(Wanganui) 1908	1	(1)
Myers R.G.	1950–	(Waikato) 1977–78	5	(1)
Mynott H.J.	1876–1924	(Taranaki) 1905–06–07–10	39	(8)
Naholo W.R.	1991-	(Highlanders) 2015–16–17–18	27	(26)
Narawa, E	1999-	(Chiefs) 2023	1	(1)
Nathan W.J.	1940–2021	(Auckland) 1962–63–64–66–67	37	(14)
Nelson K.A.	1938–	(Otago) 1962–63–64	18	(2)
Nepia G.	1905–1986	(Hawke's Bay) 1924–25; (East Coast) 1929–30	46	(9)
Nesbit S.R.	1936–	(Auckland) 1960	13	(2)
Neville W.R.	1954–	(North Auckland) 1981	4	(–)
Newell F.D.	2000-	(Crusaders) 2022-23	13	(13)
Newby C.A.	1979–	(North Harbour) 2004–06	3	(3)
Newton F.	1881–1955	(Canterbury) 1905–06	19	(3)
Ngatai C.J.	1990–	(Chiefs) 2015	1	(1)
Nicholls H.E.	1900–1978	(Wellington) 1921–22–23	7	(1)
Nicholls H.G.	1897–1977	(Wellington) 1923	1	(–)
Nicholls M.F.	1901–1972	(Wellington) 1921–22–24–25–26–28–30	51	(10)
Nicholson G.W.	1878–1968	(Auckland) 1903–04–05–06–07	39	(4)

Name	B&D	Representative Team	Games	Tests
Nonu M.A.	1982–	(Wellington) 2003–04–05–06–07–08–09–10–11–12; (Highlanders) 2013; (Blues) 2014; (Hurricanes) 2015	104	(103)
Norton R.W.	1942–2023	(Canterbury) 1971–72–73–74–75–76–77	61	(27)
O'Brien A.J.	1897–1969	(Auckland) 1922	3	(–)
O'Brien J.	1871–1946	(Wellington) 1901	1	(–)
O'Brien J.G.	1889–1958	(Auckland) 1914–20	12	(1)
O'Callaghan M.W.	1946–	(Manawatu) 1968	3	(3)
O'Callaghan T.R.	1925–2004	(Wellington) 1949	1	(1)
O'Connor T.B.	1860–1936	(Auckland) 1884	7	(–)
O'Dea R.J.	1930–1986	(Thames Valley) 1953–54	5	(–)
O'Donnell D.H.	1921–1992	(Wellington) 1949	1	(1)
O'Donnell J.M.	1860–1942	(Otago) 1884	7	(–)
O'Dowda B.C.	1874–1954	(Taranaki) 1901	2	(–)
O'Halloran J.D.	1972–	(Wellington) 2000	1	(1)
O'Leary M.J.	1883–1963	(Auckland) 1910–13	8	(4)
O'Neill K.J.	1982–	(Waikato) 2008	1	(1)
Old G.H.	1956–	(Manawatu) 1980–81–82–83	17	(3)
Oliphant R.	1870–1956	(Wellington) 1893; (Auckland) 1896	3	(–)
Oliver A.D.	1975–	(Otago) 1996–97–98–99–2000–01–03–04–05–06–07	67	(59)
Oliver C.J.	1905–1977	(Canterbury) 1928–29–34–35–36	33	(7)
Oliver D.J.	1907–1990	(Wellington) 1930	3	(2)
Oliver D.O.	1930–1997	(Otago) 1953–54	20	(2)
Oliver F.J.	1948–2014	(Southland) 1976–77; (Otago) 1978–79; (Manawatu) 1980–81	43	(17)
Orchard S.A.	1875–1947	(Canterbury) 1896–97	8	(–)
Ormond J.	1891–1970	(Hawke's Bay) 1923	1	(–)
Orr R.W.	1923–2011	(Otago) 1949	1	(1)
Osborne G.M.	1971–	(North Harbour) 1995–96–97–99	29	(19)
Osborne W.M.	1955–	(Wanganui) 1975–76–77–78–80–82	48	(16)
O'Sullivan J.M.	1883–1960	(Taranaki) 1905–07	29	(5)
O'Sullivan T.P.A.	1936–1997	(Taranaki) 1960–61–62	16	(4)
Paewai L.	1906–1970	(Hawke's Bay) 1923–24	8	(–)
Page J.R.	1908–1985	(Wellington) 1931–32–34–35	18	(6)
Page M.L.	1902–1987	(Canterbury) 1928	1	(–)
Palmer B.P.	1901–1932	(Auckland) 1928–29–32	18	(3)
Papali'i D.R.	1997-	(Blues) 2018-19-20-21-22-23	32	(32)
Parker J.H.	1897–1980	(Canterbury) 1924–25	21	(3)
Parkhill A.A.	1912–1986	(Otago) 1937–38	10	(6)
Parkinson R.M.	1948–2009	(Poverty Bay) 1972–73	20	(7)
Parsons J.W.	1986–	(Blues) 2014–16	2	(2)
Paterson A.M.	1885–1933	(Otago) 1908–10	9	(5)
Paton H.	1881–1964	(Otago) 1907–10	8	(2)
Pauling T.G.	1873–1927	(Wellington) 1896–97	9	(–)
Pene A.R.B.	1967–	(Otago) 1992–93–94	26	(15)
Pepper C.S.*	1911–1943	(Auckland) 1935–36	17	(–)
Perenara T.T.R.	1992–	(Hurricanes) 2014–15–16–17–18-19-20-21-22	81	(80)
Perofeta S.	1997-	(Blues) 2022	3	(3)
Perry A.	1899–1977	(Otago) 1923	1	(–)
Perry R.G.	1953–	(Mid Canterbury) 1980	1	(–)

Name	B&D	Representative Team	Games	Tests
Perry T.G.	1988–	(Crusaders) 2017–18	8	(6)
Petersen L.C.	1897–1961	(Canterbury) 1921–22–23	8	(–)
Phillips W.J.	1914–1982	(King Country) 1937–38	7	(3)
Philpott S.	1965–	(Canterbury) 1988–90–91	14	(2)
Pickering E.A.R.	1936–2016	(Waikato) 1957–58–59–60	21	(3)
Pierce M.J.	1957–	(Wellington) 1984–85–86–87–88–89–90	54	(26)
Piutau S.T.	1991–	(Blues) 2013–14–15	17	(17)
Pokere S.T.	1958–	(Southland) 1981–82–83; (Auckland) 1984–85	39	(18)
Pollock H.R.	1909–1984	(Wellington) 1932–36	8	(5)
Porteous H.G.	1875–1951	(Otago) 1903	3	(–)
Porter C.G.	1899–1976	(Wellington) 1923–24–25–26–28–29–30	41	(7)
Potaka W.P.	ca 1903–1967	(Wanganui) 1923	2	(–)
Preston J.P.	1967–	(Canterbury) 1991–92; (Wellington) 1993–96–97	27	(10)
Pringle A.	1899–1973	(Wellington) 1923	1	(–)
Pringle W.P.	1869–1945	(Wellington) 1893	5	(–)
Procter A.C.	1906–1989	(Otago) 1932	4	(1)
Proctor M.P.	1992–	(Hurricanes) 2018	1	(1)
Pulu A.W.	1990–	(Chiefs) 2014	2	(2)
Purdue C.A.	1874–1941	(Southland) 1901–05	3	(1)
Purdue E.	1877–1939	(Southland) 1905	1	(1)
Purdue G.B.	1909–1981	(Southland) 1931–32	7	(4)
Purvis G.H.	1960–	(Waikato) 1989–90–91–92–93	28	(2)
Purvis N.A.	1953–2008	(Otago) 1976	12	(1)
Quaid C.E.	1908–1984	(Otago) 1938	4	(2)
Ralph C.S.	1977–	(Auckland) 1998; (Canterbury) 2001–02–03	16	(14)
Ranby R.M.	1977–	(Waikato) 2001	1	(1)
Randell T.C.	1974–	(Otago) 1995–96–97–98–99–2000–01–02	61	(51)
Randle R.Q.	1974–	(Waikato) 2001	2	(–)
Ranger R.M.N.	1986–	(Northland) 2010; (Blues) 2013	6	(6)
Rangi R.E.	1941–1988	(Auckland) 1964–65–66	10	(10)
Rankin J.G.	1914–1989	(Canterbury) 1936–37	4	(3)
Rawlinson G.P.	1978–	(North Harbour) 2006–07	4	(4)
Read K.J.	1985–	(Canterbury) 2008–09–10–11–12; (Crusaders) 2013–14–15–16–17–18–19	128	(127)
Reece, S.L.	1997-	(Crusaders) 2019-20-21-22	23	(23)
Reedy W.J.	1880–1939	(Wellington) 1908	2	(2)
Reid A.R.	1929–1994	(Waikato) 1951–52–56–57	17	(5)
Reid H.R.	1958–	(Bay of Plenty) 1980–81–83–84–85–86	40	(9)
Reid K.H.	1904–1972	(Wairarapa) 1929	5	(2)
Reid S.T.	1912–2003	(Hawke's Bay) 1935–36–37	27	(9)
Reihana B.T.	1976–	(Waikato) 2000	2	(2)
Reside W.B.	1905–1985	(Wairarapa) 1929	6	(1)
Retallick B.A.	1991–	(Hawke's Bay/Bay of Plenty) 2012; (Chiefs) 2013–14–15–16–17–18-19-21-22-23	109	(109)
Rhind P.K.	1915–1996	(Canterbury) 1946	2	(2)
Richardson J.	1899–1994	(Otago) 1921–22; (Southland) 1923–24–25	42	(7)

Name	B&D	Representative Team	Games	Tests
Rickit H.A.	1951–	(Waikato) 1981	2	(2)
Ridge M.J.	1969–	(Auckland) 1989	6	(–)
Ridland A.J.*	1882–1918	(Southland) 1910	6	(3)
Riechelmann C.C.	1972–	(Auckland) 1997	10	(6)
Righton L.S.	1898–1972	(Auckland) 1923–25	9	(–)
Roberts E.J.	1891–1972	(Wellington) 1913–14–20–21	26	(5)
Roberts F.	1882–1956	(Wellington) 1905–06–07–08–10	52	(12)
Roberts H.	1862–1949	(Wellington) 1884	7	(–)
Roberts R.W.	1889–1973	(Taranaki) 1913–14	23	(5)
Roberts W.	1871–1937	(Wellington) 1896–97	8	(–)
Robertson B.J.	1952– 2023	(Counties) 1972–73–74–76–77–78–79–80–81	102	(34)
Robertson D.J.	1947–	(Otago) 1974–75–76–77	30	(10)
Robertson G.S.	1859–1920	(Otago) 1884	8	(–)
Robertson S.M.	1974–	(Canterbury) 1998–99–2000–01–02	23	(23)
Robilliard A.C.C.	1903–1990	(Canterbury) 1924–25–26–28	27	(4)
Robins B.G.	1958–	(Taranaki) 1985	4	(–)
Robinson A.G.	1956–	(North Auckland) 1983	4	(–)
Robinson C.E.	1927–1983	(Southland) 1951–52	11	(5)
Robinson J.T.	1906–1968	(Canterbury) 1928	3	(–)
Robinson K.J.	1976–	(Waikato) 2002–04–06–07	12	(12)
Robinson M.D.	1975–	(North Harbour) 1997–98–2001	8	(3)
Robinson M.P.	1974–	(Canterbury) 2000–02	9	(9)
Roigard, C.D.	2000-	(Hurricanes) 2023	5	(5)
Rokocoko J.T.	1983–	(Auckland) 2003–04–05–06–07–08–09–10	69	(68)
Rollerson D.L.	1953–2017	(Manawatu) 1976–80–81	24	(8)
Romano L.	1986–	(Canterbury) 2012; (Crusaders) 2013–14–15–16–17	32	(31)
Roper R.A.	1923–2023	(Taranaki) 1949–50	5	(5)
Ross I.B.	1984–	(Canterbury) 2009	8	(8)
Ross J.C.	1949–	(Mid Canterbury) 1981	5	(–)
Rowlands G.D.	1947–2021	(Bay of Plenty) 1976	4	(–)
Rowley H.C.B.	1924–1956	(Wanganui) 1949	1	(1)
Rush E.J.	1965–	(North Harbour) 1992–93–95–96	29	(9)
Rush X.J.	1977–	(Auckland) 1998–2004	8	(8)
Rushbrook C.A.	1907–1987	(Wellington) 1928	10	(–)
Rutledge L.M.	1952–	(Southland) 1978–79–80	31	(13)
Ryan E.	1891–1965	(Wellington) 1921	1	(–)
Ryan J.	1887–1957	(Wellington) 1910–14	15	(4)
Ryan J.A.C.	1983–	(Otago) 2005–06	9	(9)
Ryan P.J.	1950–1985	(Hawke's Bay) 1976	5	(–)
Ryan T.	1863–1927	(Auckland) 1884	9	(-)
Sadler B.S.	1914–2007	(Wellington) 1935–36	19	(5)
Saili F.	1991–	(Blues) 2013	2	(2)
Salmon J.L.B.	1959–	(Wellington) 1980–81	7	(3)
Sapsford H.P.	1949–2009	(Otago) 1976	7	(–)
Savage L.T.	1928–2013	(Canterbury) 1949	12	(3)
Savea A.S.	1993–	(Hurricanes) 2016–17–18-19-20-21-22-23	83	(81)
Savea S.J.	1990–	(Wellington) 2012; (Hurricanes) 2013–14–15–16–17	54	(54)
Saxton C.K.	1913–2001	(South Canterbury) 1938	7	(3)
Sayers M.	1947–	(Wellington) 1972–73	15	(–)
Schuler K.J.	1967–	(Manawatu) 1989–90; (North Harbour) 1992–95	13	(4)

Name	B&D	Representative Team	Games	Tests
Schuster N.J.	1964–	(Wellington) 1987–88–89	26	(10)
Schwalger J.E.	1983–	(Wellington) 2007–08	2	(2)
Scott R.W.H.	1921–2012	(Auckland) 1946–47–49–50–53–54	52	(17)
Scott S.J.	1955–1994	(Canterbury) 1980	4	(–)
Scown A.I.	1948–	(Taranaki) 1972–73	17	(5)
Scrimshaw G.	1902–1971	(Canterbury) 1928	11	(1)
Seear G.A.	1952–2018	(Otago) 1976–77–78–79	34	(12)
Seeling C.E.	1883–1956	(Auckland) 1904–05–06–07–08	39	(11)
Sellars G.M.V.*	1886–1917	(Auckland) 1913	15	(2)
Senio K.	1978–	(Bay of Plenty) 2005	1	(1)
Seymour D.J.	1967–	(Canterbury) 1992	3	(–)
Shannon H.G.	1869–1912	(Manawatu) 1893	6	(–)
Shaw M.W.	1956–	(Manawatu) 1980–81–82–83–84–85; (Hawke's Bay) 1986	69	(30)
Shearer J.D.	1896–1963	(Wellington) 1920	5	(–)
Shearer S.D.	1890–1973	(Wellington) 1921–22	8	(–)
Sheen T.R.	1905–1979	(Auckland) 1926–28	8	(–)
Shelford F.N.K.	1955–	(Bay of Plenty) 1981–84–85; (Hawke's Bay) 1983	22	(4)
Shelford W.T.	1957–	(North Harbour) 1985–86–87–88–89–90	48	(22)
Sherlock K.	1961–	(Auckland) 1985	3	(–)
Siddells S.K.	1897–1979	(Wellington) 1921	1	(1)
Simon H.J.	1911–1979	(Otago) 1937	3	(3)
Simonsson P.L.J.	1967–	(Wellington) 1987	2	(–)
Simpson J.G.	1922–2010	(Auckland) 1947–49–50	30	(9)
Simpson V.L.J.	1960–	(Canterbury) 1985	4	(2)
Sims G.S.	1951–	(Otago) 1972	1	(1)
Sinclair R.G.B.	1896–1932	(Otago) 1923	2	(–)
Sivivatu S.W.	1982–	(Waikato) 2005–06–07–08–09–11	46	(45)
Skeen J.R.	1928–2001	(Auckland) 1952	1	(1)
Skinner K.L.	1927–2014	(Otago) 1949–50–51–52–53–54; (Counties) 1956	63	(20)
Skudder G.R.	1948–2021	(Waikato) 1969–72–73	14	(1)
Slade C.R.	1987–	(Canterbury) 2010–11; (Highlanders) 2013; (Crusaders) 2014–15	21	(21)
Slater G.L.	1971–	(Taranaki) 1997–2000	6	(3)
Sloane P.H.	1948–	(North Auckland) 1973–76–79	16	(1)
Smith A.E.	1942–	(Taranaki) 1967–69–70	18	(3)
Smith A.L.	1998–	(Manawatu) 2012; (Highlanders) 2013–14–15–16–17–18-19-20-21-22-23	125	(125)
Smith B.R.	1986–	(Otago) 2009–11–12; (Highlanders) 2013–14–15–16–17–18–19	85	(84)
Smith B.W.	1959–	(Waikato) 1983–84	10	(3)
Smith C.G.	1981–	(Wellington) 2004–05–06–07–08–09–10–11–12; (Hurricanes) 2013–14–15	94	(94)
Smith C.H.	1909–1976	(Otago) 1934	2	(–)
Smith G.W.	1874–1954	(Auckland) 1897–1901–05	39	(2)
Smith I.S.T.	1941–2017	(Otago) 1963–64; (North Otago) 1965–66	24	(9)
Smith J.B.	1922–1974	(North Auckland) 1946–47–49	9	(4)
Smith P.	1924–1954	(North Auckland) 1947	3	(–)
Smith R.M.	1929–2002	(Canterbury) 1955	1	(1)
Smith W.E.	1881–1945	(Nelson) 1905	1	(1)

Name	*B&D*	*Representative Team*	*Games*	*Tests*
Smith W.R.	1957–	(Canterbury) 1980–82–83–84–85	35	(17)
Smyth B.F.	1891–1972	(Canterbury) 1922	3	(–)
Snodgrass W.F.	1898–1976	(Nelson) 1923–28	3	(–)
Snow E.M.	1898–1974	(Nelson) 1928–29	16	(3)
Solomon D.	1913–1997	(Auckland) 1935–36	8	(–)
Solomon F.	1906–1991	(Auckland) 1931–32	9	(3)
Somerville G.M.	1977–	(Canterbury) 2000–01–02–03–04–05–06–07–08	67	(66)
Sonntag W.T.C.	1894–1988	(Otago) 1929	8	(3)
So'oialo, R.	1979–	(Wellington) 2002–03–04–05–06–07–08–09	63	(62)
Soper A.J.	1936–2020	(Southland) 1957	8	(–)
Sopoaga L.Z.	1991	(Highlanders) 2015–16–17	18	(16)
Sotutu, H.C.R.	1998-	(Blues) 2020-21-22	14	(14)
Souter R.	1905–1976	(Otago) 1929	4	(–)
Sowakula P-G.N.	1994-	(Chiefs) 2022	2	(2)
Speight C.R.B.	1870–1935	(Auckland) 1893	7	(–)
Speight M.W.	1962–	(North Auckland) 1986	5	(1)
Spencer C.J.	1975–	(Auckland) 1995–96–97–98–2000–02–03–04	44	(35)
Spencer G.	1878–1950	(Wellington) 1907	5	(–)
Spencer J.C.	1880–1936	(Wellington) 1903–05–07	6	(2)
Spiers J.E.	1947–	(Counties) 1976–79–80–81	28	(5)
Spillane A.P.	1888–1974	(South Canterbury) 1913	2	(2)
Squire L.I.J.	1991–	(Highlanders) 2016–17–18	24	(23)
Stalker J.	1881–1931	(Otago) 1903	6	(–)
Stanley B.J.	1984–	(Auckland) 2010	3	(3)
Stanley J.C.	1975–	(Auckland) 1997	3	(–)
Stanley J.T.	1957–	(Auckland) 1986–87–88–89–90–91	49	(27)
Stapleton E.T.	1930–2005	(New South Wales) 1960	1	(–)
Stead J.W.	1877–1958	(Southland) 1903–04–05–06–08	42	(7)
Steel A.G.	1941–2018	(Canterbury) 1966–67–68	23	(9)
Steel J.	1898–1941	(West Coast) 1920–21–22–23–24–25	38	(6)
Steele L.B.	1929–	(Wellington) 1951	9	(3)
Steere E.R.G.	1908–1967	(Hawke's Bay) 1928–29–30–31–32	21	(6)
Steinmetz P.C.	1977–	(Wellington) 2002	1	(1)
Stensness L.	1970–	(Auckland) 1993–97	14	(8)
Stephens O.G.	1947–	(Wellington) 1968	1	(1)
Stevens I.N.	1948–	(Wellington) 1972–73–74–76	33	(3)
Stevenson D.R.L.	1903–1962	(Otago) 1926	4	(–)
Stevenson, S.T.	1996-	(Chiefs) 2023	1	(1)
Stewart A.J.	1940–	(Canterbury) 1963; (South Canterbury) 1964	26	(8)
Stewart D.T.	1872–1931	(South Canterbury) 1894	1	(–)
Stewart E.B.	1901–1979	(Otago) 1923	1	(–)
Stewart J.D.	1889–1973	(Auckland) 1913	2	(2)
Stewart K.W.	1953–	(Southland) 1972–73–74–75–76–79–81	55	(13)
Stewart R.T.	1904–1982	(South Canterbury) 1923–24–25–26–28; (Canterbury) 1930	39	(5)
Stewart V.E.	1948–	(Canterbury) 1976–79	12	(–)
Stohr L.	1889–1973	(Taranaki) 1910–13	15	(3)
Stokes E.J.T.	1950–	(Bay of Plenty) 1976	5	(–)
Stone A.M.	1960–	(Waikato) 1981–83–84; (Bay of Plenty) 1986	23	(9)
Storey P.W.	1897–1975	(South Canterbury) 1920–21	12	(2)
Strachan A.D.	1966–	(Auckland) 1992; (North Harbour) 1993–95	17	(11)

Name	B&D	Representative Team	Games	Tests
Strahan S.C.	1944–2019	(Manawatu) 1967–68–70–72–73	45	(17)
Strang W.A.	1906–1989	(South Canterbury) 1928–30–31	17	(5)
Stringfellow J.C.	1905–1959	(Wairarapa) 1929	7	(2)
Stuart A.J.	1858–1923	(Wellington) 1893	7	(–)
Stuart K.C.	1928–2005	(Canterbury) 1955	1	(1)
Stuart R.C.	1920–2005	(Canterbury) 1949–53–54	27	(7)
Stuart R.L.	1948–	(Hawke's Bay) 1977	6	(1)
Sullivan J.L.	1915–1990	(Taranaki) 1936–37–38	9	(6)
Surman J.F.	1866–1925	(Auckland) 1896	1	(–)
Surridge S.D.	1970–	(Canterbury) 1997	3	(–)
Sutherland A.R.	1944–2020	(Marlborough) 1968–70–71–72–73–76	64	(10)
Svenson K.S.	1898–1955	(Buller) 1922; (Wellington) 1924–25–26	34	(4)
Swain J.P.	1902–1960	(Hawke's Bay) 1928	16	(4)
Swindley J.T.	1876–1918	(Wellington) 1894	1	(–)
Ta'avao–Matau A.W.F.	1990	(Chiefs) 2018-19-21-22	23	(23)
Tahuriorangi T.T.H.	1995	(Chiefs) 2018	3	(3)
Taiaroa J.G.	1862–1907	(Otago) 1884	9	(–)
Taituha P.	1901–1958	(Wanganui) 1923	2	(–)
Tamanivalu S.	1992–	(Chiefs) 2016–17	5	(3)
Tanner J.M.	1927–2020	(Auckland) 1950–51–53–54	24	(5)
Tanner K.J.	1945–	(Canterbury) 1974–75–76	27	(7)
Taukei'aho S.F.S.	1997-	(Chiefs) 2021-22-23	30	(30)
Taumoepeau S.	1979–	(Auckland) 2004–05	4	(3)
Taylor C.J.	1991-	(Crusaders) 2015–16–17-18-19-20-21-22-23	85	(85)
Taylor G.L.	1970–	(North Auckland) 1992–96	6	(1)
Taylor H.M.	1889–1955	(Canterbury) 1913–14	23	(5)
Taylor J.M.	1913–1979	(Otago) 1937–38	9	(6)
Taylor K.J.	1957–	(Hawke's Bay) 1980	1	(–)
Taylor M.B.	1956–	(Waikato) 1976–79–80	30	(7)
Taylor N.M.	1951–	(Bay of Plenty) 1976–77–78; (Hawke's Bay) 1982	27	(9)
Taylor R.*	1889–1917	(Taranaki) 1913	2	(2)
Taylor T.J.	1989–	(Crusaders) 2013	3	(3)
Taylor W.T.	1960–	(Canterbury) 1983–84–85–86–87–88	40	(24)
Telea M.E.	1996-	(Blues) 2022-23	9	(9)
Tetzlaff P.L.	1920–2009	(Auckland) 1947	7	(2)
Thimbleby N.W.	1939–	(Hawke's Bay) 1970	13	(1)
Thomas B.T.	1937– 2018	(Auckland) 1962; (Wellington) 1964	4	(4)
Thomas L.A.	1897–1971	(Wellington) 1925	3	(–)
Thompson B.A.	1947–2006	(Canterbury) 1979	8	(–)
Thomson A.J.	1982–	(Otago) 2008–09–10–11–12	31	(29)
Thomson H.D.	1881–1939	(Wanganui) 1905–06; (Wellington) 1908	15	(1)
Thorn B.C.	1975–	(Canterbury) 2003–09–10–11; (Tasman) 2008	60	(59)
Thorne G.S.	1946–	(Auckland) 1967–68–69–70	39	(10)
Thorne R.D.	1975–	(Canterbury) 1999–2000–01–02–03–04–06–07	51	(50)
Thornton N.H.	1918–1998	(Auckland) 1947–49	19	(3)
Thrush J.I.	1985–	(Hurricanes) 2013–14–15	12	(12)
Tialata N.S.	1982–	(Wellington) 2005–06–07–08–09–10	44	(43)

Name	*B&D*	*Representative Team*	*Games*	*Tests*
Tiatia F.I.	1971–	(Wellington) 2000	2	(2)
Tilyard F.J.	1896–1954	(Wellington) 1923	1	(–)
Tilyard J.T.	1889–1966	(Wellington) 1913–20	10	(1)
Timu J.K.R.	1969–	(Otago) 1989–90–91–92–93–94	50	(26)
Tindill E.W.T.	1910–2010	(Wellington) 1935–36–38	17	(1)
Tiopira H.	1871–1930	(Hawke's Bay) 1893	8	(–)
Todd M.B.	1988–	(Crusaders) 2013,15–16–17–18-19	25	(25)
Toeava I.	1986–	(Auckland) 2005–06–07–08–09–10–11	37	(36)
Tonu'u O.F.J.	1970–	(Auckland) 1996–97–98	8	(5)
To'omaga–Allen J.L.	1990–	(Hurricanes) 2013–17	3	(1)
Townsend L.J.	1934– 2020	(Otago) 1955	2	(2)
Tregaskis C.D.	1965–	(Wellington) 1991	4	(–)
Tremain K.R.	1938–1992	(Canterbury) 1959; (Auckland) 1960; (Canterbury) 1961; (Hawke's Bay) 1962–63–64–65–66–67–68	86	(38)
Trevathan D.	1912–1986	(Otago) 1937	3	(3)
Tuck J.M.	1907–1967	(Waikato) 1929	6	(3)
Tuiali'i M.M.	1981–	(Auckland) 2004–05–06	10	(9)
Tuigamala V.L.	1969–2022	(Auckland) 1989–90–91–92–93	39	(19)
Tu'inukuafe G.Z.K.	1993-	(Chiefs) 2018; (Blues) 2020-21-22	27	(27)
Tuipulotu P.T.	1993–	(Blues) 2014–16–17–18-19-20-21-22	45	(43)
Tuitavake A.S.M.	1982–	(North Harbour) 2008	7	(6)
Tuitupou S.	1982–	(Auckland) 2004–06	9	(9)
Tuivasa-Sheck R.	1993-	(Blues) 2022	3	(3)
Tunnicliff R.G.	1894–1973	(Buller) 1923	1	(–)
Tupaea Q.P.C.	1999-	(Chiefs) 2021-22	14	(14)
Turnbull J.S.	1898–1947	(Otago) 1921	1	(–)
Turner R.S.	1968–	(North Harbour) 1992	2	(2)
Turtill H.S.*	1880–1918	(Canterbury) 1905	1	(1)
Tu'ungafasi A.O.H.M.	1992–	(Blues) 2016–17–18-19-20-21-22-23	59	(57)
Twigden T.M.	1952–	(Auckland) 1979–80	15	(2)
Tyler G.A.	1879–1942	(Auckland) 1903–04–05–06	36	(7)
Udy D.K.	1874–1935	(Wairarapa) 1901–03	9	(1)
Udy H.	1860–1933	(Wellington) 1884	8	(–)
Umaga J.F.	1973–	(Wellington) 1997–99–2000–01–02–03–04–05	79	(74)
Umaga-Jensen, P.I.J.	1997-	(Hurricanes) 2020	1	(1)
Urbahn R.J.	1934–1984	(Taranaki) 1959–60	15	(3)
Urlich R.A.	1944–	(Auckland) 1970–72–73	35	(2)
Uttley I.N.	1941–2015	(Wellington) 1963	2	(2)
Vaa'i, T.P.O.	2000-	(Chiefs) 2020-21-22-23	25	(25)
Valli G.T.	1954–	(Southland) 1980	1	(–)
Vanisi O.K.	1972–	(Wellington) 1999	1	(–)
Vidiri J.	1973–2022	(Counties Manukau) 1998	2	(2)
Vincent P.B.	1926–1983	(Canterbury) 1956	2	(2)
Vito V.V.J.	1987–	(Wellington) 2010–11–12; (Hurricanes) 2013–14–15	33	(33)
Vodanovich I.M.H.	1930–1995	(Wellington) 1955	3	(3)
Vorrath F.H.	1908–1972	(Otago) 1935–36	12	(–)

Name	B&D	Representative Team	Games	Tests
Waldrom S.L.	1980–	(Taranaki) 2008	1	(–)
Wallace W.J.	1878–1972	(Wellington) 1903–04–05–06–07–08	51	(11)
Waller D.A.G.	1974–	(Wellington) 2001	3	(1)
Walsh P.T.	1936–2007	(Counties) 1955–56–57–58–59–63–64	27	(13)
Walter J.	1904–1966	(Taranaki) 1925	7	(–)
Warbrick J.A.	1862–1903	(Auckland) 1884	7	(–)
Ward E.P.	1899–1958	(Taranaki) 1928	10	(–)
Ward F.G.	1900–1990	(Otago) 1921	1	(–)
Ward R.H.	1915–2000	(Southland) 1936–37	4	(3)
Waterman A.C.	1903–1997	(North Auckland) 1929	7	(2)
Watkins E.L.	1880–1949	(Wellington) 1905	1	(1)
Watson J.D.	1872–1958	(Taranaki) 1896	1	(–)
Watson W.D.	1869–1953	(Wairarapa) 1893–96	3	(–)
Watt B.A.	1939–2021	(Canterbury) 1962–63–64	29	(8)
Watt J.M.	1914–1988	(Otago) 1936	2	(2)
Watt J.R.	1935–2022	(Southland) 1957; (Wellington) 1958–60–61–62	42	(9)
Watts M.G.	1955–	(Taranaki) 1979–80	13	(5)
Webb D.S.	1934–1987	(North Auckland) 1959	1	(1)
Webb P.P.	1854–1920	(Wellington) 1884	8	(–)
Weber B.M.	1991-	(Chiefs) 2015-19-20-21-22	18	(18)
Webster T.R.D.	1920–1972	(Southland) 1947	4	(–)
Weepu P.A.T.	1983–	(Wellington) 2004–05–06–07–08–09–10–11–12; (Blues) 2013	73	(71)
Wells J.	1908–1994	(Wellington) 1936	3	(2)
Wells W.J.G.	1867–1911	(Taranaki) 1897	7	(–)
Wesney A.W.*	1915–1941	(Southland) 1938	3	(–)
West A.H.	1893–1934	(Taranaki) 1920–21–23–24–25	24	(2)
Weston L.H.	1892–1963	(Auckland) 1914	1	(–)
Whetton A.J.	1959–	(Auckland) 1984–85–86–87–88–89–90–91	65	(35)
Whetton G.W.	1959–	(Auckland) 1981–82–83–84–85–86–87–88–89–90–91	101	(58)
Whineray W.J.	1935–2012	(Canterbury) 1957; (Waikato) 1958; (Auckland) 1959–60–61–62–63–64–65	77	(32)
White A.	1894–1968	(Southland) 1921–22–23–24–25	38	(4)
White H.L.	1929–2016	(Auckland) 1953–54–55	16	(4)
White R.A.	1925–2012	(Poverty Bay) 1949–50–51–52–53–54–55–56	55	(23)
White R.M.	1917–1980	(Wellington) 1946–47	10	(4)
Whitelock G.B.	1986–	(Canterbury) 2009	1	(1)
Whitelock L.C.	1991–	(Crusaders) 2013–17–18	8	(7)
Whitelock S.L.	1988–	(Canterbury) 2010–11–12; (Crusaders) 2013–14–15–16 –17–18-19-20-21-22-23	153	(153)
Whiting G.J.	1946–	(King Country) 1972–73	31	(6)
Whiting P.J.	1946–	(Auckland) 1971–72–73–74–76	56	(20)
Wickes C.D.	1962–	(Manawatu) 1980	1	(–)
Wightman D.R.	1929–2012	(Auckland) 1951	4	(–)
Williams A.J.	1981–	(Auckland) 2002–03–04–05–06–07–08–11–12	78	(77)
Williams A.L.	1898–1972	(Otago) 1922–23	9	(–)
Williams B.G.	1950–	(Auckland) 1970–71–72–73–74–75–76–77–78	113	(38)
Williams C.W.	1916–1998	(Canterbury) 1938	4	(–)
Williams G.C.	1945–2018	(Wellington) 1967–68	18	(5)
Williams P.	1884–1976	(Otago) 1913	9	(1)
Williams R.N.	1909–2001	(Hawke's Bay) 1932	1	(–)
Williams R.O.	1963–	(North Harbour) 1988–89	10	(–)

Name	B&D	Representative Team	Games	Tests
Williams S.	1985–	(Canterbury) 2010–1–12; (Chiefs) 2014–15; (Blues) 2017–18-19	58	(58)
Williams, T.	2000-	(Crusaders) 2023	8	(8)
Williment M.	1940–1994	(Wellington) 1964–65–66–67	9	(9)
Willis R.K.	1975–	(Waikato) 1998–99–2002	12	(12)
Willis T.E.	1979–	(Otago) 2001–02	7	(5)
Willocks C.	1919–1991	(Otago) 1946–47–49	22	(5)
Willoughby S. de L.P.	1904–1985	(Wairarapa) 1928	4	(–)
Wills M.C.	1941–	(Taranaki) 1967	5	(–)
Wilson A.	1874–1932	(Auckland) 1897	8	(–)
Wilson A.L.	1927–2009	(Southland) 1951	7	(–)
Wilson B.W.	1956–	(Otago) 1977–78–79	12	(8)
Wilson D.D.	1931–2019	(Canterbury) 1953–54	14	(2)
Wilson F.R.*	1885–1916	(Auckland) 1910	2	(–)
Wilson H.B.	1957–	(Counties) 1983	3	(–)
Wilson H.C.	1868–1945	(Wellington) 1893	7	(–)
Wilson H.W.	1924–2004	(Otago) 1949–50–51	13	(5)
Wilson J.W.	1973–	(Otago) 1993–94–95–96–97–98–99–2001	71	(60)
Wilson N.A.	1886–1953	(Wellington) 1908–10–13–14	21	(10)
Wilson N.L.	1922–2001	(Otago) 1949–51	20	(3)
Wilson R.G.	1953–	(Canterbury) 1976–78–79–80	25	(2)
Wilson R.J.	1861–1944	(Canterbury) 1884	6	(–)
Wilson S.S.	1954–	(Wellington) 1976–77–78–79–80–81–82–83	85	(34)
Wilson V.W.	1899–1978	(Auckland) 1920	7	(–)
Wise G.D.	1904–1971	(Otago) 1925	7	(–)
Witcombe D.J.C.	1978–	(Auckland) 2005	5	(5)
Wolfe T.N.	1941–	(Wellington) 1961–62; (Taranaki) 1963–68	14	(6)
Wood M.E.	1876–1956	(Wellington) 1901; (Canterbury) 1903; (Auckland) 1904	12	(2)
Woodcock T.D.	1981–	(North Harbour) 2002–04–05–06–07–08–09–10–11–12; (Highlanders) 2013; (Blues) 2014–15	118	(118)
Woodman F.A.	1958–	(North Auckland) 1980–81	14	(3)
Woodman T.B.K.	1960–	(North Auckland) 1984	6	(–)
Woods C.A.	1929–	(Southland) 1953–54	14	(–)
Wright A.H.	1914–1990	(Wellington) 1938	4	(–)
Wright D.H.	1902–1966	(Auckland) 1925	7	(–)
Wright T.J.	1963–	(Auckland) 1986–87–88–89–90–91–92	64	(30)
Wright W.A.	1905–1971	(Auckland) 1926	1	(–)
Wrigley E.	1886–1958	(Wairarapa) 1905	1	(1)
Wulf R.N.	1984–	(North Harbour) 2008	4	(4)
Wylie J.T.	1887–1956	(Auckland) 1913	12	(2)
Wyllie A.J.	1944–	(Canterbury) 1970–71–72–73	40	(11)
Wyllie T.	1954–	(Wellington) 1980	1	(–)
Wynyard J.G.*	1914–1942	(Waikato) 1935–36–38	13	(–)
Wynyard W.T.	1867–1938	(Wellington) 1893	7	(–)
Yates V.M.	1939–2008	(North Auckland) 1961–62	9	(3)
Young D.	1930–2020	(Canterbury) 1956–57–58–60–61–62–63–64	61	(22)
Young F.B.	1874–1946	(Wellington) 1896	1	(–)

NZR ANNUAL AWARDS

Since 1994 the NZRU has hosted, at the end of each year, an annual awards function to honour players, personalities and teams. With the exception of the Tom French Cup all trophies were new. The Tom French Cup had been presented in 1949 by Mr J. Morris of Sydney, following the New Zealand Maori tour of Australia, in honour of the team's coach Mr T.A. French. The trophy has been awarded to the outstanding Maori player each season. No function has been held since 2019.

PLAYER OF THE YEAR

Kelvin Tremain Memorial Trophy

1994 Zinzan Brooke (*Auckland*)
1995 Jonah Lomu (*Counties*)
1996 Sean Fitzpatrick (*Auckland*)
1997 Jeff Wilson (*Otago*)
1998 Josh Kronfeld (*Otago*)
1999 Andrew Mehrtens (*Canterbury*)
2000 Tana Umaga (*Wellington*)
2001 Todd Blackadder (*Canterbury*)
2002 Chris Jack (*Canterbury*)
2003 Richard McCaw (*Canterbury*)
2004 Daniel Carter (*Canterbury*)
2005 Daniel Carter (*Canterbury*)
2006 Richard McCaw (*Canterbury*)
2007 Daniel Braid (*Auckland*)
2008 Andrew Hore (*Taranaki*)
2009 Richard McCaw (*Canterbury*)
2010 Kieran Read (*Canterbury*)
2011 Jerome Kaino (*Auckland*)
2012 Richie McCaw (*Canterbury*)
2013 Kieran Read (*Canterbury*)
2014 Brodie Retallick (*Waikato*)
2015 Ma'a Nonu (*Wellington*)
2016 Beauden Barrett (*Taranaki*)
2017 Samuel Whitelock (*Canterbury*)
2018 Kendra Cocksedge (*Canterbury*)
2019 Ardie Savea (*Wellington*)
2020 Sam Cane (*Chiefs*)
2021 Sarah Hirini (*Manawatu*)
2022 Ruahei Demant (*Auckland*)
2023 Ardie Savea (*Wellington*)

ALL BLACKS PLAYER OF THE YEAR

2019 Ardie Savea (*Hurricanes*)
2020 Sam Cane (*Chiefs*)
2021 Ardie Savea (*Wellington*)
2022 Ardie Savea (*Wellington*)
2023 Ardie Savea (*Wellington*)

SUPER RUGBY PLAYER OF THE YEAR

1996 Joeli Vidiri (*Blues*)
1997 Christian Cullen (*Hurricanes*)
1998 Andrew Mehrtens (*Crusaders*)
1999 Byron Kelleher (*Highlanders*)
2000 Scott Robertson (*Crusaders*)
2001 Deon Muir (*Chiefs*)
2002 Chris Jack (*Crusaders*)
2003 Carlos Spencer (*Blues*)
2004 Daniel Carter (*Crusaders*)
2005 Rico Gear (*Crusaders*)
2006 Daniel Carter (*Crusaders*)
2007 James Cowan (*Highlanders*)
2008 Andrew Hore (*Hurricanes*)
2009 Mils Muliaina (*Chiefs*)
2010 Alby Mathewson (*Blues*)
2011 Wyatt Crockett (*Crusaders*)
2012 Conrad Smith (*Hurricanes*)
2013 Ben Smith (*Highlanders*)
2014 Jerome Kaino (*Blues*)
2015 Lima Sopoaga (*Highlanders*)
2016 Beauden Barrett (*Hurricanes*)
2017 Samuel Whitelock (*Crusaders*)
2018 Richie Mo'unga (*Crusaders*)
2019 Ardie Savea (*Hurricanes*)
2020 Richie Mo'unga (*Crusaders*)
2021 Richie Mo'unga (*Crusaders*)
2022 Will Jordan (*Crusaders*)
2023 Scott Barrett (*Crusaders*)

TEAM OF THE YEAR

2000 New Zealand Under 21
2001 Canterbury
2002 New Zealand Sevens
2003 All Blacks
2004 Canterbury
2005 All Blacks
2006 All Blacks
2007 Auckland
2008 All Blacks
2009 Canterbury
2010 Black Ferns
2011 All Blacks
2012 All Blacks
2013 All Blacks
2014 All Blacks
2015 All Blacks
2016 All Blacks
2017 Black Ferns

NEW ZEALAND TEAM OF THE YEAR

2018 Black Ferns Sevens
2019 Black Ferns Sevens
2020 Black Ferns Sevens
2021 Black Ferns Sevens
2022 Black Ferns
2023 All Blacks Sevens

NATIONAL MEN'S TEAM OF THE YEAR

2018 Crusaders
2019 Crusaders
2020 Tasman
2021 Crusaders
2022 Wellington
2023 South Canterbury

PREMIER DIVISION PLAYER OF THE YEAR

Duane Monkley Medal from 2017

2006 Richard Kahui (*Waikato*)
2007 Isa Nacewa (*Auckland*)
2008 Jamie Mackintosh (*Southland*)
2009 Mike Delany (*Bay of Plenty*)
2010 Robbie Fruean (*Canterbury*)
2011 Aaron Cruden (*Manawatu*)
2012 Robbie Fruean (*Canterbury*)
2013 Andy Ellis (*Canterbury*)
2014 Seta Tamanivalu (*Taranaki*)
2015 George Moala (*Auckland*)
2016 Jordie Barrett (*Canterbury*)
2017 Jack Goodhue (*Northland*)
2018 Luke Romano (*Canterbury*)
2019 Chase Tiatia (*Bay of Plenty*)
2020 Folau Fakatava *(Hawke's Bay)*
2021 Stephen Perofeta (*Taranaki*)
2022 Bryn Gatland (*North Harbour*)
2023 Etene Nanai-Seturo (*Counties Manukau*)

HEARTLAND CHAMPIONSHIP PLAYER OF THE YEAR

Ian Kirkpatrick Medal from 2022

2006 Scott Leighton (*Poverty Bay*)
2007 Ross Hay (*North Otago*)
2008 Cameron Crowley (*Wanganui*)
2009 Asaeli Tikoirotuma (*Wanganui*)
2010 Peter Rowe (*Wanganui*)
2011 Jon Smyth (*Wanganui*)
2012 Peter Rowe (*Wanganui*)
2013 Jon Dampney (*Mid Canterbury*)
2014 James Lash (*Buller*)
2015 Lindsay Horrocks (*Wanganui*)
2016 Te Rangatira Waitokia (*Wanganui*)
2017 Scott Cameron (*Horowhenua Kapiti*)
2018 Brett Ranga (*Thames Valley*)
2019 Josh Clark (*North Otago*)
2020 Not awarded
2021 Willie Wright (*South Canterbury*)
2022 Sam Parkes (*Ngati Porou East Coast*)
2023 Siu Kakala (*South Canterbury*)

MAORI PLAYER OF THE YEAR
Tom French Cup

1949 Johnny Smith (*North Auckland*)
1950 Manahi Paewai (*North Auckland*)
1951 Percy Erceg (*Auckland*)
1952 Keith Davis (*Auckland*)
1953 Keith Davis (*Auckland*)
1954 Keith Davis (*Auckland*)
1955 Pat Walsh (*South Auckland*)
1956 Bill Gray (*Bay of Plenty*)
1957 Muru Walters (*North Auckland*)
1958 Pat Walsh (*Counties*)
1959 Bill Wordley (*King Country*)
1960 Mac Herewini (*Auckland*)
1961 Victor Yates (*North Auckland*)
1962 Waka Nathan (*Auckland*)
1963 Mac Herewini (*Auckland*)
1964 Ron Rangi (*Auckland*)
1965 Ron Rangi (*Auckland*)
1966 Waka Nathan (*Auckland*)
1967 Sid Going (*North Auckland*)
1968 Sid Going (*North Auckland*)
1969 Sid Going (*North Auckland*)
1970 Sid Going (*North Auckland*)
1971 Sid Going (*North Auckland*)
1972 Sid Going (*North Auckland*)
1973 Tane Norton (*Canterbury*)
1974 Tane Norton (*Canterbury*)
1975 Bill Bush (*Canterbury*)
1976 Kent Lambert (*Manawatu*)
1977 Bill Osborne (*Wanganui*)
1978 Eddie Dunn (*North Auckland*)
1979 Vance Stewart (*Canterbury*)
1980 Hika Reid (*Bay of Plenty*)
1981 Frank Shelford (*Bay of Plenty*)
1982 Steven Pokere (*Southland*)
1983 Hika Reid (*Bay of Plenty*)
1984 Michael Clamp (*Wellington*)
1985 Wayne Shelford (*North Harbour*)
1986 Frano Botica (*North Harbour*)
1987 Wayne Shelford (*North Harbour*)
1988 Wayne Shelford (*North Harbour*)
1989 Wayne Shelford (*North Harbour*)
1990 Steve McDowell (*Auckland*)
1991 John Timu (*Otago*)
1992 Zinzan Brooke (*Auckland*)
1993 Arran Pene (*Otago*)
1994 Zinzan Brooke (*Auckland*)
1995 Robin Brooke (*Auckland*)
1996 Errol Brain (*Counties Manukau*)
1997 Mark Mayerhofler (*Canterbury*)
1998 Tony Brown (*Otago*)
1999 Norman Maxwell (*Canterbury*)
2000 Daryl Gibson (*Canterbury*)
2001 Caleb Ralph (*Canterbury*)
2002 Carlos Spencer (*Auckland*)
2003 Carlos Spencer (*Auckland*)
2004 Carl Hayman (*Otago*)
2005 Rico Gear (*Nelson Bays*)
2006 Carl Hayman (*Otago*)
2007 Daniel Braid (*Auckland*)
2008 Piri Weepu (*Wellington*)
2009 Zac Guildford (*Hawke's Bay*)
2010 Hosea Gear (*Wellington*)
2011 Piri Weepu (*Wellington*)
2012 Liam Messam (*Waikato*)
2013 Liam Messam (*Waikato*)
2014 Aaron Smith (*Manawatu*)
2015 Nehe Milner-Skudder (*Manawatu*)
2016 Dane Coles (*Wellington*)
2017 Rieko Ioane (*Auckland*)
2018 Codie Taylor (*Canterbury*)
2019 Sarah Hirini (*Manawatu*)
2020 Ash Dixon (*Hawke's Bay*)
2021 Sarah Hirini (*Manawatu*)
2022 Ruahei Demant (*Auckland*)
2023 Aaron Smith (*Manawatu*)

NZ RUGBY PLAYERS' ASSN KIRK AWARD

2016 Justin Collins (*Northland*)
2017 DJ Forbes (*Counties Manukau*)
2018 Fiao'o Faamausili (*Auckland*)
Keven Mealamu (*Auckland*)
2019 Josh Blackie, Seilala Mapusua & Hale T-Pole
2020 Andy Ellis (*Canterbury*)
2021 Melodie Robinson (*Auckland*)

AGE GRADE PLAYER OF THE YEAR

1994 Taine Randell (*Otago*)
1995 Anton Oliver (*Otago*)
1996 Andrew Blowers (*Auckland*)
1997 Norman Maxwell (*Northland*)
1998 Doug Howlett (*Auckland*)
1999 Samiu Vahafolau (*Auckland*)
2000 Ben Blair (*Canterbury*)
2001 *Under 21*
Richard McCaw (*Canterbury*)
Under 19
Sam Tuitupou (*Auckland*)
2002 Luke McAlister (*North Harbour*)
2003 Ben Atiga (*Auckland*)
2004 Jerome Kaino (*Auckland*)
2005 Isaia Toeava (*Auckland*)
2006 Michael Paterson (*Canterbury*)
2007 Zac Guildford (*Hawke's Bay*)
2008 Zac Guildford (*Hawke's Bay*)
2009 Aaron Cruden (*Manawatu*)
2010 Liaki Moli (*Auckland*)
2011 Sam Cane (*Bay of Plenty*)
2012 Jason Emery (*Manawatu*)
2013 Ardie Savea (*Wellington*)
2014 Damian McKenzie (*Waikato*)
2015 Akira Ioane (*Auckland*)
2016 Jordie Barrett (*Canterbury*)
2017 Asafo Aumua (*Wellington*)
2018 Tom Christie *(Canterbury)*
2019 Fletcher Newell *(Canterbury)*
2020 Not awarded
2021 Josh Lord (*Taranaki*)
2022 Peter Lakai (*Wellington*)
2023 Harry Godfrey (*Hawke's Bay*)

SEVENS PLAYER OF THE YEAR

Richard Crawshaw Memorial Trophy from 1998

1994 Eric Rush (*North Harbour*)
1995 Jonah Lomu (*Counties*)
1996 Christian Cullen (*Manawatu*)
1997 Caleb Ralph (*Bay of Plenty*)
1998 Rico Gear (*Auckland*)
1999 Orene Ai'i (*Auckland*)
2000 Karl Te Nana (*North Harbour*)
2001 Karl Te Nana (*North Harbour*)
2002 Chris Masoe (*Taranaki*)
2003 Eric Rush (*North Harbour*)
2004 Liam Messam (*Waikato*)
2005 Amasio Valence (*Hawke's Bay*)
2006 Tafai Ioasa (*Hawke's Bay*)
2007 D.J. Forbes (*Auckland*)
2008 D.J. Forbes (*Counties Manukau*)
2009 Zar Lawrence (*Bay of Plenty*)
2010 Kurt Baker (*Taranaki*)
2011 Tim Mikkelson (*Waikato*)
2012 Tomasi Cama (*Manawatu*)
2013 Kurt Baker (*Taranaki*)
2014 DJ Forbes (*Counties Manukau*)
2015 Scott Curry (*Bay of Plenty*)
2016 Rieko Ioane (*Auckland*)
2017 DJ Forbes (*Counties Manukau*)
2018 Scott Curry (*Bay of Plenty*)
2019 Tone Ng Shiu *(Tasman)*
2020 Scott Curry *(Bay of Plenty)*
2021 Scott Curry (*Bay of Plenty*)
2022 Ngarohi McGarvey-Black
2023 Akuila Rokolisoa

WOMEN'S PLAYER OF THE YEAR

1994 Anna Richards (*Auckland*)
1995 Rochelle Martin (*Wellington*)
1996 Vanessa Cootes (*Waikato*)
1997 Louisa Wall (*Auckland*)
1998 Farah Palmer (*Otago*)
1999 Suzanne Shortland (*Auckland*)
2000 Fiona King (*Otago*)
2001 Annaleah Rush (*Auckland*)
2002 Monique Hirovanaa (*Auckland*)
2003 Monalisa Codling (*Auckland*)
2004 Stephanie Mortimer (*Canterbury*)
2005 Melissa Ruscoe (*Canterbury*)
2006 Amiria Marsh (*Canterbury*)
2007 Victoria Heighway (*Auckland*)
2008 Victoria Grant (*Auckland*)
2009 Victoria Heighway (*Auckland*)
2010 Carla Hohepa (*Otago*)
2011 Fiao'o Faamausili (*Auckland*)
2012 Rawinia Everitt (*Auckland*)
2013 Kelly Brazier (*Otago*)
2014 Rawinia Everitt (*Counties Manukau*)
2015 Kendra Cocksedge (*Canterbury*)
2016 Selica Winiata (*Manawatu*)
2017 Sarah Goss (*Manawatu*)
2018 Kendra Cocksedge (*Canterbury*)

BLACK FERNS PLAYER OF THE YEAR

2019 Charmaine McMenamin *(Auckland)*
2020 Chelsea Alley *(Waikato)*
2021 Kennedy Simon *(Waikato)*
2022 Ruahei Demant *(Auckland)*
2023 Liana Mikaele-Tu'u *(Auckland)*

SUPER RUGBY AUPIKI PLAYER OF THE YEAR

2022 Luka Connor *(Chiefs Manawa)*
2023 Lucy Jenkins *(Matatū)*

FARAH PALMER CUP PLAYER OF THE YEAR

Fiao'o Faamausili Medal

2017 Hazel Tubic *(Counties Manukau)*
2018 Kendra Cocksedge *(Canterbury)*
2019 Chelsea Bremner *(Canterbury)*
2020 Kendra Cocksedge *(Canterbury)*
2021 Krystal Murray *(Northland)*
2022 Maia Joseph *(Otago)*
2023 Krysten Cottrell *(Hawke's Bay)*

WOMEN'S SEVENS PLAYER OF THE YEAR

2013 Portia Woodman *(Auckland)*
2014 Sarah Goss *(Manawatu)*
2015 Tyla Nathan-Wong *(Auckland)*
2016 Sarah Goss *(Manawatu)*
2017 Ruby Tui *(Canterbury)*
2018 Michaela Blyde *(Bay of Plenty)*
2019 Tyla Nathan-Wong *(Auckland)*
2020 Stacey Fluhler *(Waikato)*
2021 Sarah Hirini *(Manawatu)*
2022 Michaela Blyde
2023 Stacey Waaka

NATIONAL WOMEN'S TEAM OF THE YEAR

2022 Canterbury
2023 Auckland Storm

NATIONAL WOMEN'S COACH OF THE YEAR

2022 Blair Baxter *(Canterbury)*
2023 Rawinia Everitt *(Northland)*

COACH OF THE YEAR

1994 Brad Meurant *(North Harbour)*
1995 Graham Henry *(Auckland)*
1996 John Hart *(All Blacks)*
2001 Colin Cooper *(New Zealand Under 21)*
2002 Robbie Deans *(Crusaders)*
2003 Wayne Pivac *(Auckland)*
2004 Vern Cotter *(Bay of Plenty)*
2005 Graham Henry *(All Blacks)*
2006 Graham Henry *(All Blacks)*
2007 Peter Russell *(Hawke's Bay)*
2008 Graham Henry *(All Blacks)*
2009 Dave Rennie *(New Zealand Under 20)*
2010 Gordon Tietjens *(New Zealand Sevens)*
2011 Graham Henry *(All Blacks)*
2012 Steve Hansen *(All Blacks)*
2013 Steve Hansen *(All Blacks)*
2014 Steve Hansen *(All Blacks)*
2015 Steve Hansen *(All Blacks)*
2016 Steve Hansen *(All Blacks)*
2017 Glenn Moore *(Black Ferns)*

NEW ZEALAND COACH OF THE YEAR

2018 Clark Laidlaw *(All Blacks Sevens)*
2019 Corey Sweeney & Allan Bunting *(Black Ferns Sevens)*
2020 Corey Sweeney & Allan Bunting *(Black Ferns Sevens)*
2021 Corey Sweeney & Allan Bunting *(Black Ferns Sevens)*
2022 Wayne Smith *(Black Ferns)*
2023 Corey Sweeney *(Black Ferns Sevens)*

NATIONAL COACH OF THE YEAR

2018 Alama Ieremia *(Auckland)*
2019 Scott Robertson *(Crusaders)*
2020 Scott Robertson *(Crusaders)*
2021 Ross Filipo *(Waikato)*
2022 Scott Robertson *(Crusaders)*
2023 Neil Barnes *(Taranaki)*

REFEREE OF THE YEAR

1994 Colin Hawke (*South Canterbury*)
1995 Paddy O'Brien (*Southland*)
1996 Paddy O'Brien (*Southland*)
1997 Steve Walsh jnr (*North Harbour*)*
1998 Paddy O'Brien (*Southland*)
1999 Colin Hawke (*South Canterbury*)
2000 Colin Hawke (*South Canterbury*)
2001 Kelvin Deaker (*Hawke's Bay*)
2002 Paddy O'Brien (*Southland*)
2003 Paddy O'Brien (*Southland*)
2004 Paddy O'Brien (*Southland*)
2005 Paul Honiss (*Waikato*)
2006 Paul Honiss (*Waikato*)
2007 Steve Walsh (*North Harbour*)
2008 Bryce Lawrence (*Bay of Plenty*)
2009 Bryce Lawrence (*Bay of Plenty*)
2010 Bryce Lawrence (*Bay of Plenty*)
2011 Bryce Lawrence (*Bay of Plenty*)
2012 Glen Jackson (*Bay of Plenty*)
2013 Chris Pollock (*Hawke's Bay*)
2014 Glen Jackson (*Bay of Plenty*)
2015 Glen Jackson (*Bay of Plenty*)
2016 Glen Jackson (*Bay of Plenty*)
2017 Ben O'Keeffe (*Wellington*)
2018 Glen Jackson (*Bay of Plenty*)
2019 Paul Williams (*Taranaki*)
2020 Paul Williams (*Taranaki*)
2021 Ben O'Keeffe (*Auckland*)
2022 Ben O'Keeffe (*Horowhenua Kapiti*)
2023 Ben O'Keeffe (*Horowhenua Kapiti*)

* for the Outstanding Referee Performance (Canterbury v Auckland round robin match)

STEINLAGER SALVER

For outstanding service to rugby

1999 Colin Meads
2000 Zinzan Brooke*
2001 Sir Terry McLean
2002 Fred Allen
2003 Sir Brian Lochore
2004 Peter Bush
2005 Richie Guy
2006 Stan Hill
2007 Ron Don
2008 Tane Norton
2009 John Graham
2010 Keith Quinn
2011 Jock Hobbs
2012 Ray Harper
2013 Graham Mourie
2014 Dick Littlejohn
2015 Mike Eagle
2016 Gavin Service
2017 Wayne Smith
2018 Waka Nathan
2019 Steve Tew
2020 Sir Bryan Williams
2021 Anna Richards
2022 Dr Deb Robinson
2023 Rob Fisher

* celebrating 25 years of the NPC

VOLUNTEER OF THE YEAR

Charles Monro Memorial Trophy from 2009

2002 John George (*Taranaki*)
2003 Ru Rangi (*Wellington*)
2004 Adelle Wakely (*Hawke's Bay*)
2005 Daphne Boden (*Hawke's Bay*)
2006 Jason Martin (*Otago*)
2007 Robbie Ball (*Northland*)
2008 Ken Swain (*Horowhenua Kapiti*)
2009 Blair Crawford (*Otago*)
2010 Hilton Williams (*Horowhenua Kapiti*)
2011 Andy MacDonald (*Canterbury*)
2012 Ray Watson (*Bay of Plenty*)
2013 Rob Jones (*Manawatu*)
2014 Dean File (*Horowhenua Kapiti*)
2015 Tania Karaitiana and Vio Ugone (*Wellington*)
2016 Gary Donovan (*Auckland*)
2017 Sid Tatana (*Wairarapa Bush*)
2018 Irene Eruera-Taiapa (*Horowhenua Kapiti*)
2019 Ian Spraggon (*Bay of Plenty*)
2020 Jane Chamberlain (*Horowhenua Kapiti*)
2021 Peter Chaplin (*Canterbury*)
2022 Cathy Charles (*Otago*)
2023 Allen Grainger (Waikato)

SKY FANS TRY OF THE YEAR

2013 Selica Winiata (*Black Ferns*)
2014 Malakai Fekitoa (*Highlanders*)
2015 Samu Kubunavanua (*Wanganui*)
2016 Isaiah Punivai (*Christ's College*)
2017 Portia Woodman (*Black Ferns*)
2018 Chris Hala'ufia (*St Peter's College*)
2019 TJ Perenara (*All Blacks*)
2020 Jack Jones (*Christ's College*)
2022 Stacey Fluhler (*Black Ferns*)
2023 George Dyer (*Chiefs*)

OBITUARIES

NEW ZEALAND REPRESENTATIVES

Roger John Boon (*Taranaki*) was a solidly built hooker, big by the 1960s standards for players in that position, who played his best rugby for Taranaki during its 1958-59 Ranfurly Shield defences. Boon was a non-capped All Black, who was called into the touring team in South Africa in 1960 when the original first choice hooker, Ron Hemi, was severely injured in just the fifth game in the republic. Such was the rush to get Boon to South Africa he left his travel cheques behind and he arrived in South Africa not completely fit himself, having nursed for some time back in New Zealand a suspect shoulder.

However, with the need to give the now number one hooker, Dennis Young, some relief he was quickly pressed into service, playing in six of the minor provincial matches against Rhodesian XV, Rhodesia, Eastern Province, South Western Districts, Eastern Transvaal and Western Transvaal. He, too, then was an injury casualty, suffering a displaced vertebra, which not only ruled him out of the final six games, but his representative career at just 25 years of age. A First XV player at Whanganui Collegiate School in 1951-52, Boon showed considerably early promise and was chosen in 1955 in the John Stewart-coached New Zealand Under 21 team which toured the then Ceylon. Also on this tour were the later All Blacks superstar forwards, Wilson Whineray, and Colin Meads. They also toured with Boon on the New Zealand Under 23 tour of Japan in early 1958, along with many others who were or were to become All Blacks, including Boon's Taranaki team-mate and friend, Ross Brown. It was on this trip that Boon and Brown bestowed on Meads the nickname which would become legendary, "Pinetree."

Boon played the first of 47 games for Taranaki in 1956, appearing in the province's 3-all draw with the touring Springboks. Injury meant he missed the 1957 Ranfurly Shield win over Otago, but he was a regular selection in the defences in the next two seasons. He had the first of many All Blacks trials in 1956 and during the 1959 series against the touring British and Irish Lions he was a test reserve. A carpenter by trade, Boon turned to farming near Whanganui and after coaching the Waverley club side, was Wanganui's selector-coach in 1982-84, a term which included the combined Wanganui-King Country team's match against the touring 1983 Lions. (*by Lindsay Knight*)

Roger Boon's first-class record:

For	Matches	Tries	Con	Points
Taranaki (NPHSOB) 1956(10)-57(10)-58(12)-59(14)-60	47	2	–	6
Centurions Club 1958	1	–	–	0
P.S. Burke's XV 1959	1	–	–	0
Evergreens Club 1963	1	–	–	0
North Island Colts 1955	1	–	–	0
New Zealand Colts (Under 21) 1955	4	–	–	0
New Zealand Juniors Trial 1957	1	–	–	0
New Zealand Juniors (Under 23) 1958	4	–	1	2
New Zealand Trials 1956-57-58-59(2)-60(3)	8	–	–	0
NEW ZEALAND 1960	6	–	–	0
TOTALS	***74***	***2***	***1***	***8***

At Whanganui, June 9, 2023, aged 88.

William Douglas Roy 'Bill' Currey (*Taranaki*) toured Australia in 1968 as a 23-year-old wing, he playing in seven games and scored eight tries, three being in his debut appearance, against Tasmania. On tour Currey, the 1967 Taranaki 100 and 200 yards sprint champion, showed his speed and tricky running but his hands often let him down. He was considered to be a player with promise having represented NZ Under 23 in 1967 and had taken part in two trials for selection for the end of year tour to Britain. He missed selection but in the May trials of 1968 he scored two tries which probably secured his selection for the touring squad. Currey and hooker Terry McCashin were the only players in the early trial to be selected, the leading tour contenders being placed in the second trial match including experienced All Black wing Bill Birtwistle who missed selection.

It is apparent that during the tour Currey did not perform to the selectors expectations, he did not play in either of the two tests, and on the team's return he was not included in the squads for the three-test series against France. Grahame Thorne and newcomers Mike O'Callaghan and Owens Stephens shared the wing positions when first-choice wing Tony Steel was out with injury. Even for the third test another newcomer, Northland's Dennis Panther, was brought in as a reserve ahead of Currey or his fellow tourist newcomer Michael Knight. Currey was never again given an All Blacks trial even though he showed good form for Taranaki over the following years.

Bill Currey was a member of the strong Auckland Grammar First XV in 1960-61 being vice-captain in his final year. In 1966 he made his first-class debut with two games for Auckland Colts. A schoolteacher, Currey moved to Taranaki in 1967 and immediately made an impression for Taranaki in the annual Anzac Day clash with Wanganui by scoring three tries in a narrow 22-18 victory. He became a regular in Taranaki sides through to 1972 playing mainly at centre and eight games at second five-eighth. He was captain for one game in 1970, the Almanack commenting that he 'returned to somewhere near his best form in the later matches, brilliant at times and a fine centre.'

Currey later headed overseas coaching at schools in Britain and South Africa until returning home to teach at Auckland Grammar. His father Leslie represented Auckland 1934-35.

Bill Currey's first-class record::

For	Matches	Tries	Points
Taranaki (Opunake) 1967(10)-68(11)-69(9) (NPHSOB) 1970(15)-71(12)-72(10)	67	19	59
Auckland Colts (Grammar OB) 1966	2	1	3
New Zealand Juniors Trial 1967	1	–	0
New Zealand Juniors (Under 23) 1967	1	1	3
New Zealand Trials 1967(2)-68	3	2	6
NEW ZEALAND 1968	7	8	24
TOTALS	***81***	***31***	***95***

At Auckland, February 9, 2023, aged 76.

Anthony John Kreft (*Otago*), a stalwart of Otago representative sides between 1966 and 1970, was a little unlucky in not playing more All Blacks games than the four, including just the one test, he received as a replacement prop on the 1968 tour of Australia. But he played at a time when New Zealand had an abundance of propping options and among his contemporaries were Ken Gray, Brian Muller, Alister Hopkinson, Jack Hazlett, Neil Thimbleby, and another Otago product, Keith Murdoch.

His chances of being on the 1970 tour of South Africa may have been dashed when early in that year he turned up for a pre-season festival match in Blenheim clearly out of condition. Kreft would not have been the only player in those days to have eased off their physical work over the summer months but All Black coach Ivan Vodanovich "scouted" that pre-season game and did not hide his annoyance with Kreft's lack of fitness. Tony Kreft did play in the late May trial matches but was passed over for the touring team by Hopkinson, Muller, Murdoch and Thimbleby.

Kreft, typical of the many hard-grafting forwards produced in Otago rural areas, first played for Otago in 1966 as a 21-year from the Maniototo sub-union's Ranfurly club. He had his first All Black trial the following year and played in the 1967 New Zealand Under 23 side which met Taranaki. Among his team-mates were others destined to be long-term All Blacks in Ian Kirkpatrick, Peter Whiting, Kerry Tanner and Grahame Thorne and the team's captain was another future test player in Graham Williams. Kreft reappeared in the 1968 All Black trials and after initially missing selection was summoned to Australia when two of the three chosen props, Gray and Muller, were affected by injuries. One day after arriving in Australia Kreft played against Australia Capital Territory, then the matches against New South Wales and Queensland, scoring two tries in the latter match. With Gray and Muller still unavailable he gained his one test cap partnering Hopkinson as the props in the second test at Brisbane. This was the celebrated match which was won only by the All Blacks through a controversial penalty try award near fulltime.

Kreft, however, was deemed to have acquitted himself well, both as a sturdy scrummager and for his mobility in open play. He played later that season for the South Island and was a 1969 trialist but did not make the All Blacks for the two tests that year against Wales.

After his brief stint in Australia in 1968 his only other international involvement was to play for Otago in matches against France later that season and Wales in 1969. A genial personality much liked by his Otago team-mates, he was Otago's captain in 1970, including a spirited but unsuccessful Ranfurly Shield challenge late in the season against Canterbury.

Other than a game for Otago Country in 1971, that proved to be his first-class rugby farewell. He retired when he was only 25 and for a prop still some way off from reaching his prime. Kreft, though, remained close to the game with his Ranfurly club, as a coach and selector with the Maniototo sub-union and as a radio comments man at Dunedin's Carisbrook. (*by Lindsay Knight*)

Tony Kreft's first-class record:

For	Matches	Tries	Con	Points
Otago (Ranfurly) 1966(10)-67(14)-68(8)-69(15)-70(11)	58	6	1	20
Otago Country 1967-70-71	3	2	–	6
New Zealand Juniors Trial 1967	1	–	–	0
New Zealand Juniors (Under 23) 1967	1	–	–	0
South Island 1968-70	2	–	–	0
New Zealand Trials 1967-68-69-70(2)	5	2	–	6
NEW ZEALAND 1968	4	2	–	6
TOTALS	***74***	***12***	***1***	***38***

At Dunedin, September 15, 2023, aged 78.

John Kelman Loveday (*Manawatu*) joined fellow High School Old Boys club members Mark Donaldson and Gary Knight on the 'Grand Slam' tour of Britain in 1978 playing seven games but the 29-year-old did not appear in a test. Injury in his first game kept him sidelined for the next five games. His selection was a fitting reward for his tremendous contribution towards Manawatu's Ranfurly Shield successes of 1976-78. The big lock (1.93m, 112kg) was a vigorous rucker, strong mauler, hard and determined when breaking from the pack and an excellent ball-winner in the lineout. He was not the spectacular lineout leaper of Manawatu team-mates Sam Strahan and John Callesen but he was a greater, more effective worker in the tight play.

Loveday was a member of the Ian Colquhoun-coached Palmerston North Boys' High School First XV 1964-66, teams which included future All Blacks Bob Burgess and Ian Stevens. After two games for Manawatu in 1969 Loveday went to USA to study chiropractic and captained the Palmer College of Chiropractic team to win the 1972 National Inter-Collegiate Championship.

Having attained his doctorate of Chiropractic in 1973 Loveday returned to Palmerston North and established his own practice and rejoin his club partnering Callesen. Losing 7kg he was back in the Manawatu side in 1974 and remained a regular fixture at lock until choosing to retire in 1979 to concentrate on his business. Loveday was one of three players to play in all 15 Ranfurly Shield games. He seldom had injury, the worst being against the 1977 touring Lions when he left the field with two fractured vertebrae caused by a severe kick in the back after setting up a ruck. The Manawatu locking duo of Loveday and Callesen were together in 35 games, the pairing being terminated in 1978 when Callesen was forced to retire with back injury.

With Callesen gone the responsibility during 1978 of lineout possession went to Loveday and he responded by playing the best rugby of his career, exhibiting strength and ability seldom seen in earlier years. His outstanding performance for the Ranfurly Shield holders in its 20-10 win over a test-strength Wallaby team probably secured him a place in the North Island team and All Blacks selection.

Retiring from first-class rugby in 1979 he continued with club rugby until 1981. In later years Dr Loveday practiced in Brisbane, Nelson and finally Taupo where he retired due to ill-health.

John Loveday's first-class record:

For	Matches	Tries	Points
Manawatu (HSOB) 1969(2)-74(8)-75(13)-76(15)-77(9)-78(16)-79(2)	65	5	20
Manawatu-Horowhenua 1977	1	–	0
Evergreens Club 1974-76	2	1	4
Wasps Club 1977-79	2	–	0
North Island 1978	1	–	0
New Zealand Trials 1976-77-78-79	4	–	0
NEW ZEALAND 1978	7	–	0
TOTALS	***82***	***6***	***24***

At Taupo, May 20, 2023, aged 74.

Rangitane Will Norton (*Mid Canterbury and Canterbury*) was the leading New Zealand hooker for much of the 1970s, having significant roles at national levels for both the All Blacks and New Zealand Maori. And few careers illustrate as vividly as Tane Norton's how much the hooker position has changed and evolved over the years. For Norton was one of the last of the old school hookers, whose primary roles were to strike for scrum ball, to be at the front of lineouts with wings having the task of throwing the ball in and figuring only rarely among the try-scorers.

Indeed, in the 27 tests Norton played between 1971 and 1977 he did not score one try and in the 61 All Black games he played in total there was either just the one or two tries, depending on which historical record is to be believed. He scored in the 1974 romp over South Australia in Adelaide, but while some records have him scoring against East Midlands on the 1972-73 tour of Britain, others have awarded this try to Alan Sutherland. In all his 198 first-class games Norton has been credited with just five tries.

Norton was also a prime example of a player suddenly blooming after being left to blush unseen for much of his career. As a 19-year-old Norton played three representative games for Mid Canterbury from the Methven club, the last of these appearances being against Canterbury where he was opposite another prototype of the old-style hookers, Dennis Young.

But bank transfers took him firstly to Kaikoura, where he played his senior club rugby in the old Hurunui sub-union, which came under the wing of Canterbury, and then to South Canterbury where he played his club rugby for Temuka. In the latter union he was totally overlooked at any representative level for three seasons from 1964-66, and it was only after a move in 1967 to Christchurch when he joined the famous Linwood club that he began his emergence from a rugby wilderness.

Even then, it was not until the 1969 season, and a break from first-class rugby of eight years, that he first made Canterbury representative teams making his debut ironically against South Canterbury. He played three further games for Canterbury that year and was a reserve when the Ranfurly Shield was lifted from Hawke's Bay. In 1969 he also had made the first of his many appearances for New Zealand Maori, playing in both games against the touring Tongans.

His big chance came in 1970 when Canterbury's first choice hooker in 1969, Gary Bacon, transferred to Whangarei enabling Norton to play seven of Canterbury's eight shield defences, while he also retained his New Zealand Maori position for matches against Fiji.

After playing in the 1971 trials and for the Maori against the touring Lions, Norton was surprisingly preferred to a 1970 test player in South Africa, Ron Urlich, for all four tests against the Lions. That was the beginning of an unbroken sequence in All Black tests which stretched to 27, then the record for an All Black hooker.

His All Black tenure included tours to Britain and France in 1972-73, to Australia in 1974, to Ireland in 1974 and South Africa in 1976. He succeeded an unavailable Sid Going as New Zealand Maori captain for the 1973 tour of the Pacific Islands and, having been captain on the 1976 tour in some midweek games, he led the All Blacks in all four tests against the 1977 touring Lions.

The series was won only narrowly and after the All Blacks had been forced to pack three men in a scrum because of difficulties countering the Lions' emphasis on power scrummaging. Those difficulties left Norton with a neck issue and at 35 he made himself unavailable for the upcoming tour of France and retired. Incredibly, considering his representative career didn't start properly until he was 28, he tallied nearly 200 first-class games, of which 82 were for Canterbury and 26 for the Maori. In 1973-74 he was awarded the Tom French Cup as each season's outstanding Maori player.

He then made a major contribution to the game as an administrator, becoming a life member of the Linwood club and the Canterbury union. He was New Zealand union president in 2003-04, was awarded the New Zealand Order of Merit in 2006 and for his contribution to the game won the Steinlager Salver in 2008. (*by Lindsay Knight*)

Tane Norton's first-class record

For	Matches	Tries	Points
Mid Canterbury (Methven) 1961	3	–	0
Canterbury (Linwood) 1969(3)-70(13)-71(8)-72(11)-73(9)-74(11)-75(14)-76(2)-77(10)	81	3	11
Canterbury B 1969	1	–	0
I.A. Kirkpatrick's XV 1973	1	–	0
Centurions Club 1974	1	–	0
Wasps Club 1978	1	1	4
World XV (in South Africa) 1977	3	–	0
Southern Maori 1969-70-71-72-73-74-75	7	–	0
New Zealand Maori 1969(3)-70(3)-71(2)-72-73(9)-74(3)-75(3)-77(2)	26	–	0
South Island 1971-72-73-74-75	5	–	0
New Zealand Trials 1970-71(2)-72-74-75-76-77	8	–	0
NEW ZEALAND 1971(4)-72(22)-73(3)-74(14)-75-76(13)-77(4)	61	1	4
TOTALS	***198***	***5***	***19***

At Christchurch, August 3, 2023, aged 81.

Bruce John Robertson (Counties) was a leading player in New Zealand rugby in the 1970s and into the early 80s, and would be on most short lists to be the centre in any hypothetical all-time great All Black XV. Tall, athletic and blessed with exceptional pace, Robertson brought an artistry to a position which often, even in his playing era, has been involved in the game's physical hurly-burly with the accent on brawn as much as skill.

A product of Hawke's Bay, where he played in the Hastings Boys' High School first XV and also excelled in athletics and cricket, Robertson moved to the Counties union to attend the Ardmore teachers training college, where his rare talent was soon spotted by a perceptive, innovative selector-coach, Barry Bracewell. In 1971, when only 19 years old, he was introduced into Bracewell's representative team and later that season was a surprise choice for the North Island team which played the annual inter-island fixture. Robertson's display that day was a revelation and quickly those who had criticised his selection were among his many admirers. Among that group were the then editors of the Rugby Almanack who included him among their five most promising players of the 1971 season.

Robertson became an All Black on the 1972 internal tour and made his test debut later that season against the touring Wallabies. On the 1972-73 tour of Britain and France he formed a lethal three-quarter line with two other young players, Bryan Williams and Grant Batty, though their full potential was not exploited by what generally was a conservative game plan.

A more expansive style began in the mid-1970s firstly under the coaching of JJ Stewart and more particularly by Jack Gleeson in the 1977 and 1978 seasons. Robertson was at his peak on the 1976 tour of South Africa, in the 1977 series against the British and Irish Lions and on the 1978 Grand Slammers tour of Britain, finding an ideal complement in the midfield in the rugged Bill Osborne.

There were, though, many setbacks in Robertson's career. Injuries ruled him out of several tests and the 1979 tour of Scotland and England. In 1980 he was inexplicably omitted from the tour of Australia, which must rate as one of All Black rugby's worst selection blunders. The error was soon remedied and he did join the tour as an injury replacement and in time for the second and third tests. In the second test which the All Blacks won he launched a counter attack which brought a memorable try to hooker Hika Reid.

In 1981 he joined captain Graham Mourie in making himself unavailable for the tests against the touring Springboks. Robertson, a mild-mannered and pleasant man, had been upset by what he had seen of apartheid on the 1976 tour and like many New Zealanders was aggrieved by what were obvious penalty try offences committed against him in the final test.

Earlier in 1981 Robertson had played the two tests against Scotland, and these proved to be his last All Black appearances. Appropriately, he bowed out with a try in the second test at Eden Park. In his 34 tests Robertson scored only four tries. But the measure of his worth were the many tries scored by wings outside him like Williams, Batty and Stu Wilson. His skills were also shown in the two dropped goals he landed in 1977, in the third test against the Lions and against France in Toulouse.

Robertson played in 102 All Black games, acting as captain in three minor matches on the 1977 and 1978 tours. Robertson was also a provincial centurion, revelling in the free-running style of Counties and sharing in many triumphs including winning the 1979 national provincial championship. A frustration, however, was to be in many narrow misses in Ranfurly Shield challenges.

In later years Robertson used his skills gained as a teacher as a development officer for the Auckland union and in several coaching roles with Counties Manukau, Northland, the Blues and New Zealand Colts.

Many accomplished players preceded Robertson as the All Blacks test centre and he in turn was followed by fine players like Joe Stanley, Frank Bunce, Tana Umaga and Conrad Smith. But for those of his generation Robertson will remain the benchmark. (by Lindsay Knight)

Bruce Robertson's first-class record:

For	Matches	Tries	Con	DG	Points
Counties (Ardmore College) 1971(7)-72(11)-73(3)-74(12)-75(8)-76(2)-77(10)-78(13)-79(13)-80(14)-81(14)-82(16)	123	47	1	1	189
Counties-Thames Valley) 1977	1	–	–	–	0
Barbarians Club 1972-79-80-81	4	2	–	–	8
Zingari-Richmond Invitation XV 1978	3	–	–	–	0
S.S. Wilson's XV 1984	1	–	1	–	2
World XV (in Sydney) 1981	1	–	–	–	0
North Island 1971-72-74-75-77-80-81	7	1	–	–	4
New Zealand Trials 1972-74(2)-76-77-78-79-81	8	1	–		0
NEW ZEALAND 1972(23)-73(3)-74(15)-76(17)-77(11)-78(15)-79(3)-80(13)-81(2)	102	34	–	2	142
TOTALS	***250***	***85***	***2***	***3***	***349***

At Whangarei, May 12, 2023, aged 71.

Roy Alfred Roper (*Taranaki*), one of New Zealand's fastest and best three-quarters in the years immediately after World War II, had the distinction of being the first All Black to reach 100 years, dying just 34 days after he had achieved his personal century.

Roper, by today's standards, had a brief representative career, playing only 44 first-class games and just 23 games for his provincial union, Taranaki. But it seems clear that had he been born in a later era he might have been rated among the all-time greats of All Black rugby. Some idea of his exceptional ability can be gained from the fact, despite playing only 44 games, he almost averaged a try per game, a tally of 40.

Roper's career statistics, and his international involvement, might have been greater had his early representative days not coincided with World War II, injuries and, as was the case with many players in the amateur 1940s and 50s, the need to make work and family commitments a priority.

Another insight into his rare talent can be obtained from the high rating he enjoyed from his contemporaries, men like the champion fullback Bob Scott, his team-mate in all four tests of the 1950 series against the touring British and Irish Lions. In his 1956 autobiography Scott described Roper as not only the best of the team's three-quarters in that series, but its best back. Said Scott: ". . . He was very fast, very aggressive and very, very determined, and, given the luck of a long tour, with inside backs to appreciate his skill, he could have won a reputation, I feel sure, as a three-quarter of true greatness... I wish his time in New Zealand teams had been longer."

Though not a big man at 1.73m and 72kg, Roper possessed considerable speed off the mark, as befitted his background in track and field which saw him gain a third placing in the triple jump at the national championships.

After captaining the New Plymouth Boys' High School first XV in 1941, Roper soon after entered military service and while that limited his rugby chances he did play in several services matches, both in New Zealand and overseas, while in the Navy.

He played one game for Taranaki in 1944, only becoming a regular provincial player in 1946 when he also appeared for a combined Taranaki-King Country team against the touring Wallabies, scoring a try in an 8–9 defeat. But because of injuries he missed all of the 1947 season and also the trials in 1948 to pick the All Black team to tour South Africa in 1949.

His eventual national selection came when the All Black second selection of 1949 played a Bledisloe Cup series against the Wallabies. Roper missed the first test but was brought into the team for the second test at Eden Park. He learned of his selection by telegram just after he scored Taranaki's try in its 6–5 Ranfurly Shield defeat against holders Otago. Because of the limited air travel of those years to join the All Blacks in Auckland Roper had to travel from Dunedin by train to Christchurch, by overnight ferry from Lyttelton to Wellington, and from there by overnight express to Auckland.

He played on the wing in his All Black debut, scoring the side's only try in a 16–9 defeat which gave the Wallabies the series and New Zealand its sixth test defeat from as many matches in 1949. Roper ended the 1949 season by scoring three tries for the North in that year's inter-island match in Christchurch.

Roper, who played as a wing or centre, was in the midfield for all 1950 tests against the Lions being chosen ahead of the highly regarded Johnny Smith. But despite his starring role in the series, including tries in each of the first two tests, Roper's career soon came to an end and even though he was only 27 because of a knee injury he decided to focus on his accountancy career and his family.

He later served a lengthy term (1952-71) as treasurer of the Taranaki union and a son, Guy, represented Manawatu in 1978. (*by Lindsay Knight*)

Roy Roper's first-class record

For	Matches	Tries	Points
Taranaki (Tukapa) 1944 (HSOB) 1946(5)-48(7)-49(6)-50(4)	23	17	51
Taranaki-King Country 1946	1	1	3
Barbarians Club 1952	1	–	0
2nd Brigade Group 1942	2	1	3
4th New Zealand Division 1942	3	6	18
North Services (Navy) 1944	1	–	0
New Zealand Services (in Britain) 1945	6	8	24
North Island 1949	1	3	9
New Zealand Trial 1950	1	1	3
NEW ZEALAND 1949-50(4)	5	3	9
TOTALS	***44***	***40***	***120***

At New Plymouth, September 14, 2023, aged 100.

PROVINCIAL REPRESENTATIVES

Valentine Rangiwaititi Baker (*Taranaki*) made one appearance in 1970 then six in 1973. A flanker, he represented Southern Maori 1969-70-71 and played for NZ Maori in 1970 and again the following year when the team played the touring Lions. At North Shore, August 13, 2023, aged 85.

Leslie Antonius Barbara (*Poverty Bay*) was one of a set of three brothers (Les, Graham and Gordon) to play for the union during the 1970s. a midfield back Les played 54 games 1977-82 scoring nine tries. His son Daniel also played for the union, in 2010. At Gisborne, March 22, 2023, aged 67.

Michael Roche Beveridge (*Nelson Bays*) was a loose forward appearing once for his union in 1974 and a further appearance the following year. At Nelson, July 12, 2023.

James William Bickley (*Golden Bay-Motueka*) made one appearance, at first five-eighth against Nelson, in 1950. A few weeks earlier, he played in two first-class trial matches for selection of the combined Nelson, Marlborough and Golden Bay-Motueka side to meet the touring Lions. At Takaka, November 29, 2023, aged 94.

Graeme Valentine Boness (*Manawatu*) made one appearance, as a substitute halfback, against Bush in 1969. At Palmerston North, February 8, 2023, aged 80.

Desmond Clifford Broderson (*King Country*) was a five-eighth appearing in 14 games for his union 1968-70. At Taumarunui, March 24, 2023, aged 81.

Errol Ambrose Brown (*Wanganui*) was an army corporal based at Waiouru who played eight games for Wanganui 1984-85. A first five-eighth he was a regular in NZ Services teams for five years 1984-88 playing 14 games. At Foxton, August 21, 2023, aged 63.

Robert Henry 'Bob' Cameron (*Taranaki*) played at fullback in two games 1952 and one further appearance the following year. Four brothers also represented Taranaki and a fifth, Bob's twin brother Doug, represented Manawatu. At Hawera, February 15, 2023, aged 92.

Maxwell Charles Carroll (*Taranaki*) was halfback for three games in 1953. Teacher at New Plymouth BHS 1958-91 being coach of the First XI cricket team 1960-66 and First XV 1965-79 producing several outstanding teams including future All Blacks Graham Mourie, Mark Donaldson, Geoff Old and reserve All Black Bruce Middleton. Queen's Service Medal (*QSM*) 2007 for services to education and sport. At New Plymouth, November 21, 2023, aged 91.

Raymond Lloyd Clarke (*Taranaki*) played on the wing in 49 games 1964-69 scoring 18 tries. Earlier, when at Victoria University, he made one first-class appearance for Wellington B in 1962. He had a national trial in 1967. At Hamilton, August 24, 2023, aged 82.

John Robert Dudley Coates (*Poverty Bay*) was a prop in 12 games 1983-84. He drowned during the flooding caused by Cyclone Gabrielle. At Te Karaka, February 14, 2023, aged 64.

Milton Miles Colson (*North Auckland*) played as a flanker making one appearance in 1962, six in 1963 and one further game in 1964. He moved to Malaysia in 1978. At Johor Bahru, Malaysia, April 22, 2023, aged 82.

Brett William Charles Coombe (*Taranaki*) was a first five-eighth appearing in three games in 1989 with a further four in 1991. At Darwin, Australia, November 1, 2023, aged 54.

Michael Gerald Cross (*Manawatu*) was a five-eighth playing 11 games for his union 1960-61. He served on the Manawatu RU management committee 1973-98 and made a life member in 1995. He was NZRU vice-president 1995-96 and president in 1997. At Palmerston North, January 5, 2024, aged 87.

Warwick Paul Curran (*Auckland*) became a regular flanker in Auckland teams 1967-70 appearing in 39 games. He took part in two national trials in 1970 and switched to league in 1971. At Auckland, February 16, 2023.

Robert Hunter 'Bob' Daniel (*Centurions club*) was a member of Eastern Suburbs club who played at five-eighth in a first-class game for Centurions against Horowhenua at Paraparaumu. He died just a few hours after watching the World Cup final. At Paraparaumu, October 29, 2023, aged 91.

Arthur Graham Dawson (*West Coast*) was a five-eighth in a career spanning seven seasons 1952-58 playing 33 games. He was later a West Coast selector 1980-81 and sole-selector 1982-83. At Greymouth, October 11, 2023, aged 91.

Michael Patrick 'Mick' Dennehy (*Hawke's Bay*) made one appearance in 1990 and one in 1991 before being a regular wing in seven games in 1992. At Hastings, May 27, 2023, aged 59.

Samuel Robert John Dickson (*Otago*) was a promising 19-year-old loose forward playing two games, as a substitute, in 2018, his brother Josh being at lock in both games. A NZ Schools representative in 2016 Dickson's playing career was terminated when he suffered from cancer. At Dunedin, May 27, 2023, aged 24.

Donald George St Clair Dormer (*Auckland and Wanganui*) played seven first-class games for Auckland B 1960-62 and once for the A team in 1960. In 1963 he was fullback in all 12 of Wanganui's games. He returned to Auckland to make one more appearance for Auckland in 1965. At Auckland, April 28, 2023, aged 84.

Kenneth Herbert Eglinton (*Otago*) played 27 games for Otago 1960-62 scoring six tries. In 1962 he toured California and British Columbia with the NZ Universities team. Later lived in Auckland where he became a life member of the NZ Barbarians club. Both his father Ken and brother Ron were life members of the Manawatu RU. Ron was auditor for the union for over 50 years, he passing eight weeks after Ken. At Auckland, September 26, 2023, aged 83.

Russell Henry Exeter (*Hawke's Bay*) was a threequarter playing eight games in 1960 and a further four in 1962. At Hastings, October 14, 2023, aged 83.

James Graeme 'Jamie' Francis (*Manawatu and Hawke's Bay*) was a record-breaking points-scorer for Manawatu compiling 478 points in his 55 games 1969-73. Returning to Hawke's Bay the fullback scored 165 points in his 22 games during 1974-75. In his first-class career of 81 games he compiled 669 points. He was Hawke's Bay assistant coach in 1982. A son of the Lindisfarne College rector, Jamie was educated at the college in Hastings and became head boy. He returned to the college as a teacher in 1975 and remained there until retiring in 2013 during which time he was deputy-rector for 21 years. His funeral was held at the college. At Hastings, May 26, 2023, aged 74.

Ronald Raymond Gardiner (*West Coast*) was a loose forward playing 24 games 1956-59 and appearing for the combined West Coast-Buller side that met the 1959 Lions. He also had a regional trial in 1959. At Napier, September 1, 2023, aged 86.

Kenneth Noel Grant (*Wellington and Bay of Plenty*) was hooker in Wellington sides that defeated both the 1965 Springboks and 1966 Lions. He played 29 games for the union 1964-66 and represented NZ Juniors against the Springboks. A NZ Universities representative in 1965 he toured Japan with the students in 1967. During 1968-69 he played 20 games for Bay of Plenty. At Blenheim, June 6, 2023, aged 80.

Robert Edward 'Bob' Griffiths (*Wanganui*) appeared as a midfield back in six games in 1973 with a further appearance the following year. He had played for Coventry club and Warwickshire in 1971 prior to joining the teaching staff at Whanganui Collegiate in 1972. At Taihape, April 15, 2023, aged 80.

Gordon Ralph Gray (*Manawatu*) made one appearance in 1974, at lock against Wanganui in a Bruce Steel Cup defence. At Palmerston North, March 5, 2023, aged 82.

Francis William Gugich (*West Coast*) scored 15 tries in his 31 games for the Coast 1953-57. A wing, he appeared in All Blacks trials and represented the South Island and the Rest of New Zealand teams in 1954. At Christchurch, December 5, 2023, aged 91.

Billy-John Aaron Guyton (*North Otago and Tasman*) could play in any backline position from halfback to fullback, his 116-game career commenced with North Otago with 29 games 2010-12 then with Tasman 2013-17, 52 games. One appearance for Hurricanes 2014 and one for Crusaders 2015 was followed by 24 games for the Blues 2016-17. NZ Heartland honours 2010-11-12 and NZ Maori selection in 2016 complete his varied career. He scored 21 tries and kicked 101 points. At Nelson, May 15, 2023, aged 33.

George Cuthbert Lyon Harper (*South Canterbury*) played six games as a threequarter in 1948 but was injured early in the 1949 season while playing for his Geraldine club. He had served in the navy during the war. At Geraldine, November 29, 2023, aged 98.

Teariki Ti 'Tiki' Heather (*Hawke's Bay*) made his debut in 1980 as a replacement. In his next game, against Fiji, the second five-eighth scored a try. His third, and final, game was in 1982 against Horowhenua when, playing on the wing, he again scored a try. At Hastings, September 26, 2023, aged 66.

Collier George Henderson (*Taranaki, Wellington and Poverty Bay*) was a halfback representing three unions. Firstly, Taranaki with four games 1954-55, Wellington with 10 games 1956, 58 and, finally, Poverty Bay in 1960 with eight games. He represented NZ Universities 1958-59. At New Plymouth, May 2, 2023, aged 89.

Brian William Henson (*Wairarapa*) played 26 games 1952-54, the halfback returning to the rep team in 1957 for a further five games. He was the union's selector-coach 1968-70. At Masterton, May 23, 2023, aged 92.

Edward 'Ted' Honeycombe (*Bay of Plenty*) played for Painoaiho club and made three appearances for the Bay 1965-66. At Murupara, October 6, 2023, aged 78.

Barry Winstone Johnson (*West Coast*) played 50 games for his union during a lengthy first-class career 1963-76. The halfback also played for West Coast-Buller against the 1965 Springboks. At Christchurch, November 5, 2023, aged 80.

Donald Robert Johnson (*Wairarapa*) was a five-eighth from Greytown club making two appearances for his union in 1964. A teacher at Kurunui College he coached the First XV when Grant Batty was a star player. He later coached at Westlake BHS. At Auckland, May 16, 2023.

Rawiri Toa Johnson (*King Country*) made two appearances for his union as a substitute fullback in 2003 when he was a 17-year-old pupil at Taupo Nui-a-Tia College. Died June 12, 2023, aged 36.

Lloyd Hollis Jones (*Wellington B*) was a lock appearing in five first-class games for Wellington B 1972-73. Detective Constable Jones represented NZ Services in two games in 1973. He rose to the rank of Detective Inspector in the CIB. At Melbourne, September 26, 2023, aged 79.

Tipuna Jones (*Poverty Bay*) appeared as a substitute against NZ Universities in 2016 and played on the wing against East Coast in 2017. Drowned while diving off the coast of Mahia Peninsula November 26, 2022, aged 36.

Noel Charles Kitchen (*Manawatu*) played at prop in five games in 1961 with a further three appearances in 1963. At Feilding, April 17, 2023, aged 83.

William Charles Landrebe (*Otago*) was a wing from Gimmerburn club appearing in two games for Otago in 1965, he also making two first-class appearances for Otago B that year. At Cromwell, August 20, 2023, aged 83.

Thomas Anthony 'Tom' Laurent (*Thames Valley and Bay of Plenty*) made one appearance, at fullback, for Thames Valley against Auckland in 1957. In 1959 he appeared at five-eighth in two games for Bay of Plenty. At Hamilton, May 31, 2023, aged 88.

Craig Edward McCracken (*Hawke's Bay*) played at prop in 26 games for his union 1979-81. At Gold Coast, Queensland, June 1, 2023, aged 69.

Donald George McMillan (*Thames Valley and Poverty Bay*) was a speedy wing playing 28 games for Thames Valley 1976-78 scoring 11 tries. He also scored a memorable try for the Counties-Thames Valley side against the 1977 Lions. In 1979 he made four appearances for Poverty Bay and scored two tries. Don McMillan died in Uganda on January 3, 2024, aged 71.

Kenneth Hugh Macmillan (*Manawatu and Counties*) was a goalkicking No 8 or lock who commenced his career with 51 points in eight games for Manawatu in 1963 when at Massey Agricultural College. He then had a long career with 86 games for Counties 1964-72 scoring 110 points including 12 tries and was in combined sides which played the 1965 Springboks and the Lions of 1966 and 1971. In 1964 he toured Australia with the NZ Colts side and the following year represented NZ Juniors against the Springboks. His first-class career totalled 112 games and 196 points. At Auckland, July 10, 2023, aged 79.

Malcolm Stuart MacRae (*West Coast*) appeared either as a loose forward or lock in 41 games 1963-72. He was also in the West Coast-Buller combined sides which met the 1965 Springboks, 1966 Lions and defeated the 1972 Wallabies 15-10. At Hokitika, May 5, 2023, aged 81.

Robert Patrick Magill (*Hawke's Bay*) was halfback in two games in 1949 and later president of Hawke's Bay union in 1967. At Napier, September 29, 2023, aged 96.

Augustus 'Gus' Meech (*Hawke's Bay*) was hooker during the Bay's Ranfurly Shield era, Gus playing 70 games for the union 1963-69 and had a national trial in 1966. At Hastings, April 16, 2023, aged 83.

Terence Leslie 'Terry' Mehrtens (*Canterbury*) was a regular five-eighth in Canterbury B teams 1964-69 playing in 12 first-class games but only received six callups to the A team during 1966-67. He was considered to have promise as in 1965, when aged 20, he played at first five-eighth for NZ Under 23 against the Springboks, and again was in the Under 23 team in 1967 and had a national trial in 1966. He went to South Africa and played for Natal against the 1970 All Blacks, later returning home to make a further four appearances for Canterbury in 1976. His father George was an All Black in 1928 and son Andrew 1995-2004. At Christchurch, April 9, 2023, aged 78.

Paul Bernard Mora (*Thames Valley*) played two games on the wing in 1979. He had earlier played three first-class games for Wellington B in 1972 and also four for Auckland B 1976-77. At Auckland, February 11, 2023, aged 73.

Thomas Humphrey 'Tom' Moynihan (*Canterbury*) was a loose forward from Canterbury University appearing in 42 games 1958-63 and also in the South Island Universities teams in the annual inter-island games of 1958-62-63. At Browns Bay, Auckland, February 23, 2023, aged 87.

John Patrick Murphy (*Auckland*) was a hooker in nine games during 1961. He also appeared in six first-class games for Auckland B, two in 1960 and four in 1963. At Auckland, July 31, 2023, aged 90.

Philip Francis Murphy (*Wanganui and Manawatu*) made his debut for Wanganui in 1962 but didn't reappear until 1964 with a further five games. Moving to Manawatu the hooker made 27 appearances 1969-71. At Mount Maunganui, January 2, 2024, aged 83.

Ross Cheyne Murray (*Otago*) was at fullback in six games during 1953 scoring 24 points with his boot. He also represented Otago in Brabin Shield cricket. However, golf became the sport in which he met much success, being New Zealand amateur champion in 1972 and represented New Zealand over a period of 16 years 1959-74. At Christchurch, April 4, 2023, aged 89.

Robert George 'Robin' Pearson (*Wanganui*) was a lock from Ohakune club appearing in 38 games 1972-76. At Palmerston North, April 28, 2023, aged 72.

Ihakara Porutu 'Kara' Puketapu (*Wellington*) played 23 games for Wellington 1954-58, the five-eighth also representing NZ Maori in 1955. He became prominent in Maori affairs in Wellington. At Wellington, July 7, 2023, aged 89.

Ray Wilfred Reardon (*Counties and Waikato*) was a frontrow forward playing 10 games for Counties 1960-62 and 11 for Waikato 1965-66. He also represented NZ Maori 1965-66. At Mt Maunganui, May 15, 2023, aged 87.

Francis Tony Richards (*Thames Valley*) appeared at No. 8 or at prop in 40 games for his union 1963-71 and was in the combined Counties-Thames Valley side which met the 1971 Lions. He was Thames Valley coach 1986-87. At Thames, December 17, 2023, aged 79.

Alan Arthur Riechelmann (*Hawke's Bay*) made two appearances, as a five-eighth, in 1953. The previous year, as a league player in Auckland, he toured Australia with the 1952 NZ League side. Work took him to Napier in 1953 where he was reinstated to rugby in April. He returned to Auckland in 1954 and switched back to league and represented Auckland. At Auckland, November 13, 2023, aged 93.

Trevor John Sydney Riley (*Wellington, Poverty Bay and Auckland*) had a first-class career of 85 games scoring 330 points including 17 tries. A five-eighth, he played 29 games for Wellington 1952-54, eight games for Poverty Bay 1955 and 33 games for Auckland 1956-58. In addition to several national trials he represented North Island 1953. At Tauranga, May 25, 2023, aged 90.

Oliver Henry 'Olly' Roberts (*Taranaki*) was a forward from Stratford club making two appearances in 1960. At New Plymouth, November 13, 2023, aged 85.

Jack Dickson Ross (*Auckland*) was a forward with Waitemata club making two appearances for Auckland in 1960 and six first-class appearances for Auckland B 1961-62. At Auckland, December 24, 2023, aged 91.

Trevor Huntly Ross (*Bay of Plenty and North Auckland*) was a loose forward or lock appearing in 14 games for Bay of Plenty 1954-56 and 57 games for North Auckland 1957-63. He played for combined sides against the 1955 Wallabies and 1956 Springboks and played in six trial matches for All Blacks selection in 1959-60. At Kerikeri, March 28, 2023, aged 89.

John Kay Sage (*Wellington*) was hooker in 63 games for his union 1951-59 and also had 15 games for various Wellington Colts, B and XV selections. He played for North Island 1957-58 in the annual inter-island fixture and appeared in five national trials. At Taupo, July 19, 2023, aged 94.

Raymond John 'Buster' Sharplin (*Hawke's Bay*) played in every forward position except hooker during a career of 49 games 1953-59. He had a national trial in 1959. At Hastings, April 19, 2023, aged 92.

Paul Kenneth Shorter (*Auckland*) was a loose forward playing 14 games for Auckland 1971-74. He had a NZ Under 23 trial in 1969. At Auckland, October 25, 2023, aged 76.

Clifford Simpson (*Manawatu*) was at fullback in three games for Manawatu 1955-56. In 1951 he made two first-class appearances for Otago B. He was the national 880 yards champion in 1950 and finished sixth in the 880 yards final at the 1950 Empire Games held in Auckland. At Feilding, December 10, 2023, aged 95.

Sydney Hirini Smallman (*Wanganui*) was a prop forward from the Taihape-based Moawhango Huia club making nine appearances in 1960 and two the following year. At Taihape, March 6, 2023, aged 88.

Roger Courtney Milton Spencer (*Hawke's Bay*) was a wing in 27 games 1960-62 scoring nine tries. At Hastings, April 14, 2023, aged 83.

Colin Joseph Stuart (*Nelson Bays*) was hooker in six games for his union during 1977. At Nelson, September 24, 2023, aged 68.

Michael Aidan Thomas (*Hawke's Bay*) was halfback in several games during the Bay's Ranfurly Shield era and in total appeared in 47 games 1967-72 and received a national trial in 1970 and again 1971. At Feilding, May 16, 2023, aged 76.

David Arthur Vesty (*Taranaki*) was a strong-running wing scoring 21 tries during his 48 games for Taranaki 1969-73. In 1971 he scored five tries during the game against Thames Valley. At Winton, December 15, 2023, aged 75.

Timothy William Wallis (*West Coast*) played five games in the forwards for the Coast in 1958. He became a leader in the deer industry and an aviation enthusiast collecting war planes and instigated the 'Warbirds Over Wanaka' air shows. In 1994 he was made a knight bachelor for services to deer farming, export and the community. At Wanaka, October 17, 2023, aged 85.

Graeme Eric Watt (*Otago*) made one appearance, against West Coast, in 1958. At Dunedin, July 18, 2023, aged 90.

Daniel Robert Weinberg (*Waikato and Hawke's Bay*) played 23 games for Waikato 1971-72 before moving to Hawke's Bay where the flanker played nine games 1973-75. His final first-class game was for NZ Marist in 1976 in a game against Wellington to celebrate 100 years of the Marist Brothers in New Zealand. Weinberg was Hawke's Bay coaching co-ordinator in 1981. At Piopio, May 11, 2023, aged 74.

Rangipokia Paul Wharehoka (*Taranaki*) played 95 games in a lengthy career for Taranaki 1974-82. A midfield back he also appeared for Southern Maori 1979-81-82 in the annual Prince of Wales Cup fixture. At Moerewa, November 30, 2023, aged 70.

Roger Douglas Whatman (*Auckland*) represented NZ Under 23 in 1967 before playing 61 games for Auckland 1968-73, the fullback scoring 356 points. At Auckland, January 27, 2023, aged 76.

Alan Wilkinson (*Thames Valley*) was a five-eighth appearing in 34 games for Thames Valley 1962-70. At Paeroa, January 20, 2023, aged 80.

Melita Uruinga Nicole Williams (*North Harbour*) was a prop forward who made 15 appearances for the North Harbour Hibiscus team in the Farah Palmer Cup 2021-23. At Auckland, November 25, 2023, aged 29.

Raymond Karl Wilson (*Hawke's Bay*) made his debut in 1963 against Wellington, the forward contributing a try in the Bay's 11-9 win. His only other appearance was against South Canterbury, at Timaru, the following year. At Hastings, March 19, 2023, aged 80.

Selwyn Gregory Wright (*North Auckland*) appeared at lock and loose forward in 15 games 1976-77 with one further game in 1978. At Northland, March 10, 2023, aged 73.

George Westcott Wyman (*Counties*) was a speedy loose forward playing 15 games for his union 1961-62 He also appeared for North Island Universities 1962-63. Moving to England he played for Wasps club 1965-67 and Middlesex 1967. In Canada he captained Quebec in 1967 and led Eastern Canada side against the touring 1967 All Blacks. When based in Jamaica he captained the national side 1968-71. At Auckland, October 8, 2023, on his 84th birthday.

Editors appreciate being informed of deaths of notable rugby folk. We rely on readers and unions to notify us of the deaths of former first-class players and referees and also prominent administrators and coaches. Please contact Clive Akers at akers@xtra.co.nz

FIRST-CLASS REFEREES

Lawrence 'Larry' Auckram (Horowhenua) controlled 29 fixtures between 1969 and 1982, 16 being Horowhenua home games, 10 being NPC games from 1976 and twice officiated at the National Sevens. At Levin, May 20, 2023, aged 79.

Brian Robert Bangs (Counties) controlled three of Counties home fixtures during 1982-84. After three years as Counties union secretary he was the union's CEO 1996-97, president 2003 and made a life member in 2005. At Pukekohe, December 30, 2023, aged 81.

James Robert 'Jim' Innes (Counties) had a lengthy career spanning 18 seasons 1963-80 with 41 games including three Ranfurly Shield fixtures and tour games involving Fiji, British Isles, Japan, Tonga and Samoa. At Auckland, December 19, 2023, aged 86.

Graham Francis Peach (Counties) controlled eight first-class games 1978-83 with major appointments being Thames Valley's Ranfurly Shield challenge against Waikato in 1979 and NZ Universities v All Japan in 1982. He was later a life member of Counties RRA. At Auckland, August 2, 2023, aged 85.

Colin John Pedley (Wanganui and Counties) controlled 28 games 1969-84 including 10 NPC fixtures. Moving to Counties union he controlled a further two first-class games during 1986-87. At Hamilton, December 12, 2023, aged 89.

Ronald James Pollock (Wanganui) controlled eight home games played by Wanganui between 1960 and 1969. He was later made a life member of the Whanganui Referees' Assn. At Whanganui, April 2, 2023, aged 92.

JOURNALIST

Ronald Allan Palenski was an outstanding sports journalist, especially through the 1970s and into the 90s, and as well as his high-profile role in the newspaper industry he was one of the country's foremost sporting historians. Though much of his work involved rugby, he was equally accomplished in the history and folklore of other sporting codes, particularly the Olympic and Commonwealth Games, as well as being knowledgeable on New Zealand's political, social and military history.

Always proud of his Otago origins, he began his journalism career as a cadet on the Dunedin Evening Star in 1963. He then worked for several years in Adelaide, Wellington, Auckland and in London, where he served a lengthy term as the New Zealand Press Association's UK correspondent. In between working in Adelaide, he was again with the Evening Star 1970-72, before starting his stint with NZPA, for which he had his first experience as a rugby reporter with the 1972 Wallabies on their New Zealand tour.

The first of his overseas NZPA assignments was with the Petone club on its 1974 South Africa tour, then later that year with the All Blacks in Australia and Fiji. A posting to London in 1975 led to him covering many All Blacks tours starting with the 1978 Grand Slammers. He also covered many of the momentous Olympic and Commonwealth Games in the 70s and 80s and was one of the few New Zealanders who attended the 1980 Moscow Olympics.

Returning to New Zealand in 1985, Palenski worked briefly in book publishing before joining The Dominion in 1986, working firstly in its Auckland office then moving to Wellington, where he was the paper's chief rugby writer until 1990. He covered the 1987 World Cup and All Blacks tours to Japan 1987, Australia 1988 and Wales and Ireland 1989. In 1990 he became editor of the Dominion Sunday Times and when that paper ceased early in 1994 he became assistant editor and a much-read thrice weekly columnist on the daily paper, until his return in 1997 to Dunedin.

He became executive director of the Dunedin-based Sports Hall of Fame and, having gained as a journalist an insight into sports governance, in the early 2000s had a brief term as chairman of the Otago union board. Earlier he had served as the Highlanders' media liaison officer. In November 2022, having done much to establish it, Palenski himself was inducted into the Hall of Fame.

Palenski, a fluent, concise writer, was a prolific author, penning the biographies of All Blacks Graham Mourie, Dave Loveridge and Jeff Wilson as well as many authoritative books on the game's history, including one celebrating the New Zealand union's centenary in 1992, 'Our National Game'. He updated, too, later editions of the record of All Blacks' tests, 'Men In Black', and the 'Rugby Encyclopaedia' and in more recent years had a Facebook blog focused mainly on the game's history. In all he wrote a staggering tally of almost 50 books, some being on New Zealand military history. His standing as a historian was enhanced not only by his writing skills which he developed in daily journalism but also by his academic deeds. As a mature student in 2007 he obtained a MA in history from Otago University and then a Ph.D.

Palenski earned many honours: sports journalist of the year 1987, rugby writer of the year, 1989 and NZ Order of Merit, 2002. He died in Dunedin, after battling prostate cancer, on August 22, 2023, aged 78. *(by Lindsay Knight)*

PHOTOGRAPHER

Peter George Bush achieved iconic rugby status through his deeds as a photographer. Though not the first to tour overseas, "Bushy," as he was always known, became a regular snapper on most All Blacks tours, starting with his first overseas with the 1972-73 tour of Britain and France and stretching into the 2000s, when he was in his early 80s. Though best known for his rugby photography, this was but one aspect of his craft. In his many years working for the weekly newspaper, Truth, he was involved in many other aspects of New Zealand life and among his most memorable shots were those of the 1968 'Wahine' disaster. He was also a devoted outdoorsman, a tramper and a hunter, a legacy of a West Coast childhood.

But rugby was always a passion. He came from a prominent rugby family and his uncle, Ron, was an All Black in the 1930s, co-founder of the New Zealand Barbarians club and in the 1960s a successful All Black selector. Peter himself, with his rugged build, was a more than useful tight forward, as was his late, younger brother, Barry.

Educated at Auckland's Sacred Heart College, he played in the same 1947 first XV as a later All Black halfback Keith Davis. He then played senior club rugby in Auckland with Marist and College Rifles and in Wellington for that city's Marist club. That background gave him an advantage over most of his photography colleagues. With his energy and sharp reflexes he had an ability to read a game and, coupled with an acute news sense, know what incidents would be subsequent headlines and talking points.

Bush began his newspaper career in the late 1940s as a cadet on the New Zealand Herald but for most of the 1950s worked as a merchant seaman, for the Department of Wildlife and Agriculture and as an army public relations officer in Malaya.

He returned to newspapers in 1960 beginning a long association with Truth before, in later years, working as a freelancer, with his services in demand not only in New Zealand but more especially overseas, where among the media he had many admirers.

His photography featured in many books, including some of his own, the best of which was his 1989 work, 'The Game For All New Zealand'. Much better than any words this captured New Zealand rugby in all its many strands, with an emphasis on people and community.

Surprisingly, "Bushy" won few journalistic awards, but his other honours were many: The Queen's Service Medal in 1991, The CNZM in 2011 and the Steinlager Salver for his services to the game in 2004. A natural raconteur with his distinctive gravelly voice he could have sprung from a Barry Crump novel.

Keith Quinn, as celebrated in his sphere as was "Bushy" in his, paid an apt tribute. "He will be much missed but his life's work over 60 years will live on." He was a true legend. At Wellington, December 16, 2023, aged 93. (*by Lindsay Knight*)

AMENDMENTS

to 2021 edition

Page 209 Briant did not referee game of Nov 15 Canterbury v Auckland at Christchurch. Mike Fraser was referee.

Page 210 Fraser did not referee game of Nov 14 Northland v Waikato. He was referee the next day, Nov 15, Canterbury v Auckland, a late replacement for Briant.

Page 211 Mabey was referee of Northland v Waikato fixture at Kaikohe on Nov 14, a late replacement for Fraser.

to 2022 edition

Page 339 Mackey was a substitute v Bay of Plenty.

to 2023 edition

Page 66 April 16, Hurricanes 22 Highlanders 21

Page 91 Timu, not Dawai, was a substitute v Reds.

Page 120 Rangi was hooker v Otago.

Page 131 Lienert-Brown, not Brewis, was hooker v North Harbour.

Page 151 Erickson. Correct spelling is Eriksson.

Page 162 Filimone was omitted, centre in last two games.

Page 177 Nettleton did not appear v Buller.

Page 182 Caird, not Craig, was lock v Bay of Plenty.

Page 183 Score v Wellington should read 15–6. Against Tasman Reihana and Hawkins each kicked a conversion.

Page 187 Koloamatangi was a substitute v Hawke's Bay.

Page 207 Brighouse was a substitute v Auckland.

Page 212 Matenga was a substitute v Otago. Chapman and S. Moli did not appear v Auckland.

Page 213 Nick Briant was referee v Hawke's Bay.

Page 223 Jono Bredin was referee v Southland.

Page 236 Only Wyness and Ross kicked penalty goals. Garland was a substitute v East Coast.

Page 269 Add to Williams tally. March 19 SR Moana Pasifika v Chiefs, at Auckland.

Page 315 Score was 50–6, not 56–6.

Page 318 Correct scorers for NZ were: Woodman (7), Cocksedge (2), Connor, Hirini, Holmes, du Plessis, Fluhler, Tui tries; Cocksedge (5), Holmes (4), Marino-Tauhinu conversions.

Page 323 Holmes and Demant each also kicked a penalty goal.

Page 352 Taranaki final was Clifton 28 Southern 5.

Page 364 Takimoana scored 2 tries v Canterbury, not three.

Page 376 Jensen, not Cottrell, kicked penalty v North Harbour. Cottrell kicked 3 penalties v Northland (sf).

Page 387 Ana Allen, not Johnson, was wing v Hawke's Bay in final.

Page 399 August 7 v North Harbour. Score was 42–15.

Page 412 Cogger-Orr. Add March 15 SR Chiefs Manawa v Hurricanes Poua, at Hamilton. Her game of March 20 was Matatu v Hurricanes Poua.

Page 413 Jenner. Add March 15 SR Blues v Matatu, at Hamilton. Her game of March 20 was Chiefs Manawa v Blues, at Hamilton.

Page 501 Conway died 2022.

Page 508 Vidiri died 2022.

Page 519 Leggat died 2022.